# THE HOAXERS

# THE HOAXERS
## *Plain Liars, Fancy Liars, and Damned Liars*

By
MORRIS KOMINSKY

*Boston*
BRANDEN PRESS
*Publishers*

Standard Book Number   8283-1288-5
© Copyright, 1970, by Branden Press, Inc.
Printed in the United States of America
Library of Congress Catalog Card Number   76-109134

*To*
**SOPHIE DAVIDSON**
*scholar, dedicated fighter*
*for human rights and dignity,*
*and loyal friend.*

# Preface

This is the first of a two-volume study of the trends in the United States of America towards Fascism and a Third World War.

The present volume, entitled "Plain Liars, Fancy Liars, and Damned Liars", is a special study of the use of fabrications, distortions of truth, and out-of-context quotations by the enemies of peace and freedom. It is hoped that a reading of this volume will make it easier to grasp the significance of the data presented in the second volume, entitled "America Faces Disaster", which will follow, and in which the real enemies of peace and freedom are discussed.

# Acknowledgments

Grateful acknowledgment is made for permission to include the following copyrighted items:

1. *New Republic,* July 3, 1965. Excerpts from an article by Harrison Salisbury.
2. *The Minority of One,* February, 1965. Excerpts from an article by Professor Frederick L. Schuman.
3. Prayer Book Press, Inc. Excerpts from *The High Holiday Prayer Book* by Rabbi Morris Silverman.
4. *Encyclopaedia Britannica.* Excerpt from 1937 edition, page 325.
5. *The Nation,* October 5, 1964. Excerpts from article by Alexander Werth.
6. *The Annals of American Academy of Political and Social Science* and the late Professor Pitirim Sorokin. Excerpts from article in issue of March, 1967.
7. Mr. Jack Belden. Excerpts from *China Shakes the World.*
8. William Morrow and Company, Inc. Excerpts from *The Stilwell Papers* by General Joseph Stilwell.
9. *The Progressive,* March, 1960. A letter to the editor, quoted in its entirety.
10. Martin K. Tytell. A paper presented by this distinguished criminologist at the New York Meeting of the American Association for the Advancement of Science on December 29, 1956.
11. *Los Angeles Times.* Complete essay by Gene Blake, April 28, 1967.

Deep appreciation is felt for the legal advice given so generously over a period of several years by Ben Margolis, Esq., member of the law firm of Margolis, McTernan, Smith, Scope & Herring, who have handled many important civil liberties cases. Last, but not least, thanks are due to Herbert M. Porter, Esq., who carefully read the entire manuscript from both a legal and humanitarian standpoint.

# CONTENTS

10

11

# Introduction

The dilemma that faces the American people, as well as all mankind, was very well described a few years ago by the distinguished clergyman, Dr. A. Powell-Davies: "The world is now too dangerous for anything but the truth, too small for anything but brotherhood." An obvious corollary to Dr. Davies' dictum is that the American people cannot act intelligently in a world fraught with danger, unless their opinions are formed on the basis of truthful information.

Proceeding from these assumptions, this study has been undertaken in order to show how lies and distortions of truth are systematically used to generate hysteria, to mislead the people, and to prevent a rational approach to the solution of the most pressing social problems.

In his eloquent address to the United Nations on September 25, 1961, the late President John F. Kennedy warned the world: "Every man, woman and child lives under a nuclear sword of Damocles, hanging by the slenderest of threads, capable of being cut at any moment by accident or miscalculation or by madness. The weapons of war must be abolished before they abolish us." In the light of this most sober statement, the reader will perhaps pardon me if a note of anger is detected in my writing. It is not easy to be restrained and calm when you observe evil men, ignorant men, and fanatical men daily spreading lies and hysteria—creating a climate of opinion that prepares the way for Fascism and a Third World War. The best experts tell us that such a war could very well annihilate the human species. So, the stakes are high in the task of bringing the facts to the people.

Inasmuch as a great deal of the hysteria revolves around the problem of Communism and its challenge, it becomes necessary to point out that this study is neither an attack on Communism nor a defense of Communism. It presents an analysis and exposé of the most commonly circulated falsehoods, which are used to create confusion, hysteria, frustration, and apathy. It is my belief that the people have an inalien-

13

able right to form their opinions and to make their decisions on the basis of facts rather than falsehoods. It is in this spirit that the subject matter is presented.

I frankly confess that I am biased in favor of peace, biased in favor of democracy, biased in favor of prosperity for all, and biased in favor of the brotherhood of man. Nevertheless, I am making an honest effort to present the truth, insofar as it is ascertainable.

The purpose of Volume I is to equip the reader with the factual data necessary to refute the misinformation that has become a barrier to rational thinking. Volume II gives the story of the groups, individuals, and policies that endanger the citizens of the U.S.A., as well as the rest of mankind.

If a reading of these two volumes causes people to think and to take action to reverse the present trend towards Fascism and a Third World War, I will feel amply rewarded.

MORRIS KOMINSKY

# CHAPTER I

# Poisoning the Minds of the People

## Ann Landers Was in Jail

It is almost a foregone conclusion that most readers will feel a sense of anger and outrage as the story of massive deception unfolds in the following pages. As will become apparent, there are many ways of distorting the truth. So, let us start on a light note.

In the syndicated column of Ann Landers (Riverside, California *Daily Enterprise,* February 7, 1962) there appeared the following:

Dear Ann: A friend of mine told me that you were once in jail. He said he saw you there. Is this true or false? Please answer in the paper. Your readers are entitled to know.—Corky

Dear Corky: Your friend is right. I was in jail in February, 1959. I spoke to the inmates of the Cook County jail and am delighted to report it was one of the most attentive audiences I've ever had. Not a soul walked out.

## The George Washington Hoax

The present-day purveyors of hatred and falsehoods frequently quote George Washington in an effort to "prove" that he warned the American people against the Jews. Thus we find in the January 1, 1963 issue of the anti-Semitic sheet, *Common Sense,* a picture of George Washington. Under it is the following:

George Washington's statement on the so-called "Jews": "They work more effectively against us than the enemy's armies. They are a hundred times more dangerous to our liberties and the great cause we are engaged in. It is much to be lamented that each state, long ago has not hunted them down as pests to society and the greatest enemies we have to the happiness of America."
(*Maxims of George Washington* by A.A., Appleton and Co., pages 125-6, Copyright 1894.)

jugation to another. And so, in 1863 he wrote the Emancipation Proclamation. And in 1864 he wrote that 'the restoration of the rebel States to the Union must rest upon the principle of civil and political equality of both races.' And in 1865, in the second Inaugural Address, he sought 'to bind up the Nation's wounds.'

"One hundred years later the Citizens' Councils are striving to reopen those wounds and to restore a system which has been the nation's curse. The great emancipator was never their ally and will not serve them now. History has passed them by. A new birth of freedom is dawning."

The neat little trick of quoting Lincoln's earlier views and suppressing his later and more mature philosophy, desecrates the memory of a great man who epitomized the best in the United States of America. Again it must be asked, why do so-called patriotic groups remain silent when such unpatriotic acts are committed by people who influence large segments of the population?

## The Abraham Lincoln Hoax, No. 2

One of the most widely-circulated frauds is a decalogue attributed to Abraham Lincoln. The text of the ten points is as follows.

1. You cannot bring about prosperity by discouraging thrift.
2. You cannot strengthen the weak by weakening the strong.
3. You cannot help small men up by tearing big men down.
4. You cannot help the poor by destroying the rich.
5. You cannot lift the wage earner up by pulling the wage payer down.
6. You cannot keep out of trouble by spending more than your income.
7. You cannot further the brotherhood of man by inciting class hatred.
8. You cannot establish sound social security on borrowed money.
9. You cannot build character and courage by taking away a man's initiative and independence.
10. You cannot help men permanently by doing for them what they could and should do for themselves.

The actual author of this decalogue was a Rev. William J. H. Boetcker, who copyrighted and printed it in 1916. It seems to have had some distribution by employers who wished to indoctrinate their employees. In February, 1940, the American Federation of Investors published the decalogue, under the title

18

of *Warning Signs on the Road to Prosperity,* in their periodical, *Investor America.* It was carried on the back cover, while the front cover bore a photograph of the Lincoln Memorial in Washington, D.C.

On March 14, 1941, Congressman Leland M. Ford placed the decalogue in the Congressional Record and prefaced it with these remarks: ". . . I include the following slogan of the Jeffersonian Democrats of California, 408 So. Spring St., Los Angeles, California, bearing the title of 'Warning Signs on the Road to Prosperity.' "

In the Fall of 1942 a group, calling itself the Committee for Constitutional Government, published a leaflet which bore the caption: *Lincoln on Limitation.* It carried some authentic excerpts from Lincoln's writings, and on the reverse side it carried the decalogue without attribution to its author. Nevertheless, it created the distinct impression that Abraham Lincoln was the author of the decalogue. It had a massive distribution.

In the September 15, 1943, issue of their quarterly house organ, *The Royle Forum,* John Royle & Sons of Paterson, New Jersey, printed the decalogue and ascribed it to Abraham Lincoln. This text was incorporated in a radio script and broadcast on November 30, 1948, by Galen Drake. A listener, who heard Galen Drake, carried the decalogue to Congresswoman Frances P. Bolton of Ohio. On January 25, 1949, Mrs. Bolton placed the decalogue in the Congressional Record, solemnly prefacing it with these remarks: "Mr. Speaker, certain that it never comes amiss for us to refresh our memories and perhaps clarify our thinking by recalling words once spoken by such men as Abraham Lincoln, may I read a few lines?" Thus did the Congresswoman furnish ammunition and leverage to Right-Wing and Fascistic groups; now they could "prove" the authenticity of the decalogue, because, foresooth: It comes from the Congressional Record!

On February 15, 1954, the *New York Times* carried a story, with the following headline:

"A Lincoln Hoax" Charged to G.O.P.

The *Times* published the spurious Lincoln decalogue, and went on to say: "Stephen A. Mitchell, chairman of the Democratic National Committee, said tonight Postmaster General Arthur E. Summerfield was trying to 'put over a Lincoln Hoax'

19

by quoting something Lincoln 'never said' in a speech intended for delivery Saturday night at Akron, Ohio." Further on in the *Times'* story, Democratic Chairman Mitchell is quoted as saying: "This entire passage is a fake. Mr. Summerfield has put words in the mouth of the Great Emancipator that he never said. This quotation is intended to make Lincoln sound like a modern Old Guard Senator. It is another example of the Republicans trying to rewrite history."

The Right-Wing propaganda weekly, *Human Events,* published the phoney Lincoln decalogue in its issue of October 13, 1960, quoting it from another propaganda sheet, the *Marin Tax News.*

On June 24, 1962, Dr. Ernest Wilkinson, President of the Mormons' Brigham Young University, delivered a long speech in the Palmer House, Chicago, Illinois, which he concluded by quoting the phoney Lincoln decalogue. What is even more interesting is that the educator introduced the decalogue as follows: ". . . words claimed by some, but denied by others, to have been written by Abraham Lincoln. But regardless of the authorship, they represent a philosophy which can never be dismissed as being a repetition of stale phrases, clichés of our forbears, or incantations from the forgotten past. They are the simple truths which govern all individuals and all civilizations, now and in the future." It is hardly necessary to point out the casuistry employed by the good doctor. Suffice it to say that his technique of *equivocal* disavowal of falsehood, when confronted with the truth, has been emulated by many Right-Wingers. He is indeed a most "modest" fellow, for he makes bold to lay down the rules of conduct for past, present, and future. On July 25, 1963, Senator Gordon Allott placed Dr. Wilkinson's speech in the Congressional Record. So, once again the Right-Wingers can quote the phoney Lincoln decalogue on *the authority of the Congressional Record!*

Banks are supposed to be opposed to forgery, but it is a matter of record that the Coast Federal Savings and Loan Association of Los Angeles did circulate this Lincoln forgery on a large scale. This outfit operates a propaganda division called the Free Enterprise Department, which we will examine in greater detail in Volume II. Coast Federal distributed an attractive, multi-colored 5" x 3" card, prepared by the Curt Advertising Agency. At the top appears this caption:

20

Then follows the decalogue, *signed by Abraham Lincoln.* And below it the card says:

Distributed as a public service by
COAST FEDERAL SAVINGS
JOE CRAIL, PRESIDENT

Isn't there something strange about commemorating the birthday of a great humanitarian by publishing a forgery and attributing it to him? And as "a public service"!

On November 26, 1962, I sent a letter to Mr. Thomas Cosgrove of the Coast Federal, challenging the authenticity of the decalogue used on their 5" x 3" card. On December 6, 1962, Miss Shirley Black of Coast Federal's Free Enterprise Department sent me a letter, advising me:

1. That Coast Federal took the phoney Lincoln decalogue from *Human Events* of October 13, 1960.

2. That a number of others had used the decalogue in business publications, company house organs, and other outlets.

3. That after the appearance of Coast Federal's card, former Congressman Leland M. Ford wrote Coast Federal a letter, claiming authorship of the decalogue in 1938.

4. That they are glad to acknowledge the decalogue is not authentic, but objected to my calling it a "fake," because "it implies fraudulent intent."

The letter concludes by quoting Dr. Wilkinson's remarks in justification of the use of the phoney decalogue!

On December 31, 1962, I sent Shirley Black a letter informing her that I must question the good faith of Coast Federal, unless it takes steps to publicly and extensively retract that alleged Lincoln quotation. I told her that I felt "It is incumbent upon Coast Federal Savings to place paid advertisements in leading newspapers, in order to counteract all the damage done by the hundreds of thousands of cards and leaflets you have distributed containing that alleged Lincoln quotation." I stated further that I had called to the attention of her boss, Joe Crail, in a letter of November 28, 1960, that Coast Federal was circulating a fabricated quotation attributed to a Soviet

21

leader, Dimitri Manuilsky;[1] that I had exchanged correspondence with Mr. Crail and offered proof of the fraudulent nature of the Manuilsky quotation, even offering a $500 reward if anyone could prove its authenticity; that Mr. Joe Crail had not kept his promise to advise me of the results of his investigation of my charges; that my final letter to Joe Crail, on May 5, 1961, was sent via certified mail and that I had a return receipt acknowledging that my letter was delivered to his office. On January 8, 1963, Shirley Black wrote me that they saw no point in advertising a retraction of the phoney Lincoln decalogue, because they had withdrawn it from circulation and "there have been enough newspaper and magazine articles clarifying the situation." Of course this overlooks the fact that the "clarifying" articles did not appear in sufficient number, size, and circulation to *effectively* scotch this falsehood, as we shall presently show. The letter concludes with a refusal to discuss the fraudulent Manuilsky quotation, because "we are satisfied with the findings of a duly constituted Committee of the United States Congress, on the latter." This argument, as we shall prove in our discussion of the Manuilsky hoax, is just about as valid as Coast Federal's original reliance upon *Human Events* for the Lincoln decalogue.

On February 4, 1963, I sent another letter to Miss Shirley Black of Coast Federal, challenging the validity of her previous arguments. I offered to furnish Coast Federal overwhelming documentation that the Manuilsky quotation is a fraud, providing Coast Federal would agree to publish a retraction. Then I called to Coast Federal's attention another fraudulent quotation. My concluding paragraph says: "In the Congressional Record of March 8, 1962, Senator Lee Metcalf of Montana presented proof that Coast Federal Savings is circulating a fake quotation attributed to Khrushchev. Before making the charge, he had the quotation researched by the Library of Congress, the Senate Internal Security Subcommittee, the House Committee on Un-American Activities, the FBI, and the CIA. What will you rely on now? And have you withdrawn that quotation? And will you publicly announce that it is not a bona fide quotation? I will await your comments." Needless to add, I did not receive a reply to this letter.

[1] The Manuilsky Hoax will be discussed in another chapter.

22

On March 18, 1964, fourteen months after Miss Shirley Black of Coast Federal had written me that there was no need for paid advertisements to retract the phoney Lincoln decalogue, Senator Lee Metcalf made an important speech on the floor of the Senate. It included the report from the Library of Congress regarding the genesis of the Lincoln decalogue. (Some of the facts in this chapter are based on that report, although I have corroborated each item from other sources.) Senator Metcalf related how the utilities corporations, especially the electric power groups, are still using the phoney Lincoln decalogue. Said Senator Metcalf: "However, the investor-owned-utilities— IOU's—conclude their current propaganda movie, 'The Power Within,' with a spurious quotation attributed to Abraham Lincoln. There is an emotional scene at the end of this movie where the camera focuses on a statue of Lincoln and a voice intones:

You cannot build character and courage by taking away a man's initiative and independence. You cannot help man permanently by doing for him what he could and should do for himself.

These two sentences are 'Lincoln sayings' 9 and 10 of the '10 points' erroneously attributed to Lincoln." And further on Senator Metcalf commented: "Some IOU's have paid the Committee for Constitutional Government to mail out propaganda and have contributed to the Committee for Constitutional Government. Power company officials have solicited funds for the Committee for Constitutional Government. Perhaps a fraction of the funds donated to the Committee for Constitutional Government should be invested in the works of Lincoln himself." So, Shirley Black and Coast Federal are in error if they think the Lincoln decalogue has been properly buried.[2]

The well-known preacher, Rev. Gerald L. K. Smith, quotes the Lincoln decalogue in the August 1962 issue of *The Cross and The Flag*. Following the style of Dr. Wilkinson of Brigham

2 In a speech which will be found on pages S1916-1917 of the Congressional Record, February 9, 1967, Senator Lee Metcalf stated that, with Lincoln Day approaching, it becomes necessary once more to expose the phoney Lincoln Decalogue. The Senator said: "The phoney Lincoln quotes are nevertheless circulated by some State Republican organizations, in Montana, for example, and are used by officials of leading power companies." He charged that among those using the phoney Decalogue were the President of Middle South Utilities and the Vice-President of West Penn Power Company.

Young University, Smith prefaces the decalogue with these remarks: "Below we quote ten statements accredited to Abraham Lincoln by certain people, while others insist they are not his statements. If Lincoln didn't say it, the editors of this letter would like to meet the man who did say it." In spite of Shirley Black's letter of assurance on January 8, 1963, that retraction of the phoney decalogue was not necessary, Gerald L. K. Smith became bolder by the time he got ready to publish the Lincoln decalogue again. In the December 1964 *The Cross and The Flag*, Smith put this heading over the same decalogue, about which he had expressed some doubt in his August, 1962, issue:

"ABRAHAM LINCOLN SAID"

In *The Cross and The Flag* of September 1966, the Rev. Gerald L. K. Smith says:

SAY IT AGAIN. In an earlier issue we printed the words of Abraham Lincoln uttered on a certain occasion, but we reprint them again. They cannot be uttered too often.

This is followed by the phoney Lincoln Decalogue.

One of the galaxy of retired millionaires that adorns the City of Santa Barbara, California, is a colorful chap by the name of Frank W. Ketcham, who operates a Right-Wing propaganda mill under the name of Americans for Freedom. Ketcham mails out an endless stream of leaflets, brochures, stickers, and tape recordings. During September of 1966 he mailed out a yellow 8" x 6" circular, No. 347, with a picture of a log cabin, and Abraham Lincoln next to it. Below the pictures there is our "famous" Lincoln decalogue, with Abraham Lincoln's name signed at the bottom. And you can get additional copies by sending Ketcham a stamped self-addressed envelope.

On May 16, 1963, I picked up an 8½" x 6" plastic card at the Right-Wing bookstore operated by American Freedoms Center, 139 North Maryland Avenue, Glendale, California. On one side there are a number of items, including a quotation from the late anti-Semitic General George Van Horn Moseley, who was involved in Nazi activities in this country for a number of years, and a reproduction of a propaganda advertisement of Warner & Swasey in *United States News and World Report*. On the other side there is the phoney Lincoln deca-

24

logue, with a picture of Lincoln above it and Lincoln's name signed at the bottom. In response to an inquiry, the producers of this item, Virginia Laminating Company of Amelia, Virginia, said that they obtained the Lincoln decalogue from Joseph Hulse, 814 Thirteenth Street, Washington, D.C. Hulse, who operates a blueprint and photostat service, informed us that he obtained the Lincoln decalogue some thirty years ago from a Philadelphia printer, whose name and address he could not recall.

The Rev. C. W. Burpo, a Right-Wing radio preacher, quotes the decalogue in the March 1966 issue of his *Bible Institute News,* with the heading:

## TEN GUIDELINES

Abraham Lincoln left us some guidelines too, to help us in maintaining the framework of democracy in this nation of free men.

The *Councilor,* a hate sheet published by the Citizens Councils of Louisiana, carried the phoney Lincoln decalogue in its issue of May 25, 1966.

Not to be outdone by the assorted Fascists, Right-Wingers, and hate peddlers, Mr. Harlan Gilbertson, publisher and editor of two obscure weeklies, carried the phoney Lincoln decalogue as a 5″ x 8″ block in the *Elsinore Leader-Press* of April 22, 1966. To give it emphasis, Gilbertson published it in white letters on a black background, and he had Lincoln's name at the bottom, to "prove" the authorship. On May 16, 1966, I wrote Gilbertson to advise him that the Lincoln decalogue is a fraud, that Coast Federal had disavowed it, and that he should retract it. He did not retract and did not answer my letter.

While no further proof would seem to be necessary in order to refute the Lincoln decalogue, I wish to give it a decent burial:

*Item.* In 1950, the distinguished NBC commentator, Alex Dreier, repudiated his prior use of the decalogue and said "the fact is, Lincoln never said one line of the quotes."

*Item.* The May, 1955, issue of *Ideas on Liberty,* a publication of the Foundation for Economic Education, repudiates the Lincoln decalogue, but does it in the disingenuous style of Dr. Wilkinson of Brigham Young University.

*Item.* On March 2, 1962, Mr. Morris Watson, the Editor

25

of *Dispatcher,* official organ of the International Longshoremen's and Warehousemen's Union, addressed a letter to the renowned poet and biographer of Abraham Lincoln, Carl Sandburg.[3] In the letter, a photocopy of which is in my possession, Watson quoted the Lincoln decalogue and told Sandburg that Philip Maxwell, President of the Employers Association of Hawaii, had sent him the decalogue and challenged him to publish it in the *Dispatcher.* Sandburg simply wrote on Watson's letter, at the margin next to the decalogue:

Spurious

C.S.

No one can doubt that Carl Sandburg is the supreme authority on Lincolniana.

We have by no means exhausted the list of purveyors of this hoax. Nor is there any assurance of a cessation of its dissemination. It is, however, important that we determine the significance of the fact that its distribution is by groups of capitalists, bankers, and their supporters. It is also significant that "respectable" leaders of business and industry get support in this project from the hate groups and the avowed Fascist elements. In this connection, it must be sharply emphasized that the actual transformation of the Rev. Boetcker's maxims into a Lincoln decalogue was accomplished by the sleight-of-hand in the leaflet issued in the Fall of 1942 by the Committee for Constitutional Government. The Library of Congress research report, which Senator Metcalf placed in the Congressional Record of March 18, 1964, supports this conclusion by stating that the Committee for Constitutional Government "has earned the honor of having first associated Mr. Lincoln with the maxims."

In order to round out the investigation of the launching of and widespread use of this hoax, it may be enlightening to determine the nature and aims of the "father" of the Lincoln hoax, the Committee for Constitutional Government. On September 23, 1950, Congressman Wright Patman of Texas made a most important speech, which will be found on Page A 7336 of the Congressional Record of that date. Here are some pertinent excerpts:

---

3 Mr. Sandburg passed away since this was written.

Mr. Speaker, the Committee for a Fascist Government alias the Committee for Constitutional Government, organized by and operated by E. A. Rumely, is making an all-out effort to change fundamentally our form of government. . . . Rumely and his gang are trying to make it impossible for Congress to have enough money to provide for things his Fascist group is opposed to. An effort is made to change our Constitution through petitions by 32 States as provided in Article V of the Constitution but which has never been used. This is an effort to sneak through an amendment to the Constitution that will limit to fifteen percent the income taxes on any person or corporation and not permit Congress to levy an inheritance or estate tax at all. This limitation will effectively do what this Fascist group would like to have done and that is to destroy our programs on social security, for veterans' relief, improvement of rivers and harbors, public roads, soil conservation, support prices for farmers, the Government lending its credit for an interest charge, which is repaid, the farmers and families in the city to buy farms and homes on long terms at low rates of interest, and other programs of benefit to the people. . . .

Rumely, the court records disclose, was guilty of treason against the United States during World War I. He was a German propagandist. He has been in propaganda work ever since. . . . He has carried on a persistent and ruthless campaign against labor and farmers and strictly in the direction of helping those who have the most and especially the privileged group. His whole campaign has been in the direction of making the rich richer and the poor poorer.[4]

The picture that emerges from all the data is one of indicating that the Lincoln decalogue is a propaganda device of Big Business and Right-Wing groups.


## Lenin Fabrication, No. 1

One of the most widespread fabrications is a quotation which Cold War propagandists and Ultra-Rightists persistently and repeatedly attribute to Lenin. It reads:

---

[4] In its issue of January 17, 1950, Look magazine had a full-page feature item in white letters on a completely black page. In the upper right-hand corner there is the rugged face of Abraham Lincoln. Alongside it, to the left, is the following:
LOOK thinks it's about time
for the country to remember
ABRAHAM LINCOLN
said:
Then it gives the phoney decalogue.
Time magazine of January 30, 1950, commented: "To Lincoln scholars and plain readers, there was only one thing wrong with Look's snippets of wisdom: Lincoln had never said them."

27

Promises are like pie crusts, made to be broken.

It has been quoted so widely that it is possible to fill up many pages, describing its use. A few illustrations should suffice.

The *U.S. News and World Report*, February 7, 1958, page 73, says:

Said Khrushchev in Moscow: "Agreement on many questions is possible." Said Lenin in Moscow, years ago: "Promises are like pie crust, made to be broken." Western diplomats listening to Khrushchev, remember Lenin. But diplomatic channels are open. Talking can be private as well as public.

On February 11, 1958, I sent a letter to *U.S.N. & W.R.*, asking for authentication of this alleged Lenin quotation. On February 21, 1958, Mrs. I. D. Holland, Manager, Reader Service, *U.S.N. & W.R.*, sent me the letter and accompanying memorandum, which are herewith photographically reproduced.

## U.S. News & World Report

February 21, 1958

AIR MAIL

Mr. Morris Kominsky
P. O. Box 337
Elsinore, California

Dear Mr. Kominsky:

In reply to your letter of February 11, enclosed is a memorandum covering the information requested.

We're glad to be of service.

Sincerely yours,

Mrs. I. D. Holland
Manager, Reader Service

IDH/mem
Enclosure

28

February 21, 1958

Actually Lenin was quoting the English writer Jonathan Swift —

"'Promises like pie crusts are leaven to be broken,' says the English proverb."

The quote is taken from The Collected Works of V. I. Lenin, Vol. IX, p. 290 of the Russian edition, published by the State Publishing House for Political Literature, Moscow, 1947. It was an article titled "Bourgeois Sated Bourgeois Hungary" which first appear in the Proletariat XX of October 10 (September 27) 1905.

Although Lenin did not name Swift, the quotation is actually from Swift's "Polite Conversation, Dialogue #1."

The reader's attention is directed to the behavior of *U.S. News and World Report:*

a. Insofar as I have been able to determine, no retraction was published in the magazine. Thus, hundreds of thousands of readers were misled into believing this fraudulent quotation.

b. *U.S.N. & W.R.* made its grudging admission on a blank piece of paper, with the admonitions that the information is not for attribution or distribution. I do not feel morally bound to accede to this stipulation.

Perhaps the reader is inclined to give *U.S.N. & W.R.* the benefit of the doubt and to assume that an honest error was made. If such is the case, why did not the *U.S.N. & W.R.* discharge its obligation to its readers by setting the record straight and telling its readers that the alleged Lenin quotation is a phoney? It could have done so gracefully. But this would not serve the purpose of its Cold War policy. Proof of this judgment is that three months later we find in the *U.S.N. & W.R.* (May 9, 1958) a story, quoting a speech by Secretary of State John Foster Dulles at the New Hampshire University. The following excerpt is apropos:

29

Meanwhile, the Secretary told his hearers, "the immediate problem" is: "Can we reach agreements with the Soviet Government?" There are difficulties in the way, Mr. Dulles pointed out: "Communists feel no obligation to perform their agreements. They have broken one agreement after another, confirming what Lenin said, that, to Communists, 'promises are like pie crusts, made to be broken.'"

Don't you agree that the *U.S.N. & W.R.* was morally obligated to parenthetically add at this point the memorandum it sent me on February 21, 1958?

In *The Gravediggers,* by Phyllis Schlafly and retired Admiral Chester Ward, page 64, we find the phoney Lenin quotation used as part of a plea that peaceful co-existence is impossible. A letter sent by a research assistant, brought a reply from Phyllis Schlafly on March 4, 1965. She stated that she had relied upon a letter her husband had received from the Department of State, which is reproduced on page 31.

The State Department letter shows that Phyllis Schlafly's husband had apparently read the news item in the *U.S. News & World Report* of May 9, 1958, which we have quoted. The shocking thing about the State Department letter is the sleight-of-hand perpetrated by telling Schlafly that the pie-crust quotation can be found on pages 290 and 291, volume 9, *Collected Works of Lenin* (Russian) 4th edition. They just conveniently omitted the fact that Lenin did not say it, but only alluded to it, as admitted in the memorandum from *U.S.N. & W.R.* and as we shall soon see by quoting from the above-mentioned pages 290 and 291.

The Ultra-Rightist *Life Lines,* March 5, 1965, vehemently argues against any steps toward ending the suicidal arms race. It "proves" that disarmament agreements are worthless by solemnly warning:

The U.S. somehow forgot what the communists themselves say about promises: they are like pie crust, made to be broken.

Retired Marine Corps General P. A. Del Valle, President of the Defenders of the American Constitution, presents a very shrill argument against taking any steps to end the arms race. In *Task Force,* July 1965, he trots out the old scarecrow about "the U.S.S.R. whose boast has been that treaties are made to be broken 'like pie crust.'"

August 19, 1958

Dear Mr. Schlafly:

In the absence of Secretary Dulles I am replying to your letter of August 9. The quotation "promises are like pie crusts, made to be broken" appears in the (Russian) 4th edition, volume 9 of <u>Collected Works of Lenin</u>, pages 290 and 291. The State Department's Division of Research and Analysis for the U.S.S.R. advises that the quotation was originally published in the magazine <u>Proletarian</u>, No. 20, in 1905.

I believe the speech you may be referring to in which the Secretary used the Lenin quotation was before the Atomic Power Institute at Durham, New Hampshire, on May 2. I enclose a marked copy of that speech.

I know the Secretary will appreciate your interest in writing him and <u>will be grateful for your message of confidence and support.</u>

Sincerely yours,

*D E Boster*

D. E. Boster
Staff Assistant

Enclosure:
Copy of speech.

Mr. J. F. Schlafly, Jr.,
Verlie, Eastman, Schlafly and Godfrey,
First National Bank Building,
Alton, Illinois.

Mr. G. A. Sheppard, attorney-at-law and a leader of the Freedom Club of the Rev. James W. Fifield's First Congregational Church of Los Angeles, has a list of some 56 "Communist Objectives" in the April 26, 1966, issue of *Freedom Club Bulletin*. With a reckless disregard for the most basic rules of evidence, with which attorneys are familiar, he includes item after item which he knows or should know, are untrue. Included, of course, is:

Lenin said: "Promises are like pie crusts—made to be broken."

On July 14, 1961, I asked the Library of Congress to locate the pie crust quotation which has been attributed to Lenin and a phoney quotation which had been attributed to Stalin. Page 33 is a photographic reproduction of the July 24, 1961, letter of reply and a similar reproduction on page 34 of pages 290 and 291, Volume 9 of the 1947 Russian language edition of the *Collected Works of Lenin*.

The pertinent paragraphs for our investigation are the last paragraph of page 290, which carries over to page 291, and the first paragraph of page 291. Two accomplished Russian scholars, both of whom have a better than average command of the English language, made independent translations. They did not exercise the usual literary license in translating the Russian idiom into English idiom. This accounts for a slight turgidity of style, but also obviates any distortion of the original. Both translations were almost 100% identical, which would seem to indicate the accuracy of the work. You will better understand the following passages when you realize that Lenin is here carrying on a polemical discussion with other underground revolutionaries during the barbaric regime of the Czar. Far from advocating broken promises, Lenin is here pouring scorn and bitter irony upon phoney Socialist politicians, upon precisely those people who are lacking in principle and moral stamina. In fact, he is bitterly condemning the Russian counterparts of the Quisling and Uncle Tom characters. A further word of explanation is in order. The allusion to *Yskra* refers to a revolutionary paper of that era; the allusion to *Novoe Vremia* refers to a particularly vicious anti-Semitic sheet of that period. Here are the two translated paragraphs:

# THE LIBRARY OF CONGRESS
WASHINGTON 25, D. C.

REFERENCE DEPARTMENT
SLAVIC AND CENTRAL EUROPEAN DIVISION

July 24, 1961

Dear Mr. Kominsky:

This is in reply to your letter of July 14.

The quotation from V.I. Lenin to which you refer is from his article Burzhuaziia sytaia i burzhuaziia alchushchaia (The satisfied bourgeoisie and the covetous bourgeoisie) and may be found on page 290 of volume 9 of the 1947 Russian language edition of his works. Examination of English editions of works by Lenin does not reveal a translation of this article.

The quotation from J. Stalin is taken from p. 276-277 of volume 2 of the 1946 edition of his works in Russian. It is available in English translation in volume II on page 285 of an edition of Stalin's works published in Moscow in 1953.

Your letter has been referred to the Photoduplication Service of the Library of Congress so that they may furnish you an estimate of the cost of preparing photostats of the quotations referred to above, and of the context in which they stand.

Sincerely yours,

Sergius Yakobson, Chief
Slavic and Central European Division

Mr. Morris Kominsky
400 East Franklin Street
Elsinore, California

AIR MAIL

уже не упоминается. «Решение земцев, — говорит «Le Temps, — делает им честь. Оно доказывает, что политическое воспитание наиболее просвещенных элементов русского народа прогрессирует, и что они отказываются от туманных планов политического фанкунчества, вступая мужественно на путь необходимой эволюции.

Буржуа, сытый политической властью и видавший виды по части того, к чему приводят в революциях, ни минуты не колеблется объявить сентябрьский съезд «либеральных помещиков и купцов победой эволюции над революцией.

Он хвалит «умеренность съезда. Он указывает, с каким удовлетворением, на провал резолюции о «раздроблении земель» и об «избирательных правах женщин. «Мудрость» и «умеренность» этих решений показывают ясно, что мнение крайних партий не взяли верха на этом съезде. Программа, на которой он все сошлись, достаточно демократична, чтобы обезоружить революционеров. А так как земский съезд ждет осуществления своих проектов исключительно от употребления законных средств, то его программа может присоединить и тех реформистов, которых личные споры не отделят от членов земского съезда.

Буржуа сытый поощрительно похлопывает по плечу буржуа алчущего: выставляет программу, достаточно демократичную, чтобы пустить пыль в глаза, чтобы обезоружить революционеров, и встать на легальный путь, — сиречь, говоря простым и прямым русским языком, сторговаться с Треповыми-Романовыми, вот истинная государственная мудрость.

А что надежды проницательного буржуа на простоватых революционеров не совсем «Искры», это доказали наши мудрецы из новой «Искры». Они, отпустив повода, ринулись в ловушку, запереры предлагая взымать демократические обязательства с умеренных буржуа, которые всей душой готовы теперь обещать, что угодно и обязаться на что угодно. Не только в борьбе между враждебными партиями, но и в борьбе внутри социалистических партий (шли мы после II съезда к этому!) оправдываются обещания, дитя и черту, раз затронуты сколько-нибудь существенные интересы буржуазии. The promines like pie-crust are heaven to be broken, говорят английские пословицы.

«Обещания, что корка от пирога: их на то и пекут, чтобы ломать потом».

К чему свелась искровская тактика по поводу Думы? Именно к идейному и тактическому обезоружению революционеров. «Мудрецы из оппортунистической «Искры» работали над этим обезоружением, разнося идею активного бойкота, подменивая (совершенно в духе «Нового Времени» и почти теми же словами) активный бойкот пассивным, проповедуя доверие и доверчивость к обнимающимся вместе Милюковым и Стаховичам, заменяя революционный лозунг восстания освобожденской буржуазией размашней вроде «революционного самоуправления граждан».

Только слепые могут еще теперь не видеть, в какое болото залезла «Искра». В нелегальной печати она совершенно одиноко, на ее стороне стоит только «Освобождение». Буль, которого даже Мартов с Аксельродом не занодярт в симпатии к «передовичному» арсеналу, рептильно встал за активный бойкот. В легальной печати все прохвосты и все умеренные либералы объединились в борьбе с радикальными буржуа, высказавшими сочувствие бойкоту и настроенными наиболее дружелюбно по отношению к крестьянству.

Ну, разве же неправду сказал Ленин в своих «Двух тактиках», разбирая новоискровские резолюции, что «Искра опускается до либеральных помещиков, в то время как «Пролетарий» старается поднять революционных крестьян?

Мы упомянули «Новое Время». Не только этот орган рептилий, но и «Московские Ведомости» ведут отчаянную борьбу против идеи бойкота, показывая этим всем каждому реальное политическое значение Думы. Вот для образчика одна характерная выходка «Нового Времени», из которой мы тем охотнее остановимся, что она проливает новый свет на всю безалу буржуазной подлости даже такого «отечественного либерального органа, как «Русские Ведомости».

Известный берлинский корреспондент этой последней газеты, г. Иоллос остановается в № 247 на Иенском съезде. Мещанская душа прежде всего возмущается тем, что там немного добрый и справедливый буржуа-либерал богач Аббе, который подарил городу Иене миллион дом

And that the hopes of the sated bourgeois, placed on the naive, foolhardy Revolutionaries, were not altogether without foundation, was proved by our own "sages" from the new *Yskra*. Reins released, they rushed into a trap, in the interim proposing to raise all democratic responsibilities and obligations from the moderate bourgeois, who are now themselves eager and ready to oblige, holding out any and all promises. Not only in struggles with adversary parties, but also inside the Socialist Parties (as we had occasion after the Second Congress, to convince ourselves on the spot), all promises fall by the wayside, as soon as it affects in a measure the essential interests of the toiling masses. To quote an English proverb: "The promises like pie-crust are leaven to be broken."

What did the tactics of the *Yskra* lead up to in connection with the Duma? Just to disarm the Revolutionaries ideologically and tactically. The wise men of the opportunistic *Yskra* have done their share in helping disarm the Revolutionaries, by distorting the idea of the active boycott. They have substituted (quite in the spirit of the *Novoe Vremia* and almost in the same words) the passive boycott for the active one. They preached trust and confidence in those embracing Miliukow and Stachwitz, thus replacing the revolutionary slogan of an uprising with the bourgeois liberation illusion, the so-called slogan, Citizen's Revolutionary Self-Government.

It is, of course, shocking that the Department of State of the United States Government and Secretary of State John Foster Dulles were actively spreading a deliberate forgery of Lenin's remarks. It is shocking that the *U.S. News & World Report* was a party to spreading this falsehood and to concealing the truth. It is shocking that a prominent church group spreads this canard. It is shocking that hundreds of Ultra-Rightist groups peddle this swindle. But what is even more shocking is that it is used to instill fear and distrust—thus endangering the peace of the world. A case in point is that, during the 1963 Congressional debate on the Nuclear Test Ban Treaty, it became a formidable weapon in the hands of the war mongers, who worked hard to block the ratification of the Treaty. There is the real danger that death—nay more, death of the entire human race—may become the wages of the sin of bearing false witness.

## Lenin Fabrication, No. 2

Lawyers are supposed to be trained in the art of carefully scrutinizing evidence in the course of a court trial. This universal rule was flagrantly violated by the Special Committee on Communist Tactics, Strategy and Objectives of the American Bar Association, the highest body among the lawyers. This Committee presented a report to the bar association's house of delegates in August of 1958, which included a number of

35

fabrications attributed to Lenin, Stalin, Khrushchev, and others. The Report was placed in the *Congressional Record* on March 1, 1962 by Senator Everett McKinley Dirksen, a member of the Senate Internal Security Subcommittee, the counterpart of the House Committee on Un-American Activities. Thus was a double-barreled weapon furnished to the purveyors of false-hood—the combined "seal of approval" of the American Bar Association Committee and the *Congressional Record!*[5]

The Report not only quoted the phoney pie-crust story, which we have called Lenin Fabrication No. 1, but quoted the following words, allegedly written by Lenin:

First, we will take Eastern Europe, then the masses of Asia, then we will encircle the United States, which will be the last bastion of capitalism. We will not have to attack. It will fall like an overripe fruit into our hands.

A footnote in the Committee's Report tells us that the quotation comes from *Collected Works of Lenin*, vol. 10, p. 172. Sounds authentic, doesn't it?

Not to be outdone by others in the dissemination of false quotations, the Free Enterprise Department of Coast Federal Savings & Loan Association of Los Angeles used Lenin Fabrication, No. 2 on page 5 of a manual for study groups, which they have brazenly entitled *The Truth About Communism*. Coast Federal tells us that the quotation comes from *Collected Works of Lenin*, Vol. 10, p. 172, "as printed in the *Congressional Record* of August 22, 1958, p. 4." There is a very shrewd device employed here. If the quotation does not appear in the quoted volume of Lenin, Coast Federal can always claim innocence, because they relied upon the *Congressional Record!* However, this maneuver will not suffice. First of all, there is no page 4 in the *Congressional Record* of August 22, 1958. The pages are numbered from 19015 to 19325. Secondly, if Coast Federal were interested in the truth, it could have researched the authenticity of the alleged quotation as well as I did. Furthermore, having twice visited the Free Enterprise Department of Coast Federal, I can testify that they have an

---

5 One of the earliest uses of this hoax was by the late Chairman of the House Committee on Un-American Activities, Congressman Francis E. Walter, in a series of articles he wrote for the Philadelphia Inquirer, March 3-9, 1958. Walter's articles were reprinted as an official document of his Committee.

adequate library of Communist books, including the works of Lenin.

In the "bible" of the John Birch Society, the Blue Book, page 10, Robert Welch quoted Lenin Fabrication No. 2. Mr. Welch prefaced the false quotation with the following, which sounds so "scholarly" to his dupes:

Lenin died in 1924. But before he died he had laid down for his followers the strategy for this conquest. It was, we should readily admit, brilliant, far-seeing, realistic, and majestically simple. It has been paraphrased and summarized as follows.

Then follows the phoney quotation, exactly as it was used in the Report of the Committee of the American Bar Association. Welch also used a device to give him an "out," when he said: "It has been paraphrased and summarized as follows." But then he gives the phoney Lenin statement in quotation marks. Even Welch's former public relations man, John Rousselot, knows that a statement in quotation marks must be the exact words, not a paraphrase or a summary. Rousselot repeatedly told audiences that no one, just no one, has ever found any factual error in Mr. Welch's writings.

There is a widely circulated pamphlet entitled *A Business Man Looks at Communism*. Underneath the title on the outside cover we are told that it is "By An American Business Man." On the title page we learn that the author is Fred Koch, and that by January, 1964, it had gone through ten editions. On page 2, it says that Koch is president of two corporations, chairman of the board of another corporation, and a director of a bank and of five other companies. Koch wrote this booklet in 1960, many years after he had built fifteen oil-cracking plants in the Soviet Union and after having traveled, according to his own admission, with one of the old Bolsheviks. I find it necessary to supply some information not given in the booklet:

A. Fred C. Koch is one of the founders of the John Birch Society.
B. Fred C. Koch is listed as a member of the Executive Committee of the John Birch Society.

Among other falsehoods contained in this booklet is the Lenin Fabrication, No. 2, which Koch solemnly proceeds to prove is the basis for a program now in progress.

Hate peddler Gerald L. K. Smith uses this phoney quotation in *The Cross and The Flag,* October, 1955, assuring his dupes that it is "the prophecy made by Lenin in 1923."

The Rev. Howard Kershner, who operates a Right-Wing propaganda outfit called Christian Freedom Foundation, says on page 27 of a booklet entitled *The Hangman's Rope:* "Lenin said we would fall like a ripe apple into their basket."

Marie Larson, in *Freedom Club Bulletin* of Rev. Fifield's First Congregational Church in Los Angeles, issue of June 16, 1966, has her own version of the phoney Lenin quotation. Marie's inventive genius is expressed in the following manner:

Lenin decreed: "Demoralize, degenerate, and if necessary devastate the United States . . . it will fall like an overripe fruit into our hands."

A Right-Wing outfit calling itself The Patrick Henry Group, operates from a postoffice box in Richmond, Virginia. Its sponsor is former Internal Revenue Commissioner T. Coleman Andrews, who has been prominent in many Right-Wing causes. A circular that this group sent out in August of 1965 advertises a book attacking the U.S. Supreme Court. The title of the circular is the phoney Lenin quotation.

That compendium of falsehood and distortion of truth, which the Right-Wing circulated in the millions during the 1964 election campaign, "None Dare Call It Treason," followed Robert Welch's style in its use of the phoney quotation. On page 26 it says:

After only seven years at the head of the world's first communist state, Lenin died in 1924. Before he died, he formulated a plan for world domination. Summarized and paraphrased, Lenin's plan stated:

"First, we will take eastern Europe, then the masses of Asia, then we will encircle the United States which will be the last bastion of capitalism. We will not have to attack. It will fall like an overripe fruit into our hands."

I first ran across this "overripe fruit" fabrication in the May, 1964, issue of a little Right-Wing propaganda monthly, issued by a group calling itself California Liberty Bell, Inc. in San Diego, California. I sent a letter to the author of the article,

Col. Fred S. Stevers, U.S. Air Force, Retired, challenging him to prove the authenticity of the quotation he had attributed to Lenin. The Colonel replied cordially that the quotation comes from the *Collected Works of Lenin,* Russian Edition; that I might have some difficulty locating the Lenin volume in my home town of Elsinore; that he was enclosing a U.S. Senate Document containing the quotation. It is a publication of the Senate Internal Security Subcommittee. It simply reprints, as part of a Hearing of the Subcommittee, a fantastic document submitted to the Committee by a Colonel Tom Hutton, retired Air Force intelligence operative. Hutton called his document "The Supreme Court as an Instrument of Global Conquest." Hutton and the group that he heads up will be discussed in another chapter; and we shall also come back to Colonel Stevers.

A close examination of the document shows that Colonel Stevers had no basis for relying on "a Senate Document." The Senate only printed Colonel Hutton's statement as part of the Report of its Hearings. It is therefore Colonel Hutton who is furnishing the phoney Lenin quotation in a footnote on page 1077, prefacing it with the words: "Lenin's exact language." Incidentally, on the same day that Colonel Stevers' letter arrived, I received a letterhead of the American Committee to Free Cuba. Listed on the Advisory Board is the name of Colonel Stevers and such Right-Wing worthies as John Rousselot of the John Birch Society, Kent Courtney, Jose Norman, Walter Knott, Phyllis Schlafly, Congressman James B. Utt, and others.

We are now ready to examine the proof that Lenin Fabrication, No. 2, the "overripe fruit" yarn, is a fraud.

In 1950, the Bureau of Intelligence and Research of the United States Department of State published a large volume entitled *Soviet World Outlook, a Handbook of Communist Statements.* In its own words, it is "a handbook of major statements by Communist leaders from Marx to Khrushchev." Inasmuch as we have already shown that the State Department was slyly spreading the Lenin Fabrication, No. 1, the "piecrust" fraud, one can be sure that this document would not omit anything that the Cold Warriors of the State Department could use in its anti-Soviet propaganda campaign. A careful examination of the third revised edition, released in July,

1959, shows that Lenin Fabrications, No. 1 and No. 2, *are not quoted.* The reason is very obvious. Not only can these statements not be found in any of Lenin's writings and speeches, but they are so out of character that the State Department would discredit itself if it used them in a document prepared by its Bureau of Intelligence and Research.

On May 21, 1964, I asked the Library of Congress to institute a search for the "overripe fruit statement." The following reply was received from Robert H. Land, Chief of the General Reference and Bibliography Division of the Library of Congress.

### THE LIBRARY OF CONGRESS

WASHINGTON, D. C. 20540

REFERENCE DEPARTMENT
GENERAL REFERENCE AND BIBLIOGRAPHY DIVISION                    June 11, 1964

Dear Mr. Kominsky:

    According to Mr. Pistrak of the United States Information Agency, an expert on Communist statements, it is extremely improbable that Lenin ever made the statement you quote. The Library of Congress, Mr. Pistrak, and others have searched fruitlessly for verification of this quotation. In addition, according to Mr. Pistrak, since Lenin was almost wholly uninterested in the United States (his interest lay in the hope of a Communist revolution in Europe), it is unlikely he would have made such a statement.

Very truly yours,

Robert H. Land
Chief
General Reference and
Bibliography Division

In order not to leave any loopholes in my research, I sent a letter on September 21, 1964, to Mr. Donald H. Holmes, Chief of the Photoduplication Service of the Library of Congress. I asked him to send me a photocopy of page 172 of Volume 10, *Collected Works of Lenin*. I explained that I especially wanted the quotation attributed to Lenin:

First we will take Eastern Europe, then the masses of Asia, then we will encircle the United States, which will be the last bastion of capitalism. We will not have to attack. It will fall like an overripe fruit into our hands.

On October 20, 1964, Mr. Holmes sent me a report which stated that the alleged Lenin quotation is "not identified in available Russian and English editions." Mr. Holmes also sent me the following memorandum which he received from Robert V. Allen, Area Specialist (USSR) of the Library of Congress.

UNITED STATES GOVERNMENT

# Memorandum

LIBRARY OF CONGRESS

TO        Donald H. Holmes, Chief          DATE: October 20, 1
          Photoduplication Service

FROM      Robert V. Allen, Area Specialist (USSR)
          Slavic and Central European Division

SUBJECT: Attached photocopy of letter from Morris Kominsky

> This Division has been asked a number of times about the quotation given by Mr. Kominsky, stated to be found on page 172 of volume 10 of the Collected Works of V.I. Lenin. We have examined that page in the tenth volume of all editions of the works of V.I. Lenin available in LC and have not found the quotation.

Mr. Bryan W. Stevens, teacher at San Marino (California) High School and former Lieutenant in the U.S. Navy, discusses the "overripe fruit" quotation in his book, *The John Birch Society in California Politics, 1966*. On page 111 Mr. Stevens says:

41

Now, there is no record that Lenin ever wrote or said this. Research scholars at Stanford University have pored over Lenin's works, the Curator of the Slavic Room of the Library of Congress has tried to track the quotation down. Even Louis Budenz, now fairly discredited professional anti-Communist, wrote in the March-May issue of the *Communist Line Bulletin,* that this quote from Lenin is one of the "many questionable quotations from Lenin that are floating around in ill-informed anti-Communist circles."

We can give the final burial to this fabrication by quoting from an article by Kenneth D. Robertson, Jr. in the Ultra-Rightist *Task Force* of October, 1964. Mr. Robertson tells us that the "overripe fruit" story is "a popular quotation spuriously attributed to Lenin." Despite its fraudulent nature, this phoney story is continually used to poison the minds of unsuspecting and gullible citizens.

## Lenin Fabrication, No. 3

Tom Anderson is the owner and publisher of *Farm and Ranch* magazine with circulation of over 1,300,000. He also publishes a number of other farm magazines, and writes an editorial column entitled "Straight Talk," which is carried in many publications across the country. A 1962 brochure of the John Birch Society lists him as one of the founders of the Society. In a notice inserted with the August and October, 1961, Bulletins of the Birch Society, it was announced that the Birchers were launching An Essay Contest for the American Undergraduate. The subject was Grounds for Impeachment of Earl Warren. Among the five judges for the contest was Tom Anderson. Anderson is also a participant in a number of other Ultra-Rightist groups.

In his "Straight Talk" column, *Farm and Ranch* magazine, August, 1960, Anderson tells us:

Lenin said: "We will find our most fertile field for infiltration of Marxism within the field of religion, because religious people are the most gullible and will accept almost anything if it is couched in religious terminology."

On May 2, 1963, the Committee of Christian Laymen of Woodland Hills, California, issued a reprint of Tom Anderson's August, 1960, column, and called it "More Straight Talk Regarding the National Council of Churches of Christ." On

July 19, 1963, a research assistant of mine wrote to Tom Anderson, asking where in Lenin's writings this quotation could be found. In his letter of reply, dated August 30, 1963, Anderson wrote, in part:

With respect to the quotation used in my August 1960 "Straight Talk" editorial, a reprint of which is enclosed, I find that the statement attributed to Lenin was made by him shortly after the Bolshevik Revolution in Russia, and was taken by me from the tract, "How the Communists Are Penetrating Our Churches," by Captain Edgar C. Bundy, Executive Secretary of Church League of America, Wheaton, Illinois, one of the outstanding authorities on Communist infiltration. Captain Bundy's statement will be found on p. 4, of the tract referred to, and which I am enclosing. I must ask that the tract be returned to me, since I have only the single copy.

An inquiry addressed to Bundy, who is also known as Major Bundy, brought a terse reply on September 26, 1963:

With regard to your question concerning Lenin's statement, the quote was given to Mr. Bundy by Joseph Zack Cornfeder.

Aside from the fact that Kornfeder's name was misspelled, Kornfeder died on May 2, 1963, and it was no longer possible to check with him. However, as we shall see when we examine the Manuilsky hoax, Kornfeder was not among the most trustworthy of witnesses.

On December 4, 1964, I sent the following letter to Ex-FBI Agent Dan Smoot:

On page 381 of your issue of *Dan Smoot Report* of December 1, 1964, you attribute to Lenin the following: "We will find our most fertile field for infiltration of Marxism within the field of religion, because religious people are the most gullible and will accept anything that is couched in religious terminology." I challenge the authenticity of this quotation. I have seen this used before, and I know that it is a fabrication. Furthermore, it is in diametrical opposition to anything that Lenin ever said or wrote about religion. Even if you consider that your use of the quotation is a paraphrase, due to the fact that you did not use quotation marks, it is a fake. The fact that you used bold-faced type, in effect makes its use a direct quotation. Please advise me what you are relying upon?

On January 6, 1965, Mr. Smoot sent me a long letter, from which I quote the first two paragraphs:

43

The Lenin material has been used by numerous persons for many years. The actual text varies widely in the many places where I have seen it. Yet, the meanings is always the same. I summed up the meaning and presented it in paraphrased form. I do not have time to do your research for you, but can quickly give you leads for a start toward proving to yourself that Lenin did order infiltration of churches so that they could be destroyed from within.

Smoot then goes on with some out-of-context quotations and references to writings of Lenin which do *not* prove his point. In fact, the first two paragraphs of his letter, which I have quoted, prove the following:

1. Smoot is evasive. He refers to the "Lenin material" rather than the specific quotation.

2. Smoot admits to tampering with quotations attributed to Lenin by second-hand sources and admits that *he* "summed up the meaning and presented it in paraphrased form."

3. Smoot is arrogant and petulant when he answers that he does not have time "to do your research for you." I did not ask him to do research for *me*. I asked him to do research to prove that Dan Smoot is an honest man.

Dan Smoot is thoroughly familiar with the writings of Lenin, and could easily find evidence that Lenin never wrote such atrocious nonsense. Smoot might have considered the following from page 22 of Volume 7 of *Little Lenin Library*, where Lenin writes:

We must not only admit into the Social-Democratic Party all those workers who still retain faith in God, we must redouble our efforts to recruit them. *We are absolutely opposed to the slightest affront to these workers' religious convictions. We recruit them in order to educate them in the spirit of our programme, and not in order to carry on an active struggle against religion.* (Emphasis is mine— M. K.)

The Rev. G. Archer Weniger is Professor of Practical Theology at the San Francisco Conservative Baptist Theological Seminary and pastor of the Foothill Boulevard Baptist Church in Oakland, California. In addition to his vociferous defense of the House Un-American Activities Committee, Dr. Weniger has compiled a brochure entitled *Has Communist Thought Penetrated the Church?*, in which he has used the phoney Lenin quotation.

On February 4, 1966, I sent Rev. Weniger a letter from which I quote the two most pertinent paragraphs:

Inasmuch as Lenin never wrote or said this, I would appreciate your advising me where you obtained this alleged quotation.

May I also suggest that, unless you can produce documentation to prove that Lenin ever said or wrote this, you should publish a retraction in accordance with the Commandment: Thou Shalt Not Bear False Witness Against Thy Neighbor.

On February 11, 1966, Rev. Weniger wrote me:

Thank you so kindly for your letter of February 4 bringing to my attention your assertion with respect to the widely reported statement by Lenin. We appreciate your bringing this to our attention. We will be glad to look into it.

On April 1, 1966, I sent Rev. Weniger the following letter, for which I hold a postal receipt signed by a member of his staff, Chuck Baker:

Dear Dr. Weniger:

On February 4, 1966, I wrote to you advising you that you had used an alleged Lenin quotation, which Lenin had never said or written.

In response to my challenge to retract this falsehood, you simply stated in your letter of February 11, 1966, that you would "look into it."

I consider this an inadequate and unresponsive reply to my challenge.

Please advise whether or not you intend to publish a retraction.

I am writing you again before closing my file on this matter, because I do not wish to do you an injustice in my forthcoming book.

*Cordially yours,*
MORRIS KOMINSKY

I have not received a reply from the Rev. G. Archer Weniger. Perhaps he will claim that it is God's will that falsehood and deceit are necessary means to combat Communism. One cannot help wondering why truth is not used!

## Lenin Fabrication, No. 4

The Ultra-Rightists have derived considerable "mileage" from a bogeyman story which appeared in the *American Mercury*, February, 1961, p. 106:

We have it on the word of no less than Nikolai Lenin himself that a small number of persons with their eyes open could have nipped Communism in the bud 44 years ago. "If there had been in Petrograd in 1917 a group of only a thousand men who knew what they wanted, we never could have come to power in Russia."

The *American Mercury* headlined the story: "Eyes Open," and stated that it was being quoted from *Christopher Notes*.

On August 30, 1964 I asked the Library of Congress to check the authenticity of this alleged Lenin quotation. The reply, which is herewith reproduced, shows the difficulty of tracking down fake quotations.

**THE LIBRARY OF CONGRESS**

WASHINGTON 25, D. C.

REFERENCE DEPARTMENT
SLAVIC AND CENTRAL EUROPEAN DIVISION

SEP 9 1964

Dear Mr. Kominsky:

This is in reply to your letter of August 30.

The pressure of official duties for the Congress and other government agencies does not permit us to undertake an extensive search of Lenin's voluminous writings. To authenticate an isolated Lenin quotation is often akin to finding a needle in a haystack.

A very cursory examination of some portions of the third edition of Lenin's works in Russian has failed to disclose any statement resembling the one about which you inquired. However, obviously we cannot state that such a statement was not made by Lenin.

Sincerely yours,

*Sergius Yakobson*

Sergius Yakobson
Chief, Slavic and Central
European Division

Mr. Morris Kominsky
400 East Franklin Street
Elsinore, California 92330

Airmail

46

On September 1, 1964, a research assistant, who must remain anonymous for the present, sent a letter to Father James Keller, director of The Christophers, asking that he furnish proof of the authenticity of the alleged Lenin quotation. The reply, which is here presented, is not only evasive, but employs a common Right-Wing dodge. When caught using a phoney quotation, they offer something that "means the same" to *them!* In this case, the "similar quotation" is also a fake. (In photocopying Father Keller's letter, we have deleted the name of our research assistant. See page 48.)

We are safe in branding Father Keller's Lenin quotation as a fake, because it definitely clashes with Lenin's known ideological and philosophical posture.

The State Department's *Soviet World Outlook—A Handbook of Communist Statements,* 1959 edition, does *not* contain this alleged Lenin quotation. It would tax one's credulity to expect that the Cold Warriors of its Bureau of Intelligence and Research would overlook such a "juicy" item. In fact, on page 80, they give a quotation from Lenin which definitely disproves the validity of the phoney quotation. Lenin wrote:

To be successful, insurrection must rely not upon conspiracy and not upon party, but upon the advanced class. That is the first point. Insurrection must rely upon the revolutionary spirit of the people. That is the second point. Insurrection must rely upon the crucial moment in the history of the growing revolution, when the activity of the advanced ranks of the people is at its height, and when the vaccilations in the ranks of the enemies and in the ranks of the weak, half-hearted, and irresolute friends of the revolution are strongest. That is the third point. . . .

The final proof of the impossibility that Lenin ever made the statement attributed to him by Father Keller and *The American Mercury* is in the actual historical facts of the two Russian revolutions of 1917. Harrison Salisbury, who spent some years as a reporter in the Soviet Union and who is now the Assistant Managing Editor of the *New York Times,* summarized it excellently and succinctly in the *New Republic* of July 3, 1965:[6]

Russia's February (non-Communist) Revolution occurred because the existing Czarist Government disintegrated. No revolutionary

[6] Quoted by permission of *The New Republic,* copyright 1965, Harrison-Blaine of New Jersey, Inc.

16 East 18th Street. New York. N.Y. 10017

September 9, 1964

Dear Mr.

It was good to hear from you. Would that we could
supply you with the information on the statement by Lenin,
but unfortunately, we no longer have this data since it
was first used many years ago. Should it ever come to light
again, we'll be happy to let you know. Meanwhile, we are
typing off a similar quotation with references which may interest
you as well as the enclosed Christopher News Notes.

Blessings to you, Mr.

Sincerely in Christ,

*James Keller*

Father James Keller, M.M., director                    Phone PLaza 9-1050

"Without doubt, an oppressed multitude had to be liberated.
But our method only provoked further oppressions and atrocious
massacres. You know that my living nightmare is to find myself
lost in an ocean red with the blood of innumerable victims. To
save our Russia, what was imperative to have...but it is too late
now to alter the past...was ten Francis' of Assisi. Ten Francis'
of Assisi and we would have saved Russia." Lenin.

Msgr. M. d'Herbi ny, "Le Message du Christ." Lecture given at
La Semaine Sociale de Versailles. Quoted in Lettres de Rome Sur
l'Atheisme Moderne, 1937, pa, e 173. Published by the Pontificio
Instituto Russo, Piazza Santa Mag iore, Rome, Italy/

48

leader of consequence was even in the country (Lenin was in Switzerland, Trotsky in New York and Stalin in Siberia). None of them had the faintest notion that Russia was on the brink. Lenin, indeed was despondent.

But, under the impact of war, the Czarist system fell apart. It succeeded in alienating its strongest defenders—the nobility, the army, the industrialists. Even the Imperial family had begun to line up against the Czar. Thus, the February Revolution occurred without plan, without conspiracy, without leaders.

But what of the Communist seizure of power following November 7? Surely, this was a skillful coup d'etat carried on by a secretive group of revolutionary plotters with Lenin at the head. Again, the reality bears little resemblance to the legend. Everyone in Petrograd knew the coup was to be attempted. The plans had been published in the Petrograd press (several leading Bolsheviks had quit the party in a public row over Lenin's proposal). The Bolsheviks won not because of their skill but because the feeble Kerensky regime was staggering toward collapse.

I think that the only error in Salisbury's analysis is that he has underestimated the importance of Lenin's political perspicacity and psychological acumen: his ability to judge the proper timing of the coup d'etat which ushered in the Communist (Bolshevik) assumption of state power. Otherwise, Salisbury is eminently correct.

In order to leave no stone unturned in our documentation, I sent a letter on August 4, 1966 to Dr. Herbert Aptheker, Director of the American Institute for Marxist Studies, who is probably the foremost authority in this country on the writings of Lenin. I asked Dr. Aptheker about Lenin Fabrication, No. 4 and also about Father Keller's "similar quotation." Dr. Aptheker replied bluntly:

Certainly, neither written nor spoken by Lenin!

Now that we have given Lenin Fabrication, No. 4 a decent burial, the reader can be sure that the Ultra-Rightists will continue to resurrect the corpse. It is very effective in scaring the daylights out of the Birchers, Birchsymps, and their followers. A case in point is a long letter in the *San Diego Tribune* of April 21, 1966. The writer raves about *Red Nazis* and Godless tyranny. His entire tirade is predicated upon the Lenin Fabrication, No. 4. But the readers of the *San Diego Tribune* have no way of knowing that the foundation of the monologue is a

49

falsehood. Nor do the readers have any way of knowing who Mr. Tedis Zierins is, and why he writes from 2118 West Schiller Street, Chicago, Illinois to a San Diego, California paper. This is as good a time as any to introduce the reader to a new social phenomenon in the United States—a network of Ultra-Rightists, who write propaganda letters to newspapers, magazines, public officials, broadcasting stations, and other places where they want to inject their doctrines. One such group is the Network of Patriotic Letter Writers, with headquarters in Pasadena, California, about which more will be told in another chapter.

## Lenin Fabrication, No. 5

Dr. Robert Henderson Kazmayer of Rochester, N.Y., a Methodist Episcopal minister, left the ministry in 1939 to devote full time to writing and lecturing. He is a 32nd Degree Mason. He is a member of the Rotary Club, Union League Club, Adventurers Club, Overseas Press Club, and the American Academy of Political Science. His loyalty to the status quo is attested by the fact that in 1961 he was awarded the George Washington Honor Medal by that most unique propaganda organization of Big Business, Freedoms Foundation at Valley Forge. Kazmayer has travelled extensively.

In *This Week* magazine, which is a Sunday supplement to many newspapers, we find on February 7, 1965 an article entitled "Lincoln versus Lenin" by Robert Kazmayer. Senator Frank Carlson of Kansas saw it while reading the *Washington Star*, and he was so enamoured of it that he placed it in the *Congressional Record* on February 11, 1965, page 2564. In singing hosannas to the Rev. Kazmayer, Senator Carlson said:

"Mr. Kazmayer, a publisher, lecturer, and world traveler recently returned from a trip to Russia, where a visit to Lenin's tomb inspired the following thoughts, which I shall read into the *Record*. These are Mr. Kazmayer's words:"

I thought of the contrast between the two. You go down into the darkness in Lenin's tomb. At the Lincoln Memorial you ascend the steps in the light. You look down on Lenin; you raise your eyes to Lincoln. I don't want to be melodramatic about this thing, but there is a contrast between those two leaders, Lenin and Lincoln. Lenin spent his whole life setting class against class. Abraham Lin-

50

coln said, "You can't help the poor by attempting to destroy the rich. You can't raise up the wage earner by pulling down the wage payer."

Lenin said: "One would like to caress the masses, but one doesn't dare; like a dog they will turn and bite." Abraham Lincoln said, "God must have loved the common people; he made so many of them."

Lenin said, "This is a fight to the end, to their extinction"—and yours and mine and all who will not bow to the hammer and sickle. Abraham Lincoln said, "With malice toward none; with charity for all."

Lenin said, "There's nothing right or wrong in the world, there's nothing false or true except as it furthers the revolution." That's dialectical materialism for you. Abraham Lincoln said, "With firmness in the right as God gives us to see the right."

The first quotation from Abraham Lincoln, the one about helping the poor and destroying the rich, is of course taken directly from the phoney Lincoln decalogue, which we exposed under the heading of *Lincoln Fabrication, No. 2.*

Taking the remaining Lenin quotations in sequence, we will call them Lenin Fabrication No. 5, Lenin Fabrication No. 8, and Lenin Fabrication, No. 14. For the present, we shall deal with No. 5, and come back to the other two a little later.

On February 20, 1965, a research assistant sent a letter to Dr. Kazmayer, asking for the source of the three Lenin quotations. On March 27, 1965, Kazmayer wrote from the Miyako Hotel in Kyoto, Japan:

> The quotations from Lenin are taken from his Collected Works. This is a many-volumed set . . . at the moment I can't remember how many . . . was printed in England and I found it in the British Museum . . . which as you probably know contains the equivalent of our Library of Congress.
>
> These quotations have been in my notebook for a number of years now. In fact I put them in originally only because they were such a contrast to the statements of Lincoln.

Then our scholar goes on to assure us that we can probably find the Lenin quotations without his help.

With the help of Library of Congress, we were able to determine the source of the phoney Lenin quotations which Dr. Kazmayer used. On May 17, 1965, we sent a long letter to Dr. Kazmayer, giving him the documentation to prove that these three Lenin quotations are phoney. We received a letter, dated

May 21, 1965, from his Rochester, New York office, signed by his secretary, Mrs. Arline Greenwell:

Dr. Kazmayer is still on his trip around the world. I am forwarding your letter that it may have his personal attention.

We did not hear from Dr. Kazmayer in reply to our letter of polite, but firm, criticism.

The Lenin Fabrication, No. 5, as given by Dr. Kazmayer is:

Lenin said: "One would like to caress the masses, but one doesn't dare; like a dog they will turn and bite."

Lenin, of course, never uttered such balderdash. Kazmayer has presented a garbled version of something from a book, entitled *Lenin and the Russian Revolution* by Christopher Hill, published in London during 1947 by Hodder and Stoughton, Ltd. On page 220, Mr. Hill writes:

Lenin once said to Gorky, after enjoying a Beethovan Sonata: "But I can't listen to music too often. It affects your nerves, makes you want to say stupid, nice things, and stroke the heads of people who could create such beauty while living in this vile hell. And now you mustn't stroke anyone's head—you might get your hand bitten off. You have to hit them on the head, without any mercy, although our ideal is not to use force against anyone. H'm, h'm our duty is infernally hard."

Skipping an unimportant small paragraph of Mr. Hill's, which follows immediately after the above, Mr. Hill observes:

Hatred of tyranny and oppression because of their degrading effects on oppressors and oppressed alike was the moral force behind Lenin's loathing for tsarism, for any system of economic exploitation or national subjugation.

It is clear that there is nothing in the above quotations to justify the Rev. Robert Kazmayer's Lenin quotation. And it is clear that the meaning of all this is:

1. Lenin expressed amazement that musicians could compose beautiful music, even under conditions of poverty, deprivations, oppression, and civil war.

2. Lenin found it difficult to relax and enjoy music while he saw so much human suffering around him.

3. Lenin expressed regret and sorrow that the civil war which followed the revolution, demanded stern and Draconian measures to suppress the counter-revolutionary conspirators.

4. Lenin's remarks that "You have to hit them on the head, without mercy," is, of course, metaphorical. This is easily understood from his qualifying remark that "our ideal is not to use force against anyone," and that it is done only when necessary.

The headline and first paragraph of a story by Frank Finch in the *Los Angeles Times* of August 6, 1966 illustrate a point:

### SHADES OF ALAMO!
### DODGERS, KOUFAX
### MASSACRE ASTROS

HOUSTON—The undermanned Astros, their ranks decimated by injuries and defections, underwent Texas baseball version of the Alamo when they were massacred Friday by the Dodgers, 12-1, before 46,555 eyewitnesses to the bloodletting.

Just imagine what a Russian counterpart of Dr. Kazmayer could do by a *literal* translation of the American idiom, contained in this colorful description of a peaceful activity!

## Lenin Fabrication, No. 6

Millions of people believe the *Reader's Digest* almost as much as their Bible. They hardly suspect its Right-Wing bias, its planted articles, and its shocking falsifications. A classic example of the *Digest*'s method is an article entitled "How the Reds Make a Riot," by Eugene Methvin, in its issue of January, 1965. The reader is told that Methvin is a member of its Washington staff and that the article is "based on four years of research." The article is given an air of authenticity by the *Digest*'s claim that: "It represents scores of case studies of Red riots, plus hundreds of interviews with the FBI, CIA, Secret Service, police experts, academic and military-intelligence authorities, and former communists who have personally organized strikes and riots."

The *Digest* depends on the fact that most of its faithful readers would not discern the obviously tendentious nature of an article based almost entirely on secret police sources. It is hardly research when one starts with a premise and seeks out only those sources that will help confirm a preconceived notion.

Some people liked Methvin's article. The Right-Wing *Fire and Police Research Association* of Los Angeles sent out reprints, along with the January 1965 issue of its monthly publication, *FIPO News*. The speed with which FIPO was able to get reprints from the *January* issue of the *Digest* in time to send them out with the *January* issue of *FIPO News* suggests that FIPO may have collaborated with Methvin. Harding College, at Searcy, Arkansas, is considered the "West Point" of the Ultra-Right. It is a veritable propaganda mill of pamphlets, brochures, films, tapes and maps. Its *National Program Letter* of April 1965 devotes a full page to lavish praise of Methvin's article.

As usual, an article of this kind in the *Digest* inspires a series of ponderous editorials, quoting the "authoritative" *Reader's Digest*. The *Courier* of Madison, Indiana, January 18, 1965, told its readers that Methvin's article, "Based on 4 years of research," "discloses that so-called 'spontaneous demonstration' in many parts of the world are in fact carefully staged by Communists and their dupes." In similar vein there were editorials in the *Post Tribune*, Jefferson City, Missouri, January 4, 1965 and the *Daily Plainsman* of Huron, South Dakota on May 2, 1965. This is only a small part of the total number of solemn warnings, but these are the ones placed in the *Congressional Record* by Senator Karl Mundt on May 14, 1965. The Senator is noted as a Red-hunter and an advocate of repressive legislation.

The article consists largely of a rehash of the usual charges made by the witch-hunters of the House Un-American Activities Committee and its retinue of professional stoolpigeons. At the very outset Methvin says:

A communist leader knows that if he chooses proper slogans, gathers a crowd and agitates it, he can create a riot. The techniques of starting a riot are as simple, as scientific and as systematic as that.

Not only is this completely untrue, but it is an insult to the intelligence of the readers. How does Methvin know that "a communist leader knows"? Does he produce one Communist leader who ever said this? Does he name one Communist leader who told him this? Methvin does not do so, because it is strictly a Methvin-FBI invention. (Methvin had the help of the FBI in the preparation of his opus). Furthermore, any competent psychologist, psychiatrist, or sociologist could have told Methvin that riots are not started in this fashion; human behavior is quite different from the pattern suggested by the sage of *Reader's Digest*. Methvin and the *Digest* can peddle such nonsense under the guise of research, because no one can talk back to the *Digest*; it does *not* print letters-to-the-editor. All you can do is stop buying it.

Methvin proceeds to blame every demonstration, every struggle, every riot on to the Communists. It never dawns on him that human beings struggle against oppression, injustice, and poverty in the only way open to them. One wonders how Methvin would have described the Boston Tea Party of the American Revolution! The nearest Methvin comes to understanding the struggles of hungry people is his reference to "food marches in India"! What a cute description of a horrible state of affairs, where people die of hunger in the streets of this vast country! A story by Rudy Abramson from Washington in the *Los Angeles Times*, February 1, 1966, quotes testimony before the House Agriculture Committee by Dr. W. H. Sebrell, Jr. of Columbia University school of public health, regarding conditions in India:

It is estimated 70% of the children in developing areas suffer from malnutrition and upwards of 3 million children die annually from malnutrition. This fact is hidden because these deaths often are recorded as being from diarrhea, parasites and infectious diseases. If these children were well nourished, they would not die of these diseases.

Abramson summarized the testimony by reporting that:

Estimates have been made that 10 to 15 million Indians will die of starvation this year.

What shall we say about a man's four years of "research" that can only see protests against such horrors as "food marches" and as riots created by Communist leaders using "proper slogans"?

Throughout his essay Methvin makes statements without furnishing proof, excepting to quote anonymous and faceless characters, such as: 1. "Experts, reconstructing the Panama explosion, unearthed these facts." 2. "An amazed American witness stood beside a radio commentator. . ." 3. "A Panamanian carrying a camera . . ." 4. "Reliable authorities identified . . ."

All this leads us to the Methvin discovery of the century. With perfect safety from a libel suit, Methvin explains that the riots of 1964 and 1965 really began in Longjumeau, France. Yes indeed, Methvin traces our trouble to a "clandestine communist school" where Lenin allegedly taught in 1911! Referring to Lenin, Methvin says:

His bold boast: "When we have companies of especially trained worker-revolutionaries who have passed through a long course of schooling, no police in the world will be able to cope with them." Today, from a worldwide collection of data, including captured documents and interrogations of defectors from training schools, the step-by-step stages of Red-manipulated violence can be fully revealed.

On February 10, 1965, my research assistant addressed a letter to Eugene Methvin, asking for the source of this alleged Lenin quotation. On February 15, 1965, Mr. Eugene Methvin replied, with a very cordial letter, stating:

The Lenin quote which you inquired about is from his pamphlet *What Is To Be Done?* which he wrote in 1901. One version of the quote can be found in *Lenin: Collected Works* (Moscow: Foreign Languages Publishing House, 1961, Volume Five, page 473). In this book the translation is slightly different from the one I used, which I took from the article by J. Edgar Hoover in the *American Bar Association Journal,* February 1962. This translation of the quote, according to the FBI, was taken from a translation of *What Is To Be Done?* published in New York by a communist publishing house around 1926.

So far, the following conclusions emerge: a. Methvin reveals that he had FBI collaboration in the preparation of his essay. b. Methvin admits that he took his alleged Lenin quotation from a second-hand source, in spite of his awareness of the original source. c. His reference to different versions of the quotation lays the groundwork for some subsequent squirming out of a tight situation. d. Methvin seems to see nothing wrong in trying to explain social phenomena of 1964 by quoting something written by Lenin 63 years earlier, under conditions of Czarist oppression!

A comparison of the Lenin quotations as given by Eugene Methvin and John E. Hoover should prove enlightening:

| Methvin version in Reader's Digest, January 1965 | John E. Hoover version in American Bar Association Journal, February 1962 |
|---|---|
| When we have companies of especially-trained worker-revolutionaries who have passed through a long course of schooling, no police will be able to cope with them. | When we have companies of special trained worker-revolutionaries who have passed through a long course of schooling . . . no police in the world will be able to cope with them. . . . |

At first glance it appears that both versions are identical, but a closer examination reveals an essential, and even a crucial, difference. *Mr. Methvin omitted the multiple dots in the two places where Mr. Hoover had used them to indicate omissions.* And a *responsible* writer is duty-bound to check out the original sources, when confronted with multiple dots. Otherwise, he risks a repetition of another person's error or deliberate misrepresentation. In four years of research, Mr. Methvin apparently did not check the original source, but was satisfied to rely upon the authority of the head of a secret police organization. We shall soon see how valid is this criticism.

| From What Is To Be Done? page 221 | From Lenin: Collected Works, Foreign Language Publishing House, 1963, Vol. V, page 473 |
|---|---|
| As the spontaneous rise of the working-class masses becomes wider and deeper, they promote from their ranks not only an increasing number of talented agitators, but also talented organizers, propagandists and "practical workers" in the best sense of the term (of whom there are so few among our intelligentsia who, for the most part, in the Russian | As the spontaneous rise of their movement becomes broader and deeper, the working-class masses promote from their ranks not only an increasing number of talented agitators, but also talented organizers, propagandists, and "practical workers" in the best sense of the term (of whom there are so few among our intellectuals who, for the most |

manner, are somewhat careless and sluggish in their habits). When we have detachments of specially trained worker-revolutionaries who have gone through extensive preparation (and, of course, revolutionaries "of all arms"), no political police in the world will then be able to contend against them, for these detachments of men absolutely devoted to the revolution will themselves enjoy the absolute confidence of the widest masses of the workers.

part, in the Russian manner, are somewhat careless and sluggish in their habits). When we have forces of specially trained worker-revolutionaries who have gone through extensive preparation (and, of course, revolutionaries "of all arms of the service"), no political police in the world will then be able to contend with them, for these forces, boundlessly devoted to the revolution, will enjoy the boundless confidence of the widest mass of the workers.

(This pamphlet, *What Is To Be Done?*, is a series of essays taken from Volume V, *Lenin: Collected Works*, Fourth Russian Edition; translated from the Russian by the Institute of Marxism-Leninism, and distributed by Foreign Languages Publishing House. These essays were written in February of 1902).

A close examination reveals some slight differences in translation, but nothing of an essential nature. The two translations convey almost precise meanings. A comparison with John E. Hoover's version shows a definite and shocking *exercise in deception* by the author of *Masters of Deceit*, the man who called Dr. Martin Luther King "this country's most notorious liar."

Hoover's deceptions are many-folded. First of all, Hoover's version is not a quotation from Lenin, but rather it is Hoover's *paraphrasing* of Lenin's remarks. Therefore, it was literary deception to place his paraphrase in quotation marks, when he planted it in his article in the *American Bar Association Journal* of February, 1962. Secondly, Hoover deliberately changed "political police" to "police," dropping the word "political." This is most shocking, because Hoover knows, or should know, that Lenin was not discussing police in general, as Herr Eugene Methvin tries to make the *Reader's Digest*'s followers believe. Lenin was writing in 1902 to inspire Russian workers and peasants to revolt against one of the world's most brutal and tyrannical despotisms and its *political police*, the dreaded Ochrana, which was the precursor of Hitler's Gestapo. The third Hoover deception is the omission of the words that follow his second series of multiple dots, to wit:

". . . for these forces, boundlessly devoted to the revolution, will enjoy the boundless confidence of the widest masses of the workers."

In other words, Lenin was advocating the training of revolutionary cadres that would be so integrated with the broad masses of the people that the Ochrana would not be able to destroy them. But Hoover deceitfully twists and garbles Lenin's words to serve his need of hysteria, behind which he is able to get increased appropriations each year and maintain his position of Mr. Untouchable!

On March 5, 1965, my research assistant wrote Eugene Methvin again, calling to his attention the discrepancies of both Hoover and Methvin. All the above documentation was given in the letter. On March 12, 1965, Methvin replied in a lengthy and petulant letter. Methvin advanced some new and novel justifications for the practice of journalists' misrepresentation:

1. "It is a common and perfectly ethical journalistic practice to pare away the verbal underbrush in popular magazines such as ours so long as the original meaning of the quote is not changed or distorted. (Writing for the *American Scholar* or *Foreign Affairs* or even the *American Bar Journal* is another matter.)"

*Comment*: It is indeed a common journalistic practice of Right-Wing partisans of the Cold War to twist and distort and fabricate. Methvin calls this: paring away "verbal underbrush." And he ignores the point that the Methvin-Hoover quotation was a flagrant and shocking misrepresentation! It *did* change and distort Lenin's clear meaning.

2. Methvin opines further in his letter that "people often argue about the fairness of some quote taken out of context; but don't you realize the utter absurdity usually involved in this kind of logic? It would mean, ultimately, that nobody could ever quote anything since the 'original context' would not be perfectly preserved, too."

*Comment*: The sophistry employed here by Methvin hardly

59

needs comment, excepting to point out that an honest and reasonable person can determine how to quote another person without doing violence to the self-evident meaning of the quoted passage. Methvin is here trying to obscure truth by making a simple matter sound hopelessly complex.

3. Methvin argues next that Lenin's remark about "no political police in the world" proves that in 1902 Lenin was planning to build a "world-wide organization" in order "to subvert *every* nation, democratic, monarchial, or what-have-you."

*Comment*: For the purpose of his letter, Methvin speaks of Lenin's reference to "political police," but conveniently over-looks the crucial point that Methvin and Hoover had previously changed "political police" to "police" per se, when they were quoting Lenin! And how inconsiderate Lenin was in misleading poor Mr. Methvin by referring metaphorically to "no political police *in the world*"! By the Methvinian system of logic, when-ever a woman remarks that she has the "best husband in the world," she must come under suspicion. For the rest, it is clear that Methvin's attempts to extrapolate from Lenin's remarks have a close resemblance to Robert Welch's conspiracy theory of history.

4. Methvin's next point is that you cannot trust the Moscow government translations of Lenin's works from Russian into English; that Lenin and his followers use "Aesopian jargon" to disguise their real meaning and intent; and "I have read enough of Lenin's works and studied his operations sufficiently to say quite emphatically that the quotation as we published it was a fair and accurate reflection of his meaning."

*Comment*: No, I did *not* invent the above quotation. That is exactly what Methvin wrote and it is not quoted out of context. Nor is this a novel approach in Right-Wing circles. It is custom-ary for Right-Wing propagandists to give their own definitions of words and their own explanations of other people's philos-ophies. By Methvin's logic you can prove anything you want to prove about anyone. All you need do is set yourself up as the infallible interpreter of another person's writings and, after setting up a straw man, you proceed to demolish it with specious arguments and fallacious reasoning.

5. Methvin's final point, after advising that my research assistant should "study Lenin a little more closely and broadly," was:

Let me add, too, that you are simply flat wrong in accusing J. Edgar Hoover of misquoting Lenin, since he took his quote directly and verbatim (except for those dots you get so dithered about) from a different English translation of *What Is To Be Done?* published by a communist publishing house in New York. There is nothing so mysterious, insidious or invidious about this difference in translations. You'll find such differences in every translation of the same original work, be it Marx, Lenin, Jesus Christ or Chaucer.

*Comment*: On May 11, 1965, my research assistant sent Mr. Methvin a long letter, embodying all of the comments I have made so far and pointing out that Methvin was arguing against Methvin. Methvin had said that you couldn't easily understand Lenin's true meanings; then he had urged a further study of Lenin's writings. In order to meet his challenge of alleged inaccuracy of the Moscow translators of Lenin's works, we offered to obtain a Library of Congress photocopy of the pertinent page from the original *Russian* edition of Lenin's writings and then obtain an independent translation by a competent scholar of repute in this country.

On May 17, 1965, Methvin sent my research assistant an angry letter of reply, again harping on the differences in translations. What is most interesting, however, is a rather novel ploy. Methvin now referred to a pamphlet published in Chicago in 1926, entitled *Lenin on Organization,* in which he claims they quote Lenin as saying merely "police" instead of "political police." Not having access to this pamphlet I can only say that it is not an official translation of Lenin's works, but most likely a compendium. In any case, I cannot check the accuracy of Methvin's claim; nor am I inclined to accept his statement at face value. But even if he is telling the truth this time, it is completely irrelevant to our discussion. Methvin stated very distinctly in his letter of February 15, 1965, that the Lenin quotation that he used was taken from John E. Hoover's article in the *American Bar Association Journal* of February, 1962; that "This translation of the quote, according to the FBI, was taken from a translation of *What Is to Be Done?* published in New York by a communist publishing house around 1926."

During the 1920's the only authorized English translations available in the U.S.A. of Lenin's writings were an 8-volume set entitled *Collected Works of V. I. Lenin,* issued by International Publishers, New York, in 1929, and a 12-volume set entitled *Selected Works of Lenin,* printed in the U.S.S.R. and distributed by International Publishers. In Volume IV of the *Collected Works* the quotation in question is on page 206; in the *Selected Works,* it is on pages 147-148. These translations are almost 100% identical with the one we quoted previously from page 221 of the pamphlet, *What Is to Be Done?* The same essay, under the identical title, is contained in both volumes. With exception of such insignificant variations as saying "labouring masses" instead of "working-class masses," all four versions of *What Is to Be Done?* use the term "political police" and contain the other qualifying sentences, which John E. Hoover chose to omit.

Therefore, in recapitulation, I charge John E. Hoover with perpetrating a gross deception and Mr. Eugene Methvin with using Hoover's deception without any attempt at verification. Furthermore, Methvin has stubbornly refused to publish a retraction or even to admit any guilt in the matter.

Returning to Methvin's *Digest* article. After quoting the truncated version of Lenin's writings in juxtaposition to a story about "a clandestine school at Longjumeau, France," where Lenin was a teacher, he tells about Communist techniques for agitating a crowd. His "proof" is "based largely on documents captured from the Iraqui Communist Party." Who captured the documents and how Methvin obtained them and how authentic they are—these questions are left unanswered. We simply have to believe Methvin and the *Digest.* One wonders how Methvin would feel if I told some stories about him, based on alleged documents obtained mysteriously thousands of miles away.

Further along in his article, Methvin admits that an "FBI investigation of the riots that swept Harlem and five eastern cities uncovered no systematic national organization or planning behind them," but this does not satisfy our expert. With the same specious arguments that he used to justify out-of-context quotations and distorted versions of another's writing, Methvin goes on to argue that it is not important whether or not Communists incited Negro revolts against inhuman conditions. "The lesson of Harlem," Methvin says, "is that Red wreckers *can* move in on any controversy, and every thinking person must be aware of their methods and objectives." Of course, it can just as easily be argued that Methvin can also move in on any controversy. There are many things that *can* transpire, but this is not the stuff of which one constructs a report "based on four years of research."

The most harmful aspect of the Methvin-Hoover-*Digest* school of sociology is that it diverts so many good citizens from a sensible and honest approach to the solution of social evils. As long as the "solution" to all problems is to blame it onto the Communists, it is obvious that this kind of propaganda is not in the best interests of our country. It partakes of the nature of the cancer quack whose greatest harm is the causing of delay in obtaining proper diagnosis. A case in point is an incident that occurred on Saturday night, June 19, 1965, in Laconia, New Hampshire. Several thousand motorcyclists converged on the city, after attending the races that were held on the shore of nearby Lake Winnipesaukee. A riot began when a group of leather-jacketed motorcyclists tipped over an auto and set it afire. They also set fire to a couple of buildings and a boardwalk. The police arrested and brought to court 32 youths. Public Safety Commissioner Rhodes stated that the riot was started by members of a group from California calling themselves Hell's Angels. This group has a record of causing trouble in many communities and has been linked in some places with the American Nazi Party. The Mayor of Laconia, Peter Lessard, 28 years of age, had apparently read the *Digest* article which appeared five months earlier. Giving evidence of having learned well the Methvin-Hoover-*Digest* formula, Lessard said that the rioting "was Communist-inspired." While Methvin traced rioting in 1965 to Lenin's alleged teachings at Longjumeau, France, in 1911, Mayor Lessard charged that Hell's Angels had been in Mexico "for special training on how to start riots." While Methvin based part of his story on documents "captured" in Iraqui, Mayor Lessard had "reliable reports" that instigators of the Saturday night riot were Communist-trained "riot mongers." The Mayor went on to say that he would ask the FBI to investigate. Nothing was said by the Mayor about turning over his "reliable reports" to the FBI. The U.P.I. dispatch in the *Los Angeles Times* of June 22,

1965, punctured Mayor Lessard's balloon by reporting that the Governor of New Hampshire "had no evidence to support Lessard's charge." Anyway, Mayor Lessard obtained some easy and cheap publicity by slandering people who, in the present climate of opinion, cannot retaliate.

Lest the reader think that my judgment of the Methvin-Hoover-*Digest* alliance is too harsh, a summary of the concluding section of Methvin's article should dispel such a notion. Just as Lenin wrote *What Is to Be Done?* Methvin concludes with *What Can Be Done?* Among other things, Methvin advises readers to get in touch with three Right-Wing Cold-War propaganda outfits. Another bit of advice is that citizens should "emulate the inspiring" example of the Brazilians who helped usher in the present Fascist dictatorship. Of course, Methvin does this under the guise of a call to defeat the Communists. Strange, isn't it, that the ultimate remedy of the anti-Communist crusaders is a Fascist dictatorship? Another Methvin recommendation is that Congress pass legislation establishing a so-called Freedom Academy. This is a thinly disguised plan for a stepping-up of the Cold War. Finally, Methvin shows his true colors by this piece of sage advice:

Wherever Red agents of violence set up party units or front groups, citizens must organize specific attack forces to wreck the wreckers before their organizations are deployed for action.

I can hear Methvin scream that I have taken his words out of context, that I should have quoted some sentences that followed the above quotation. I would have to reject such a protest on the ground that *in any context* Methvin's use of such terms as "citizens must organize attack forces to wreck the wreckers" is the same violent language used by Der Fuehrer of the Birch Society in the Blue Book of that Society. We have a right to consider such language "Aesopian jargon" to incite violence, especially when Methvin has urged his readers to emulate the dupes who helped establish Fascism in Brazil.

It is axiomatic that all Fascist drives begin with an anti-Communist crusade. They all use fake stories and phoney quotations. The Methvin-Hoover-*Digest* alliance owes the American people some better explanations than have been forthcoming from Mr. Methvin so far.

# Lenin Fabrication, No. 7

The Rev. Billy James Hargis operates the Christian Crusade, with headquarters in Tulsa, Oklahoma. Hargis tells the world that he is for "God and our children" and for "Christ-Centered Americanism." Under the cloak of religion, the Hargis propaganda mill grinds out a never-ending stream of Ultra-Rightist messages.

Seventy-four hours after the tragic death of President John F. Kennedy, Hargis wrote a long essay about the assassination; it appeared in the December, 1963, issue of *Christian Crusade* magazine.[7] It would seem from this essay that President Lyndon Johnson could have saved the taxpayers the expense of the Warren Commission investigation, because the Rev. Hargis had all the answers in this twelve-page essay. After stating that any man who would assassinate the President is *an anarchist* and that he holds anarchists in as much contempt as he holds the Communists, Hargis tells his readers at least sixteen times that the assassin was *a Communist*. And in the midst of all this he reiterates that a man "who would take the law into his own hands and become judge and jury is not a conservative—he is *an anarchist*." Billy has made it clear that he knows there is an essential difference between anarchists and Communists. Nevertheless, he calls Lee Harvey Oswald both a Communist and, inferentially, an anarchist. Nor is Hargis in any way disturbed by the fact that Lee Harvey Oswald was not convicted in a court of law by the "due process" which Hargis claims to uphold. In his frenzy of hate for the Communists, Hargis sets out to prove that President Kennedy was assassinated by an agent or a dupe of the Communists. How does he do it? By the simple device of reaching up to a shelf in his headquarters' library for Volume II of *Selected Works of Lenin* to get a quotation from page 17. In this essay, which he entitled "Reflections on the Death of the President," Hargis quotes the following:

We have never rejected terror on principle, nor can we do so. Terror is a form of military operation that may be usefully applied, or may even be essential in certain moments of the battle, under certain conditions, and when the troops are in a certain condition. The

---

[7] Hargis himself boasted about writing the essay within the seventy-four hours after the assassination.

point is, however, that terror is now advocated, not as one of the operations the army in the field must carry out in close connection and in complete harmony with the whole system in fighting, but as an individual attack, completely separated from any army whatever. . . .

Then he proceeded to gleefully cite this as proof that a Communist assassinated President Kennedy, blithely ignoring the fact that no proof had been presented that Lee Harvey Oswald actually was a Communist and the further fact that Lee Harvey Oswald was never tried and convicted in a court of law, but rather by propaganda issued by law enforcement officers. He followed the use of the Lenin quotation with these remarks:

From the days of Lenin up to this day, the communist conspirators have lived up to Lenin's instructions to use terror as a "form of military operation" in harmony with "the whole system of fighting" and also as "an individual attack completely separated from any army whatever."

These comments are a complete distortion of the truth. Had Hargis placed the Lenin quotation in proper context, he could not possibly get away with this, even with the most stupid and most ignorant of his followers. But even the quotation standing by itself is not susceptible of any such interpretation. Lenin is simply saying here that terror is sometimes used and is sometimes necessary as part of a military operation. He is trying to dissuade some hotheads from engaging in individual deeds of terrorism, deeds which would not be connected with a planned military operation. Lenin is not instructing anyone at this point to engage in acts of terrorism. He is simply stating some self-evident truths about the nature of most military operations.

Lenin is definitely *not* instructing anyone, in the quotation that Hargis used, to consider terror as "an individual attack completely separated from any army whatever." He is *reproaching* others for advocating such procedures. This is very clear, but Hargis brazenly put the words in Lenin's mouth and accused him of advocating something that he is categorically and explicitly condemning!

This essential departure from the truth is further compounded by a sin of omission. He did not tell his readers that the quotation he used was from something Lenin wrote in

66

May, 1901, under conditions of preparing a revolution against one of the worst tyrannies in human history. Furthermore, he left out the following sentence which comes right after the quotation that he used, and is in the same paragraph from which he quoted:

That is why we declare that under present circumstances such a method of fighting is inopportune and inexpedient; it will distract the most active fighters from their present tasks, which are more important from the standpoint of the interests of the whole movement, and will disrupt, not the government forces, but the revolutionary forces.

In addition, on the next page, Lenin wrote:

We would not for one moment assert that individual strokes of heroism are of no importance at all. But it is our duty to utter a strong warning against devoting all attention to terror, against regarding it as the principal method of struggle, as so many at the present time are inclined to do. Terror can never become the regular means of warfare; at best, it can only be of use as one of the methods of a final onslaught.

Now, in the context of a struggle against a brutal and tyrannical regime and under conditions where, in desperation, thousands of people are goaded into preparing to use terroristic tactics, here is Lenin wisely inveighing against such actions. But it did not serve Hargis' propaganda needs to tell the truth.

Finally, on page 19 of the Lenin volume from which Hargis quoted, Lenin points out that the most important task of the hour is *not terror, not violence, not assassination—but education!* Here are his exact words, which Hargis so conveniently left out:

In our opinion, the starting point of all our activities, the first practical step towards creating the organization we desire, the thread that will guide us in unswervingly developing, deepening and expanding that organization, is the establishment of an all-Russian political newspaper. A paper is what we need above all; without it we cannot systematically carry on that extensive and theoretically sound propaganda and agitation which is the principal and constant duty of the Social-Democrats in general, and the essential task of the present moment in particular. . . .

It is quite clear that the Rev. Billy James Hargis deliberately misrepresented Lenin's writings, which were right in front of him as he wrote his article. On June 23, 1964, a research assistant sent the Rev. Hargis a letter, pointing out the errors, distortions, and omissions; and it was suggested that an explanation should be forthcoming, as well as a full retraction and confession of sin.

The "God-fearing" staff at Hargis' propaganda mill tore our letter in half, stapled the halves together, and typed across the outside:

> Send your letter on to Russia. They
> could not agree with you more.

On the envelope, they addressed my research assistant by name, but prefaced it with:

## Mr.?

## Lenin Fabrication, No. 8

The Cold War propagandists who wish to oppose the idea of peaceful coexistence frequently quote Lenin, as follows:

As long as capitalism and socialism exist, we cannot live in peace; in the end, one or the other will triumph—a funeral dirge will be sung over the Soviet Republic or over world capitalism.

With some slight variations this quotation from Lenin is trotted out to "prove" that Lenin taught the inevitability of war and that this proves that the Soviet Union intends to attack militarily the U.S.A. The quotation, as given here, is exactly as quoted on page 96 of the State Department's document, *Soviet World Outlook: A Handbook of Communist Statements*. It correctly attributes it to page 297, Volume VIII, *Selected Works of Lenin* (International Publishers, New York, 1943).

The Cold Warriors of the Bureau of Intelligence and Research of the Department of State, as well as others who use this quotation, quote it out of literary context. Just by adding two short succeeding sentences, the correct meaning becomes clear. Here it is in proper context:

As long as capitalism and socialism exist, we cannot live in peace;

in the end, one or the other will triumph—a funeral dirge will be sung either over the Soviet Republic or over world capitalism. *This is a respite in war. The capitalists will seek pretexts for fighting.*
(Italics are mine—M.K.)

It is clear that Lenin was not advocating aggression. He was predicting aggression against the Soviets by their enemies! Furthermore, it was part of a speech delivered on November 26, 1920, under conditions which have little relevance to present-day realities. The speech was delivered after the Soviet Union had signed a peace treaty, which brought about a suspension of armed attacks by other countries. Consequently, its use by the Cold Warriors is deceitful, because it is taken out of historical context, in addition to being quoted out of literary context.

The Rev. Dr. Kazmayer had his own special version of Lenin Fabrication, No. 8. His article in the *This Week* supplement to the February 7, 1965 issue of the *Washington Sunday Star,* which we have previously discussed, solemnly declares:

Lenin said: "This is a fight to the end, to their extinction"—and yours and mine and all who will not bow to the hammer and sickle.

Of course, Lenin never wrote this, and the Rev. Dr. Kazmayer should know it.

## Lenin Fabrication, No. 9

Lenin is often quoted as advocating the use of ruses, subterfuges, and stratagems as a matter of Communist policy. Again the device of quoting out of context is used. An interesting sidelight is presented by Father James Keller, Director of *The Christophers,* which carries on a special kind of Cold War campaign. In *Christopher News Notes,* No. 134, March 1964, Father Keller exhorts his readers to lead an honorable life by "a constant awareness of God's presence and the avoidance of self-deception by an occasional checkup like this: . . ." The good Father lists 14 points of self-criticism, among which is:

Do I take words or facts out of context, or indulge in half-truths, thus giving a slanted, distorted or biased interpretation?

Did Father Keller forget that a few weeks earlier, in *Christopher News Notes*, No. 119, he quoted Lenin out of historical and literary contexts? As part of a number of false or unproved statements and garbled quotations, Father Keller quotes Lenin as saying:

> . . . It is necessary to be able to withstand all this, to agree to any and every sacrifice, and even—if need be—to resort to all sorts of stratagems, maneuvres and illegal methods, to evasion and subterfuges in order to penetrate the trade unions, to remain in them, and to carry on Communist work in them at all costs.

Father Keller correctly notes that the quotation is in *Selected Works of Lenin, Vol. 1*. Turning to this volume, we find, among others, a lengthy essay written on July 4, 1920, entitled *"Left-Wing" Communism, An Infantile Disorder*. (This essay has also been published as a separate pamphlet.) Lenin is here sharply criticizing a segment of the German Communists who were refusing to belong to trade unions that were corrupt and reactionary. Lenin proceeds to advise them how to work in unions that are led by and/or infiltrated by gangsters, crooks, hoodlums, agents-provocateur, opportunists, and spies. In this historical context, and considering Lenin's remarks in the relationship of time, place, and circumstances, we can better understand this quotation from page 95 of volume X:

*Undoubtedly, Messieurs the "leaders" of opportunism will resort to every trick of bourgeois diplomacy, to the aid of bourgeois governments, the priests, the police and the courts, in order to prevent Communists from getting into the trade unions, to force them out by every means, to make their work in the trade unions as unpleasant as possible, to insult, to bait and to persecute them.* It is necessary to be able to withstand all this, to agree to any and every sacrifice, and even—if need be—to resort to all sorts of stratagems, manoeuvres and illegal methods, to evasion and subterfuges in order to penetrate the trade unions, to remain in them, and to carry on Communist work in them at all costs. (I have italicized the portion which Father Keller omitted, because it did not serve his purpose. —M.K.)

Lenin goes on to point out how his strategy had successfully combatted the dirty work of the Russian counterpart of the Ku Klux Klan, the infamous Tsarist "Black Hundreds."

There is a poetic justice in a little error that Father Keller makes. Inadvertently, to be sure, he stated that the Lenin quotation is on pages 93-94. (It is actually on page 95.) When you turn to pages 93-94, you find something which completely discredits Father Keller's insinuations:

In order to be able to help "the masses" and to win the sympathy, confidence, and support of "the masses," it is necessary to brave all difficulties and to be unafraid of the pin-pricks, obstacles, insults and persecution of the "leaders" (who, being opportunists and social-chauvinists, are, in most cases, directly and indirectly connected with the bourgeoisie and the police); and it is imperatively necessary to *work wherever the masses are to be found.*

In the State Department document, *Soviet World Outlook: A Handbook of Communist Statements,* page 118, there is another type of tampering with the same quotation that Father Keller used. They quoted more than Father Keller did, but omitted some crucial lines, which they indicated by multiple dots. Thus, they presented another garbled version of what Lenin actually said.

It should also be noted that Father Keller knew that he was omitting the crucial explanatory remarks, because his version of the quotation begins with multiple dots to indicate omission.

## Lenin Fabrication, No. 10

One of the widely-used scarecrows is a slogan attributed to Lenin:

The Road to Paris leads through Peking.

This is supposed to prove that there is a Communist plot for world conquest. Thus the Ultra-Rightist columnist, George Todt of the *Los Angeles Herald Examiner,* pontificated on July 28, 1966:

It was the infamous—but correct—Nicolai Lenin who once told his Bolsheviks: "The Road to Paris Lies Through Peking."

The U.S. Government, as part of its Cold War propaganda campaign, issues a bi-monthly journal called *Problems of Communism,* edited by Abraham Brumberg. In an article that he wrote for the *New Republic,* August 29, 1960, Brumberg states that Lenin *never* made that statement. Brumberg argues: (1)

71

That world conquest "is hardly a *stated* Communist aim" and (2) that liberty and justice *"are* stated Communist goals." Brumberg takes the position that, even if "world conquest" were a Communist aim, Lenin would not say so openly.

The State Department's *Soviet World Outlook: A Handbook of Communist Statements,* in its foreword, points out that the business of paraphrasing Lenin's writings has "frequently assumed an unwarranted degree of authenticity." Continuing, it tells us:

Lenin is often quoted as saying:
"We will come to Paris by way of Peking."

or

"The road to Paris lies through Hong Kong and Calcutta."

or

"The way to Europe is through Asia."

or

"Asia is the key to Europe."

The State Department document then offers this astounding comment:

While none of these "quotations" can be documented, Lenin did say: "In the last analysis, the outcome of the struggle will be determined by the fact that Russia, India, China, etc. constitute the overwhelming majority of the population of the globe. It is precisely this majority of the population that during the past few years, has been drawn into the struggle for its emancipation with extraordinary rapidity, so that in this respect there cannot be the slightest shadow of doubt what the final outcome of the world struggle will be. In this sense, the final victory of socialism is fully and absolutely assured."—Lenin—"Better Few, But Better" (1923), *Selected Works* (International Publishers, New York, 1943), Vol. IX, p. 400.

There is, of course, not the slightest justification in the above quotation for any of the variations of the Road-to-Paris-via-Peking fabrication.

## Lenin Fabrication, No. 11

In a speech to the New York Republican Club on July 12, 1960, Governor Nelson Rockefeller quoted Lenin as having said the following:

Our immutable aim, is, after all, world conquest. Soviet domination recognizes neither liberty nor justice. It is erected knowingly upon the annihilation of the individual will, upon unconditional submission to the work relationship as in other human relationships. We are, after all, the masters. Repression is our right. It is our duty to employ absolute severity and in accomplishment of such a task great cruelty can signify supreme merit. By employment of terror and its auxiliaries, treason, perjury, and the negation of all truth, we shall reduce humanity to a state of docile submission to our domination.

It will be noticed by the discerning reader that this phoney quotation bears a resemblance to some of the others. It embodies the concepts of world conquest, deceitfulness, brutality, and repression—it makes good propaganda for justifying a war "to save freedom"! There is one thing wrong: it is a complete fabrication. The proof is: 1. The *style* of writing cannot be found in any of Lenin's voluminous writings. 2. It clashes with everything Lenin ever spoke or wrote. 3. The State Department document, which has been alluded to several times, does *not* quote it. 4. U.S. Government expert, Abraham Brumberg, in his *New Republic* article of August 29, 1960, labeled it spurious and tells us how it originated.

Governor Rockefeller obtained the quotation from Adolph A. Berle, Jr. Berle, in turn, obtained it from "a Swiss scholar," Claude Meyer. And this latter worthy picked it up in some now-defunct Swiss newspaper. It is also worthy of note that Governor Rockefeller finally admitted that the quotation could not be documented, and he dropped it from his list of quotations. 5. David Shub, who wrote a biography of Lenin in 1948, was quoted by the *New York Times* as labeling this Lenin quotation "a fraud." 6. Victor Lasky, a well-known free-lance writer told the *New York Times* that this quotation is "a hoax" and that "there are factories in Europe that manufacture quotes of this sort." To which we can add, that there are some lie factories in this country too!

On December 28, 1966, we sent a letter to Governor Rockefeller's press secretary, Mr. Leslie Slote, in which we asked the following questions with respect to *Lenin Fabrication, No. 11:*

Where and under what circumstances was this quotation obtained? Has the Governor retracted this statement publicly? If so, where does the retraction appear?

We prefaced these questions by stating that we knew the quotation is phoney. No reply was received.

After sending two more letters, to which we did receive replies, Mr. Leslie Slote finally wrote, in a letter dated April 4, 1967, that "in regard to a quotation used by Governor Rockefeller in 1960, the quotation used by the Governor was used in good faith and to the best knowledge of our researchers and was believed to be accurate." This reply, is, of course, not responsive to the questions we asked. Furthermore, we obtained this reply only after we sent the Governor's secretary some of our proof of the phoney nature of that Lenin quotation.

## Lenin Fabrication, No. 12

According to the operators of the anti-Communist lie factories, Lenin is supposed to have written the following in 1919:

We shall force the United States to spend itself to destruction.

This scarecrow is frequently trotted out by opponents of welfare programs and foreign aid programs. Right-Wing scribes and orators wax eloquent when "disclosing" this "secret" strategy of Lenin and his disciples.

In an excellent essay that appeared in *Harper's* magazine of March, 1961, Professor David Spitz of Ohio State University tells an hilarious story of trying to establish the truth about this alleged quotation. What follows is a summary of the professor's story.

On February 22, 1960, the Columbus *Dispatch,* which modestly calls itself "Ohio's Greatest Newspaper," carried a half-page advertisement of the Timken Roller Bearing Co., one of America's giant corporations. It featured a picture of Lenin with a hammer-and-sickle on either side of his head. Superimposed on his chest was:

"WE SHALL FORCE THE
UNITED STATES
TO *SPEND* ITSELF
TO DESTRUCTION"

Nikolai Lenin
(Red Boss 1917-1924)

In addition to stating that Timken had first used this propaganda item some ten years earlier (in an advertisement on September 3, 1950) Timken asked this question:

Is Lenin's Prophecy Coming True?

Professor Spitz wrote a letter to the Timken Company, requesting the volume and page number in Lenin's writings where the alleged quotation could be found. Almost immediately he received this reply from the *Superintendent of Labor Relations* of the Timken Company:

I am told by our Public Relations Department in Canton that this is a literal translation of a speech by Lenin, made before the Soviet Presidium in 1919. It can be found in Volume 21, of Lenin's Collected Works.

Professor Spitz teaches political science, and he thought that he was familiar with Lenin's writings. Moreover, he found it somewhat incongruous that Lenin would be plotting a devious conspiracy against the world's most powerful nation at a time when he was faced with the superhuman task of prosecuting a revolutionary struggle and simultaneously rebuilding a country that was largely in ruins. Nevertheless, the professor searched Volume 21 in both the English and Russian editions. All to no avail! So, the tenacious professor wrote Timken again, pressing for more specific information. Receiving no reply within the next two weeks, Professor Spitz wrote Timken a third letter, this time in a more stern tone. In reply, the Manager of Public Relations for Timken wrote:

Our investigations into the subject show that while Lenin may not have said verbatim "We shall force the United States to spend itself to destruction," the substance of what Lenin writes in Volumes 21 and 22 of his Collected Works amounts to substantially the same thing. Thank you very much for your interest and concern in the Timken Company's institutional advertising.

Professor Spitz writes that he "sat for a time in numbed amazement staring at this unapologetic statement." The professor is, of course, somewhat naive. He would not have been so startled had he been aware of the fact that, this particular gambit of inventing quotations and then retreating to a previously prepared position of interpreting the writings of an-

75

other person, is the line laid down by the Cold Warriors of the Bureau of Intelligence and Research of the Department of State and is followed by many of the propagandists in the Ultra-Rightist camp.

There is a sequel to the saga of this search for truth. Professor Spitz sent copies of the entire correspondence, together with a letter, to the Managing Editor of the Columbus *Dispatch*. He requested the editor's assurance that the *Dispatch* would not accept this misleading Timken advertising in the future. He received a perfunctory reply that the matter was being turned over to the Director of Advertising for consideration. Twice more did the doughty professor write to the *Dispatch* in an attempt to elicit a definite reply to his request. But his efforts were in vain with "Ohio's Greatest Home Newspaper," which Professor Spitz describes as a paper that "wages daily war against political sin and intellectual heresy." The professor adds wryly that by these the *Dispatch* means any views or practices not favored by hard-shell Republicans.

There is an interesting postscript to this story which illustrates the ruthless disregard for truth by the Ultra-Rightists. The July, 1966, newsletter of the Network of Patriotic Letter Writers advises the faithful:

Write to President Johnson demanding deep cuts in government spending. Remind him that Karl Marx predicted that Communism would spend Capitalism to death.

This, of course, is a switch from Lenin to Marx. Needless to point out, Marx also never wrote such nonsense. The cuts in government spending, which the diligent ladies of the Network prefer, are any and all welfare programs that affect the lives of the poor people.

Additional research has disclosed that Lenin Fabrication No. 12 first appeared in Professor John Maynard Keynes' book, *The Economic Consequences of the Peace,* published in 1920. Later it was picked up by Senator William A. Jenner of Indiana, a member of the Republican Party's Right Wing. In voting against the Marshall Plan, in March 1948, Jenner argued that it would "please Stalin to have the United States spend itself into bankruptcy." Subsequently, President Eisenhower and his Secretary of the Treasury, George M. Humphrey, used this scarecrow fabrication repeatedly. The irony of this story is that Keynes himself, fifteen years later, advocated huge programs of government spending to shore up the economy, and as a result the Ultra-Rightists have written books and tracts accusing him of being a stooge of the Communists or a crypto-Communist!

In the John Birch Society magazine, *American Opinion*, November 1967, Garey Allen quotes from an item in the *Chicago Tribune* of September 3, 1967, which discusses the delegates to the National Conference on New Politics:

> They recall Lenin's dictum that the United States someday would be forced to spend itself into a financial crisis which would make it vulnerable to a Communist-led revolution.

Neither the *Chicago Tribune* nor the *American Opinion* explain how the delegates can recall a non-existent dictum! Like "Ole Man River," the Big Lie Keeps Rolling Along!

## Lenin Fabrication, No. 13

One of the propaganda lies of the wealthy physicians who control the American Medical Association was neatly exposed by Congressman Andrew Biemiller of Wisconsin on July 13, 1950 (*Congressional Record,* page 10117):

> There is the slander campaign against national-health insurance which calls it socialized medicine despite the fact that the AMA well knows it is not socialized medicine at all. Part of this campaign is the attempt to use the completely discredited alleged quotation from Lenin that "socialized medicine is the keystone of the arch of the Socialist state." The AMA has been called upon to either document or stop using that quotation, many, many times. Its officials have admitted that the quotation cannot be documented. Experts at both the Library of Congress and the University of Chicago have declared there is no such statement in the known works of Lenin. Yet the quotation continues to be used in published material, in public speeches, and in political assaults. The use of such falsehoods is typical of the AMA approach to issues of public health, and they can no longer be defended on the lame grounds of ignorance of the truth. *They are willful perversions of the truth.* (Italics are mine.—M.K.)

Isn't there something monstrous about the idea that men of power and wealth will try to block much-needed health insurance for the poor by dangling the scarecrow of a phoney Lenin quotation? And even if Lenin had said this, what would be its relevance forty or forty-five years later? Must millions of Americans be barred forever from adequate medical care because of something Lenin wrote? How crazy can we become?

## Lenin Fabrication, No. 14

A phoney quotation, used in many variations, is calculated to scare religious people especially. It is to the effect that Communists have no morality. Thus Dr. Robert H. Kazmayer, as we pointed out before, wrote in his *This Week* article, which appeared as a supplement to the Washington *Sunday Star* of February 7, 1965:

Lenin said: "There's nothing right or wrong in the world, there's nothing false or true, except as it furthers the revolution." That's dialectical materialism for you.

This is neither a quotation from Lenin nor a part of the philosophy of dialectical materialism. *It is a distorted and garbled version of something Lenin wrote.* It is the concoction of a man who is less than honest. The sheer lunacy of such a doctrine should be very obvious. The truths, that water is $H_2O$, that peroxide is $H_2O_2$, that sulphuric acid is $H_2SO_4$, are independent of any relationship to revolution. The famous Einstein equation that ushered in the nuclear age, $E = MC^2$, is truth independent of social revolutionary theory. Heart surgery embodies techniques whose truth does not affect philosophies of revolution. Thousands of such examples could be cited, but these should suffice.

Pursuant to the advice contained in Kazmayer's letter, from which we quoted previously, we checked the writings of Lenin and discovered the source of the Rev. Dr.'s fabrication. In *Selected Works of Lenin,* Volume IX, pp. 467-483, we find that Lenin delivered a speech to the Young Communist League on October 2, 1920. On page 474 Lenin is quoted as saying:

But is there such a thing as Communist morality? Of course there is. Often it is made to appear that we have no ethics of our own; and very often the bourgeoisie accuse us Communists of repudiating all ethics. This is a method of shuffling concepts, of throwing dust in the eyes of the workers and peasants.

Sounds like Lenin anticipated the Rev. Dr. Kazmayer, doesn't it?

On page 475 Lenin elucidates further the changes of moral concepts that take place when an old social order is overthrown and a new one struggles to supplant it. On page 475 Lenin summarizes all this as follows:

That is why we say that for us there is no such thing as morality taken outside of human society; such a morality is a fraud. For us, morality is subordinated to the interests of the class struggle of the proletariat. What is this class struggle? It is—overthrowing the tsar, overthrowing the capitalist class.

There follows additional discussion in which this quotation is clearly and distinctly spelled out to mean that Communists must work tirelessly to wipe out illiteracy, ignorance, unsanitary conditions, and poverty; that the goal is a better life *in this world*. Central to the entire polemic is the concept that those who seek to advance the struggle against injustice cannot be bound by the ground rules or morality taught to them by their oppressors. More specifically, Lenin was exhorting his listeners not to follow the slave ethics taught to them by the Tsarist society and its subsidized church. A simple analogy will make this clear. During the American Revolution, Thomas Paine, Thomas Jefferson, Patrick Henry, George Washington, James Madison and others of similar caliber called upon the people to disregard the old ground rules and the philosophy of the divine right of kings, and they set forth instead the world-shaking revolutionary principles embodied in the Declaration of Independence.

There is a bi-weekly Red-Baiting sheet called *Tocsin*,[8] edited by George H. Keith, professor on the Davis campus of the University of California and published by Charles Fox, former instructor on the Berkeley campus. The issue of August 10, 1966 contains two phoney quotations attributed to Lenin. One is *Tocsin's* special version of Lenin Fabrication, No. 9, regarding the use of ruses and stratagems to outwit and outmaneuver crooks, gangsters, hoodlums, and agents-provocateur who get control of labor unions. The other phoney quotation, as given by *Tocsin* is:

---

[8] Since this was written, *Tocsin* has suspended publication.

79

(The) solid Communist principle as laid down by Lenin, who wrote: "We say that our (Communist) morality is entirely subordinated to the interests of the class struggle."

Aside from the fact that this quotation is torn out of both literary and historical context, Dr. Keith has deliberately altered the wording, shifting words from one sentence to another and adding the word "entirely," so that it reads "entirely subordinated." We sent a letter via certified mail, requesting that Keith tell us where we could find in Lenin's writings the version of Lenin Fabrication, No. 9 he had quoted. Our postal receipt bears the signature of George H. Keith by Charles Fox. No reply was received!

## Lenin Fabrication, No. 15

The Information Council of the Americas, a New Orleans-based Ultra-Rightist propaganda organization, vigorously participates in the Great Crusade. Its newsletter, *Victory*, of March 3, 1965 quotes Eugene Methvin of the *Reader's Digest* staff as saying that Lenin once commented:

Give me an organization of professional revolutionaries and I will turn the world upside down.

Following this, this "expert" on Communism observes: "and he has turned our century upside down."

Mr. Methvin is a specialist of sorts in the use of Communist "quotations," as we have shown in the discussion of Lenin Fabrication No. 6. Mr. Methvin made just a little change when he quoted Lenin. Lenin actually said: "Give us an organization of professional revolutionaries—and we will overturn Russia." This may be found in Lenin's *Collected Works*, volume 5, Foreign Languages Publishing House, 1961, p. 467.

The change from "we will overturn Russia" to "I will turn the world upside down" is not the only deception in this innocent-appearing item by Mr. Methvin. The greater deception lies in quoting *out of historical context*. Mr. Methvin is no fool. In fact, he is a pretty shrewd hombre. He is fully aware of the fact that Lenin was talking about overthrowing the brutal Czarist regime, and no matter what he said *in this context* some forty-five or fifty years ago, it has little or no relevance to

80

the problems in the age of the thermonuclear bomb. At a time when humanity teeters on the brink of the precipice of total annihilation, we have a right to expect our journalists to refrain from flippancy and/or downright irresponsibility. And so, we can now add *Lenin Fabrication, No. 15* to our "collection."

## Lenin Fabrication, No. 16

The August, 1967, edition of *National Program Letter,* issued by Harding College, the "West Point" of Ultra-Rightist propaganda, carries a front-page article, entitled "The Great Deception." The main thrust of the essay is an attempt to prove "the duplicity of World Communism." It begins with an alleged quotation from Lenin. The reader can judge who is guilty of duplicity by comparing the "quotation" given in the essay with the actual words that Lenin wrote in 1913:

| *National Program Letter* | Lenin, *Collected Works,* volume 19, page 28.[9] |
|---|---|
| People always have been and they always will be stupid victims of deceit and self-deception in politics. . . . | People always have been the foolish victims of deception and self-deception in politics, and they always will be until they have learnt to seek out the *interests* of some class or other behind all moral, religious, political and social phrases, declarations and promises. |

The reader will note that Lenin does not use the word "stupid," and that he *qualifies his prediction.* This qualification was deleted by *National Program Letter,* which shows the deletion by the use of multiple dots after the word "politics." The garbled version presented by the sages of Harding College is a little less than honest! The justification for this statement is that the secretary of the author of the *NPL* article wrote us a letter, in which she told us exactly where we would find Lenin's words. And the Library of Congress furnished a photocopy of the page in which those words appeared.

9 Foreign Languages Publishing House, Moscow, 1963.

# Lenin Fabrication, No. 17

*Freedom's Facts* is the monthly bulletin of the All-American Conference to Combat Communism. In its issue of November, 1967, an "Intelligence Brief" says, in part:

> War between the U.S. and Communist China is now a major goal of the Kremlin. This is unconfirmed, but from a usually reliable source from inside the Communist bloc.
>
> The tactic is not new for Moscow. Lenin boasted in 1920 that he had "set Japan and America at loggerheads" and that Russia had gained an advantage from this. He added: "By all means, defeat America."

Nowhere in the State Department publication, *Soviet World Outlook,* can one find anything resembling these alleged quotations from Lenin or anything suggesting a boast by Lenin. A search by the Library of Congress determined that in a Moscow regional conference of the Russian Communist Party, Lenin did say, in the course of a speech on November 21, 1920:

> ... today I read a communication which said that Japan is accusing Soviet Russia of wanting to set Japan against America. We have correctly appraised the intensity of the imperialist rivalry and *have told ourselves* that we must make systematic use of the dissension between them *so as to hamper their struggle against us.*[10]

It is clear that the words "set Japan and America at loggerheads" and "By all means, defeat America" were not used by Lenin. The language that he did use is understandable when one recalls that in 1920, memories of invasion of Soviet territory by some nineteen Capitalist countries were still fresh in the minds of Soviet leaders.

Another fact that should have been considered by the editor of *Freedom's Facts* is that the Soviet Union fought on the side of the United States *against Japan,* since Lenin made that speech! Which is a case of actions speaking louder than words. Finally, if the gentleman were to consider facts rather than *unconfirmed* reports from his mysterious "usually reliable source from inside the Communist bloc," he would tell his readers that war between the U.S.A. and China would involve the

---

10 Lenin, *Collected Works* (Moscow, Progress Publishers, 1966) volume 31, pages 442-443. Emphasis has been added.

U.S.S.R. and that the Soviet Union wants peace above all other things.

## Lenin Fabrication, No. 18

In the September, 1967 issue of *Freedom's Facts,* the editor quotes "an old dictum of Lenin":

Why should freedom of speech and freedom of the press be allowed? Why should a government which is doing what it believes to be right allow itself to be criticized? It would not allow opposition by lethal weapons. Ideas are much more fatal things than guns.

In response to our query of October 11, 1967, Donald L. Miller, the editor, replied that he had obtained the quotation from "Lenin, quoted in *Nieman Reports,* Jan. 1956." After considerable difficulty, we obtained a copy of that issue of *Nieman Reports,* and found that it is not *Nieman Reports* which quotes Lenin, but rather that *Nieman Reports* carries a speech delivered by United States Solicitor General Simon E. Soboleff. The alleged Lenin quotation is in Soboleff's speech. This is a crucial difference which Donald L. Miller and other anti-Communist crusaders continually ignore.

We addressed an inquiry to the Hon. Simon E. Soboleff, who is now Chief Judge of the United States Court of Appeals at Baltimore, Maryland. We pointed out to Judge Soboleff that the alleged Lenin quotation does not appear in *Soviet World Outlook, A Handbook of Communist Statements,* issued by the Bureau of Intelligence and Research of the State Department, and that an inquiry sent to the Library of Congress brought a reply, which said: "A number of guides to Lenin's life and views were consulted without finding this quotation." Judge Soboleff wrote to us on February 27, 1968:

I do not have the notes from which I prepared the speech which was published in the *Nieman Reports,* and I am unable to cite the source of the quotation you mentioned. Of one thing I can assure you, I did not invent it. I read it somewhere, and not anticipating the necessity of documentation, I did not retain the notation.

I am very sorry that I cannot be more helpful in clarifying the matter.

On the basis of the known public record of Judge Soboleff,

we are certain that he speaks the truth, but it is a sorry state of affairs that even honorable people will pick up Lenin "quotations" from dubious sources and, by using them, give them the stamp of authenticity. This furnishes ammunition to the Ultra-Rightists in their campaigns of fear and smear.

Following the receipt of Judge Soboleff's letter, we wrote Donald L. Miller on March 6, 1968, giving him a full and detailed report of our research. We challenged him to publish a retraction. His reply, dated March 8, 1968, was cordial, conciliatory, and somewhat facetious. He said, in part:

We are grateful to you for your scholarship in respect to the quote, or, should I now say, alleged quote from Lenin on the subject of free speech. . . .

Ours is not a scholarly journal, and not everyone can work from original material on every item. As a popular publication we must depend in some cases upon the scholarship of others.

We assumed that the *Nieman Reports* would be a dependable source for this quote. Your painstaking research proves that while there is now at hand no proof that Lenin did not say or write the alleged quote, there is no proof that he did.

I will be happy to inform our readers that due to your research we have learned that the said quote may not be authentic. While this specific quote may not be authentic, and cannot be authenticated, in letter, it is in spirit.

On March 14, 1968, we wrote Mr. Miller a letter, which said, in part:

You do not seem to be responsive to the essential thrust of my criticism, viz: that you quoted the phoney Lenin statement in *ex cathedra* fashion, without giving the source upon which you are relying. Consequently, you must bear the responsibility and cannot mitigate your error by pleading the necessity of reliance upon scholarship of others. Nor can you plead for justification by citing the reliability of *Nieman Reports,* which I cheerfully concede is a reputable publication. *Nieman Reports* did *not* use the alleged Lenin quotation. It simply *reported a speech* by Solicitor General Soboleff, in which the alleged Lenin quotation was used. This is *not* tantamount to accepting responsibility for the accuracy of the speech, unless it contained clearly obvious fraud.

I cannot accept your argument that a phoney quotation (or a dubious quotation) becomes transformed into an authentic quotation, when you quote something that, in your opinion, conveys the "spirit" of the questioned quotation. I consider this kind of argument pure and unadulterated sophistry. A quotation must be a quotation, and it must be exactly as it was spoken or written by the person to whom it is attributed.

To his credit, Mr. Miller replied, agreeing substantially with our position, and said, in part:

Nor do I argue that a phoney quote can be made true by the discovery of similar quotes. Even considering the loose ends that come up in various translations, and I expect you read Russian as I do, a quote either is there or it isn't.

This is certainly a more forthright acceptance of our criticism than was displayed by Eugene Methvin of *Reader's Digest*. In the April, 1968, issue of *Freedom's Facts*, Mr. Miller did publish a retraction of the phoney Lenin quotation, but vitiated its value by a tendentious series of statements, which, in effect, carry out the idea of presenting the "spirit" of the phoney quotation. We find this procedure quite akin to the charge of "spectral murder" that was used against some of the victims of the Salem witchcraft delusion. It is difficult to answer such irrationalities, even when one uses truth as a weapon.

## Lenin Fabrication, No. 19

Of all the dragon-slayers on the House Committee on Un-American Activities, none is more prolific in discovering "secret" documents with which to expose the "witches" than Congressman John M. Ashbrook of Ohio. The Congressman, who has links with Fascist groups in other countries, placed a document in the Congressional Record, November 21, 1966, which he obtained from a propaganda mill in Munich, Germany, that calls itself the Institute for the Study of the U.S.S.R. It consists of excerpts from an article that appeared in a 1961 issue of an obscure Russian magazine, *Novy Zhurnal*, which is published in New York City. The author, one Yury P. Annenkov, relates a tale which consists, in summary, of: 1. That three weeks after Lenin's death on January 21, 1924, he had access to "a mass of photographs, printed articles and manuscripts," which included "some brief, fragmentary notes hurriedly jotted down by Lenin in his own hand with many of the words unfinished. . ." 2. That these notes were dated 1921. 3.

That he copied them surreptitiously into his notebook just in the nick of time, because soon afterwards "these pages of Lenin's jottings disappeared from the Institute and were hidden away in Party archives. . ." 4. That he carried this notebook in his pocket when he came to France. 5. That thirty years later he decided that these notes should be published, and he therefore translated them in French. 6. That Parisian newspapers, to whom he proffered his copied notes, all declined to accept them for publication in the absence of any documentation to prove their authenticity.

Mr. Annenkov relates that he told the editors of these newspapers that "it was up to the Soviets to prove that Lenin had not written the notes." As we have previously noted, this is just like challenging a person to prove that he is not guilty of "spectral murder." Mr. Annenkov can chalk up at least one victory: His tale made the Congressional Record both on November 21, 1966, and March 1, 1967. For the second insertion, Mr. Ashbrook found a neat little alibi. He explained that one paragraph had been omitted from the first insertion.

What was it that warmed the cockles of Mr. Ashbrook's heart so much that he was eager to place in the Congressional Record a dubious item from an obscure publication in New York by way of Munich, Germany? The alleged notes say that Lenin referred to Western intellectuals, who could not comprehend the situation in Russia during 1920, as "deaf-mutes"; that Lenin advocated the use of a number of ruses and stratagems "to placate the deaf-mutes"; that Lenin said: "Speaking the truth is a petty-bourgeois prejudice"; and Lenin said that, if Capitalist countries grant the Soviets commercial credits, the coffers of the respective Communist parties would receive ample funds.

The reader can easily appreciate that these alleged notes from Lenin's writings are simply a rehash of several of the Lenin Fabrications that we have already exposed. Is it any wonder that no reputable Parisian newspaper would touch Mr. Annenkov's discoveries? But anything, even from the gutters, is grist for the mill of the House Committee on Un-American Activities. As usually happens, Mr. Ashbrook's items in the Congressional Record furnished ammunition for Ultra-Rightists. One of these, the hate sheet, *Common Sense*, in its issue of January 15, 1968, gave its readers a garbled and doctored version of the Annenkov-Ashbrook "quotations" from Lenin, under the heading of:

## LENIN EXPRESSED IT AS FOLLOWS

It was all put neatly between quotations marks, and with no attribution to its source.

## Lenin Hoax No. 1

In *Parade* magazine, a Sunday supplement to many newspapers, there appeared on its *Intelligence* page on June 7, 1964, the following:

*Q.* Was Lenin financed by the Germans in World War I—George McCready, New Haven, Conn.

*A.* The Germans gave him $10,000,000 to incite rebellion in Russia.

On September 26, 1964, we sent a letter to *Parade's* editor, asking in the most courteous fashion for proof of this statement. *Parade's* office is at 285 Madison Avenue, New York City. In an envelope postmarked October 18, 1964, at Beverly Hills, California, we received in return a photocopy of *our* letter. Scribbled diagonally across the top, there was written in red crayon:

All the biographies on Lenin and also releases of German Foreign Office, Bonn.

Above this the writer had written his name, and then apparently tore off part of the sheet, so that all we could read was: L. Shen or L. Shin. Of course this is a most evasive and disingenuous reply. The German Foreign Office can hardly be a trustworthy source of information about Lenin. At best it would be as biased as the American Legion or the Central Intelligence Agency. And when the gentleman suggests that all the Lenin biographies tell that yarn, he is compounding the original falsehood. It just isn't true!

The historical facts behind this hoax are interesting. The yarn about Lenin being a paid German agent is a hoary and moth-eaten canard. It originally started with a much smaller sum of money, and by constant repetition the amount was finally upped to $10,000,000. You see, the lying business has its inflationary pressures too. As a matter of fact, the Imperial German government had its back to the wall and was desperate for finances. It just did not have the $10,000,000 to give Lenin. The only element of truth in the hoax story is that the German government did permit Lenin, who was an exile, to travel back to Czarist Russia. At the time it was German policy to let *every* political exile go back to Russia, hoping they would make trouble for its Czarist enemy. Lenin and his comrades arrived in Russia, by way of Finland, desperately broke. A wag has suggested that he donated the $10,000,000 to the Finns! At any rate, the imaginary $10,000,000 did *not* show up in Russia. But *Parade* and others can still peddle this hoax, because they know that no one will sue them for libel and, in the present climate of opinion, it is considered "subversive" to challenge the veracity of any anti-Communist fabrication!

## Lenin Biographies

A lucrative business has been developed since the Communists took power in Russia. It consists of "exposing" Communism and Communists. Any lie, any falsehood, any concoction, any hoax—there is a profitable market for all these and there is no shortage of gentry of elastic morals, who are looking for a fast buck.

In addition to the business of fabricating statements that Lenin never made, there is the profitable enterprise of grinding out biographies of Lenin. There appeared on the American scene during 1964: *The Life and Death of Lenin* by Robert Payne, selling for $8.50; *Lenin: The Compulsive Revolutionary* by Stefan T. Possony, selling at $7.95; and *The Life of Lenin* by Louis Fischer, with a price tag of $10.00. The best evaluation of these books, in this writer's opinion, comes from the pen of Dr. Frederick L. Schuman, one of this country's most distinguished political scientists. Dr. Schuman held the Woodrow Wilson Professorship of Government at Williams College, and has taught at the Universities of Chicago, Harvard, Cornell, Columbia, and California. He is the author of many books and magazine articles. The following are excerpts from an article in *The Minority of One*, February 1965, one of the most courageous magazines in the country:

I deem it deplorable that all three of these lengthy and laborious "biographies" of Lenin should begin by trying to discredit him on "racialist" grounds. This is a sad commentary on contemporary America, not on Lenin or on Russia. I take it for granted that after almost two decades (actually almost five decades) of Cold War no writer could find a publisher for a "favorable" biography of Lenin. Nor would I hail such a work, since I have never been a "Leninist." Yet devotion to truth is a value worth cherishing. All three of these works, dedicated to defaming Lenin, depart from truth at many points. And all three go through elaborate rituals of setting up straw men and knocking them down, with the straw all too obvious.

The worst offender is Robert Payne. His objective is not veracity but sensationalism—to make the best-seller list, if possible. He "proves" that Lenin had several mistresses, ordered the killing of German Ambassador von Hirbach and of the Romanov family in the summer of 1918, and was finally murdered by Stalin. In my judgment, all of this is fiction presented as fact with pretended "documentation" in "Chapter Notes" at the end of the book. The method is simple: any materials including Tsarist police records, French scandal sheets, German archives, etc., which denigrate Lenin are cited as valid authorities; any materials of opposite import are ignored or denied.

. . . His ignorance of the import of Lenin's books and articles is profound and comprehensive. His non-knowledge of Party history is colossal—*e.g.*, he calls Congress V of the Party (1907) the "London Conference." The disturbing fact is that his book is a Book-of-the-Month Club selection and has been "reviewed" by reputable journals as if it were in fact a biography of Lenin.

Stefan Possony's contribution to Leninist mythology requires less attention. He is part of the Cold War "Establishment"—Princeton, Georgetown, National War College, Naval War College, Air University, University of Pennsylvania, erstwhile colleague of Robert Strauz-Hupe, Goldwater enthusiast, and "political studies director" of the Hoover Institution of War, Revolution, and Peace at Stanford. His book on Lenin is the kind of book you would expect him to write. He is better informed and more sophisticated than Payne. . . .

Possony's conclusion: "Lenin's monstrous policies could not but beget worse monstrosities. In retrospect, the best that can be said about V. I. Lenin is that, had he recovered, he would have been purged by J. V. Stalin." No evidence, apart from prejudice, is offered to support this speculation. Indeed all the evidence points to exactly the opposite conclusion.

Regarding Louis Fischer's book, Professor Schuman says, in part:

The bulk of his book is devoted, quite rightly, to Lenin as political leader of the Soviet Union from 1917 until his death. In an appendix he demolishes Payne's myth that Lenin was poisoned by Stalin.

For the rest, Fischer's book is an impressive contribution to what we would like to know about Lenin. He does not "buy" the scandal stories. Yet I wonder why he writes: "He loved one woman—Inessa Armand." There is ample evidence that Lenin dearly loved his mother and his wife, Krupskaya. I also wonder why Fischer seeks to catch Lenin in contradictions in his voluminous writings and speeches. Contradictions are inevitable and necessary in all political leadership. Fischer's book is once more an anti-Lenin book, but an honest one.

All of these volumes assert or imply that the Stalinist totalitarian police state was implicit in Lenin's conception of the Party. This is a falsehood. The Soviet regime of 1917-18 was a coalition functioning democratically and with a minimum of repression. As the price of survival, it became a totalitarian police state, the first of our era, in the summer of 1918 only after it had been attacked with guns by its internal enemies and by American and allied interventionist armies bent upon its destruction. No reader of Payne or Possony or Fischer would ever guess this unless he already knew the facts.

It is important to emphasize once more that the purpose of setting the record straight regarding the entire field of anti-Communist crusading is two-fold: 1. As Professor Schuman has pointed out, decent people must indeed cherish truth. It has been said: "And ye shall know the truth, and the truth shall make you free." 2. We cannot achieve a peaceful world in an atmosphere of saints and devils, with the devils (Communists) being painted as sub-human creatures worthy of annihilation. This can only pave the way for annihilation of the human race in this era of the thermonuclear bomb. As the late President John F. Kennedy put it: "Mankind must put an end to war, or war will put an end to mankind." It is urgently necessary to understand unequivocally that the choice today is peaceful co-existence with the Communist countries or no existence for the entire human race. Accordingly, the record must be set straight and the truth must be told about the Communist countries and indeed about the Communist movement. It is going to take much intellectual courage and moral stamina for the American people to face the truth.

In view of the many lying stories and phoney biographies about Lenin, perhaps the following will serve as an antidote:

Perhaps the greatest man of modern times was Vladimir Ilyich

90

Ulianov. He took the name of Lenin, spent most of his fifty-four years in exile from his country, and gave the world the biggest new political fact of our era, the federal Union of Soviet Socialist Republics under a form of Communism.

The impression of integrated force he gave in life may be sensed in the portrait above, taken not long before his great step to power. Lenin was that rarest of men, an absolutely unselfconscious and unselfish man who had passionate respect for ideas, but even more respect for deeds. He had mastered the trick of complete concentration. He had a fantastic capacity for work and was scrupulous and thorough about the smallest, as well as the biggest, duties of his life. He spoke English, German and French, as well as Russian, and could read Italian, Swedish and Polish. He was a normal well-balanced man who was dedicated to rescuing 140,000,000 people from a brutal and incompetent tyranny. He did what he set out to do.

Lenin did not make the Revolution in Russia, nor did any one group of men. But he made the Revolution make sense and saved it from much of the folly of the French Revolution. It is impossible to imagine what the history of Russia and the world would have been had he not lived.

No, the above quotation is not from *Pravda,* is not from the *Daily Worker,* and is not from the *People's World.* You will find it on page 29 of *Life* magazine, March 29, 1943. That was the period when the Communists were our allies in the war against the Fascist countries, and *Life* devoted an entire issue to telling the truth about the U.S.S.R.! How times have changed!

## The Israel Cohen Hoax

Just as it was customary during the era of the Salem witchcraft delusion to label opponents as witches (or wizards), so in the period of the Cold War it has become standard procedure to label opponents "Communist," without defining the term. The free-wheeling style of attributing all the evils of the world to the Communists, makes it unnecessary to do any thinking about how to solve real problems. It has the same devastating effect as that of consulting a quack practitioner—it postpones the day of accurate diagnosis, often with disastrous results. All that is necessary in order to discredit anything is to label it "Communist." A case in point is the attempt of Congressman Thomas G. Abernathy of Mississippi to explain the Negro struggle for human dignity as a Communist plot.

91

On June 7, 1957, Mr. Abernathy delivered a speech on the floor of Congress in order to block the pending Civil Rights Legislation. After working himself up to the usual emotional pitch of the segregationists, the honorable gentleman delivered the following solar-plexus blow:

This civil-rights business is all according to a studied and well-defined plan. It may be news to some of you, but the course of the advocates of this legislation was carefully planned and outlined more than 45 years ago. Israel Cohen, a leading Communist in England, in his *A Racial Program for the 20th Century,* wrote in 1912, the following:

> We must realize that our party's most powerful weapon is racial tension. By propounding into the consciousness of the dark races that for centuries they have been oppressed by the whites, we can mould them to the program of the Communist Party. In America we will aim for subtle victory. While inflaming the Negro minority against the whites, we will endeavor to instill in the whites a guilt complex for their exploitation of the Negroes. We will aid the Negroes to rise in prominence in every walk of life, in the professions and in the world of sports and entertainment. With this prestige, the Negro will be able to intermarry with the whites and begin a process which will deliver America to our cause.

What truer prophecy could there have been 40 years ago of what we now see taking place in America, than that made by Israel Cohen? The plan was outlined to perfection and is being carried out by politicians who have fallen into the trap. Many thousands in America today who are in no sense Communists are helping to carry out the Communist plan laid down by their faithful thinker, Israel Cohen. Truly, vigilance is the price of liberty.

Congressman Abernathy's presentation was the inspiration for a rash of statements, speeches, and editorials "proving" from "official documents" that the Negroes would not think of fighting injustice, oppression, and humiliation, were it not for the diabolical plotting of the Communists.

The only things wrong with Congressman Abernathy's story are:

1.  There was no Communist Party in England, the United States of America, or anywhere else in 1912!

2.  At the request of the *Washington Star,* the Library of Congress conducted a search in 1958, and could find no record of the alleged book entitled *A Racial Program for the Twentieth Century;* nor could the Library find the quotation attributed to Israel Cohen by Mr. Abernathy. It is perhaps super-

fluous to point out that the research facilities of the Library of Congress are unexcelled, and if such a book were ever published, the Library of Congress would know about it.

3. The British Museum Catalog of Printed Books and all the other catalogs published in England from 1911 to 1915 contain no reference to the Israel Cohen book.

4. The National Union Catalogue, which summarizes the listings of 800 principal libraries in the United States, has never listed this alleged book.

5. The British *Who's Who* did list an Israel Cohen who was born in England in 1879. In response to an inquiry, he wrote a letter to the *Washington Star,* from which the following is excerpted:

I have never written a book, pamphlet or article under the title "A Racial Program for the Twentieth Century," or under any title resembling this or any subject relating to it . . , I have never been a Communist or had any sympathy with the movement . . . I am credited with a long list of books, pamphlets, etc., but none of them has anything to do with Communism or the Negro question.

To the above, it should be added that Israel Cohen openly campaigned for the election of Winston Churchill. And even John E. Hoover never called Churchill a Red.

6. The internal evidence of the quotation proves its fraudulent nature. The words "Communist Party" were not used in the English language in 1912, and only came into usage after 1916. The term "guilt complex" is a psychiatric term that did not come into usage until many years *after* 1912.

All the above evidence of refutation will be found in a presentation by Congressman Abraham Multer in the *Congressional Record,* August 30, 1957, page 16777, and a three-column full-length article on the editorial page of the *Washington Star* of February 18, 1958. It is strange that Ultra-Rightists and anti-Semites quote Abernathy's presentation in the *Congressional Record* of June 7, 1957, and ignore the incontrovertible refutation in the *Congressional Record* of August 30, 1957, some eleven weeks later. And the excellently researched article in the *Washington Star* some eight months later has meant nothing to the professional liars.

On September 3, 1963, I sent Congressman Abernathy a letter, asking him the following three questions:

1. Where did you get this story about that leading Communist in England, Israel Cohen?
2. Did you ever see any documentary proof of the existence of his "A Racial Program for the 20th Century"?
3. Did you ever retract your story after Congressman Abraham Multer's refutation in the *Congressional Record* of August 30, 1957, page 16777?

On September 6, 1963, Mr. Abernathy wrote:

Replying your letter of September 3, the quotation included in my speech delivered in the House of Representatives on June 7, 1957, to which you referred, was taken from the Letters to the Editor column of the *Washington Evening Star* newspaper. This is the only source we had for the quotation.

On September 11, 1963, another letter was sent to Mr. Abernathy, reminding him that he had answered only one of the three questions I had addressed to him. On September 14, 1963, his secretary, Clair Stevens, wrote me that Mr. Abernathy was away and that the letter of September 11th would be brought to his attention upon his return. On December 19, 1963, I sent Mr. Abernathy another letter, calling to his attention the previous letters, recapitulating their contents, and especially reminding him of Congressman Multer's refutation of the Israel Cohen Hoax. My final sentence asked: "In the event that you did not retract, don't you think that it is the decent and honorable thing to do, even at this late date?"

There was no reply received, as the reader can well imagine. Consider the utter irresponsibility of a Congressman who solemnly places something in the *Congressional Record* that he picks up in the letters-to-the-editor column and presents it as though he has a documented discovery. Consider his further irresponsibility in not asking the Library of Congress to check its authenticity. Like most of the noisy segregationists, Congressman Abernathy doesn't care what weapons he uses to keep the Negro "in his place," even if the weapon is falsehood from the underworld of bigotry. Surely Mr. Abernathy knew that, within a few weeks after he had placed that hoax item in the *Record,* Congressman Multer had placed an effective refutation in the *Record.* And surely he knew that the *Washington Star,* from which he picked up the hoax story, carried a devastating exposé eight months after he had placed the hoax in the *Con-*

*gressional Record.* When challenged almost six years later to retract the hoax, the Honorable Congressman Abernathy met the challenge with a deafening silence.

Mr. Abernathy speaks on the floor of Congress on many subjects, usually expressing the reactionary philosophy of the Southern big business interests. The Ultra-Rightist *Americans for Constitutional Action* gave him a correct voting rating, by their reactionary standards, of 87 for 1963 and 100 for 1965. On December 19, 1963, he placed in the *Congressional Record* his Newsletter, in which he had all the answers about the Kennedy assassination. He was absolutely sure that Lee Harvey Oswald was the assassin; absolutely sure that: "There is not the slightest shred of evidence that it was associated with or sprang from an alleged wave of racial hatred or racial bigotry." He "explained" the Civil Rights struggle on the floor of Congress, February 4, 1964 in this fashion:

Mr. Speaker, there are thousands, perhaps millions, of Negroes in America who live in good homes, have good jobs, and who educate their children. There are many Negro millionaires in this country. They did not achieve success by being cry-babies. They got there by the same means that some white people achieve success; that is by personal initiative and hard work.

The Negro leaders who are causing so much unrest in America are misleading their people. They are trying to substitute political pressure for personal achievement. It will not work.

With this exquisite logic, a physician would treat a patient's complaints about symptoms in one part of the body by enumerating the list of healthy organs the patient possesses. It should come as no surprise that Abernathy is a staunch supporter of the House Un-American Activities Committee, which has an unbroken record of racist tendencies. Abernathy concluded a speech full of rationalizations, on the floor of Congress, January 14, 1965, with: "I urge the House to stand strong in support of this great committee."

The *Washington Star* article of February 18, 1958 reflects such a huge amount of painstaking research that it seems worthwhile to relate some of its findings. In March of 1957 the *Star* published a letter-to-the-editor from R. A. Hester, chairman of the Montgomery County Chapter of the Maryland Petition Committee, which contained the Israel Cohen quotation. In

June the *Star* received a letter from the director of the Washington Anti-Defamation League, which branded the Israel Cohen quotation as spurious and pointed out that there is no record of an Israel Cohen, British Communist leader. In July the *Star* received a letter from a reader, not for publication, disputing the Anti-Defamation League's letter. The writer gave information which resulted in the *Star* doing some real detective work. The phoney quotation was finally traced to a notorious peddler of fake stories about Jews, Negroes, Communists, and Liberals, one Eustace Mullins. Among his distinctions are that he wrote an article in one of the hate sheets, *Women's Voice,* June 1955, warning his dupes that "Jonas Salk, Yiddish inventor of a so-called polio vaccine" is a part of a plot of the Jews to "Mass Poison American Children." His other distinction is that he was on the staff of the late Fascist Senator, Joe McCarthy.[11]

The Israel Cohen hoax has been carried in many Right-Wing publications. The *Richmond News Leader* of June 26, 1957, published a letter, with Congressman Abernathy's picture, quoting his Israel Cohen speech from the *Congressional Record.* The magazine, *South,* quoted the statement in an editorial, October 21, 1957. The racist Citizens' Council of America quoted Abernathy's statement from the *Congressional Record* in its newsletter of September 5, 1957, and it was quoted again in a radio broadcast on January 19, 1958.

The ex-FBI Agent, Dan Smoot, in his *Report* of July 22, 1963, wrote:

Have you seen this? In 1912, Israel Cohen, a leading communist in England, outlined what he called "A Racial Program for the 20th Century." Cohen said:

Then follows the same quotation used by Abernathy, and Smoot credits Abernathy's presentation in the *Congressional Record* of June 7, 1957, page 7633. (Smoot made an error. It is actually on page 8559.)

On December 19, 1963, I wrote Dan Smoot a four-page single-space, typewritten letter, calling to his attention four

11 Eustace Mullins is also the author of an article entitled "Adolph Hitler: An Appreciation," which appeared in the October 1952 Bulletin of a Fascist Group, the National Renaissance Party. He has also participated in outdoor rallies of this Fascist outfit.

phoney stories that I had discovered in recent issues of *Dan Smoot Report,* including the Israel Cohen hoax. No reply was received from Smoot. However, in his *Report* of February 3, 1964, Smoot told his readers that he had quoted the Israel Cohen hoax from Abernathy's insertion in the *Congressional Record,* and said Smoot:

I was subsequently advised that Mr. Abernathy got the quotation from a letter-to-the-editor in a Washington newspaper, and that a more authentic source could not be found. I have tried in vain (through libraries in the United States and in Europe) to identify the "Israel Cohen" in question.

I therefore apologize to readers of this *Report* for having published an item that I cannot authenticate.

Aside from the fact that Smoot was not gracious enough to credit me with having called to his attention both the *Washington Star* and *Congressman Multer* research items, he brags about his allegedly checking "libraries in the United States and in Europe." I suggest that Smoot is here taking credit for exactly what the Anti-Defamation League had done, and which had been reported in the *Washington Star* article.

On February 15, 1964, I sent Dan Smoot the following letter via certified mail:

On Dec. 19, 1963, I sent you a 4-page typewritten letter, documenting some of the erroneous stories, distortions of fact, and outright fabrications that you have used in your *Reports.*

With the exception of your equivocal retraction of the Israel Cohen canard, you have not replied to my letter and its challenge.

Inasmuch as my typist made two carbon copies of my letter of Dec. 19, 1963, I am herewith sending you a carbon copy of my letter, and I again ask you to reply to it point by point, and what is more important, publish corrections, and retractions. I am sending this via certified mail, return receipt requested, so that you will be unable to say that you did not receive it.

A receipt for the letter was received, but Smoot did not reply and did not retract the other phoney stories, for which documented refutation was sent to him.

Jack Moffitt, who writes the syndicated "Cracker Barrel" column, is the film critic of the John Birch Society's monthly, *American Opinion.* Moffitt quotes part of the Israel Cohen hoax in the October 1963 issue, assuring his readers that it was

97

written by Israel Cohen in 1912. For reasons best known to Moffitt, he does not refer to Cohen as a British Communist. A letter from one Robert M. Beren, in the January 1964 issue of *American Opinion* challenged the authenticity of the Israel Cohen canard and referred the editor to the research article in the *Washington Star* of February 18, 1958. *American Opinion's* editor appended this comment: *"Mr. Beren is perfectly correct."* Two months later, Mr. Tom Anderson, member of the National Council of the John Birch Society quoted the Israel Cohen hoax in his syndicated column, "Straight Talk." Anderson referred to Israel Cohen as "a leading English Communist." The question is: Does Tom Anderson neglect to read *American Opinion* or does he deliberately spread falsehood?

The American Coalition of Patriotic Societies, in its "Report to America," June, 1961, quoted the Israel Cohen hoax in its entirety, with the notation that it is from the *Congressional Record*, June 7, 1957. This is a common device of the Ultra-Rightist propagandists—to quote from the *Congressional Record*, without stating who inserted it in the *Record*. This serves to place a sort of imprimatur on the quoted item, thus misleading the dupes into believing that it has the backing of the U.S. government. Is it possible that Mr. Milton M. Lory, President of the American Coalition of Patriotic Societies, did not know that his quotation had been completely discredited four years earlier?

In Burney, California, there is a character by the name of Hal W. Hunt, who edits and publishes a hate sheet which duplicates the ravings of Julius Streicher in the former Nazi sheet, *Der Stürmer*. Hunt's *National Chronicle*, March 11, 1965, quotes the Israel Cohen hoax, changing the name of the alleged book to *Social Problems For the Twentieth Century* (instead of *A Racial Program for the 20th Century*).

A leaflet was circulated throughout the South in the Spring of 1965 under the title of *Views of a Southern Negro*. It was issued by something called Mississippi Publishers, P.O. Box 668, Meridian, Mississippi and 41 Kentucky Street, Delhi, Louisiana. The depths of depravity reached in this message from the gutter can be judged from this excerpt:

Patrick Henry saw the evils of Communism when he spoke these

98

words, "Is life so dear or peace so sweet as to be purchased with the price of chains and slavery?" Communism is the road back to slavery and the way is crowded with people who are looking for something for nothing.

That there was no Communist movement in 1776 makes no difference to the hate-peddling liars. In fact, Karl Marx, the founder of the modern Communist movement, had not yet been born when Patrick Henry made that speech.

Immediately following the above quotation there is served another delectable morsel:

Leo Kahn, the head of the Communist Party in Great Britain, said these words 52 years ago: "The Racial Question is the most potent weapon that the Communists have. If we can convince the Black People of the world that they are the oppressed and the white people are the oppressors, there is the great possibility of getting the Negro on our side."

Not only has the name of the phantom Communist leader been changed from Israel Cohen to Leo Kahn, but the alleged quotation is a garbled version of a fake quotation from a non-existent book!

The March 22, 1965 issue of *The Councilor* reprinted the leaflet completely, giving the name and address of the publisher. *The Councilor* is the official organ of the rabidly segregationist Citizens Council of Shreveport, Louisiana.

On April 2, 1965 my research assistant sent a letter to Mr. Robert Beals of Mississippi Enterprises, asking him where he obtained the Leo Kahn quotation. On April 20, 1965, Robert Beals replied:

We appreciate your letter and we are very happy to send you the book of Leo Kahn, but due to the circumstances I haven't been able to look up the book. But I found that statement in a book on Communistic by the Grate Britain press.

I hope that these answers are satisfactory. In addition, you will find one of my pamphlet.

Yours truly,
ROBERT BEALS

It is apparent that not only is Robert Beals a liar, but he is abysmally ignorant, as can be seen from his atrocious spelling and infantile sentence structure.

On April 28, 1965 we sent Robert Beals another letter, asking him to give us the name of the book, pamphlet, or publication from which he obtained the Leo Kahn quotation. There was no reply, because Beals fabricated the story from a previous fabrication.

*The White American,* issued by American States Rights Party, an offshoot from the Fascistic *National States Rights Party,* carried a front-page story in its issue of April-May 1965, entitled "National Council of Churches and Jews United to Destroy White Race." Turning to page three we find the Israel Cohen hoax, and we are informed that it is "taken from the Congressional Record." Again it is made to appear that a fraudulent statement is the truth, by authority of the U.S. Government!

Myron C. Fagan, a former henchman of the Rev. Gerald L. K. Smith, operates an Ultra-Rightist outfit called Cinema Educational League. In his News-Bulletin No. 116, issued January 1966, we are told that the United Nations is a conspiracy and that the Civil Rights Movement is a Communist conspiracy. He claims that the Supreme Court's desegregation decision of 1954 and Ike's "Civil Rights Bill" were designed to carry out the plans of the "Communist Conspiracy." Then he adds:

To further remove all lingering doubts in anybody's mind that Ike's "Civil Rights Bill" and Warren's "Desegregation Decision" were designed to implement that feature of the Communist Conspiracy, I will quote verbatim from yet another official Communist Party document of directives, written by one Israel Cohen, A Communist Party top functionary in England. The following excerpt is from his book, *A Racial Program for the 20th Century,* setting forth the Communist policy:

Then, after quoting the Israel Cohen hoax, Fagan says:

Note: To remove all doubts about the authenticity of the above quotation, it was entered into the *Congressional Record* of June 7, 1957, by Rep. Thomas G. Abernathy.

That directive was written in 1913, simultaneously with the birth of NAACP.

There you have it. A professional liar quotes a fraudulent statement from a non-existent book, "proves" it by quoting the *Congressional Record,* and then slyly changes the 1912 date of

Israel Cohen's alleged statement to 1913, so that he can tie Israel Cohen to the NAACP. This is no isolated phenomenon. It is typical of the so-called educational work of the Ultra-Rightists and the professional anti-Communists.

In his News-Bulletin No. 122, issued in November, 1966, Myron C. Fagan claims to have met Israel Cohen and that Cohen told him he was writing a book which was to be titled: *A Racial Program for the 20th Century.* This, of course, is a story made up out of the whole cloth. Then Fagan explains that he did not get a copy of the book, but that it was brought to his attention by an article in the *Washington Star.* Here again Fagan has invented a story, because the *Washington Star* did *not* carry a story initially about the alleged Israel Cohen book. It did carry a letter from a reader, which quoted from the alleged book. This was followed by an article in which the *Star* exposed *the fraudulent nature of the story* about the Israel Cohen book! Fagan's prolific imagination produced a third lie in this News Bulletin. Following his yarn about how he had learned that Israel Cohen had written *A Racial Program for the Twentieth Century,* Fagan says:

Following the publication of that story, Congressman Abernathy, after checking with the "Star," and himself reading the book, published the same quote in the Congressional Record.

That book was published in 1913 . . . the NAACP and the ADL were created almost simultaneously to carry out those directives. *That was more than a half century ago. Can there be any doubt that that was intended to launch our present Negro upheaval for a Black Revolution?*

Quite apart from the ridiculousness of Fagan's smears against the National Association for the Advancement of Colored People and against the Anti-Defamation League, there are two things wrong with his story: 1. Congressman Abernathy could not have read a non-existent book. 2. In a letter to a research assistant, Abernathy admitted to us that his *sole source* of information about the alleged Israel Cohen book was a letter-to-the-editor in the *Washington Star.*

Fagan has a "cover story" to cope with the exposure of the Israel Cohen hoax. He makes the lying allegation that two years elapsed before anyone challenged the authenticity of the Israel Cohen hoax. Then he adds that "the ADL and similar groups had ferreted out ALL copies of the book and destroyed them. . ." From all this it is clear that Fagan is an inventive "genius."

One of the more violent of the indigenous Fascist groups is a Cleveland, Ohio outfit called the Right Brigade, operated by a fanatical hate-peddler, Allan Dawson. In a Bulletin issued January 5, 1966, Dawson quotes part of the Israel Cohen hoax and says: "See Congressional Record for June 7, 1957," and then adds:

Patriots! Arm yourselves with information and keep defensive weapons close to hand. Treason, is abroad in the land! Don't let the conspirators take your guns away! Know your enemy—and be prepared!

The *Cincinnati Enquirer,* July 26, 1961 ran a long editorial entitled "The Peril to Racial Progress." It revolved around the fake "A Racial Programme for the Twentieth Century," allegedly written by Israel Cohen, which it quoted from the *Congressional Record* of June 7, 1957. It is interesting that, four years after this canard appeared in the *Congressional Record,* a large metropolitan daily newspaper could resurrect it and be completely oblivious of the fact that it had been refuted over and over again in the intervening period. On August 3, 1961 the *Enquirer* ran a large editorial entitled "No Book, No Author," in which it sheepishly admitted that the Israel Cohen book is a hoax, but then went on to "prove" the same doctrines by quoting Louis Budenz and John E. Hoover.

This seems to be a pattern in Right-Wing circles. When their sources of information are proven to be false, they come up with substitutes that are used to minimize the immorality of using fabrications.

We have by no means heard the end of the Israel Cohen hoax. It will be revived and used again and again. There are thousands of Right-Wingers who have this in their scrap books, and when the opportunity arises they will quote it in letters to the editor and in leaflets and speeches. Typical of this is a letter in the now-defunct *Los Angeles Mirror-News* of October 1, 1958, which starts off with:

It would seem that the plan for integration is going exactly according to schedule—the Communists' schedule, that is. The following paragraph comes from a book entitled, "A Racial Program For the 20th Century," written in 1912 by Israel Cohen, an English Communist:

After the famous quotation, which needs no further repetition here, the writer confidently concludes:

This is a very familiar picture of exactly what is going on in the United States today.

On September 20, 1966, Hubert Eaton, a member of the Sons of the American Revolution, died in his Beverly Hills, California home, after a lingering illness. Mr. Eaton had the distinction of glamorizing death and making millions of dollars doing it. Founder and Board Chairman of Forest Lawn Memorial-Park, Eaton applied the principles of modern advertising and salesmanship to the undertaker business, and developed in Southern California a chain of glorified cemeteries, euphemistically called memorial parks. As an intensely class-conscious capitalist, Eaton joined the ranks of those whose feelings of insecurity drive them to conduct frenzied propaganda campaigns. Mr. Eaton delivered a speech on May 7, 1964 at the Beverly Hilton Hotel in Beverly Hills, entitled, "Have We Reached the Point of No Return?"

Mr. Eaton stated that former FBI agent Dan Smoot had recommended that a study should be made of "the communist blueprint for the South, written in 1955 by Victor Perlo. Victor Perlo was a communist spy who worked for the NRA in 1933 and later became an economic analyst for the Treasury Department." He followed this up by quoting the Israel Cohen hoax, prefacing the quotation by saying: "Israel Cohen, another communist leader, foreshadowed Perlo's words when he wrote *A Racial Program for the 20th Century*." Further on, Eaton ventures into the realm of anthropology by stating: "Segregation is a natural instinct of all animals (including man)."

On April 26, 1965, I sent a three-page single-space, typewritten letter to Mr. Eaton, and I have a receipt showing it was delivered to his office. I asked Mr. Eaton:

Please tell me where and in what court of law Victor Perlo was tried and convicted of violation of the espionage laws of the United States of America.

Then I gave him all the essential proof that the Israel Cohen quotation he had used is a palpable fraud. My letter concludes with the following:

Apparently you have not done your homework, because you used the phoney Israel Cohen story *three months after Dan Smoot disavowed it.* I suggest that you now show evidence of good faith by placing a paid advertisement in the *Los Angeles Times* retracting the spy charge against Victor Perlo and disavowing the Israel Cohen canard.

In the opening remarks of his speech, Eaton told his audience: "Every statement I shall make tonight is well documented, well authenticated and supervised by Forest Lawn's Legal Department composed of four able attorneys." Indeed!

Mr. Eaton did not accept the moral challenge of my letter. He did not even show me the elementary courtesy of a reply. This is most interesting, because near the end of his speech Eaton waxed eloquent, telling his audience: "Without religion we cannot have morality; without morality we cannot have social safety; and without social safety we cannot have civilization."

Such is the morality of the pillars of our society that they see nothing wrong in telling lies and assassinating character, as long as it is against Communism.

One additional bit of information should be added to our exposé of the Israel Cohen Hoax. In its February 15, 1958 story, entitled "Story of a Phony Quotation," the Washington, D.C. *Evening Star* expressed its exasperation with Eustace Mullins. The *Star* had attempted to pin down Mullins for some proof of the authenticity of that fraudulent "A Racial Program for the Twentieth Century." It finally concluded that Mullins' letter of reply was "a revealing evasion to the question of where he got the quotation." In a companion editorial entitled "Running Down a Hoax," the *Star* said: "Certainly one innocent victim of this fraud has been Israel Cohen of London, a journalist and writer of excellent reputation, whose name seems to have been gratuitously exploited as part of the fabrication." There is some sort of irony in the fact that Mullins' letter to the *Star* was on stationery of the American Humane Church of Huntley, Illinois, and Mullins was listed on the stationery as

104

"Rev. Eustace Mullins, director, Society for the Propagation of the Human Faith."

Appropriately enough, the Israel Cohen hoax was repeated in the Summer of 1967 edition of *Stormtrooper* magazine, issued by the American Nazi Party.

## Hedda Hopper Tells the Truth

The late Hollywood gossip columnist cut quite a swath for many years with her peephole journalism. In 1963 she brought out a book entitled *The Whole Truth and Nothing but the Truth*. British-born actor, Michael Wilding, didn't believe the implications of the title, and alleged that Hedda had told a few things about him that were *not* the truth. Wilding figured that he should get $3 million for the damage done by Hedda's venture into the realm of The Truth. He sued, and according to his attorney, he received more than $100,000 in an out-of-court settlement. The Truth and Nothing but the Truth!

## The Oscar Wilde Hoax

In his little hate sheet, *National Chronicle,* May 14, 1964, Hal Hunt delivered a "haymaker" to the Soviet Union. He quoted the British author and poet, Oscar Wilde, as saying:

A Russian who lives happily under the present system of government in Russia must either believe that man has no soul, or that, if he has, it is not worth developing.

That is quite an indictment against the Soviet system, and it sounds as if it is spoken from a high moral plane. Mr. Hunt neglected to tell his readers that Oscar Wilde was born in Dublin in 1854; and that he died in 1900, *seventeen years before the Soviet Union was founded!*

## The Rabbi Wise Fabrication

The propaganda sheets of anti-Semitism have circulated for a long time a statement which they have attributed to the late, distinguished Rabbi Stephen Wise:

> Some call it communism;
> I call it Judaism.

After they heard this phoney story in an interview with the American Nazi, George Lincoln Rockwell, the editors of *Playboy Magazine* checked it out and reported in the issue of April 1966, that research into Rabbi Wise's speeches and writings disclosed no evidence of that statement. Said *Playboy:* "Confronted with this evidence, Rockwell later retracted the allegation."

## Pious Fakery of *"Free Enterprise"*

*Free Enterprise* is the monthly tabloid paper issued by the Ultra-Rightist *We, The People*. It was formerly published in Chicago, and is now based in Phoenix, Arizona. Its editor, Harry Everingham, is president of *We, The People* and editor of another Ultra-Rightist sheet called *Fact Finder*.

*Free Enterprise* is written in that shrill, frenetic style which characterizes most of the Ultra-Right propaganda. It promotes confusion and obscurantism, which are essential ingredients of all pro-Fascist propaganda. On the last page of each issue there is a list of about 100 names of something called *Wake Up America Committee,* which presumably is the steering committee of *We, The People*. Among the names are such well-known Right-Wing activists as attorney Robert B. Dresser; manufacturer Robert Dilley; Walter Knott; J. Bracken Lee, the Mayor of Salt Lake City; Birch Society member and former Congressman, Edgar W. Hiestand; and the Rev. Charles S. Poling.

In its issue of December, 1965, *Free Enterprise* said:

Students who call themselves *Christian Liberals* were allowed to give out a publication at Arizona State University on Nov. 4, 1965 ("I. F. Stone's Weekly" of 10/25/65) which bore the following front page headline:

IF WE COULD ONLY GET RID OF CHRIST
AND CONSTITUTION

Directly underneath this headline, *Free Enterprise* placed the last paragraph of *another* article from page 3. This had no relationship to the quoted headline. Alongside this paragraph from page 3, *Free Enterprise* placed *the last paragraph* of page 1, omitting all of the preceding two paragraphs of page 1. In

106

addition, there were two sentences omitted from the end of each of the quoted paragraphs.

Thus, by garbled quotations, truncated quotations, and sleight-of-hand juxtaposition, the *Wake Up America* crowd gave its readers an impression that was diametrically opposed to the clear intent of Mr. I. F. Stone, one of the country's most honest and courageous journalists. In order that the reader may judge the enormity of the pious fakery of *Free Enterprise*, the entire front page of *I. F. Stone's Weekly* is reproduced on p. 108. It is very apparent that Mr. Stone's headline and story constitute a most reverent approach to both Christ and the Constitution.

## The Housing Bill Fabrication

Sylvester Petro is a law professor at the University of New York, and is considered one of the "respectable" theoreticians of the Right-Wing. He is active in New York's Conservative Party, is on the advisory board of the Right-Wing "Freedom School" (Ramparts College, Larkspur, Colorado), and is a member of the Advisory Assembly of the American Conservative Union. A thinly-disguised employers' propaganda outfit, the Labor Policy Association, distributes two of his books. He has also served as a member of the Citizens Committee to Preserve Taft-Hartley.[12]

With the credentials possessed by the good professor, it should come as no surprise that he appeared as an opposition witness before a Senate Subcommittee hearing on the proposed Civil Rights Act of 1966. The main thrust of Professor Petro's argumentation was that freedom is destroyed by passing legislation which restricts racial discrimination in housing. After some oratorical flights of fancy, the professor attacked the previous testimony of Attorney General Nicholas Katzenbach, saying in part:

When one removes the tortured indirectness from the Attorney General's language, what remains is this assertion: "The policy of this administration is to favor a compelled amalgamation of all races, colors and creeds in residential areas; individual preferences,

---

[12] His book, *The Kohler Strike,* is a featured item of the John Birch Society in its "One Dozen Candles" group.

### Despite Heavier Bombings and Bigger Boloney

"Saigon—The number of Vietcong fighting in South Vietnam increased sharply in September despite near-record battle losses and defections, according to American High Command estimates. Neither bombing of infiltration starting points nor sea-patroling apparently has interfered seriously with the continuing Vietcong buildup, although some of its increased strength may be due to forced recruiting* of young men in areas where guerrillas hold sway. The number of main force insurgents—those who are full-time fighters in organized units—is estimated by American intelligence sources at 80,000 an increase of 15,000 over a month ago.

"The number of part-time guerrillas—farmers by day and raiders in black pajamas by night—has increased from an estimate of 80,000 to 100,000 in August to from 100,000 to 120,000 in September. Growth of the Vietcong as learned today was in sharp contrast to the flurry of favorable numerical indicators that the enemy is losing personnel faster than ever before."

—*Jack Foisie, Washington Post, Oct. 17 (abridged).*

\* Isn't it just barely possible that one or two might have joined up in protest against our indiscriminate slaughter?
—IFS

# I. F. Stone's Weekly

VOL. XIII. NO. 35   ·OCTOBER 25, 1965   101    WASHINGTON, D. C.      15 CENTS

## If We Could Only Get Rid of Christ and Constitution

Those who remember how the Romans felt about the Christians will not be surprised that one of them should have burned his draft card. Christians have always claimed to render unto Caesar what is Caesar's, but this may be Aesopian language. Under apparent submission to authority lies encouragement to civil disobedience since the saying leaves unanswered who is to determine what is Caesar's. If each man insists that his conscience be his guide, the end result is anarchy. Thoughtful men have long recognized the peril in the Christian doctrine of the primacy of conscience. Defense counsel tried to make the West see what openings this gave Moscow but their warnings were brushed aside at the Nuremberg trial. Der Fuehrer saw the danger and wanted to replace this pacifistic religion with a more virile Germanic creed, but his efforts were frustrated by the need to placate the Papacy, which is again showing its true colors. When the Pope virtually advocates admission of Red China to the United Nations, little wonder that a devout young Catholic refuses to fight in Asia.

### Most Catholics Loyal

We do not wish to suggest that Roman Catholics are not to be trusted. Most of them are loyal citizens. Their priests often preach the most invigorating sermons in wartime. But judge and jury at the trial of David J. Miller for burning his draft card must be made to see, in extenuation, that the religious doctrines to which this young man was exposed left him unfit to understand practical realities. The Church itself in the Middle Ages, by keeping the laity from reading the Gospels, acknowledged that they might have an unsettling effect on immature minds. We would be the first to protest if this led the government to take hasty action against churchgoing. But it is not without proper means for dealing with those who abuse freedom of religion. The Internal Security Act was framed to cope with the Communist menace but its provisions are general enough to cover any international movement which takes positions paralleling those of the Commu-

> ### Perhaps the Next Step Will Be to Seize Papers Which Print Lippmann at Home
>
> "SAIGON, Oct. 17—The Saigon English-language Daily News was ordered to halt publication for five days for infringing the country's censorship laws. The newspaper was told it infringed the laws by publishing articles without first submitting them to the censor. It was understood that an article by the syndicated American columnist Walter Lippmann displeased the government. The article published Oct. 12, described the South Vietnamese army as war-weary and said it had too little morale to occupy territory that American forces seized from the Vietcong."
>
> —*Reuters, Washington Post, Oct. 18.*

nists. Their members, their financial contributors, their printing presses and publications, must be disclosed to the Subversive Activities Control Board by registration. This is clearly usable against Roman Catholic pacifist groups, opposing the war in Vietnam, in concert with the Vatican.

Next to the problem of Christians who take their Gospel too seriously is that of Americans who take the Constitution too literally. McCarthy taught us to look with suspicion on "Constitution-lovers." We must be on our guard against constitutionalist infiltration. The day before Attorney General Katzenbach spoke in Chicago of prosecutions against the student peace movement, the Associated Press asked Justice Department for comment on Senator Stennis's demand for action. "One top level lawyer" said (*Washington Star*, Oct. 16), "You just can't make a snap judgment on what you would do if someone should put out a pamphlet or make a speech exhorting others to be draft dodgers. Sure we're keeping an eye on this thing, and we know what the law is, but we also keep an eye on the First amendment." Katzenbach had better begin his investigation right in his own Department. How are we going to make Asia safe for democracy if we allow all this subversive talk about free speech?

the right of private property, and personal freedom must all be sacrificed to this overriding policy."

Verbal by-play must not be allowed to conceal the real meaning of the Attorney General's statement.[13]

In reporting on the subsequent use of Petro's testimony by

[13] *Congressional Record,* June 21, 1966, page 13135.

some Right-Wing groups, the Washington columnists, Evans & Nowak, said:

Word for word, this is the statement now attributed directly to Katzenbach. What Petro claimed to see in the mind of the attorney general now has been put in his mouth by direct quotation.[14]

Evans & Nowak then go on to report the following sequence of events: In the early part of July, 1966, Kent and Phoebe Courtney brought out a pamphlet, which was mailed out across the country. They quoted Petro's statement which we have given above, and preceded it by this remark: ". . . Professor Petro said that, in essence what the attorney general meant was. . . ." A few days later Phoebe Courtney threw all cautions to the wind, and in a fund-raising letter of appeal she asked:

How many Americans know that the attorney general of the United States of America made the following statement before a congressional committee in urging passage of the "forced housing" section of L. B. J.'s civil rights bill?

Then followed the statement of Professor Petro, after which our Phoebe asked, "Does that shock you?" Phoebe answered: "It does me. This is the kind of news that the left-wing-controlled press carefully hides from the American people. I found it only after laboriously researching the Congressional Record."

Kent and Phoebe Courtney edit and publish a monthly Ultra-Rightist newspaper called *Independent American*. In 1962 Kent Courtney was reported to be president of something called Free Men Speak, Inc. and national chairman of Conservative Society of America. Both Courtneys were reported to be members of the John Birch Society.

Willis E. Stone is the national chairman of the Liberty Amendment Committee. Mr. Stone followed Phoebe Courtney's lead, and, in a fund-raising letter for his operation, scared the daylights out of his followers by telling them:

Attorney General Katzenbach, in pleading for the "civil rights" bill, said: ". . . individual preference, the right of private property and personal freedom must all be sacrificed. . . ."

14 *Los Angeles Times,* Sept. 8, 1966.

Followers of the Courtneys and Willis Stone started a barrage of letters-to-the-editor, and as a result the Ultra-Rightist network generated enough hysteria to bury the pending legislation. Evans & Nowak summarized it very well:

> Ironically, in its present form, the open housing provision does not even apply to individual homeowners. But by now it is probably impossible to convince many of them that Katzenbach did not tell Congress that "personal freedom" must be sacrificed. Through the technique of the big lie, the spurious Katzenbach quote has become inseparably entwined with hysterical opposition to open housing.

While Evans & Nowak seem to absolve Professor Petro of any wrongdoing, we feel that the cardinal sin was committed by the professor. In our opinion, no one has a right to paraphrase another person's words and then put quotation marks around them. Quotation marks should be reserved for *exact* quotations. It is hard to believe that a sophisticated person like Professor Sylvester Petro was not aware of the possibility that his paraphrase of Attorney General Katzenbach's *thinking* would result in Ultra-Rightist exploitation. His use of quotation marks around the paraphrase made it almost a foregone conclusion that it would be used for dishonest purposes.

### The Thomas Jefferson Hoax

The propagandists of the race-hatred groups frequently quote Thomas Jefferson to bolster their Hitlerian philosophy of White Supremacy. What they fail to tell their dupes is that Thomas Jefferson *repudiated* his previously-held views about Negro inferiority. On February 25, 1809, Jefferson wrote the following letter to a French author, Monsieur Gregoire:

> Sir,—I have received the favor of your letter of August 17th, and with it the volume you were so kind as to send me on the "Literature of Negroes." Be assured that no person living wishes more sincerely than I do, to see a complete refutation of the doubts I have myself entertained and expressed on the grade of understanding allotted to them by nature, and to find that in this respect they are on a par with ourselves. My doubts were the result of personal observation on the limited sphere of my own State, where the opportunities for the development of their genius were not favorable and those of exercising it still less so. I expressed them therefore with

great hesitation; but whatever be their degree of talent it is no measure of their rights. Because Sir Isaac Newton was superior to others in understanding, he was not therefore lord of the person or property of others. On this subject they are gaining daily in the opinions of nations, and hopeful advances are making toward their re-establishment on an equal footing with the other colors of the human family. I pray you therefore to accept my thanks for the many instances you have enabled me to observe of respectable intelligence in that race of men, which cannot fail to have effect in hastening the day of their relief; and to be assured of the sentiments of high and just esteem and consideration which I tender to yourself with all sincerity.

It is a measure of the greatness of the immortal Thomas Jefferson that, not only was he willing to openly admit his previous error, but he clearly discerned the basic truths which were later established by the research of the world's most renowned anthropologists. Thomas Jefferson clearly belongs in the ranks of the Civil Rights movement. The Ku Kluxers, the Nazis, the Birchers, the James Eastlands, and the Strom Thurmonds cannot, in truth, call him one of their own. Jefferson's letter can be found on page 429 of Volume V, *The Writings of Thomas Jefferson,* edited by H. A. Washington.

## The Alaska Mental Health Hoax

A sizeable segment of the Ultra-Right conducts a relentless campaign against the professions and sciences of psychology and psychiatry, and as a corollary, it sees a Communist plot in every mental health program. Three distinguished psychiatrists, Drs. Marmor, Bernard, and Ottenberg, have observed: "The reactions of some of these individuals seem to reflect a fear that any psychiatric insights may expose their own underlying mental instability, much as a patient who fears that he has cancer of the lung may be terrified of a chest X-ray."[15] There is abundant evidence to show that leaders and promoters of Ultra-Rightist groups exploit the fears of such people and prepare them to act as the storm-troopers of the Fascist movement in the U.S.A.

The Territory of Alaska (before it was admitted to Statehood) was for many years without facilities for the care of

---

[15] *The American Journal of Orthopsychiatry,* April, 1960.

mentally ill patients. The procedures that were followed are shocking. Anyone could sign a declaration that another person is insane. The nearest U.S. Marshal was then obliged to incarcerate such a person until a jury of six men could pass upon the sanity complaint. If the "jury" pronounced the hapless person "guilty," the Marshal would transport him to a private mental hospital in Portland, Oregon, which was under contract to the Department of Interior of the U.S. Government. At no point in this procedure was a medical and/or psychiatric examination required. And quite often the "guilty" one was kept in an Alaskan jail until the Marshal found it convenient to make a trip to Portland.

In 1955 Congresswoman Edith Green and Senator Richard Neuberger, both of Oregon, sponsored a bill, known as the Alaska Mental Health Act (H.R. 6376). It provided that the Federal Government would give the Territory of Alaska 12½ million dollars during the ensuing ten years, in order to finance a mental health program and build the necessary hospitals. There were, however, two provisions of this bill which sent the Ultra-Rightists into orbit, even before the advent of Sputnik I. The bill provided that the Governor of Alaska could enter into reciprocal arrangements with the Governors of other states, so that Alaskans who became mentally ill when traveling outside the territory, would be properly treated until they could be returned to Alaska; and likewise, when residents of the states became mentally ill while traveling in Alaska, they could be returned to their respective states. The second provision which excited the Ultra-Rightists was made to order for the operators of the Right-Wing propaganda mills. It so happened that the Federal Government owned about 99 percent of the 375 million acres in the Territory of Alaska. The bill provided that the Federal Government would turn over one million acres to the Territory of Alaska, to provide revenue for the support of the mental hospitals and the mental health program. Thus, if the Territory sold, leased, or developed any portion of or all of the million acres of land, the income would go to the mental health fund. There was nothing new in this proposal, as it had been common American procedure for the Federal Government to provide land grants for the support of mental hospitals, schools, colleges, and other public facilities when other territories achieved statehood.

112

On January 18, 1956, the House of Representatives *unanimously* passed HR 6376, The Alaska Mental Health Bill, and it was on its way to passage by the Senate. Then all Hell broke loose when the Senate Subcommittee started its hearings on February 20, 1956, under the chairmanship of Senator Henry Jackson. The anti-Semitic and pro-Fascist *National Economic Council* issued its Letter No. 377, dated February 15, 1956, which gave the signal to the other Ultra-Rightists who feed at its ideological trough. The Letter asked "why is it necessary to give a million acres to this proposed hospital?", conveniently omitting the *known* reason for the land grant. The following are representative excerpts from succeeding paragraphs of the Letter, and are fairly quoted without destroying the contextual integrity:

1. ". . . H.R. 6376 would build the counterpart in Alaska of what Soviet Russia has in Siberia."
2. "Are they, consciously or unconsciously, following an invisible blueprint of a pattern that would be useful when the moment comes, to take the 'nonsense' out of any persons who disagree in the slightest manner with the plans for the taking the United States into a world government?"
3. The Letter winds up with: "These provisions in H.R. 6376 could take care nicely of many persons who have been warning the country about the socialistic and communistic phases of our own Government which they don't like. Troublesome dissenters can be silenced by a determined Palace Guard. What better scheme than an American Siberia?"

Here you have the classic conspiratorial theory of Robert Welch and his John Birch Society: the solemn allegation that the Communist masters of the United States Government are preparing to railroad all anti-Communists to a mental hospital type of concentration camp in Alaska. It is no secret that Robert Welch was an avid reader of the National Economic Council Letters.

In Burbank, California, there was a group of women, estimated to be about 100, who called themselves the American Public Relations Forum, Inc. It was incorporated under the laws of California on May 13, 1952, and was formed, according to its Articles of Incorporation, "To do any and all proper things to maintain and preserve the Republic of the United States and its form of representative government. . . ." We

113

shall see what "proper things" these lady vigilantes were capable of doing. Its president, Mrs. Stephanie Williams, had gone through a dress rehearsal for her role as hatchet woman in the attack against H.R. 6376. In 1955, a year earlier, she had been in the leadership of a fight that defeated a bill in the California legislature to establish mental health clinics in local communities. Allied with Stephanie Williams in the fight to "save" California was the notorious anti-Semite, former State Senator Jack Tenney, who made a career out of Red-Baiting for many years. Additional help came from a group of super patriots, Pro America, and from a professional Red-Baiter and purveyor of anti-Semitism, retired Air Force Major, Robert H. Williams of Santa Ana.

Shortly after H.R. 6376 passed in the House of Representatives on January 18, 1956, someone sent a copy of the bill to the lady vigilantes of the American Public Relations Forum, Inc. Their "research" committee "analyzed" the bill and quickly discovered a Communist plot to establish a concentration camp in Alaska, where "patriots" would be confined. In their January, 1966, bulletin, the lady vigilantes issued a Paul Revere style call to arms! They said that the bill "could apply to all Americans who have been active against the New Dealers and their schemes to make this country into a member of world government and reduce us to slavery." That old standby of the Ultra-Rightists, the *Santa Ana Register,* screamed in an editorial headed "Now—Siberia, U.S.A.":

Is it the purpose of H.R. 6376 to establish a concentration camp for political prisoners under the guise of treatment of mental cases? The answer, based on a study of the bill, indicates that it is entirely within the realm of possibility that we may be establishing in Alaska our own version of the Siberia slave camps run by the Russian government.

Within days of the appearance of the January bulletin of the American Public Relations Forum, Inc., the Ultra-Rightists mounted a formidable campaign. Ex-FBI Agent Dan Smoot pitched into the fight, warning in his solemn, "scholarly" fashion that H.R. 6376 "would permit seizure, incarceration and treatment of 'mentally ill' people without trial by jury and without due process of law prescribed by our Constitution."

Others who jumped into the fray were the Rev. Gerald L. K. Smith; Women for God and Country; For America League;

114

the Women's Patriotic Conference on National Defense; the Right-Wing Catholic weekly, the *Brooklyn Tablet*; and retired Army General Herbert C. Holdridge, who constantly finds the Vatican behind plots and this time said that behind H.R. 6376 were "the black forces of the Jesuits who dominate the Vatican and, through its affiliates in our government, dominate our policies."

Mrs. Stephanie Williams testified at the Senate hearings that H.R. 6376 was an Internationalist thought-control scheme that had the backing of Ford Foundation financing. Moreover, opined the embattled Stephanie: "There is nothing to prevent Russia from buying a whole million acres or renting it or leasing it. You remember she has always maintained that Alaska belonged to her and that it is *very near*." Stephanie's chum, Mrs. Leigh F. Burkeland, who has been credited with inventing the slogan "Siberia, U.S.A.," wrote in an article, which became part of the report of the Senate Hearings: "This legislation . . . will place every resident of the United States at the mercy of the whims and fancies of any person with whom they might have a disagreement, causing a charge of 'mental illness' to be placed against them with immediate deportation to Siberia, U.S.A.!"

That violent peddler of hate against Negroes and Jews, John Kasper of Merchantville, New Jersey, testified that H.R. 6376 is a Jewish plot, because "about 80 per cent of the psychiatrists are Jewish." Most remarkable of all was the support given to the fight against H.R. 6376 by the Right-Wing-oriented Association of American Physicians and Surgeons, which issued a number of bulletins denouncing the bill in the most general terms. Even when their political adviser, Dr. Marjorie Shearon, patiently explained to this group that they had been hoaxed into joining a most atrocious campaign, they refused to retract, apparently because of their loyalty to other Right-Wing groups. As the psychiatrists Marmor, Bernard and Ottenberg have pointed out: "Sometimes the general public is misled when opponents to health legislation carry the insignia of esteemed authorities. Thus, an M.D. or a Ph.D. degree is not always a reliable indicator of scientific objectivity when borne by individuals *whose personal bias outweighs their rationality*." (Emphasis has been added.—M. K.)[16] As a matter of keeping

16 *The American Journal of Orthopsychiatry*, April, 1960.

the record straight, it should be noted that the American Medical Association, which is the main body of organized medicine, *did* support H.R. 6376. This was also true of the American Psychiatric Association and the National Association for Mental Health.

As far as the record shows, not a single Senator had expressed any objections to H.R. 6376. Contrary to the lies assiduously spread by ex-FBI agent Dan Smoot and the rest of the Ultra-Rightist cabal, the bill very explicitly provided that any person who believed himself unjustly committed to a mental hospital would have the right to be represented by an attorney, the right of habeas corpus, and the right to trial by jury. How these principles, which we like to include in definitions of Americanism, could be equated with "Siberia, U.S.A." is something that the "scholar," Mr. Dan Smoot, may perhaps explain.

The violent campaign of this organized minority was not adequately combatted by the democratic and progressive forces of our society, with the result that the Senate passed H.R. 6376, only after it had accepted a cowardly amendment, *which deleted the very safeguards against a "Siberia, U.S.A."* and placed the matter of legislation about such safeguards in the hands of the Alaskan Territorial Legislature. It was Senator Barry Goldwater who introduced the amendment that finally insured passage of the bill, giving Alaska the Federal grant of money to build mental hospitals and clinics and giving it the grant of a million acres of land as a source of income to pay for the mental health program. Some of the more virulent of the Fascist scribes have never forgiven Barry Goldwater for this bit of "treason" to the cause, and every once in a while one of the sheets of the Ultra-Rightists taunts Barry for his "double-cross" of the faithful.

This episode is not an isolated phenomenon. It is typical of the Ultra-Right campaign against scientific programs designed to cope with the ever-mounting problem of mental illness.

Up to this point we have presented a sampling of the different kinds of fabrications and hoaxes being used by the Ultra-Rightists and other reactionary groups to poison the minds of the people and to mislead them into acting contrary to their own best interests. In the pages that follow, the subject matter is being presented in a systematic manner, according to a classified arrangement.

116

# CHAPTER II

## The Anti-Semitic Liars

For centuries anti-Semitism has been the weapon used by tyrants and ruling classes to stay in power: by diverting the attention of the people from the real enemy, and by keeping the people fighting among themselves. Whatever motivation may be ascribed to any particular anti-Semitic agitator, the fact remains that our society does not cleanse itself of these elements. It will be shown that a certain portion of the present-day Ultra-Right does overtly spread anti-Semitism; that another portion spreads anti-Semitism covertly; and that rich and powerful members of our society do *encourage and subsidize* anti-Semitic activities. Contrary to the philosophy held in certain quarters, we believe that anti-Semitic falsehoods should be met head-on and thoroughly discredited, that people of goodwill should be equipped with *the answers* to the anti-Semitic hate-peddlers, and that a massive campaign of *pitiless exposure* of the anti-Semites should be instituted. Some of the most common poison pellets will now be examined.

### The Ben Hecht Hoax

One of the most active of the anti-Semitic pamphleteers is Elizabeth Shepherd, who operates something in New York City called the National Citizens Union. In March of 1964 she circulated a leaflet entitled *Who Are The Haters?*, which employed a device used by the Nazi propaganda wizard, Dr. Paul Joseph Goebbels. This consists essentially of "proving" that the originators of hate doctrines are Jews and Communists. As part of her proof, Elizabeth stated that Ben Hecht, Zionist writer of *A Jew in Love*, said:

One of the finest things ever done by the mob was the crucifixion of Christ. Intellectually it was a splendid gesture. But trust the mob to bungle. If I had charge of executing Christ, I would have

117

handled it differently. You see what I would have done was had him shipped to Rome and fed to the lions. They never could have made a saviour out of mince meat.

*Councilor*, the semi-monthly hate sheet of the Louisiana White Citizens Councils, never misses an opportunity to say something in derogation of Negroes; it is also not averse to spreading some anti-Semitism, along with its anti-Communist crusade. Thus, on the front page of its October 22, 1965 issue, *Councilor* says:

New York—Some of his fans cried when TV celebrity Ben Hecht died.
What they may not have known: Hecht's attitude toward the death of others.
Hecht, a dedicated Red, said in a book, "One of the finest things ever done by the mob was the crucifixion of Christ." He added that the mob should have fed Christ to the lions, however, because "They (Christians) never could have made a Savior out of mince meat."

Tom Anderson, member of the National Council of the John Birch Society and associate editor of its monthly *American Opinion*, included the following in his syndicated newspaper column (*Santa Ana Register*, Nov. 28, 1966):

The late Ben Hecht, television celebrity and darling of the "liberals," wrote in his book, *A Jew in Love*, page 120: "One of the finest things ever done by the mob was the Crucifixion of Christ. Intellectually it was a splendid gesture. But trust the mob to bungle. If I had been in charge of executing Christ, I'd have handled it differently. You see, what I'd have done was had him shipped to Rome and fed to the lions. They never could have made a Savior out of mince meat."

Then Anderson referred to the author as "hater Hecht" and complained that no one had called Hecht "an extremist or a hater." All this was part of an essay, in which Anderson tried to clean up the image of the Ultra-Rightists, by imputing to others the actions of the Ultra-Rightists. His final sentence was:

Is it all right to hate Christ but a mortal misdemeanor to hate Bobby Kennedy?

In response to a letter challenging his remarks about Hecht, Anderson wrote to us on February 12, 1967, that he read *A Jew in Love after* receiving our letter, thus admitting that he was using a second-hand quotation when he wrote his column. His main comment about our criticism was: "Since when can an author say anything he wants to, then blame the character he created?"

The truth of the matter is that Ben Hecht never said what the hate peddlers attributed to him. In his novel, *A Jew in Love*, one of the characters he portrays is a very offensive, reactionary, anti-Communist degenerate by the name of Boshere, who at one point in *his* dialogue with a writer, says:

> One of the finest things every done by the mob was the crucifixion of Christ. Intellectually it was a splendid gesture. But trust the mob to bungle. If I'd have been there, if I'd have charge of executing Christ, I'd have handled it differently. You see, what I would have done was had him shipped to Rome and fed to the lions. They could never have made a savior out of mince meat. I would do the same thing to the radicals today."

The first thing to be noticed is that the hate peddlers have omitted a portion of one sentence and completely deleted the last sentence. A careful reading of the entire quotation reveals that one of the characters in Hecht's book is pointing out in somewhat irreverent fashion, to be sure, that the method of executing Christ made him a martyr and that the character (Boshere) is in favor of Draconion measures against present-day radicals. Just imagine what confusion and dishonesty there would be in attributing to Shakespeare himself all the utterances of characters in any of his plays. Or consider if the same line of reasoning would be applied to the novels or plays of Tolstoy, Upton Sinclair, Balzac, Arthur Miller, George Bernard Shaw, and other giants of literary history. As we shall see later, this is a common form of deception by the Ultra-Rightists.

## The Fascist Ghouls

If there can be anything to equal or surpass the bestialities of Hitler's Nazis, it is the macabre spreading of stories by some sections of the Ultra-Right, denying or minimizing the atrocities perpetrated against the Jews by the Nazis.

119

The *National Economic Council,* whose offices are at 156 Fifth Avenue, New York City, asked these two questions in its Letter of April 15, 1961: 1. "If there were six million Jews within reach of Hitler, which number is widely questioned, and if they have all disappeared, where are they?" 2. "Is it not likely that many of these six million, claimed to have been killed by Hitler and Eichmann, are right here in the United States and are now joining in the agitation for more and more support for the State of Israel . . . even if the American Republic goes down?"

It is, of course, no surprise that George Lincoln Rockwell,[1] der Fuehrer of the American Nazi Party, spreads doctrines emanating from the neo-Nazis of West Germany, as well as the doctrines of the old Nazi leaders, Hitler, Goebbels, and Streicher. When he was interviewed by a reporter for *Playboy* magazine,[2] the Nazi said: "I don't believe for one minute that any 6,000,000 Jews *were* exterminated by Hitler. It never happened. You want me to prove it to you?"

Rockwell's "proof" is not only interesting, but is typical of Fascist intellectual dishonesty. It so happens that Hanson W. Baldwin, the military affairs editor of the *New York Times,* referred to "the 15 to 18 million Jews of the world" in an article which appeared in the *Times* on February 22, 1948. *Rockwell* decided that 18 million is the correct figure for 1948. To this he adds the 6 million Jews exterminated by Hitler, and comes up with a total of 24 million. Then he compares 24 million with the 1939 World Almanac figure for world Jewish population: 15,688,259. Rockwell argues that this difference of some $8\frac{1}{4}$ million for a span of nine years is a biological impossibility. The only thing that it wrong with Rockwell's logic is that it proceeds from a false premise, the figures given by Baldwin. Had Rockwell used Baldwin's low figure, his argument would not have so much force; but it so happens that Baldwin was in error about the figures. *Playboy* obtained the following figures from the Population Reference Bureau in Washington, D.C., which is obviously a better authority on demography than Mr. Baldwin:

---

1 Mr. Rockwell was assassinated by one of his own followers since this was written.

2 *Playboy,* April, 1966.

| YEAR | WORLD JEWISH POPULATION | EUROPE'S JEWISH POPULATION |
|------|------------------------|----------------------------|
| 1939 | 16,600,000 | 9,700,000 |
| 1945 | 11,400,000 | 3,700,000 |

As further evidence to support the accuracy of the figures given by Population Reference Bureau, it may be of some significance that the 1965 *Britannica Book of the Year* gives a world Jewish population figure of 13,016,000, and in January of 1966 the World Jewish Congress concluded from the survey that the 1965 world Jewish population had risen to 13,887,000. The latter two figures are consistent with a 1945 figure of 11,400,000. (The 1965 *Britannica Book of the Year* figure is probably the figure of 1963). (Hanson W. Baldwin's admission, that he was in error about the world Jewish population, is given in our discussion of the Khazar Canard.)

The hate sheets, such as *The Cross and The Flag, Common Sense, Women's Voice, National Chronicle, Thunderbolt, National Christian News*, and others of similar character use another method of statistical juggling to "prove" to their dupes and suckers that the 6,000,000 Jews were not exterminated. They quote the figure of the total *German* Jewish population at the time of Hitler's accession to power, and then ask how Hitler could exterminate 6 million Jews out of a population of half a million or so. Some of the dupes are so ignorant of history that they accept the "logic" of this argument; others accept it with tongue-in-cheek, as a justifiable form of deception in fighting Jews and Communists. Of course, any person with a knowledge of history knows that the Nazis exterminated Jews in Germany, Poland, Czechoslovakia, Austria, Hungary, Soviet Union, France, Belgium, and wherever they could apprehend them. Millions were shipped to extermination centers, and there is ample documentary evidence, assembled from the Nazis' own records by U.S. army specialists. The Nuremberg Trials and the many trials that have been held even in West Germany have uncovered overwhelming evidence beyond any possibility of refutation. A case in point is a story in the *Catholic Universe Bulletin* of May 29, 1964, which, in turn, quotes from an article in *La Parrochia*, a Catholic monthly published in Rome. The article in *La Parrochia* is written by Father Pirro Scavizzi, the chaplain who was stationed with Italian troops on the Russian front during World War II.

Father Scavizzi reports that he told Pope Pius XII: a high Nazi official had cynically informed Father Scavizzi that about six million Jews had been eliminated, and that "we hope to finish with eight million—the others will die of hunger by themselves."[3]

The John Birch Society, and especially its public relations director, John H. Rousselot, would vehemently deny that it is a Fascist organization. It should then explain why its official organ, *American Opinion*, in the issue of January 1965 carried an article entitled "Atrocities Which The 'Liberals' Hide" by Michael F. Connors. The author's qualifications are that he teaches history at a Roman Catholic academy for women, Gwynedd-Mercy College, and that he has written articles for such Ultra-Rightist publications as *Wanderer, University Bookman,* and *American Mercury*.[4] An examination of his footnotes reveals that he relies for the raw material of his article almost exclusively on Right-Wing and pro-Fascist sources, including *Human Events,* the House Un-American Activities Committee, the Senate Internal Security Subcommittee, the Bonn regime of West Germany, and two books by Professor Austin J. App of Philadelphia. App is a contributing editor of the Ultra-Rightist *American Mercury* and is national president of the Federation of American Citizens of German Descent. App also writes for the notorious neo-Nazi publication, *National-Zeitung und Soldaten-Zeitung,* which circulates in West Germany. Its issue of October 14, 1966, carried an article by App, telling of a meeting in Philadelphia to celebrate the "Week of Oppressed People." App also spoke at a meeting of expellees at Kiel, West Germany in mid-August 1966.

Connors follows the line of the more "respectable" apologists for the Nazis. This line consists of minimizing the extent and scope of the Nazi bestialities and creating a diversionary movement to focus attention on real (and imaginary) Communist atrocities. In fact, the pile-it-on technique is used to make Nazi atrocities look relatively insignificant. Thus Connors begins his article:

For the past thirty-odd years, spokesmen for American "Liberalism"

3 *The Catholic Universe Bulletin* is published in Cleveland, Ohio.
4 Mr. Connors is also a member of the National Council of the John Birch Society and the head of the Wanderer Forum Foundation.

have had a field day recounting the misdeeds of the Nazis and Fascists.

Note the clever use of "misdeeds."

After complaining that there is too much discussion about Auschwitz and the Gestapo rather than the alleged Soviet massacre at Katyn forest and the crimes of Lavrenti Beria, Connors discovers the reason for the attacks against "Germany." Not the Nazis, you understand, but "Germany." Connors discovers that there is a plot to divide the West and deter the rearmament of Germany. Thus he proves himself a good student of Professor App and Robert Welch. And to bolster his argument that the Russians are the real perpetrators of atrocities, he quotes a 1945 statement of that great champion of human rights and Christian womanhood, Senator James O. Eastland. It was consistent with the Birch Society whitewash of Nazi atrocities that in the same issue with Connors' masterpiece, Martin Dies, the veteran witch-hunter became a contributing editor of *American Opinion*.

In the February 1965 issue of *American Opinion*, Martin Dies pursues the sly technique of minimizing Nazi atrocities, repeating the Hitlerian lies that the Communists killed 25 million people in Russia and that the Soviets were the "sworn ally" of Japan up to their entry in the war against Japan. Then he adds the biggest of the Hitler-Goebbels swindles: "Remember, Hitler and the Fascists were Socialists."

In the April 1965 *American Opinion* the Texas dragon slayer returns to the arena with more lies from the Nazi propaganda arsenal. Emboldened by the accolades from the Birchers for his previous performance, Dies now tells us that the Communists killed 25 million people in Russia and 35 million in China. Then he refers to the Hitler atrocities as "the crimes of a Nazi regime deposed twenty years ago." This sleight-of-hand performance is, of course, designed to sell a "let bygones be bygones" attitude with respect to the Nazis and to whip up hysteria against Communists, but more especially against liberals.

This line, of covertly or overtly defending Nazism and absolving it of its crimes against humanity, has become part and parcel of the ideology of the Ultra-Right.

123

# Meet Mr. Hal Hunt

Hal Hunt's weekly hate sheet, *The National Chronicle*, has a circulation of less than 1000, but it is a force to be reckoned with, because it is one of the pacemakers of the incipient U.S.A. Fascism. It furnishes the ideological ammunition for a host of other Fascist sheets and individuals, including some gentlemen in high positions, who for reasons of political and financial expediency conceal their pro-Fascist sympathies. Typical of Hunt's fulminations is his issue of March 11, 1965. It consists of four pages, of which 3⅔ pages are devoted to a vile concoction entitled *A History of "Uncle Sam" and the Zionist-Jews*. It is redolent of the ravings of Hitler's hate-peddler, the late and unlamented Julius Streicher. The final ⅓ of page 4 contains three advertisements of the Fascist *National States Rights Party*, one advertisement of the Fascist *Minutemen*, and the advertisement of a book, *We will Survive*, written by Art and Kay Westerman. The book, incidentally, is an Ultra-Rightist treatise on how to prepare for the "coming Negro Revolution or attack from enemy forces."

According to Hunt, the Federal Reserve System is run solely by "privately owned Jewish banks," and "Talmud Jews thus acquired control over the means of livelihood of the American people." That American banking is about 95% Gentile-controlled and that there is flagrant discrimination against Jews throughout the banking industry—these easily documented facts do not in any way inhibit professional anti-Semites from spreading the lie of Jewish control.

As a "historian," Hunt introduces some novel theories. He claims that "President Truman never issued any official order for dropping the bomb," but rather that it was the fault of the late J. Robert Oppenheimer, the physicist who was head of the Los Alamos laboratory, which developed the first atomic bomb. Why does Hunt shift the responsibility to Oppenheimer?[5] The reason, of course, is that Oppenheimer is Jewish, and in the lexicon of the Fascists, a lie is not a lie, if it is told about Jews, Communists, and Negroes. In addition, Hunt claims that the atomic bomb was developed by Jewish physicists working with unlimited funds provided by Jewish government officials, who saw this as a means of intimidating the world.

[5] Dr. Oppenheimer has passed away since this was written.

It is to be expected that a Fascist "historian" would accord special treatment to President Franklin D. Roosevelt. Hunt seems to have mastered well the writings of that eminent "historian" and Fuehrer of the Birch Society, Robert Welch. For Hunt uses the one devastating word that Welch used against Eisenhower: Hunt accuses Roosevelt of *Treason!* And not to be out-done by Welch, Hunt also accuses F.D.R. of being a Communist conspirator: "There is no denying the truth—the United States was brought under a Communistic regime in 1932 and has ever since been administered as such, growing worse day by day, rapidly approaching totality." Of course sane people understand that far from being a Communist, Franklin D. Roosevelt introduced his New Deal measures to rescue Capitalism from its most disastrous crisis, precipitated by the stock market crash of 1929 and its ensuing depression.

## The *"Jewish World"* Fabrication, No. 1

Hal Hunt, like all rabid anti-Semites, knows no bounds to his sadistic frenzy. He "proves" that the Jews were responsible for World War I by quoting the following alleged statement from the *Jewish World* of January 16, 1919:

International Jewry forced Europe into this war not only in order to get possession of a great quantity of gold, but also to prepare, by means of this war, a new Jewish war.

It requires no research to prove that this is a fabrication, a forgery. For only an insane Jew or an agent-provocateur would write such tripe. In the first place, there is no such entity as International Jewry, politically or otherwise. Jews fought and died on both sides in World War I, as in all wars. Some Jews on both sides opposed the war and were jailed for their efforts. How do the anti-Semites like Hal Hunt get away with such lies? In the first place, they aim at an audience that wants to believe anti-Semitic lies. In the second place, no one systematically refutes their lies, because of the paralyzing "hush-hush" policies in certain quarters. Thirdly, the anti-Semites frequently "quote" stuff that is very difficult to check out. Hal Hunt can safely "quote" the *Jewish World* of *January 16, 1919,* in his issue of *March 11, 1965*, because the *Jewish World* is out of business. There were two publications with this name. The first one, a daily in Cleveland, Ohio, was established in 1908 and *suspended in 1952*. The second *Jewish World* was published daily in Philadelphia from 1913 until 1941, when it became a weekly. It finally *suspended in 1945*.

## The *"Jewish World"* Fabrication, No. 2

*Common Sense* of January 15, 1962, quotes the *Jewish World* of March 15, 1923, as saying:

Fundamentally, Judaism is Anti-Christian.

Lyrl Van Hyning uses the same quotation in her collection of anti-Semitic lies and forgeries, *Key to the Mystery*, page 13. Victor Marsden, translator of that masterpiece of forgery, *The Protocols of the Learned Elders of Zion*, uses the same quotation on page 7 of the March, 1958 edition of *World Conquest Through World Government*, under which name the notorious Protocols were published in London by the Britons Publishing Society.

In checking out this obviously phoney quotation, we carried on considerable correspondence until we finally determined that a file of the Philadelphia *Jewish World* was in the archives of the New York Public Library and that a file of the Cleveland *Jewish World* was in the archives of the Midwest Inter-Library Center in Chicago. In reply to our inquiry regarding "Fundamentally, Judaism is Anti-Christian" we received a negative report from the New York Public Library, one of the world's finest research libraries (see page 127).

On June 21, 1962, we visited the Midwest Inter-Library Center in Chicago, a most unique research institution, whose facilities are available only to faculty members of the thirteen supporting universities and to research scholars. To our surprise we found that they had files of both the Cleveland and the Philadelphia *Jewish World*. A most painstaking search failed to reveal any trace of the quotations allegedly appearing in the January 16, 1919 issue and in the March 15, 1923 issue.

One week later we again checked the Philadelphia *Jewish World* in the archives of the New York Public Library, and

126

FIFTH AVENUE & 42ND STREET
NEW YORK 18, N.Y.

March 21, 1962

Mr. Morris Kominsky
400 East Franklin St.
Elsinore, Calif.

Dear Mr. Kominsky:

I have examined the "Jewish World" of Philadelphia from March 15, 1923, but could find no reference to the statement you quote.

Sincerely yours,

*Abraham Berger*

Abraham Berger
Chief, Jewish Division

personally verified the report we had received from Mr. Berger. In the four days that we spent in the New York Public Library, we explored every possibility of finding any evidence of authenticity of these quotations. But both phoney quotations are still receiving widespread circulation—internationally—while occasionally there are weak and insipid refutations on a very limited and inadequate scale.

## The Rabbi Emanuel Rabinovich Hoax

In the same issue of his hate sheet, "historian" Hal Hunt serves his dupes an exotic morsel of more recent vintage. He quotes from "the address of Rabbi Emanuel Rabinovich before a special meeting of the Emergency Council of European Rabbis

127

in Budapest Hungary, on January 12, 1952." Nowhere does our historian tell us how or where he obtained this report of a speech at a secret conference. As he does quite often, Mr. Hunt leads his dupes to believe that he has secret pipelines to special intelligence sources. Needless to point out, this secret meeting never took place. Neither the *New York Times* Index nor any other source that we researched had any of this special information, miraculously acquired by this small-town hate peddler.

Any person of average intelligence can readily see from the internal evidence of the item itself that it is a fraud; providing, of course, that the intelligent person is free of paralyzing and blinding prejudices. For instance, in Hunt's report of the rabbi's speech, the rabbi begins with: "Greetings, My Children!" This form of salutation is used only by clergymen who are addressing laymen, but never at a gathering of fellow clergymen. Then the rabbi is quoted as saying: "Within five years this program will achieve its objective, the Third World War, which will surpass in destructiveness all previous contests." According to this prognostication, the Third World War was scheduled to break out in 1957. Strangely enough, neither Hunt nor any of his readers questioned the validity of this purported report of the Rabinovich speech. No one stopped to consider that it is eight years later and the plot of the International Jews has not materialized. It is quite a lengthy speech, and it is quite apparent that it follows the pattern of the ugly and notorious "Protocols of the Elders of Zion," which we will consider presently.

The inventor of the Rabbi Emanuel Rabinovich Hoax is that damned liar, Eustace Mullins, who invented the Israel Cohen Hoax. Mullins launched the Rabbi Rabinovich Hoax in the May 1952 issue of *Women's Voice.* It was picked up by the September 1952 issue of the Canadian Intelligence Service, a Fascist propaganda outfit with a misleading name that causes some people to consider it an official agency of the Canadian Government. From there it was reproduced in a pamphlet entitled *The Seed of the Serpent vs. The Seed of the Woman,* issued by an anti-Semitic propaganda outfit in Vancouver, The British-Israel Association. As usual, this Fascist-minded group operates behind the facade of an innocent-sounding name. The alacrity with which the merchants of hate will utilize any fraudulent material and palm it off as religious doctrine is illustrated by the heading given to the Rabbi Rabinovich "speech" in this pamphlet:

Plans of The "Synagogue of Satan"

Mullins' own account of how he allegedly obtained the Rabbi Rabinovich speech was given, as a footnote to the speech, by *Women's Voice*:

This transcription of Rabinovich's speech was given to me by a former Bulgarian diplomat who broke with the Communist regime and reached Budapest, Hungary, where he hid out with anti-Communist friends until March. While there, be obtained a copy of this speech, and was then smuggled to Hamburg, Germany, finally making his way to this country. A gentleman in Hamburg gave him my name, and he met me and urged me to distribute this speech at once. I sincerely hope that it will give the American people a better picture of the force arrayed against them.—Eustace Mullins.

Yes, there are people ready to believe Mullins' nursery tale, but for sensible people this story is not believable, especially from the inventor of the Israel Cohen Hoax and the slanderer of the great Jewish benefactors of children throughout the world, Dr. Jonas Salk and Dr. Albert Sabin. The Rabbi Rabinovich Hoax is still making the rounds of the underworld of hate peddlers. It cropped up in a leaflet issued in October, 1966 by Helen Courtois' propaganda mill, Keep America Committee. And it will continue to fan the flames of prejudice until the climate of public opinion makes these people the outcasts of society, to be shunned by all decent people.

## The Polio Vaccine Hoax

Mrs. Lyrl Van Hyning has made a career of peddling anti-Semitism, and it is therefore fitting that one of the stars of her hate sheet, *Women's Voice*, is the irrepressible story teller, Eustace Mullins. In the June, 1955, issue is an article by Mullins entitled "Jews Mass Poison American Children." Some excerpts are quoted here at length, in order to preserve contextual integrity:

One of the most shocking and sadistic episodes in the history of

129

the world is now being carried out in the United States by Jewish mass poisoners of children. Jonas Salk, Yiddish inventor of a so-called polio vaccine, is directing the inoculation of millions of American children with this sinister concoction of live polio germs. All that is known is that it CAUSES polio in an alarming percentage of children injected with it, while its effectiveness in preventing polio is a myth of Jewish propaganda.

Meanwhile, commentator Paul Harvey warns his radio audience of millions of listeners that he is NOT going to have his little boy injected with this poison.

The press prints testimonial after testimonial in FAVOR of the Jew vaccine from the filthy immoral rats in the U.S. Public Health Service in Washington, which is nothing but a publicity bureau for Jewish poisons such as fluorine in water. How can they be so heartless as to go on day after day urging American citizens to poison their children with the Jewish vaccine?

The answer lies in the multi-million dollar charity racket known as the March of Dimes, which kept the late demented cripple F. D. Roosevelt in clover most of his life.

If these atrocious statements sound shocking, how much more shocking is it that the author of these poison darts was on the staff of a U.S. Senator, the late Joseph McCarthy, the hero of the John Birch Society and William F. Buckley, Jr. and his *National Review* staff? It seems almost gratuitous to refute the ravings of the inventor of the Israel Cohen hoax and the Rabbi Rabinovich Hoax, but for the sake of any readers who are victims of the Fascist propaganda mill a few facts would be in order.

On March 25, 1965, almost ten years after Mullins' masterpiece appeared, U.S. Senator Lester Hill (of Alabama) introduced a concurrent resolution in the Senate, which pointed out:

1. That in the ten years since the Salk vaccine had been introduced there has been a 99% reduction in the number of cases of poliomyelitis.

2. That this dread disease once attacked as many as 57,000 Americans in a single year and made the summer months a time of fear and apprehension for parents.

3. That this victory against polio had been won by a partnership of Dr. Jonas Salk, the National Foundation of March of Dimes, and the U.S. Public Health Service.

Subsequent to Dr. Salk's crowning discovery, another type of polio vaccine was developed by Dr. Albert Sabin, who also

130

happens to be Jewish. But what sends the Fascist propagandists into paroxysms of hysteria is the fact that Dr. Sabin came here from the U.S.S.R. in 1921. What further proof is needed by Eustace Mullins and Lyrl Van Hyning that the polio vaccine is a Jewish-Communist plot? To a large extent the Sabin vaccine has superseded the Salk vaccine, but humanity will be everlastingly grateful to both of these great medical scientists who continue their researches in microbiology and immunology. In September, 1962, Professor Nikolai Blokhin, president of the Soviet Academy of Medical Sciences reported that since 1956 the Sabin polio vaccine had been taken orally by more than 100,000,000 Soviet children and young adults, virtually wiping out poliomyelitis in that vast country. This presents a strange problem for the anti-Semitic propagandists who argue that the Jews run the Soviet Union. Now, if the polio vaccine is a poison, are the Jews poisoning themselves and the people they supposedly rule and exploit?

## The Marcus Eli Ravage Fabrication

Marcus Eli Ravage, a well-known Jewish-American writer, author of several books and formerly on the staff of the *New York Times,* wrote a couple of satirical articles which appeared in *Century Magazine,* January and February 1928. The dishonesty of the anti-Semitic mind does not permit the idea of a Jew saying something ironically or jocularly. So, the professional anti-Semites have had a field day quoting Marcus Ravage out of context and even misquoting him. A few years ago Lyrl Van Hyning compiled a 16-page tabloid of anti-Semitic hate items under the title of *The Key to the Mystery.* It is a compendium of imaginary quotations from real people, imaginary quotations from imaginary people, out-of-context quotations from real authors and publications, and outright fabrications. Van Hyning has dredged the sewers of anti-Semitism throughout the world and prepared this handbook for hate peddlers. Some of the "quotations" go back to 1489!

Van Hyning's technique is very deceptive, and cannot be detected unless one is willing to go to the trouble of digging for the truth. Her method consists of a selective presentation of excerpts from both articles, placed in such juxtaposition as to distort and destroy what Mr. Ravage is saying, but above all, it twists the author's satire into *Jewish self-incrimination*. The reader is urged to look up the two articles of Mr. Ravage and enjoy his satirical thrusts at the Van Hynings, the Eustace Mullins, and others of the hate-peddling fraternity. Mr. Ravage has produced the reductio ad absurdam par excellence, and the reader will understand the angry reaction of the anti-Semites. One little sample of the Van Hyning technique should suffice. In the left-hand column, we give a quotation as Van Hyning presented it, and in the right-hand column is the quotation as it appears on page 477 of *Century Magazine,* January, 1928.

| VAN HYNING'S VERSION | MARCUS RAVAGE'S WORDS |
|---|---|
| You go on prattling of Jewish conspiracies and cite as instances the Great War and the Russian Revolution! Can you wonder that we Jews have always taken your antisemites rather lightly, as long as they did resort to violence? | *And then* you go on prattling of Jewish conspiracies and cite as instances the Great War and the Russian Revolution! Can you wonder that we Jews have always taken your anti-Semites rather lightly, as long as they did *not* resort to violence? |

We have italicized the three words that Madam Van Hyning so conveniently omitted. The "And then" would furnish the clue to the fact that the quoted paragraph is taken out of context! And the omission of the word "not" is, of course, downright falsification. Van Hyning solemnly assures her dupes that she is carrying on a fight for Christianity!

In the March 11, 1965, issue of *The National Chronicle,* Hal Hunt has also quoted a satirical paragraph from the Marcus Ravage articles, in a manner calculated to make it sound like Jewish self-incrimination! Another professional anti-Semite, Major Robert H. Williams, has written a booklet entitled *Know Your Enemy*. Williams has made a profound discovery: all of the world's troubles are caused by the Jews. No lie is too big and no story too silly for Williams to use against the Jews and the Communists. On the front cover of this opus, we are shown four pictures. From left to right: Stalin; U.S. Senator Herbert Lehman; U.S. Supreme Court Justice Felix Frankfurter; and Secretary of the Treasury Henry Morgenthau, Jr. Underneath these pictures, it says:

And, of course, the three Jews are the "secret government." Major General Edward F. Witsel, Adjutant General of the U.S. Army, stated in a letter on January 8, 1951, that after an investigation "it has been determined that the termination of Major Williams' commission would be in the best interest of the service. He has, accordingly, been discharged from his commission." The letter was sent to the Washington, D.C. Director of the Anti-Defamation League. Williams quotes from Marcus Ravage as follows:

We (Jews) have been at the bottom . . . not only of the Russian but of every other major revolution in your history.

In quoting this, the question arises if Williams seriously believes this boast, and if he does, he must believe that the Jews were the organizers of the American Revolution circa 1776. And does Williams regret that the American Revolution was engineered by the "Jews"?

Actually Williams has not only taken something out of context, but he has made some alterations. This is the exact quotation from page 476 of *Century Magazine*, January, 1928:

You call us subverters, agitators, revolution-mongers. It is the truth, and I cower at your discovery. It could be shown with only the slightest straining and *juggling of the facts* that we have been at the bottom of all the major revolutions in your history.

Now, Williams is either a damned liar or he is too stupid to understand irony and satire. For immediately, following the above quotation, Mr. Ravage lists some more of the charges usually made against Jews, and then points out that all this is petty stuff and that if the anti-Semitic propagandists had any brains, they would charge the Jews with the biggest crime of all—foisting a new religion on a bunch of heathen. Ravage puts it this way:

But even these plots and revolutions are as nothing compared with the great conspiracy which we engineered at the beginning of this era and which was destined to make the creed of a Jewish sect the religion of the Western world.

All throughout his two articles Ravage uses devastating satire to demolish the myths and the lies of the anti-Semites; but Williams, Van Hyning, Hunt and Company choose to twist Ravage's writings into Jewish self-incrimination. Needless to point out, the Marcus Ravage Fabrication has been used hundreds of times and will continue to be used as long as there is a market for bigots' tonic!

There are those who believe that the best way of coping with the professional hate-peddlers is to ignore them, because, forsooth, they appeal only to the crackpots, the malcontents, the lunatic fringe. Unfortunately, there are two things wrong with this theory. In the first place, it ignores the fact that the followers of the hate-peddlers *spread* the poisonous doctrines and prepare the minds of the stormtroopers of incipient Fascism. Secondly, it ignores the fact that "respectable" segments of our society covertly and overtly encourage and support the hate-peddlers. If you think that Major Robert H. Williams' anti-Semitic lie about the "secret Government of the United States" can be ignored, what will you say to the fact that the powerful *Chicago Tribune* carried a front-page story on May 29, 1950, with the same canard? It was written by Walter Trohan, one of the darlings of the Ultra-Rightists. Trohan, who is chief of the *Tribune's* Washington Bureau, attacked and slandered Senator Herbert Lehman, Supreme Court Justice Felix Frankfurter, and former Secretary of the Treasury, Henry Morgenthau, Jr.—all Jews—as the "secret Government of the United States." Trohan covered himself from a libel suit by "quoting" anonymously a high official in the State Department.

Trohan's columns are carried by a number of Ultra-Rightist publications, and he is quoted from time to time by others. The hate sheet of the Louisiana (White) Citizens Councils, *The Councilor* of March 6, 1967, carried the following item:

### THE SECRET GOVERNMENT OF THE UNITED STATES

Chicago—The Chicago Tribune on May 29, 1950, published the pictures of three men, Felix Frankfurter, Henry Morgenthau, Jr. and Herbert Lehman, along with this caption: "A person with highest state department connections identified these three figures as the secret government of the United States." Morgenthau was related to Lehman by at least one mariage on this side of the Atlantic, and probably through many other connections in Bavaria. Of the three, Lehman apparently had final authority.

This illustrates one of the techniques of the Ultra-Rightists. A story that is seventeen years old is repeated in the form of a dispatch from Chicago, as if it is a current news item.

## The Benjamin Franklin Hoax

In its December, 1966, issue, *Thunderbolt*, the hate sheet of the Fascistic *National States Rights Party*, resurrected a stale and discredited canard. It quoted the following remarks, allegedly made by Benjamin Franklin at the Constitutional Convention of 1787 in Philadelphia:

In whatever country Jews have settled in any great numbers, they have lowered its moral tone, depreciated its commercial integrity, have segregated themselves and have not been assimilated, have sneered at and tried to undermine the Christian religion, and have, when opposed, tried to strangle that country to death financially.

If you do not exclude them from the United States in the Constitution, in less than 200 years they will have swarmed in such great numbers that they will dominate and devour the land and change our form of government.

If you do not exclude them, in less than 200 years our descendants will be working in the fields to furnish the substance while they will be in the counting house rubbing their hands. I warn you, gentlemen, if you do not exclude the Jews for all time, your children will curse you in your graves. Jews, gentlemen, are Asiatics; they will never be otherwise.

The professional hate-peddlers have, from time immemorial, produced forged documents to "prove" the very simple thesis that the Jews are responsible for all the ills and crimes of humanity. The Benjamin Franklin speech has been assiduously spread through the use of such "documents," and even though these "documents" have been pronounced forgeries by the Benjamin Franklin Institute and a host of reputable historians, the hoax keeps marching on! It is not uncommon to find hate sheets resurrecting this hoax at least once a year, on a continuing basis.

It is interesting to examine the *internal evidence* that proves the fraudulent nature of this Benjamin Franklin speech:

1. Franklin was a very learned man, an inventor, a scholar, and a philosopher. This alleged speech clashes will all the known writings and speeches of Franklin.

135

2. Such a speech on the floor of the Constitutional Convention would certainly have brought forth comments by other delegates. Our document forgers overlooked this little item, and they failed to forge speeches by other delegates in response to Franklin's "speech."

3. The very last sentence of the speech gives away the entire game: "Jews, gentlemen, are Asiatics; they will never be otherwise." It desecrates the memory of the immortal Franklin when anyone attributes such nonsense to him. The Jews, of course, are not Asiatics. This line—about Asiatics—was invented more than a hundred years later by professional anti-Semites. So, aside from the fact that the learned Franklin would not utter such a falsehood, the notion itself was not extant in 1787. It should be noted, of course, that there is nothing shameful about being an Asiatic, excepting to the promoters of national hatreds.

4. There is an obvious contradiction between the charge that Jews do not assimilate and the prognostication that in 200 years the Jews would dominate the country. Of course, with respect to the latter item, professional anti-Semites always claim falsely that Jews control the country.

5. In the face of the prophecy in the alleged Franklin speech that, unless Jews were excluded from the country, the others would be working in the fields to support the Jews who would be rubbing their hands in the counting houses—one can only wonder how the anti-Semitic hate merchants peddle such nonsense! Obviously, the American people are not living as slaves of Jewish masters, except in the hallucinatory essays of Eustace Mullins, Gerald L. K. Smith, George Lincoln Rockwell, Charles Coughlin, Paul Joseph Goebbels, Lyrl Van Hyning, Marilyn Allen, Robert Williams, and the other traffickers in hate.

The Benjamin Franklin hoax was first circulated in the United States during 1934 by professional anti-Semite, William Dudley Pelley, who was the leader of the Fascist *Silver Shirts*. He attributed it to the private diary of Charles Pinckney of South Carolina, who was a delegate to the Constitutional Convention of 1787. When challenged, Pelley claimed to have taken it from a copy of the diary which was the property of an unidentified descendant of Pinckney. The eminent historian, Dr.

Charles Beard, researched very thoroughly and could find no trace of the Pinckney diary, and finally he stated that the so-called prophecy of Benjamin Franklin is "a barefaced forgery."

Other anti-Semites have claimed that the original copy of the Pinckney diary, with the Benjamin Franklin prophecy in it, can be found in the Franklin Institute at Philadelphia, Penn. In August, 1938, the librarian, Mr. Henry Butler Allen, issued a statement, from which the following are excerpts:

Reports have been widely circulated, for several years, off and on, saying that Dr. Franklin made a speech during the Constitutional Convention against the Jewish race. The purported speech is printed, and said to be quoted in full, from a "private diary" kept by Charles Pinckney of South Carolina, who was a fellow delegate with Franklin at the Convention in 1787.

But this "private diary" has not been produced. Historians and librarians have not been able to find it or any record of it having existed. The historians have said further that some of the words and phraseology used in the quoted speech cast doubt on its colonial origin. In plain English, they have claimed it a fake. The Charles Pinckney "private diary" containing Franklin's vitriolic speech is now reported to be in possession of the Franklin Institute.

The truth is, we *do not* possess the notorious diary. In fact we know no more about its whereabouts than we did before, and that was nothing.

Further on Mr. Allen points out that when the Hebrew Society of Philadelphia sought to raise money for a synagogue building, *Franklin signed an appeal to "citizens of every religious denomination" asking for contributions, and Franklin himself gave five pounds to the fund.* And Mr. Allen points out that *this story is historically authenticated.* Hardly the type of man who would deliver an anti-Semitic speech!

## The Xmas Hoax

The spewing of hatred—at a handsome profit—has become the way of life with Gerald L. K. Smith to such an extent that he virtually celebrated the Christmas season of 1966 by a special newsletter of hate, which reached many of his dupes and "suckers" on December 23. In the middle of this long anti-Semitic diatribe, Smith has cunningly placed a special item in such juxtaposition as to leave the impression that this also is a Jewish "crime":

Years ago the campaign to take the word "CHRIST" out of the word Christmas was lubricated by introducing the figure "X" so that people would be tempted to abbreviate Christmas by the blasphemous omission of the name of Christ from the word Christmas, leaving it Xmas. Furthermore, in the mathematical vocabularly of modern life, the figure "X" is referred to as being symbolical of the unknown quantity.

This, of course, sends his fanatical and delirious followers into a high state of emotional intoxication. And his rich supporters, who understand the sociological role of anti-Semitism as a device for propping up the status quo, applaud Gerald's cunning and imaginative use of every opportunity to cause discord. The truth of the matter can easily be ascertained.

Webster's New International Dictionary, Second Edition, 1949, tells us that the "X," as used in Xmas, does *not* represent the "X" of the mathematical vocabulary; but rather it represents the Greek letter "chi," which is like "X" in form. "Chi" is the initial letter of "Christos." Thus, the "X" is used, alone or in combination, to denote the word "Christ," and therefore Xmas means Christmas, with no irreverent connotation.

The American College Dictionary, 1963 edition, gives the following definitions:

| X. | 1. Christ. | 2. Christian |
|---|---|---|
| Xt. | Christ | |
| Xn. | Christian | |
| Xtian. | Christian | |
| Xnty. | Christianity | |
| Xty. | Christianity | |
| Xmas. | Christmas | |

In the same hate message, Smith accuses the Jews of introducing the concept of Santa Claus in order to drown out the Biblical story of Christ; he claims further that the United Nations was designed and blueprinted by "world Jewry" and that the United Nations "has outlawed the name of Christ." Strange as it may seem, there are people who believe this kind of rubbish to be God's truth, because Smith says it is the word of God!

The original source of this Xmas Hoax seems to be an article, entitled "X= The Unknown Quantity," which appeared in the December 1957 issue of *News and Views*, the monthly newsletter of the Ultra-Rightist *Church League of America*.

138

# The Bilderbergers

The story of the Bilderbergers has relevance to our study of anti-Semitism as a weapon of the forces of reaction and Fascism, only because of the sly innuendoes in the publications of the hate mongers, which hint that The Bilderbergers are part of a Jewish plot. The very name lends itself, because to the ignoramuses, who are the "privates" in the "armies" of anti-Semitism, Bilderberger sounds Jewish. To the followers of anti-Semitic racketeers that is usually sufficient proof of something sinister.

On April 11, 1964, Senator Jacob Javits placed a statement in the *Congressional Record*, which fairly well explains the true nature of The Bilderbergers. As is well known by all informed people, the advent of Communist-controlled governments has presented a challenge to the stability of Capitalist society throughout the world, and despite the rivalries between respective Capitalist groups and nations, there are constant attempts made to establish unified efforts in the struggle against the spread of Communist ideas and influence. There is a school of thought among the supporters of Capitalism which believes that Fascism is the only solution to the Communist challenge. And much as the Fascists and crypto-Fascists try to deny it, the overwhelming evidence proves that they are traveling in the direction of a dictatorship of militarists and monopolists, as well as a third world war to "crush" Communism. There is another school of thought among the supporters of Capitalism which has not yet succumbed to this insanity, and which has confidence that somehow Capitalism will "muddle through." This, of course, is a somewhat oversimplified analysis, but is sufficiently adequate for present purposes.

Although it is cloaked in the usual high-sounding phraseology of the public relations fraternity, the first two paragraphs and paragraphs 6, 7, and 4 of the official statement in the *Congressional Record* are worth quoting:

The idea of the Bilderberg meetings originated in the early fifties. Changes had taken place on the international political and economic scene after World War II. The countries of the Western World felt the need for closer collaboration to protect their moral and ethical values, their democratic institutions, and their independence *against the growing Communist threat.* (Emphasis added.—

M. K.) The Marshall plan and NATO were examples of collective efforts of Western countries to join hands in economic and military matters after World War II.

In the early 1950's a number of people on both sides of the Atlantic sought a means of bringing together leading citizens, not necessarily connected with government, for informal discussions of problems facing the Atlantic community. Such meetings, they felt, would create a better understanding of the forces and trends affecting Western nations; in particular, they believed that direct exchanges *could help to clear up differences and misunderstandings that might weaken the West.* (Emphasis added.—M. K.)

Bilderberg is in no sense a policy-making body. No conclusions are reached. There is no voting and no resolutions are passed.

The meetings are off the record. Only the participants themselves may attend the meetings.

The first meeting that brought Americans and Europeans together took place under the chairmanship of Prince Bernhard at the Bilderberg Hotel in Oosterbeek, Holland, from May 29 to May 31, 1954. Ever since, the meetings have been called Bilderberg meetings.

The propaganda sheets of anti-Semitism, of course, have never brought this information to their followers, who dote on esoteric tales of Jewish intrigue. Nor are they ever told that Bilderberg is a Dutch name, and not necessarily Jewish. Consequently, they get quite a bit of "mileage" out of "profound" and "learned" discussions of The Bilderbergers, in the context of anti-Semitic innuendo.

One of the leading ideologists of the Ultra-Right is Phyllis Schlafly, Research Director of the Cardinal Mindszenty Foundation and President of the Illinois Federation of Republican Women. Her husband is a Director of Eversharp, Inc., parent company of Schick Safety Razor Co., Inc., whose President, Patrick Frawley, Jr., is a leading supporter of Fred Schwartz' Christian Anti-Communism Crusade, Moral Re-Armament, and the American Security Council. She is the author of *A Choice Not an Echo.* Professor Revilo P. Oliver said in the November 1964 issue of the Bircher's magazine, *American Opinion,* that this book "was undoubtedly the *one* publication that contributed most to the nomination of Senator Goldwater in San Francisco."

In this book, Mrs. Schlafly "reveals" something that every knowledgeable person knows: that most of the essential political decisions are made behind the scenes of our various legislative bodies and that the effective control of the country is in the hands of a plutocracy. Long before Phyllis Schlafly became an expert, a leading historian wrote:

We know that something intervenes between the people of the United States and the control of their affairs at Washington. It is not the people who have been ruling there of late.
An invisible empire has been set up above the forms of democracy.
The masters of the government of the United States are the combined capitalists and manufacturers of the United States.

Those words were written in 1913, probably before Phyllis Schlafly was born, by Professor Thomas Woodrow Wilson, President of Princeton University and subsequently President of the United States. There are hundreds of sociological studies that expound the same thesis, but in true Sherlock Holmes style, Phyllis makes two world-shaking discoveries:

Several years ago, the author of this book stumbled on clear evidence that very powerful men actually do meet to make plans which are kept secret from American citizens.

As previously noted, this is not a Schlafly discovery, and her manner of presentation is only sensationalizing some known facts and giving them an aura of mystery. Continuing, she tells us:

While visiting at Sea Island, Georgia, this writer discovered the details of a secret meeting on nearby St. Simons Island, Georgia, held at the King and Prince Hotel, February 14-18, 1957.

Then she describes this Bilderberger conference, giving some of the names of the bankers, industrialists, journalists, and Government officials who participated. She tells the story in a manner which shows her displeasure with the fact that the participants are not sufficiently Ultra-Rightist to suit her. In fact, she slyly Red-Baits some of them by linking one to Alger Hiss and by complaining that "these secret meetings are heavily weighted in favor of the liberal foreign viewpoint and loaded with Americans who have important financial and business contacts and investments abroad—to the exclusion of persons with a pro-American viewpoint." A couple of pages later Phyllis tells us that President Johnson is using Henry Cabot Lodge "to cover for the Administration's sellout to the Communists in South Viet Nam."

141

What emerges from all this is that Mrs. Schlafly demagogically raises the question of plutocratic control of our Government, as a means of pushing for the Ultra-Rightist position, which means moving closer to Fascism and a "preventive" war against the countries of the Sino-Soviet bloc. Why did Mrs. Schlafly wait until 1964 to announce her 1957 discovery? Did it take seven years to work up the patriotic spirit necessary to "expose" The Bilderbergers? Is it not because she needed this story as another political weapon to build an image for General Barry Goldwater as the knight in shining armor who would defeat the plutocrats?

The Ultra-Rightist position vis-a-vis The Bilderbergers is more clearly revealed in an article by Jim Lucier in the November, 1964 issue of *American Opinion*. He begins with a wise-acre's title:

## BILDERBERGERS
### Served With Mustard

Lucier's essay makes the following points, which may be considered the official Birch Line:

1. "The Bilderbergers are men without integrity", using that word "in the deepest sense of philosophical analysis."

2. "They are ready to study, discuss, and adjust differences rather than settle them."

3. They believe that "every problem can be adjusted," and horror of horrors, they would even sit down to discuss matters with Khrushchev.

Like Schlafly, Lucier advocates a "tough guy" policy in foreign relations, a policy of "settling" differences rather than adjusting them. Lucier doesn't quite come out and say that a few nuclear bombs would "settle" matters faster and more effectively than talking, but one can only wonder what else he is driving at with his sneers and jeers.

The 1964 Bilderberger conference was held at Williamsburg, Virginia, in March. It included such "Leftists" as David Rockefeller, president of one of the world's largest banks, Chase Manhattan of New York; Gabriel Hauge, president of Manufacturers Hanover Trust Co.; Lawrence Litchfield, Jr., chairman of the board of the Aluminum Co. of America; Robert D. Murphy, president, Corning Glass International; Emilio G.

142

Collado, vice-president, Standard Oil of New Jersey; Congressman Gerald Ford; Senator Henry M. Jackson; Senator Jacob Javits; Senator J. William Fulbright; Henry J. Heinz II, chairman of the board of Heinz Co.; Hans Speidel, Nazi war criminal, who was one of the leaders of Hitler's invasions; and other representatives of Government, industry, finance, and militarists from this and other countries. All this information was available to Jim Lucier months before he wrote the article for *American Opinion*, but the Birch line requires pushing farther and farther to the Right. And The Bilderbergers remains a good scarecrow story for the Ultra-Rightist agitators to use on their followers.

## The Khazar Canard

If all the lies and libelous stories being circulated by the anti-Semitic underworld were listed and presented in a classified arrangement, it would amaze any rational person with the striking fact that they cancel each other out. Such is the contradictory nature of the stories which are presented with a show of profundity and alleged documentation. Not the least among these is the cunningly devised Khazar canard.

Stated briefly, the Khazar canard is a theory that present-day Jews are not the descendants of the Jews mentioned in the Bible, but rather they are descendants of an Asiatic people, who occupied Southern Russia during the seventh century and became converted to Judiasm. One would expect that, having proved the present-day Jews are not Jews after all, the anti-Semites would cease and desist from hurling the ugly lie: Christ-killer. Strangely enough, the dupes and followers of the anti-Semitic racketeers can simultaneously believe both the Khazar and the Christ-killer canards. Even stranger than fiction is the additional fact that the Khazar canard was originated by an apostate Jew, one Benjamin Harrison Freedman.

Freedman was born in New York City on October 5, 1890 of Jewish parents who came to the U.S.A. from Hungary.[6] His father was a successful manufacturer of clothing. Reports from a number of sources indicate that Freedman has from early childhood been at war with society and himself, and above all

6 Biographical data taken from *The Trouble Makers* by Forster and Epstein of the Anti-Defamation League.

he seems to have hated himself for being born a Jew. There are, of course, other examples of this in the history of Jews, Catholics, Buddhists, Germans, Italians, and other religious and national groups. At age 43, Freedman married a Catholic divorcee.

He openly revealed himself to be a Fascist and an "honorary Aryan," when World War II broke out, by categorically declaring himself a supporter of Hitler's campaign to expand Fascist control, and by predicting that Hitler would win the war. He expressed himself as desirous of doing business with Hitler, that "it would be a splendid business opportunity." When proposals were made to resettle in Palestine 100,000 tragic survivors of Nazism, Freedman held conferences in his New York apartment with Arab leaders to plot a campaign of opposition, using pro-Arab and anti-Zionist propaganda. For more than two years, beginning May 2, 1946, Freedman ran full-page newspaper advertisements in New York and Chicago to thwart this humanitarian rescue operation. Such was the hatred for himself and his people! Although he pretended to have organizational backing, actually his vendetta was a one-man operation behind the facade of a paper organization, the League for Peace with Justice in Palestine.

Freedman had retired from business in 1944, and found himself with plenty of money to spend and plenty of time in which to do mischief. Embracing the doctrines of a small, but wealthy group of anti-Zionist Jews, who operate as the American Council of Judaism, Freedman found the ideological and philosophical outlet for his all-consuming hatred. He wrote and paid for a series of truculent advertisements, proclaiming to the world that through original research he had discovered that the Jews of the present day are only "so-called Jews" and they are really descendants of a Mongol tribe called the Khazars.

By the time he was ready to embark on the campaign against a rescue operation for the pitifully few of Hitler's victims, his publicizing of the Khazar canard had so endeared him with the Arab propagandists that he was soon a part of the pro-Arab propaganda apparatus in the U.S.A. In 1947, when the leader of the Egyptian Fascist "Green Shirts" arrived, Freedman wined him and dined him, despite the fact that the Fascist Egyptian was appearing on the same platform with some known Nazis at anti-Jewish rallies. Freedman was the principal speaker at the

144

farewell party for the Egyptian Fascist and paid half the cost of the farewell banquet. The discussions that Freedman had with the Egyptian Fascist on ways and means of defeating the Jews caused a number of Egyptian publications to hail Freedman as an "alright Jew" and a "Brother."

Freedman was one of the principal actors in a real life drama, which partially lifted the curtain which sometimes obscures the machinations of the Fascist elements of our society. On November 9, 1950, Secretary of Defense George C. Marshall, announced the appointment of a distinguished Jewess, Mrs. Anna M. Rosenberg, as Assistant Secretary of Defense, in charge of manpower. The next day, Fulton Lewis, Jr. did a Red-Scare smear against Mrs. Rosenberg on a nation-wide radio network, basing his alleged facts on a dossier supplied him by Dr. Joseph B. Matthews, a professional anti-Communist and formerly chief counsel for the Dies Committee, the precursor of the House Un-American Activities Committee. At the same time, the network of hate-peddlers mounted a massive anti-Semitic and Red-Scare campaign against the nomination of Anna M. Rosenberg to this Government post. Such professional hate-mongers as Rev. Gerald L. K. Smith, Rev. Wesley Swift, Rev. Gerald Winrod, Edward James Smythe, Major Robert H. Williams, and Conde McGinley got into the act. The latter's hate sheet, *Common Sense*, in its September 1950 issue, screamed in big headlines:

YIDDISH MARXISTS PLOT USA DEFEAT BY USSR

When Mrs. Rosenberg appeared before the Senate Armed Services Committee on November 29, 1950, she effectively rebutted all the phoney charges. The Committee voted unanimously to recommend to the full Senate that her nomination be approved. The Senate, however, could not act at once on this recommendation, because it was in recess. This gave the hate-peddlers additional time to re-deploy their forces. Mr. Benjamin Harrison Freedman came to Washington on December 1,1950, where he conferred with Rev. Gerald L. K. Smith, Rev. Wesley Swift, and Congressman John Rankin of Mississippi. Rankin's credentials were that he was a blatant hater of Jews and Negroes, and had the dubious distinction of having introduced the motion in Congress on January 3, 1945, which transformed the temporary Dies Committee into the permanent House

145

Committee on Un-American Activities. This quartet hatched a plot to block Mrs. Rosenberg's appointment.

Freedman went back to New York, conferred with an attorney, and came up with a witness against Mrs. Rosenberg, one Ralph De Sola. On December 4, 1950, Freedman came back to Washington and conferred with Congressman Ed Gossett of Texas, who also had dabbled in anti-Semitism. Gossett helped Freedman bring pressure to have the Senate Armed Services Committee re-open the hearings. Additional pressure was engineered through the offices of Senator William B. Knowland and the late Senator Joseph McCarthy. After considerable behind-the-scenes maneuvering, Freedman and Gerald Smith met in Congressman Rankin's office, where two affidavits of charges against Mrs. Rosenberg were prepared, and Freedman signed them.

The next day, December 5, 1950, the Rev. Wesley Swift presented the Freedman documents to the Senate Armed Services Committee. The first document charged that Dr. J. B. Matthews had told Freedman that the FBI files contained information "to prove that Anna M. Rosenberg is the least desirable person in the entire United States to be appointed to that position." Furthermore, that the FBI files would support the allegations of Mrs. Rosenberg's ties to Communist and Communist-front organizations. The second document quoted information from Ralph De Sola, who, with his wife, had been a member of the Communist Party; that the De Solas had met Mrs. Rosenberg at the John Reed Club in New York; and that Mrs. Rosenberg had given Mrs. De Sola an assignment to plant Communist agents in the New York educational system.

As a result of all this pressure, the Senate Armed Services Committee subpoenaed a number of witnesses and re-opened its hearing on December 8, 1950. De Sola proved to be a very erratic and contradictory witness. His ex-wife, who testified a few days later, blew up his entire story, and asked to testify additionally about her ex-husband, in executive session. The story that emerged was that De Sola was a pathological liar. Dr. J. B. Matthews testified that the statements attributed to him by Freedman were not his statements and that Freedman had already sent him an abject letter of apology. When placed on the stand, Freedman proved to be a slippery and evasive witness, as well as an unmitigated liar. Under the withering cross-examination of Senator Estes Kefauver, Freedman admitted all his charges were phoney and withdrew them.

In the course of the hearings it developed that among those involved in this gigantic smear of a great American woman of the Jewish faith, in addition to those already mentioned, were ex-FBI Agent Don Surine, who was an employee of Senator Joseph McCarthy, and Edward K. Nellor, who was a reporter for Fulton Lewis, Jr. It is also significant to note that Lewis devoted broadcast after broadcast to "prove" his case against Mrs. Rosenberg. Lewis led with gusto the wolf-pack which was engaged in the public pillorying of a person who had committed no crime, but who was *suspected* of holding certain beliefs. Verily, the modern witch hunters have learned nothing from the lessons of history. After a subcommittee read the FBI files on Anna M. Rosenberg and after the full Committee listened to many additional witnesses, the Senate Armed Services Committee voted again unanimously to approve her nomination. Finally, the United States Senate confirmed Mrs. Rosenberg's appointment as Assistant Secretary of Defense.

Freedman followed this up by sending the Committee several lengthy statements correcting his previous testimony, probably as a move to obviate prosecution for perjury, which he richly deserved. Thus did a vicious frameup blow up in the faces of the conspirators, but other victims of the Fascist and anti-Semitic forces are not always as fortunate as Mrs. Rosenberg.

Over the years, Freedman has been a prolific producer of anti-Semitic statements, tracts, and pamphlets. His material has been used by most of the well-known anti-Semitic racketeers, and he has seemingly gloried in the fact that he has been able to torment the Jewish people, who have endured an ordeal unprecedented in all history. Freedman imagines himself as a martyr who is being persecuted for his sacrifices in fighting the "forces of evil." On one occasion, Freedman told a friend: "Since the death of Hitler I am the most hated man in the world."

A "monument" to Freedman's efforts is his support of the late Conde McGinley, publisher of the violently anti-Semitic and anti-Communist sheet, *Common Sense*. This bigot would probably have remained relatively harmless had it not been for Freedman's massive financial suuport, sometimes consisting of the purchase and gratis mailing of 400,000 copies of a single issue. At the hearings of the Senate Armed Services Committee, Freedman admitted that he had purchased 50,000 copies of the November 1950 issue of *Common Sense*, which was devoted to the Red-Baiting smear of Anna M. Rosenberg. Largely as a result of Freedman's contributions of money and phoney research items, *Common Sense* became the most widely circulated hate sheet in the country, furnishing the ideological ammunition for bigots, racketeers, and Fascists all over the country.

Freedman's crowning "achievement" is the launching of the Khazar canard. This delusion has been for years the grand passion of Freedman's life. Whenever he starts on this subject, he can keep going for hours without time out for a breath of fresh air. On one occasion, Freedman expatiated on his Khazar delusion to a group of seven or eight Congressmen for five hours without surcease. Freedman claims that he announced his great discovery to a waiting world in 1945. He claims that his revelations were sensational.

The May 1, 1959, issue of *Common Sense* has all of its four tabloid-size pages filled with an article by Benjamin Freedman that explains his discovery of the Khazar story. The upper portion of the front page, which always contains its masthead, is photographically reproduced on page 149.

The lying nature of the paper itself can be seen from the juxtaposition of two items: "The Truth, The whole Truth, and nothing but the Truth" and the Big Lie that "Communism is treason." This latter statement cannot be supported either by any dictionary definition of treason or by the data in any encyclopedia or reputable textbook on political science; nor is it compatible with the definition of treason in the Constitution of the United States. The next lie is that it is "The Nation's Anti-Communist Newspaper." A careful scrutiny of the contents, year after year, shows that it consists mainly of anti-Jewish and anti-Negro diatribes and lies, as well as propaganda against almost any kind of welfare legislation. It is therefore not surprising that the body of Freedman's article does not support his headline and sub-headline.

Freedman begins by quoting the Apostle Paul and quickly strikes a charismatic pose, telling his readers: "Prompted by Paul's inspired faith in the Divine power of truth, the facts here assembled are submitted to U.S.A. Christians hoping this knowledge added to their present wisdom will insure victory

★ communism is treason! ★ fight it with common sense!

The Nation's Anti-Communist Newspaper

# Common Sense

Copyright Registered 1948 United States Patent Office.

Issue No. 322 (14th Year)      Union, New Jersey, U.S.A.   May 1   1959

SUBSCRIPTION RATES:
(24 issues annually)
Plain envelope, unsealed .... $1.
Plain envelope, sealed ....... $3.
Foreign & Canada, (10 mos) $1.

"The Truth, the whole Truth, and nothing but the Truth"

Without fear or favor,
Conde McGinley
PUBLISHER AND EDITOR

FIVE CENTS

## CHRISTIANS DUPED BY UNHOLIEST HOAX IN ALL HISTORY!

### "Big lie" technique pushing U.S.A. to the brink of World War III.

By Benjamin H. Freedman

KHAZAR (CHAZAR) KINGDOM OF SO-CALLED "JEWS" IN 960 A.D.
'Khazar and 'Chazar are pronounced the same, histories use both spellings!

for the U.S.A. in the nameless war now silently raging against an unseen enemy, the prologue of World War III, in which the U.S.A. will again sacrifice the most, *as in the last three wars.*"

This mixture of religiosity, mysticism, prophecy, obscurantism, and patriotism comes from a man who has been proven, over and over again, to be a liar, especially at the hearings of the Senate Armed Services Committee, where he had tried to frame Mrs. Anna M. Rosenberg. But Freedman is a clever propagandist, and in the above quotation he establishes his "holiness," his mission as God's representative, and therefore supposedly believable.

The next step in his article is to make a perfectly sane and valid plea for the urgency of preventing World War III. Thus, he immediately establishes a degree of rapport with the reader, and prepares the reader for this exotic morsel:

The "big lie" technique of the unholiest hoax in all the recorded history of mankind brainwashed U.S.A. Christians that so-called "Jews" throughout the world today are the historic descendants of the so-called "chosen people" of the Holy Land in Old Testament history. The consensus of leading authorities on the subject stresses the fact to their best knowledge so-called "Jews" throughout the world today are not historic descendants of the so-called "Jews" of the Holy Land in Old Testament history. They furthermore feel that the threat of World War III hanging over the U.S.A. is the result of the "big lie" technique of the unholiest hoax in all the recorded history of mankind, a deception responsible for agitation far and wide the world little suspects.

The additional quotations that follow are not in organic sequence, but are presented without impairing contextual integrity:

The U.S.A. Christians continue being brainwashed by the U.S.A. media of mass-communications that so-called "Jews" of throughout the world today are the actual historic descendants of the so-called "Jews" of the Holy Land in Old Testament history. The U.S.A. Christians have been brainwashed by so-called "Jews" of historic Khazar ancestry, *and by their servile Christian stooges,* as they have been brainwashed by them for many years with the unholiest hoax in all the recorded history of mankind, *betraying the confidence of Christians.*

Incontestible facts supply the unchallengable proof of the historic accuracy that so-called "Jews" throughout the world today of eastern European origin are unquestionably the historic descendants of the

150

Khazars, a pagan Turco-Finn ancient Mongoloid nation deep in the heart of Asia according to history, who battled their way in bloody wars about the 1st B.C. century into eastern Europe where they set up their Khazar kingdom. For some mysterious reason the history of the Khazar kingdom is conspicuous by its absence from U.S.A. text-books on history, and from history courses in the schools and colleges.

The "big lie" technique of the unholiest hoax in all the recorded history of mankind brainwashed U.S.A. Christians into believing that Jesus Christ was actually a Jew in the sense that so-called Jews call themselves Jews now to bamboozle Christians.

Freedman also has a simple explanation for the anti-Semitism and the systematic massacres of Jews (pogroms) in Czarist Russia:

The root of all troubles between so-called "Jews" and Christians in Russia since the conversion of Vladimir III in 986 A.D. is not difficult to understand. So-called "Jews" of historic Khazar ancestry inside and outside Russia have never forgiven nor forgotten, firstly, the liquidation of the Khazar kingdom as a great independent, autonomous and sovereign body politic in Europe, and secondly, Vladimir III's rejection in 986 A.D. of the overtures to become a so-called "Jew" ...

Freedman makes this preposterous claim:

The so-called "Jews" of historic Khazar ancestry make up 92% of the total population of so-called "Jews" throughout the world today.

His final point is the one we have considered under the heading of "The Fascist Ghouls," wherein we showed how our native Fascists are trying to "disprove" that the Nazis murdered six million Jews. We quoted the April 15, 1961, newsletter of the Fascist *National Economic Council*, which had a cunning argument to "prove" that the six million Jewish victims of Hitler are really alive and that many of them are right here in the U.S.A. Freedman seems to be the source of this macabre joke, for not only does he present all the arguments used by the other Fascists, but he quotes Mr. Hanson W. Baldwin, the military editor of the *New York Times*, just as George Lincoln Rockwell did in the interview published in *Playboy*, April, 1966. And Freedman did this not only in this essay of May 1, 1959, but also in publicity issued as early as 1948.

151

Freedman makes his essay very plausible, especially to people who lack scientific training, by brazenly quoting or referring to a whole galaxy of authorities and scientists. Before we examine the proofs of Freedman's meretriciousness, it is important that the reader understand why so much attention is being devoted to such a character. It may be comforting for some people to say that Benjamin Freedman should be ignored, but Freedman's poison keeps spreading, for the same reason that cancer spreads when it is not checked early.

Although hundreds of examples of the use of Freedman's Khazar canard could be cited, a few examples should suffice:

1. Hal Hunt, in *National Chronicle*, March 11, 1965, tells his dupes:

Like Poland and Germany, Russia harbored many Khazar Jews. Some of these Jews came to America but stayed only long enough to obtain citizen papers, then returned to Russia and engaged in political intrigue.

2. *Councilor*, official organ of the racist Citizens Councils of Louisiana, in its issue of July 15, 1965, has an article entitled: "Old Documents Show Early U.S. Khazars Were Active As Slave-Traders In All Parts of America." It starts off by saying that Jews, as well as Gentiles, were involved in the African slave trade, but manages to shift most of the onus onto the Jews:

But the big money from slavery went to Khazar merchants and Boston shipowners. In many instances, the Boston ships were fianced by Khazars at usurious rates of interest and the big profits ended in the same pockets.

*Councilor* then gives an impressive list of documentary references, but its own synopsis of the contents of each item reveals the usual anti-Semitic sleight-of-hand, *the selective presentation of data*, by which it is possible to prove anything. All you need do is present the evidence to support a thesis and ignore all evidence to the contrary, and you can prove anything. But the dim-witted characters who believe *Councilor* are not concerned with the rules of evidence or the criteria of scientific proof. The hoodlum mentality which gravitates to the Fascist movements

152

cannot tolerate any proof which upsets its paranoidal assumptions.

3. In October of 1966, Helen Courtois' hate-peddling Keep America Committee issued a four-page brochure. The first page consists entirely of excerpts from the articles in *Common Sense* of February 1, 1953 and May 1, 1959 by the "Historian—Researcher—Scholar, Benj. H. Freedman." The heading is:

### JESUS WAS NOT A JEW

Christians Duped By The Unholiest Hoax in All History, By So-Called Jews. This is Considered Their Most Effective Weapon.

Pages two and three contain a number of the stock slanders and libels of the anti-Semitic underworld, and on page four we read:

### THOSE SIX MILLION JEWS—ANOTHER HOAX

The author of this last item, taken from *Common Sense* of January 1, 1961, is Holten Whitney, "author and investigator," who may very well be a fictitious character; he seems to plagiarize Benjamin Harrison Freedman.

Perhaps the most pernicious use of the Khazar canard was perpetrated by an Ultra-Rightist, Professor John O. Beaty, who served as a Military Intelligence officer in World War II. We shall deal later with Beaty's book, *The Iron Curtain Over America*, but the Khazar Jew canard, which Beaty espouses, requires immediate scrutiny.

Basing ourselves on the fact that Freedman was promoting his Khazar hallucination as early as 1948 and that Beaty's book was first published in 1951, it would appear that Beaty derived his inspiration for the Khazar canard from Freedman. It is also significant that Beaty reports, with approval, some statements made by Freedman in a full-page advertisement on January 14, 1947, in the New York *Herald-Tribune*. Beaty's responsibility and reliability as a researcher can be judged by the following comment of his regarding the Freedman advertisement:

The long documented article is signed by R. M. Schoendorf, "Representative of Cooperating Americans of the Christian Faiths"; by Habib I. Katibah, "Representative of Cooperating Americans of

153

Arab Ancestry"; and by Benjamin H. Freedman, "Representative of Cooperating Americans of the Jewish Faith," and is convincing.

It may be convincing to Beaty, but it should be noted that the R. M. Schoendorf was the maiden name of Benjamin Freedman's wife, and she represented no one but herself; that Habib I. Katibah was an Arab propagandist who represented an Arab lobbying outfit; and that Benjamin Freedman represented no organization of Jewish people. It was a fraudulent and misleading advertisement; which fact should have been easy to ascertain if this former Intelligence Officer and professor were really researching for the truth.

One of the best exposés of Beaty's opus comes from the pen of a Right-Wing scholar, who just cannot swallow Beaty's style of scholarship. Dr. V. Orvall Watts has been on the staff of Freedom School at Colorado Springs, Colorado, a Right-Wing school with several prominent Birchers on the board; and he has also been on the advisory committee of the National Economic Council, which was prominent in spreading the falsehood that six million Jews had not been exterminated by the Nazis. With these credentials, he can hardly be considered prejudiced against Professor Beaty on ideological or philosophical grounds. In an article which appeared in the Ultra-Rightist *Santa Ana Register*, November 6, 1963, Dr. Orval Watts criticizes Beaty's slipshod research methods, and then he adds:

But far more serious than his hit-or-miss listing of references is his flagrant abuse of such references as he does give for the basic points of his theory. For example, anyone who troubles to check his references will find that Beaty's whole Khazar story has little more historical foundation than the legend of King Arthur and his Knights of the Round Table.

Furthermore, Beaty does not do justice even to the legends, for he omits the various details that suggest the ancient Khazar Jews were a comparatively enlightened people, *although a minority among the Khazars as a whole.*

No better founded than his story of the origin and character of the ancient Khazars is Beaty's notion that nearly all Russian Jews are direct descendants of these "Judaized Khazars." The authors to whom he refers indicate that the Khazars were scattered to the four winds many hundreds of years ago. They state also that *the Jews of Russia seem to have come from every sort of race and region. In fact quite contrary to Beaty's theory, these authors point out that the*

154

*Khazar Jews themselves probably included Palestinian Jews.* (Emphasis throughout added.—M. K.)

In short, as far as Beaty's listed sources show, there is no more reason for assuming that a Russian Jew is a Khazar than to assume that an American Episcopalian is a Celtic descendant of King Arthur's knights.

Inasmuch as both Beaty and Freedman have quoted mostly from the same sources, Dr. Orval Watts' criticism applies equally to Freedman. Both Freedman and Beaty have presented garbled and distorted versions of the writings of reputable scholars. Freedman's charlatanism is easily recognized by any well-informed person. The internal evidence is the *excessive* use of deletions in almost every quotation given by him, as shown by the number of multiple dots used in each quotation to represent deletions. As Professor Watts said in the quoted article: "But quotations and references mean nothing unless the author selects them with care and uses them with integrity." While all reputable writers make use of multiple dots to represent deletions which do not destroy contextual integrity, it certainly cannot be considered honest reporting when a writer does what Freedman has done in his four-page diatribe in *Common Sense* of May 1, 1959. In the 53 lines of quotations from other authors, he made 33 deletions, which are represented by multiple dots!

With extraordinary brazenness, Freedman quotes *The History of the Jewish Khazars* by Professor D. M. Dunlop, to bolster his Khazar canard. Freedman is lavish in his praise of Professor Dunlop's scholarly attainments, and that is about the extent of truth in Freedman's article. However, Freedman relies on the fact that not one person in a thousand will check his references. So he feels safe in misrepresenting Professor Dunlop, quoting him as saying the exact opposite of what the professor says in his book. A few points made by Professor Dunlop will illustrate the difference between an honest scholar and a propagandist with an axe to grind.

1. With respect to Freedman's insinuation that dupes of the Khazar Jews have censored history textbooks, resulting in our having little or no knowledge about the Khazar Jews, Professor Dunlop points out in Chapter VIII that, the lack of familiarity is caused by the difficulty of dealing with the existing sources

of information, which are written in a variety of languages, with much obscurity and with many contradictions. Some of the languages are Greek, Arabic, Hebrew, Syriac, Armenian, Georgian, Russian, Persian, Turkish, and even Chinese.

2. Contrary to the Freedman-Beaty thesis, Professor Dunlop points out that the Khazar people were not converted completely to Judaism. While the ruling class of Khazaria did convert to Judaism, other religions were practiced extensively. Turks, Jews, and Arabs, as well as people of Slavic and Finnish origin, were represented in Khazaria. *This conglomeration of people and creeds was presided over by an aristocracy consisting of a relatively small number of Judaized Turks.*

3. With respect to the Freedman-Beaty story that the modern Jews of eastern Europe, and more particularly those in Poland, are the descendants of the medieval Khazars, Professor Dunlop concludes that *there is little evidence which bears directly upon it and it unavoidably retains the character of a mere assumption.*

Benjamin Harrison Freedman, George Lincoln Rockwell, and the rest of the Fascistic peddlers of hate have based their argument, in their cunning attempt to absolve the Nazis of the crime of exterminating six million Jews, on an inadvertent error, in giving the world Jewish population, by Hanson W. Baldwin in the *New York Times* of February 22, 1948. According to these erroneous figures, no six million Jews were missing, and if they were not missing, so the argument goes, they could not have been murdered by the Nazis.

By the simple expedient of writing a letter to the *Times*, the truth was ascertained, and the whole anti-Semitic syllogism collapses, as witness the letter on the opposite page.

An examination of the files of the *New York Times* reveals two things in this connection:

1. Mr. Baldwin did in fact make the correction on February 26, 1948, exactly as noted in his letter to this writer.

2. In his article on a preceding Sunday, February 22, 1948, the erroneous figures of world Jewish population were mentioned *incidentally*, while writing on the subject of a possible Arab-Israeli conflict.

Is it possible that Freedman did not see or hear about Baldwin's correction? Before jumping to the conclusion that Freed-

November 25, 1966

Dear Mr. Kominsky:

The correction appeared in The Times on February 26, 1948 as follows:

"Last Sunday's article incorrectly estimated the Jewish population of the world at 15 million to 18 million. No census has been conducted since the war, and estimates are only approximate, but most authorities agree that Hitler's wholesale massacres of Jews during the war reduced the Jewish population to perhaps 12 million today".

Sincerely,

Hanson W. Baldwin
(Military Editor)

man made an honest error, it is well to consider another of his yarns. In his May 1, 1959 article in *Common Sense*, Freedman strikes a pose of the meticulous researcher:

On February 22, 1948, the *New York Times* published figures taken from their 1947 secret census indicating a minimum of 16,150,000 and a maximum of 19,200,000 so-called "Jews" in the world in 1947. Through the courtesy of Mr. Arthur Hays Sulzberger, publisher of the *New York Times* this author conferred on February 23, 1948 with Commander Baldwin in his office where this author examined documents fully supporting the figures published by the *New York Times* on February 22, 1948. This author was allowed to examine the file containing the results of the searching investigations conducted by the *New York Times* through its own offices throughout the world and with the collaboration of governments and religious bodies in these foreign countries.

In answer to a further query, Mr. Hanson W. Baldwin sent

157

us another letter on January 10, 1967, which is here photographically reproduced:

January 10,1967

Dear Mr. Kominsky:

        Thank you for your letter of inquiry of January 6.

        The world Jewish population figures printed in the story came from the 1948 edition of the World Almanac. Later we checked with the American Jewish Committee and other sources and said in the correction, as I noted to you in my previous letter, that the authorities agree that Hitler's wholesale massacres of Jews during the war reduced the Jewish population to perhaps 12 million today. (2/26/48.)

        If Mr. Freedman met with me I do not remember it. The problem of course is that you are talking about events that took place 19 years ago. I see hundreds of people per year, many of them only for a few minutes so I could not swear that I did not see Mr. Freedman but if I did it made no impression either upon me or upon my assistant.

        I do not know what Mr. Freedman means by examination of documents but to my knowledge we had no particular documents bearing on the issue in question.

        I hope this answers your questions; if there is anything else you wish to know please do not hesitate to write again.

Sincerely,

Hanson W. Baldwin
(Military Editor)

Commander Baldwin's letter is an obviously honest one, and the following facts emerge from reading it:

1. There was no "searching investigation conducted by the *New York Times* throughout the world and with the collabora-

tion of governments and religious bodies in these foreign countries."

2. There were no "documents fully supporting the figures published by the *New York Times* on February 22, 1948."

3. It is questionable that Freedman ever talked to Mr. Baldwin, because by his own statement he went to the *Times* office the very next day after the February 22, 1948 article and was introduced to Baldwin through the courtesy of Mr. Arthur Hays Sulzberger, and was immediately given access to secret documents which did not exist. This was pretty fast footwork, and in real life is quite unlikely.

4. If Freedman did go to the *Times* office, the only document he was probably shown was the 1948 edition of the World Almanac, which apparently was the source of Baldwin's erroneous population figures.

5. Freedman does have the ability to make up a story out of the whole cloth!

In his article that we have under review, Freedman adds to his cunning posture of the careful researcher by making it sound as if he went to great lengths to uncover the allegedly suppressed data regarding the Khazar Jews:

In an original 1903 edition of the *Jewish Encyclopedia* in New York's Public Library, and in the Library of Congress, Volume IV, pages 1 to 5 inclusive, appears a most comprehensive history of the Khazars, and the interesting map of the Khazar Kingdom in the 10th century reproduced here.

The facts are that the "original" 1903 edition of the *Jewish Encyclopedia* is available in many of the older public libraries and it is not necessary to go to the Library of Congress in order to consult it. We found a perfectly good set in the Los Angeles Public Library, where it is catalogued as R

296.03
J 59.

A careful perusal of pages 1 to 5 fully substantiates Dr. V. Orvall Watts' critique of Professor John Beaty's *The Iron Curtain Over America* and corroborates Professor D. M. Dunlop's *The History of the Jewish Khazars*.

Before leaving the Khazar canard it is pertinent to our theory, that Freedman inspired at least the Khazar canard portion of

*The Iron Curtain Over America,* that Professor Beaty's widow, Josephine Powell Beaty, stated in a letter January 8, 1967, to a research assistant:

Mr. Freedman made available to my husband certain books in his library. Some of these may be ones from which he quoted.

Mrs. Beaty, incidentally, is the vice-president of the Ultra-Rightist *Defenders of the American Constitution.*

It taxes one's credulity that there should be people in the world, so hate-ridden and so blinded by prejudice, that they would be willing to disregard the mountain of evidence which proves the Nazis' guilt in the extermination of six million Jews. There are the records of the world-famous Nuremburg Trials. There are the records of the numerous postwar trials of Nazi war criminals in West German courts. There is the record of the Eichmann trial. Finally, the Messieurs Anti-Semites should bear in mind that, in acordance with German tradition of long standing, the Nazis kept methodical statistics, which corroborate the story of extermination of six million Jews. These records were captured by the U.S. Army and its allied forces.

So, we must conclude that the Khazar Jews theory is a palpable fraud, that Professor John Beaty was an irresponsible and unreliable writer, and that Benjamin Harrison Freedman is a proven liar!

In *Common Sense* of April 15, 1967, Freedman has an article in which he justifies Nazi anti-Semitism and, in general, offers an apologia for Hitlerism. At one point Freedman brags:

The author of this article had the honor of being a protege of the Hon. Mr. Henry Morgenthau, Sr., between 1912 and the time of his death on November 25, 1946, only on matters of international significance.

. . . The author of this article was privy with Mr. Morgenthau, Sr. to the meeting in New York City of leading Zionists and other Jews on December 25, 1916 to give effect to the 1916 London agreement between the British War Cabinet and the World Zionists Organization shortly implemented by them.

. . . The author of this article had the privilege of serving in a confidential capacity under Mr. Morgenthau, Sr. as Chairman of the Finance Committee of the National Democratic Committee in the 1912 election which installed President Woodrow Wilson in the White House.

On June 28, 1967, we sent a letter to Henry Morgenthau, Jr., the former Secretary of the Treasury in 1934, under the Roosevelt Administration. At the time, we had forgotten that Henry Morgenthau, Jr. had passed away. We gave the entire quotation, as above, and asked: "Would you be good enough to tell me how much of the above is truth and how much is figment of Freedman's imagination?"

The following reply, dated July 24, 1967, was received from Robert M. Morgenthau, son of Henry Morgenthau, Jr. and grandson of the man Freedman claimed as his close associate:

ROBERT M. MORGENTHAU
4725 INDEPENDENCE AVENUE
NEW YORK 7 NEW YORK

July 24, 1967

Mr. Morris Kominsky
400 E. Franklin
Elsinore, California   92330

Dear Mr. Kominsky:

I have your letter of June 28, 1967, addressed to my father, who died in February.

I have no information that Mr. Benjamin H. Freedman ever had any relationship with my grandfather, Henry M. Morgenthau, Sr.  I have discussed your letter with other members of the family, and they do not recall any relationship between Freedman and my grandfather.

Sincerely,

ROBERT M. MORGENTHAU

161

# The "Kol Nidre" Hoax

The apprehension, trial and execution by the State of Israel of the Nazi beast, Adolph Eichmann, brought the Fascists and Fascist sympathizers into a mood of orgiastic frenzy. This writer talked with many of these people during this period, and was amazed at the extent of their identification with and sympathy for Eichmann. Typical was the attitude of a Birchite dentist, who tried to conceal his Birchite connections and his anti-Semitic prejudices, but who pleaded almost frenetically with this writer for an expression of at least the hope that Eichmann would not be executed. Needless to point out, one cannot argue effectively with the fellow who is at the moment drilling your tooth!

The hate sheet, *Common Sense*, in its issue of May 15, 1961, "made" the following points:

1. That no proof had been adduced to prove Eichmann had killed even one person!

2. That Nazi Germany was compelled to put the Jews in concentration camps, because they were sabotaging the government.

3. That the Nazis did not exterminate six million Jews!

4. "Not one Jew was burned alive in Germany."

5. That the Jews have fabricated the stories of Nazi atrocites, and that Jews cannot be trusted, because it is a part of their religion to be able to break promises.

On page 1, *Common Sense*, screams:

Read the Kol Nidre prayer which absolves them from all oaths!

On page 4, next to a column which attempts to "prove" that the extermination camp at Dachau was staged by the Jews, *Common Sense* tries to bolster its lies by printing a garbled version of the Kol Nidre prayer.

The sly trick of presenting the Kol Nidre prayer, as a means of discrediting Jews, is used by many of the professional anti-Semites. *National Cronicle*, in the issue of March 11, 1965, quotes the Kol Nidre prayer, as given in the *Jewish Encyclopedia*. It is presented here exactly as *National Chronicle* published it, and alongside we give the garbled version published in *Common Sense*, May 15, 1961.

## KOL NIDRE
### A Jewish Prayer to absolve All Vows

## KOL NIDRE
### (All vows)

All vows, obligations, oaths or anathemas, pledges of all names, which we have vowed, sworn, devoted, or bound ourselves to, from this day of atonement until the next day of atonement, (whose arrival we hope for in happiness) we repent, aforehand, of them all, they shall all be deemed absolved, forgiven, annulled, void and made of no effect; they shall not be binding, nor have any power; the vows shall not be reckoned vows, the obligations shall not be obligatory, nor the oaths considered as oaths.

All vows, obligations, oaths, anathemas, whether called 'konan', 'konas', or by any other name, which we may vow, or swear, or pledge, or whereby we may be bound, from this Day of Atonement unto the next, (whose happy coming we await), we do repent. May they be deemed absolved, annulled, and void and made of no effect. They shall not bind us or have power over us. The vows shall not be reckoned vows, and the obligations shall not be obligatory, nor the oaths be oaths.

After this, editor Hal Hunt comments:

Let it be impressed upon the minds of all good men that this vow removes the keeping of obligations from the realm of honor, integrity, justice and equity, and places it squarely on the basis of expedience, whereby a Talmudist may either keep or break a contract, as best serves his interests, without a queasy feeling.

Kol Nidre totally disqualifies a Talmud Jew from holding any position of trust or authority anywhere in the world, or to act as advisor or consultant to any public or private official or citizen, and should be rigidly excluded from such positions, his sworn oath to tell the truth, the whole truth and nothing but the truth, being good for nothing.

There is a certain plausibility to the charges of the anti-Semites, but as we shall soon see, the appearances are deceiving. The professional hate peddlers thrive because very few people can take the time to research their clever fabrications and hoaxes. And as the French mathematician and religious philosopher of the seventeenth century, Blaise Pascal, observed: "Men never do evil so completely and cheerfully as when they do it from religious conviction."

163

In *The High Holiday Prayer Book*,[7] compiled and arranged by Rabbi Morris Silverman, we find on page 206:

## NOTE ON KOL NIDRE PRAYER

Though the author and the date of the Kol Nidre are unknown, the prayer was in use as early as the Gaonic period in the eighth century. In ancient times, as in our day, vows unto the Lord were often rashly made. In the precarious eras in which our forefathers lived, circumstances beyond their control frequently denied them the opportunity of fulfilling their vows. Because of the unusual stress and exigencies of their lives, these vows at times were forgotten and thus violated. Recognizing that the broken word profaned the soul, they developed the earnest desire to have such vows nullified on the Day of Atonement, when men yearned to be at peace with God and their fellowmen. The following legal formula, known as the Kol Nidre, was the result. In those lands where Jews, under duress, made vows to accept another faith, the recital of the Kol Nidre often brought relief to their tormented consciences.

Judaism always recognized and taught that the Kol Nidre cannot release anyone from a juridical oath or from any promise, contract or obligation between man and man. It applies only to those vows which an individual makes to his God and in which no other persons are involved. Sins between man and man are not forgiven until amends have been made for the wrong.

The underlying motives of the Kol Nidre prayer, the sincere longing for a clear conscience, the release from the feeling of guilt, the recognition of the sacredness of the plighted word, and the desire to be absolved from vows which could not be carried out or which would make for enmity and rancor, still possess significance for us today.

As famous as the legal formula, is the appealing melody which grew up around the words. Through the words and the melody of Kol Nidre, the Jew expressed his deepest feelings and emotions. Altogether apart from the meaning of the words and their significance, the plaintive chant has captivated and charmed the heart of the Jew to this day.

On page 207 Rabbi Silverman presents the authoritative translation of Kol Nidre from the original Hebrew, with the addition of two parenthetical qualifications. Rabbi Silverman points out that, in this translation, "The legal formula of Kol Nidre has been retained in its archaic form."

All vows, bonds, promises, obligations, and oaths [to God] wherewith we have vowed, sworn and bound ourselves from this Day of

7 *The High Holiday Prayer Book* is published by Prayer Book Press, Inc., 410 Asylum St., Hartford, Conn., 06103.

Atonement unto the next Day of Atonement, may it come unto us for good; lo, of all these, we repent us in them. They shall be absolved, released, annulled, made void, and of none effect; they shall not be binding nor shall they have any power. Our vows [to God] shall not be vows; our bonds shall not be bonds; and our oaths shall not be oaths.

Rabbi Silverman comments further:

Whereas the Hebrew text does not specify what vows are meant, it was clearly understood by Jews at all times that the recital of the Kol Nidre could not release one from vows and obligations made to his fellowmen. This is evident from the following selection of the Mishna, the authoritative code of law which antedates the Kol Nidre by at least five hundred years. Only willful enemies of the truth persist in distorting the meaning of the Kol Nidre:

"For transgressions between man and God, repentance on Yom Kippur brings atonement. For transgressions between man and man, Yom Kippur brings no atonement, until the injured party is appeased." (Mishna Yoma, Chapter 8.)

The professional anti-Semites are well aware of the existence of the passage in the Mishna that Rabbi Silverman has quoted, but it does not serve their purpose, which is the *selective* and one-sided presentation of data, so as to mislead. The truth of the matter is that only persons of ill will can find in the Kol Nidre prayer anything for which to be critical of the Jewish people.

Finally, it comes with poor grace for Roman Catholics like Conde McGinley to use the Kol Nidre prayer as a bludgeon over the Jews, because the Catholic doctrine embodies something which is quite akin to the Kol Nidre motif. In a little leaflet bearing the imprimatur of Archbishop Albert G. Meyer (later elevated to Cardinal) at Milwaukee, January 13, 1958, we read:

Because holy water is one of the Church's sacramentals, it remits venial sin. Keep your soul beautifully pure in God's sight by making the Sign of the Cross carefully while saying,
"By this holy water and by Thy Precious Blood wash away all my sins, O Lord."

Would Jews be justified in condemning Catholics as being deceitful, untrustworthy and habitual liars? Of course, only bigots and hate-peddlers would put such an interpretation upon the Catholic ritual. It is high time that the Kol Nidre hoax be completely buried.

## Falsifiers of the Talmud

The Talmud has always served as a sort of happy hunting ground for professional anti-Semites. The dishonest and misleading use of quotations and the manufacture of phoney quotations are the standard procedures used to inflame religious prejudices and to exploit the fears of the ignorant—usually forming the basis for a lucrative business operation in the guise of a religious crusade. An intelligent approach to understanding the problem must begin with a description of what the Talmud is and is not.

The *Universal Jewish Encyclopedia,* 1943 edition says:

The Talmud consists of two parts: the Mishnah, and its commentary, the Gemara. The Mishnah, complied and edited by Judah Hanasi about 200 C.E.,[8] was the first Jewish code of laws since the Torah.[9] There are two Gemaras, known as the Babylonian and the Palestinian. The former, completed about 500 C.E., is the record of the discussions of the Palestinian scholars. The Mishnah plus the Babylonian Gemara is known as the Babylonian Talmud; the Mishnah plus the Palestinian Gemara is known as the Palestinian Talmud. The two Talmuds have always been printed separately, and never together.

One of the best and most honest evaluations of the Talmud will be found in *The Encyclopedia of Religion and Ethics,* 1955 edition. Turning to Volume 12:

*Page 185.* ". . . Talmudic references to ancient paganism were misinterpreted as being attacks on the [Christian] Church."
*Page 186.* ". . . Modern anti-Semitism has displayed much energy in seeking in the pages of the Talmud grounds for attacks on the Jews. Those pages contain enough and to spare of superstition, narrowness, folly, and intolerance. *But the faults are superficial, the merits fundamental;* and it is because of the latter that the Talmud retains its permanent worth. (Emphasis has been added.—M. K.)
*Page 187.* ". . . the Talmud is a work of most manifold interest. It concerns itself with every phase of human activity. To read it intelligently—and it was assuredly so read—was a liberal education

8 Common Era.
9 The Pentateuch (the first five books of the Old Testament).

in the arts and sciences and philosophies. So wide is its range that a student of the Talmud is perforce acquainted with very many subjects which nowadays are regarded as distinct disciplines. . . . The Talmud breathes with vital freshness."

Page 187. "Ridicule was cast on its trivialities; fault was found with its trivialities; fault was found with its religious conceptions; objection was taken to its attitude to Gentiles. These unfavourable criticisms were not at all unfounded, for the Talmud contains much of inferior value, and *bears the marks of the different ages and strata of thought in which it grew up.* (Emphasis has been added.—M. K.) Nevertheless, some of the attacks on the Talmud were absolutely false; in others the assailants confused the attitude towards the Rome which destroyed the Temple with the attitude to the Rome which became the seat of the papacy. Often, too, overmuch importance was attached to the obiter dicta of isolated Rabbis."

Before leaving the experts, it is important to note that most of the editorial staff and research scholars of *The Encyclopedia of Religion and Ethics* are not of the Jewish faith and that, contrary to another slander of the hate-peddlers, the Talmud is not a secret collection of documents, but is available in theological seminaries, colleges, and universities everywhere. The Talmud has been carefully studied by non-Jewish scholars who would quickly refute any inaccuracies in the statements quoted here from *The Encyclopedia of Religion and Ethics.*

The professional anti-Semites have all kinds of books, pamphlets, and tracts which "expose" and "unmask" the Talmud. Typical is the work of Mrs. Lyrl Van Hyning, editor and publisher of *Women's Voice,* which featured Eustace Mullins' vile attack against the polio vaccine. Several years ago Van Hyning issued a long leaflet entitled:

## WHO ARE THE REAL "HATE-MONGERS"?
## THE TALMUD UNMASKED

In our research of Van Hyning's claims, we consulted a Hebrew scholar, Mr. Shimeon Brisman, formerly librarian of the Los Angeles Jewish Community Library and presently bibliographer of Hebraica and Judaica at the Research Library of the University of California at Los Angeles. Together we worked almost a whole day checking the statements of Van Hyning. We are devoting much time and space to her leaflet, because it is so *typical* of the Falsifiers of the Talmud.

## Van Hyning Leaflet

The Babylonian Talmud is the Jewish holy book, used in the training of rabbis, taught in the synagogues by the rabbis and studied by the Jews from an early age until death. Without any question, the Talmud stands as the SUPREME AUTHORITY of Jewish law, philosophy and ethics, containing the unchanging moral code by which the religious and social life of the Jews has been regulated to this day. The Jews believe in the teachings of the Talmud and act in accordance with its commands.

The teachings of the Christian Bible are available to all, for it is to be found everywhere. On the other hand, only a very few non-Jews even so much as heard of the Talmud, and still fewer know of its teachings, for it is scores of volumes in length and shrouded in secrecy by the Jews.

## Research Findings

The *Jewish Encyclopedia,* 1925 edition, says: "Modern culture, however, has gradually alienated from the study of the Talmud a number of the Jews in the countries of progressive civilization and it is now regarded by most of them merely as one of the branches of Jewish theology, to which only a limited amount of time can be devoted, although it occupies a prominent place in the curricula of the rabbinical seminaries. . . . The study of the Talmud has even attracted the attention of non-Jewish scholars; and it has been included in the curricula of universities."

The Hebrew Bible, which is called the Old Testament, is available in all religious book stores and in most libraries; and probably in many Christian Churches. Van Hyning has here performed some intellectual sleight-of-hand by posing the New Testament against the Talmud. The Talmud is *not* a Bible. Any individual or institution can purchase the Talmud, and it is available for study by anyone. The Talmud has been expertly translated into good English, and is obtainable in most good public libraries. It has also been translated into German, French, and other languages. When Chief Justice Earl Warren took a course of study in the Talmud several years ago, the professional anti-Semites screamed to the high heavens. Perhaps one of the reasons is that it upsets the "shrouded in secrecy" nonsense.

## Van Hyning Leaflet

"The Talmud refers to Jesus Christ as the bastard son of a harlot (Kallah, 1b, 18b)."

*Kallah, 1b, 18b.* The quotation does not exist in this volume. This is a complete fabrication, and even the reference numbers are fabricated.

## VAN HYNING LEAFLET

"Jesus is blasphemed as a fool (Schabbath, 104b), a conjurer (Toldoth Jeschu), and idolater. (Sanhedrin 103a) and a seducer (Sanhedrin 107b)."

## RESEARCH FINDINGS

*Schabbath, 104b.* The correct spelling for the name of this volume is Shabbath. It does not make an evaluation of anyone, but rather reports a dialogue: "It was taught, Rabbi Eliezer said to the Sages: But did not Ben Stada bring forth witchcraft from Egypt by means of scratches (in the form of charms) upon his flesh? He was a fool, answered they, and proof cannot be adduced from fools."

The professional anti-Semites are relying here on the theory that the Talmudic scholars meant Jesus when they referred to Ben Stada. A British scholar, R. Travers Herford, gives it as his opinion in "Christianity in Talmud and Midrash" (p. 37) that Ben Stada means Jesus of Nazareth. Further on, however, he says: ". . . The Talmud has preserved only a very vague and confused recollection of Jesus" (p. 83). And he points out that some people argue "that there are in the Talmud two persons called Jesus, neither of whom is the historical Jesus of Nazareth" (p. 347).

*Toldoth Jeschu* is a book from the Middle Ages. It is *not* a part of the Talmud.

*Sanhedrin, 103a.* Van Hyning's claim that it calls Jesus an idolater is a complete fabrication.

*Sanhedrin, 107b.* This distortion of the truth by Van Hyning is based upon a legendary story in this portion of the Talmud. As it is actually related, Jesus and his teacher met a woman at a wayside inn; Jesus admired her extreme beauty. For this the teacher severely admonished him and dismissed him as a pupil. The rabbis in the Talmud sharply criticized the teacher for his harshness and severity towards Jesus.

## VAN HYNING LEAFLET

"The Talmud teaches that Jesus died like a beast and was buried in that 'dirt heap' . . . where they throw the dead bodies of dogs and asses, and where the sons of Ssau (the Christians) and of Ismael (the Turks), also Jesus and Mohammed, uncircumsized and unclean like dead dogs, are buried (Zobar, III, 282)."

## RESEARCH FINDINGS

*Zobar, III, 282.* This is a cabalistic work that came into being during the Middle Ages. It is *not* a part of the Talmud. The entire "quotation" is a complete fabrication.

## VAN HYNING LEAFLET

"One of the basic doctrines of the Talmud is that all non-Talmudists rank as non-humans, that they are not like men, but beasts (Kerithuth, 6b, p. 78)".

## RESEARCH FINDINGS

*Kerithuth, 6b, p. 78.* Even the numbering system is a fabrication. 6b means page 6, side 2. Consequently, page 78 can have no relation to 6b. This claim is based upon a particular dialogue in which reference is made specifically to heathens in a fashion comparable to that of the many Christian preachers who today still thunder away with the doctrine that only those who accept Jesus Christ will be "saved." Obviously no sane person with a semblance of decency would condemn present-day Jews for the dialogue of some individual religious philosophers 1700 years ago. Rabbi Morris Joseph summarizes very well the present-day religious posture of the Jews in his *Judaism as Creed and Life*: "Judaism teaches not only that the Divine Love is freely offered to all men, whatever their religion may be, but that their religion is itself the instrument by which they may win it. They are sure of the Divine fellowship if only they will follow the good way that their conscience points out to them." The professional anti-Semites, who assiduously scrutinize Jewish writings for something they can twist to their special needs, somehow manage to overlook the writings of scholars like Rabbi Morris Joseph.

## VAN HYNING LEAFLET

"A JEW WHO KILLS A CHRISTIAN COMMITS NO SIN, BUT OFFERS AN ACCEPTABLE SACRIFICE TO GOD. 'Even the best of the non-Jews should be killed.' (Abhodah Zarah, 26b Tosepoth)."

*Abhodah Zarah, 26b, Tosepoth.* Tosepoth is not a part of the Talmud. It is a collection of commentaries on the Talmud. In the passage alluded to by Van Hyning, Tosepoth quotes a Talmudic source as stating that the command of killing all Canaanites was applicable *only* during the war against them.

### VAN HYNING LEAFLET

"The following quotations from and about the Talmud should be of interest to all Christians. Note: 'GOY' means non-Jews; 'GOYIM' is plural for Goy."

"Jehovah Himself studies the Talmud standing, he has such respect for that book (Tract Mechilla)."

### RESEARCH FINDINGS

*Tract Mechilla.* No such book exists in the Talmud. Furthermore, the internal evidence in the alleged quotation suggests crude fabrication. The Talmud is not "that book"; it is a *collection of volumes.*

### VAN HYNING LEAFLET

"Every goy who studies the Talmud and every Jew who helps him in it, ought to die. (Sanhedrin, 59a Abhodah Zarah 8-6)."

### RESEARCH FINDINGS

*Abhodah Zarah 8-6.* Insofar as this volume is concerned the quotation is a complete fabrication. Even the reference number is incorrect. It should read "Abhodah Zarah, 8a or 8b." A number such 8-6 can never exist in the Talmud.

*Sanhedrin, 59a.* Here there is reported a dialogue between two Rabbis, the first of whom does indeed fanatically advocate death for a heathen who studies the Torah (the Pentateuch, not the Talmud). The second Rabbi effectively demolishes his colleague's argument by pointing out that the heathen who studies the Torah succeeds in elevating himself to the status of a High Priest.

### VAN HYNING LEAFLET

"To communicate anything to a goy about our religious relations would be equal to the killing of all Jews, for if the goyim knew what we teach about them they would kill us openly. (Libbre David 37)."

*Libbre David 37.* This is a complete fabrication. No such book exists in the Talmud or in the entire Jewish literature. Here again there is some internal evidence of the work of the fabricator. Libbre is probably a corruption of Liber, which is part of "Liber David", the Latin for Book of David (the psalms of the Bible).

### VAN HYNING LEAFLET

"A Jew should and must make a false oath when the goyim asks if our books contain anything against them. (Szaaloth-Utszabot, The Book of Jore Dia 17)."

### RESEARCH FINDINGS

*The Book of Jore Dia 17.* No such statement appears. This is a complete fabrication.

*Szaaloth-Utszabot.* There is no such book in the Talmud. These two words are *part* of the title of some 1500 books, but by themselves they mean only "responses."

### VAN HYNING LEAFLET

"The Jews are human beings, but the nations of the world are not human beings but beasts. (Baba Mecia 114-6)."

### RESEARCH FINDINGS

*Baba Mecia 114-6.* This quotation is a complete fabrication. Even the numbering is incorrect. There can be no 114-6; it has to be 114a or 114b.

### VAN HYNING LEAFLET

"When the Messiah comes every Jew will have 2800 slaves. (Simeon Haddarsen, fol. 56D)."

### RESEARCH FINDINGS

*Simeon Haddarsen, fol. 56D.* There is no such book in the Talmud. It is actually the name of a 10th century Bible commentator. The "fol. 56D" is an invention.

### VAN HYNING LEAFLET

"Jehovah created the non-Jew in human form so that the Jew would not have to be served by beasts. The non-Jew is consequently an animal in human form, and condemned to serve the Jew day and night. (Midrash Talpioth, 225-L)."

*Midrash Talpioth, 225-L.* This is not a volume of the Talmud. It is something composed by a Turkish Jew in the 18th century. His name was Elijah ben Solomon Abraham, ha-Kohen.

## VAN HYNING LEAFLET

"As soon as the King Messiah will declare himself, He will destroy Rome and make a wilderness of it. Thorns and weeds will grow in the Pope's palace. Then he will start a merciless war on non-Jews and will overpower them. He will slay them in masses, kill their kings and lay waste the whole Roman land. He will say to the Jews: 'I am the King Messiah for whom you have been waiting. Take the silver and the gold from the goyim.' (Josiah 60, Rabbi Abarbanel to Daniel 7, 13)."

## RESEARCH FINDINGS

*Josiah 60.* This is not a volume from the Talmud. There is no book of that title in existence. The last sentence of the alleged quotation, "Take the silver and gold from the goyim", clashes head-on with the basic teachings and philosophy of Judaism. The rest of the alleged quotation differs very little from hundreds of similar reverse statements that are being made daily by fundamentalist Christian preachers. In these statements, the second coming of Christ is predicted as being imminent, and many precise details are predicted, including a thermonuclear war that will wipe out all except those who accept Jesus.

## VAN HYNING LEAFLET

"A Jew may do to a non-Jewess what he can do. He may treat her as he treats a piece of meat. (Nadarine, 20, B; Schulchan Aruch, Choszen Hamiszpat 348)."

## RESEARCH FINDINGS

*Nadarine 20.* This is a falsified version, designed to inflame passions in the same manner as the Southern Racists try to promote the idea that every Negro man will rape white women. The actual quotation is: "The Rabbis say: That whatever a man wants to do with his wife he may do; just as he can prepare meat to suit his fancy." This concept of male superiority of 1700 years ago bears no relationship to the *philosophy and conduct of present-day Jewry.* To represent this as the teachings of Judaism in the twentieth century is to perpetrate a palpable fraud. Van Hyning perpetrated the additional fraud of twisting it into a Jew vs. Gentile problem.

### Van Hyning Leaflet

"A Jew may rob a goy—that is, he may cheat him in a bill, if unlikely to be perceived by him. (Schulchan Aruch, Choszen Hamiszpat 348)."

### Research Findings

*Schulchan Aruch, Choszen Hamiszpat 348.* This is not a part of the Talmud. It is actually part of a collection of Biblical commentaries composed in the sixteenth century. The actual text in this volume says that *it is forbidden to steal even a small item from Jew or non-Jew, from children or from adults.* One of the commentators remarks that in dealing with an idolater it would be permissible to use artifice or stratagem to effect *repayment of a loan.* He then adds that others say that to do it intentionally is forbidden, but if the idolater makes a mistake in one's favor, it is proper to accept the advantage that accrues. However, it is pointed out that the famous Rabbi Maimonedes is vigorously opposed to such procedures.

### Van Hyning Leaflet

"All property of other nations belongs to the Jewish nation, which consequently is entitled to seize upon it without any scruples. An orthodox Jew is not bound to observe principles of morality towards people of other tribes. He may act contrary to morality, if profitable to himself or to Jews in general. (Schulchan Aruch, Choszen Hamiszpat 348)."

### Research Findings

*Schulchan Aruch, Choszen Hamiszpat 348.* This is a complete fabrication.

### Van Hyning Leaflet

"On the house of the goy one looks as on the fold of cattle. (Tosefta, Erubin VIII, 1)."

### Research Findings

*Tosefta, Erubin VIII, 1.* This is a complete fabrication. Tosefta is not a part of the Talmud.

## Van Hyning Leaflet

"How to interpret the word 'robbery'. A goy is forbidden to steal, rob or take women slaves, etc., from a goy or Jew. But the Jew is NOT forbidden to do all this to a goy. (Tosefta, Abhodah Zarah VIII, 5)."

## Research Findings

*Tosefta, Abhodah Zarah, VIII, 5.* This is a complete fabrication. Tosefta is not a part of the Talmud.

## Van Hyning Leaflet

"All vows, oaths, promises, engagements, and swearing, which, beginning this very day of reconciliation, we intend to vow, promise, swear, and bind ourselves to fulfill, we repent of beforehand; let them be illegalized, acquitted, annihilated, abolished, valueless, unimportant. Our vows shall be no vows, and our oaths no oaths at all. (Schulchan Aruch, Edit. 1, 136)."

## Research Findings

*Schulchan Aruch, Edit. 1, 136.* This is not from the Talmud. This is actually a garbled version of the Kol Nidre prayer. The reference to "Edit. 1, 136" it completely meaningless.

## Van Hyning Leaflet

"At the time of the Cholhamoed the transaction of any kind of business is forbidden. But it is permitted to cheat a goy, because cheating of goyim at any time pleases the Lord. (Schulchan Aruch, Orach Chaim 539)."

## Research Findings

*Schulchan Aruch, Orach Chaim 539.* This is a complete fabrication.

## Van Hyning Leaflet

"If a Jew be called upon to explain any part of the rabbinic books, he ought to give only a false explanation. Who ever will violate this order shall be put to death. (Libbre David 37)."

## Research Findings

*Libbre David 37.* There is no such book, as previously noted.

If the reader's sense of decency and propriety has been outraged by this collection of lies and fabrications, what is to be said about the rest of Van Hyning's leaflet which follows immediately after her list of charges against the Jews? It may tax the reader's credulity, but Van Hyning did have the brazen effrontery to say the following right after telling such shocking lies:

Is it necessary to give any more of these quotations, to show the average intelligent American citizen that these Jewish people are not to be trusted? THERE ARE THOUSANDS OF SIMILAR PASSAGES IN ALL OF THE JEWISH WRITINGS, but after reading these few, they ought to be enough to bring these questions to the mind of patriots:

How can a Jew take the oath of naturalization and become an American citizen? And, is it unjust to observe he may be valueless if not dangerous to American society?
How can a Jew legally and morally take the oath of Public Office? How can a Jew be expected to act as a worthy and ethical leaven in the capacity of publisher, editor, correspondent; theatrical producer or director; banker, statesman, congressman, or educator of American Youth?

## "HATE-MONGERING"

Much has been said about so-called anti-Jewish "hate-mongering". While a great many self-sacrificing Christians have been smeared, persecuted and falsely branded as "hate-mongers," the masters of "hate-mongering," the TALMUDIC JEWS, have gone unchallenged.

Talk about "hate-literature"! Could there possibly be any more vicious "hate-literature" than that Jewish cesspool of filth and hatred, the Talmud? And when it comes to inciting to violence, the Talmud, with its commands to kill Christians is unsurpassed.

We will leave it up to any impartial jury to decide. Who are the real "hate-mongers"—the Talmudic Jews, or the Christian patriots who seek to expose them?

Will you help in the distribution of this important leaflet? Order as many copies as you can and distribute them to ministers and public officials and to all your friends and relatives.

Far from unmasking the Talmud, the leaflet unmasks Van Hyning and the techniques commonly used by the hate-peddling fraternity.

The Rev. Gerald L. K. Smith distributes *free,* a tract in which is quoted most of the Van Hyning fabrications. The tract states that it is a reprint from *The Cross and The Flag.* Smith has added some additional chamber-of-horrors items, which are obvious frauds. It is hard to tell whether Smith has

176

cribbed from Van Hyning or vice versa. One thing is certain: once a fabrication or forgery gets started, it travels with lightning speed from one hate sheet to another across state and national boundaries.

*Common Sense* of June 15, 1964, carried a falsification of the Talmud, which had some elements of humor, in a perverse sort of way:

> A single sentence near the end of a long, rambling column in the Los Angeles *B'nai B'rith Messenger* of October 25, 1957, is more thought-provoking than many a book. The columnist, Rabbi Charles W. Steckel, PhD., Temple Beth Israel, Sierra Madre, California, writes:
> "According to Jewish tradition the universe, our world, survives because of the 36 righteous men (Lamed-Vovenic) who are hidden so that no one knows about them."
> Rabbi Steckel added that he was "deeply convinced" that a certain Swedish Jew, Raoul Wallenberg, now dead, was one of them. As he was taken to the Soviet Union after the war and never was heard of again, till, ten years later, the Soviet said he had died in 1947.

Conde McGinley, the editor of *Common Sense,* found something incriminating in the sentence he quoted from Rabbi Steckel's article, although it should be clear, without further research, that Rabbi Steckel was relating a *legendary* story at the conclusion of his article, in order to pay tribute in allegorical form to the memory of Raoul Wallenberg. But McGinley saw an opportunity *almost seven years later* to strike another blow at the Jews. Apart from his gratuitous speculation that Raoul Wallenberg "May have been a Communist", McGinley placed this headline over his story:

### RABBI SAYS 36 JEWS RULE JEWISH WORLD

There you have it, the old canard about secret Jewish power! On page 512 of *The Universal Jewish Encyclopedia* we find:

LAMED VAV ZADDIKIM, "the thirty-six righteous men," who, according to Jewish legend, live unrecognized and unsuspecting in the world, and to whose piety the world owes its continued existence (Suk. 45b). The popular term for them is Lamed-Vovnik or Nistar, "hidden saint." They are generally humble people unostentatiously plying their trade as artisans, usually tailors or shoemakers, until some untoward calamity threatening the Jewish community arouses

177

them to their appointed duty. They then emerge from their obscurity, perform some act by which the calamity is averted, and retire into obscurity in some town where they would not be recognized.

There is, of course, nothing in this legendary story of folk heroes to justify the headline about 36 Jews ruling the Jewish world. Every people, every nation has its legends and its legendary heroes. Imagine some rabid anti-American agitator, who would take the story of George Washington (chopping down a cherry tree in his youth) and build that legend into a grotesque theory that all Americans are vandals!

It so happens that Rabbi Steckel's article in the *B'nai B'rith Messenger* of October 25, 1957 is a beautiful tribute to the heroism of Raoul Wallenberg, the special emissary of King Gustav V of Sweden. It was largely through his perseverance and dedication that over 100,000 Hungarian Jews were rescued from extermination by the Nazis. Rabbi Steckel entitled his article: "Wallenberg—A Saint." There are 22 column-inches of narrative before you arrive at the sentence McGinley pounced upon, and distorted. At the end, Rabbi Steckel did say:

According to Jewish tradition the universe, our world, survives because of the 36 righteous men (Lamed-Vovenic) who are hidden so that no ones knows about them. I am deeply convinced that Raoul Wallenberg is one of them.

When you read the entire story with its headline, "Wallenberg—A Saint," it is clear that Rabbi Steckel's final sentence about Wallenberg is a metaphorical tribute in the context of a legendary and allegorical story about thirty-six pious men who perform deeds of heroism without fanfare. Surely, such a beautiful legend should not be sullied.

Another American used the legend of Lamad-Vovenic for honest purposes. At the Democratic National Convention in August of 1964, the late Ambassador Adlai Stevenson paid a beautiful tribute to the memory of Eleanor Roosevelt. The following are the opening three paragraphs of his speech:

She was a lady—a lady for all seasons. And like her husband, our immortal leader, she left "a name to shine on the entablatures of truth—forever."

There is, I believe, a legend in the Talmud which tells us that in any period of man's history the heavens themselves are held in place by the virtue, love, and shining integrity of 12 just men. (Stevenson was in error. It is 36 men.—M.K.) They are completely unaware of this function. They go about their daily work, their humble chores—doctors, teachers, workers, farmers (never, alas, lawyers, so I understand), just ordinary devoted citizens—and meanwhile the rooftree of creation is supported by them alone.

And I think perhaps there are times when nations or movements or great political parties are similarly sustained in their purposes and being by the pervasive, unconscious influence of a few great men and women. Can we here, in the Democratic Party, doubt that Eleanor Roosevelt, throughout her selfless life, had in some measure the keeping of the party's conscience in her special care? That her standards and integrity steadied our own? That her judgment persuaded the doubters and "too-soon despairers"? That her will stiffened the waverers and encouraged the strong?

Too bad that Conde McGinley died before Adlai Stevenson made that speech. Imagine with what gusto McGinley could have written a story about that speech, using the following headline:

ADLAI STEVENSON REVEALS
Eleanor's Secret Ties to the 36 Jewish Rulers!

Some twenty-five years ago a very brilliant Roman Catholic scholar, Dr. Joseph N. Moody, wrote an essay entitled "What Is The Talmud?" which appeared in a publication called *Wisdom*. It was reprinted in pamphlet form by the Trinity League of the Paulist Fathers' educational division in New York City. The following excerpts from Dr. Moody's pamphlet summarize our discussion very well:

*Page 7.* Since the emancipation and the entrance of the Jew into the cultural activities of the West, the importance of the Talmud has diminished, and today it is regarded as a branch of theological learning, and its study is relegated to the rabbinical seminaries.

*Page 8.* Although later Christian scholars have come to appreciate it and to study it objectively, modern anti-Semites of the pagan variety have made it one of their chief objectives in their campaign of slander.

*Page 9.* It was the fruit of more than twenty-five hundred separate authors and its production took a thousand years. Hence it contains the most diverse, and often contradictory, opinions on a great variety of subjects and includes "the most varied shades of piety and ethical-thinking, casual dialogues of a general nature, private

utterances of teachers totally devoid of any binding implication."
Selected quotations from this huge storehouse of fact and thought,
law and fancy, must be made cautiously. It is obviously unfair to
take a few passages and say: "Behold this is the book," or "These
are thy Gods, O Israel."

*Page 13.* When we examine the Talmud for references to Christ or
Christianity, we are struck by the remarkably few references to subjects which must have been of profound interest to the authors of
the work. There are no contemporary references to Christ, and the
few found are all late and legendary. There is no mention of either
Christ or the Christian religion in the Mishna, and only casual ones
in the Gemara.

The misuse of real and imaginary quotations from the Talmud is only effective with people who believe the nonsense
about an international Jewish conspiracy. It is incredible, but
true, that there are many people who believe in the monolithic
nature of Jews. According to this theory, Jews work in unison
and follow a central leadership from some mysterious, hidden
world headquarters. The anti-Semites, who spread this canard,
will quite often spread another falsehood, which contradicts
the concept of a monolithic Jewish people. As the anti-Semites
tell it, there is not and cannot be unity among Jews, because
when six Jews get together they want to start seven synagogues,
so that everyone can be the president of a synagogue.

The facts of life, of course, disprove the monolithic nature
of the Jews. Under comparable economic and social conditions,
Jews function the same as other members of the human race.
In the normal course of living, only an infinitesimal portion of
the Jews come in contact with the Talmud, and most assuredly
none of them would be guided by anything written hundreds
of years ago that would clash with their present-day code of
ethics and morality. One can frankly admit that there are some
things in the Talmud which modern people would reject, and
one can also concede that some of the ancient Talmudists
expressed some ideas that are repugnant to people in the
present era. To argue that present-day Jews are responsible for
and are guided by everything written hundreds of years ago,
is to display either ignorance or malevolence. Modern Jews,
who study the Talmud, are just as selective as any other people
who study ancient documents. They accept that which makes
sense to them and reject that which is unwise, untenable, and
outmoded.

# The Illuminati Hoax

One of the most effective weapons in the arsenal of anti-Semitic and Fascistic rabble-rousers is the Illuminati hoax. Aside from the fact that certain types of people enjoy being regaled with stories about secret societies, secret oaths, secret rituals, secret plans, and secret agents—the very name Illuminati, seems to be cloaked with an aura of mystery. Consequently, it lends itself to a variety of interpretations and phoney conspiracy stories.

The Rev. Gerald L. K. Smith, in the January, 1965, issue of *The Cross and The Flag,* advises his readers that they have thirteen enemies, and he lists them in the order of importance. First on the list is the International Bankers, promoted by the Rothschilds, Warburgs, Kuhn, Loeb and Co. (In the world of Gerald L. K. Smith there are no powerful Gentile bankers.) Second on his list are the Illuminati. Third is Zionism. Fourth is Bilderberger Conferences. And the Soviet Union is listed as the thirteenth!

The Rev. Oren Fenton Potito, in his hate sheet, *National Christian News,* of January, 1965, has a rip-roaring exposé of "Satan's organization, The Illuminati." Potito avers that the Illuminati was founded on May 1, 1776 by "the renegade Jew Weishaupt." To a world breathlessly awaiting his great discoveries, Potito announces:

Indeed, the Jews, Karl Marx and Friedrich Engels, in their nefarious works on Socialism and the instigation of the first International, incorporated the Illuminati program bodily. The fact that communism is nothing but the Jew Weishaupt's satanism has not been generally revealed. The point that we are getting at is, that the Jews had in Illuminism exactly the weapon they needed to effect their world takeover.

Potito emerges as an original discoverer of "hidden" items of history, when he declares:

George III did not have the English Soldiers requisite to fight a successful war with the Colonies, yet was egged on by predatory and scheming Jews in the New World, of whom American historians are careful to make no mention.

The reader will perhaps appreciate the thrust of Potito's dia-

181

tribe by learning that on the next page Potito reprints in its entirety the long and infamous letter of the Nazi leader, Hermann Goering, to Winston Churchill. The reason, of course, is that Georing's ranting bolsters Potito's anti-Semitic Illuminati story.

The hate sheet of the Louisiana (White) Citizens Councils, *The Councilor,* in its issue of February 1, 1965, quoted data from an editorial in the *Christian Science Monitor* of June 19, 1920. According to *The Councilor,* the editorial stated that Adam Weishaupt is really the father of Communism, not Karl Marx; that there is an international conspiracy which aims to erect a world despotism ruled by anti-Christians. *Councilor* states that the editor of *Christian Science Monitor* was replaced for indulging in this venture into Illuminism.[10]

In its issue of April 9, 1965, *The Councilor* amused its readers with a thrilling mystery story, which says in part:

A confession written 78 years ago may shed new light on the role of a secret society in the assassination of American presidents—including Abraham Lincoln.

Even before the death of Kennedy, the Councilor had clues which pointed to the existence in New Orleans of a secret society organized nearly 200 years ago in Bavaria. This society uses political assassination as a method of controlling world money markets.

Other historians have linked this group to Jacobism, Bolshevism and Communism. Councilor investigations seek to determine its role in:

a. Starting the U.S. Civil War,

b. The death of American presidents from Lincoln forward, and

c. Its part, if any, in U.S. money policy and favoritism in such matters as military procurement and federal contracts.

The organization was the Bavarian Illuminati.

The Reverend Kenneth Goff told his followers in *The Pilgrim Torch,* July 1965:

Many have requested from our office the information as to whom has taken the place of Bernard Baruch who died during the past month. The new head of the World's Illuminati is Sidney Weinberg.

---

10 In a letter to the author, Mr. Erwin D. Canham, the distinguished editor of the *Monitor,* points out that in 1920: "Our Board of Directors had lost actual operating control and the then Editor was writing editorials reflecting his own ideas. This particular editorial crops up in anti-Semitic literature from time to time."

Colonel Walter L. Furbershaw, chairman of the committee on un-American and subversive activities of the swanky Union League Club of Chicago and former U.S. Army intelligence officer, wrote an essay entitled "International Communism: Its Origin and Growth," which is based on the Illuminati hoax. Congressman Ralph E. Church dignified this nonsense by placing it in the *Congressional Record* on February 24, 1949. Frank Capell, in turn, quoted it from the *Congressional Record* in his *Herald of Freedom* of December 2, 1966, Religious News Edition.

Rev. Gerald L. K. Smith got into the act again, in *The Cross and The Flag* of February, 1967. He published an article by Frank Capell, entitled "The Temple of Understanding." It seems that a group representing the six major world religions are planning to build a Temple of Understanding in an area just south of Washington, D.C. Capell begins his smear attack by quoting the Ultra-Rightist columnist, Edith Kermit Roosevelt, who referred to the leaders of this project as "the Illuminati, Masters of Wisdom." Then Capell takes us through a Red-Baiting attack on many of the clergymen who are involved in this undertaking, and finally advises:

The plan of the Illuminati, doing Satan's work, is to destroy religion by combining the religions of the world into a "Brotherhood of Man."
The Temple of Understanding, an occult Illuminati enterprise, is a major step in the direction of establishing this single religion of the Brotherhood of Man.

Apparently Capell considers the Brotherhood of Man to be a dangerous doctrine; in fact he considers it an attack upon religion. He reports that at the Annual Presidential Prayer Breakfast on February 5, 1964, President Johnson said that "a fitting memorial to the God that made us all" should be established in Washington. All of which impels Capell to inquire:

Is the Temple of Understanding what he had in mind? Does it signify the death of God and the rise of illuminized man?

Myron C. Fagan, impresario of the Ultra-Rightist propaganda outfit, Cinema Educational Guild, states in his November 1966 News-Bulletin that the "United Nations is [the] spawn of the Illuminati" and that:

The UN is today's culmination of a plot that was launched back in the 1760's when it first came into existence under the name of The Illuminati. This Illuminati was organized by one Adam Weishaupt, a Catholic priest, who defected at the behest (and financed) of the Rothschilds.

There you have the great historical discovery of the century. Fagan lets you in on information not available elsewhere. His followers delight in getting the "inside dope." And while the Rev. Oren Potito stated that Adam Weishaupt was a Jew, Myron Fagan says he was a Catholic Priest. Weishaupt was actually a Catholic, so Fagan uses him against the Jews by claiming he was a tool of Jewish bankers. Fagan has the resourcefulness to turn anything and everything into a Jewish and/or a Communist conspiracy. Fagan announces further that the Council on Foreign Relations, which consists largely of people prominent in business, banking, industry, government, journalism, and education, is actually the Illuminati of the United States.

The following month Fagan became emboldened, and he devoted his entire December, 1966, issue to the theme that the Council on Foreign Relations is being "Completely unmasked as 'Illuminati' in U.S." Briefly summarized, his mental gyrations produced the following points:

1. That the original plans for the Council on Foreign Relations were created by Col. E. M. House, chief advisor to President Woodrow Wilson. According to Fagan, Col. House was the chief errand boy for the Jewish banker, Jacob H. Schiff.

2. That the idea of One-World Government was outlined in "Philip Dru: Administrator," a novel writtten by Col. House.

3. That the "CFR is the heartbeat and provides the inspiration and motive power necessary to maintain the Illuminati in the United States."

4. That the graduated income tax was originated by Karl Marx for the purpose of impoverishing the American people and forcing Communism upon them; that all of Karl Marx' writings were derived from original Illuminati texts.

5. That for a number of years J. Edgar Hoover has been trying to alert the American people to the subversion of youth by Communists and the Council on Foreign Relations.

6. That forty years ago, Lenin, "oracle of the Russian Communists and protege of the Rothschilds and Jacob H. Schiff," stated:

184

First we will take Eastern Europe, next the masses of Asia, then we shall encircle the last bastion of Capitalism, the United States of America. We shall not have to attack—it will fall like overripe fruit into our hands."

(This is, of course, the Lenin Fabrication No. 2, that we have previously discussed.)

Fagan concludes his "unmasking" of the Council on Foreign Relations by giving a list of the alleged Illuminati conspirators in the U.S.A. In addition to naming more than a dozen prominent Jewish bankers, Fagan names Winthrop Aldrich, Henry Luce, John Rockefeller, David Rockefeller, Leland Stowe, Hubert Humphrey, and Brooks Hays.

The Rev. Billy James Hargis has written a book attacking *America's Liberal Press,* by which he means the newspapers, magazines, and broadcasting stations that have not completely adopted an outright Ultra-Rightist position. In his "Distortion by Design," he slyly insinuates that newspaper columnist Walter Lippmann may be allied with the Illuminati order. Then he manages to insinuate that Lippmann derived some inspiration for some of his ideas from "Philip Dru: Administrator," which was written by Col. House, whom Hargis calls "that master conspirator of all time."

Robert Welch and his public relations expert, John J. Rousselot,[11] have loudly proclaimed that they and the John Birch Society are not anti-Semitic. If their claims are to be accepted as valid, it would seem to be essential that they explain why Welch wrote a long essay in the Birchite magazine, *American Opinion,* November 1966, entitled "The Truth in Time."

Welch begins by quoting John E. Hoover, who is the most widely-quoted person by almost all of the Ultra-Right groups. Then Welch makes the following major points:

1. That the Illuminati had much to do in the planning and initiating of the French Revolution, which Welch calls "the holocaust."

2. That the Communist movement is only the tool of something that Welch calls "the total conspiracy." According to Welch, this "total conspiracy" has given birth to "an inner core of conspiratorial power," which is able to direct and control world-wide subversive activities. Welch says he is not quite

---

11 Since this was written, Mr. Rousselot publicly announced his resignation.

sure that all this is caused by the machinations of the Illuminati, so he has decided to play it safe and just call this "inner core": the INSIDERS.

3. That by 1914 the INSIDERS brought about the adoption of the Federal Reserve System, the graduated income tax, and the direct election of U.S. Senators—all of which Welch views with suspicion.

4. *That ever since Adam Weishaupt founded the Illuminati, the INSIDERS have conspired to effectuate his stated policy.*

5. That in the Nineteenth Century the most important split among mankind was between Jew and Gentile; that in the present era the most important split is along the color line.

6. That the Communists have planted agents-provocateurs to persuade John Birch Society members that Communism is simply a Jewish conspiracy, and that therefore John Birch Society members are wasting their time in an organization which refuses to name *the real enemy,* the Jews.

7. That the INSIDERS instigated World War I; and simultaneously the INSIDERS were plotting to convert our constitutional republic into a democracy. Prominent in this plot, according to Welch, was President Wilson's assistant, Col. E. M. House.

8. That in 1917 the INSIDERS of Europe and the United States financed the seizure of power in Russia by "Lenin, Trotsky, and a relative handful of ruthless criminals."

9. That, as matters stand now, we need to fight the enemy by concentrating our efforts against "the Communist conspiracy." At this point Welch has executed a neat bit of intellectual sleight-of-hand, in a leap from his original premise about the Communist movement being only the tool of something he calls "the total conspiracy."

10. That in 1933 President Franklin D. Roosevelt saved the Soviet regime from financial collapse by extending diplomatic recognition, thus signaling the start of "the alliance between Washington and Moscow which has steadily grown stronger ever since. . ."

11. That, with "plenty of help" from the INSIDERS within a number of governments, Stalin brought on World War II.

12. That Stalin was able to forge an alliance with other

countries to combat Hitler through the work of Stalin's agents and the influence of the INSIDERS.

13. That the Communist principle of reversal came fully into play at this point in history, and that "everything about Communism is part of one Big Lie."

14. That Communism is not a movement of the masses against the ruling classes. Welch at this point propounds a doctrine similar to that of the Australian medicine man, Dr. Fred Schwarz of the Christian Anti-Communism Crusade. According to Welch:

Communism is, in every country, a drive for absolute power on the part of a closely-knit gang of megalomaniacs. In most countries these treasonous criminals come largely from the top social, educational, economic, and political circles.

(Apparently, Welch is too dull to realize what a left-handed compliment he has handed the Communists in this last sentence.)

15. That the U.S.A. foreign aid program was instigated by the Communists as a means of building up world Communism, but was sold to the American people as a means of blocking Communist advance—all this Welch explains, was done in accordance with the Communist principle of reversal, a political concept invented by Welch. It is not known if he owns a copyright.

16. That another example of the Communist principle of reversal is the establishment of the United Nations, which Welch claims was originated by Communists, is controlled by Communists, and increasingly carries out Communist programs.

17. That since 1945 "the most powerful single force in promoting Communism everywhere" has been the United States Government.

18. That in 1945 "Stalin's longtime agent, Charles de Gaulle," established himself as dictator of France.

19. That in the U.S.A. the Communists are using an ancient Chinese strategy in full force against the anti-Communists: breaking down the will to resist.

20. That the INSIDERS have the advantage of "almost two hundred years of cumulative experience," and that the Communists have established *formal* rule over almost half the pop-

ulation of the globe; and that the Communists have established *informal* but preponderant influence over the rest of the governments, except Spain, Portugal, West Germany, South Africa, Nicaragua, Paraguay, Nationalist China, New Zealand, and Australia. As for the U.S.A., Welch informs us that the Communists and the INSIDERS "now have full working control over our government."

21. That the INSIDERS, with the help of "our government, which the Communists already own," have devised a strategy which includes the deliberate breaking down of all morality, the distortion and destruction of religious influences, the gradual change of our republic into a democracy (which Welch claims will lead to "a mobocratic dictatorship"), the carrying on of a phoney war in Vietnam (which Welch claims is being run on both sides by the Communists), and the surrender of American sovereignty to the United Nations (which Welch claims will "police" our country with foreign troops).

22. That "today Moscow and Washington are, and for many years have been, but two hands of one body controlled by one brain."

We hasten to caution the reader against jumping to the conclusion that Robert Welch is a psychotic. There is, in our opinion, a better explanation for his dissemination of so much confusion, misinformation, and obscurantism. This will be dealt with in Volume II, under the heading of the role of the John Birch Society. For the present, three observations are in order:

a. The bibliography that Welch gives at the conclusion of his essay shows that he follows the pattern of most zealots—he reads mostly that which bolsters and reinforces his own prejudices (many of his reference books are written by unreliable authors). b. The INSIDERS thesis can easily give support to the anti-Semitic propagandists. c. Welch's INSIDERS thesis sounds suspiciously like a parody on the ILLUMINATI hoax.

The truth about the Illuminati, like other matters, is not difficult to acquire. It needs only a little time and a modicum of integrity. It appears that the first use of the name, Illuminati, was by the anti-Nicene Church Fathers, who applied it to those who agreed to be baptized. The idea was that a person who received the instruction for baptism in the Apostolic faith had become an enlightened or "illuminated" person. It is from this metaphorical use of language that demagogues, rabble rousers, and opportunists have concocted a weird, conspiratorial theory of history.

Another Illuminati group was called the Alumbrados. It originated in Spain about 1492, and was sometimes called Aluminados. For almost a hundred years, members of this group were victims of the Spanish Inquisition, which considered its philosophical tenets heretical. Around 1623 the principles of this group seem to have been adopted by a Frenchman, Pierre Guérin, whose followers were called Guérinets. An international philosophical order, known as the Rosicrucians, has also been called the Illuminati. It is believed to have been founded in 1422, and was first established in the U.S.A. in 1693. Benjamin Franklin and Thomas Jefferson were among its early officers.

The Illuminati group which seems to furnish the most ammunition to the rabble rousers is the one founded by Adam Weishaupt in Germany, on May 1, 1776. Weishaupt was a former Jesuit priest, who was professor of canon law at Ingolstadt. His philosophical principles had attraction for many prominent people, including the poet, Goethe. Branches of the order of Illuminati were established in most of the European countries. Internal problems and dissensions, as well as an edict by the Bavarian government in 1785 to outlaw the order, finally caused the Illuminati to virtually disappear, except as a scarecrow to frighten the gullible.

## The Baruch Levy Hoax

Professional anti-Semites are continually discovering secret Jewish "conspiracies" with which to inflame the passions of their ignorant followers. Simple-minded people avidly accept the simple-minded explanation that all of the world's troubles are caused by the Jews. There is a regular business of producing forged Jewish documents, and it is very plain to any serious student that hate peddlers have scoured the earth in search of "documents," which are then placed in files, for use at appropriate times. Thus we find that a reactionary magazine, *Revue De Paris*, in its issue of June 1, 1928, carried a long and boring article in French, whose translated title is "The Secret Origins of Bolshevism: Henry Heine and Karl Marx." It is a

189

vicious, anti-Semitic article, which tells of a Jewish "conspiracy" to conquer the world and then ties this imaginary conspiracy to Communism. As part of its "proof," it quotes from an alleged letter from one, Baruch Levy, to Karl Marx, the co-founder of the modern Communist movement. Nowhere in the article is there any inkling of who Baruch Levy could possibly be, excepting that he is referred to as a Neo-Messianist (whatever that is supposed to denote). The Baruch Levy "letter" outlines a Jewish plan to take over the world. Nowhere in the writings of Karl Marx is there any mention of Baruch Levy and/or his alleged letter. In fact, one can be reasonably certain Marx would have consigned it to the incinerator, if such a letter had reached him. *Revue De Paris* does not state where it obtained the alleged letter. The obvious reason—that it is a fraud—can easily be deduced from the internal evidence. Its *leitmotif* is almost identical with the central theme of the Rabbi Rabinovich fabrication (which we have already discussed) and the fraudulent Protocols of the Elders of Zion (which we will soon examine). In other words, any sane person, who has a knowledge of history, can readily recognize the Baruch Levy letter as a palpable fraud.

Thirty-seven years later, Hal Hunt quoted the Baruch Levy letter on the front page of his hate sheet, *National Chronicle* of March 11, 1965, along with the Kol Nidre hoax and other fraudulent items. How did the editor of a small-circulation sheet obtain an article from a Parisian magazine and how did he obtain an English translation of this essay? The answers are obvious to anyone who does research into the propaganda techniques of the hate publications: it is a stock item, which travels from one hate publication to another, because the members of this fraternity read and dote on each other's fulminations. The Baruch Levy hoax has appeared periodically, and will probably continue to be used until there is no longer a market for this kind of merchandise.

We asked Dr. Herbert Aptheker, Director of the American Institute for Marxist Studies, to do some additional research about the alleged letter from Baruch Levy to Karl Marx. In a letter, dated September 5, 1967, Dr. Aptheker stated:

I have examined five of the biographies of Marx . . . including those by Mehring, Ruhle, Postgate, Eastman, Lewis . . . and find no mention of anything in any way resembling the material you quote from Baruch Levy. In all my reading in Marxism . . . considerable for about 33 years . . . I have never seen anything remotely like that. Let me add that I have examined the indexes of all 6 volumes . . . Volumes 27 through 32 . . . of the Marx-Engels Werke (Dietz Verlag, Berlin, 1963-1965) and find no mention of a Baruch Levy or any indication of any letter in any way similar to that you mention. These are the volumes which contain the letters . . . Briefe . . . of Marx and Engels, commencing in 1842 and going through 1870 (all so far published). I think one may therefore say with great confidence that the letter is a hoax, as one would believe in any case from its contents.

## The Blood Libel

For upwards of a thousand years the Jews have been plagued, tortured, and murdered as a result of the circulation of the myth that they indulge in ritual murders of two kinds. The first is supposed to be a blood sacrifice, in observance of alleged Jewish religious teachings. This is supposed to require the secret murder of a Christian, usually an adult, and the draining of his blood onto the ground. An examination of the literature of the professsional anti-Semites would seem to indicate that the inspiration for this canard comes from the Old Testament story of Abraham agreeing to kill with a knife his first-born son, Isaac, as an offering to God, who had commanded him to do so. It never occurs to the dim-wits who believe the blood libel myth that, if God commanded Abraham to slay his son, they can hardly blame Abraham, and certainly not his descendants of thousands of years later. The dim-wits hardly realize that they come pretty close to accusing God of advocating ritual murder, when they use the Biblical story to prove the "original sin" of the Jews. Competent Biblical scholars consider this story in a symbolic, rather than a literal sense. The writer keenly remembers that, when he studied the Old Testament in his boyhood days, the rabbi explained it as God's way of testing Abraham's loyalty and that God would not have permitted Abraham to consummate the sacrifice and that he did have an angel order Abraham to call off the slaying of Isaac.

The gentlemen who circulate the ritual murder canard in this country—yes, it is being circulated openly right now—never explain how the Jews could be so clever that they have not been convicted of one single ritual murder these past 191 years, since the founding of the Republic! Can it be possible that all the police and detectives in this country are inferior to Czarist police and others, who have in past eras framed Jews on such charges? The anti-Semitic gentlemen have an explanation: the Jews buy up all the police, all the detectives, all the prosecutors, all the judges, all the juries, and all the media of communications! Yes, there are people who believe this nonsense.

Perhaps the reader thinks that frame-ups on ritual murder charges can happen only in backward countries, but that it can't happen here. Not only can it happen here, it did happen here! In Atlanta, Georgia, during 1913, Leo Frank, a young Jewish manager of a pencil factory, was arrested and charged with the rape murder of a fourteen-year old employee of the factory. Incited by a flood of inflammatory anti-Semitic tracts and pamphlets, a lynch mob surrounded the court house where the hapless Leo Frank was being tried. With guns pointed directly at the judge and jury, the mobsters shouted repeatedly: "Hang the Jew!" The mob's leaders threatened to kill the judge and the jury unless Leo Frank was sentenced to hang. He was sentenced to hang!

Newspapers all over the country protested that the trial was a farce, a mockery of justice. Even the *Atlanta Journal* editorially protested that Leo Frank had not had a fair trial. Distinguished lawyers throughout the country, who reviewed the trial record and the evidence, protested that the sentencing of Leo Frank was contrary to the weight of evidence, that it was a gross miscarriage of justice. In spite of ugly threats and the mounting pressures generated by professional anti-Semites, Governor John M. Slaton courageously commuted the death sentence to life imprisonment. As a protection against the lynch mobs, Governor Slaton ordered Frank moved to the maximum security prison at Millidgeville.[12] But prison walls are no barriers to the poison of prejudice, and Leo Frank was repeatedly assulted by white and Negro prisoners, who believed the blood libel canard: that Leo Frank, the Jew, had performed a ritual murder of a Christian girl. Finally, one of the convicts slashed

[12] When his term of office expired, Governor Slaton had to leave the state in order to save his own life from the mob.

Frank's throat, and he had to be transferred to the prison hospital.

On August 15, 1915, while Frank was still confined to a hospital bed, about thirty vigilantes marched onto the prison grounds, without encountering any resistance from the prison warden or the prison guards. Apparently, they were able to march through an open gate. They abducted Frank, chained him to the back of a car, dragged his body some fifty miles and then strung up the broken body to a tree. Leading newspapers denounced the lynching, but no official attempt was made to investigate the lynching or to apprehend the lynchers. The notorious bigot, Tom Watson, waxed eloquent in his personal hate sheet about the glory of teaching a lesson to those who attack Christian women. One of his articles, approving the act of the lynch mob, was headed:

## A VIGILANCE COMMITTEE REDEEMS GEORGIA

The second part of the blood libel hoax pretends that Jews murder Christian children and drain the blood from their victims for use in the ritual baking of matzos (unleavened bread) for the Passover holidays. The charge is so preposterous, that it would seem to be an insult to the reader's intelligence to adduce arguments and evidence in refutation. However, inasmuch as this hoax is presently being circulated by Fascist groups in this country, it would seem to be appropriate to present facts, which persons of goodwill can use to combat the liars. But first, let us examine a few of the classic cases that have become part of the historical record.

In the year 1475 a three-year old Christian boy named Simon was found murdered, in the city of Trent, Italy. Twelve Jews were arrested on a charge of ritual murder and immediately put to death. It was a frame-up, engineered by some leaders of the Roman Catholic Church in collaboration with city officials. For almost 400 years anti-Semites have cited the "confession" of the Jews that the boy had been ritually murdered, in order to obtain Christian blood for use in the baking of Passover matzos. That the "confessions" were obtained by torture seems to make no difference to the anti-Semitic scribes. Sometimes the wheels of justice grind at an excruciatingly slow speed, but finally the truth has come out. Several years ago, a priest of the diocese of Trent undertook a painstaking study of the murder

193

of Simon, the Christian lad, and as a result, both he and his Archbishop have labeled the trial of the twelve Jews "Judicial Assassination." As a further result of this study, the Vatican has officially admitted that *the twelve Jews were innocent,* and has banned the further veneration of Simon of Trent, who had previously been considered a martyr of Christendom and an object of veneration. The story is told in a front-page story in the *New York Times* of November 1, 1965.

In 1911, the entire civilized world was rocked by the story of the trial in Kiev, Russia, of an obscure Jewish worker, Mendel Beiliss, on a charge of killing a Christian boy in order to obtain blood for the baking of matzos. Despite a carefully planned conspiracy by Ultra-Rightists, anti-Semites, a dishonest professor, a cynical religious figure, a bribed physician, Czarist police, and a crooked prosecutor, Beiliss was acquitted. The acquittal came about, because the frame-up was so palpable that it backfired. Even the brother of one of the anti-Beiliss officials served as a member of Beiliss' legal staff. The pressure of worldwide protests and demonstrations also helped to insure the release of Beiliss, who finally came to this country, where he lived the rest of his life. After the revolution of 1917, it was proven by examination of the pertinent documents that Beiliss was framed in order to inflame public opinion with a showcase trial, so that two purposes could be served: a. To instigate massacres of the Jews (pogroms). b. To create a diversionary move in hopes of thwarting pressures for social and political reforms. When the Communists took over state power in the latter part of 1917, many of the conspirators were apprehended and executed.

Let us come back from Czarist Russia to the good old U.S.A., where such things just can't happen. On September 23, 1928—the eve of Yom Kippur, the Jewish Day of Atonement—a four-year-old Christian girl disappeared in Massena, New York. The local mayor promptly told a state trooper to inquire of the local rabbi if the little girl had been ritually murdered for *Yom Kippur.* This ignorant bigot apparently forgot his lines, because the usual cock-and-bull story is the ritual murder to obtain blood for the matzos of *Passover.* Fortunately, the girl showed up and a possible pogrom was averted.

That the blood libel myth is more widely disseminated in this country than many people are willing to believe, was proven more recently, when a professor in a New Jersey university was asked by a sophomore student if it is really true that Jews use blood in baking matzos for Passover.

On September 21, 1936, an Englishman, Arnold S. Leese, was sentenced to six months in a British prison for circulating an essay he had written, containing allegations against the Jews about the practice of ritual murder. In 1938 Leese published his views and his "proofs" in a booklet entitled *Jewish Ritual Murder*. In 1962, the Hitler-oriented National States Rights Party, which now has its headquarters in Savannah, Georgia, brought out a second edition of the Leese booklet, after obtaining permission from his widow. So now, we can say to those apathetic people who think that it can't happen here: "Wake up! It *is* happening here. The *Jewish Ritual Murder* booklet and copies of Julius Streicher's *Der Steurmer* are being circulated widely by the National States Rights Party and other Fascistic groups across the length and breadth of this country."

In ordinary times one would hesitate about spending the time to refute such atrocious nonsense, but these are not ordinary times. Evil men are sedulously spreading these poisonous doctrines, and the way to prevent a recrudescence of Hitler's racist ideology is to put it on the dissecting table *now*!

*Item.* Historically, the Jews have been, on the whole, a peaceful people. In fact, the universal and traditional greeting of the Jew is: Shalom! or Shalom Aleichim! Translated from the Hebrew, it means Peace or Peace be with You. Criminologists are all aware of the fact that there is a very low incidence of homicides and other crimes of violence among Jews. Such a people would hardly be prone to the murder of people in order to drain blood for ritual purposes. Furthermore, as we have already mentioned, no such crime has ever been officially charged, prosecuted, or proved in the entire history of this republic. To the Jewish people the Commandment, Thou Shalt Not Kill, has always been a meaningful precept of its religious philosophy.

*Item.* The Jewish religion expressly prohibits the ingestion of blood. Thus we find in the Old Testament:

If the sanctuary which the Lord your God chooses as the seat of his presence is far away from you, as I have instructed you, you may slaughter for food purposes in your own communities whenever you wish any of your herd or flock which the Lord has given

195

you. You are to eat it just as you would a gazelle or a deer, the unclean and the clean eating it together; *only be sure never to partake of the blood; for the blood is the life, and you must not eat the life along with the flesh; you must not eat it;* you must pour it out on the ground like water. (Emphasis added—M.K.)

—Deuteronomy, 12: 21, 22, 23, 24

It may come as a surprise to many readers, but it is a fact that the orthodox Jewish religion requires that any meat to be consumed by a person of the Jewish faith must be prepared as follows:

1. It must be soaked in water for one-half hour.

2. Then the water is poured off, and a heavy coating of coarse salt is applied all over the meat, in order to absorb the blood.

3. After the salt has been on the meat for an hour, the meat is washed with cold water three times.

This is hardly consistent with the notion that Jews use blood in the baking of matzos.[13]

It is a matter of historical record that it was customary for Jews in Czarist Russia to hire a Gentile and have him present when they were baking matzos, so that he could testify that no blood was used. Such were the defensive measures that Jews had to adopt against the blood libel story that was spread by Ultra-Rightists of that era. One wonders why the professional anti-Semites have not been successful in finding blood in the hundreds of thousands of pounds of matzos sold on the open market each year in this country, as well as other countries. It is very probable that, when confronted with this argument, the hate merchants will reply that only The Insiders can buy the matzos in which Christian blood is an ingredient.

The extent to which Jews avoid the ingestion of blood was shown in an advertisement of the orthodox rabbis of greater Los Angeles, which appeared in the *California Jewish Voice,* March 6, 1964. The following are some excerpts from that advertisement:

## BEWARE OF POULTRY
## CONTAMINATED WITH BLOOD

Dressing poultry in heated
water causes blood to be
absorbed into the flesh.

13 The Hebrew Bible, in Levicitus, 19:26, admonishes: "You must not eat anything with the blood."

## THE HOLY TORAH PROHIBITS
## THE CONSUMPTION OF BLOOD

## BE SURE TO BUY ONLY KOSHER POULTRY

Arnold Leese begins on page 1 of his booklet with the Biblical story of Abraham offering to slay his first-born son, Isaac, and states that this is a typical Semitic idea, without offering any proof of this statement. On page 2, Leese expounds the quintessence of Hitler's racist ideology: "All is Race; there is no other truth." This statement in itself discredits the man in the eyes of anyone with the slightest knowledge of science in general and anthropology in particular. Before uttering that gem of wisdom, Leese remarks:

According to the *Jewish Encyclopedia*, 1903, Vol. IV, p. 99, when performing the operation of circumcision on children, the mohel (operator) "takes some wine in his mouth and applies his lips to the part involved in the operation, and exerts suction, after which he expels the mixture of wine and blood into a receptacle provided."

It is this custom, which arose in antiquity, that Leese uses as one of the pillars of the structure of falsehood that he erects in his book. A brief examination of this argument is in order.

First, it must be pointed out that some credit must be given to the people of antiquity for having perceived, in rudimentary form, the importance of suction and mild alcohol application (in the wine) as a means of preventing infection. Secondly, the operator fills his mouth with wine first in order to prevent ingestion of blood. Thirdly, he quickly expels the mixture of blood and wine. Considering these elements of procedure, one can only marvel at the impudence of Arnold Leese when he insinuates that this, in any way, proves that Jews have a predilection for ritual murders.

The essential dishonesty displayed by Leese, in his quoting from page 99, Volume IV of the 1903 edition, *Jewish Encyclopedia*, can be seen by the fact of his omission of something on page 100 of the very same volume. Here it tells of the fact that many modern Jews have strenuously objected to the oral suction procedure, and that much discussion has taken place. The upshot of the controversy is reported by the *Jewish Encyclopedia*, as follows:

197

As a compromise, which has received satisfactory ecclesiastical authority, a method has been adopted which consists in the application of a glass cylinder that has a compressed mouthpiece, by means of which suction is accomplished.

It does not serve the purpose of an anti-Semitic liar to admit that Jews, like other peoples, have moved away from some of the customs of antiquity. The anti-Semite cannot tolerate any evidence that clashes with his attempt to depict the Jew as some sort of sub-human creature.

The Arnold Leese method of documentation is best illustrated by what he does on page 5 of his booklet. Says Leese:

Bernard Lazare, a Jew who was stated (*Jewish Encyclopedia,* 1904, Vol. VII, p. 650) to be "without any religious convictions," wrote what he himself described as "an impartial study of the history and sociology of the Jews," calling his book *L'Antisemitisme;* in the 1934 edition of this, Vol. II, page 215, he writes, after mentioning the accusations against the Jews of Ritual Murder:

"To this general belief are added the suspicions, often justified, against the Jews addicted to magical practices. Actually, in the Middle Ages, the Jew was considered by the people as the magician *par excellence;* one finds many formulae of exorcism in the Talmud, and the Talmudic and Cabbalistic demonology is very complicated. Now one knows the position that blood always occupies in the operations of sorcery. In Chaldean magic it had a very great importance. . . Now, it is very probable, even certain, that Jewish magicians must have sacrificed children; hence the origin of the legend of ritual sacrifices."

Quite apart from the fact that Leese has performed a feat of selective presentation of sentences torn out of context, he is obviously relying upon the fact that the reader is likely to overlook the internal evidence, in the above quotation, which disproves the ritual murder thesis. Note that Bernard Lazare does not speak of Jews in general, but only of "the Jews *addicted to magical practices.*" (Emphasis added.—M. K.) This sharply limits the scope. Notice also that Bernard Lazare speaks not of the *fact of ritual murder,* but of *the legend of ritual sacrifice.* A *legend* is quite different from a *fact.*

Even in introducing Lazare, Leese departs from the truth. He quotes the *Jewish Encyclopedia*'s characterization of Lazare as a Jew "without any religious convictions." The *Jewish En-*

*cyclopedia,* 1904, Vol. VII, page 650, which Leese says he is quoting, says of Lazare:

Although without any religious convictions he avowed himself a Jew, and was always ready to defend his brethren.

It should be noted that in quoting from *L'Antisemitisme,* Leese gives his readers what purports to be a translation from the French, but does not state who did the translating or where he obtained the translation. In order that a fair comparison may be made between what Lazare actually said and what Leese attributes to Lazare, we shall quote extensively from the official translation of Lazare's book. It was published in 1903 by the International Library Publishing Company, under the title of *Anti-Semitism, Its History and Causes.*

Discussing the anti-Semites' charge "that human sacrifice is a Semitic institution," Lazare points out that human sacrifice "is found among all peoples at a certain stage of civilization." Then Lazare continues:

In this manner we would prove, as has in fact been proven, that *the Jewish religion does not demand blood.* Can we, however, prove, in addition, that no Jew ever shed blood? Of course not, and throughout the Middle Ages there must have been Jewish murderers, Jews whom oppression and persecution drove to avenge themselves by assassinating their persecutors or even perhaps their children. Nevertheless, this does not afford a sufficient explanation for the popular belief which has its real origin in the widespread conviction that the Jew was irresistibly impelled every year and at the same time to reproduce exactly the murder of Christ. It is for this reason that in the legendary acts of the Infant martyrs the victims are always shown as crucified and undergoing the agony of Jesus: sometimes even they are represented as wearing a crown of thorns and with their sides pierced. To this general belief there were added the accusations, often justified, which were brought against the Jews as being addicted to the practice of magic. Throughout the Middle Ages the Jew was considered by the common people as the magician *par excellence.* As a matter of fact, a number of Jews did devote themselves to magic. We find many formulas of exorcism in the Talmud, and the demonology both of Talmud and the Kabbala is very complicated. Now it is well known the blood played always a very important part in the arts of sorcery. In Chaldean magic, it was of the utmost consequence; in Persia it was considered as a means of redemption, and it delivered all those who submitted themselves to the practices of Taurobolus and Kriobolus. *The Middle Ages were haunted by the idea of blood* as they were haunted by the idea of gold; for the alchemist, for the enchanter blood was the medium through which the astral light could work. The elemental spirits, according to the magicians, utilized outpoured blood in fashioning a body for themselves, and it is in this sense that Paracelsus speaks when he says that "the blood lost by them brought into being phantoms and larvae." To blood, and especially to the blood of a virgin, unheard of powers were assigned. Blood was the curer, the redeemer, the preserver; it was useful in the search for the Philosopher's Stone, in the composition of potions, and in the practice of enchantments. Now it is quite probable, certain, in fact, that Jewish magicians may have sacrificed children, and thence the genesis of ritual murder. *The isolated acts of certain magicians were attributed to them in their character as Jews.* It was maintained that the Jewish religion which approved of the Crucifixion of Christ, prescribed in addition the shedding of Christian blood; and the Talmud and the Kabbala were zealously searched for text that might be made to justify such a thesis. *Such investigations have succeeded only through deliberate misinterpretation,* as in the Middle Ages, *or through actual falsifications* like those recently committed by Dr. Rohling, and proven spurious by Delitzch. *The result, therefore, is this, that whatever the facts brought forward, they cannot prove that the murder of children constituted, or still constitutes, a part of the Jewish ritual* any more than the acts of the maréchal de Retz and of the sacriligious priests who practised the "black mass" would prove that the Church recommends in the books assassination and human sacrifice.

Are there still in existence in the East sects maintaining such practices? It is possible.[14] Do Jews constitute a part of such societies? *There is nothing to support such a contention. The general accusation of ritual murder, therefore, is shown to be utterly baseless.* The murder of children, I speak of cases where murder was actually proved, *and these are very rare,*[15] can be attributed only to vengeance or to the practice of magicians, *practices which were no more peculiar to Jews than to Christians.* (Emphasis throughout, added. —M. K.)

At the risk of boring the reader, we have given this lengthy quotation from Bernard Lazare, because it shows how Arnold

14 In 1814 a Christian sect arose in Bavaria, known as the Brothers and Sisters of Prayer, the members of which brought human sacrifices to God. The founder of this sect was called Poeschl. In Switzerland, in 1815, a certain Joseph Ganz, founded a similar association, to which he gave the same name, and which practiced the same rites.

15 Consult the report of Ganganelli, afterwards Pope Clement XIV, which, after an investigation into the charges of ritual murder brought against the Jews, arrives at the conclusion of their absolute falsity. (*Revue des Etudes Juices,* April-June 1889). It may be observed here that the bodies of children murdered for the purpose of magical practices were never found, the magician having prudently burnt them.

Leese quoted from Lazare in a manner to make him appear as a supporter of the ritual murder hoax. This procedure is typical of the rest of Leese's booklet and of all the anti-Semitic slanderers.

Arnold Leese concedes on page 5 of his booklet that "the Mosaic Laws and the Talmud do not demand Ritual Murder, and *even forbid the use of blood."* (Emphasis added.—M. K.) But then he argues that people steal in spite of the Eighth Commandment and that Jews commit ritual murder surreptitiously, and successfully conceal it. No proof is offered, excepting the stories where Jews have been victims of frame-ups. One of the cases that he cites to prove his point is the case of Simon of Trent, Italy. Too bad Arnold Leese died before the Catholic Church itself finally admitted that the Jewish "confessions" were phoney and that the twelve Jews were victims of "Judicial Assassination."

It would be a waste of time to refute the entire booklet point by point, although it can easily be done. It is enough to point out that Leese relies for some of his proof on one of the worst degenerates in all human history, Julius Streicher, editor of the pornographic hate sheet, *Der Sturmer.* Leese refers to Streicher as "a gallant and faithful German officer" and complains that Streicher was a much-maligned person. Faithful he was indeed to Hitler's murder machine, which Leese finds acceptable, despite the murders and bestialities on a scale unprecedented in all history. Thus, Leese comes into the court of public opinion with his hands dripping with blood and is in no position to point the finger of accusation against Jews or anyone else. His booklet can be summarized as a compendium of lies, slanders, distortions, and innuendoes. Nevertheless, the Leeses and others of this ilk must be vigorously exposed and refuted, lest the poison spread to dangerous proportions.

The subject of ritual murder is very well summarized in the 1937 edition of the Encyclopaedia Britannica, page 325:

. . . the revival of the myth by the anti-Semite in modern times is a deplorable instance of degeneration. That there is no foundation whatsoever for the belief is proved in the classical treatise on the subject by Hermann L. Strack, regius professor of theology at the University of Berlin. Several of the popes have issued bulls exonerating them, and temporal princes have often taken a similar step. Many Christian scholars and ecclesiastics have felt it their duty to utter protests against the libel, *including the most eminent Gentile students of Rabbinism of modern times. Indeed, the vast majority of the literature refuting the charge comes from non-Jewish pens.* That on the other side is entirely anti-Semitic, and in no case has it survived the ordeal of criticism. (Emphasis added.—M. K.)

## The "Protocols" Hoax

With the possible exception of Hitler's *Mein Kampf,* no single book has caused the spilling of more Jewish blood than the "Protocols of the Learned Elders of Zion." In fact, it furnished some of the inspiration for the writing of *Mein Kampf,* and it was required reading in Hitler Germany. In this country, it was given massive circulation by the late Henry Ford, Sr., together with a specially prepared pamphlet, entitled *The International Jew.* Ford ran the latter item serially in his paper, *The Dearborn Independent.*[16] Faced with a huge libel suit, that had been filed in a Detroit court in 1927, Ford publicly apologized and admitted that the "Protocols" is a fake and that "The International Jew" is based upon falsehoods and distortions of truth. His apology, however, did not completely undo the damage that he had done. He was responsible for the spread of anti-Semitic propaganda throughout this country, Germany, and Latin America. In a very real sense, it can be said that Ford and other Americans helped to prepare the ideological soil for Hitler and his Fascist regime. Ford is dead, but the evil that he committed lives on to plague mankind. In the 1930's, the Roman Catholic radio preacher, Father Charles Coughlin, resurrected both the "Protocols" and *The International Jew.* He spread the Fascist doctrines by way of a national radio hookup, by pamphlets, and by serialization in his magazine, *Social Justice.* During the national election contest of 1936, the "Protocols" was used in a whispering campaign against both Alf Landon and Franklin Delano Roosevelt. In May of 1948, the Rev. Gerald L. K. Smith sent a copy of the "Protocols" to every member of Congress. Smith's outfit, the Christian Nationalist Crusade, pushes vigorously the sale of both the "Protocols" and *The International Jew.* This is also true of the American Nazi Party, the National States Rights Party, Rev. Oren F. Potito's *National Christian News,* and

---

[16] At one time, it had a weekly circulation of 700,000.

other groups of similar nature. In addition, the National States Rights Party, the Christian Nationalist Crusade, the *National Christian News,* and others have run "The International Jew" serially in their periodicals.

The "Protocols" is quoted continually by hate sheets and leaflets throughout the country. Thus, in its issue of March 1, 1962, *Common Sense* stated:

Rabbi Epstein living in Africa wrote a letter to the *Brooklyn Tablet* back in the late thirties stating that he attended the Lectures of which the "Protocols of the Elders of Zion" are but a synopsis and that their contents are True.

In reply to a letter of inquiry from the writer, *The Tablet* editor, Patrick F. Scanlan wrote on April 13, 1962:

Unless you can give us the approximate date of the alleged publication of the Epstein letter we could not track it down. The "late thirties" covers so many issues, and since our volumes for that period are in a vault outside the building, it would be a time-consuming and expensive task to endeavor to locate the communication.

On April 17, 1962 we sent a letter to Mr. Conde McGinley, editor of *Common Sense,* in which we asked the following questions:

1. What is the full name of Rabbi Epstein?
2. What city and country did he live in?
3. In what month of what year did the Rabbi send the letter?

We are still waiting for a reply! And it is more than of little significance that editor Patrick Scanlan referred to "the *alleged* publication of the Epstein letter." The whole story is a fraud, as will soon be obvious to the reader.

According to the "Protocols," there are three hundred Wise Men of Zion, who gather in secret conferences at intervals of 100 years. At these conferences they plot to overthrow all governments and impose a Jewish super-government. The "Protocols" is supposed to be the minutes of the secret conferences. A rational, well-informed person can easily detect the internal evidence of the fraudulent nature of this story. For instance, who are these three hundred Wise Men of Zion? Where do they live? Who appoints them? How are successors chosen when some die? How do they earn a living? How is it possible that the identity of one single member of this group has never been disclosed?

According to the "Protocols," the Jews are in control of most of the world's gold, real estate, commerce, and industry. At the same time, they are supposed to be planning to create economic panic in order to achieve power. What is not made clear is how the Jews could avoid hurting themselves by creating an economic panic. And of course, the Jews have never controlled most of the world's wealth, in the past or the present.

In the "Protocols" the Jews claim to have achieved great power through their control of most of the world's gold, and at the same time they are supposed to be advocating the destruction of their power by calling for the abandonment of the gold standard.

The "Protocols" quotes the Jews as boasting that the French Revolution "was wholly the work of our hands." It is a matter of historical record that there were very few Jews in France at the time of the revolution; that the Jews did not enjoy political rights in France at the time; that there was not a single Jew among the top leaders of the revolution; and that Jews had little or no part in the revolution.

The "Protocols" falsely claims that in ancient times the Jews coined the slogan, "Liberty, Equality, Fraternity." It is a matter of historical record that the slogan was coined by a Frenchman, a Gentile by the name of Antoine François Momoro.

One could go on and on with citations of the mutually incompatible statements contained in this document, and it could be hilarious entertainment, if it were not so tragic. For this masterpiece of fraud has been used to inflame the passions of ignorant and fanatical mobs for well over sixty years and is still being circulated by evil men under the protection of freedom of the press. In its simplest terms, the "Protocols" was designed to divert the attention of exploited and frustrated people, away from their real oppressors, and turn the wrath of the people against the Jews. Thus, the Jews would become the easy scapegoat.

Whenever the "Protocols" have had to meet the test of civilized judicial process, it has been discredited and denounced. As previously mentioned, Henry Ford, Sr., backed down rather than face a libel suit in 1927. At the Rathenau murder trial in 1924 (before the advent of the Nazi regime), the German Supreme Court at Leipzig termed the "Protocols" the "Bible of the Rathenau Murderers." In pronouncing judgment, the Court said: "Behind the Rathenau murder was fanatical anti-Semitism, which found expression in *the libelous legend* about the Elders of Zion. This has engendered murderous instincts in the hearts of men." (Emphasis added—M. K.)

In August of 1934, during the course of a trial which resulted in the conviction of some local Nazi leaders, the Supreme Court of South Africa said: "The 'Protocols' are an impudent forgery, obviously published for the purpose of anti-Jewish propaganda."

In 1934, the Jewish Community of Berne, Switzerland brought a suit against certain editors for circulating the "Protocols." In announcing its verdict of guilty against the defendants, the court declared on May 14, 1935, that the "Protocols" are forgeries. On appeal, the Swiss Court of Criminal Appeal overruled the judgment and dismissed the fines levied against two of the defendants. The anti-Semites have argued that this was a victory for the "Protocols," but actually the judgment of the Appeals Court was on a technicality which in no way contravened the findings of forgery. The legal loophole, through which the defendants slipped out, was that under Swiss law, as of that date, the "Protocols," even though they be forgeries, could not be classified as *salacious* literature. It is interesting that at the close of the trial in the lower court, the judge declared the "Protocols" to be "nothing but ridiculous nonsense."

In 1864, a Parisian lawyer, Maurice Joly, published in Brussels a satirical novel entitled: *Dialogue in Hell Between Machiavelli and Montesquieu; or the Politics of Machiavelli in the Nineteenth Century.* The book was such an obvious attempt to condemn and ridicule the government of Napoleon III that Joly was prosecuted and sentenced to fifteen months in prison; a fine of 300 francs was imposed; and his book was confiscated. Through the painstaking work of the Constantinople correspondent of the *London Times*, Mr. Philip Graves, it was proven that whoever forged the "Protocols" had plagiarized Joly's novel. Sitting in his office in Constantinople during the summer of 1920, Graves was handed a tattered French book by a former officer of the Czar of Russia's army. Graves, who happened to be a student of French literature, immediately discovered a similarity between large portions of this French book and the "Protocols" (which were issued some fifty years after the French book had been published). A search of the British Museum in London produced another copy of this French book. During the famous trial at Bern, Switzerland in 1934-1935, Dr. Arthur Baumgarten, professor of criminal law at the University of Basel, testified that 176 passages of the "Protocols," taken from some fifty pages, were plagiarized from Maurice Joly's novel. Thus, the forger of the "Protocols" *transferred to the mouths of Jewish Leaders* the aims of world conquest, which Joly had attributed to Napoleon III in his novel!

In 1868, a blackmailing German journalist, Hermann Goedsche, published a novel entitled *Biarritz*. A careful examination of Goedsche's novel by scholars revealed that he had plagiarized some portions of Maurice Joly's novel. In a lurid chapter entitled, "On the Jewish Cemetery in Prague," Goedsche describes an imaginary meeting of the princes of the twelve tribes of Israel, who have assembled from all the capitals of Europe to plot for subduing the Gentile world. The scheme later outlined in the "Protocols" bears a striking resemblance to the plot that is hatched at this imaginary meeting. Goedsche later converted some of the material from this imaginary episode and palmed it off as a speech supposedly delivered by a rabbi at Lemberg. These imaginary speeches by non-existent rabbis are a common device employed by professional anti-Semites, as we have previously shown.

In 1869, a Frenchman, Gougenot des Mousseaux, published an anti-Semitic book which outlined an alleged Jewish plot to conquer the world and destroy Christianity.

In 1897, the dreaded Czarist secret police, the Ochrana, claimed that it had obtained a copy of the report of a secret meeting of Jewish leaders allegedly held in Basel, Switzerland. This alleged secret report, the "Protocols," was published as an appendix to a book published in Moscow by Professor Sergei Nilus in 1905. Other editions of the book appeared in 1911, 1912, and 1917. Prior to the appearance of the "Protocols" in Nilus' book, it had been published in a condensed version by the Russian newspaper, *Znamia,* whose editor, Krushevan, stated that he was not sure of its authenticity.

Professor Sergei Nilus was a lawyer without clients, who lived off the largesse of his mistress. When her resources were exhausted, although he had been an atheist, he turned religionist and lived on the bounty of the Church, which in those days was an adjunct of the corrupt Czarist regime. In 1901, Nilus wrote his autobiography, and in 1905 a second edition was published. It was in this second edition that Nilus included the "Protocols" as an appendix.

The year 1905 was a year of uprisings against Czarist oppression and a year of revolution. The Ultra-Rightist officials and leaders sent paid agitators across the country, using the "Protocols" and other hate literature as tools for stirring mob violence against the "alien Jews." There were 690 pogroms, carefully synchronized, immediately after the distribution of Nilus' book containing the "Protocols." When the Communists came into power in 1917, it was proven by documents found in the archives of the Czarist police that the "Protocols" were actually issued in 1905 in order to enable Chief of Police Trepow to instigate pogroms, making the Jews the scapegoats for all the ills of Czarism.

The 1912 edition of Nilus' book triggered a series of pogroms in 1913 and served as a springboard for the Mendel Beiliss frame-up, about which we have already taken notice. During World War I, Czarist secret police agents brought the "Protocols" to the secret service agencies of the Allied Powers, who refused to treat the document seriously. In 1917 the "Protocols" were *openly circulated by the Czarist police* in what came to be known as the *Pogrom Edition*. The results can be summarized in one sentence: Oceans of Jewish blood flowed. Meanwhile, like a vulture feasting on carrion, Nilus derived a huge income from the distribution of his book. In 1917, shortly after the Pogrom Edition had done its damage, the Communists (Bolsheviks) came into power in Russia and a decree was issued, making mere possession of the "Protocols" punishable with a sentence of death.

In 1907, two years after Nilus launched the distribution of the "Protocols," a political associate of his, Mr. C. Butmi, published a book entitled *The Enemies of Mankind*. The thesis of his book revolved around the "Protocols." In the introduction, Butmi says:

These "Protocols" were procured with great difficulty in Decem-

207

ber 1901, and were translated into Russian. It is impossible to return to the secret vaults where they are concealed, and therefore *they cannot be confirmed by definite assertions about place and time, where and when they were written.* (Emphasis added.—M. K.)

In 1919, Captain Mueller von Hausen, writing under the pen name of Gottfried zur Beek, published a book entitled: *The Secrets of the Elders of Zion.* It was based upon the "Protocols," which were in the appendix of Professor Nilus' book. Gottfried zur Beek added more "proof" and expanded upon the "Protocols." Some of his additional proof consists of *the speeches of the princes of Israel.* Not so strangely, these are almost identical with the speeches, "On the Jewish Cemetery in Prague," which appeared fifty-one years earlier in Hermann Goedsche's novel, *Biarritz.* Another "proof" zur Beek adduced was the imaginary speech of a non-existent rabbi in Lemberg, which Hermann Goedsche had concocted after he published his novel. Zur Beek's book was researched exhaustively by Otto Friedrich, a scholarly German Senator, who summarized his findings as follows:

What, according to Gottfried zur Beek, the Elders of Zion had decided in 1897, was already part of a trashy German novel in 1868 and part of a French satire in 1864.

Perhaps the most significant aspect of the "Protocols" story is that neither Nilus nor Butmi has been able to name one single member of the alleged Elders of Zion who were supposed to have composed the manuscript. Furthermore, both Nilus and Butmi admitted that they have never seen the original manuscript, but only a copy which had passed through many hands. Both Nilus and Butmi were violently anti-Jewish in their public pronouncements, and consequently must be considered psychologically prone to the acceptance of a hoax planted on them or overt participants in a conspiracy to circulate genocidal doctrines.

In the 1905 edition of his book, Professor Nilus claims that the meetings of the Elders of Zion referred to in the "Protocols" took place in 1902-1903. Nevertheless, through a quirk of memory, which often causes the downfall of criminals, he claims to have acquired the "Protocols" in 1901! This is quite a feat, and to rational people it should be sufficient to prove the spurious nature of the "Protocols." But there is more, and overwhelming, proof of its fraudulent nature.

In the introduction to the 1911 edition of his book, Professor Nilus says:

In 1901, I succeeded through an acquaintance of mine (the late Court Marshal Alexei Nicolayevitch Sukhotin of Tchernigov) in getting a manuscript that exposed with unusual perfection and clarity the course and development of the secret Jewish Freemasonic conspiracy, which would bring this wicked world to its inevitable end. The person who gave me this manuscript guaranteed it to be a faithful translation of the original documents that were stolen by a woman from one of the highest and most influential leaders of the Freemasons at a secret meeting somewhere in France—the beloved nest of Freemasonic conspiracy.

In the introduction to the 1917 edition, Nilus repeats the explanation of how he acquired the manuscript and adds that the late Alexander Nicolayevitch Sukhotin gave him the name of the woman from whom the manuscript had been obtained, but he has forgotten her name. (This is indeed strange, considering Nilus' otherwise vivid memory of minutiae.) Whereas in the 1911 edition he claimed that the manuscript was stolen by a woman who gave it to his friend Sukhotin, in 1917 Nilus says that "this lady had gained possession of the manuscript in a somewhat mysterious way—I believe by theft." Thus, his explanation has changed from a categorical position to an equivocal one.

In the 1917 edition, Nilus also claims that he has secret information, proving that the "Protocols" were presented to the Council of the Elders of Zion, at the first Zionist Congress at Basel, Switzerland in 1897, by Theodore Herzl. Nilus refers to a statement by Herzl that he found in "circular 18." As far as can be ascertained, no one else has ever heard of or seen "circular 18." Aside from the fact that the first Zionist Congress at Basel was not supported by large segments of world Jewry, the sessions were open to the public and were attended by representative Christian clergymen and political figures. Inasmuch as no one has produced any evidence of any secret sessions during the Basel Congress, one wonders how it was possible to read the 69 pages of the "Protocols" without having it leaked to the press in particular and to the Gentile world in general. Only Nilus seems to have out-foxed the Jews, according to his nursery tale!

While there are over 175 passages in the "Protocols" that are taken bodily from Maurice Joly's novel, a few examples should be sufficient to prove with finality the fraudulent nature of the "Protocols."

| MAURICE JOLY'S DIALOGUE IN HELL (From Brussels Edition, 1864) | NILUS' PROTOCOLS OF THE LEARNED ELDERS OF ZION (From the English translation) |
|---|---|
| "The evil instinct in man is more powerful than the good; man leans more toward the evil than the good; fear and power have more control over him than reason. . . . All men seek power, and there is none who would not be an oppressor if he could; all, or nearly all are ready to sacrifice the rights of others to their own interests. . . . Political liberty is only a relative idea." (page 8) | "Men with bad instincts are more in number than the good, and therefore the best results in governing them are attained by violence and terror, and not by academic discussions. Every man aims at power, every one would like to become a dictator, if only he could, and rare indeed are the men who would not be willing to sacrifice the welfare of all for the sake of securing their own welfare. . . . Political freedom is an idea, but not a fact." (page 1) |
| "The political has nothing in common with the moral." (page 19) | "Has politics anything to do with morals?" (page 19) |
| "I would institute . . . huge financial monopolies, reservoirs of the public wealth, on which depends so closely the fate of all the private fortunes that they would be swallowed up with the credit of the state the day after any political catastrophe." (page 75) | "We shall begin to establish huge monopolies, reservoirs of colossal riches upon which even large fortunes of the *Goyim* will depend to such an extent that they will go to the bottom together with the credit of the states on the day after the political smash." (page 22) |
| "It is useless to add that the perpetual upkeep of a large army continually exercised by foreign wars must be the indispensable comple- | "The intensification of armaments, the increase of police forces—are all essential for the completion of the afore-mentioned plans. . . . |

ment of this system; it is necessary to arrive at the existence in the state only of proletarians, several millionaires and soldiers." (pages 76, 77)

There should be . . . besides ourselves, only the masses of the proletariat, a few millionaires devoted to our interest, police and soldiers." (page 24)

"Like the God Wishnu, my press will have one hundred arms, each hand of which will feel all shades of public opinion." (page 141)

"Like the Hindu God Wishnu, they will have one hundred hands, each one of which will feel the pulsation of some intellectual tendency." (page 43)

We could go on and on, but it is very obvious that the "Protocols" is nothing more or less than a forgery, perpetrated by a religious fanatic who became a stool-pigeon for the Czar's secret police, the Ochrana.

It is interesting to compare Gottfried zur Beek's *The Secrets of the Elders of Zion* with Hermann Goedsche's novel, *Biarritz*, which, in turn, had plagiarized Maurice Joly's *Dialogue in Hell*.

### GOEDSCHE'S "BIARRITZ" (1868)

### ZUR BEEK'S "THE SECRETS OF THE ELDERS OF ZION" (1919)

"The insecurity of monarchical governments increases our power and influence. Therefore, we always stir up disturbances. Every revolution yields interest to our capital and brings us nearer to our goal." (page 178)

"Every war, every revolution, every political and religious change brings us nearer to that moment, when we shall attain the high goal for which we are striving." (page 32)

"All commerce that is connected with speculation and profit must be in our hands. Above all, we must have the commerce in alcohol, oil, wool, and corn. Then we shall have agriculture and the country under our control." (page 180)

"Commerce and speculation, two productive sources of profit must never be snatched from the hands of the Jews. Above all, the commerce in alcohol, butter, bread, and wine, must be protected, for by doing so, we shall become the absolute masters of agriculture." (pages 32, 33)

211

| "By controlling the stock exchange, we are masters of the wealth of the states. Therefore, we must make it easy for the governments to contract debts, in order to gradually gain more control over the states. If possible, capital must get a mortgage on the institutions of the state, such as trains, revenues, mines, franchises, domains." (page 173) | "The stock exchange records and regulates these debts (of the states) and we are the masters of the stock exchange almost everywhere. Therefore, we must strive to involve the governments in debt, in order to be in a position to dictate prices, and we must take from the countries to which we lend our capital, their trains, mines, forests, smelting works, and factories as a mortgage." (page 32) |

When confronted with the overwhelming evidence of the fraudulent nature of the "Protocols," its exponents invariably reply that its "prophesies" have come to pass, or as Henry Ford, Sr. put it, "they fit in with what is going on."[17] This argument is so preposterous that many intelligent people become either infuriated or stultified in their efforts to cope with it. This, however, is not the way to handle this argument. In the first place, the argument is a classic example of what is known in the realm of logic as the *non sequitur*. That is to say, the conclusion does not necessarily follow from a given set of facts. For instance, if John Jones is found dead from a bullet wound and William Brown's revolver with a spent cartridge is found alongside Jones' body, it does not necessarily prove that Brown murdered Jones, unless other evidence can be adduced. Similarly, if one finds some resemblance between happenings in the world and "prophesies" or statements in the "Protocols," it is not proof that the Jews caused them or planned them. In fact, if we are to use the anti-Semites' line of reasoning, the blame for the conditions, against which they complain, should be lodged against *a Gentile* by the name of Maurice Joly, the

17 The *Wiener Library Bulletin,* published in London, England, in its Summer of 1967 issue, tells of a recent English edition of the *Protocols of the Learned Elders of Zion,* which was edited by a Muslim writer and published in Karachi, Pakistan. In addition to the editor's essay, there are contributions by two other Muslim writers who are natives of Pakistan. It is issued under the title of "Jewish Conspiracy and the Muslim World: With the complete text of the Protocols of the Learned Elders of Zion of the 33rd Degree."

In addition to the usual lies and slanders, this concoction accuses the Jews of being part of a conspiracy with the Masonic order. Simultaneously, the Jews are accused of having formed a conspiratorial alliance with the Catholic Church to combat the Muslims.

author of *Dialogues in Hell*. It was Joly who furnished the raw material for the "Protocols" and the other fraudulent concoctions. Of course, it can be conceded that Joly could not foresee the use made by corrupt people of his satirical novel.

The attempt to link statements in the "Protocols" with current social phenomena makes use of another fallacious procedure: the *selective* presentation of data and the suppression of any contrary evidence. Thus the followers of crystal ball gazer, Mrs. Jeanne Dixon, will cite her "hits" and neglect her "misses." There are fundamentalist preachers who spend long hours finding "prophecies" in the Bible about the atomic and thermonuclear bombs and just about anything else that suits their fancy. Some of these gentlemen have even cited some weird combination of numbers taken from the Bible to "prove" that Pope Paul VI is the anti-Christ of Bible prophecy! This illustrates the fallacy of trying to find any links between the "Protocols" and current world conditions. It is bad enough if people do this with the Bible, but when they do it with a forged document, they are traveling towards a psychotic dream world.

The Ultra-Rightist *National Review* pointed out editorially on November 20, 1962: "The Protocols are a fraud, from beginning to end." It pointed out further that in one state of the Union copies of this fraud are being widely distributed. The truth is that it is being circulated widely throughout the country and it is preparing the minds of potential storm troopers. The question that should be asked is why these groups and individuals are not vigorously exposed and condemned by John E. Hoover, the House Un-American Activities Committee, the Senate Internal Security Subcommittee, the American Legion, and the California Un-American Activities Committee. The usual alibi, that publicity helps these people, is just a cover up, as we shall see when we explore this matter further in Volume II. It should be clear that individuals and/or groups who circulate *The Protocols of the Learned Elders of Zion, The International Jew,* Arnold Leese's *Jewish Ritual Murder,* and anti-Semitic and anti-Negro literature of any kind must be classified as enemies of humanity, and should be mercilessly subjected to the spotlight of public exposure. Nothing less will effectively cope with this growing menace.

(Note: In addition to our own research into the "Protocols" fraud, we gratefully acknowledge the help derived from Benjamin Segel's book, *The Protocols of the*

213

*Elders of Zion—The Greatest Lie in History;* two excellent articles in *Liberty Magazine,* Feb. 10 and 17, 1940; and a study done by the Library of Congress, which was placed in the Congressional Record on June 1, 1948 by Senator Harley M. Kilgore.)

## The Fraud of Deicide

The doctrine of deicide expresses itself in its simplest terms when the charge of Christ-Killer is hurled at a person of Jewish heritage. The devastating effect of this charge in terms of human suffering almost defies description. The psychic trauma inflicted upon Jewish people, especially children, is something that has been described in many books, including such excellent novels as *Gentleman's Agreement.* There is a direct political, sociological, and psychological path from the original launching of this charge to the extermination of six million Jews by Hitler and his minions. What is not so generally known is a fact that was pointed out by Rabbi Jay Kaufman: "Through the centuries, some seven million Jews were killed by religious anti-Semitism—as many as were killed by the ethnic, racist anti-Semitism of the Nazis."[18]

The persistence of this story up to this age of enlightment, in the "Land of the Free and the Home of the Brave," is attested by some recent happenings. In the Mormon pavilion of the New York World's Fair, in September of 1964, there was a mural depicting the crucifixion of Christ. Beneath the picture of Christ was the inscription: "They crucified the Son of God." When asked who the "they" means, an elder of the church said that it referred to the Jews. A study made several years ago by the Survey Research Center of the University of California showed that 53% of the large, liberal church congregations blamed Jews for the crucifixion; and that 72% of the fundamentalist congregations believed the same story.

The responsibility of the Church for the propagation of this fraud is something that is proven by incontrovertible evidence. In 1442, Pope Eugenius IV issued this statement:

We decree and order that from now on, and for all time, Christians shall not eat with Jews, nor admit them to feasts, nor cohabit with them, nor bathe with them. Christians shall not allow Jews to hold civil honors over Christians, or to exercise public offices in the state.[19]

[18] *ADL Bulletin,* November 1965.
[19] Quoted in *Christian Beliefs and Anti-Semitism* by Glock and Stark.

As a concomitant of this policy, the Vatican maintained a Ghetto in Rome until 1870.

The Spanish Inquisition, established in 1478, wrote another ugly chapter in the history of anti-Semitism. As so frequently happens, the persecution of a small minority evolved into a form of thought control that soon engulfed the entire nation, and from which no citizen was safe. Nor has Spain yet fully recovered from its effects.

The story of Simon of Trent, which we discussed under the heading of "The Blood Libel" (the Jewish ritual murder canard), has some additional aspects which deserve examination. When three-year-old Simon Unberdorben disappeared in 1475, Bishop Hinderbach of Trent instigated a series of atrocities. At least one-half of the Jewish population was subjected to unspeakable tortures. Some were sent to the gallows or beheaded. Others were burnt alive. A "confession" of ritual murder, obtained from an eighty-year-old Jew after prolonged torture, was the signal for atrocities against the Jews of Trent and other cities. Although a bishop of the Church, who made a thorough investigation on behalf of the Vatican, reported that the Jews were innocent, Pope Gregory XIII chose to listen to an anti-Semitic investigator, and on June 20, 1478, he issued a "bull" declaring the Jews guilty and declaring Simon a martyr. Later Simon was made a saint, as was Bernardius de Feltre, the Franciscan monk who had told the Pope that the Jews were guilty.

It was only after a courageous and distinguished Catholic historian, Father W. R. Eckert, proved that the Jews of Trent were victims of a monstrous frame-up and after he reported strong indications that the real murderer blamed the Jews in order to distract attention from himself—it was only then that Archbishop Allessandro Maria Gottard of Trent issued a pastoral letter on October 28, 1965, which acknowledged the innocence of the Jews. At the same time, he abolished the "cult of Simon." This is all very fine, but Christians in general and Roman Catholics in particular have some tall explaining to do. During some 390 years, the embalmed body of Simon of Trent was on display in a special "chapel," the object of reverence along with pictures and sculpture showing Simon's alleged murder by the Jews. Meanwhile, for 390 years this poison was allowed to spread, forming the justification for hatred and suffering and bloodshed. How do Christians explain the fact that it took 390 years to ascertain the truth? And why are there no public exposure and open denunciation of the distribution in this country at this very moment of *The Jewish Ritual Murder* book by the National States Rights Party? Why is similar action not taken against Rev. Gerald L. K. Smith, the American Nazi Party, Rev. Oren F. Potito, National States Rights Party, and others who are at this very moment distributing the *Protocols of the Learned Elders of Zion* and Henry Ford's *The International Jew*? Would it not be in order for Mr. John Edgar Hoover to expose these "Masters of Deceit,"[20] these "most notorious liars in the United States?"[21] Would it be amiss for the House Un-American Activities Committee to investigate these activities and to expose them thoroughly, and to name names? And how about the American Legion, the Daughters of the American Revolution, and the others who uphold "our way of life" and wave the flag vigorously?

Progress along these lines is being made slowly and painfully. In 1959, the late Pope John XXIII ordered the removal from the Good Friday liturgy of allusions to "the perfidious Jews" and the removal of the prayer that "They may be rescued from their darkness." In 1960 he ordered removed from the ritual-of-baptism-for-converts the formula: "You should abhor Hebrew perfidy and reject Hebrew superstition." Even so, Pope John was forced to halt the prayers during Good Friday services in St. Peter's Basilica, in 1963, because of an erroneous mention of the "perfidious Jews." The Pope ordered the prayers recited a second time, purged of the poison which he had previously forbidden.

The Protestants have little right to point the finger of accusation against the Roman Catholics in the matter of anti-Semitism. While it is possible to quote many passages from his writings, that condemn anti-Semitism, it is nevertheless true that on other occasions, Dr. Martin Luther, the leader of the Protestant Reformation, did utter anti-Semitic remarks that are shocking. In fact, several anti-Semitic groups are currently circulating a book, supposedly consisting of quotations from Dr. Martin Luther, under the title of *The Jews and Their*

[20] Title of a book by John E. Hoover, which is widely circulated by Ultra-Rightist groups.

[21] Mr. Hoover once referred to Dr. Martin Luther King as "the most notorious liar in the country."

*Lies.* Among the verifiable quotations from Dr. Martin Luther, these two stand out as particularly inflammatory:

> Jews and papists are ungodly wretches; they are two stockings made of one piece of cloth.
> Heretics are not to be disputed with, but to be condemned unheard, and whilst they perish by fire, the faithful ought to pursue the evil to its source, and bathe their hands in the blood of the Catholic bishops, and of the Pope, who is the devil in disguise.[22]

Protestants who taunt Roman Catholics with the fact that Adolph Hitler was brought up in the Roman Catholic Church, should take a good look at the justification for the burning alive and slaughtering of human beings that is contained in the remarks of Dr. Martin Luther.

The Greek Catholic Church bears a heavy responsibility for the massacres (pogroms) in Czarist Russia, for the forging and distribution of the *Protocols of the Learned Elders of Zion,* and for a major role in keeping the Russian people steeped in ignorance, superstition, and vodka. An incident that epitomizes the posture of the Church is worth recalling. During the infamous Kishinev massacre of 1903, *the pogrom procession* was led by Greek Catholic Sisters, who had about fifty of their pupils with them. They carried ikons or pictures of Jesus and sang "God Save the Czar!"

Among the courageous and principled clergymen who have taken steps to openly debunk the deicide doctrine, and to show its harmful effects, was the Right Rev. James A. Pike, who, at the time, was Bishop of the Episcopal Diocese of California. In an excellent article that he wrote for *Look* magazine, March 14, 1961, Bishop Pike said:

> Actually, the responsibility for Jesus' death is a complex matter. While He had vivid disagreements with the Pharisees, *those primarily responsible for His undoing were the Jewish ecclesiastical leaders, who belonged to a tiny minority group known as the Sadducees.* (There were perhaps not more than 2,000 at the time.) *Jesus threatened their income and status* because He opposed the Temple abuses and because His teaching presented a direct pathway to God, bypassing the system they ran. Also, the Sadducees were collaborating with Israel's Roman oppressors. *Both the Sadducees and the Romans feared Jesus as a threat to the status quo.* (Emphasis added.—M. K.)

[22] See *The Great Quotations* by George Seldes, pages 446, 447.

The National Council of Churches, at the opening of its triennial assembly in Philadelphia on December 1, 1963, announced a project which would seek to remove the deicide charge against the Jews. Father Edward Flannery, editor of the *Catholic Visitor* of Providence, Rhode Island, delivered a most remarkable speech in Boston, Massachusetts, on December 1963, at a conference held at Boston College. Father Flannery emphasized the following points:

1. That Jews and Gentiles must learn to *understand* one another much better.
2. That it is necessary to establish recognition of the historical basis of anti-Semitism, its nature, and its causes.
3. That Popes, Saints, and Church fathers have contributed their share to anti-Semitism, and that consequently the task of arriving at an understanding of the history and harmful effects of anti-Semitism *is one primarily for Christians.*

Even more outspoken in his denunciation of Christians who regard Jews as responsible for the crucifixion of Christ was Cardinal James McGuigon, Archbishop of Toronto, Canada. In a signed column that appeared in the *Toronto Telegram* during August of 1964, Cardinal McGuigon declared:

If there ever was a stain on the conscience of the Christians, it must surely be our scandalously ambiguous attitude toward the Jew.
Christians today are slow to realize that hatred of the Jew has been fostered in a certain type of facile theological reasoning that makes a Jew a Christ-killer, an accursed race rejected by God.
*This basically un-Christian notion has existed too long* in the unspoken level of many a Christian conscience. (Emphasis added.— M. K.)

On October 14, 1964, the House of Bishops of the Protestant Episcopal Church forthrightly declared:

The charge of deicide against the Jews is a tragic misunderstanding of the inner significance of the crucifixion. Furthermore, in the dimension of faith, the Christian understands that all men are guilty of the death of Christ, for all have in some manner denied him.

On October 15, 1965, the Ecumenical Council of the Roman

Catholic Church, meeting in Vatican City, adopted a declaration by a vote of 1,763 to 250, which set a new course for the Church in its relations to non-Christian religious groups. This change did not come without a formidable behind-the-scenes struggle. Three years earlier, when the Ecumenical Council started its deliberations, every delegate was sent a copy of a book published by a neo-Nazi group called the "New Order" movement. The "New Order" movement has affiliates in many of the European countries, including Italy. The 600-page book was well-printed and beautifully bound, and was published in an edition of some 4000 copies. It bore the signature of Maurice Piney, whom no one has yet identified. It contained the standard anti-Semitic quotations that are used by Lyrl Van Hyning, Rev. Gerald L. K. Smith, Rev. Oren F. Potito, Rev. Wesley Swift, Rev. Dennis Fahey, Conde McGinley, and others in this line of business. As was to be expected, the book contained copious excerpts from *The Protocols of the Learned Elders of Zion*. Most interesting, however, is the title of the book: *The Plot Against the Church*. This may sound incredible, but the book actually explains the "plot" against the Roman Catholic Church on the basis of a supposed "Jewish fifth column" *among the Catholic clergy!* It is known that heavy pressure was exerted against Pope Paul VI by some sections of the administrative apparatus in Rome, as well as by some bishops in Italy, Spain, and the Middle East. Despite all this, it was announced during the latter part of October, 1965, that the Pope accepted the Declaration and promulgated it as the official policy of the Church.

The Declaration was not as courageous and as forthright as it might have been. It did not *confess* the errors and crimes of the Church with respect to the 1900 years of anti-Semitic suffering, tortures, and massacres. The original text condemned the doctrine of deicide, but "deicide" was finally deleted by a vote of 1,821 to 245. On the question of anti-Semitism, the Council voted to "deplore" it instead of "condemn" it, by a vote of 1,905 to 199. It would have been appropriate that the confessional procedure be followed by the Church leaders who require it of their followers. Nevertheless, the Declaration does contain a renunciation of the deicide doctrine and the anti-Semitic myths that have plagued mankind for so many generations. The principal stands taken are as follows:

*On deicide:* "Although the Jewish authorities and those who followed their lead pressed for the death of Christ, nevertheless what happened to Christ in his Passion cannot be attributed to all Jews without distinction, then alive, nor to the Jews of today."

*On anti-Semitism:* "Moreover the Church, which rejects every persecution against any man, mindful of the common patrimony with the Jews and moved not by political reasons but by the Gospel's spiritual love, deplores hatred, persecutions, displays of anti-Semitism directed against Jews at any time and by anyone."

*On race hatred:* "We cannot call on God, the Father of all, if we refuse to treat in a brotherly way any man, created as he is in the image of God. Man's relation to God the Father and his relation to men his brothers are so linked together that Scripture says: 'He who does not love does not know God.' "

*On discrimination:* "The Church thus reproves, as foreign to the mind of Christ, any discrimination against men or harassment of them because of their race, color, condition in life, or religion."

A study of the New Testament makes one wonder why so many Christians ignore its teachings. For instance, in the Gospel according to Saint Luke we find in verses 31, 32, and 33 of the 18th Chapter that Jesus is referred to as the "Son of man" and that he prophesied that he will be delivered unto the *Gentiles* who will mock him, mistreat him, torture him, and put him to death; and that he will rise again on the third day. Clearly, the Bible here speaks of the *Gentile* role in the crucifixion of Christ. And the question is: why has this been soft-pedaled all these centuries?

Turning to the Gospel according to Saint Matthew, it is crystal clear, in reading Chapters 26, 27, and 28, that Jesus was put to death by a ruling clique of Jewish priests and elders who were in league with Roman officials. The assistant editor of *Christianity Today,* Mr. James Daane, points out that Jesus was tried in a Roman court, and "was crowned with thorns by Romans and condemned under Pontius Pilate, a Roman judge. He died at the hands of Roman soldiers, in the Roman manner, on a cross. And the Romans were Gentiles. Although Pilate was reluctant and his wife uneasy, no Gentile rose to protest the injustice of Christ's condemnation."[23]

The real clue to the execution of Christ is found in the Gospel according to Saint John, Chapter 11, verses 47 and 48:

[23] *The Anatomy of Anti-Semitism* by James Daane, page 23.

Then gathered the chief priests and the Pharisees a council and said, What do we? for this man doeth many miracles.

If we let him thus alone, all men will believe on him; and the Romans shall come and take away both our place and nation.

Clearly, Jesus was a "subversive" in the eyes of the ruling clique, who suddenly became super-patriotic towards the Roman officials, in order to get rid of this "trouble maker." It can easily be understood why Jesus was a threat to both the rich Jews and the rich and powerful Romans. For, when we turn to Luke, Chapter 18, we find Jesus telling a rich man that he must sell all his holdings and distribute the proceeds unto the poor. Moreover, he preached sheer "sedition" and "un-American" doctrine when he proclaimed:

For it is easier for a camel to go through a needle's eye, than for a rich man to enter into the kingdom of God.

Finally, it should be pointed out that the ugly charge of deicide is completely anti-Christian in nature. Our authority for this statement is the description of the crucifixion in the Gospel according to Saint Luke, Chapter 23, verse 34, where Jesus asks forgiveness for his executioners and for the lynch mob:

Father, forgive them; for they know not what they do.

Clearly, anyone who professes to be a follower of Christ and at the same time practices anti-Semitism, especially the use of the Christ-Killer slander, has not learned the basic teaching of Christ, as epitomized in his final words. The compassion and love which are inherent in his teaching cannot be reconciled with the fraudulent charge of deicide and the devastating doctrine of anti-Semitism. If Christ could ask forgiveness while on the Cross, by what kind of logic and what kind of justice do some of his professed followers deign to condemn and villify and massacre descendants of his own people for over nineteen hundred years?

The Republican candidate for President of the United States in 1940, the late Wendell L. Wilkie, understood very well the danger of anti-Semitism. In his forceful manner, Wilkie said in 1940:

The desire to deprive some of our citizens of their rights—economic, civic or political, has the same basic motivation as actuates the fascist mind when it seeks to dominate whole people and whole nations.

I consider Anti-Semitism in America as a possible criminal movement and every anti-Semite as a possible traitor to America.[24]

One of the most interesting and promising developments, in the fight against anti-Semitism in general and the deicide doctrine in particular, was the publication in 1966 of a set of 6 pamphlets by the John XXIII Center of Fordham University. Produced under the editorial supervision of the distinguished Catholic scholar, Father Edward Flannery, who is also the author of *The Anguish of Jews*, this set of pamphlets constitutes a powerful message of clarity and sanity. Typical of its philosophical posture is this message in one of the pamphlets, entitled *The Outline of Truth*:

Yet Christ was slain, the crime was committed. He was slain by Romans, gentiles and Jews. But not all the gentiles, not all the Romans and not all the Jews. The tears of Jews and Christians mingled at Calvary, as they have mingled many times since then for many other crimes.

The blame for the death of Christ belongs not to the Jews but to the sins of all men everywhere. He came for us all . . . Jew, gentile and those without any faith. He came in love and died in forgiveness.

Specifically, the Church speaks out about the death of Christ and the charge of Deicide, which for nearly 2,000 years has been a source of so much hate, bloodshed and violence directed against the Jewish people.

The outline of this terrible event has been distorted and twisted for all these centuries through misunderstanding, misinterpretation and plain lack of knowledge.

Unfortunately, up to September 28, 1967, only 30,000 sets of these pamphlets have been distributed out of an original press run of 250,000 sets. Would it not be in order for some group or combination of groups to arrange for massive distribution . . . in the tens of millions . . . of this powerful plea for truth and justice?

People of good-will could demand of all Christian churches an active, aggressive campaign to completely wipe out every

<hr />

[24] See *The Great Quotations* by George Seldes, page 749.

vestige of the deicide doctrine. A public pronouncement once a year will not suffice. A forthright, meaningful, and energetic campaign could be mounted, in order to rid mankind of the disease of anti-Semitism, especially the deicide fraud. Sincere Christians could demand that the pastors of their respective churches preach sermons periodically to help bury the deicide charge. If such a course of action were to be followed by one single denomination on a national scale, it would probably inspire all the other denominations to emulate that policy. This could hasten the day of justice for the Jews and the rehabilitation of the Christian conscience.

# CHAPTER III

## The Racist Liars and Myth-Makers

Racism may be defined as a system of beliefs which confuses hereditary traits with traits that are derived from our social, economic and cultural environments. The cardinal error in racist pseudo-science is the attempt to transfer the data and methodology of biology to sociology, economics, and psychology.

While the inherited traits predetermine that a fish will swim in water, that a bird will fly in the air, and that an ant will live underground, man can and does alter his *natural environment*. Man differs from the rest of the animal kingdom in a number of respects, among which are:

1. He is a tool-making and tool-using animal.
2. He has the capacity for abstract reasoning.
3. He can transmit the heritage of the past—the accumulated wisdom of all mankind—through spoken languages and written records. From date of birth, man *acquires* traits from his social environment: family influences, schools, radio, television, books, newspapers, churches, theaters, and other forms of social intercourse.

One of the factors that accounts for belief in racist doctrine is, of course, prejudice. The essential nature of prejudice is an attitude, toward people or toward problems, that is taken without careful examination of the facts. Such an attitude is usually charged with strong emotions. Many of the racists fit the description given by the late American humorist, Henry Wheeler Shaw, who wrote under the pseudonym of Josh Billings: "The trouble with some folks is not that they are so ignorant, but that they know so much that isn't so." Some racist-minded people are suffering from such deep-seated feelings of insecurity and/or inferiority that they need to denigrate others in order to build up their own egos. Such prejudices form a barrier to a rational solution of problems, causing harm to both the prejudiced person and the object of his scorn.

Racism is historically a late arrival on the social scene. While religious differences provided the camouflage behind which struggles for power and wealth were conducted in past eras, racism is rapidly displacing it as a device to indoctrinate the masses for the benefit of ruling classes who need cannon fodder for wars of conquest. Dr. Alfred Metraux, in an essay prepared for the United Nations Educational, Scientific and Cultural Organization (Unesco) in July 1950, summarized it very well:

Racism is one of the most disturbing phenomena of the great revolution of the modern world. At the very time when industrial civilization is penetrating to all points of the globe and is uprooting men of every colour from their age-old traditions, a doctrine, *treacherously scientific in appearance,* is invoked in order to rob these men of their full share in the advantages of the civilization forced upon them. (Emphasis added.—M. K.)

The late Professor Ruth Benedict, one of the world's greatest anthropologists, summarized the nature of racism as follows:

Desperate men easily seize upon some scapegoat to sacrifice to their unhappiness; it is a kind of magic by which they feel for the moment that they have laid the misery that has been tormenting them. In this *they are actively encouraged by their rulers and exploiters,* who like to see them occupied with this violence, and fear that if it were denied them they might demand something more difficult. So, Hitler, when his armament program cut consumers' goods and increased hours of work and lowered real wages, exhorted the nation in 1938 to believe that Germany's defeat in 1919 had been due to Jewry, and *encouraged racial riots.* And this served two purposes: *It gave an undernourished people an outlet harmless to the government, and it allowed the government treasury to appropriate the wealth of the Jews.*[1] (Emphasis added.—M. K.)

We Americans cannot be very proud of our own racism, for it is a matter of historical record that the U.S.A. was a racist society from its very inception. Many of the founding fathers were owners of chattel slaves. Our genocidal treatment of the natives, whom we arrogantly termed Indians, is something that is partly concealed by falsifiers of history, who have used both real and phoney atrocity stories to rationalize and justify our crimes against the Indians. And to this very day, our denial of elementary human rights to Negro-Americans, Mexican-Ameri-

[1] *Race: Science and Politics* by Ruth Benedict. Viking Press, New York. 1959.

225

cans, and Puerto Rican-Americans is a cancer that eats away at the vitals of our society. The poison of racism permeates and infects every aspect of our lives, and is reflected in our political pronouncements and in our cultural activities.

Abraham Lincoln's Emancipation Proclamation, his immortal Gettysburg Address, and the 14th and 15th Amendments to the U.S. Constitution have remained largely scraps of paper as far as millions of Negroes are concerned. Through the use of a variety of subtle economic and political pressures, as well as overt acts of violence and terror, the Negroes have been cruelly oppressed, "kept in their place." On October 23, 1901, U.S. Senator Benjamin R. Tillman of South Carolina said in a public speech:

The action of President (Theodore) Roosevelt in entertaining that Negro Booker T. Washington will necessitate our killing a thousand Negroes in the South before they will learn their place again.

Senator Tillman and his ilk were not idle boasters, for there were 3,426 Negroes lynched between 1882 and 1947, according to the records of Tuskegee Institute. Since 1947 the number of open lynchings has decreased, but other forms of "judicial lynching" have supplanted the crude and more obvious methods. Those who play the numbers game, and minimize the horror of the lynchings by arguing that only a small percentage of the Negroes have been murdered, should bear in mind that every time a Negro lynching is reported millions of Negroes "die a thousand deaths." Nor should one overlook the beatings, the bombings, the unjust jailings, the savage court decisions, and the innumerable forms of oppression visited upon these people.

The late William Faulkner, winner of the Nobel Prize in literature for 1949, was born in Mississippi and knew the South. In a refreshingly frank interview with the *London Times* of February 21, 1956, Faulkner was asked if there was an economic basis for Southern prejudice against Negroes. His reply was:

Absolutely. To produce cotton we have to have a system of peonage. That is absolutely what is at the bottom of the situation.

The next question that was asked of Mr. Faulkner was: "Are

the psychological rationalizations for prejudice something grafted on to the economic roots?"

Again with refreshing frankness, Faulkner replied:

Yes, I would say that a planter who has a thousand acres wants to keep the Negro in a position of debt peonage, and in order to do it he is going to tell the poor class of white folks that the Negro is going to violate his daughter. But all he wants at the back of it is a system of peonage to produce his cotton at the highest rate of profit.

Another distinguished writer, the late Thomas L. Stokes, a Pulitzer Prize winner, wrote in the New York *World-Telegram and Sun*, November 16, 1951:

The truth is beginning to be suspected—that there is some selfish purpose behind the appeal to racial prejudice. The trick is for the politician, in league with the privileged, to rally the underprivileged interests by stirring up racial prejudice. That is disclosed if you inquire who provides the big chunks of money for the Dixiecrats. *It is great corporate interests, many headquartered far from the South.* (Emphasis added.—M. K.)

Both Faulkner and Stokes were part of that small, but growing section of the white race, that has the courage and integrity to strike a blow against the cruel myth of racism. Similarly, at the Southern California Psychiatric convention held at San Diego, California on November 2, 1963, a joint paper was presented by Dr. Bernard Teitel, chief of the Long Beach Memorial Hospital, and Dr. George Demos, dean of counseling and testing at Long Beach State College. Pertinent to our investigation are the following excerpts:

Caucasians who have a basic feeling of inferiority cope with it by projecting the Negro into a false position of inferiority.

In certain cultures, as in the South, racial myths of Negro inferiority have become institutionalized to reinforce the social, economic, and political system and to maintain the status quo.

It is clear from all the evidence that racism is an ideology which serves the following purposes:

1. It furnishes an emotional crutch for people with feelings of inferiority and/or insecurity, who assuage their own feelings by denigrating others.

2. It serves as "a bribe" by which ruling classes, crooked politicians, and some corrupt clergymen are able to mislead whole populations.

Even if there were any semblance of scientific truth to the racist ideology, decent people would have to consider the dissemination of its doctrines as immoral and cruel. Fortunately, it can be proven, beyond peradventure, that racism is entirely false and completely without merit. Before proceeding with an examination of the scientific pretensions of the racist philosophers, we cannot resist the temptation to quote again the distinguished assistant editor of *Christianity Today*, Mr. James Daane:

> In this exercise of racial prejudice a man stands godlike astride humanity and selects himself and some of his fellows. What is this but a proud assertion that one is—together with those one chooses—the elect, the favored of God? Racial prejudice is a secular version of divine election—a sinful usurpation of prerogatives that belong to God alone.[2]

Racist ideology is exceedingly dangerous and extremely difficult to combat for a number of reasons. It panders to man's most primitive emotions. It pretends to furnish simplistic answers to complex problems. Above all, its most important danger stems from the fact that some of the ideologists of racism have M.D. or Ph.D. next to their names. The warning (previously quoted in our discussion of the Alaska Mental Health Hoax) of psychiatrists Marmor, Bernard, and Ottenberg is worth repeating: that "an M.D. or a Ph.D. degree is not always a reliable indicator of scientific objectivity when borne by individuals whose personal bias outweighs their rationality." We are all familiar with the unspeakable crimes perpetrated by the "doctors of infamy" under Hitler's regime—the excruciatingly painful experiments conducted on live human beings. It is high time that the pseudo-scientific basis for racism be dissected.

A considerable amount of the propaganda being distributed by Southern racists bases itself upon a distortion of the theories of Dr. Carleton S. Coon, professor of anthropology at the University of Pennsylvania. In a book entitled *The Origin of*

2 *The Anatomy of Anti-Semitism* by James Daane. Wm. B. Eerdmans Publishing Co.

*Races,* in a book entitled *The Races of Man,* and in an article appearing in *Harper's Magazine,* December, 1962, Dr. Coon divides the human species into five different races, each having a different origin and each one having reached the "Homo sapiens" (wise man) state at a different stage in time. According to Dr. Coon's estimate, the Caucasian race arrived at the "Homo sapiens" stage about 200,000 years before the Negroes. Much to the dismay and chagrin of Professor Coon, the racists have seized upon this hypothesis and exploited it for the propaganda of alleged Negro inferiority. Professor Coon, being a man of great scientific stature and great personal integrity, has roundly denounced this perversion of his writings. Whatever the truth about the validity of Dr. Coon's theories, no honest person can use his theories to bolster racist pseudo-science. And Dr. Coon has affirmed this conclusion in unequivocal terms.

An important source, upon which racist propagandists rely, is Professor Henry E. Garrett of the University of Virginia. Dr. Garrett is the author of a number of standard works on psychology and was president, in 1946, of the American Psychological Association. His racist views are summarized in a pamphlet entitled *How Classroom Desegregation Will Work.* It should be noted at the very outset that Dr. Garrett gives evidence of a departure from scientific methodology by the very title of his pamphlet. Scientists do not usually undertake to make a prognostication with such an air of finality as is implicit in the phrase *"will* work." The true scientist is cautious; he makes his prognostications on a tentative basis, using words such as *probably* or *likely.* Dr. Garrett begins his booklet by dismissing as "wishful thinking" all the evidence contained in newspapers, magazines, and various books that in any way contradicts his philosophy. Thus, Dr. Garrett suggests that his prejudices compel him to ignore evidence that clashes with his preconceived notions. He frankly admits that all the contrary evidence has been deliberately omitted from his booklet.

Dr. Garrett's pamphlet is in four parts. The first part uses a system of comparative intelligence tests, which, we shall show, is now discredited. In the second part, he gives three examples of desegregation in the school systems. He tells of some of the problems encountered in overcoming the handicaps of Negro children when they are placed in integrated schools. He tells it in the style to which one becomes accustomed in reading such racist hate sheets as *Thunderbolt,* the organ of the National State Rights Party, and *The Councilor,* the organ of the Louisiana (White) Citizens Councils. It is no accident that the resemblance in style is apparent, for it is no secret that Dr. Garrett has contributed articles to *The Citizen,* official organ of the (White) Citizens Councils of Mississippi. Moreover, it was reported in November of 1965 that his pamphlet was being reprinted by the (White) Citizens Councils. It has also been reprinted by a racist propaganda group in Richmond, Virginia, that calls itself the Patrick Henry Group. In the latter part of 1965 the Patrick Henry Group sent out free sample copies of Dr. Garrett's pamphlet, and sent along a form letter inviting the recipient to order as many copies as possible in order to spread the "truth." In December of 1965, it was reported that Dr. Garrett was expected to participate in a Citizens Councils Leadership Conference in Chattanooga, Tennessee, January 7 and 8, 1966.

In giving some alleged data about integration of schools in Washington, D.C., Los Angeles, California, and New York City, Dr. Garrett uses the method of *selective presentation of data,* a procedure he confessed to employing, at the very beginning of his pamphlet. In dealing with Los Angeles, he relies entirely upon a book written by a school teacher who tells of his own experience in one single school. How much truth there may be in this book we cannot tell, but we do know that Ultra-Rightists and racists have been promoting its sale. Even Dr. Garrett concedes that one should not rely too much on one experience, for he grudgingly admits:

Kendall's book is not representative of every desegregated school, to be sure, but it shows clearly to what lengths deterioration can go when there is no effort to face facts.

May we politely suggest that Professor Garrett is contradicting himself? For if Kendall's book "is not representative of every desegregated school," why does Dr. Garrett rely *solely* on it for his story about desegregation of schools in Los Angeles?

The circulars that are used by the Patrick Henry Group to advertise "White Teacher in a Black School" by Robert Kendall, give us some clues to an understanding of Kendall's views. Kendall grew up in Michigan. He was not interested in his

230

family's hotel business, so he went to Hollywood. He replaced Sabu in "Song of Scheherazade" and appeared later in several TV and screen productions. In the course of his work in a Youth-for-Christ movie, Mr. Kendall became interested in the problems of juvenile delinquency. His thinking led him to the conclusion that his career should be that of a teacher, where he felt he could make the best contribution to human welfare. He obtained a position as a teacher in a Los Angeles High School, which had a preponderance of Negro students. According to Kendall, he had some rough experiences which led him to the conclusion that desegregation will not work. He also had some difficulty with the principal of the High School, a white man, who told Kendall that "it has become apparent that you are basically a rabble-rouser." Kendall also had some difficulties with the principal because of an apparent desire to indoctrinate his students with his particular religious views.[3] The principal found it necessary to inform Kendall that he could no more teach Christian doctrine than he could Buddhist doctrine, because in this country we have a separation of church and state. Kendall also found it important, in narrating his experiences, to make much ado about a parody on the Pledge of Allegiance, which was recited in a private party at the home of his principal.

It should be clear from all this that whatever percentage of truth there may be in Kendall's book, it is nevertheless one man's experiences, one man's prejudices, one man's petulance. This is not the stuff of which scientists arrive at conclusions about human behavioral problems. It is, therefore, regrettable that Professor Garrett chose to rely so much on this book.

In a letter to the *Los Angeles Times*, July 21, 1967, William C. Ward praises his teacher-colleagues who *choose* to continue working in a predominantly Negro school, because of their dedication to the needs of these children. He says:

I myself teach an afternoon class in reading enrichment and a Saturday class in Negro history. My being white has been no handicap as far as I am concerned, and my fondest wish is that I might someday consider myself the peer of these fine teachers. They not

---

3 Subsequently, Kendall was dismissed as incompetent by the Pinecrest Ranch School in Woodland Hills, California. Kendall claimed it was because of his book. He sued for $127,250 damages, and settled for $2,450.

only teach the academic subjects but impart far more to the children through love and caring.

Here you have *another* teacher's experience—which seems to contradict Mr. Kendall's report. Could it be that Mr. Kendall saw exactly what he had decided to see?

Contrary to usual procedure, Professor Garrett summarizes his views in the third chapter of his booklet, instead of the fourth one, which is the final one. In this General Summary, he makes four points, which we give here verbatim, with our comment in parentheses:

1. Judging the probable future from the known past, wholesale desegregation of public schools will lead, first, to demoralization, next to disorganization, and eventually to ruin or complete ineffectiveness. (Dr. Garrett backs away from the positive prediction contained in the title of his pamphlet when he speaks of "probable future." Inasmuch as no one has advocated "wholesale desegregation," his entire argument falls flat on its face. Every responsible leader, Negro and White, realizes that desegregation must proceed by a series of steps. It cannot be instantaneous, wholesale, or overnight. But it should be carried out in good faith by men and women of goodwill.)

2. It is painfully evident that desegregation and "quality" education are incompatible. (Dr. Garrett does not give the reason for his quotation marks around the word "quality," giving it some kind of implication. Perhaps by "quality" he means the kind of education calculated to teach Negroes to "stay in their place." Whatever the interpretation, Dr. Garrett has not proven his thesis, because it cannot be proven.)

3. The Federal agencies are deliberately sacrificing the country's talent in a futile attempt to accomplish the impossible: To "equalize" the Negro child of 80 IQ with the White child of 100 IQ. (Dr. Garrett has again set up a straw man and knocked it down. Perhaps this is why he uses quotation marks around "equalize." Aside from the fact that his use of the statistics of intelligence tests is grossly misleading, no one is trying to "equalize" the Negro child of 80 IQ with the White child of 100 IQ. What is being attempted is to give the Negro child an equal *start* in life, and, of course, it requires improved social environment, improved home environment, *and* elimination of discrimination in all facets of life, including the schools.)

4. Intermarriage, a primary goal of the integrationist, will lead inevitably to a loss in the intellectual and cultural assets of this country. Such loss could make the difference between victory and defeat in any future conflict. (Bringing in the scarecrow argument about intermarriage would seem to indicate the frantic nature of

232

Dr. Garrett's search for something to justify discrimination and segregation. His assumption, that integration of schools necessarily leads to more mixed marriages, is not proven. Nor has he proven that intermarriage is biologically or socially harmful. He only says so, but he does not prove it.)

The final chapter of Dr. Garrett's pamphlet presents arguments and alleged facts to "prove" the innate inferiority of the Negro. Inasmuch as we shall examine these arguments in great detail in a general discussion of racist pseudo-science, we shall conclude the commentary on Dr. Garrett only by pointing out that one of the sources he relies upon to prove his position is Dr. Carleton Coon's *The Origin of Races*. Inasmuch as Dr. Coon has strongly denounced this misuse of his research findings, Dr. Garrett should have at least pointed out this fact in a footnote. One does not strengthen his position by quoting a witness who contradicts one's thesis.

Probably the most widely distributed book expounding the racist philosophy is *Race and Reason: A Yankee View* by Carleton Putnam. *Playboy* magazine, of April, 1966, said: "Putnam, a former president of Delta Airlines, has no academic credentials in sociology, anthropology or genetics." Another source of support of the racist position comes from the work of a psychologist, Professor Audrey Shuey. Her specialty is cataloguing the results of intelligence tests and constructing charts to prove Negroes are innately inferior in intelligence and aptitude. Still another support for the racist viewpoint is a book published in 1962 *under the sponsorship of Alabama's Governor John Patterson,* entitled *The Biology of the Race Problem,* by Dr. Wesley George. Obviously, the book's findings were a foregone conclusion.

In 1958 the American Association for the Advancement of Science established a Committee on Science in the Promotion of Human Welfare. This committee consisting of scientists of great repute, including the internationally famous anthropologist, Dr. Margaret Mead, issued a report which appeared in the November 1, 1963 issue of *Science*. The report took notice of the fact that racists were using alleged scientific data to prove the innate biological inferiority of Negroes, in an attempt to block school desegregation. Although professional patriots missed the point, the committee made it clear that the racist doctrines are distinctly un-American, because the U.S. Constitution confers the benefits of citizenship on all citizens. *The committee specifically condemned the writings of Carleton Putnam and Dr. Wesley George.* It went on to say:

We know of no scientific evidence which can challenge this axiomatic political principle. The use of purported scientific evidence to justify non-compliance with the Constitution debases both science and the human conscience.

At its 1961 convention in Philadelphia, the American Anthropological Association approved by a vote of 192 to 0 a resolution which said that the group "repudiates statements now appearing in the United States that Negroes are biologically and in innate mental ability inferior to whites, and reaffirm the fact that there is no scientifically established evidence to justify the exclusion of any race from the rights guaranteed by the constitution."

One of the most interesting aspects of the fraternity of racist philosophers is the extent to which they quote each other as authority for statements and conclusions. The methodology may well be described as intellectual incest, a condition which prevails throughout the ranks of the Ultra-Rightist intellectuals. A case in point is the list of footnote references given by Robert Welch in *The Politician,* sometimes referred to as "The Black Book" of the John Birch Society. In 1959, there was established the International Association for the Advancement of Ethnology and Eugenics. While using what the public relations men call the "soft sell" approach, the orientation of this group is racist and elitist. Listed among its members are Professor Henry E. Garrett and the late Professor Charles C. Tansill. Tansill wrote articles for the John Birch Society's magazine, *American Opinion,* and for the now-defunct *Western Destiny,* a quarterly magazine expressing the philosophy of racism and Ultra-Rightism. Professor Tansill also was a member of the Textbook Evaluation Committee of the Ultra-Rightist group, America's Future. The Committee serves as a sort of watchdog, to make sure that school textbooks contain material that makes the student safe for Capitalism. A columnist in the *New Republic* of March 27, 1965, refers to him as "the late Charles C. Tansill, who was dropped by American University after an *outspoken defense of Hitler and the Nazis.*" (Emphasis added.—M. K.) In a full-page eulogy of Tansill, in

*American Opinion* of May 1965, associate editor Francis X. Gannon averred that Tansill "was devoted to his religion" and that he "imparted his love for God and our nation."

A discussion of race must of necessity begin with an understanding of what constitutes a race. The Germans are a nationality, not a race. The French are a nationality, not a race. The Jews in Israel are a nationality, not a race. Elsewhere in the world, Jews are a religious and cultural entity, within the nationality framework of the specific country in which they live, and are usually members of the white race. (There are about 50,000 black Jews in Ethiopia, and there are some black Jews in the U.S.A. There is at least one synagogue of the black Jews in New York City.)[4] Race, at best, is a rough and imprecise method of classifying divisions within the human species according to such features as color and texture of hair, color of the skin, and shape of the skull. Most anthropologists now roughly divide the human species into three generalized color categories: white (Caucasoid), yellow (Mongoloid), and black (Negroid).

Skin color is determined by two chemicals, *both of which are present in the skin of all human beings.* Melanin is the chemical which gives us the brown color, and carotene is the chemical which gives us the yellow color. A greater or lesser amount of each chemical determines a person's complexion, and *not any characteristic of the blood or the brain.* There are so many different shades of complexion within each racial group that color, by itself, becomes only a very loose way of classifying people. Indeed, there are some groups of Whites whose skin is darker than some groups of Negroes.[5]

The racist philosophers, using arguments and data which are, in the words of Dr. Alfred Metraux, "treacherously scientific in appearance," try to prove that Caucasoids are further removed from apes than Negroids. In the first place, Charles Darwin and the biologists that followed him have not claimed that man is descended from the ape, but rather that both man and ape are descended from a common ancestor, which was

[4] There are also Black Jews in India; in Mexico among some of the aboriginal tribes; and in the Bukharian region of the Uzbek Republic of the Soviet Union. The latter show some evidences of Turko-Mongolian mixture.
[5] Racists have never explained why so many of them make the effort to get a sun tan, which often makes their complexion approximate that of light-skinned Negroes.

neither man nor ape. Through long and patient study of fossil remains, the paleontologists have traced the history of man back some 30,000,000 years. It is obvious that in this context it becomes somewhat silly to argue that one race is closer to the anthropoids than another. Nevertheless, the pseudo-science of the racists can be refuted by the evidence at hand.[6]

*Item.* The anthropoids have a hairy coat on their skin. *The Whites have more hair on the skin than do the Negroes.* The skin of the Mongoloids is the freest of body hair.

*Item.* The anthropoids have thin lips. The racists, who ridicule the Negroes' thick lips, conveniently ignore the fact that the thick lips move the Negro further from the anthropoid than the more "primitive" lips of the Whites.

*Item.* The world-renowned Columbia University anthropologist, Professor Franz Boas, pointed out, in *The Mind of Primitive Man,* another superior physical characteristic that the Negro possesses. "The proportions of the limbs of the Negro," said Professor Boas, "are also more markedly distinct from the corresponding proportions in the higher apes than are those of the European."

It is clear from the evidence that the racists "prove" the superiority of Whites over Negroes by *the selective presentation of data.* Using the same procedure, it is possible to prove Negro superiority over White, but the truth is that *no race has a monopoly of superior traits.* Evolution has favored each race with some distinctive features, but none of them prove the superiority of one race over another.

An argument that racist philosophers find very attractive is the admitted fact that the average weight of the brain in the White race is greater than the average weight of the brain in the Negro race. The argument sounds plausible until it is subjected to critical analysis. It is well known that scientists, working with the best microscopes available, cannot tell from examination to what race a brain belonged. It is also well known that some of the most gifted members of the human race were proven by autopsy to have had very small brains, and it was also shown that the world's largest brain belonged

6 Racists who resort to pseudo-biological arguments, should be reminded that mating of Negroes or Whites with anthropoids will not produce offspring, whereas mating between Whites and Negroes does produce offspring. Nature provides the best answer to the racists.

to an imbecile. Anatomical research has long ago established the basic truth that the shape and the convolutions of a brain are more important than its weight. It has been proven that, as a brain develops more convolutions, the surface area of the brain increases. Mere weight is of no discernible advantage.

Perhaps the most erroneous of the racist claims is that of difference in blood among races. Actually, scientists recognize four blood types: O, A, B, and AB. All the races of mankind have all these blood types, and it has been proven incontrovertibly that all human blood is the same. Operators of medical blood banks are well aware of this basic truth.

A favorite argument of racists is that Negroes are more prone to commit crime than Whites. Criminologists and sociologists are well aware that this is "proven" by the juggling of statistics, by *selective presentation of data,* and by ignoring the oppressive social, economic, and political conditions under which most Negroes live in this country. It would be more truthful to state that, under the conditions, it is a wonder that the incidence of crime is not greater among Negroes. A few facts will illustrate the point. In answer to a question asked by a reader, *Parade* magazine on December 20, 1964 pointed out that in Phoenix, Arizona, where the population is 95% White, the crime rate was one-third greater than in Washington, D.C., which has a population of 54% Negro. A United Press International dispatch, which was carried in the Riverside, California *Daily Enterprise* on February 28, 1964, is something for the racists to ponder:

Suicide is almost exclusively a "white man's disease" in San Francisco, according to statistics gathered by the city's health director.

Among Negroes the suicide death rate was 2.6 per 100,000 population—while among Whites it is 33.5 per 100,000.

It would be interesting to inquire what Professor Henry E. Garrett would have to offer by way of explanation of this phenomenon. Or perhaps some of the racist philosophers would care to give us some value judgments as to the superiority of one race over another from the following Associated Press dispatch of April 7, 1963:

Birmingham, Ala. Thirty-two Negro marchers were arrested

yesterday as they knelt to pray for segregationist Police Commissioner Eugene Connor, who has vowed to fill the jails with integrationists.

A staunch white supremacist, Connor stood nearby ordering, "Let's get this thing over with . . . Call the wagons, sergeant. I'm hungry."

Another facet of the Negro crime myth was pointed up by Mr. Roy Wilkins, executive secretary of the National Association for the Advancement of Colored People, in his syndicated column, *Los Angeles Times*, May 8, 1967. Contrary to the impression created by sensational news stories and screaming headlines, the crime statistics show that most of the crimes of violence by Negroes are committed against other Negroes. Of the murder cases that were solved in New York City during 1966, *those committed by Negroes* averaged one against a White for every seven against Negroes. In Washington, D.C., there was a total of 172 murders in 1966. Only twelve were of Whites by Negroes. On the other hand, in some areas of this country five times as many Negroes are murdered by Whites as Whites by Negroes. In Washington, D.C., 88% of the rapes were confined to persons within the same race. And, if the truth were made known, it would probably show that more Negro women are raped by Whites than White women by Negroes.

Racist philosophers rely to a considerable extent on intelligence tests which purport to show that Negroes are inferior to Whites. Disregarding the pseudo-scientists who prepare tendentious reports for a price or to satisfy prejudice, it can be said that any such findings are based upon faulty and unscientific methods of investigation, as well as erroneous interpretation of data. In 1935, Professor Otto Klineberg published a study entitled *Race Differences*, in which he summarized the results of mental testing:

Intelligence tests may therefore not be used as measures of group differences in native ability, though they may be used as measures of accomplishment.[7]

Another scientist, who had previously fallen into the trap of

_____
[7] Professor Klineberg is quoted by Professor Ruth Benedict in *Race: Science and Politics*.

interpreting army intelligence tests in 1921 as proving racial superiority of the Nordic peoples, finally confessed his error, as an honorable scientist must. Dr. C. C. Brigham wrote in 1930:

Comparative studies of various national and racial groups may not be made with existing tests. . . . In particular one of the most pretentious of these comparative racial studies—the writer's own—was without foundation.[8]

In September of 1961, the Society for the Psychological Study of Social Issues, a section of the American Psychological Association, issued a report which was a direct reply to Professor Henry E. Garrett. The report said categorically that there is no direct evidence that Negroes are innately inferior to Whites in intellect.

On October 1, 1964, a group of twenty-two biologists, geneticists, and anthropologists from seventeen countries issued a statement which was published by the United Nations Educational, Scientific, and Cultural Organization. Among the conclusions in the Report are the following:

Neither in the field of hereditary potentialities concerning the over-all intelligence and the capacity for cultural development, nor in that of physical traits, is there any justification for the concept of "inferior" and "superior" races.

The biological data (given in the report) stand in open contradiction to the tenets of racism. Racist theories can in no way pretend to have any scientific foundation.

It has never been proved that interbreeding has biological disadvantages for mankind as a whole. On the contrary, it contributes to the maintenance of biological ties between human groups and thus to the unity of the species in its diversity. . .

The biological consequences of a marriage depend only on the individual genetic makeup of the couple and not on the race. Therefore, no biological justification exists for prohibiting intermarriage between persons of different races, or for advising against it on racial grounds. . .

The peoples of the world today appear to possess equal biological potentialities for attaining any civilization level.

Among the signers of the report was *Professor Carleton S.*

---

[8] Dr. Brigham is quoted by Professor Ruth Benedict in *Race: Science and Politics.*

*Coon,* whose writings the racists try to misrepresent as a confirmation of their ideology. His signing of the Report of the twenty-two scientists *proves* that Professor Coon does not support the pseudo-science of the racists.

On December 29, 1964, a very distinguished and courageous Southern psychologist made a landmark report to the meeting, in Montreal, Canada, of the American Association for the Advancement of Science. Dr. Susan W. Gray, of George Peabody College in Nashville, Tennessee, told of a scientific experiment, which confirms what the reputable scientists have been saying about Negro innate intelligence and capabilities.

Dr. Gray worked with Negro children who lived in shed-like houses, who usually had many brothers and sisters, and most of whose mothers were domestic workers. Almost half of the children had no fathers in the homes. Dr. Gray began the experiment by taking twenty of these children at age 3½ into a pre-school summer program *where they were encouraged to talk and express curiosity.* They were allowed to do finger painting, to examine their own hands under a magnifying glass, and to work with jigsaw puzzles. They were taken on visits to farms, to an airport, and to libraries. This program of activities was carried on with the group for three successive summers. During the rest of each year, program teachers made weekly visits to the children's homes.

Another group of twenty children was given the same help, but only for two summers and the same weekly visits during the rest of each year.

Two control groups of children, from the same general kind of environment, were studied at the same time, but were not helped in the manner of the first two groups.

When all the children entered school in the Fall of 1964, the following results were observed:

1. The 20 children in the first group (who had been helped for three summers) increased their IQs from 86 to 95.
2. The 20 children in the second group (who had been helped for two summers) increased their IQs from 91 to 96.
3. The children in the two control groups (who had not received any pre-school help) had *a decrease* in IQs from four to six points lower than when they were tested at 3½ years of age.

These tests confirm studies published by Professor Thomas

Russell Garth in 1931, which showed that Negro children, tested in Northern cities where they were being educated under better conditions than in the South, achieved results averaging about one-third higher than Negro children in the South and in some cases they were slightly above the white children with whom they were compared.

In his syndicated column (*Los Angeles Times*, May 18, 1967), Joseph Alsop tells of the "more effective schools" program introduced in 21 of New York City's schools, to help overcome the handicaps of children from the Negro ghetto. These handicaps, Alsop says, are the result "of broken homes, of homes without books and of homes, too, where the common English of the outer world is sometimes hardly spoken." The more effective schools at present cover the period of pre-kindergarten through grade six. As a result of this special attention to their needs by providing excellent schools, excellent facilities, and excellent teachers, these children from the Negro ghetto "are now scoring on a level with the children in middle-class schools." This gives added confirmation to the findings of Dr. Susan W. Gray.

Dr. Leonard R. Bullas, an internationally known Australian scientist, who is professor of microbiology and pathology at Loma Linda University, told the Rotary Club in Sun City, California, on September 20, 1966:

There is no true genetic reason for people of one race to be more intelligent than those of another race. Environment and development through the years are the keys to intelligence.

In a speech delivered on March 31, 1967, at the Commonwealth Club of San Francisco, California, Dr. Sherwood L. Washburn, professor of anthropology at the University of California, told his audience:

Discrimination, by denying equal social opportunity to the Negro, made his progress lag approximately 20 years behind that of the White.

A very persuasive argument used by racists is that the White race is superior, because it has developed a higher civilization. This argument overlooks the fact that not all sections of the White race have developed a higher civilization. Consequently, race does not explain social evolution, but rather a combination of complex historical factors. Civilizations develop with great intensity in some areas and decline in others. No race and no nation has a monopoly on achievement. Every race and every nation has made some important contributions to the advancement of the human species.

In surveying human achievement, it is well to consider how much we owe to the invention of a rudimentary form of *the wheel* during the Bronze Age, some 4000 years ago. It took some 300 years more before the spoked wheel was developed, and it staggers the imagination to think how much of what we call civilization would disappear if suddenly we were forbidden the use of all applications of the wheel.

From ancient Chinese civilization we acquired the use of movable type and the art of printing. Likewise, the use of gunpowder was first developed by the Chinese. It may surprise Americans, who are proud of our huge production of automobiles, that the principles of the internal combustion engine were evolved from experiences of the Chinese with firecrackers. Our use of paper also must be credited to the Chinese. Sugar was first made in India.

A visit to the museum in the Mesa Verde National Park, in southeastern Colorado, is usually a sobering and humbling experience. For there one learns that the original 100% Americans, whom we call Indians, had domesticated corn, potatoes, beans and tobacco. Little do most people in the rest of the world realize that they owe the use of these four commodities to the American Indians. In the same museum one learns that the Navajo tribe of Indians had developed the use of analgesic drugs, a rudimentary form of skull surgery, a highly developed art of basket weaving, fascinating forms of dancing, and distinctive styles of music. In addition, the Navajos were skilled sheep raisers and makers of woolen garments and blankets.

Steel was invented in India or Turkestan. Much of our mathematics depends upon two Asian inventions, the Arabic numeral system and algebra. When an Englishman, James Watt, patented the steam engine in 1769, he worked from principles first applied by Heron of Alexandria almost 2000 years earlier.

Although it is not generally known to most Americans, the continent of Africa has made substantial contributions to the main stream of human culture. The Negroes of East Africa had a working economic system, a well-developed governmental structure, a system of justice courts, and a system of roads long before they were brought over here in chains. After all the atrocities committed by the White race against the Negroes of Africa, it ill behooves the White man to condemn them for not making more progress. Had they been left alone, most assuredly they would have made more progress. Given the opportunity, the Negro can rise to greater heights of achievement. Even under conditions of oppression, they have made singular contributions to American society. It is well to recall that a Negro, Crispus Attucks, was the first to give his life in the American Revolution. It was a Negro, George Washington Carver, who was one of the world's greatest agricultural chemists of all time. He discovered many uses for peanuts, soybeans, and sweet potatoes. He developed techniques of soil improvement, crop diversity, and utilization of cotton wastes. Who has not been thrilled by listening to the singing of Marian Anderson, Leontyne Price, and Paul Robeson? Who has not enjoyed the superb performances of Dick Gregory, Sidney Poitier, and Harry Belafonte? Negro performance in the field of sports can hardly be squared with the concept of Negro inferiority. The world's heavyweight championship has been held by such Negroes as the late Jack Johnson, by Joe Louis, and now by Cassius Clay. It is more than amusing to see the racists shout themselves hoarse with applause at international sports events, where American Negro participants win trophies time and time again, often becoming the major factor in the winning of high scores for the American teams. The racists have never explained why they never complained about the dark skin when they enjoyed Jackie Robinson's performance on the baseball fields or Duke Ellington's musical performance. Negroes have acquitted themselves very well as lawyers and as judges. One of the most distinguished of the Federal judges is a Negro, Justice William Henry Hastie of the Third Circuit Court of Appeals. A Negro, Edward W. Brooke, after serving successfully as Attorney-General of the State of Massachusetts, sits today in the U.S. Senate. In many state legislatures, in many city councils, and in every field of endeavor Negroes have proven their capacity to achieve. Such outstanding personalities as the late Dr. W. E. B. Dubois, Dr. Ralph Bunche at the United Nations,

Thurgood Marshall as Solicitor-General of the United States,[9] Robert C. Weaver as Secretary of Housing and Urban Development, and the Nobel Laureate, Dr. Martin Luther King, Jr.,[10] are the harbingers of the rich contributions that Negroes can and will make to American civilization, if the barriers of prejudice, hate, poverty, unemployment, and segregation are removed. It is of utmost importance that we should neither forget nor underestimate the contributions of the unsung heroes and heroines, black and white, who do the useful work of the world and keep our interdependent society functioning.

Science does not recognize the concept of race superiority. There is no such thing as a racially pure nation. In fact, it can be demonstrated that every civilized nation has made advances precisely because of racial mixing. What else is meant by the much-vaunted "melting pot" of the United States of America? The phenomenal achievements of the U.S.A. can be attributed to a continent blessed with an abundance of natural resources, a variety of climatic conditions, and the settling here of wave after wave of "foreigners" of all races, all religions, all nationalities. Nor should one overlook the very important heritage of American Indian achievements, from which the White settlers benefited immensely. These are the factors that account for America's greatness. In just one achievement alone—the development of atomic energy—one can easily see that this country profited immensely from the contributions of scientists from Germany, Sweden, Italy, and England.

The Nordics of Europe, about whom Nazi propagandists wrote so many panegyrics, actually were a backward and barbaric group for thousands of years, until they came in contact with the culture of the peoples inhabiting the Mediterranean area. It was this stimulus that started them on the road to building a higher civilization.

For many centuries Japan was one of the most stable countries from a racial standpoint. With the opening of Japan to Western influences following the visit of Commodore Perry in 1854, the Japanese rapidly adopted Occidental methods and became a modern, highly industrialized power. Japanese technological achievements are quite formidable and are the envy of many

---

9 Since above was written, he has been appointed Justice of the U.S. Supreme Court.

10 Dr. King was assassinated in Memphis, Tennessee, on April 4, 1968.

nations. In 1946, the new constitution that was adopted, after Japan's defeat in World War II, gave the vote to women. Thus, in this and many other respects, the Japanese (Mongoloids) have surpassed the Swiss (Caucasoids). These developments cannot be explained by theories of race. Our explanation has to come from a study of historical development. Race theorists will be hard put in explaining why the high fertility rate of Japanese drops considerably when they move to another country, even though they do not intermarry.

It is perfectly clear that concepts of inferior and superior races are purely value judgments, with no basis in objective scientific criteria. From one standpoint, it may be argued with considerable cogency that White civilization is inferior. The perennial slaughter and maiming of people on our highways, the pollution of the air we breathe, the contamination of the water we drink, the ugly poverty in the midst of affluence, the rapid increase in deaths from cancer—these and other problems, which our White civilization has been unable to conquer, raise the question of whether we have the intelligence to use rationally our technological innovations. And if the White race should blunder into a nuclear war, the mutual destruction may well prove the inferiority of the White race, and quite conceivably the future of civilization may rest in the lap of the Negroid and Mongoloid races.

The final stumbling block, in the minds of the racists and those who are influenced by them, is the question of miscegenation, the interbreeding of races. Many of the racists imagine that all Negroes are extremely anxious to marry Whites. The truth is that most Negroes do *not* wish to marry Whites. Furthermore, the argument comes pretty late in history, considering the number of mulattoes fathered by White men, forcibly in a large percentage of cases. In any case, it cannot and should not be used as an excuse for the prolongation of the oppression of the Negroes in America. As of April 1967 there were 40,000 American Negroes fighting America's dirty war in Vietnam, and in 1966 some 750 American Negroes died in Vietnam. Nowhere, in all the racist literature, have we been able to find any arguments and propaganda against sending Negroes to fight and die in Vietnam.

In a beautifully written book, "For Human Beings Only," Sarah Patton Boyle, a White scholar, points out that most experts believe that integration will not speed amalgamation much or soon. Mrs. Boyle states the case in a manner that may startle some people:

Indeed, some experts think that segregation more than integration leads to intermarriage. Anthropologists have estimated that about 20 thousand Negroes who are light enough to pass for white "cross over" every year to escape the handicaps of segregation. They marry unsuspecting whites.

"The irony of it," a social psychologist commented, "is that Negroes who cross over often pretend to be rabid segregationists as a safeguard against detection. The result is that they attract genuine rabid segregationists as mates—people who would be utterly horrified if they knew."

One of the logical replies to the question "Do you want your daughter to marry a Negro?" might well be "Do you want your daughter to know a Negro suitor when she sees one?"

The findings of biology, anthropology, sociology, psychology, and history support the concept of universal kinship. The dream of the brotherhood of man, rather than doctrines of hate, finds support in scientific research. Dr. Bayard Brattstrom, Chairman of the Biology Department at California State College at Fullerton points out that "no peoples on the earth are much more distantly related than 71st cousins!" The racists should start weeping now, because they are really distant cousins of the people against whom they hurl their invectives.[11]

It would be interesting to conduct the following experiment. Line up thirty people on a raised platform in front of an audience of racists. At one end of the line, place the darkest-skinned Negro available, and then have fourteen more Negroes lined up from that end of the line to the center of the stage, each one being progressively lighter. At the other end of the stage, place the lightest-complected White person available, and then have fourteen more White people lined up from that end to the center of the stage, each one being progressively darker in complexion. By this method, the lightest-skin Negro at the center of the stage would be almost identical in complexion with the darkest-skin White man at the center of the stage and

11 A wag has asked what some of the fundamentalist racists would do, upon arriving in heaven, if they found that God is a Negro. The Rev. Malcolm Boyd has pointed out that Jesus undoubtedly had a dark skin, despite the usual portrayal of him with a very light complexion.

from one end of the lineup to the other there would be a progression of difference in pigmentation. A challenge should then be issued to the racists to point out at which particular shade of pigmentation they develop hostility. This experiment should prove conclusively that a difference in skin shading is an irrational basis for disliking anyone.

A more satisfying and elevating philosophy of life than that of the racist ideologues was expressed by the great scientist and humanitarian, the late Dr. Albert Einstein:

Man is here for the sake of other men . . . above all, for those upon whose smile and well-being our own happiness depends, and also for the countless unknown souls with whose fate we are connected by a bond of sympathy. Many times a day I realize how much my outer and inner life is built upon the labors of my fellow-men, both living and dead, and how earnestly I must exert myself in order to give in return as much as I have received.

# CHAPTER IV

## The Anti-Soviet Liars

### A Prologue to Mendacity

In March of 1917, the imperial regime of Czar Nicholas II of Russia was overthrown, and in July of the same year, a young moderate Socialist, Alexander Kerensky, became the provisional premier. Due to widespread shortages of food, weariness of the people with the war, and the vacillations of Kerensky, his government was overthrown in November by a coup d'état, which brought into power the Communists (Bolsheviks). Among the prominent leaders of the newly established Soviet government, which several years later assumed the name of Union of Soviet Socialist Republics, were V. I. Lenin and Leon Trotzky.

When the Bolsheviks announced to the whole world that they were taking Russia out of World War I and that they were confiscating the wealth of the capitalists and of the owners of huge tracts of land, it became the signal for what was probably the most venomous campaign of lies and villifications in all history. Not only did some nineteen Capitalist nations, including the U.S.A., send troops illegally into Russia to support counter-revolutionary groups, but an entire new industry came into being, the lucrative business of concocting and spreading anti-Soviet lies. The business still thrives, even as this book is being written fifty years later. There were established veritable lie-factories in the principal cities of Europe, as well as in New York, Chicago, Mexico City, and Buenos Aires. Staffed largely by former counts, dukes, kings, princes, and their female counterparts, they found a ready market for their atrocity tales and slanders in a frightened Capitalist class and its controlled media of communications. The extent of the fear that gripped the newspaper Capitalists at the time, may be gauged from a fact reported in Upton Sinclair's *The Brass Check*: ". . . one great newspaper in Chicago has already purchased half a dozen machine guns and stored them away in its cellar!" (This was in 1919.)

Upton Sinclair summed it up very well, when he pointed out: "They published so many inventions that they couldn't keep track of them. Here are two paragraphs from a single issue of one newspaper:"

Nicolai Lenin, the Bolshevist Premier, is the only prominent Bolshevist left who appears to lead an austere life. . . *New York Times,* February 26, 1919.

Premier Lenin, refugees say, is not affected by the food problem. His bill for fruit and vegetables in a recent month amounted to sixty thousand rubles. . . *New York Times,* February 26, 1919.

Dr. Evans Clark, an instructor at Columbia University, prepared a monograph in 1920, entitled *Facts and Fabrications about Soviet Russia.* From the headlines in the *New York Times,* Dr. Clark prepared the following "Times Biography of Lenin and Trotzky":

*1917*

| | |
|---|---|
| May 10. | Lenin Reported Missing in Petrograd. |
| May 22. | Lenin Still Alive. |
| June 25. | Lenin's Real Name Said to Be Zederbluhm. |
| July 31. | Lenin Still Missing. |
| August 13. | Lenin Reported in Capital. |
| September 1. | Lenin in Switzerland. |
| September 28. | Lenin Reported in Petrograd. |
| November 11. | Lenin Heads New Russian Cabinet—Trotzky in the Foreign Office. |
| November 16. | Lenin's Power Waning. |
| November 19. | Lenin Government Split. |
| November 30. | Coalition Cabinet Forced on Bolsheviki. |

*1918*

| | |
|---|---|
| January 16. | Lenin in Sanitarium. |
| January 17. | Four Shots Miss Lenin. |
| February 18. | Attempt to Kidnap Lenin Foiled. Bolshevist Power Wanes and Anti-Semitism Is Growing. |
| February 20. | Heard Lenin Had Fled. Rumour in Finland Bolsheviki Had Been Overthrown. |
| February 22. | Party Turns on Trotzky and He May Resign. |
| March 10. | Trotzky Resigns Office. |
| March 12. | Lenin Dismissed Trotzky. |
| March 31. | Lenin Has Pneumonia. |

| | |
|---|---|
| April 28. | Revolt in Russia. Grand Duke Michael Emperor. |
| April 29. | Repeat Reports of Russian Revolt. Stockholm Now Hears Alexis is Chosen Ruler. |
| June 23. | Lenin Ready to Resign. Czecho-Slovak Success in Russia Upsetting His Regime. |
| June 23. | Moscow Reported Taken. New Czar Named. Red Leaders in Flight. |
| August 12. | Lenin May Seek Refuge in Berlin. Prepares for Flight with Trotzky as Red Regime Totters. |
| August 13. | Red Leaders Reach Kronstadt. Entire Bolshevist Government Escaping from Moscow, German Papers Announce. |
| August 16. | Bolsheviki Flee Moscow. |
| August 16. | Allies' Movements Hearten Russians. Washington Sees in Increasing Activity a Speedy Rout of Bolsheviki. |
| August 18. | Report Kronstadt Seized by Germans. French Hear Lenin's Refuge Is in Foe's Possession. |
| August 20. | Red Power Wanes as Allied Troops Push into Russia. |
| August 20. | Bolshevist Chiefs Reported on Warship at Kronstadt Ready to Flee. |
| August 27. | Recent Reports That Both Moscow and Petrograd Had Been Virtually Abandoned by the Principal Bolshevist Leaders Appeared to Be Confirmed by Information Reaching the State Department Today from Sweden. |
| September 1. | Lenin Twice Wounded by an Assassin. |
| September 2. | Lenin Reported Dead. Was Shot by a Girl. |
| September 3. | Lenin Not Dead. |
| September 5. | Lenin Has a Relapse. |
| September 7. | Lenin Reported Weaker. |
| October 17. | Reports New Attack on Premier Lenin. Amsterdam Hears Bolshevist Leader Was Shot by a Member of Soviet Bureau. |
| December 9. | Red Leaders Ready to Flee to Sweden. |
| December 16. | Lenin Reported Ready to Give Up. His Plan to Abandon the Red Regime Was Barely Defeated at Central Council Ballot. |

*1919*

| | |
|---|---|
| January 3. | His Train Captured, Lenin Escapes. |
| January 9. | Trotzky Dictator—Arrests Lenin—Ousts Bolshevist Premier and Now Rules Alone in Russia, Copenhagen Hears. |
| January 11. | Kremlin Is Lenin's Prison. Trotzky, Red Dictator, Holds Deposed Premier in Moscow. |

| | |
|---|---|
| January 11. | Lenin Abolishes Money. (On another page of same issue of the *Times*.) |
| January 18. | Lenin Is Reported to Have Arrived in Barcelona. |
| January 24. | Trotzky's Forces Quit Petrograd. Admit Cause is Beaten. "Nikolai Lenin, the Bolshevist Premier, and Trotzky, speaking recently before the Moscow Soviet, confessed that the Bolshevist regime was bankrupt." |
| January 25. | Assert Trotzky Was Taken. Libau Advices to Switzerland Say He Did Not Escape from Narva. |
| January 27. | Trotzky Not Captured. |
| February 19. | Red Leaders Are at Odds. |
| March 15. | Bullet Hits Trotzky's Hat. |
| April 3. | Trotzky Opposes Lenin. Break Between the Bolshevik Leaders Said to Be Definite Over Policy Against Allies. |
| April 22. | Red Rule Totters as Kolchak Wins. Troops and People in Revolt. |
| April 22. | Proletariat Plots Against Lenin. Premier Blames Trotzky. |
| June 7. | Lenin Tired of Struggle. |
| July 3. | Trotzky Nearly Captured. |
| August 2. | Talk That Lenin Intends to Retire. |
| September 26. | Says Lenin Is Captive in Kremlin at Moscow. (Copenhagen dispatch.) |
| September 26. | Rumor That Lenin is Slain. (Paris, A.P.) |
| October 9. | Thirteen Red Leaders Killed by Bomb. Moscow in Revolt. |
| October 31. | Lenin Plans to Lie Low. Says Reds Must Await Another Chance When Soviet Regime Falls. |
| November 23. | State Department Gets News of Revolts All Over Red Russia. Rumor Soviet Has Given Up. Copenhagen Hears Lenin Has Agreed to Turn Power Over to United Socialist Parties. |

*1920*

| | |
|---|---|
| January 26. | Rumor of Moscow Revolt. Soviet Also Reported to Have Moved to Tver Because of Plague. |

Dr. Clark's monograph contains a similar chronological listing of *New York Times* headlines about Petrograd, but we can best summarize their content by quoting the concluding paragraph of that portion of his study:

A writer in a recent issue of the *Nation* has summed up the

Petrograd fabrications in a sentence: Petrograd has "thus far fallen six times, been burned to the ground twice, been in absolute panic twice, has starved to death constantly, and has revolted against the Bolsheviks on no less than six different occasions—all in the columns of the *Times*."

Walter Lippmann and Charles Merz pointed out in an article published in the *New Republic*, August 11, 1920 that "one of the major themes in the news from Russia was prophecy that the Soviets were tottering. Not once or twice—but ninety-one times—in the two years from November, 1917 to November, 1919, it was reported in the *Times* that the Soviets were nearing their rope's end, or actually had reached it. Naturally this steady repetition left its effect upon the reader."[1]

We would not want to leave the impression that the *Times* was the sole offender. The performance of the *Times* was typical of the entire Capitalist press, radio, theater, pulpit, and school system. Nothing was too vile or too fantastic to be charged against the Bolsheviks and the new society they had set out to build. Feeding the lies and distortions to the various media of communications were the "Lusk Committee" of the New York State Legislature and the "Overman Committee" of the United States Senate. Of recent years, the reports of these Committees have been reprinted and are being sold by Ultra-Rightist groups.

The "Lusk Committee" was appointed in March, 1919, as a result of pressure by the Union League Club of New York, a group of rich, socially prominent, and politically powerful Republicans, many of them with national ties. The guiding light of the "Lusk Committee" was a member of the Union League Club, Archibald E. Stevenson. Reading the reports of the hearings conducted by Lusk and Stevenson is about as enlightening as the *Times'* headlines we have quoted. The Committee managed to capture the headlines by its "sensational" disclosures and by the kind of smear tactics later made famous by

[1] In a special supplement to the *New Republic*, Aug. 4, 1920, Walter Lippmann and Charles Merz reported results of a careful scrutiny of the *New York Times* from March 1917 to March 1920: some one thousand issues. Among their conclusions were the following: "In the large, the news about Russia is a case of seeing not what was, but what men wished to see." And further: "From the point of view of professional journalism the reporting of the Russian Revolution is nothing short of a disaster. On the essential questions the net effect was almost always misleading, and misleading news is worse than none at all."

Senator Joseph McCarthy. It did succeed in keeping millions of people from finding out the truth about what was happening in Russia.

## An Exercise in Wholesale Obscenity

Senator Overman's Committee ran extensive hearings in Washington, D.C., giving a libel-free forum for any former Czarist supporter that could tell an atrocity story. Many of the newspapers, including the *New York Times*, published almost verbatim accounts of the hearings, usually with sensational and blaring headlines. Among the scare-crow stories spread by the Overman hearings was the obscene story about the alleged nationalization of women in Russia. In the *New York Times* of February 12, 1919 there appeared these headlines over two different stories:

BOLSHEVISM BARED BY R. E. SIMONS
WOMEN ARE NATIONALIZED
OFFICIAL DECREES REVEAL DEPTH TO WHICH
THEY ARE SUBJECTED BY REDS

DESCRIBE HORRORS UNDER RED RULE
R E. SIMONS AND W. W. WELSH TELL
SENATORS OF BRUTALITIES OF
BOLSHEVIKI—STRIP WOMEN IN
STREETS—PEOPLE OF EVERY CLASS
EXCEPT THE SCUM SUBJECTED
TO VIOLENCE BY MOBS

The yarn about the nationalization of women became the subject of thousands of editorials, thousands of "patriotic" speeches, and thousands of thunderous denunciations of the "godless Bolsheviki" from thousands of pulpits. There was only one thing wrong with this holy crusade: it was based upon a damned lie!

The story of the origin of this canard is well told in Upton Sinclair's *The Brass Check*. A comic paper in Moscow published a "skit" on Bolshevism, and the result is shown in a story which appeared in the official government newspaper, *Isvestija* of May 18, 1918:

Moscow Soviet Decision.—The Moscow newspaper, "The Evening Life" for printing an invented decree regarding the socialization of women, in the issue of the 3rd of May, No. 36, shall be closed forever and fined 25,000 rubles.

An additional source of this hoax was the work of a prankster in the city of Saratov, in central Russia. As a means of discrediting some Anarchists who had become troublesome, the prankster invented an elaborate decree establishing that women were henceforth public property. The phoney decree was signed "The Free Association of Anarchists of Saratov," and was posted in several places around the city. The decree, of course, was meaningless, as any knowledgeable reporter could tell, because the Anarchists were not in power and could not enforce any decree, phoney or otherwise.

Upton Sinclair told the story of the ensuing events, pointing out that from one end of this country to the other the alleged decree took the front pages, and:

> The "Los Angeles Times" published it with a solemn assurance to its readers that the authenticity of the decree might be accepted without question. And forthwith all our capitalist clergymen rose up in their pulpits to denounce the Bolsheviki as monsters and moral perverts, and a good part of the moving picture machinery of Southern California has been set to work constructing romances around this obscene theme.
>
> The *New Europe,* which had first published the story, made a full retraction and apology. Harold Williams, who had sent the story to England, also apologized. The American State Department denied the story officially, February 28, 1919. Jerome Davis, of the American Red Cross, denied it from first-hand knowledge in the *Independent,* March 15, 1919. But did you read these apologies and denials in American capitalist newspapers? You did not! It would not be too much to say that nine people out of ten in America today[2] firmly believe that women have been "nationalized" in Russia, or at any rate that the Bolsheviki attempted it.

Upton Sinclair pointed out further that *McClure's Magazine* hired a preacher, Rev. Newell Dwight Hillis, to villify the Russian Soviets. In an article which he contributed to its June 1919 issue, this man of the cloth wrote: "It is now conceded that the interior towns and cities of Russia have gone over to this nationalization of Russia." Considering that this was written several months after reputable sources had both retracted and denied the yarn, the reader can appreciate the editorial state-

2 Upton Sinclair is writing this in 1920, in *The Brass Check.*

ment which accompanied the Rev. Hillis' article: "He writes as he preaches, fearlessly, truthfully." And what shall we say about Senator Overman holding official hearings, with false witnesses, to "prove" something which had been officially denied by the Department of State of his own government? The Report of the Overman Committee has been reprinted and *is being sold currently* by a Clerical Fascist group, Soldiers of the Cross, which is operated by a renegade Communist, Rev. Kenneth Goff.

The lies, that were told about the Soviet regime during the first few years, included so many false atrocity stories that it became next to impossible for most Americans to understand what was going on. In various forms, this has continued up to the very present. When the truth was presented, the class solidarity of the capitalist owners of the media of communication prevented its being made available to the American people. A story from the official records of the U.S. Government will illuminate this point.

## Blockading the Truth

On September 12, 1919 the Senate Foreign Relations Committee convened, under the chairmanship of Henry Cabot Lodge, Senior.[3] Testifying was Mr. William C. Bullitt, a former Philadelphia journalist, who had become a State Department attaché. He was a member of the American Commission that accompanied President Woodrow Wilson to the Paris Peace Conference on December 4, 1918. On February 22, 1919, he was sent on a confidential mission to Russia by Secretary of State Robert Lansing. Accompanying him in an unofficial capacity were Captain W. W. Pettit of the U.S. Army and the renowned author and journalist, Lincoln Steffens.

On or about April 1, 1919, Bullitt gave copies of his Report to Secretary of State Robert Lansing, President Woodrow Wilson, Colonel E. M. House, General Bliss, and Henry White; the latter three, in addition to Lansing, being members of Wilson's confidential staff of advisers. The following are excerpts from the Report:

The destructive phase of the revolution is over and all the energy of the Government is turned to constructive work. The terror has

[3] Grandfather of the present Ambassador Henry Cabot Lodge.

ceased. All power of judgment has been taken away from the extraordinary commission for suppression of the counter-revolution, which now merely accuses suspected counter-revolutionaries, who are tried by the regular, established, legal tribunals. Executions are extremely rare. Good order has been established. The streets are safe. Shooting has ceased. There are few robberies. Prostitution has disappeared from sight. Family life has been unchanged by the revolution, the canard in regard to "nationalization of women" notwithstanding.

The theaters, opera, and ballet are performing as in peace. Thousands of new schools have been opened in all parts of Russia and the Soviet Government seems to have done more for the education of the Russian people in a year and a half than Czardom did in 50 years.

Bullitt began his report by pointing out that economic conditions were extremely bad in all of Russia, and he blamed it onto the capitalist countries. His exact opening remarks were:

Russia today is in a condition of acute economic distress. The blockade by land and sea is the cause of this distress and the lack of essentials of transportation is its gravest symptom.

He went on to point out that starvation and disease were rampant throughout the country. It is important to note this as one of the great crimes against humanity perpetrated with due deliberation by Capitalist governments, in order to crush a new type of society, a new idea in social and economic relationships.

In an appendix to his Report Mr. Bullitt stated:

*Terror.*—The red terror is over. During the period of its power the extraordinary commission for the suppression of the counter-revolution, which was the instrument of the terror, executed about 1,500 persons in Petrograd, 500 in Moscow, and 3,000 in the remainder of the country—5,000 in all Russia. These figures agree with those which were brought back from Russia by Maj. Wardwell, and inasmuch as I have checked them from Soviet, anti-Soviet, and neutral sources I believe them to be approximately correct. It is worthy of note in this connection that in the white terror in southern Finland alone, according to official figures, Gen. Mannerheim executed without trial 12,000 working men and women.

*Order.*—One feels as safe in the streets of Petrograd and Moscow as in the streets of Paris or New York. On the other hand, the streets of these cities are dismal, because of the closing of retail shops whose functions are now concentrated in a few large nationalized

256

"department stores." Petrograd, furthermore, has been deserted by half its population; but Moscow teems with twice the number of inhabitants it contained before the war. The only noticeable difference in the theaters, opera, and ballet is that they are now run under the direction of the department of education, which prefers classics and sees to it that working men and women and children are given an opportunity to attend the performances and that they are instructed beforehand in the significance and beauties of the productions.

*Morals.*—Prostitutes have disappeared from sight, the economic reasons for their career having ceased to exist. Family life has been absolutely unchanged by the revolution. I have never heard more genuinely mirthful laughter than when I told Lenin, Tchitcherin, and Litvinov that much of the world believed that women had been "nationalized." This lie is so wildly fantastic that they will not even take the trouble to deny it. Respect for womanhood was never greater than in Russia today. Indeed, the day I reached Petrograd was a holiday in honor of wives and mothers.

*Education.*—The achievements of the department of education under Lunacharsky have been very great. Not only have all the Russian classics been reprinted in editions of three and five million copies and sold at a low price to the people, but thousands of new schools for men, women, and children have been opened in all parts of Russia. Furthermore, workingmen's and soldiers' clubs have been organized in many of the palaces of yesteryear, where the people are instructed by means of moving pictures and lectures. In the art galleries one meets classes of working men and women being instructed in the beauties of the pictures. The children's schools have been entirely reorganized, and an attempt is being made to give every child a good dinner at school every day. Furthermore, very remarkable schools have been opened for defective and over-nervous children. On the theory that genius and insanity are closely allied, these children are taught from the first to compose music, paint pictures, sculpt and write poetry, and it is asserted that some valuable results have been achieved, not only in the way of productions but also in the way of restoring the nervous systems of the children.

*Morale.*—The belief of the convinced communists in their cause is almost religious. Never in any religious service have I seen higher emotional unity than prevailed at the meeting of the Petrograd Soviet in celebration of the foundation of the Third Socialist Internationale. The remark of one young man to me when I questioned him in regard to his starved appearance is characteristic. He replied very simply: "I am ready to give another year of starvation to our revolution."

Face to face Lenin is a very striking man—straightforward and direct, but also genial and with a large humor and serenity.

The Report of Lincoln Steffens corroborated the findings of

Bullitt in every respect, and the same is true of the Report of Captain Pettit. The following are excerpts from Captain Pettit's Report:

It is needless for me to tell you that most of the stories that have come from Russia regarding atrocities, horrors, immorality, are manufactured in Viborg, Helsingfors, or Stockholm. The horrible massacres planned for last November were first learned of in Petrograd from the Helsingfors papers. That anybody could even for a moment believe in the nationalization of women seems impossible to anyone in Petrograd. Today Petrograd is an orderly city—probably the only city of the world its size without police. Bill Shatov, chief of police, and I were at the opera the other night to hear Chaliapin sing in Boris Gudonov. He excused himself early because he said there had been a robbery the previous night, in which a man had lost 5,000 rubles, that this was the first robbery in several weeks, and that he had an idea who had done it, and was going to get the men that night. I feel personally that Petrograd is safer than Paris. At night there are automobiles, sleighs, and people on the streets at 12 o'clock to a much greater extent than was true in Paris when I left five weeks ago.

Most wonderful of all, the great crowd of prostitutes has disappeared. I have seen not a disreputable woman since I went to Petrograd, and foreigners who have been there for the last three months report the same. The policy of the present government has resulted in eliminating throughout Russia, I am told, this horrible outgrowth of modern civilization.

Begging has decreased. I have asked to be taken to the poorest parts of the city to see how the people in the slums live, and both the communists and the bourgeoisie have held up their hands and said, "But you fail to understand there are no such places." There is poverty, but it is scattered and exists among those of the former poor or of the former rich who have been unable to adapt themselves to the conditions which require everyone to do something.

Terrorism has ended. For months there have been no executions, I am told, and certainly people go to the theater and church and out on the streets as much as they would in any city of the world.

During the hearing, Mr. Bullitt was asked by Senator Knox if he had made his Report public. This was Bullitt's reply:

I attempted to. I prepared a statement for the press based on my report, giving the facts, which I submitted to the commission to be given out. No member of the commission was ready to take the responsibility for publicity in the matter and it was referred to the President. The President received it and decided that he did not want it given out. He thought he would rather keep it secret, and in spite of the urgings of the other commissioners he continued to adhere to that point of view, and my report has never been made public until this moment.

Not only did President Woodrow Wilson keep the Bullitt Report on Russia from the American people, but an attempt was made to suppress the *Report of the Hearing before the Senate Committee on Foreign Relations*. This document contained the Bullitt testimony at the hearing, the suppressed Bullitt Report on Russia, the Report on Russia by Lincoln Steffens, the Report on Russia by Captain W. W. Pettit, the peace proposals of Lenin, and other documents. It was rumored, at the time, that when approximately 1,000 copies of the Report of the Hearing had been printed, a mysterious order to the Government Printing Office stopped the presses. This charge seems to be borne out by the fact that a courageous publisher, B. W. Huebsch, obtained a copy and reprinted it privately. But very few of the American people learned of the truth in this document, because the capitalist media of communication showed their class solidarity and almost completely ignored it. There were, of course, a few honorable exceptions.[4, 5]

## Documenting a Lie!

Quite apart from the class hatred directed against the Soviet Government, there was the need to cover up a previous fabrication perpetrated by the United States Government against the fledgling government of Russia. We were at war with Imperial Germany and Austria-Hungary. Imperial Russia had been one of our allies, and now Soviet Russia was denouncing the war and withdrawing from it. In our country, the war hysteria was so great that it was just as devastating to call one pro-German as to call one a witch during the Salem witchcraft days. Our Government, with the help of the media of communication, set out to prove that the Communist regime was pro-German. That was supposed to be the solar plexus blow. Accordingly, in October of 1918, the wartime propaganda agency, the Committee on Public Information, distributed in

---

[4] The Bullitt-Steffens-Pettit Reports were published in the International Relations Section of the *Nation* magazine, October 4, 1919.

[5] Honorable mention must be made of a series of articles by William Hard in *New Republic*, July 2 through August 13, 1919.

pamphlet form the "Sisson Documents." In its introduction, it stated:

> The documents show that the heads of the Bolshevik Government —Lenin and Trotzky and their associates—are German agents. They show that the Bolshevik revolution was arranged for by the German Great General Staff and financed by the German Imperial Bank. They show that the treaty of Brest-Litovsk was a betrayal of the Russian people by the German agents, Lenin and Trotzky. . . . They show, in short, that the present Bolsheviki Government is not a Russian government at all, but a German government acting solely in the interests of Germany, and betraying the Russian people . . . for the benefit of the Imperial German Government alone.

The editors of the capitalist newspapers had a Roman holiday, regaling their readers with sensational stories based on the "Sisson Documents." It was not unusual for these stories to be accompanied by cartoons showing the Communists (Bolsheviks) as wild-eyed characters with shaggy hair and black beards, a dagger between the teeth, and a bomb poised for immediate hurling. It was considered the height of political sophistication to say directly or by innuendo that Bolsheviks never used soap! The reader can best judge the extent to which this avalanche of lying propaganda poisoned the thinking of the American people by the fact that a remnant of that campaign is still making the rounds: the lie that the Germans gave Lenin $10 million, which we discussed in Chapter I under the heading of Lenin Hoax No. 1.

Among the early exposures of the fraudulent nature of the "Sisson Documents" was a book published in 1919 by Charles Scribner's Sons, New York, entitled *Russia's Ruin*. The author, E. H. Wilcox, had been the Petrograd correspondent of the London *Daily Telegraph*, and was noted for his anti-Soviet views and sentiments. Referring to the U.S. Government pamphlet containing the "Sisson Documents," Mr. Wilcox says on page 248:

> The pamphlet includes some fifteen or sixteen facsimiles by way of corroboration. One of these facsimiles purports to be a circular sent out on November 28, 1914 by the "General Staff" of the German High Sea Fleet. Now, such a body as a "General Staff" does not exist in the German Navy. What corresponds in the Navy to the General Staff of the Army is the "Admiral Staff." The circular itself consists of eighteen lines. In these eighteen lines are two mistakes

in grammar, seven mistakes in spelling and seven mistakes in phrasing. An expert on the German language has given the following opinion: "This circular was most certainly not written by a German. It would appear to be a very poor attempt to copy German official language." That, it is true, is only one of the documents; but its inclusion in the pamphlet undoubtedly shows a failure so gross to apply the most rudimentary tests that in itself it throws grave doubts on the authenticity of the whole collection.

Upton Sinclair commented regarding the "Sisson Documents": "These documents had been examined and rejected as forgeries by Raymond Robins,[6] also by the British Embassy, none too favorably disposed to the Bolsheviks; but matters like that do not trouble Hearst editors, who have learned to think in headlines. The "Sisson Documents" were shipped to Washington, and issued under authority of the United States government, and published in every newspaper in America."[7]

Edgar Sisson was formerly an editor of William Randolph Hearst's *Cosmopolitan Magazine*, receiving a salary of $25,000 per year, which one may consider an enormously high salary for the period around 1917. Sisson was stationed in Petrograd during the winter of 1917-18 as a special representative of the official American propaganda apparatus, euphemistically called the Committee on Public Information.

The best analysis of the "Sisson Documents" was made by George F. Kennan, a lifelong career diplomat and a former U.S. Ambassador to Russia, in a lengthy article written for *The Journal of Modern History*, June, 1956. We summarize some of the salient features of his article:

1. Sisson purchased the documents for a sizable amount of cash from a Petrograd journalist, Eugene Semenov, on March 3, 1918.

2. Sisson arrived in Washington, D.C. with the documents, in May of 1918.

3. The Department of State showed very little enthusiasm for the documents, and refused to authorize publication under its aegis.

4. In September of 1918 the Committee on Public Information went directly to President Woodrow Wilson and obtained

6 Colonel Raymond Robins, who was the head of the American Red Cross mission in Russia.—M. K.

7 *The Brass Check* by Upton Sinclair.

his permission to publish the documents, in spite of the protests from the State Department.

Kennan adduces incontrovertible evidence to prove the fraudulent nature of the documents. He is little short of devastating in his attack, leaving no doubt whatsoever of the correctness of his position. We quote three statements from different portions of his essay:

> The state of affairs suggested in the main body of the documents is of such extreme historical implausibility that the question might well be asked whether the documents could not be declared generally fraudulent on this ground alone.

> Both individually and collectively, the documents abound in specific suggestions that are irreconcilable with historical fact.

> The Sisson documents were plainly drawn up by someone who had something more than a good Petrograd-newspaper-reader's knowledge of historical fact; and an impressive effort was made to weave this fact in with abundant fiction. The result remains nevertheless unconvincing. At every hand one finds serious discrepancies between circumstances suggested by the documents and known historical fact.

Kennan traces the origin of the documents, revealing that Semenov had confessed to Sir Basil Thomson, the head of Scotland Yard, that he had obtained the documents from another journalist, Anton M. Ossendowski. Kennan indicates that Ossendowski was a professional propagandist, whose elastic morals were on a par with those of some of our advertising specialists, who sing the praises of various brands of cigarettes, despite abundant evidence of the relationship of cigarette smoking to cancer, heart diseases, and other ailments.

## Keeping Up to Date—With Lies!

It is, of course, useful that Ambassador Kennan exposed the fraudulent "Sisson Documents" thirty-eight years after the damage was done, but the point is that there has been systematic, organized lying about the Soviet Union for the past fifty years. As soon as one lie is exposed, another one shows up on the political scene. Thus on February 28, 1921, the London *Daily Herald* revealed that Sir Basil Thomson, the Director of Scotland Yard, had been circulating *forged* copies of *Pravda*,

262

the official organ of the Communist Party of the Soviet Union. Just as his American counterpart, FBI Director John E. Hoover, was trying to block ratification of the Consular Treaty with the USSR in 1967, so the British Director of Intelligence was trying to sabotage the negotiations being conducted by the Foreign Office in 1921 for an Anglo-Soviet trade agreement.

In order to illustrate the point about the fifty years of consistent and persistent lying about the Soviet Union, let us temporarily skip some of the chronicle of events. Shortly after the death of Joseph Stalin, the now-defunct New York *World Telegram* ran two stories in its March 5, 1953 issue, with the following headlines:

|  |  |
|---|---|
| Heir to Stalin<br>May Need War<br>To Hold Power | Kremlin's New Rulers Need<br>Peace to Solve Problems |
| (Page 7) | (Page 8) |

As a sort of obituary, the now-defunct *Los Angeles Mirror* said on March 6, 1953:

Incidentally, it should be noted that some of the world's newspapers officially killed Stalin off five times since 1926.

First time was in 1926, when British newspapers had him assassinated. Four years later this was echoed by some papers in Latvia.

He also was disposed of assertedly in 1930, when some papers had him dying from a stroke suffered the year previous. In 1945, rumors of "sickness" had become so widespread that the Soviet Embassy in Paris had to issue an emphatic denial. Three years later, the London Embassy likewise retorted "nonsense" to similar reports in Swiss newspapers.

*In 1949, too, he was supposed to have died from a heart attack— and some fanciful editors had his place in the Kremlin filled by a "double."*

Stalin himself quipped once to newsmen that since he was supposed to have been dead, why didn't they let him rest—a Stanlinist interpretation to Mark Twain's celebrated retort.

The Ultra-Rightist group that calls itself Young Americans for Freedom apparently learned a lesson from Sir Basil Thomson's forgery of an issue of *Pravda* in 1921. In June of 1966, this group produced and circulated a *forged* edition of the New York Communist paper, *The Worker*. And it throws some light on the moral values in certain quarters that the Ultra-Rightist

*Human Events* carried an article in its issue of July 9, 1966, in which the circulation of this forgery is told with gusto and with kudos for the perpetrators. The writer is Phillip Abbott Luce, another convert to "freedom," who earns his living "exposing" anything and everything to the Left of Barry Goldwater.

On May 16, 1967, Congressman John M. Ashbrook of Ohio, one of the most active members of the House Committee on Un-American Activities, brought the fifty years of Anti-Soviet lies right up to date. He placed in the Congressional Record an article from *National Observer*, dealing with the use of terror in the Vietnam war. We are not concerned at this point with the merits or demerits of the article. However, we do find interest in Ashbrook's "celebration" of the 50th anniversary of the Bolshevik revolution. As a preface to the article, Ashbrook stated:

The use of terror in South Vietnam is, of course, but the latest in communism's long history of brutality. As far back as 1901 V. I. Lenin stated that—
We have never rejected terror on principle nor can we do so.

The essential dishonesty of quoting this sentence, torn out of context, can easily be seen by going back to *Lenin Fabrication, No. 7* in Chapter I, where we showed that Lenin openly and vehemently opposed the senseless and unnecessary use of terror, but pointed out that, in *military* campaigns, terror is a part of warfare. Of course, Congressman Ashbrook says nothing about the fact that the U.S.A. invaded Vietnam without a declaration of war; that we have intervened in a civil war, contrary to international law and the United Nations Chapter; that we have used such fiendish devices as the multiple anti-personnel bombs, which scatter thousands of steel pellets onto human bodies indiscriminately; that we have used gas against people on their own territory; that we have used chemical warfare to destroy crops and foliage; and that we have burned human beings alive by the use of jellied gasoline (Napalm).

Ashbrook continues:

Now, fifty years after the 1917 October revolution inaugurated the greatest bloodbath in history, the use of the official policy of terror is being employed every day in South Vietnam.

264

This falsification of history is, of course, disproven by the Reports of Bullitt, Steffens, Captain Pettit, Colonel Raymond Robins, and many other reliable observers. The atrocity tale is a typical Ultra-Rightist propaganda device. In its simplest terms, it consists of charging the Communists with atrocities of such astronomical proportions that the Nazi bestialities and mass extermination pale to insignificance. It is an oblique way of whitewashing Hitler and his associates.

## The American "Zinoviev Letter"

President Woodrow Wilson and his Secretary of State, Robert Lansing, started on a course of hostility toward the new Soviet republic, not only by blocking the publication of the truth contained in the Bullitt-Steffens-Pettit Reports, but also by sending troops into Russia to bolster the counter-revolutionary White Guard armies of Kolchak, Denikin, Wrangel, and Yudenitch. This attitude of hostility and a refusal of diplomatic recognition were carried on by his next Secretary of State, Bainbridge Colby. In 1923, sentiment began to mount among some business and industrial leaders, as well as among some members of Congress for diplomatic recognition and establishment of trade relations. Calvin Coolidge was President at the time, and his Secretary of State was Charles Evans Hughes, who had served in the same capacity under President Warren G. Harding. A way had to be found to scotch the pressure for diplomatic recognition of the Soviet government. Suddenly, on December 19, 1923, Secretary of State Hughes issued a press release, which appeared with screaming headlines in the morning papers of December 19, 1923. It began with the following statement:

The Department of State made public today the text of instructions given by Zinoviev, President of the Communist International and President of the Petrograd Soviet, to the Workers Party of America,[8] the Communist organization in the United States. The Department of Justice has assured the Department of State of the authenticity of these instructions.

The alleged instructions from Zinoviev to the American Communists included the following items:

8 The name was later changed to "Communist Party, U.S.A."

265

1. The Party's activity was to be concentrated among the workers in basic industries.

2. The Party was to be organized in units of ten.

3. The leader of each unit must "report everything direct to the central committee of the Party."

4. Not less than three members of each unit must be a fighting unit and be given instructions once a week in shooting and in trench and fortification techniques.

5. The hope was expressed that the Communists would "in the not distant future raise the red flag over the White House."

The internal evidence that this was a phoney document, forged by the Bureau of Investigation[9] of the Department of Justice, becomes clear from the following facts:

1. The Department of State admitted that the Justice Department had vouched for the authenticity of the "Zinoviev letter."

2. The Bureau of Investigation of the Department of Justice was in charge of undercover work in the ranks of Communists and other radicals.

3. The head of the Bureau of Investigation, a young lawyer by the name of John Edgar Hoover, had already achieved notoriety for his direction of the infamous "Palmer raids" of 1919.

4. Neither the State Department nor the Justice Department has ever produced, from that day on, *the original document* or a photocopy of the original document.

5. The Communist forces in the U.S.A. were so small at the time that their presidential ticket during the following year attracted only 36,000 votes nationally. It was therefore the height of absurdity to talk about their raising the red flag over the White House in the not distant future.

6. The Communists were just beginning to recover from the repressive measures of the previous few years and were fighting hard to achieve legality.

7. It has always been the contention of John E. Hoover and those who follow his school of thought that the Communist leaders are very shrewd, nay more, diabolically cunning. It is therefore unlikely that they would send such secret instruc-

---

[9] The name was later changed to "Federal Bureau of Investigation."

tions *in writing* and risk interception, when the same purpose could be achieved through a trusted courier who would deliver the message orally. In fact, such a trusted potential courier was available in the person of James Peter Cannon, who returned to the United States several weeks before the release of the alleged "Zinoviev letter," after he had spent six months in Moscow with the executive committee of the Communist International. If one is willing to believe that Zinoviev sent such instructions in writing instead of through James Peter Cannon, one has to adopt the thesis that Zinoviev et alia were both stupid and reckless.

8. A proposal for training small insurrectionary units in the absence of a revolutionary situation is either the product of an irrational mind or the work of agents-provocateurs. The reason we can make this categorical statement is that the Communists in the U.S.A. and in Russia must have been aware that John E. Hoover's agents had infiltrated the ranks of the Workers Party of America. Consequently, they would have to be incredibly stupid to start military drilling and risk easy detection and punishment.

The additional evidence that the "Zinoviev letter" was a forgery was the fact that no date for the issuance of the alleged letter was given. Neither was there any mention of any identifying data to prove its authenticity. Senators William E. Borah and George Norris challenged the State Department to present proof of authenticity. Finally, it should be mentioned that Russia's Foreign Minister, George Chicherin, denounced the "Zinoviev letter" as an obvious "clumsy forgery," and he openly challenged the United States Government to submit the question of authenticity to an "impartial authority" for evaluation. This challenge was never accepted.

## The British "Zinoviev Letter"

Not to be outdone by the intelligence agencies of the U.S.A., one year later British Intelligence produced a "Zinoviev letter" of its own. In fact, the letter was "discovered" on October 10, 1924, one day after it was announced that the British Parliament had been dissolved and that the government of Prime Minister Ramsay MacDonald would have to stand for a vote of the electorate on October 29, 1924.

267

The story is told on the front page of the *New York Times*, October 25, 1924. It relates that the government of Great Britain had addressed a note of protest to the government of the U.S.S.R., charging that the U.S.S.R. was sending propaganda into Great Britain, in violation of treaties. The *Times* explained further:

With the Foreign Office protest is published a letter from Zinoviev, head of the Red International, marked "very secret." This document, addressed to the British Communist Party, openly orders and incites violence, sedition, subversion of the army and navy, the formation of a nucleus of a Red army and general preparations looking to crippling the nation in war and thus giving the "proletariat the opportunity to turn an imperialist war into a class war."

According to the *Daily Mail* copies of the letter were delivered to the Foreign Secretary of Premier MacDonald immediately after it was received several weeks ago. It goes on to say: "On Wednesday afternoon copies were officially circulated by the executive authorities to high officers of the army and navy. A copy of the document came into the possession of the *Daily Mail* and we felt it our duty to make it public. We circulated printed copies to the other London morning newspapers yesterday afternoon. Later on the Foreign Office decided to issue it together with the protest dated yesterday."

Christian Rakovsky, the Russian Chargé d'Affaires here, suggested tonight that the Zinoviev letter "at first glance looks like a crude forgery."

Two days later, on October 27, 1924, the *Times* carried a front page wireless dispatch from Moscow, which quoted the Soviet Government as stating: "In view of the fact that this forgery has been made use of in an official document, the Soviet Government will insist upon an adequate apology by the British Government and the bringing to trial of both the official and the private persons involved in the forgery." The *Times* dispatch continues:

In order to avoid the serious consequences from this forgery which might result for both countries, the Soviet Government proposes to have recourse to an impartial arbitration court for establishing the fact that the alleged letter of the Communist International dated Sept. 15 is a forgery.

There were some strange circumstances surrounding the British "Zinoviev letter." The British Foreign Office acquired a copy dated September 15, 1924, signed "Zinoviev" and "Mc-

Manus." Arthur McManus was the delegate of the British Communist Party to the Communist International, was a member of its presidium, and was known to have been living in the same bungalow with Zinoviev in the suburbs of Moscow during September 1924. The British Foreign Office released its copy to the *London Times* for publication on October 10, 1924. The *London Daily Mail* obtained two copies independently from a businessman, who in turn obtained it from some mysterious source. The *Daily Mail* claimed that it received its two copies on October 9, 1924. One of these copies *was identical with the Foreign Office copy*. The second copy was signed *only by Zinoviev*, and instead of McManus' name as a co-signer, *it was addressed to McManus*. Which raises the question of why Zinoviev would address a letter to McManus in England when McManus was practically a member of his household in Moscow. And how could there be two versions of the same letter—one with a single signature, the other with two signatures? The obviousness of this forgery did not prevent the *Daily Mail* from splashing it across its front pages three days before the elections of October 29, 1924, when it would serve to hurt the Ramsay MacDonald slate of candidates.

There was abundant internal evidence of the fraudulent nature of the document. It is now known that all the intelligence agencies had examined the document and pronounced it a forgery, but not one of the intelligence agencies advised Prime Minister Ramsay MacDonald of this fact. The evidence is clear that there was a Right-Wing cabal among the intelligence agencies which conspired with leaders of the Conservative Party to defeat the Labor Party. Had MacDonald been told the truth, he would not have sent a protest note to the U.S.S.R. and thus, in effect, accepted the genuineness of the document. Indeed, he would have been able to publicly denounce this crude forgery. By the time he found out the truth, it was too late. His party was defeated in the elections. It seems to be certain that the chief organizer of the conspiracy was the head of the intelligence division of the Foreign Office. After his defeat, MacDonald obtained admissions from all the intelligence agencies that they knew the "Zinoviev letter" was a forgery. The conspirators had taken advantage of MacDonald's preoccupation with the election campaign. In fact, the Conservative Party could not afford to have the spotlight turned on to this episode, as was shown less than four years later when the House of Commons defeated a Labor Party motion for a full-scale investigation, by a vote of 326 to 132.

An interesting sequel to this story appeared in a dispatch filed from London to the *Los Angeles Times*, December 26, 1966, by Robert C. Toth. It says, in part:

The "Zinoviev Letter," which was to the British leftists what McCarthy's original list of card-carrying Communists is to American liberals, was a blatant fake, according to the wife of one of the men who concocted it.

It was written in Berlin by White Russian emigres at the request of "a person of authority in London," Mrs. Irma Bellegarde told the *Sunday Times*.

The newspaper also discovered that the Conservative Party paid 5,000 pounds (then worth $20,000 to someone still unknown for a copy of the letter which it then exploited in the election via the press.

And the man who served as intermediary in the sale, C. Donald Im Thurn, later asked the Conservative government for a knighthood. He never got the honor but Baldwin in 1928 identified him publicly as the "honest and patriotic" citizen who passed the letter to the equally patriotic *Daily Mail* newspaper.

Mr. Toth points out that in 1928 the Soviet Government named the plotters, including Bellegarde and a Soviet official in Berlin who had stolen the official stationery on which the Zinoviev letter was written; that the Soviet Government charged that the forgery was committed with the connivance of British intelligence. Mrs. Bellegarde, the dispatch discloses, was not only the wife of the conspirator, Bellegarde, whom the Russians had named, but was the sister of a second conspirator and a close friend of a third conspirator. Mr. Toth observes that "there seems little doubt that the [Zinoviev] letter was an ingenious fake" and that the British Foreign Office does not now have the letter in its files. The reason is obvious. It never had an authentic letter. It had a forgery, which it dare not submit to an impartial investigation.

## "TIME" MARCHES ON—UNDER THE BANNER OF A HOAX!

In an editorial on page 37 of its issue of April 12, 1948, *Time* magazine made some sneering references to a lecture delivered in Moscow by Professor V. N. Kolbanovsky on the subject of

270

"Love, Marriage, and Family in Socialist Society." After referring to Kolbanovsky as the "sleek-haired, glib philosophy professor," *Time* gave the following quotation from his lecture:

Ugly psychological leftovers of bourgeois ideology concerning marriage and love still exist here. . . Bourgeois marriages are business marriages where love gets dirtied and trampled. . . . In bourgeois countries the working girl, in order to get and hold a job, often has to pass through the boss' bed. . . In the bourgeois state children are not wanted in great numbers. (Multiple dots are exactly as in the *Time* quotation.)

Another portion of the professor's lecture was quoted by *Time,* and is of interest:

The time will never come when parents are reduced to the function of producing children and handing their babies over to the state. . . Love under Communism will become even more beautiful. (Multiple dots are exactly as in the *Time* quotation.)

How does an anti-Communist journalist go about discrediting the sensible remarks of a scholar who happens to be a Communist? This was no hardship for *Time,* because it had on its staff, at the time, Mr. Whitaker Chambers, a renegade Communist who achieved fame and fortune by writing "exposés."[10] The following footnote, given with the editorial, accomplished the purpose:

In the 100 years since Karl Marx's *Communist Manifesto* espoused "an open, legalized community of women" few subjects have been more frequently disputed by Marxists. Lenin, in one of his sharpest departures from Marxism, vehemently rejected "free love" on the ground that "love is more than drinking a glass of water". . .

Here is what Marx and Engels actually said in the *Communist Manifesto,* published in 1848:

But you Communists would introduce community of women, screams the whole bourgeoisie in chorus.
The bourgeois sees in his wife a mere instrument of production.

[10] In a letter to the writer, dated July 17, 1963, *Time* admitted that Whitaker Chambers was on its staff when the editorial was written, but attributed its authorship to Craig Thompson.

He hears that the instruments of production are to be exploited in common, and, naturally, can come to no other conclusion than that the lot of being common to all will likewise fall to the women.

He has not even a suspicion that *the real point aimed at is to do away with the status of women as mere instruments of production.*

For the rest, nothing is more ridiculous than the virtuous indignation of our bourgeois at the community of women which, they pretend, is to be openly and officially established by the Communists. The Communists have no need to introduce community of women; it has existed almost from time immemorial.

Our bourgeois, not content with having wives and daughters of their proletarians at their disposal, not to speak of common prostitutes, take the greatest pleasure in seducing each other's wives.

Bourgeois marriage is in reality a system of wives in common and thus, at the most, what the Communists might possibly be reproached with is that they desire to introduce, in substitution for a hypocritically concealed, an openly legalised community of women. For the rest, *it is self-evident, that the abolition of the present system of production must bring with it the abolition of the community of women* springing from that system, i.e., of prostitution both public and private. (Emphasis added.—M. K.)

It is quite clear that Marx and Engels had no business indulging in political satire back in 1848. Didn't they realize that sixty years later *Time* magazine would make their words mean the opposite of what they had intended? From the first lie, *Time* marched on to the lie about Lenin's "sharpest departure from Marxism." The truth is that Lenin did not depart from Marxism, because Marxism had *never* included the concept of promiscuous sex relations. It is interesting to trace the origin of this second lie. The truth will be found in *Clara Zetkin's Reminiscences,* in which the late Clara Zetkin tells of a discussion with Lenin about sexual morality.

It appears that some irresponsible and shallow-minded theoreticians were circulating a theory that in Communist society, it would be as simple as drinking a glass of water to satisfy one's sexual needs and craving for love. Lenin stated very vehemently: "I do not consider the famous 'glass-of-water' theory as Marxist at all and besides it is anti-social." He emphasized this point again by saying: "Drinking water is really an individual matter. But in love-making two take part and a third, a new life, comes into being. Herein lies a social interest; a duty to the collective body arises. As a Communist I do not like the 'glass-of-water' theory in the least despite its beautiful

272

label: 'emancipated love.' Moreover, it is neither new nor Communistic."

Lenin then proceeded to outline his philosophy with respect to sex, love, and the problems of youth:

Communism ought to bring with it not asceticism but joy of life and good cheer called forth, among other things, by a life replete with love. However, in my opinion the plethora of sex life observable today brings neither joy of life nor cheerfulness, but on the contrary diminishes them. In revolutionary times this is bad, very bad, indeed.

The youth is particularly in need of joy of life and cheerfulness. Healthy sports: gymnastics, swimming, excursions, physical exercise of every description; also a diversity of intellectual pursuits: teaching, criticism, research; and all of this in combination as far as possible. That will mean more to the youth than eternal lectures and discussions on sex problems and so-called "utilisation of life."

Lenin made two additional points in elucidating his philosophy: "Laxity in sexual matters is bourgeois; it is a sign of degeneration." "Self-possession, self-discipline are not slavery; they are necessary also in love. . ."

It is clear that the hoax story of the nationalization of women in Russia has its historical roots at the very inception of the modern Communist movement. It is a bogeyman story that has been used against Communists and Socialists for almost 125 years. Somewhere around 1914, a renegade Socialist and renegade Jew, David Goldstein, saw an opportunity to achieve fame and fortune. So, he became a Roman Catholic and was toured around the country under the auspices of the Knights of Columbus to scare people into believing that Socialists would usher in an era of "free love," a scarecrow term that he used to denote promiscuous sex relations. In collaboration with another renegade Socialist, Martha Moore Avery, Goldstein wrote a shameful book, entitled *Socialism: A Nation of Fatherless Children*. The proofs adduced were of the same calibre as those in the *Time* magazine editorial footnote: distortions of truth and out-of-context quotations. This obscene compendium was circulated widely and placed in the libraries from coast to coast. Little did the readers of the Goldstein-Avery book suspect that they were being fed outright lies behind a religious facade. And little did the readers of *Time* magazine suspect that they too were being told a couple of bald-faced lies. It is most difficult to ascribe the *Time* performance to inadvertency. Not only did it have an expert, Mr. Whitaker Chambers, on its staff, but the alleged quotations from Marx and Lenin could easily have been checked out in any public library. But *Time* chose to march on with a latter-day version of the nationalization of women hoax.

### Brazil's "Zinoviev Letter"

On December 2, 1963, two newspapers in Rio de Janeiro, *O Jornal* and *O Globo*, published a document purporting to be a letter from a Soviet diplomat in Havana to a Soviet diplomat in Rio de Janeiro. Among the gems in this alleged letter are the following:

1. Regarding the Cuban beauties: that "they never take a bath, they smell like dogs."
2. That Cuba "seems like an island inhabited by savages."
3. "All our help seems to fall into a ditch without a bottom."
4. The author of the letter asks his friend in Rio to intervene on his behalf in Moscow so that he may get out of Cuba alive.

The evidence that this document is a clumsy forgery is as follows:

1. It clashes with all the known facts about Moscow-Havana relations.
2. No Soviet diplomat in his right mind would put such nonsense in writing, when even if he expressed such views privately he would risk dismissal from his post.
3. No Soviet diplomat needs help to "escape" from Cuba.
4. The letter was addressed to V. Khabitikin. The Brazilian Foreign Office records did not contain any record of a Soviet diplomat in Rio de Janeiro by that name. There was, however, one by the name of Vladimir Khalioutine, who had returned to the Soviet Union in July, six months before this alleged letter was publicized. Who was in possession of it for six months? And is it likely that diplomats misspell the names of close friends and associates?
5. The Soviet ambassador to Brazil branded the letter a forgery, pointing out:

a. That the letter was written in poor Russian, which is unlikely for a Soviet diplomat.

b. That the envelope bore the *Portuguese* imprint "via aerea" instead of the *Spanish* imprint "correo aereo." This would seem to indicate that the envelope was bought in Brazil rather than in Cuba.

It would appear that the Brazilian "Edgar Sisson" was more of a novice than his American predecessor.

## "News Makers"

A journalist friend of the writer once described the qualifications of a fellow journalist: "He is an excellent reporter. He can make a story out of nothing." It seems that Mr. John Scali, the Washington diplomatic correspondent of the American Broadcasting Company, has the same extraordinary ability. In the fall of 1965 he reported that a power struggle is raging in the Kremlin that could result in a shakeup of the leadership. He based this story "on a flood of reports reaching Washington." Strangely enough, the chief of ABC's Moscow news bureau, Sam Jaffe, was at the same time transmitting broadcasts to ABC's New York office calling Scali's reports "unfounded." When ABC did not broadcast Jaffe's denial stories, the Soviet Government told him to go home.[11] This, of course, was no reflection on Jaffe's integrity. It was the Soviet Government's way of letting ABC know that its handling of the news was unsatisfactory.

## The Iron Curtain Hoax

The use of the term "Iron Curtain" is a classic example of the tyranny of words that are used deceptively. This was a handy little device for creating a distorted image of life in the Soviet Union and its allied countries. It was used effectively by Winston Churchill in his famous speech at Fulton, Missouri on March 5, 1946, which was the signal for the grand opening of the Cold War. What is not generally known is that in this drastic maneuver to break up the anti-Fascist wartime alliance,

11 The story is told in a UPI dispatch, *Los Angeles Times,* October 1, 1965.

Churchill plagiarized the terminology of Hitler's minister of propaganda, Dr. Paul Joseph Goebbels.

Right-Wing columnist Max Freedman, in a column that appeared in the *Los Angeles Times*, April 20, 1964, tells some of the details of how Churchill received the invitation to speak at Fulton, Missouri. Freedman relates how Churchill had told Sir Denis Brogan that he intended to talk about the "iron curtain" that divided Europe. "The phrase, 'iron curtain,' " writes Freedman, "had been used earlier in a totally different context by Dr. Goebbels in a Nazi broadcast."

Another Right-Wing source, *Western Destiny,*[12] a now defunct quarterly magazine that openly espoused the Hitlerian racist doctrine, said in an editorial deploring the fact that Churchill had taken a stand against Hitler:

Perhaps the most famous "Churchillism" is his phrase "iron curtain," which he is supposed to have coined in his famous Fulton, Missouri speech. Even this is a fraud. The phrase, "iron curtain," was coined by an even better propagandist, Dr. Josef Goebbels, some three or four years before Churchill plagiarized it!

Ernest K. Bramsted, in his book, *Goebbels and the National Socialist Propaganda, 1924-1945,* published in 1965 by the University of Michigan Press, says:

It is not generally recognized that it was Goebbels who first, in February 1945, coined the term "the iron curtain," which he said was about to be clamped down on Russian-occupied Europe by the Soviet Forces. This he did in one of his last articles designed to put the fear of Bolshevism into the minds of the Germans and the Western Allies. "Should the German people lay down their arms," predicted Goebbels, "according to Yalta the Soviets would occupy the whole Eastern and South Eastern Europe, plus the largest part of the Reich. In front of these territories which, if one includes the Soviet Union, are gigantic, an *iron curtain* would come down at once behind which the mass-slaughter of the people would take place, probably amidst the applause of the Jewish Press in London and New York."

In a footnote, Ernest K. Bramsted points out that Goebbels' article appeared in the February 22, 1945 issue of *Das Reich*. In a letter, which appeared in *The Minority of One,* October

---

12 Issue of March 1965.

1965, Mr. John Peet, editor of the *Democratic German Report*, an East German publication, reveals a further interesting fact. An obscure journalist wrote a story in the Nazi newspaper, *Frankfurter Anzeiger*, February 12, 1945, which placed this headline over it:

BEHIND THE IRON CURTAIN—NEUTRAL REPORTS ON
EVENTS IN BULGARIA AND RUMANIA

Ten days later Goebbels plagiarized the catchy phrase from the provincial newspaper, and gave it widespread publicity. Thirteen months later, Sir Winston Churchill used this Nazi slogan as an ideological battering ram and gave it world-wide publicity. In a certain sense, this was very appropriate for the launching of the Cold War, which is rapidly propelling the U.S.A. in the direction of Fascism and a Third World War!

Actually there is not and never has been an iron curtain around any of the countries in the Soviet orbit. Admittedly certain travel restrictions had to be imposed because of the elaborate network of spies and saboteurs which the Central Intelligence Agency was using against them. Secondly, the real iron curtain was the ring of military and naval bases the U.S.A. and its allies built up around the Soviet Union and its allies, openly boasting of the number of thermonuclear bombs poised for delivery on pre-selected targets. Thirdly, the desperate need to rebuild a war-torn economy made it essential that Soviet citizens concentrate on that task rather than travel abroad. Recently, many of these restrictions have been progressively eased, but the iron curtain label sticks like glue. A case in point is a long dispatch from Syria by Joe Alex Morris, Jr. in the *Los Angeles Times,* November 7, 1965. The reporter tells of a ship leaving the harbor of Aleppo, Syria with 400 Armenians who are leaving Syria. He explains it this way:

They are willingly returning behind the Iron Curtain to Soviet Armenia—part of 2,000 scheduled to be voluntarily repatriated from Syria this year.
They are living proof that crossing the Iron Curtain is a two-way affair. Not everyone is trying to get out from behind it. These people are anxious to get in.

And further on in his story, Mr. Morris adds:

277

This year there was a reported 18,000 applicants to return, but the Russians felt they could handle only 2,000 comfortably. Other shipments of repatriates are coming from Egypt, Iran and Cyprus.

. . . for the poorer Armenians, the lure of free public education is enough by itself to make them pack up and leave for the Soviet Union.

. . . Armenians are impressed by the fact that an Armenian named Anastas Mikoyan is president of the Soviet Union.

Is it not about time that this Nazi propaganda phrase be dropped from continual usage in our media of communication? Is it not time for us to realize the truth of Voltaire's dictum: "Prejudice is the reason of fools"? Is it not time for us Americans to look at ourselves in the mirror and honestly answer the question of where, in fact, there is an Iron Curtain?

Since 1949, when the Communists came to power in mainland China, there has been a ban on American citizens visiting that country. We have had to depend upon newsmen from other countries in order to get some factual information about the doings of one-quarter of the human race. What are we afraid of? Who put up that Iron Curtain?

Since Dr. Fidel Castro and his followers overthrew the regime of Fulgencio Batista, our State Department has kept a ban on travel to that country by American citizens. It was only after expensive litigation that it was possible to get a ruling from the U.S. Supreme Court on January 10, 1967 that citizens who went to Cuba could be punished by having their passports revoked, but could not be jailed. Even our champion chess player, Bobby Fischer, was prevented from going to Cuba to participate in an international chess tournament in August of 1965, and finally he arranged to participate by telephone! We have similar bans on travel by our citizens to North Korea, North Vietnam, and Albania. What are we afraid of? And who put up those Iron Curtains?

In July, 1963, an 81-year old British citizen expressed a desire to visit his 75-year-old sister in Chicago, who had just undergone major surgery. This threw the huge bureaucracy of our State Department into a dither. First, a visa was denied. Next, it was granted. Then, it was revoked. Finally, it was granted, but only after fifty members of the British Parliament had petitioned our State Department to grant a visa to William Gallacher, a British Communist and former Member of Parliament. Similarly, the provisions of the McCarran-Walter Immigration Act of 1952 and the Ultra-Rightist posture of Miss Frances Knight, head of the passport division in the State Department, have discouraged and interfered with the holding of scientific conferences on American soil. Is it not sheer hypocrisy for us to taunt the Soviet Union about an Iron Curtain?

Mr. Vincent Burke, in a Moscow dispatch to the *Los Angeles Times,* March 4, 1966, summarizes very well the true state of affairs:

This is the story of a wall of fear which Congress built around the United States. This is a plea to tear down the wall.

Mr. Burke goes on to point out that *in 1965,* some 20,000 American tourists visited the Soviet Union, while only 260 Soviet citizens visited the United States; that even if permission were granted by the Soviet Government, the U.S.A. would not grant visas to additional Soviet visitors. Senator Stephen Young of Ohio, in a speech on the floor of the Senate, August 17, 1965, stated that *in 1964* there were 12,000 American visitors to the Soviet Union and only 204 Russian tourists in the United States.

*Newsweek* magazine, May 2, 1966, reported: "More than 1 million Soviet citizens traveled abroad last year, roughly half of them to purely capitalist countries. And even those who don't travel have some access to the ideas and tastes of the capitalist world; they can listen to the Voice of America or the BBC without a qualm, do the twist in a local restaurant or buy French cognac in a local store."

*Life* magazine, September 13, 1963, stated: "The American tourist encounters many surprises in the sprawling land that is the subject of this special issue—but the greatest, perhaps, is the ease with which he can come and go about the U.S.S.R. All it really takes is money." Of course, what *Life* has left out of the story is the part that *Life* and the rest of the media of communication played in spreading the lie about an Iron Curtain.

Yes, indeed, the Iron Curtain should be removed, but first we must be informed of its precise location. Is it not time to rid ourselves of the tyranny of this Nazi propaganda slogan?

# Is There Forced Labor in U.S.S.R.?

For years the American people have been deluged with stories of forced labor and slave labor camps in the Soviet Union. The stories have been told in a manner that makes the Nazi concentration camps and extermination centers almost vanish from one's consciousness. We are not attempting an assessment of the merits or demerits of the restrictive labor laws that once prevailed in the Soviet Union. We are concerned here only with the fact that the trend towards more freedom and improved living conditions in the Soviet Union is partly concealed or blurred by the media of communication. Consider the fact that hardly anywhere in the media would one find this admission: that "the compulsory labor laws" of the Soviet Union "were abolished piecemeal beginning in 1956." This appeared in the October 7, 1963, issue of *Washington Report,* the newsletter of the American Security Council, an organization of monopolists, militarists, ex-FBI agents, and professional anti-Communists. Their guarded admission is significant, but millions of Americans still believe that there is forced labor in the Soviet Union.

# The U-2 Aftermath

On May 1, 1960, a U-2 spy plane of the United States Central Intelligence Agency crashed deep inside the Soviet Union. For several years thereafter, editors and columnists wrote "think pieces" in order to disprove Khrushchev's claim that a Soviet missile had hit the plane that was piloted by Francis Gary Powers. Following a pattern that has been followed for some fifty years, the truth gradually seeped out after a barrage of lies, ridicule, and scorn had been laid down, all in an effort to make it sound as if Soviet missiles lacked the capability of shooting down a U-2 plane. First we noticed that Stewart Alsop, the editor of *Saturday Evening Post,* in an editorial on September 28, 1963, in which he called for U.S. bombing of China, referred to the Soviets' "SA-2 missile which can shoot down the U-2." (Alsop is known to have some intimate relationships with top brass in the Pentagon.) Next was a disclosure by his brother, Joseph Alsop, in his syndicated column of July 12, 1965: "In brief, Soviet SAM-2s have a range of about 35 miles and are reasonably accurate to altitudes of 60,000 feet (where they got the famous U-2) and above."[14] The final item is a Washington dispatch to the *Los Angeles Times* of May 5, 1965, in which we are told that Powers was downed near Sverdlovsk, deep inside the Soviet Union, and that CIA concluded he was hit by a Soviet SA-2 missile." Thus has another anti-Soviet fairy tale gone with the wind!

## Those Poor Oppressed Russians

The picture of life in the Soviet Union, as painted by Dr. Fred Schwarz of the Christian Anti-Communism Crusade, Dr. Carl McIntire of the 20th Century Reformation Hour, Dr. Billy James Hargis of the Christian Crusade, John Edgar Hoover of the FBI, the House Committee on Un-American Activities, and many other self-proclaimed experts on Communism and the Soviet Union, is one of horror and incredible human suffering. Mr. Barry Mather, in the *Vancouver Sun,* November 8, 1950, told the story very well about the systematic lying of the anti-Soviet Crusaders:

Here are eight facts Explaining Russia which I got by reading the last eight books Explaining Russia:

1. The Russian economic system is so inefficient that, in the last few years, Russia has become the most formidable power in the world.
2. The bureaucrats who run Russia have crippled industry to such an extent that Russia has made astounding industrial progress.
3. The men in charge of Russian foreign policy are so stupidly ignorant of world conditions that they are always two jumps ahead of anybody else.
4. Russia is such a godless country that drunkenness is at a minimum, prostitution is nil and the papers wouldn't know a sex story if they saw one.
5. Under the stifling confines of Communism the Russian people have so little interest in culture that every town has an opera and a symphony orchestra.
6. Under the Bolshevik bureaucracy chaotic conditions have laid waste the country, resulting in such widespread famines and other disasters that the population has increased by leaps and bounds.
7. The poor Soviet worker has been so exploited that he has now little left except economic security from the cradle to the grave.

---

[14] The parenthetical qualification is by Alsop.

8. So heartily do the Russian masses detest their present way of life that, given a chance, they will wipe out anybody who tries to liberate them.

The correctness of Barry Mather's observation is proven by reports that have been made by reputable observers, most of whom have been shocked upon discovery of the extent to which they have been misled. Thus Mr. Norman Smith, associate editor of the *Ottawa Journal,* reported his impressions of a short visit to the Soviet Union in 1956: "I was overwhelmed by the ignorance of my preconceived notions. . ."[15] Smith prefaced this remark by stating that "the lively state of the U.S.S.R. stunned me." Two other statements in his report are worthy of note:

The food stores had plentiful stocks of attractive goods being rapidly bought at reasonable prices by ordinary and even poorer-seeming citizens.
Here was a people with more individuality, more spirit, more pride in country, better health, and greater energy than I had been led to believe.

Ten years later Mr. Vincent Burke, the *Los Angeles Times'* Moscow correspondent reported in depth on life in that vast country:

Today, on the eve of the Soviet Union's 49th birthday, its factories are turning out quantities of consumer goods that would have been deemed fantastic only a few years ago.
Today the U.S.S.R. is an industrial Goliath, second only to the United States."[16]

In his next dispatch Mr. Burke tells of a Soviet family with one child that was asked to keep a record of its expenditures for one month. It broke down as follows: Food 39.5%, clothing 11.9%, entertainment of guests 6.3%, kindergarten fee 5.3%, income tax about 5%, housing (rent, electricity, gas and heat) 4.9%, entertainment 3.3%, barber 2.6%, and 16% unaccounted for.[17] The importance of this report is that it shows how mis-

15 A Reuters dispatch from Ottawa, Canada in *Los Angeles Times,* April 22, 1956.
16 *Los Angeles Times,* November 6, 1966.
17 *Los Angeles Times,* November 27, 1966.

leading comparisons of living conditions can be, if one uses American criteria, which usually include installment payments, interest payments, automobile maintenance, etc. Furthermore, in the U.S.S.R. all medical and dental care are free, as well as a number of other social benefits, including free education, paid vacations, and special maternity benefits.

One of the best and most qualified reporters on conditions in the Soviet Union is U.S. Senator Allen J. Ellender of Louisiana. The Senator is by no means a partisan of the Soviet Union; nor is he in the least sympathetic to Communism as a philosophy or as a social system. He is forceful in his belief in the superiority of Capitalism, and is known in political circles as a Conservative. He does, however, have the merit that he is *a keen observer and an honest reporter.* He has traveled extensively in many countries on behalf of the Senate Committee on Appropriations, reporting by means of a day-to-day diary, which is incorporated in each case in a Report entitled *A Review of United States Foreign Policy and Operations.*

In the introduction to his 1957 Report, Senator Ellender makes reference to "an increasing awareness among our people that the traditional concept of the Soviet Union as a backward, semideveloped nation is incorrect. . . ." In the introduction to his 1961 Report, the Senator refers to "a general lack of knowledge among our people in regard to the industrial, as well as the agricultural developments of the U.S.S.R."

In the 1957 Report, Senator Ellender says:

This is my third successive report to the committee about Russia. For the third time in as many years, I traveled extensively through the most important areas of this enigmatic country. During the course of my most recent trip I spent 33 days inside Russia's borders. I visited cities never before seen by an American Government official, and talked, and came in contact with, literally thousands of Russian people.

In 1957, as in 1956, my conversations with the people of Russia were facilitated by my having at my side an official of the United States Embassy at Moscow who spoke and understood the Russian language.

In the 1961 Report, the Senator tells us that this time he spent *seven whole weeks* inside the Soviet Union. In 1957 he was allowed to take pictures, and he reported: "With more film I could have taken as many pictures as I desired." In 1961 the

Senator reported: "I had my camera along and I took, at my own expense, 6,750 feet of 16-millimeter movie film within the U.S.S.R., plus 1,500 feet in other countries I visited." This, of course, does not support the Iron Curtain image, but even more devastating to this myth is the Senator's description of his movements within the U.S.S.R. In the 1957 Report, the Senator states:

On this trip I was able to see all I asked to visit, with one exception, and that was a shipyard at Gorki.

I was never treated better and more friendly and cordially in any part of the world than I was on this trip, by the Russians I met, particularly in Siberia. I know it was not prearranged. I attribute my success to my manner and method of approaching my hosts in various cities. There was some hesitation at first, but I always ended in seeing all that I asked to see, except in the one instance heretofore mentioned. Almost in all places visited I was asked if I desired to see more, and I had to decline because of lack of time. Invariably, my hosts expressed regrets that I could not stay longer. (Page 76.)

In the 1961 Report, the Senator tells us that, when he landed at the Moscow airport, he went through customs, passport check, and medical requirements. Furthermore: "None of my bags were opened, and no questions were asked." (Page 4.) Reporting further, the Senator states:

I was not followed by anyone that I could observe, and I went along as though I were a native, without being questioned or stopped from taking movies. (Page 17.)

I walked the streets of Minsk this morning and took many movies. (Page 27.)

Regarding progress and improvements of living standards:

1957 Report. Almost uniformly, I found improvements in Russian conditions as contrasted with my findings of last year (1956) and the year before (1955).

Generally speaking, I found a much higher degree of contentment among the peoples of Russia than on my previous visits. (Page 6.)

1961 Report. I was very much impressed with the industrial expansion which has obviously taken place in four years in the area I had visited before. As to those areas I had not seen before, I was surprised at what I found in the way of old cities being modernized, new cities springing up, housing being constructed at phenomenal

284

speed, and all sorts of industries being fostered where formerly there had been little if any industrial development. . . . True, there is still a long way to go before Soviet industry can approach our own industrial facilities and capabilities, but when one considers that only a few years ago the new areas I visited were some of the most backward in Russia, it is a revelation to find there thriving industries which are for the most part being operated and managed by local people. (Page 2.)

*1961 Report.* The people were well dressed, as a whole, as can be seen from the pictures I took of crowds on the streets. No one objected to my taking pictures.

Generally speaking, I found this city making fine progress since my last visit in 1956. People talk more. They seem happier. They look better in every way. There are doubtless more clothes and food available. (This refers to the city of Leningrad.) (Page 17.)

*1961 Report.* I was surprised to note the larger variety of goods and the cheaper retail prices since my last visit.

I was really surprised at the apparent progress made. (This refers to the city of Stalingrad.) (Page 46.)

*1961 Report.* I visited the Stalingrad hydroelectric power plant, the largest in the world. It was a real thrill, since I was here in 1956, shortly after the work was resumed on the project, and I took movies of the work then in progress. (Page 47.)

*1961 Report.* It was quite an experience, one I shall not forget.

I do not see how the Russians did such a job so quickly. (This refers to an inspection trip beneath the huge generators at the Stalingrad hydroelectric plant.) (Page 49.)

*1961 Report.* The city is modern with wide boulevards lined with trees. I was amazed at the progress made. There is bound to be much teamwork among the people. They seem to work unceasingly. (This refers to the city of Stalingrad.) (Page 49.)

*1961 Report.* There is no doubt that the average Russian is better housed than he has ever been. The people seem to cooperate to the *n*th degree in building parks, planting trees, shrubs, and flowers and, generally, in beautifying vacant grounds, including squares, parks, and neutral grounds throughout urban Russia. (This refers to the city of Tibilsi in Georgia, a constituent Republic of the U.S.S.R.) (Page 52.)

*1961 Report.* I visited a new area that is now being built, and it is amazing to see so many apartments and homes being constructed in such a period of time. These new homes will be a great asset to the workers. The rentals are very low. A three-bedroom apartment, with gas, electricity, water, and heat will rent from 9 to 11 rubles per month, and the smaller ones in proportion. The undertaking in this city, as well as many others, in the construction of new and better homes, is a stupendous task, and it is hard to realize that so much is being done in such a short time. In addition, there are many institutes, schools, and colleges being constructed. In the light of the deplorable conditions which are said to have existed here and in other cities less than 30 years ago, it is obvious that progress is being made. (This refers to the city of Alma-Ata in Kazakhstan, a constituent Republic of U.S.S.R.) (Page 85.)

## Regarding cultural activities in the Soviet Union:

*1957 Report.* The factory's theater has 560 seats and each workshop employee attends a show at least once a month, I was informed. The workers have their own theatrical performers, as well as dancing and movies. All of those are free except when special artists perform.

In connection with this plant, a Pioneer camp was erected last year to which boys and girls from 9 to 14 years come each summer from June through August. (This refers to an electronic components factory in Novosibirsk.) (Page 38.)

*1957 Report.* Novosibirsk is the proud possessor of the largest opera house in Russia. In the evening we attended a performance in one of its huge concert halls with a seating capacity of 1,000. The main concert hall, however, where ballets and operas are given, seats 2,200. We were told that it required 14 years to build this huge structure, where over 700 people—including the casts—are employed. (Page 43.)

*1961 Report.* On the premises are clinics to take care of the workers, a hospital, and a technical school. Some of the workers attend this school to become more proficient in their work. There is a cultural center on the grounds, as well as cafeterias to take care of most of the workers. (This refers to the Leningrad Metal Works, which employs 11,000 workers.) (Page 14.)

*1961 Report.* This circus business is more or less a permanent institution in all the larger centers of Russia, I was informed. Circuses are housed in specially constructed arenas in many of the large cities of the U.S.S.R. (Page 23.)

*1961 Report.* After a fine supper of various native dishes and melon, I attended a concert at the local Turkmenian State Theatre of Opera and Ballet. Our party occupied front seats in this large theater. Most of the singers and ballet dancers were trained locally, and I was again surprised to find such a variety of good talent in this part of the U.S.S.R. Only two of the singers were from other republics. Arias from "Carmen," "Rigoletto," the "Barber of Seville," and other operas were rendered, with a few folk songs also included in the program. I enjoyed the evening very much. (This refers to the city of Ashkhabad, capital city of the constituent Republic of Turkmenstan.) (Page 67.)

## Regarding educational developments:

*1961 Report.* The school system is being expanded to take care of the increased population, and one must be impressed at the progress made by the U.S.S.R. in the field of education, considering the extremely high level of illiteracy that existed less than three decades ago. (Page 32.)

*1961 Report.* The claim is that Armenia has awakened in the last 30 years since it became a part of the U.S.S.R. Schools and colleges have been built, and illiteracy is almost at zero. There is no doubt that much physical progress has been made. (Page 55.)

*1961 Report.* The lodging, per student, is 1.5 rubles per month. The students are given a scholarship and a stipend from the Government of 22 rubles per month. The more proficient students get 20 percent additional per month. Each year the base stipend increases. The stipend is used to pay expenses at school, such as food and lodging. The scholarships above mentioned cover tuition, laboratory fees, and books. This school is a far cry from what existed here before the revolution according to Mr. Azimor [the rector of the University]. After visiting the new campus, I could not help but agree that it was most modern. (This refers to the Gorky-Turkmen State University at Ashkhabad.) (Page 65.)

## Regarding health and medical problems:

*1957 Report.* I visited a very fine hospital. It appeared to be very clean and fairly well equipped. It had 75 beds, and is 1 of 10 hospitals in Kazan, although some are larger than the one I visited. I was told that there were many small clinics throughout the area from which doctors visit sick patients at home.

There were 30 doctors, 28 of whom were women, and 54 women nurses, who operated the hospital. The 2 male doctors were surgeons. . . . No doctors or nurses are allowed to do any work outside the hospital.

I was informed that 75 percent of all doctors in Russia are women; that 50 percent of the lawyers are women; that 38 percent of all engineers, chemists, agronomists, and veterinarians are women. (Page 26.)

*1957 Report.* Every year a certain number of workers are sent by the trade unions to the Crimea, for a rest I was told. Shortly after my visit 120 were to leave. Some 200 were also to go to a local rest home situated only a few kilometers from the city. All this without any expense to the lucky workers who are selected on a basis of performance, except in cases where the worker must have rest because of illness. Some others are permitted to rest at these specially erected resthouses upon paying 30 percent of the cost. I was told that well-paid workers pay their own way. (This refers to an electronic parts factory in Novosibirsk.) (Page 38.)

*1957 Report.* The plant has an auditorium, dormitories, and all the usual facilities. Each room in the dormitory has six beds—crowded, but clean and tidy. We were told that each worker is examined by doctors four times per year.

We ate a big dinner in the dining room, which was very good.

287

I was told that employees get 2 to 4 weeks' vacation with pay. They get 30 percent of the cost of sanitarium rest visits, while 1 out of 5 gets free sanitarium rest facilities. The unions bear a part of the cost, while the factory pays the balance. (This refers to a visit in an electric test-meter factory, in the city of Omsk.) (Page 53.)

*1961 Report.* I then visited the Stalinabad Medical Institute. I was escorted by the assistant director, Dr. Kalinicheva, a lady surgeon, and the chief surgeon, Dr. Todzhiev. Both were cordial and anxious to show me around. I met with and talked to quite a few students.

The school was completed only 6 years ago. It has a student body of 1,800, with a faculty of 250. The students study for 6 years after completing the 10-year preparatory courses. Graduates may practice after 6 years of study and training. Even surgery may be engaged in after 6 years of study.

I visited the hospital, operated in connection with the institute. It has a total of 400 beds. Some rooms have 8 to 12 beds, others from 4 to 6 beds. The director said the hospital was overcrowded. This institute, as well as the hospital, would be a credit to any city of a comparable size. (Page 81.)

## Planning Aggression—Soviet Style

*1961 Report.* There is no doubt in my mind that we are highly thought of by the Russian people and that peace with us is their paramount desire. (Page 88.)

*1961 Report.* These people have been conditioned for peace. That is all they talk about and toast about. I believe they are sincere.

All the people I met seem to like Americans. (Page 102.)

## The Trend to Democratization of Society

*1957 Report.* It is my firm belief that the average Russian is convinced that his form of government is the best, that it provides him with the best living he has ever experienced or enjoyed. He simply knows of no better form of government. His Government, through propaganda, shows him what can be done through hard work. He is rewarded for hard work. He is rewarded for hard work by being put on the honor roll, if he is a factory worker. If he is very good, he climbs up the ladder on his own.

Newsreels are extensively used to show the great progress being made by the Government in agriculture and industry. For instance, a whole show will tell how better seed has improved wheat production, or how fertilizer increases yields, or how cattle breeding has been progressing in the last few years.

Complete programs depicting the construction of a dam from the beginning to its completion are shown. I saw one of them. It began by showing thousands of people assembled at ground-breaking exercises. The next scene depicted when the river was closed. Then the placing of the first turbine was shown. Finally, pictures were shown of the facility as completed.

The people are given credit for accomplishing such projects, and men and women are rewarded and honored at each function by presentation of certificates and medals. They are made conscious of the part they play in developing all projects.

The same approach is carried through in the building of a new school or in the developing of an area for apartments. Parks and cultural centers are stressed, and the people are given the credit for much of what is accomplished in that direction.

Women are recognized as being the equal of men in all professions. They are encouraged to study and become proficient. (Page 75.)

### Juvenile Delinquency

*1957 Report.* Juvenile delinquency, as we in the United States know it, is almost unknown in Russia. The reason is simply that the children are kept busy and occupied. (Page 34.)

I was told that child delinquency was not a problem in practically all parts of Russia and I am inclined to believe it.

All the children I met on the streets and other places are well behaved and polite. That also applies to the ones I met on collective farms. They seem to keep busy and are well taught and taken care of in these camps as well as in schools. (Page 59.)

We visited the House of Pioneers [in Novosibirsk], originally an old mansion owned by a former Russian capitalist, which was put into the hands of pioneers in 1937 who later enlarged and improved it. Now some 4,000 children from 140 separate clubs use it. These clubs are organized, I was told, in separate fields, such as painting and sculpture, music, dancing, machine work, tooling, carpentering, botany, zoology, and travel, to name but a few.

There is a garden in connection with this center containing 4 hectares where flowers, fruit, and other produce are grown by the children, depending on the projects undertaken.

The first room we visited was elaborately painted with very fine works depicting Russian fairy tales.

We also visited a group that was being told of the Soviet film industry. The children, all fine looking and well dressed, ranged in age from 10 to 14 years.

I was presented with a pin and neckerchief making me an honorary member of their club. I spoke to them for a few minutes and I was enthusiastically applauded. (Page 58.)

In the fall and winter of 1968, Senator Ellender spent 53 days within the borders of the Soviet Union, representing his fifth visit since 1955. For the sake of brevity, we quote a few important excerpts from his Report to the Committee on Appropriations of the United States Senate.

*Page V.* Generally, I was allowed free movement and was

able to see many new industrial facilities that have been constructed in all parts of the country, particularly in Siberia.

*Page XIII.* The U.S.S.R. is today second only to the United States in manufacturing output. Its people, like our own, have become almost universally literate.

*Page XIV.* Whatever the faults of present Russian society, its people are living incomparably better than at any time in their history. In every city, there are hundreds of apartment buildings being constructed, and industry is booming in all parts of the country. . . . I saw more consumer goods available than at any time in the past and it was easily apparent that the people were well fed and content. No one expressed any desire to turn against the Government.

In presenting these copious quotations from the Reports of U.S. Senator Allen J. Ellender and the reports that follow, it may be well to point out that we are concerned only in proving that the American people have been deceived for some fifty years about what is going on in the Soviet Union and the other Socialist countries. It is not within the purview of this study to determine whether Communism and Socialism are good, bad, or indifferent. Our interest is that the truth be known, that barriers of misunderstanding be removed, and that mankind be spared from the horrors of a thermonuclear holocaust. We seek to remove the Iron Curtain of hate and vituperation. In this spirit, we present the reports of some other dependable observers.

Alxander Werth was the Moscow correspondent of the London *Sunday Times* and the British Broadcasting Corporation during the war years of 1941-1946. He has made several visits to the U.S.S.R. since then. He speaks the Russian language fluently. Among his observations in a two-month trip, reported in the *Nation* magazine of October 5, 1964, were the following:

Medical services in Russia are completely free to everybody, and there are more doctors—most of them women—per capita than in any other country.[18] There are no pharmaceutical rackets: if, without consulting a doctor, you buy medicine in a drugstore, you pay a few cents for what would cost you a few dollars in the West.

Rents are very low; a friend of mine, a Leningrad writer, pays

18 *Parade* magazine, Aug. 1, 1965, said: "There is 1 doctor for every 714 people in the U.S., 1 doctor for every 350 persons in the Soviet Union."

only $16 a month for a four-room apartment with central heating. Smaller apartments in the vast newly built areas of Leningrad can be had for between $5 and $10 a month. Since 1959, more than 250,000 apartments have been built in Leningrad alone, 42,000 of them in the current year. . . Building on a similar scale is going on in practically every city in the Soviet Union. All cultural activity is cheap enough to be available to everybody—whether theatres, cinemas, books or phonograph records; the finest large LP records cost $1 apiece.

The abolition of fear is certainly the greatest thing that has happened in Russia in the last ten years, and the intelligentsia appreciates it more keenly than anyone else.

One of the most revealing reports is in an article in the *Saturday Evening Post,* February 27, 1965, by George Feifer, entitled "Communism Is Not What We Think." Mr. Feifer *has made four extended visits* to the Soviet Union and is the author of *Justice in Moscow,* a study of the Soviet Courts, which has been widely praised for its scholarly objectivity.

Mr. Feifer makes some incisive observations, which can be summarized as follows:

1. That the American people possess very little factual information about the Soviet Union, but they do have an image of that country based upon prejudices and platitudes.

2. That the daily life of the Russians is more comparable to that of the Americans than to some of the backward countries that we consider as our friends.

3. That the American press gives its readers a distorted and unbalanced image of life in the U.S.S.R.

4. That, when one sees the U.S.S.R. at first hand he can hardly reconcile it with what he reads in the American press.

5. That the stories about the Russians being on the verge of a revolt against oppressive rulers and inhuman conditions, are just so much nonsense, with no relationship to reality.

6. That after living in the Soviet Union for a year and a half he finds the people relatively contented, secure, optimistic, and loyal to their government.

All in all, Mr. Feifer challenges the hoax story about the 200 million slaves living in fear and degradation.

Mr. Feifer tells in his article that he had testified several months earlier before the House Committee on Foreign Affairs. After telling the Congressmen that the students he had met at Moscow University believed in Soviet Socialism and were confident of building a Communist future, *he was asked how we could subvert this belief, how we could put obstacles in their path, how we could exploit dissatisfactions, and how we could contaminate their ideology.* Mr. Feifer points out that the Russian people are making rapid strides, that they have their ideals, their hopes, and their aspirations. And he comments: "We ought to encourage such hopes and ideals, not scheme to destroy them."

*Newsweek* magazine of May 2, 1966, which we have previously quoted on the subject of Soviet citizens traveling abroad, tells of many of the accomplishments that our other witnesses have reported. An interesting additional commentary on Soviet life is the following:

As of last year the Soviet Union boasted 10,000 movie theaters, 500 professional dramatic companies and some 126,000 theatrical groups . . . and nearly all of them operated to capacity houses at every performance.

*U.S. News & World Report* has never been accused of being "soft on Communism," not even by the Birchites. In its issue of June 5, 1967, it presents a 4-page study entitled *A New Look at Today's Russia.* Worthy of note are these observations:

Now Russians are eating better. Following a year of record harvest, 1967 has started out as a year of abundance. Even imported food . . . such as juicy Moroccan oranges . . . is available in increasing amounts.

It is interesting to point out at this time that for several years Russia was plagued by a severe drought. This was the signal for all the hostile scribes and commentators to compose their prejudicial "think" pieces. Hundreds of columns were ground out, telling of Communism's failure to feed its people. Thus Ernest Conine's column in the *Los Angeles Times,* August 27, 1965, tells us that the Soviet economy is slowing down and is in trouble, and that it is doubtful if Russia will overtake America in this century. The knockout blow by Conine is: "The greatest Communist power on earth has shown itself incapable, for two years out of the past three, of feeding its own people." And furthermore says our journalistic

292

sage: "The political shock within the Soviet Union, once the facts soak in, could jeopardize the jobs of Premier Alexi Kosygin and party chief Leonid Brezhnev."

As this is being written, in September of 1968, Kosygin is still the Premier and Leonid Brezhnev is still the First Secretary of the Communist Party of the Soviet Union. As a prophet, therefore, Ernest Conine scores pretty low. As a reporter, he told less than the truth. The shortage of food had little to do with Communism. Its primary cause was an unprecedented drought. Moreover, no one went hungry in the Soviet Union. The government used its gold reserves and its credit to buy millions of bushels of wheat from Canada and the United States. By any standard of truth and logic this should be proof of strength, not weakness.

The article in *U.S. News & World Report* tells further about "the brightening picture of Soviet life," and correctly summarizes: "These changes are not marked by dramatic breakthroughs, but by modest, and so far steady advances." Lest some Right-Wing zealots start questioning the impeccable anti-Communist posture of the *U.S. News & World Report,* we hasten to add that, as usual, it "balances" every grudging admission of progress in the Soviet Union with some snide comments or some lugubrious prediction.

Sue Davidson Gottfried is a brilliant Seattle High School teacher, a Quaker, an ardent peace worker, and the author of many magazine articles. In the course of our own research work in the Seattle area in 1965 we discovered that many people consider her "the conscience of Seattle." In the *Progressive* magazine of June 1967, Mrs. Gottfried reports on her trip to the Soviet Union, as part of a delegation, in July of 1966. We summarize her findings:

1. They found it easy to talk with Soviet Citizens wherever they went, in large groups or in private. People were eager to talk, were very outspoken about conditions in their country, and were not afraid to voice nonconforming views.

2. Eight Soviet trade unionists who wanted to visit the United States in 1966 were denied visas by our State Department, in response to pressure from AFL-CIO President George Meany and his foreign affairs expert, Jay Lovestone, a renegade Communist. (Who put up that Iron Curtain?)

293

3. The delegation, which included teachers, was very impressed with a Soviet educator, who stated in the course of a lecture on the central tasks of education: "Before you shape a chemist, an engineer, a cosmonaut, you must shape a *man*. And it is the humanities which do *this*."

4. There is no glorification of war in the U.S.S.R. in the ways that are common in the U.S.A. In fact, war toys are not manufactured there.

5. One night she and two other young women went strolling through the streets, parks, and alleys of Moscow, striking up conversations with everyone they met. She points out that many of her group would not risk such an adventure in a large city in the U.S.A., but they somehow felt perfectly safe in Moscow.

From all the reliable data available we can safely conclude that the people of the Soviet Union and their leaders are neither witches nor angels, that the country is neither an utopia nor a hell, and that peaceful coexistence is in the best interests of both the Soviet Union and the United States of America.

## Education for the Russian "Slaves"!

In thousands of pamphlets, books, tracts, columns, and sermons, as well as in radio and television programs, the American people have been deluged with stories about the Russian "slaves." In evaluating this image, it is important to take a good look at the educational program of Soviet society, for it must be considered axiomatic that a well-informed populace cannot long be kept in slavery: that people who are trained *to think* will not remain slaves. Consequently, the findings of reputable educators should provide some important insights.

Dr. Lawrence Derthick, U.S. Commissioner of Education, was the head of a ten-man delegation of educators who studied the Soviet educational system at first hand. In a speech at the National Press Club, Dr. Derthick said:

What we have seen has amazed us in one particular: We were simply not prepared for the degree to which the U.S.S.R., as a nation, is committed to education as a means of national advancement. Everywhere we went we saw indication after indication of what we could only conclude amounted to a total commitment to education.

Our major reaction therefore is one of astonishment—and I

choose the word carefully—at the extent to which this seems to have been accomplished. For what it is worth ten American educators came away sobered by what they saw.[19]

In the official report of his 1958 trip, which can be found in *Bulletin 1959, No. 16* of the U.S. Department of Health, Education, and Welfare, Dr. Derthick said, in part:

Everywhere we went in the U.S.S.R. we were struck by the zeal and enthusiasm which the people have for education. It is a kind of grand passion with them.

Down on the borders of China where only a half-century ago the people were almost 100 percent illiterate, we saw thriving schools, an impressive scientific academy, and other institutions that have reduced illiteracy and advanced knowledge to an astonishing degree. From the shores of the Black Sea to remote Siberia we found the attitude summed up in the expression of a Soviet education official: "A child can be born healthy, but he can't be born educated."

There seems to be equality between men and women. The relationship between boys and girls in school appears to be characterized by dignity and mutual respect for each other.[20]

In 1959 another official delegation of educators went to the Soviet Union, and is reported in *Bulletin 1960, No. 17* of the U.S. Department of Health, Education, and Welfare. In the introduction to the report made by the three specialists, whom Dr. Derthick sent on this mission, it says:

In the school classroom and workshop, in the machine building plant, in the countryside, and wherever we went, we felt the pulse of the Soviet Government's drive to educate and train a new generation of technically skilled and scientifically literate citizens.

For us, traveling and observing in the U.S.S.R. were thrilling cultural experiences. Our hosts in Moscow, Kiev, Tbilisi, Leningrad, and outlying points were most attentive to our interests and helped us take note of long-established traditions and ancient monuments that mark the way their peoples have trod across the centuries. They took us to musical concerts, theatrical performances, and art exhibits that testified to their many accomplishments in these fields. We left their country with many new impressions and with some added assurances about the usefulness of cultural exchange.

19 Reported in *New York Times,* June 14, 1958.
20 In his column of September 15, 1959, Drew Pearson reported that, shortly after Dr. Derthick made his speech at the National Press Club, he was ordered to stop making speeches about the sensational developments of Soviet education. Furthermore, the written report of his 1958 trip to the U.S.S.R., which we have quoted, was suppressed for fifteen months.

A report, which was termed "one of the most thought-provoking studies of U.S.S.R. education that I have ever seen," was placed in the Congressional Record in 11 installments by Congressman Bernard F. Grabowski of Connecticut. It was written by William H. Benton, former Assistant Secretary of State and former U.S. Senator; presently U.S. Ambassador to UNESCO; and publisher and chairman of the board of Encyclopaedia Britannica.

Some highlights of Ambassador Benton's report, as taken from respective issues of the Congressional Record, are presented:

*May 12, 1965.* The visit was my fifth to the U.S.S.R. in nine years. I found the highest Soviet officials eager to talk.

In some areas of technical training the Soviets are already ahead of us—for example, by nearly 3 to 1 in the quantity of output of engineers.

*May 13, 1965.* Education is at the very core of the Communist system.

The reappraisal of science education within the United States following the sputnik largely contributed to the passage by Congress of the National Defense Education Act of 1958—and to its amendment and extension in 1964 for another three years.

. . . it seems ironic that a Soviet scientific and technical success was required to galvanize public interest in our American schools.

With occasional exceptions in one or two fields, Soviet scientific researchers are as precise, as probing and as curious as any in the world.

On Moscow subways and buses every second or third passenger may be reading a book.

*May 17, 1965.* The Soviet universities train teachers. They also train research scientists "at the theoretical level." There were 33 Soviet universities when I first visited the U.S.S.R. in 1955. Now there are 40. This is almost one new university a year.

Engineers, physicians, agricultural experts, and other professionals are trained in specialized institutes. There are over 700 of these. They also train scholars in basic research. Only about 10 percent of Soviet students in advanced education attend the universities. The rest attend the institutes.

*May 26, 1965.* In the U.S.S.R. education continues to get the intellectual priorities and the budget. Each student is not merely permitted to develop his talent to the fullest. He is pushed and prodded to develop it (provided, of course, that his talent is of the kind that the state values).

In the installment of Ambassador Benton's report, which

appeared in the May 20, 1965 Congressional Record, he discusses the elaborate plans that were being put into effect to utilize television for culture, enlightenment, and education: "This promises to be education at a much more formal and higher level than almost all educational TV in the United States."

Dr. John MacDonald, president of the University of British Columbia, presented a comprehensive view of the Soviet educational system in an article prepared for United Press International,[21] upon his return from a trip of inspection. The following are excerpts:

The most striking thing about Russian education is the enthusiasm with which the people of all walks of life have accepted the idea that education should have the nation's top priority.

Everyone is interested in education in the Soviet Union. In Moscow, 500,000 students are engaged in studies beyond the high school level. At the University of Moscow, 30,000 are studying in the arts and sciences.

A majority are in institutes that specialize: institutes for medicine, for engineering, for law, for foreign languages. Some institutes are very large. The institute of aeronautics, for instance, has an enrollment of 14,000.

The sciences are highly popular, but the humanities do not appear to be neglected. Every student must take courses in history, philosophy, economics and a foreign language. Half of them choose English as their foreign language.

Striking evidence of the interest in education is the reading. There are bookstores everywhere, and invariably they appear to be crowded. The university has 119 bookstalls scattered around the campus.

The huge Lenin Library, one of the world's finest, serves 9,000 readers a day. It increases its book collection by 500,000 volumes a year—comparable to adding the University of British Columbia's entire library each year.

The Lenin Library has eight million volumes in English—a number that exceeds the total collection of the famous Harvard Library.

People in Moscow and Leningrad display an avid interest also in art and history. The galleries and museums are well attended, the superb hermitage galleries in Leningrad are crowded.

Russian students are lavishly supported financially by the state. Residence charges to 9,000 students living at the University of Moscow range from $1.50 to $3.00 a month. The accommodation I inspected was good—a private bathroom for every two students.

Meals are inexpensive, averaging about $1 a day. . .

21 Riverside, Calif. *Daily Enterprise,* November 26, 1964.

The Soviet accomplishment in education to date is impressive.

Dr. Robert Hutchins, the distinguished educator and President of the Center for the Study of Democratic Institutions at Santa Barbara, California, reported on his inspection tour of the Soviet educational system in the *Los Angeles Times,* September 13, 1965, from which the following is excerpted:

One has the impression of 200 million people grimly learning under forced draft. They all seem to be preparing for some examination that will get them a better job. Everything is connected with a better job; the way to rise in the society, and the only way, is to learn.

The great park in Moscow is laid out as an adult education project, in which the earnest Russian, instead of wasting his time in a pleasant stroll on a Sunday afternoon, can learn all about how to operate machinery and grow crops. The same solemnity characterizes Russian television.

Still the Soviet Union is the first learning society of modern times. It may be learning some wrong things in the wrong way, for the wrong purposes. But the learning habit is a good one, and the Russians are forming it on a scale never before attempted. The learning society is the society of the future.

Vice Admiral H. G. Rickover, the chief designer of the nuclear-powered submarine, was a member of Vice President Nixon's party that toured the Soviet Union in 1959. When he visited Novosibirsk, he told the correspondent of United Press International on July 30, 1959, how impressed he was that he had seen under construction a scientific complex that would consist of 35,000 scientific personnel, of whom 2,000 would be scientists and engineers, 4,000 teachers, and the rest staff members. Admiral Rickover's comment was: "We better change our school system and do it fast."

In an article written specially for the Associated Press, Admiral Rickover said, in part:

Russia's real threat to us will come through their educational and not through their military processes. Military systems and techniques are transitory—they now change every few years. An intelligent and well-educated body of citizens is something you will have forever.

This is where the Russians are smarter than we. They have recognized the full value of a good education and are hell-bent on giving it to as many of their youngsters as they can coax into taking it.

This is about the best comparison I can make: Almost half of Russia's children, graduating at 17 after but 10 years of schooling, do as well—by the record—as many of our children after 14 years of schooling, two of them in college.[22]

In 1961, a book was published in this country, entitled *What Ivan Knows That Johnny Doesn't*. It created something of a sensation in American educational circles. Written by Dr. Arthur S. Trace, Jr., professor of English and member of the Institute for Soviet and East European Studies at John Carroll University in Cleveland, it was the first comprehensive attempt to compare the non-science subject content of school curricula. These are some of the findings of the research done by Professor Trace:

1. That fourth-grade Russian children successfully use books with a vocabulary of approximately 10,000 words. American children in the same grade are using so-called "basic readers" with a vocabulary of less than 1,800 words.

2. That American schools lag seriously behind Soviet schools, not only in mathematics and science, but also in reading, literature, history, and geography.

3. That contrary to the notion that Soviet education is weighted excessively with the physical sciences and mathematics, fifth-grade Russian students read extensively such literary giants as Pushkin, Tolstoy, Gorky, and Chekhov.

4. A first-grade primer in Russia contains about 130 selections and a vocabulary of about 2,000 words—considerably higher than books used in the fourth grade in American schools.

An interesting sidelight to the image of the Russians as "slaves" of a Communist hierarchy is the experience of Dr. B. F. Skinner, professor of psychology at Harvard University. Professor Skinner invented a machine to speed up the teaching of a variety of subjects. His machine and other machines of similar nature are being adopted in American schools. Upon his return from a tour of Europe in 1962, Professor Skinner reported great interest in his machine and modalities, excepting among Soviet educators. Invariably they would say: "Yes, yes. But what does it do to the individuality of the child?" It

[22] Riverside, Calif. *Press-Enterprise*, August 21, 1960.

would seem that this is hardly consistent with an attempt to encourage a psychology of docility or to indoctrinate with a set of slave ethics!

Our number one super-spy, Mr. Allen W. Dulles, former Director, U.S. Central Intelligence, also took cognizance of Soviet Education, in his Commencement Day address at Columbia University in June of 1965. In spite of his position as number one organizer of Cold War activities and in spite of his penchant for issuing anti-Soviet statements, Dulles recognized the progress of Soviet education as a liberating force, and somewhat churlishly concluded: "In introducing mass education, the troubled Soviet leaders have loosed forces dangerous to themselves." It would seem appropriate to suggest that, unless one assumes that the Soviet leaders are incredibly stupid, their program of educating a whole nation at a "forced draft" pace must be motivated by a desire to make the people masters of their own destiny. Another thought worthy of consideration is that Soviet education is introducing some other freedoms: freedom from superstition, freedom from ignorance, freedom from poverty, freedom from fear, and freedom from drudgery. These conclusions are borne out by the testimony of our next witness.

Dr. Pitirim Sorokin,[23] professor-emeritus and former head of the sociology department at Harvard University, came originally from Russia, where he was a professor under the Czarist regime. He was hostile to the Bolshevik revolution and left the country. For many years he was less than enthusiastic, to put it very mildly, about developments in the Soviet Union. For this reason, and also for the reason that he was considered by many to be the ranking American sociologist, an excellent recent essay is very remarkable for its penetrating analysis and for its forthright statement of the facts about the changing scene in the Soviet Union. The following are some of Professor Sorokin's conclusions:[24]

The policy of a rude force and merciless terror of the Soviet government toward all its Russian opponents has been gradually supplanted by the rule of law.

[23] We deeply regret that Professor Sorokin passed away on February 10, 1968.
[24] *The Annals of American Academy of Political and Social Science,* March, 1967.

The unlimited totalitarian, dictatorial regime of the Soviet government has been increasingly limited in favor of a political, economic, social, and cultural democracy. The rights of individuals, their free pursuit of "life, liberty, and happiness," have been enlarged and progressively secured by the constitution and by the new codes of civil, criminal, and constitutional laws, as well as by increasing implementation of these laws in actual practice and social life. . . . In science, philosophy, religion, ethics, law, literature, music, drama, painting, sports, and other fields of cultural creativity, the Russian nation now occupies a position second to none of the existing nations and peoples.

Of these cultural achievements, special mention should be made of the moral renaissance of the population of the Soviet Union. Utter demoralization of the first phase of the Revolution is now largely overcome and replaced by the "new Communist ethic" defined as "the ethics of solidarity, of unselfish help and support in the struggle for liberation of man from the burden of exploitation and oppression," as the ethics of collective protection of dignity, freedom, and self-realization of the individual as the supreme end-value. These ethics are opposite to that of bourgeois selfish individualism. In their essentials these "new ethics" are a reiteration and modification of the perennial and universal moral principles expounded by all great religions and systems of ethics including the ethics of the Sermon on the Mount and the Beatitudes of Jesus.

These ethics have been increasingly realized during the constructive period of the Revolution, though this realization is, of course, only partial and relative. As a behavioral sign of this realization, we can mention a striking decline of criminality of the Soviet population—its rates of criminality in grave as well as lesser crimes is now one of the very lowest among those of other nations.

. . . In brief, ideologically and behaviorally, today's morality of the Russian nation suggests that, all in all, it is possibly better rather than worse in comparison with the state of most of the nations of the world.

If no world war explodes, there is hardly any doubt that the Soviet Union, still led by the Russian nation, can hopefully look to its future. It has successfully overcome "the abomination of desolation" wrought by the world wars and the civil war, has already become a constructive leader among all nations, and is likely to continue its leadership in the decades, even centuries, to come.

In the *Nation*, 10-30-67, Alexander Werth reports on his latest 2-month visit, during the celebration of fifty years of Soviet existence:

Yes, the Russia of Stalin and the Russia of today are two very different countries. As the Soviet jubilee budget shows, for the first time in the country's history the production of light industry, that is, consumer goods, will exceed that of heavy industry. Also, there have been sensational gains in this year of celebration in wages, pensions and hours of work. If it goes on like this, without a major war, Soviet Russia should be a remarkable country indeed on its sixtieth birthday.

Dr. Milton J. E. Senn, director of the Yale University Child Study Center, made a trip to the Soviet Union to study Russian methods of rearing and educating children. Together with Ernest Haveman, a veteran newspaper reporter, magazine writer, and photographer, Dr. Senn visited Moscow, Leningrad, Kiev, and rural areas of Russia. They visited hospitals, clinics, churches, nurseries, schools, and institutes of higher education. In addition, they interviewed teachers, administrators, and scientists. They also took great pains to observe children under conditions which no one could possibly prearrange. He tells of his experiences in the October 1958 issue of *McCall's* magazine. We find this remark of his very pathetic: "I went to Russia expecting the worst. What I found surprised and fascinated me."

Dr. Senn observes that the Russian children "seem to fear no one," that the boys and girls play in the parks much like American children. Dr. Senn was very much impressed by the government's network of nurseries, kindergartens, and children's homes—quite unlike anything he had seen in the U.S.A. Describing an orphan home that he visited, he tells us that there were 110 children living there. To his utter astonishment, Dr. Senn discovered that the staff of nurses, nurses' aides, physicians, and attendants consisted of 98 people! The staff of physicians—each one working a six hour shift—is available around the clock.

Dr. Senn describes the Russian children in this manner:

They are good-humored, easygoing, carefree and friendly. Yet they are remarkably well behaved. They are not given to yelling, fighting or breaking things. They play together in notable harmony, even when there is a considerable disparity in their ages. They never seem to whine; they cry only when they hurt themselves, and then only briefly. They are warm, spontaneous, polite and it is impossible, from one's hiding place on the park bench, to keep from falling in love with them.

Perhaps the reader will now understand why we made the

remark about finding Dr. Senn's attitude pathetic—his going to Russia "expecting the worst." And now it comes out that he essayed the role of a Sherlock Holmes, in order to find out the truth about bringing up and educating children in the U.S.S.R. Such is the prejudice generated in this country against a country with advanced ideas in education, pediatrics, and public health programs!

## Perplexities of the News

It may very well be asked how we can reconcile the charge of consistent and persistent lying about the Soviet Union with the fact that we were able to quote so many favorable reports about life in the Soviet Union. The answer is twofold:

1. Many reports, such as those of Senator Ellender, Dr. Derthick, and Ambassador Benton, get little or no publicity. Only a handful of people know about these reports. One can safely state that less than 1% of the American adults have ever heard of Senator Ellender's reports.

2. Every favorable report published by the media of communication is drowned out by a hundred or more lying reports, fabricated stories, distortions of the truth, and sneering editorials. The result is that an *image* has been created, which is completely misleading and which provides the rationale for provoking a third world war. Aside from the fact that truth is an attribute that should be cherished for its own sake, it is of the utmost urgency that the truth—the whole truth—be made known about the conditions of life in the Soviet Union. Experience has shown that most people are not ready to accept the truth while their minds are clouded by prejudice and untruth. For these reasons we consider it necessary to present more illustrations of mendaciousness in news reporting about the Soviet Union.

On September 28, 1961 the Riverside, California *Daily Enterprise* carried this U.P.I. dispatch from Washington on the front page of its *first* section:

Eighteen Soviet technicians have been arrested in Guinea for stealing diamonds from Guinea mines, a high administration official said last night.

The official said the technicians were showing Guineans how to mine diamonds with one hand and taking the gems with another.

On September 30, the *Daily Enterprise* carried an A.P. dispatch from Conakry, Guinea. This time the dispatch was carried on the front page of the *second* section:

The Guinea Mines Ministry denied Friday reports that 18 Soviet technicians have been jailed in Guinea for taking diamonds they were supposed to be mining for the Guineans. Western diplomatic sources also said the reports were without foundation.

The first story, on the front page of the *first* section, carried this headline:

GUINEA JAILS 18 REDS FOR DIAMOND THEFTS

The second story, on the front page of the *second* section, two days later, carried this headline:

SOVIETS CLEARED

Which story left the lasting impression?

On August 6, 1962 The *Los Angeles Times* carried on its front page an exclusive Reuters dispatch, with this headline:

500 REPORTED
SLAIN IN SOVIET
FOOD RIOTING

This food riot never happened, as proven by the fact that no confirmation for the yarn could be found anywhere. Furthermore, people do not riot during a period when wages are rising and food prices are being lowered. Any person with a slight knowledge of journalistic techniques can recognize the phoney nature of the dispatch and can see that it is strictly a "think piece." With a typewriter, and a bottle of gin to drown out moral scruples, any journalist in need of a sensational story to file can concoct such a story. It quotes a *London newspaper,* which, in turn, had quoted "reports reaching Helsinki" from an unnamed source that 500 Russians were killed in this alleged riot near Rostov-on-Don. In the second paragraph the newspaper is identified as the *Daily Express* and we are told the alleged riot "took place at Novocherkask." While the two cities are close to each other, in 1962 Rostov-on-Don had a population of 500,000 and Novocherkask had a population of 81,286. Both cities are close to huge agricultural areas and would hardly be plagued with excessive food prices.

Congressman John M. Ashbrook, probably the most vociferous member of the House Un-American Activities Committee, seldom passes up an opportunity to spread a tall story about the Communists in general and the Soviet Union in particular. In the light of the reports about the steady and significant improvements in living standards in the Soviet Union—reports made by reputable observers—one can only wonder at the brazenness of Congressman Ashbrook's speech, reported in the Congressional Record, June 29, 1967, in which he said:

Any responsible person longs for true world peace. But all prudent people recognize that for the past 50 years there has been festering among the nations of the world a cancerous international growth which has spread havoc over a large portion of the globe.

The Congressman can get away with this loaded and irresponsible statement only because people have been conditioned to refrain from challenging such untruths, for fear of being branded Communist or subversive. Such statements furnish ammunition for innumerable Right-Wing groups who quote it as coming "from the Congressional Record."

For years it has been a pastime for editors, columnists, and orators to sneer at the fact that approximately 98% of the eligible voters turn out on election day in the Soviet Union to cast their ballots. The critics usually find something sinister in the heavy turnout and offer it as proof that the Soviet people are driven like cattle by their masters. This is, of course, pure speculation and is known in the realm of logic as the non-sequitur, the oldest of logical fallacies. In the *United States News & World Report,* November 17, 1960, there is a full-page advertisement of the Metropolitan Life Insurance Co., urging people to vote. It gives the following percentages of voters who exercised that right in the previous election:

| | |
|---|---|
| Australia | 95.48% |
| West Germany | 88.2% |
| Israel | 82.8% |
| Canada | 80% |
| Great Britain | 78.7% |
| Sweden | 77.4% |
| United States | 60.4% |

Nowhere could we find any denunciation of Australia or any other country for the much higher turnout of voters than in the U.S.A. Nowhere did we find any "think pieces" on this subject by the carping critics.

In the *Santa Ana Register,* June 13, 1967, we find a dispatch from New York by Fred Sparks of NEA (Newspaper Enterprise Association). He tells us:

The Soviet high command has updated and is prepared to put into effect—in the event of emergency—Nikita Khrushchev's four-year-old plan to destroy Peking's nuclear capacity and missile sites.

Further on, Sparks says "let's call it 'Operation Khrushchev,'" and he says:

During my recent assignments in Moscow I heard Russians, on all levels, mention Khrushchev's foresight. And I was told about Operation Khrushchev by seasoned Western diplomats.

Here you have the classic example of a synthetic story made up out of nothing. There is nothing unusual or sinister about Russian citizens talking about Khrushchev's foresight. On the contrary, it would seem to indicate a high degree of freedom of expression and absence of fear. The other ingredient in Mr. Spark's story—the information from "seasoned Western diplomats"—could mean some barroom habitués, Central Intelligence Agency Operatives, professional tipsters, or a figment of Mr. Spark's imagination. In any case, it serves only the purpose of heating up the Cold War and adds to the confused picture Americans already possess of the Soviet Union.

Dr. Melvin Munn is a dentist, turned radio commentator for the network program of the Life Line Foundation, a Right-Wing propaganda project operated by oil tycoon H. L. Hunt of Dallas, Texas. About a quarter of his programs are devoted to homilies which suggest that any attempt to change the status quo is the work of Satan, that capitalism is an integral part of Christian doctrine, and that the Soviet Union is the incarnation of evil. His repeated quoting of Scripture and his continual preaching of the eternal verities hardly prepare one for this distortion of the truth, which was a part of his radiocast on June 21, 1967:

A number of people with whom we have talked after they had visited Communist countries have remarked how expressionless the faces of people on the streets seemed to be. They very rarely smiled or showed any sign of pleasure or humor. They seemed to go stolidly about their affairs—their actions saying eloquently that they do not have a happy life.

If Dr. Melvin Munn did not manufacture this yarn, if he did indeed talk to some people who told him some cock-and-bull stories, Dr. Munn is in a position to ascertain the truth. Surely he has seen some television programs which have shown Soviet people in all walks of life, and he knows better than to repeat such twaddle. Accordingly, we propose to do some preaching to preacher Munn, coming directly to the point:

> Thou Shalt Not Bear False Witness
> Against Thy Neighbor!

*National Review,* edited by the millionaire, William F. Buckley, Jr., carried an article in its issue of June 13, 1967, which presented a picture of life in the Soviet Union that could only be pleasing to William F. Buckley, Jr. It is written by a Mr. Edward Diedrich, who is identified as one who made a recent visit to the Soviet Union and "has been in the radio broadcasting business, and likes to move quietly in New York as in Moscow."

Mr. Diedrich describes life in the Soviet Union in terms that are quite original and that are contradicted by hundreds of reputable and scholarly observers and trained reporters. He claims that when he arrived at the Leningrad Airport, the customs official who examined his baggage called him aside and asked: "Is there anything in it that you would like to sell?" Next he tells us that people roam Gorky Street trying to buy anything a tourist has for sale. He goes on to state that food is also in short supply. He bemoans the fate of the Russians, who, he avers, are deprived of their essential human dignity because of the housing shortage. Somehow Mr. Diedrich forgets to mention the huge construction program for new homes and apartments that is being carried forward at a fantastic pace in every principal city of the country. Every honest observer has noted this, and one can only wonder if Mr. Diedrich really visited the U.S.S.R. And, when one talks of a housing shortage in the Soviet Union, does not elementary honesty require that

307

one point out the devastation and destruction caused by the Nazi invasion? Diedrich claims that tourists who patronize the Intourist restaurants receive slow service because the waiters and cooks have to fill out so many government forms. Whereas hundreds of scholars have heaped lavish praise on the famous Lenin Public Library in Moscow, Diedrich complains that he he had to fill out some forms in order to use the reading room. Whether this is true or not, perhaps Diedrich will feel better if he is told that this writer has had to fill out forms and obtain an admission card in order to use the facilities of several university research libraries in this country. Another story Diedrich tells is that the Lenin Library files books by physical size instead of by subject matter and that sometimes one has to wait three to four hours for a book.[25] Inasmuch as a library that did not index and file books by subject matter and by name of author could not possibly function as a public library, Diedrich's story must be rejected out of hand as a flight of fantasy. As for waiting sometimes three to four hours for a book, the key word here is "sometimes." It could be once a month or once a year and still be "sometimes." This writer has experienced some inordinate delays at times in libraries in various cities across the country, but never thought of complaining to the Russians about slow service in libraries of the U.S.A.

After an intensive investigation, we came to the conclusion that *National Review* had misled its readers when it described Diedrich as one who "has been in the radio broadcasting business, and likes to move quietly in New York and Moscow." Letters to radio and television editors, to the industry publications, to unions of the industry, and to broadcasting networks brought the uniform reply: no one had heard of Edward Diedrich. Finally, after a 4-month delay, we received a letter from Diedrich, dated December 17, 1967, from which we quote, and we leave it up to the reader to decide how much credence to place in Diedrich's report or in *National Review:*

To answer your query, I would be willing to answer any questions you may have on my *National Review* article. There will, however, be certain limitations to this. Some of the information

---

[25] Contrast this claim with Dr. MacDonald's report that the Lenin Library serves 9,000 patrons each day and has over 8 million volumes in English alone.

that I obtained in Russia came from correspondents who would like to remain anonymous. For obvious reasons I also cannot mention any names or addresses having to do with the "New People" referred to in my article.

There is one other point that I would like to clear up. *National Review* described me as being in the "radio broadcasting business," and while this was technically true, I'm afraid that this has misled a good many people including yourself. Actually, I did work for CBS for a period of four years, but my work there had nothing to do with radio broadcasting, and I was never a part of the CBS news staff. When I went to Russia, it was as a tourist.

*Look* magazine of May 22, 1962, which stated on its front cover that its circulation exceeds 7 million copies per issue, had also on its front cover a picture of the head of Lenin. Superimposed on one half of his face is a fire-engine-red coloring, which makes Lenin look like a grotesque monster. Along with this trick photography, we are treated to this blurb:

> The chilling story
> behind the man who
> created the
> Communist threat
> to our world
> LENIN
> A new
> pictorial history
> complete
> in this issue.

The authors are Richard Harrity and Ralph G. Martin, who subsequently "did a job" on Khrushchev in *Look* of November 19, 1963, with which we will deal a little later.

Turning to page 33, we find a faithful photograph of Lenin, which shows his head and his body to a point a little below the shoulders. This occupies the upper half of the page. With a white horizontal line across the middle of the page, the lower half shows 28 black airplanes, in battle formation, deployed in fire-engine-red clouds. In large white letters, positioned half on Lenin and half on the red clouds, we are asked:

> Who was
> this man
> who put
> a red star
> in the sky?

309

On page 34, we are shown the takeoff scene of a rocket. This occupies the right half of the page, from top to bottom. To the left it shows Khrushchev addressing a session of the United Nations; and a likeness of Lenin's head is superimposed on the upper section of the background. Towards the lower portion of this side of the page, we are asked, in fire-engine-red letters:

Who was this man . . . who created an empire so strong and so powerful that it now threatens to destroy the world?

On page 35 there is a picture of Lenin on a podium, in a posture suggesting that he is addressing a mass meeting. At the top of the page, partly resting on Lenin's fur hat, we find in fire-engine-red, in letters one-inch tall:

## LENIN

Just below the position where his hand rests on a lectern, the following is placed in white letters on the front surface of the lectern:

> The true story of
> the evil genius who launched
> the Global Red threat

Below this picture, the story by the authors begins in a space about three inches wide. The very second sentence is a lie which *Look* would not dare print if it thought it might be subject to a libel suit. It reads: "He was a master terrorist who marched to supremacy over the bodies of thousands of his countrymen." To the right of this opening portion of the article there is a fire-engine-red section, $6\frac{1}{4}$ inches wide and $3\frac{1}{4}$ inches high. In black letters against this red background we are treated to "Lenin's Ten Commandments of Revolution." On May 22, 1962, we sent the following letter to the editor of *Look:*

Your tendentious article on Lenin in your issue of May 22, 1962 is something you need not be proud to have produced.

I challenge you to prove the accuracy and veracity of "Lenin's Ten Commandments of Revolution." Every single one of these is a fraud, a deception perpetrated on your readers. Some of these alleged quotations from Lenin were never uttered or written by Lenin; others are mutilations by lifting out of context.

The only purpose served by this hate-piece is to heat up the Cold War.

I don't think you have the "guts" to publish this letter.

*Look's* silence after we sent this letter was deafening! It neither published the letter nor sent an individual reply.

There are sixteen more pages of this sorry performance, with more dubious quotations and more torturing of historical truth. Shrewd writers are aware of the fact that there is a ready and lucrative market for anti-Soviet and anti-Communist slanders, and they know that they are practically immune from libel suits in the present climate of opinion. And no matter what they write and no matter what they fabricate, they are sure of little or no effective challenge. So, we conclude by saying that *Look* did indeed take a "look" at Lenin! And *Look's* 25 million readers were given a huge dose of deception.

Ofttimes, when the Cold Warriors of the typewriter run out of phoney quotations and fairy tales, they find that sneers and jeers can also be the source of a fast buck. Thus for a long time, columnists and editors were solemnly assuring their readers "from confidential sources" that the Russians were not giving us as much information about their exploits in space exploration as we were giving them. With an air of injured innocence, hundreds of these stories were spread through our media of communications. Finally, the balloon was punctured by the world-renowned astrophysicist, Dr. James Van Allen, whom the scientific community has honored for his discovery of what is now known as the Van Allen radiation belt in outer space. In testimony before the House Appropriations Committee, which was released for publication on May 14, 1961, Dr. Van Allen defended the amount of scientific information released by the Soviets on their space shots. He told the Committee: "I feel that the common statement that the Russians do not tell us the results of their scientific work is really plain wrong." Of course, what should be added to Dr. Van Allen's statement is the explanation of the origin of the erroneous "common statements."

The difficulty the American people experience, in getting the truth about Soviet developments, is exemplified by the following sequence of events:

1. *July 1957*. The press carried stories from "authoritative sources" that the Soviet Union was far behind the U.S.A. in rocket and missile developments.

2. *August 1957*. Soviet space scientists announced that they

had developed a powerful intercontinental ballistics rocket and missile. The announcement was met with derision in Washington and in the press.

3. *October 4, 1957.* The Soviet Union launched Sputnik I, the first earth satellite in history.

4. *November 1, 1957.* The *U.S. News & World Report* intoned: "Facts show that U.S. is actually taking the lead now in big missiles, despite Russian boasts."

5. *November 4, 1957.* The Soviet Union launched Sputnik II, with a larger payload than Sputnik I and with a rocket motor so powerful that scientists the world over acclaimed it as "fantastic."

6. *November 8, 1957. The U.S. News & World Report* trotted out a Dr. S. F. Singer, whom it characterized as "one of the world's leading authorities on space vehicles," who said that the U.S. had had a space vehicle ready for quite some time and could send it up any day.

7. *December 1957.* The U.S. attempted to launch a satellite, which was labeled "Vanguard." It blew up. The *London Daily Herald* called it "The Flopnik."

8. *December 2, 1957.* The former top rocket expert in the Nazi military machine, now securely ensconced as the top missile expert for the U.S.A., Dr. Wernher Von Braun, gave an interview to United Press. From the time of the launching of Sputnik I, the typewriter generals of the Cold War had been solemnly assuring the American people that the dumb Russians could not possibly have developed a space technology of their own. The explanation that was repeated over and over again by editors, columnists, commentators, political orators, and assorted tub thumpers was that the Russians captured some top Nazi scientists who developed space technology for them. Leading the procession of enlightenment in this matter was former President Harry Truman, who churlishly commented on Sputnik I that he wouldn't believe the reports until more proof was adduced. In the interview, Dr. Von Braun stated that "the Russians had made foolish use of the German specialists they had captured." Furthermore, stated Dr. Von Braun, the German rocket men were kept "isolated from the real Soviet rocket program" and the truth is that "they obviously did not even know such a program existed."

9. *January 1958.* Despite the disclosures in the Von Braun

312

interview a month earlier, *Look* magazine carried a highly sensational article in which it claimed that the U.S.A. gave the *secrets* of rocket-building to the Soviet Union when we allowed it to capture some German rocket experts! (It was similar mythology that formed the basis for the lie that the Soviet Union had stolen the "secret" of the atomic bomb and which resulted in sending innocent people to the electric chair. Proof of this charge will be presented in volume II.)

10. *December 29, 1957.* Unfortunate for *Look's* masterpiece of rocket intelligence, about the time that this January 1958 issue was arriving on the news stands the Associated Press released a long dispatch from Frankfurt, Germany by Reinhold Ensz.[26] It tells of an interview with three German rocket experts, who had worked in the Soviet Union after being captured by the Russians. Mr. Ensz says, in part:

They paint a picture of German scientists playing a kind of blind man's buff because the Russians evidently didn't trust their unwilling collaboration too far.

One individual research station staffed by Germans didn't know exactly what the others were doing, the scientists said. Then, in 1951, the Russians barred virtually all German scientists from work on secret rocket projects altogether.

Since 1952, when most of the Germans were released and sent home, the Russians obviously made major strides on their own, the three experts said.

11. *July 1967.* The American Security Council,[27] a membership organization of some 4000 corporations, which we consider to be the spearhead of the Cold War drive, issued a report entitled "The Changing Strategic Military Balance: U.S.A. vs. U.S.S.R." On page 24 is a chart entitled "Soviet Space Firsts."

These are the "Soviet Firsts," as listed in the report, but which we present in paraphrased, non-technical language:

1. *Oct. 4, 1957.* First earth satellite (Sputnik I).
2. *Nov. 3, 1957.* First satellite with live animal.
3. *Jan. 2, 1959.* First satellite placed in solar orbit.
4. *Sept. 12, 1959.* First satellite to reach the moon.

26 Riverside, Calif. *Press-Enterprise,* December 29, 1957.
27 Not to be confused with the National Security Council of the U.S. Government or the Security Council of the United Nations.

5. *April 12, 1961.* First human being to travel in outer space (Yuri Gagarin).

6. *August 11-12, 1962.* First manned flight with two space vehicles "in tandem."

7. *Nov. 1, 1962.* First satellite to probe the planet Mars.

8. *October 12, 1964.* First 3-man space flight.

9. *March 18, 1965.* First astronaut to step out into space (Leonov).

The report omitted two very important Soviet space achievements. On June 19, 1963, Valentina Tereshkova, a 26-year-old blonde Russian woman returned to earth, after completing 48 orbits for a distance of 1.2 million miles in 70 hours and 50 minutes—the first woman astronaut to travel in space, and so far the only one. On March 1, 1966, a Soviet spacecraft became the first man-made object to reach another planet. After a voyage of 105 days, traveling millions of miles, the Soviet Union landed a 1-ton spacecraft on Venus in another major "space first." And since the American Security Council report was issued, the Soviet Union, in September 1968, achieved another technical triumph by being the first to get back to earth safely a spaceship that had circled around the moon.

There is another achievement of Soviet space technology which the journalistic pundits seem to soft-pedal. Soviet astronauts all descend safely on the ocean or *on land*, without ballyhoo or fanfare. U.S.A. astronauts all descend *on the ocean only*, and each landing is serviced by an armada of naval vessels and helicopters, accompanied by tremendous publicity and anxiety. Obviously, Soviet space technology has solved some problems that still await solution in this country. Our astronauts cannot yet descend safely on land.

Is it not time that the nonsense, about Germans having developed Soviet astronautical science, be abandoned? Is it not patently clear that Soviet astronautics made its greatest advances *after* the German specialists were sent home? And is it not equally clear that at no time did the Germans make any significant contributions to Soviet space technology?

The Cold Warriors of the typewriter have come up more recently with a most ingenious, albeit equally disingenuous, explanation for Soviet superiority in astronautics. They explain it on the basis that the Soviet Union considers human lives

314

more expendable than does the U.S.A., and consequently it advances more rapidly by paying with lives lost in daring experiments. A U.P.I. dispatch from Washington on July 23, 1965[28] points out:

1.  That the C.I.A. has never been able to authenticate the tales that were spread about dead Russians circling the earth in spacecraft that went astray.
2.  That some of these stories may possibly have been deliberate spoofs broadcast by a clandestine station somewhere.
3.  That one U.S. official said that "as far as I know this government has never caught Russia in a flat lie about a space launch."

Perhaps the best answer to the hoax story about alleged wanton disregard for human lives is a statement by Alexei Leonov, the first astronaut to walk in outer space. In an interview given to Associated Press in Sofia, Bulgaria,[29] Leonov pointed out that, when American astronaut Edward H. White stepped into space, he passed directly from the capsule into the vacuum of space. When Soviet astronauts step into space, they first enter a sealed airlock, which is made possible by a lock-gate system that is isolated from the ship's cabin. "Why should the tremendous vacuum at the moment of exit be felt by the whole crew?" Leonov asked. This additional safety factor that is built into Soviet space ships is obviously more costly and involves some intricate design engineering. Above all, it adds to the total weight of the space ship, and this additional weight is acceptable to the design engineers because of the superior lifting powers of Soviet rocket engines.

It took an accident, with the tragic loss of the lives of three American astronauts, to finally establish the truth about the relative safety factors of space ships. On January 27, 1967, a flash fire snuffed out the lives of three American astronauts in an Apollo space ship that was about to be launched. Subsequently it was shown that Russian space ships are safer in this respect than American space ships, because U.S.A. craft were using an all-oxygen atmosphere while the Russian craft were using an oxygen-nitrogen system. The equipment for providing the all-oxygen atmosphere is simpler, lighter, and

28 *Los Angeles Times,* July 23, 1965.
29 *Los Angeles Times,* June 7, 1965.

cheaper than the equipment necessary to provide the oxygen-nitrogen atmosphere. It was also charged that American space authorities had pushed ahead with the Apollo program despite the fact that inspectors from the National Aeronautics and Space Administration had found defects in factory tests of the craft.

The utter absurdity of the fairy tales about undisclosed accidents in Soviet space ventures is apparent when one considers these facts:

1. Every Soviet rocket launching is thoroughly monitored by tracking stations of the U.S.A., Great Britain, France, and other countries, as well as by U-2 spy planes and American spy satellites.

2. These tracking stations are equipped with sophisticated devices that record every detail of a Soviet rocket's activity from launching to landing.

3. No accident could possibly escape detection by these monitoring stations.

4. Since each launching of a rocket involves hundreds of specialists, all of whom have relatives and friends, it would be next to impossible to keep secret any serious accident.

5. Recently, when a Soviet astronaut did meet with an accident which was fatal, it was promptly disclosed.

Is it not time that the purveyors of the falsehood about Soviet disregard for human lives explain how they can square that story with the facts we have given here?

The perplexity of sifting out fact from fiction in the news about the Soviet Union did not prevent one prominent American from discerning the truth:

Who will gainsay that most of the Russian people are not better off today than they've ever been before? And to what must the credit be given? The system they've been working for, of course.

Those words were spoken in the course of a speech to the 10th Annual Junior College World Affairs Day, held in Los Angeles on May 14, 1966. The speaker was General David M. Shoup, retired Commandant of the U.S. Marine Corps.[30]

Christian Freedom Foundation is an Ultra Right-Wing

30 Congressional Record, February 20, 1967, page S2280.

propaganda machine, headed by Dr. Howard Kershner and financed principally by oil tycoon J. Howard Pew. Operating behind a facade of religion, it sends its monthly magazine, *Christian Economics*, to most of the clergymen in the country, without charge. Dr. Kershner and associates present a philosophy which makes a reactionary capitalist out of Christ, makes Capitalism a system ordained by God, and makes the war in Vietnam and any anti-Communist war the will of God. Therefore, it is no surprise to read the following collection of outright lies in a front-page article by Lawrence Sullivan in the August 1, 1967 issue:

Communists are always hungry. And Russia has less housing per capita today than at the time of the Red Revolution in November 1917. Poverty, hunger, and dirt are the universal legacy of communism. No nation proves the exception.

The point that we wish to emphasize again and again is that the central problem confronting humanity today is to avoid a third world war, which could annihilate the human species. The catchy slogan—"Better Dead than Red"—can only be acceptable to irrational persons and/or political desperadoes. It requires only the intellectual and emotional level of a ten-year-old child to realize that whatever aspirations a person, a group, or a nation may have, nothing can be accomplished by dead people. Consequently, the first and foremost task is to keep the human species alive! Only then can we begin to cope with whatever problems confront us. And a corollary to this position is that the hate campaign against the Soviet Union and the other Communist countries must be combatted by people of goodwill. It is not a question of approval or disapproval of these countries and their social systems. It is a question of the survival of the human race. There is no alternative: we must either practice peaceful coexistence or there will be no existence for anyone. Any other proposal is a chimera, a delusion. Sane people must choose a program that is not predestined to failure.

# CHAPTER V

## China Disappears

### The Great Prestidigitators

Since the Communists came into power in China in 1949, the Cold Warriors of the State Department of the U.S.A. have had the problem of making China disappear, of pretending that it doesn't exist, and of persuading the American people that it doesn't exist. The problem that was (and still is) so vexatious to the State Department is best expressed in this ditty:

> Last night I saw upon the stair,
> A little man who wasn't there.
> He wasn't there again today;
> Oh, how I wish he'd go away.

The problem was to take a rump government, that exercised an iron-clad military dictatorship over some 10,000,000 people on an island of 13,886 square miles, and claim that it had superseded a government that had under its jurisdiction some 650,000,000 people—one-fourth of the human race and occupying 2,279,134 square miles of territory.[1] In the entire history of legerdemain, it is doubtful that any prestidigitator ever attempted a feat of such fantastic proportions.

After the Chinese people drove Generalissimo Chiang Kai-shek and his corrupt cabal from the mainland of China, he set up a military dictatorship on the island of Taiwan (Formosa) with the help of American bayonets. He has remained in power ever since, mainly because of American economic and military assistance and because of the protection of one of the most formidable armadas in history—the U.S. Seventh Fleet and its complement of thermonuclear-armed units of the U.S. Strategic Air Command.

[1] The population figures are for 1949. By 1966, the estimated populations were 12,819,000 and 773,119,000, respectively.

318

The first element in the State Department's feat of magic was to call the rump regime of Chiang Kai-shek the "Republic of China," causing people to confuse it with the real government of China, the People's Republic of China which has one-fourth of the human race under its jurisdiction. It will, of course, be argued that the State Department must call Chiang's rump regime by whatever name he chose for it. This argument overlooks the fact that Chiang is our puppet and dances to the tune of the financial, political, and military support that we give him.

The second trick was to persistently refer to the capital city of mainland China as Peiping instead of its correct name of *Peking*. Under the ancient Ming Dynasty, the capital city was called Peiping. In 1420, the name was changed to *Peking*. In 1928, while he was still the ruler of mainland China, Chiang restored the ancient name of Peiping. In 1949, when the Communists came into power, they changed the name of the capital city back to *Peking*. In every country of the world, with one exception, the government and the media of communication refer to *Peking* as the capital city of mainland China. That one exception is the United States of America, which persists in using *Peiping* as a means of bolstering the ridiculous myth that Chiang Kai-shek is the legal head of mainland China. This Cold War ploy has made us look silly in the eyes of informed people everywhere. It makes as much sense as if some living descendant of Peter Stuyvesant were to persist in calling New York by its original name of New Amsterdam, as a protest against the British stealing of New Amsterdam from the Dutch in 1664 and as a means of asserting the Dutch claim to the city. In 1962, the *New York Times* decided to end the comedy and adopted a policy of referring to *Peking* in all its stories. Most of the reputable newspapers and the Associated Press followed the lead of the *Times,* but not the State Department and its propaganda agency, the Voice of America.

The third item in the State Department's bag of tricks has been the keeping of the *Peking* regime—representing one-fourth of the human race—out of the United Nations under the phoney charge of aggressor. Not only does Chiang's rump regime "represent" China in the United Nations, but it also occupies one of the five permanent seats on the Security Council of that body. Thus does our State Department, in its blind hatred of the Chinese Communists, make a mockery of the United Nations and of international law. For it is obvious that, if world peace is to be preserved, one cannot exclude from the councils of deliberation a fourth of the human race.

The fifth trick in the "disappearing" act was to erect an "Iron Curtain" around mainland China, thus preventing the American people, and especially journalists and scholars, from learning the truth about the spectacular advances made in China since 1949. While shouting loudly about an alleged "Bamboo Curtain," the State Department has maintained its own "Iron Curtain" around China by keeping *A Curtain of Ignorance*[2] around the American people.

## The Aggression Hoax

By far the most effective of the tricks used to make China "go away" has been the steady barrage maintained by the "Plain Liars, Fancy Liars, and Damned Liars." The basic lie, which was launched by the late Senator Joseph McCarthy, was that "we" had "lost" China because of Communists who had allegedly infiltrated the State Department. This theme was repeated so often and by so many molders of public opinion that the sheer lunacy of it was overlooked, viz: that China was never ours to lose! The Right-Wing yarn, that aims at explaining the Communist defeat of Chiang Kai-shek and the Communist acquisition of political power in China, has been effectively demolished by Jack Belden in his monumental book, *China Shakes the World,* and also by Felix Greene in his excellent book, *A Curtain of Ignorance.* Even some Right-Wingers have begun to shy away from this nonsense, among whom is William F. Buckley, Jr. In his syndicated column,[3] Buckley refers to "the general corruption that was greatly responsible in bringing down into ineffectuality the government of Chiang Kai-shek after the Second World War, and then led to universal contempt for his leadership." A considerable portion of the Right-Wing camp, however, still purveys the McCarthyite myth in an endless stream of books, pamphlets, tracts, speeches, film productions, and tape recordings.

[2] This is the title of a book by Felix Greene, which we strongly urge everyone to read.

[3] *Los Angeles Times,* April 6, 1966.

The second big lie in the State Department's "holy crusade" against Communist China was getting it labeled as an aggressor. This started at the time China sent troops into North Korea, when American armed forces were getting too close for comfort to the Chinese border. This happened after China had warned the U.S.A. not to go beyond the 38th Parallel. After the Chinese forces pushed back across the 38th Parallel the so-called United Nations forces (in reality United States forces under MacArthur), the State Department forced a resolution through the United Nations General Assembly branding China as an aggressor. Actually, the Chinese Government had acted as any prudent government would have acted under comparable conditions. The charge of Chinese "aggression" was aptly disposed of by Robert Vaughn, the star of the television series, "Man From U.N.C.L.E." In a speech at Portland, Oregon on May 8, 1966, he said, in this respect:

China has not one soldier outside her boundaries. Hanoi has had a Communist Government for a dozen years and China has not taken over. The Burma and India confrontations with China were border disputes based on British colonial maps delineating frontiers. Chiang Kai-shek openly supported Peking in the border dispute with India and he also supported the Chinese occupation of Tibet. When Chiang was ruler of China he talked of Tibet as part of China. The Rand Corporation[4] study entitled "China Crosses the Yalu" defends China's entry into the Korean War as a "rationally motivated" defense of its power plants which fed electricity to the Chinese factories in Manchuria. Thus the record shows no "aggression" of any kind by the Chinese to date.

## Mao's Expendable Millions

The Chinese Communist leader, Mao Tse-tung, has been quoted in thousands of articles, columns, editorials, speeches, radiocasts, telecasts, and sermons from the pulpit, as saying:

What does it matter if three-quarters of the world is destroyed, if the remaining one-quarter is Communist?

With variations, additions, and embellishments, this story has been told to prove that Mao Tse-tung would welcome a ther-

---

4 The Rand Corporation is a research institute largely dependent upon Defense Department grants for its existence.

monuclear war and that he is an unspeakable monster who threatens the peace of the world.

In tracing the evolution of this story, Felix Greene makes a very significant observation:

A thorough search through the Chinese press has not revealed any speech or comment of this kind by any Chinese leader. Its origin? A comment by Marshal Tito of Yugoslavia in 1958 at a time when Belgrade and Peking were engaged in verbal assaults against each other. Of several Western Correspondents present at the time, only one apparently thought Tito's remark sufficiently interesting to report. But it was quickly seized upon and disseminated. The original remark was embroidered and enlarged.[5]

On June 16, 1958, *The New York Times* reported:

Without mentioning names or places Marshall Tito said the Chinese liked to boast that their population of 600,000,000 was a guarantee of victory in war. According to President Tito, Peiping calculated that "if 300,000,000 were killed there would still remain 300,000,000 Chinese."

It should be noted that the *Times* was still calling the capital city *Peiping* instead of *Peking*. Most important, however, is the fact that Mao's name does not appear in this initial story about the expendable millions.

On the next day, June 17, 1958, the *New York Times* ran an editorial solemnly advising its readers that the *Times* knew about the bloody past history of how the Chinese Communists achieved political power, but that no one was prepared for such callous disregard of human lives as Tito's revelation that they would consider 300,000,000 lives of little consequence. Nowhere did the *Times* mention about our bloody conquest of the Indian tribes and nowhere did the *Times* mention about our bloody Revolutionary War and our bloody Civil War.

Eleven days later, on July 28, 1958, Joseph Lash wrote in the New York *Post:*

At the Communist "summit" meeting in Moscow Mao is said to have remarked that another world war might well mean the

---

[5] *A Curtain of Ignorance*, pages XVII-XVIII. In presenting the sequence of events, we acknowledge our indebtedness to Mr. Greene's research, as reflected on pages 213-216 of his book.

death of 1,500,000,000 people, but of the 600,000,000 who would survive half would be Chinese and they would rule the world.

In this strictly "think piece" it should be noted that "Mao is said to have remarked." Who reported Mao's remarks is not made clear. Instead of 300,000,000 getting killed, it is now 1,500,000,000—five times the original figure. This is galloping inflation, with a vengeance! And now a new element is introduced: the Chinese "would rule the world."

Two months later, on September 23, 1958, the editors of the New York *Herald Tribune* got into the "expendable millions" act by writing an authoritative-sounding editorial, in which the reader is informed that the Chinese Communist leaders look with favor on the population increase, because it furnishes manpower for the industrialization program, as well as for cannon fodder. And, the editors opined:

> This new view of the population as a military asset has led the Chinese to boast (as Tito has revealed) that they can win a war even if atomic weapons are used: "Even if 300,000,000 Chinese were killed in an atomic war, there would still remain 300,000,000."

The editorial went on with a number of moral pronouncements on the Chinese Communists, and at no point did the editorial come to grips with the reality that the entire argument is based upon a flimsy rumor that originated in the heat of a political squabble!

One month later, on October 28, 1959, Drew Pearson wrote that Mao "doesn't worry about atomic war because (China) could lose half its population." Ironically enough, some Right-Wing agitators call Pearson a pro-Communist, a crypto-Communist, and even a card-carrying Communist.

On October 17, 1962, the New York *Herald Tribune* shed some editorial tears for "Red China's bleak prospect for 1980." Continuing its deep concern for the Chinese people, the *Herald Tribune* said:

> The plight of people never bothered Mao. He said that in case of nuclear war, Red China would emerge best off in the world. Why? Even if 200 million lives were lost on the mainland, there'd be more people left in China than perhaps the rest of the world combined.

If the reader is not dizzy by now from the involved mathematics of these reports, perhaps Mr. Lucius Beebe's statement in the San Francisco *Chronicle* of January 28, 1963 will produce that effect:

The Chinese Government approves war, agitates for war, and predicates its entire existence on war . . .

The late Mr. Beebe's qualifications to hand out moral preachments to the Communists can be appreciated by reading some of his columns. Thus on July 30, 1961 Beebe wrote:

The happiest day that might be foreseen for the American taxpayer is that on which his miserable representatives in government begin to live in physical fear for their lives and persons and give some consideration to the constituency for whom their contempt is commensurate with their availability to looting.

An American congressman fleeing from a mob of taxpayers while his house burned would be the heartening sight of a lifetime.

An election every four years isn't as effectual as would be the assassination of a legislator every four minutes, because the enemy isn't always in Moscow. He's much nearer home.[6]

On November 19, 1961, Beebe concluded a column with his "solution" of the Cold War:

A 1000-megaton bomb and the means and complete readiness to deliver and detonate it, and not against any "military objectives" either, would seem about the only solution. It's time Americans woke up and it's time Americans became murder-minded, just like everybody else.[7] (The largest known bomb in existence is rated at 65-megatons, and Beebe wanted a 1000-megaton bomb!)

On March 18, 1963, Beebe's column in the San Francisco *Chronicle* was a thinly disguised apologia for the John Birch Society, in which he asserted that the doctrines of the Birchers are just "plain American patriotism." He compared the Birch Society to the early Christian martyrs, and lest anyone have any doubt about his philosophy, Beebe stated that it is his firm belief "that any five persons gathered together for any purpose whatsoever more urgent than a floating crap game are a mob and should be dispersed with fire hoses."

6 Riverside, California *Press-Enterprise.*
7 Riverside, California *Press-Enterprise.*

Assuming even that Mao Tse-tung said what he is credited with saying, the critics in this country had better clean up their own dirty back yards first. For years and years, stories have been carried in all the media about our Defense Department's calculations of 50,000,000, 75,000,000, 100,000,000, and other estimates of American deaths in the first 24 hours of a nuclear war. A number of "strategic thinkers," led by Dr. Herman Kahn,[8] have made calculations on whether 50,000,000 deaths or some other figure is an "acceptable" risk to this nation. And Defense Secretary Robert S. McNamara has made speeches and delivered testimony to Congressional Committees along these same lines. This does not seem to evoke a stream of moral strictures from our journalists and commentators.

In carrying our research farther than did Felix Greene, it becomes apparent that in the squabbles between Communist leaders over ideological differences, both Tito and Khrushchev saw fit to exploit and extrapolate on something that Mao Tse-tung said in a speech in Moscow during 1957, a year before Tito was reported to have made that original remark. An Associated Press dispatch from Tokyo[9] quotes the Chinese theoretical journal, *Red Flag,* which gave an answer to the charge that the Peking leaders would welcome a nuclear war. The dispatch summarized the *Red Flag's* 2,000-word article as follows:

Mao, in his then secret speech, said that if war should break out a third of the world's population might be lost, but that "imperialism would be razed and the whole world would become socialist." That did not mean China wanted a nuclear war, only that there was no need to be afraid if the West launched one, the article said.

An earlier dispatch from Tokyo by United Press International[10] quoted an editorial from the official Communist *People's Daily:*

If imperialism dares to unleash an all-out nuclear war, the result can only be the destruction of imperialism while the victorious peoples will build a beautiful future for themselves on the debris of the dead imperialism.

8 Author of "On Thermonuclear War."
9 *Los Angeles Times,* September 10, 1963.
10 Riverside, California *Daily Enterprise,* December 11, 1961.

In one of a series of articles, Simon Malley relates the story of an interview with a Chinese youngster:

Thirteen-year-old Yen Pao-Yu, who said both his parents are high school teachers, quoted Mao in reply to my questions: "Chairman Mao taught us that China wants peace and is against war, but that if war comes, we must not be afraid of it."[11]

The same point of view is expressed in another portion of the editorial previously quoted from the Chinese Communist *People's Daily:*

What is the use of being afraid of nuclear war? Is it conceivable that the enemy would turn benevolent because we are frightened out of our wits? If we take fright we shall be disarmed spiritually, the enemy will become more rabid, and the danger of nuclear war will increase.

Edgar Snow, the author of several books on China and considered one of the ablest and most reliable of the correspondents who have actually traveled extensively in China, interviewed Mao Tse-tung on January 9, 1965. He asked Mao about the 300,000,000 expendable story attributed to him. (It should be borne in mind that, in the report of his 1957 Moscow speech, there is no mention of 300,000,000 expendables.) From Mr. Snow's transcript of the interview,[12] we learn:

He doubts that atomic bombs ever will be used again, and said China does not want a lot of bombs—a few will suffice for scientific experiments. He said he can not recall but may have made the controversial statement attributed to him that China *has less fear* of the bomb than other nations because of her vast population. (Emphasis added—M.K.)

The *New Republic* of February 27, 1965 carried a dispatch from Peking by Mr. Snow, who, incidentally, was formerly a correspondent for *Look* magazine and formerly an associate editor of the *Saturday Evening Post.* In further clarification of his January 9, 1965 interview with Mao, Snow reports about his questioning him on the 300,000,000 expendable story:

11 *Los Angeles Times,* May 22, 1967.
12 Reported in the *Los Angeles Times,* February 14, 1965.

He answered that he had no recollection of saying anything like that but he might have said it. He did recall a conversation he had with Jawaharlal Nehru, when the latter visited China (in 1954). As he remembered it, he had said *China did not want a war*. They didn't have atom bombs, but if other countries wanted to fight there would be a catastrophe in the whole world, meaning that many people would die. As for how many, nobody could know. He was not speaking only of China. (Emphasis added—M.K.)

Writing in the *Nation* magazine of October 4, 1965, Charles Taylor summarizes very succinctly the tendentious nature of the expendable story: "Contrary to both American and Soviet propaganda, the Chinese have never said that they would welcome a nuclear war."

It is crystal clear that one or two "off the cuff" remarks by Mao Tse-tung have been distorted and blown up to ludicrous proportions by propagandists with an axe to grind. To illustrate the point, here is what the press said about a speech delivered in Atlanta, Georgia by the Nobel Prize Laureate, Dr. Martin Luther King, who was discussing the Vietnam war:

If Red China enters the war, he said "there is no way to win. We would kill 300 million and it would be an act of birth control for them—they would still be the largest nation in the world."[13]

Applying the same criteria to Dr. King's remarks as were used with respect to Mao Tse-tung's remarks, will the pundits of the press now accuse Dr. King of advocating the extermination of 300,000,000 Chinese as an act of birth control?

The late Ernest T. Weir, chairman of the National Steel Corporation, was long regarded in many circles as reactionary and as far from a pacifist as it is possible to be. In a brochure he issued on January 5, 1951, entitled *Statement on Our Foreign Situation*, he said: "We certainly must realize that we cannot eliminate communism by war. On the contrary, I am sure that a third World War would increase communism, because the war would be so long drawn out and so disastrous that there would be a greater degree of dissatisfaction among the peoples of all nations than exists today."

Is there not a similarity between Mr. Weir's views and some of the statements attributed to Mao Tse-tung and some of

13 *Los Angeles Times*, May 11, 1967.

the editorial in the Chinese Communist *People's Daily*? Can it therefore be argued that Mr. Weir was suggesting another war in order to advance the influence of Communism? The asking of this question is no more ridiculous than the distortions of Mao's views.

Great Britain's World War II hero, Field Marshal Viscount Montgomery, paid a visit to China in 1961. His report illustrates the difference between what an honest observer can contribute to truth and the misleading "think pieces" and outright fabrications with which the American people have been deluged since 1949. The *Los Angeles Mirror* (now defunct) reported on October 5, 1961:

> Field Marshal Viscount Montgomery says Red China's Mao Tsetung is a "great guy—an uncommon man in an age of common men."
> The 73-year old British World War II Commander arrived in Toronto Wednesday night from a visit to Red China, where he met the Communist leader and received a red-carpet reception.
> Montgomery said western press reports that the Chinese are starving and have lost confidence in the Communist regime are "totally untrue."
> The retired field marshal said he did not see a single case of malnutrition during his three-week visit to the Chinese mainland but saw "bags of it" in Hong Kong, the British Crown Colony filled with Chinese refugees.

The next day the *Los Angeles Mirror* ran an editorial to discredit General Montgomery's report. It was a mean, sneering attack, conveying the impression that Montgomery had been swindled by a confidence man, one Mao Tse-tung. The last laugh was on the *Mirror,* because subsequent reports from reliable foreign journalists and scholars, plus the reports of a handful of Americans, proved Montgomery was eminently correct.

*Parade* magazine, a Sunday newspaper supplement read by millions from coast to coast, in its issue of February 13, 1966, carried a vicious, war-inciting column. It used the hoax story of Mao's 300,000,000 expendables as a take-off for justifying a so-called "preventive" war, which is one of the euphemisms of the militarists who dream about and plot for a war to annihilate the Communist countries.

Dr. W. S. McBirnie, Jr. is pastor of the United Community

Church of Glendale, California. He also is the head of an Ultra-Rightist propaganda operation called Voice of Americanism, which features him on a radio network and distributes pamphlets written by him. One of these pamphlets is entitled *Red China's Secret Plans for Destroying America*. Anyone who is willing to believe the truthfulness of the title of the pamphlet must be prepared to believe that the Rev. McBirnie has been able to discover secrets that neither the Defense Intelligence Agency nor the Central Intelligence Agency have been able to discover. No such secret plans can be found in the pamphlet, because no such plans can be proven to be in existence. Rev. McBirnie "proves" his case mainly by innuendo.

On page 23 of this pamphlet, the Rev. McBirnie quotes from a *New York Times* news service dispatch of May 13, 1965, in which Max Frankel gives a summary of the views expressed by a Chinese Communist general. The general had suggested that the Chinese people must be prepared, especially from a morale standpoint, for the possibility that a hostile power will attack them. Immediately after the quotation, McBirnie says:

This is in concert with Mao Tse-tung's infamous declaration concerning his *willingness* to accept enormous losses in an atomic war with the U.S.A. (Emphasis added.—M.K.)

This is a shocking departure from the truth, because Mao Tse-tung has never declared a *willingness* to accept enormous losses in an atomic war. One is tempted to ask Dr. McBirnie to tell us how, in the event China is attacked, Mao could effectively express his unwillingness to accept enormous losses. Does the Rev. McBirnie mean that Mao should meekly surrender? McBirnie continues:

His statement has often been quoted to the effect that he would be willing to accept the loss of half the people of China (population now over 700,000,000 and destined to be one billion by 1985) if he could in the process defeat "capitalist imperialism." More recently this quotation was submitted to Mao, and he corrected it to say (even more shockingly, if possible) that he would accept the destruction of half the population of the *whole world*—for then the half that would remain would go firmly communist and it would be better for those fortunate enough to survive.

329

The reader will, of course, recognize that the Rev. McBirnie has presented a garbled and distorted version of Edgar Snow's interview with Mao Tse-tung. It is difficult to believe that McBirnie is innocent of wrong-doing in this instance. The item we have quoted appears on pages 19-20 of his pamphlet. On page 7 of that same pamphlet McBirnie quotes from a book, which *refutes* McBirnie's conclusion. The book quotes a spokesman for the Chinese government as saying on September 1, 1963, that Mao Tse-tung had stated:

What about the people who will die if a war broke out? Out of a world population of two billion, seven hundred million, a third and perhaps more, half could be destroyed . . . I have discussed the question with a foreign statesman, who thought that humanity would be annihilated in an atomic war. I told him that *if the worst took place* and half of humanity perished, the other half would still remain, whereas imperialism would be destroyed and the entire world would become Socialist: after a certain number of years, there would again be two billion, seven hundred million men and even more. (Emphasis added.—M.K.)

In the Rev. McBirnie's system of standing logic on its head, if Mao Tse-tung speaks of war breaking out, it means Mao will be responsible for it. If Mao expresses the idea that a nuclear war would not necessarily wipe out all of humanity, McBirnie interprets this as *accepting* the destruction of half the world. (McBirnie thereby neatly absolves of responsibility our indigenous atomaniacs who openly advocate a third World War.) If Mao expresses the idea that another World War would cause more countries to go Communist, McBirnie interprets this as wishing for a World War in order to defeat Capitalism. What will the Rev. McBirnie say about Ernest T. Weir's opinion—that a third World War would cause a spread of Communism? Would McBirnie, perchance, have accused the late president of the huge National Steel Corporation of being a crypto-Communist, a Maoist, or a "pseudo-liberal"?

To any reasonable person, the quotation from that book cannot be reconciled with McBirnie's conclusion. But there are other distinctive features in McBirnie's pamphlet, besides his bombastic and misleading title. He dedicates the pamphlet to the Fascist dictator of Taiwan, Chiang Kai-shek, and Madame Chiang Kai-shek. On page 1 he refers to another hero whom he admires, the late William Randolph Hearst. For the benefit of posterity, it must be stated that Hearst is the man who made yellow-journalism a big business and that the great American historian, Professor Charles A. Beard, said that no decent person would touch Hearst with a ten-foot pole. Another of Hearst's accomplishments was his role in stampeding this country into the war with Spain in 1898. Hearst had sent one of his staff artists to Cuba to take pictures of the war. When Frederick Remington sent word that there was no war, Hearst cabled back to him:

> You furnish the pictures
> and I'll furnish the war.

This is the man whom the Rev. McBirnie calls "a clear-headed analyst of world affairs."

McBirnie likes to advertise himself as a "news analyst," and with William Randolph Hearst and Chiang Kai-shek as his idols, one can understand his performance in concocting "Red China's Secret Plans for Destroying America." For, it is done in the approved Hearstian style. And it surely meets with the approval of Chiang Kai-shek.

There is a tragicomic aspect to the Right-Wingers' dissemination of the 300,000,000 expendables hoax. No better illustration of the utter recklessness and irresponsibility of the Anti-Communist crusaders can be presented than the fact that a considerable segment of the Right-Wing attributes the expendables yarn to Lenin instead of Mao Tse-tung.

Fred C. Koch of Wichita, Kansas is the author of a pamphlet, *A Business Man Looks at Communism,* published in 1960. By 1964 it had gone through 10 editions. On page 2 we are told that Mr. Koch is:

1. President of the Rock Island Oil & Refining Co., Inc.
2. Chairman of the board of the Koch Engineering Co., Inc.
3. President of the Koch Oil Corporation, Inc.
4. A director of the First National Bank of Wichita.
5. A director of the Coleman Company of Wichita.
6. A director of the Great Northern Oil Co.
7. A director of the Minnesota Pipe Line Co.
8. A director of the South Saskatchewan Pipe Line Co.
9. A director of the Great Northern Oil Purchasing Co.

On page 3 of his pamphlet, Mr. Koch quotes *Lenin* as saying:

What does it matter if three quarters of the world perish, if the remaining one quarter is Communist?

In addition to all his leading positions in industry and finance, it should be noted that, although it is not mentioned in his pamphlet, Mr. Koch has these distinctions:

1. He is a founder of the John Birch Society.
2. He is a member of the National Council of the John Birch Society.
3. He is an endorser of the Ultra-Rightist *Manion Forum*, which is operated by a member of the National Council of the John Birch Society.
4. In 1961 he was listed as a member of the National Advisory Committee of the Christian Crusade, the Ultra-Rightist propaganda operation of the Rev. Billy James Hargis.

The Rev. M. L. Dye, in a pamphlet entitled *The Murderous Communist Conspiracy*, which is published by Anchor Bay Evangelistic Ass'n, Inc., quotes Lenin with just a slight variation from Mr. Koch's version:

It would not matter a lot if three-quarters of the human race perished; the important thing is that the remaining quarter should be Communists.

*Divine Love*, a quarterly publication of the Ultra-Rightist group in Fresno, California, that operates as the Apostolate of Christian Action, quotes Lenin as saying:

What does it matter if three-quarters of the world is destroyed, if the remaining one-quarter is Communist?[14]

Harry Everingham was the founder of an Ultra-Rightist group called We, the People. At one time the Rev. Billy James Hargis served as president. Everingham is the editor of *Free Enterprise*, monthly paper of We, the People, and he is also the editor of a small newsletter he calls *The Fact Finder*. In the November 15, 1965 issue he quotes Lenin exactly as the quotation in *Divine Love*.

Frank W. Ketcham is a Santa Barbara, California millionaire

14 Vol. 8, No. 1, issued in winter of 1964-1965.

who operates an Ultra-Rightist propaganda mill called Americans for Freedom. He spends huge sums sending out leaflets, pamphlets, brochures, stickers, and tape recordings to save us from Communism. In a brochure entitled "Are We at War with Communism?," which he circulated in January of 1966, Ketcham quotes Lenin as saying:

It would not matter a lot if ¾ of the human race perished; the important thing is that the remaining quarter should be Communists.

He gives as his source for this "Lenin" quotation the radio network program of the oil tycoon H. L. Hunt, which is called Life Lines. In addition to the phoney Lenin (or Mao Tsetung) quotation, the brochure contains seven more fabrications attributed to Marx, Khrushchev, Manuilsky, and other Communists. The obvious intent of all this use of falsified quotations is to prepare the mind of the reader for the desirability and inevitability of a war with the Communist countries.

Lenin, of course, never made such a statement or anything like it. It is perfectly clear that the 300,000,000 expendables story is one of many hoaxes and fabrications used by the professional Anti-Communists. The examples we have used are only a small part of what could be shown to illustrate the extent to which this hoax has been used to poison the minds of the American people. As we have pointed out before, the Right-Wingers copy and quote from each other by what we have called a system of intellectual incest, which eliminates the necessity to do any research for verification purposes. Their fanaticism and blind hatred lead them to eagerly accept as truth the most preposterous and irrational statements. But what shall we say about Professor Stefan T. Possony, who wrote the following in the July 10, 1967 issue of *Washington Report*, the weekly newsletter of the Ultra-Rightist *American Security Council*?

Early in 1954 Marshal Lin Piao expounded to an English laborite visitor that even if 200 million Chinese were killed, 400 million would still remain. In October 1954, Mao told Nehru that China could afford to lose 200 or 300 million people: hence, China is the nation which has the least reason to fear nuclear war. Furthermore, Mao said that even if one-third or one-half of the world population were to perish, imperialism would be annihilated and the entire world would become socialist.

Whatever excuses other Right-Wingers might pretend to have for writing such garbled and distorted summaries of another person's statements, Professor Possony cannot honestly avail himself of these excuses. He was formerly on the staff of the Foreign Policy Research Institute at the University of Pennsylvania. He is at present the director of the International Political Studies program of the Hoover Institute at Stanford University. The point is that Prof. Possony has excellent research facilities and can easily ascertain the truth. But in the era of the Cold War the truth is not accepted as truth by the Cold Warriors of the Right-Wing and their allies among the militarists who dream of "Der Tag," the day they can unleash a nuclear war of annihilation against the more than 1 billion human beings in the Communist countries. We can better understand Professor Possony's brand of truth and his ideological posture when we take note of these facts:

1. He is a former special advisor to the Assistant Chief of Staff, Air Force Intelligence.
2. He is a member of the National Strategy Committee of the American Security Council, which is the spearhead in the Cold War drive towards a hot war.
3. He is the Strategy and Military Affairs Editor of American Security Council's *Washington Report.*

In his article, which we must consider as a thinly disguised call for war against China and an hysterical plea against a non-proliferation treaty, he says:

We are inviting countries threatened by Mao's nuclear weapons to sign the non-proliferation pact *but we are able to defend them only if we are willing to fight nuclear wars with China.* Since we don't want to do this, why do we insist on keeping those countries disarmed? (Emphasis added.—M.K.)

Professor Possony is very well aware of the fact that his central premise in the above polemic is false—there is no country being threatened by Mao's nuclear weapons! There are no Chinese soldiers slaughtering people of another nation. There are no Chinese airplanes dropping jellied gasoline (Napalm) to incinerate men, women, and children. Possony cannot produce a scintilla of evidence to support his slanderous statement about "countries threatened by Mao's nuclear weapons." The fact is that Possony is not willing that this country shall take the slightest step in the direction of ending the suicidal arms race. In his strident campaign to *expand* the arms race, Possony wants larger military appropriations. The present astronomical budget of 70 billion dollars is not enough for Possony. So, he joins the campaign to push Defense Secretary McNamara into recommending a new phase in the arms race, development of a so-called anti-ballistic missile and its deployment around the principal cities of the country. So, after misrepresenting Mao Tse-tung's views, Possony says:

In his posture statements to Congress during January 1966 and 1967, our Secretary of Defense was just as calmly talking about a possible U.S. population loss of 135 million.

So now the Ultra-Rightists have made Robert McNamara a member of the "Mao Tse-tung club"!

### Looking Down the Barrel of a Gun

A frequent device of the Cold War propagandists is to scan the writings and speeches of Lenin, Marx, Mao Tse-tung, and other Communist theoreticians for something that can be used as a scarecrow. Whenever they run out of false reports of living conditions in the Soviet Union and China, it becomes profitable to take some statement out of historical and literary context and use it to scare the wits out of an unsuspecting reading audience. On November 6, 1938, in the midst of conducting a war against both the Japanese invaders and the armies of the corrupt Chiang Kai-shek cabal, Mao Tse-tung delivered a 5,000 word speech at a meeting of the Central Committee of the Communist Party of China. In the course of a discussion of military strategy, Mao said: "Every Communist must grasp the truth: 'Political power grows out of the barrel of a gun!'" Any honest scholar can realize that this statement had application to *a specific time, place, and set of circumstances.* When it is lifted out of context and quoted, along with the 300,000,000 expendables hoax, as a means of scaring people into believing that Mao Tse-tung threatens the security of the American people, it becomes a device for justifying a third World War behind the euphemism of a "preventive" war.

Felix Greene[15] tells how Professor A. Doak Barnett quoted this barrel-of-a-gun statement and a couple of other statements, all strung together. But one of the statements was picked up from a point three pages away from its preceding sentence. This kind of synthetic quoting is essentially unethical and misleading. In the course of quoting Mao Tse-tung in garbled fashion, in order to depict him as a monster who is eager for war, Professor Barnett left out this sentence, which is at the beginning of Mao's essay:

War, this monster of mutual slaughter, will be finally eliminated through the progress of human society, and in no distant future too.

Little did Mao Tse-tung dream that 28 years later the Rev. W. S. McBirnie, Jr. would be misrepresenting his views by quoting a garbled and out-of-context version of his statement about the barrel-of-a-gun.[16] Perhaps we can teach a lesson to McBirnie and his kind by a vivid illustration of dishonesty, by out-of-context quoting. The Bible says that Cain murdered Abel. The Bible also says: "Go thou and do likewise." But it is a shabby and dishonest trick to run the two statements together, even if multiple dots are used to indicate separation, because there are several hundred pages in the Bible between the two items.

## Mao's Fabulous Literary Agents

Ambitious writers all over the world can look with envy upon Mao Tse-tung. Here is a man who has been the recipient of an unprecedented amount of free service by volunteer "literary agents." As everyone knows, literary agents work on a commission basis. But not Mao's volunteer agents. In *Interview with Mao,* which we have previously quoted,[17] Edgar Snow relates that, during his previous interview with Mao in 1960, he had asked him if he had ever written his autobiography or if he intended to do so. Mao replied that he had *not*

15 *A Curtain of Ignorance,* pages 219-220.
16 McBirnie's pamphlet, *Mao Tse-Tung.*
17 *New Republic,* February 27, 1965.

written his autobiography. Snow adds wryly: "Nevertheless, learned professors had discovered 'autobiographies' written by Mao. The fact that they were fraudulent did not in the least effect their documentary terminology." Can anyone ask for better literary agents than these Cold War professors, who publicize books that Mao never wrote?

Snow points out, in addition, that the learned China "experts" have also discovered a philosophical treatise entitled "On Dialectical Materialism," which they attribute to Mao. He told Snow that he had not the faintest recollection of having written such an essay; that, if he had written it, he would surely have remembered it.

## Chiang Gets a Face-Lifting

It has been the custom for many years to present Chiang Kai-shek as a benign, mild-mannered, Christian gentleman, who is doing God's work in smiting the Devil (Communism). For reasons that the reader will have to guess, parts of his biographical data have been all but suppressed. Perhaps the reason is that he does not have such fabulous "literary agents" as does Mao Tse-tung. The first item that has been neglected is his "Red" record. As everybody knows, for many years the House Un-American Activities Committee, the Senate Internal Security Subcommittee, the Federal Bureau of Investigation, and all the Ultra-Rightist groups, who use the information furnished by these agencies, have been exposing Communists and former Communists. It would seem appropriate that we too display our patriotism, our 100% Americanism, by exposing Chiang's Communist past. The story is told in a thick volume entitled *United States Relations with China,* an official report of the State Department to the President of the United States, July 30, 1949. It comprises some 1050 pages and is generally known as the "White Paper" on China, in the language of the diplomats.

Up to 1927, the political party of which Chiang had become the leader—the Kuomintang—and the Chinese Communist Party had cooperated. Chiang had traveled to Moscow where he had met Lenin, Trotsky, and other Russian Communist leaders. He studied Communist ideology, strategy, and tactics, and he sought aid and support from the Russian Communists.

Chiang's eldest son by his first wife—Ching-kuo—is the head of the dreaded secret police of the Taiwan regime. During the period when Chiang was a collaborator with the Communists, Ching-kuo was sent to the Sun Yat-sen University in Moscow. He joined the Young Communist League and graduated into full membership in the Communist Party. After his courses in the Sun Yat-sen University were completed, Ching-kuo enrolled in the Lenin University. Upon completion of a rigorous training course, he was assigned to work in Russian factories and rose to the position of general manager of one of the factories.

Sometime in 1927, a powerful group of Shanghai bankers, industrialists, and business tycoons became frightened at the steady increase of Communist strength and influence. They approached Chiang Kai-shek with an offer of huge sums of money and continued financial support for his political ambitions, if he would sever his relations with the Communists and purge the Kuomintang of Communist members and influence. Chiang accepted the deal; and it should be made clear that Chiang changed his politics for the same reason that all corrupt politicians sell out their principles—money. It was not because he suddenly became a "born-again Christian."

The Thomas Jefferson of the Chinese people was the great patriot, Dr. Sun Yat-sen. He outlined the principles to guide the struggle of the Chinese people to rid themselves of feudal lords and military dictators. Just as the American Revolution sought aid from France and other foreign countries, so Dr. Sun Yat-sen made appeals for foreign aid. The only country that responded was the Soviet Union. In partial fulfillment of its offer of help, the Soviet Union sent one of its specialists, Michael Borodin, to meet with Dr. Sun Yat-sen in September 1923. Under the guidance of Borodin and other Soviet advisers, the Kuomintang was reorganized so that a shift could be made from conspiratorial tactics to those of revolution. Quoting from the State Department's "White Paper":

The Kuomintang assumed the leadership over the new forces that had been unleashed by the spread of nationalism in China. Through the use of propaganda among the peasant and working masses, the Kuomintang was able to turn its military campaigns into popular uprisings. *Its army was put under the leadership of officers trained according to Soviet methods* at the newly established Whampoa

338

Academy, *and achieved a degree of efficiency never before* equaled in modern China.

Following the death of Dr. Sun Yat-sen in 1925, General Chiang Kai-shek, director of the Whampoa Academy, became the leading figure in the Kuomintang. In 1926 he commanded the "Northern Expedition," a campaign to unify China by destroying the power of the warlords in the north. The revolutionary forces, preceded by the propaganda corps, made rapid progress, and toward the end of the year the Kuomintang capital was established at Hankow. A split in the party between the left wing at Hankow and *the right wing under the leadership of General Chiang*, however, was becoming increasingly evident. *The latter was anxious to obtain the support of the middle classes, particularly the commercial and banking community of Shanghai*, while the Communists were attempting to turn the Nationalist revolution into social revolutionary channels. In April 1927 the Generalissimo set up a government at Nanking rivaling that of the left faction of the Kuomintang which had gained dominance in Hankow. Following the capture of Shanghai *in March 1927 he carried out a purge of the Communists in Shanghai, and somewhat later conducted a similar one in Canton. These purges involved several hundred thousand deaths.* (Emphasis added—M.K.)

It should be added that Generalissimo Chiang Kai-shek unleashed the savage attacks against his former associates without the slightest warning. *The New York Times,* December 12, 1927 reported Chiang's orgy as follows:

Canton has been quite aptly described as a "city of the dead" since the suppression of the Communist peasant and labor uprisings of Sunday.

Photographs confirm the ruthless slaughter that occurred. There are pictures available of trucks loaded with bodies, piled three and four deep, as they were driven through the streets to burial places.

Long rows of bodies on pavements provided gruesome evidence of the vengeance wreaked upon those suspected of Communist leanings when the Nationalists recaptured the city later in the week.

That is only a small part of the story of the treachery and wholesale atrocities by which the gentle, "Christian" gentleman came into power. His eldest son, Ching-kuo, who had not yet gone over to the Fascist camp, bitterly denounced Chiang's 1927 purge of the Communists and the working people in general. He called his father "an evil warlord bent on oppressing the laboring and peasant classes." (Ching-kuo remained in the Soviet Union until 1939.)

*The New York Times* reported further on December 16,

1927 regarding Chiang's atrocities in Canton that ". . . stringent methods are being used to see that every suspicious character, man, woman or child, is placed in custody. Gruesome tales continue to permeate through from Canton . . ."

In the face of the Japanese aggression against China, beginning with the occupation of Manchuria in 1931, the Chinese Communist Party called for a patriotic united front of all elements to resist the invaders. They even "turned the other cheek" and made overtures to Chiang and the Kuomintang. Some of Chiang's generals were opposed to his fighting the Communists instead of the Japanese invaders. Quoting again from the State Department's "White Paper":

By the end of 1936 the army of Chang Hsueh-liang, the former warlord of Manchuria, was in no mood to fight against the Communist forces. In December 1936 the Generalissimo and his staff visited Sian in Shensi Province to map out a sixth "Bandit Suppression" campaign. Rather than carry out Nationalist orders to resume operations against the Communists, Chang Hsueh-liang decided to "arrest" the Generalissimo. In this move he was acting in league with the commander of the "Hsipei" (Northwestern) troops, Yan Hu-ch'eng, and the subordinate commanders of both the Hsipei army and his own "Tungpei" (Manchurian) army.

The "White Paper" explains further on that the representatives of the Chinese Communist Party were called to Sian immediately after the capture of Chiang Kai-shek by his own generals. At first the Communists favored the execution of Chiang, but "apparently on orders from Moscow, shifted to a policy of saving his life," as one step in the direction of forging a patriotic united front against the Japanese invaders of their homeland.

It appears that the Communist Party strategy worked, resulting in an informal working agreement with the Kuomintang. On September 22, 1937 the Chinese Communist Party issued a manifesto declaring that unity had been achieved with the Kuomintang for the purpose of resisting Japanese aggression. The next day Generalissimo Chiang Kai-shek issued a formal statement approving the Manifesto of the Communist Party and its united front policy. During 1937 and 1938 the working alliance between the Chinese Communist Party and the Kuomintang of Chiang Kai-shek progressed to a point that areas of jurisdiction were allocated to the Chinese Communist Army; and for a period of some three years the Communist armies received a financial subsidy and allotments of ammunition from Chiang's Nationalist government. The Communist leader Chou En-lai was appointed a member of the presidium of the March 1938 Extraordinary National Congress of the Kuomintang. In addition, Chou En-lai held the position until 1940 of Vice-Minister of the Political Training Board of the National Military Council. As late as September 1943 Chiang had made a public statement saying that the Chinese Communist "problem" should be solved by peaceful, political measures.

Such is the "Red" record of the man whom many of our native anti-Communist crusaders hold up as the perfect anti-Communist warrior. The historical facts prove that he was and is an opportunist, an unprincipled person who finally embraced Fascism as a philosophy after "playing ball" with the Communists. The rest of the story is recent history, that the Communists conducted a struggle against his corrupt military regime and drove him from the Chinese mainland in 1949, and that Chiang took up residence on Taiwan (Formosa).

Our evaluation of Chiang is corroborated in a memorandum prepared by American Ambassador Stuart, which is included in the State Department's "White Paper." It is a story of treachery and atrocities perpetrated upon the people of Formosa. Quoting Ambassador Stuart:

The Formosan Chinese greeted the surrender of Japanese authority to the Chinese with immense enthusiasm on October 25, 1945. After fifty years under Japanese control and intensive economic development they welcomed a return to China, which they had idealized as the "Mother Country." (Page 923.)

Economic and political conditions worsened for the people of Formosa after Chiang's regime took over from the Japanese at the conclusion of the World War II. On February 27, 1947, a parade of Formosans was marching to present a petition to the Governor for a redress of grievances. Ambassador Stuart tells us what happened:

Without warning a machine gun mounted somewhere on the government building opened fire, swept and dispersed the crowd and killed at least four. (Page 926.)

Public resentment and anger mounted. So, Chiang's Governor invoked martial law on the next day. And as Ambassador Stuart tells it: "Armed military patrols began to appear in the city, firing at random wherever they went." (Page 927.)

A few days later a delegation of prominent citizens called on the Governor. Ambassador Stuart explains what happened:

They urged the Governor to lift martial law so that the dangers of clash between the unarmed civil population and the military would be averted. This the Governor agreed to do at midnight, March 1, meanwhile forbidding meetings and parades.

On that day busses and trucks, filled with squads of government troops armed with machine guns and rifles, began to sweep through the streets, firing indiscriminately. Machine guns were set up at important intersections. Shooting grew in volume during the afternoon. At no time were Formosans observed to have arms and no instances of Formosan use of arms were reported in Taipei. Nevertheless, the military were evidently allowed free use in what appeared to be an attempt to frighten the people into obedience. (Page 927.)

On March 8, 1947, the military commander for the Taipei area called at the headquarters of the citizens committee, entreated them to cooperate with the Central Government of Chiang Kai-shek, and solemnly assured the people that the Central Government would not dispatch troops to Taiwan and would not take any military actions against the people of Taiwan. Ambassador Stuart tells what happened *the very next day* (Pages 931-933):

Foreign observers who were at Keelung March 8 state that in mid-afternoon the streets of the city were cleared suddenly by machine gun fire directed at no particular objects or persons. After dark ships docked and discharged the troops for which the Governor had apparently been waiting. . . .

Beginning March 9, there was widespread and indiscriminate killing. Soldiers were seen bayonetting coolies without apparent provocation in front of a Consulate staff residence. Soldiers were seen to rob passersby. An old man protesting the removal of a woman from his house was seen cut down by two soldiers. . . .

Anyone thought to be trying to hide or run was shot down. Looting began whenever the soldiers saw something desirable. . . .

On March 11 it was reported that a systematic search for middle school students had begun during the night. School enrollment lists were used. A broadcast earlier had ordered all youths who had been members of the Security Patrol or the Youth League to turn in their weapons. Concurrently, all middle school students were ordered to remain at home. If a student was caught on the street while trying to obey the first order he was killed; if searchers found a weapon in his house, he met a like fate. If a student was not at home his brother or his father was seized as hostage. . . .

After three days in Taipei streets, government forces began to push out into suburban and rural areas. Mounted machine gun patrols were observed along the highroads 15 to 20 miles from Taipei shooting at random in village streets in what appeared to be an effort to break any spirit of resistance. Manhunts were observed being conducted through the hills near the UNRRA hostel. Foreigners saw bodies in the streets of Tamsui.

Ambassador Stuart concludes his report:[18]

The following developments have been reported as occurring during the end of March and the first part of April:

The continuing presence of fresh bodies in Keelung Harbor and other evidence indicate that the elimination of the informed opposition is continuing . . . It is reported at Taipei that although shots and screams in the night have become less frequent, they continue, and that there is no palpable difference in the tense atmosphere of the city . . . (Page 938.)

Thus did Chiang Kai-shek crush the hopes and aspirations and freedom of the Formosan people who had trusted him. Thus did he prepare in 1945 for the police state over which he would reign after the Communists drove him out of mainland China, Lest anyone think that his wife is any different in her attitude towards the essential dignity of human beings, it is enough to recall that, on a nationwide television program in the U.S.A. on September 20, 1958, Madame Chiang Kai-shek called for dropping of atomic bombs on the people of mainland China. Madame Chiang, as well as our own trigger-happy Cold Warriors, tries to justify such monstrous proposals by spreading an endless chain of atrocity stories about Communist China, making it sound as if the Chinese people are groaning under horrible conditions of oppression. But consider the following from Drew Pearson's column of May 1, 1957:

Generalissimo Chiang Kai-shek has sent a frantic message to President Eisenhower, pleading that he not allow American reporters to visit Red China.

18 Ambassador Stuart's memorandum was submitted to Chiang Kai-shek on April 18, 1947. Consequently, it must be considered a courageous and forthright document.

The cable followed on the heels of Dulles' revelation that he is ready to lift the travel ban which has been keeping newsmen away.

Chiang warned that visits by reporters would be disastrous to his prestige in the Far East.

Why is Chiang Kai-shek afraid to let American reporters see the "horrors" of Communist China with their own eyes? What is there about conditions in China that would be disastrous to his prestige in the Far East? Perhaps we can learn the answers.

One of the great military leaders of all time was the late General Joseph W. Stilwell, affectionately called by his men, who fairly worshipped him, "Uncle Joe" and "Vinegar Joe." General Stilwell was commander of the China-Burma-India theater of operations in World War II, and, as part of his job, he had to try to keep Chiang Kai-shek fighting the Japanese. In the *Stilwell Papers,* made up of his confidential field diaries and letters to Mrs. Stilwell, we find the General repeatedly showing his utter contempt for Chiang Kai-shek by repeatedly referring to him as "the Peanut" and "the little squirt." The General wrote about Chiang:[19]

No one tells him the truth . . . no one. He will not listen to anything unpleasant, so nobody tells him anything but pleasant things. It is impossible to reason with him . . . one could with Sun Yat-sen . . . but this man! He flies into a rage if anyone argues against him. (N.B.: All the multiple dots appear in the original.) (Page 214.)

Peanut knows only what goes on immediately around him, and the country is so big that he will not be able to control it.[20] Obstinate, pigheaded, ignorant, intolerant, arbitrary, unreasonable, illogical, ungrateful, grasping. (Page 215.)

I judge Kuomintang and Kungchantang (Communist Party) by what I saw:

*Kuomintang.* Corruption, neglect, chaos, economy, taxes, words and deeds. Hoarding, black market, trading with the enemy.

*Communist program.* Reduce taxes, rents, interest. Raise production and standard of living. Participate in government. Practice what they preach. (Page 316.)

In time of war you have to take your allies as you find them. We were fighting Germany to tear down the Nazi system—one-party government, supported by the Gestapo and headed by an un-

19 *The Stilwell Papers* by General Joseph Stilwell. Published by William Sloane Associates, Inc., New York, 1948. Copyright by Winifred E. Stilwell.

20 One year after these remarks were published, Chiang had been chased out of mainland China.—M. K.

balanced man with little education. We had plenty to say against such a system. China, our ally, was being run by a one-party government (the Kuomintang), supported by a Gestapo (Tai Li's organization) and headed by an unbalanced man with little education. (Page 320.)

The cure for China's trouble is the elimination of Chiang Kai-shek. (Page 321.)

It is interesting to get a glimpse of the man, Mao Tse-tung, whom we are trying (in alliance with "Peanut") to depose. Edgar Snow concludes his "Interview with Mao"[21] by telling us that, at the conclusion of his long interview, Mao insisted on walking with him to his waiting car, going out coatless into the subzero night air to bid him farewell. Snow was deeply impressed, not only by Mao's friendliness and simplicity, but also by the fact that there were no security guards at the entrance of the building. And then it suddenly dawned on him that he had not seen a single armed bodyguard in the entire vicinity all evening.

We believe that this requires no further comment!

Our thesis that Chiang Kai-shek is an egregiously evil man, whom our media of communication have given a "face-lifting," is borne out by General Stilwell's reference to the Chiang regime as a government whose "titular head had been built up by propaganda in America out of all proportion to his deserts and accomplishments" (page 320).

Felix Greene[22] tells the story of how the great China expert, Professor John King Fairbank, gave Chiang a "face-lifting." In the *1948 edition* of his book, *The United States and China,* Professor Fairbank says of Chiang: "He treacherously crushed the vigorous labor movement in Shanghai . . . The new Nanking Government expelled the Chinese Communists from its ranks and instituted a nation-wide white terror to suppress the Communist revolution."

In the *1958 edition* of his book, Professor Fairbank gives a perfumed version of Chiang's rise to power by changing the "treacherously crushed" to plain "crushed," by changing the "vigorous labor movement" to "Communist-led labor movement," and by changing "a nation-wide white terror" to "a nation-wide effort." On another page Professor Fairbank

21 *New Republic,* February 27, 1965.
22 *A Curtain of Ignorance,* Page 173.

changes from "white terror" in his 1948 edition to "military campaigns" in his 1958 edition!

It is fitting that we conclude our study of the "face-lifting" given Chiang by presenting the story of a man who really knew Chiang as no other man knew him. An Associated Press dispatch from Tokyo[23] tells of the arrival at the Peking airport of a distinguished visitor and his wife, who were greeted at the airport personally by Premier Chou En-lai. The dispatch said, in part:

> Li Tsung-jen, Nationalist China's vice president for six years and its acting president for one, threw in his lot with the Chinese Communists today. He fired a parting blast at the United States which had sheltered him since 1949.

Here is a man who fled from China to escape the wrath of the Communists when they overthrew the government in which he was the number two man. Here is a man who did *not* defect because of bad treatment by the U.S.A.; nor was he lured away by a huge Communist bribe. This is a case of a man swallowing his pride and downing a huge dose of "crow." He stated upon arrival at Peking that he was renouncing his past mistakes and that he had made his choice because he was impressed with China's nuclear developments and "the wise leadership of Communist Party chairman Mao Tse-tung.

Two questions seem appropriate:

1. How much longer will our government keep up its partnership with the Fascist dictator of Taiwan?
2. How much longer are we going to pretend that the Peking government is non-existent and that the tragic farce on Taiwan is the government of China?

## The Family "Disappears" in China

The prestidigitators of the Cold War alternate between making the real China disappear and reappear. During the periods when China exists, the practitioners of journalistic sleight-of-hand make the institution of the Chinese family disappear— in the minds of millions of Americans.

23 Santa Barbara, Calif. *News-Press,* July 20, 1965.

*Item.* The late Marguerite Higgins reported in the New York *Herald Tribune,* November 25, 1958:

It is not only Washington that is appalled by the regimentation, which finds women "liberated" from their homes and placed in barracks separated from their husbands and everyone from teenage youth to oldster trained to put gun worship over ancestor worship.

*Item. Time* magazine, December 1, 1958, regaled its readers with a story about the "Saturday-night system":

. . . under which a married woman worker lives in a factory dormitory, is alone with her husband only on the odd Saturday night when she has the use of a dormitory room all to herself.

*Item.* The *New York Times,* October 3, 1953, thundered about "the assault upon the mores and morals of the good Chinese family."

The world famous American journalist, Anna Louise Strong, who has traveled extensively in the Soviet Union and China and has resided in both countries for long periods of time, tells the story in the *New World Review* of March 1961 of how this hoax originated.[24]

One last slander has spread very widely: the tale that the people's Communes in China are "slave labor camps" and specifically, that they separate men from their wives, and ration sex relations by the half hour under control. *Life* of December 1958, was one of the first promoters of this story; their article originated in Macao. It was full of grotesque inventions about the adjacent Chinese areas in Kwangtung province. When I visited that province I took some pains to check these tales with the help of thirty people over a period of a month. I proved them lies and sent the proof to *Life.* My letter was never acknowledged.

Families still live together in their former homes or in new ones and their sex life is far more normal than it used to be in China's "old society," when men often had to leave their wives for years either for army duty or for jobs.

For a period of eighteen months, Charles Taylor was the resident correspondent in China for *The Globe and Mail* of Toronto, Canada. As a Canadian citizen, he does not have to fear prosecution from the State Department as does Mrs. Strong

24 Mrs. Strong examines a number of hoax stories in this article.—M. K.

if she should venture to return to the U.S.A. Regarding the "disappearing family" yarn, Mr. Taylor writes in *Progressive* magazine, December 1966:

Actually, the Communist rulers have never tried to wipe out the family unit, as scare stories in the West have often stated. For centuries the Chinese family was the main stabilizing factor in a nation that was often wracked by political and economic turmoil. But it was also often an instrument of injustice and tyranny, with the old dominating the young and the men dominating the women. As such it was under attack and starting to disintegrate several decades before the Communist victory.

As a conservative force in society, the family was a prime target for the Communists; but they have sought to eliminate its reactionary influence, not to eradicate the whole system.

Marc Riboud is a European journalist and photographer who visited China in 1957 for the first time. In 1965 he returned, and traveled some 16,000 miles inside China during a period of four months, using jeeps, trains, and airplanes. *Look* magazine, November 2, 1965, published eighteen pages of pictures of Chinese life taken by Riboud. One of *Look's* senior editors comments about some of the pictures that deal with women:

Women, their feet surely unbound, have new roles. They work in all professions. They can get birth-control information. They vote, they march, they travel abroad. And if women find their husbands incompatible, they can sue for divorce.

Under another photograph the editor comments:

Women won equal status under the Communists and one is an army general.

It is clear then that the same blind hatred of Communism, that inspired the hoax story in 1917 about the nationalization of women in Russia, also inspired the hoax story of the disappearing family in China. Reactionaries always look upon increased freedom for the toiling masses as a loss of freedom for themselves. But the really serious aspect of the massive campaign of lies about the Soviet Union and about China is that it furnishes "justification" and rationalization for incipient American Fascism. As an example, we can cite the use of this fabrication by Robert De Pugh, founder and national leader of the Minutemen. In a book he issued in 1966, entitled *Blueprint for Victory*, De Pugh writes:

After the Chinese conquest of Tibet families were systematically broken up and separated. Adults over fifty were killed or turned out to starve. Children under fifteen were shipped to China for Communist indoctrination. Married couples were separated. Most men were castrated to make them docile then sent to slave labor camps. Women were systematically impregnated to start raising a new generation of half-breed communists.

There are at least six outrageous lies in this quotation, but it serves the purpose of deluding, and working into a frenzy, those elements of the population who can become the storm-troopers of the emerging Fascist movement in this country. The molders of public opinion must begin to face the consequences of their anti-Communist crusades, which utilize fabrications and distortions of truth. There is, of course, legitimate criticism of Communists and Communism, and no one can deny the right of anyone to voice such criticism. However, when criticism degenerates into witch-hunting, Red-Baiting, and hysterical campaigns to divert the people from the real problems that press for solution—this type of anti-Communism becomes the ideological and psychological battering ram of Fascism. Every Fascist dictator has come into power under the slogan of saving the people from Communism. This is the lesson of history that we must learn if the U.S.A. is not to go the way of Hitler's Germany, Mussolini's Italy, and Franco's Spain!

## Sixty Million Chinese Disappear

Another act in the repertoire of the Cold War prestidigitators makes 60,000,000 Chinese disappear, allegedly murdered by Mao Tse-tung and associates. Sometimes the figure is scaled down to 40,000,000 or 30,000,000 or even 20,000,000, depending upon how big a whopper the particular storyteller cares to tell. Before examining the evidence, a few observations are in order.

Not counting combat casualties, Hitler's murder teams exterminated some 6,000,000 Jews and 2,000,000 Gentiles. If

349

people can be made to believe that the Chinese Communists murdered between 20 and 60,000,000 civilians, Hitler becomes by comparison a Christian gentleman. In addition, one must consider that many of the Ultra-Rightists attempt to deny or to minimize the Hitler atrocities. The net result is to inflame passions and to heat up the Cold War. Even more dangerous is the mood that is created, one of acquiescence in anything that the government does under the pretext of fighting Communism or "Communist aggression." It becomes possible for our government to conduct *undeclared wars* against the peoples of the Dominican Republic, Vietnam, Thailand, Cambodia, and other countries—all in the name of fighting "Communism," a term that is seldom clearly defined and which remains, at best, an illy-understood concept in the minds of most people.

Typical of the Ultra-Rightist propaganda technique of "piling it on" with atrocity tales is a brochure entitled *The Facts That Will Save America*. It was issued by American Intelligence Research, Incorporated, of Des Moines, Iowa, which is operated by Robert D. Dilley. On page 13 we read:

I'm for explaining that to make Socialism (called Nazism) work, Hitler had to murder six million Germans. To make Socialism (called Communism) work in Russia, Stalin had Khrushchev murder 20 million souls and place 20 million more in slave labor where they toil today. I'm for making it clear that to make Socialism work in China, Mao Tse-tung had to murder 37 million good Chinese citizens and he still retains 24 million more in slave labor camps. I'M FOR LETTING THE WORLD KNOW THAT WE DON'T WANT THIS TO HAPPEN HERE.

Brave words these be, but unfortunately based upon a series of lies, which we will examine briefly:

*Lie # 1.* Nazism is not Socialism, and Socialism is not Nazism. In order to capitalize upon the widespread acceptance of Socialist doctrine by the German people, Hitler and Goebbels demagogically called their Fascist program by the deceptive name of National Socialism. It was an obvious device for deluding the German people into supporting a movement towards Fascist dictatorship and world war. When our indigenous Ultra-Rightists adopt as their own a propaganda swindle invented by Hitler and Goebbels, it would seem that they are demonstrating an affinity for the Hitler brand of Fascism (Nazism).

*Lie # 2.* In the world of Robert Dilley, the six million Jews

350

whom Hitler exterminated—most of whom were not Germans—become "six million Germans." The facts are that, aside from the murder of millions of people as part of combat operations, Hitler's extermination squads murdered two million Gentiles and six million Jews in the so-called death camps.

*Lie # 3.* There is a distinction between Socialism and Communism, which is not within the purview of this book. We mention it only as another example of free-and-easy disregard for the facts.

*Lie # 4.* Khrushchev did not murder or order the murder of "20 million souls" or 20 million people. If the Soviet Government murdered 20 million people, Mr. Dilley and the other Ultra-Rightists must produce documentation that there existed a network of extermination camps such as Buchenwald, Maidanek, Dachau, Treblinka, and the rest of the Nazi torture and murder establishments. It would be impossible to murder 2½ times the number that Hitler wiped out in the murder camps, without having some evidence leak out to the world. There is, however, documentary evidence proving overwhelmingly that more than 20 million Russians were killed during the Nazi occupation. The Ultra-Right, with the help of the House Un-American Activities Committee, has been trying for many years to switch the blame for the Hitler atrocities onto the Russian Communists.

*Lie # 5.* When we challenged Dilley to produce proof of the 20 million murders and the 20 million in slave camps in the Soviet Union, he replied vaguely that we should check various documents, especially some notoriously dishonest reports of the House Un-American Activities Committee entitled "The Crimes of Khrushchev," which were concocted especially to combat the goodwill effects of Khrushchev's visit to this country in 1959. Dilley's brochure was issued in 1963, and, as we have previously pointed out, even the American Security Council admitted in its *Washington Report* of October 7, 1963 that the compulsory labor laws in the Soviet Union "were abolished piecemeal beginning in 1956."

*Lie # 6.* There are no slave labor camps in China with even 24 slaves. The "24 million slaves" story is either a Dilley invention or Dilley is repeating someone's fabrication. Can anyone comprehend what facilities and manpower it would take to imprison 24 million people?

*Lie # 7.* When we challenged Dilley to provide some proof that Mao Tse-tung had murdered 37 million "good Chinese citizens," he replied:

1. "Mao Tse-tung boasted of this at the Geneva Conference. I can't find my documentation right now."
2. "Write to Dr. George Benson, National Education Program, Harding College, Searcy, Arkansas."

The extermination of 37 million "good Chinese citizens"—4½ times the number that perished in Hitler's monstrous death camps—would require a huge network of extermination camps and facilities. No one—not even Mr. Dilley—has ever located one of these or even mentioned the name of the city or town where it might be located. Surely, Mr. Dilley will admit that such a gigantic project could not possibly remain secret indefinitely. The C.I.A.'s U-2 spy planes and spy satellites-in-the-sky would long ago have discovered them. Furthermore, Mao Tse-tung did *not* boast of this alleged wholesale murder at the "Geneva Conference," because he positively did *not* attend such a conference. He has left China only twice in his entire life—both times to visit Moscow, prior to 1953.[25] Dilley cannot find his documentation, because he cannot find anything of probative value. As for his "good Chinese citizens," couldn't it be possible that there would be a few thieves, swindlers, burglars, rapists, and murderers among those 37 million? Why would they all be good?

Mr. Dilley's qualifications for reporting the truth about the Soviet Union and about China, and his qualifications to give us "The Facts That Will Save America" deserve some scrutiny. Robert D. Dilley is the founder and president of the Dilley Manufacturing Company of Des Moines, Iowa. It produces book covers and advertising specialties. The brochure that was designed to "save America" was obviously designed to make some money for Robert Dilley. On the front cover we are told that the brochure and its "facts" are "Your Key to Profit and the Preservation of Liberty." On the back cover it says:

Here's What You've Been Waiting For. . . .
PATRIOTISM
AT A PROFIT

[25] *Life* magazine, November 2, 1965, says of Mao: "Apart from several visits to Moscow, he has not been known to leave the country."

Earn a Profit While Saving The Profit System
Be Able to Support Your Favorite Organizations
YOU CAN SELL BOOKS ON LIBERTY
AND EARN MONEY IN THE PROCESS

As one reads the brochure it becomes clear that it is a sales manual to promote the sale of $50.00 worth of Ultra-Rightist books and to promote membership in a monthly book club, to receive an Ultra-Rightist book each month. We are told that Dilley's American Intelligence Research "provides an invaluable service by making it possible for you to have many books that up to now have been suppressed from the American people." Of the 28 books whose outside covers are reproduced on two pages of this brochure, we could not find a single one that is not available from Ultra-Rightist bookstores and organizations. In the lexicon of the Ultra-Rightists, a book is considered "suppressed" if it is not enthusiastically praised by all the media and on sale at all the stores.

One of the books that is given considerable publicity in Dilley's brochure is a book written by Dilley, entitled *Message for America*. It is advertised on the jacket cover as "A Hand-Book For Those Who Will Defend Freedom." On page 81, Dilley expounds the philosophy that unemployment is caused by minimum wage laws, laws limiting the working hours, and laws limiting production. On page 150, we are told: "It is the author's belief that if people were given the facts, social security and all socialism would disappear." It is clear that, when Dilley speaks of liberty and of saving America, he is yearning for the return of the 16 and 18-hour working day and a minimum wage for unskilled labor of 25¢ per hour. Oh for the good old days of American freedom! It is also clear that Dilley's brochures, books, and publications are designed to make a profit.

The *Des Moines Tribune* reported on August 11, 1961, that Robert D. Dilley is a member of the John Birch Society and that he helped to organize two Birch chapters. He was also reported to be a member of Iowans for Effective Citizenship, Greater Des Moines Chamber of Commerce, and the National Association of Manufacturers. The *Weekly Crusader*, February 8, 1963, reported that he is a member of the National Advisory Board of Billy James Hargis' Christian Crusade. Subsequently, Dilley ran for Governor on the Conservative Party ticket.

Dilley has also been active in the Congress of Freedom, an Ultra-Rightist group that attempts to unify the competing Ultra-Rightist groups under the banner of super-patriotism. At its Board of Directors meeting in Birmingham, Alabama, in the early part of 1967, Merle Thayer was chosen as its Executive Director. Thayer is the advertising manager for *True News,* a monthly pictorial magazine started by Robert D. Dilley, presumably to help "save America." Among the speakers at this meeting were George Wallace, former Governor of Alabama, and Mrs. Opal Tanner White, assistant to the veteran hate-peddler, Reverend Gerald L. K. Smith. Dilley is also a member of a virulent Ultra-Rightist group, Wake Up America Committee, which seems to be a front for another group called We, the People.

Pursuant to the second suggestion in the letter that Dilley wrote to us, we sent a letter of inquiry to Dr. George Benson, who operates the Ultra-Rightist National Education Program at Harding College, Searcy, Arkansas. We asked for authentication of the story about Mao Tse-tung murdering "37 million good Chinese citizens," the story about 24 million in Mao's slave labor camps, and the story about Mao's boasting at the "Geneva Conference" about his alleged atrocities. On October 29, 1965, Dr. James D. Bales, an assistant to Dr. Benson, sent us a letter of reply.

Dr. Bales begins his letter with the statement: "Communists use terror as a weapon." He gives as documentation a number of professional anti-Communist writers and some reports of the House Committee on Un-American Activities, all of which are of very dubious value. But the deceptive aspect of Dr. Bales' statement is the implication that only Communists use terror as a weapon. Historically, it has been proven over and over again that the anti-Communist terror—especially that of the Fascist regimes—outperforms the Communist by at least 10 to 1. This was proven by the Bullitt Report of the Civil War after the overthrow of the Czar of Russia, and by the fact that nowhere in history has the ferocity and the bestiality of the Hitler regime been equaled.

Dr. Bales goes on to say in his letter that *he does not have any verification of Robert Dilley's story about Mao's alleged bragging at an alleged "Geneva Conference."* Dr. Bales is a more cautious Right-Winger than Dilley. He is more suave,

354

and attempts to "prove" the same thing by another method. Says Dr. Bales:

In 1938 Stalin told Chiang Kai-shek that if he wanted to establish firm control he should kill four million people as matter of policy.

One would expect that the Reverend Dr. Bales, Professor of Christian Doctrine at Harding College, would be very cautious with the truth before making such a categorical statement. This may tax the reader's credulity but Dr. Bales gives his source for such an impossible occurrence:

I take this from a mimeograph copy of a speech by Dr. Hollington K. Tong, "Why Red China should not be admitted to the United Nations," December 3, 1964. Tong was a close friend of Chiang Kai-shek's. Tong went on to say that Mao Tse-tung had killed over 20 million; this is in the same speech."

We suggest that no reputable scholar would accept any statement by Chiang Kai-shek or his ambassador without obtaining corroboration from independent sources. We are asked to believe that Stalin gave advice to Chiang in 1938, eleven years after Chiang began butchering his former Communist allies. We are asked to believe that Chiang, whose bloody record is only surpassed by that of Hitler's, needed some advice about methods of repression. We are asked to believe that Stalin calculated that precisely four million people should be killed. In any case, what relevance would this have about the charge that Mao Tse-tung killed 37 million "good Chinese citizens?" Is Dr. Bales, perchance, suggesting that Stalin gave advice to Chiang, and that Chiang relayed the advice to Mao, and that Mao took the advice and applied it with a gusto that raised the 4 million victims to 20 million? In any case, we were greatly elated by this portion of Dr. Bales' letter. Robert Dilley, the Des Moines prestidigitator, had made 37 million "good Chinese" disappear and Dr. Bales helped us to find 17 million, because he solemnly quotes Chiang's ambassador that Mao had killed about 20 million.

In the next paragraph Dr. Bales seeks to bolster the charge of 20 million murders by Mao (reduced from 37 million) by referring to a speech by Dr. Clark Kerr, President of the University of California. Dr. Bales says that Dr. Kerr "estimated in 1959 that the Chinese Communists had killed perhaps as many as 20 million people." The key word here, of course, is *perhaps*, indicating that Dr. Bales may be getting ready to settle for less than 20 million people.

Dr. Clark Kerr delivered the speech in question at Pomona College on February 12, 1959. It was placed in the Congressional Record of March 11, 1959, pages A 2033-2035, by the late John F. Kennedy, who was at the time a Senator from Massachusetts. We quote the pertinent section of Dr. Kerr's speech:

In Calcutta it is common to see a refugee family literally living on a 3-by-5-foot mat spread out on a public sidewalk. This mat, this small rectangle of space, is home. The babies, often unclothed, crawl on the sidewalk beside the destitute mother. The small brother or sisters beg. Flies settle on the sacred cow standing nearby or on a vendor's cart.

Travelers returning from Peking report that there are no babies living on the sidewalks of that city and almost no flies anywhere in China. These travelers also report that, in a land that has known starvation for centuries, agricultural production has risen quite significantly. India also has known starvation—and still knows it. As yet India's agricultural production is rising very slowly. (This last sentence may be termed the understatement of the century. On September 3, 1957—6½ years after that statement—*Parade Magazine* reported about India: "In Bihar province there are 40 million Indians on the edge of starvation. In other provinces it is almost as bad."—M. K.)

It is risky for a $35,000-a-year President of the largest university in the country to say that conditions of life in Communist China have improved spectacularly and that a nearby neighbor of the "free world" allows millions of people to die of starvation every year. Especially is this so, when in the same speech he points out that 40% of the students attending the University of Calcutta are undernourished. What will the California Un-American Activities Committee say about such a speech? And the House Un-American Activities Committee, the American Legion, and John Edgar Hoover? How does one protect oneself from the criticism (and possible loss of job) of the millionaires on the University Board of Regents? The formula is very simple: You tell an atrocity story that makes it sound as if the Chinese have paid too big a price for wiping out hunger, filth, ignorance, unemployment, prostitution, and foreign interference; you make it sound as if the agonizing

356

deaths by starvation of up to 15 million people in India each year are a fair price to pay for "freedom." Dr. Clark Kerr followed the remarks we have quoted with this qualification:

This, of course, is only part of the story. Perhaps 2 or even 20 million people have been killed in China by the new regime; in India, none. China knows the rigid discipline of the anthill—blue-clad ants toiling ceaselessly at their alloted tasks. India is a free country.

On November 28, 1965, we sent a perfectly courteous letter to Dr. Clark Kerr, in which we asked for proof of the killing of 2 million or 20 million people. No reply was received. On February 4, 1966 we sent the following letter:

400 East Franklin St.
Elsinore, Calif. 92330
Feb. 4, 1966

Dr. Clark Kerr, President
University of California
Berkeley, California

Dear Dr. Kerr:

I know that you are a very busy person. For this reason, I hate to intrude, but it is important that I have the proof that I called this matter to your attention. Therefore, I am sending this letter via "certified mail, personal receipt requested".

On November 28, 1965, I sent you a letter, to which I have had no reply. Therefore, I take this opportunity of calling this matter to your attention again.

Reference is made to your speech at Pomona College, February 12, 1959, which was printed in the Congressional Record of March 11, 1959, pages A 2033-A 2035. In this speech you stated: "Perhaps 2 or even 20 million people have been killed by the new regime; . . ."

In a book which I am writing, I intend to challenge the accuracy of this statement. As a matter of fair play, I am attempting to get your side of the story, and for this reason I ask the following questions:

1. Do you have any proof or valid documentation in support of this statement?
2. How do you explain the disparity between the figures of 2 million and 20 million?
3. Whatever the figures, what was your frame of reference with respect to "killed in China by the new regime"?

357

Did you mean in the course of fighting the civil war before the Peking government was established or did you mean terrorist actions after the regime was established?

A reply at your earliest convenience would be deeply appreciated. Thank you.

Respectfully yours,

MORRIS KOMINSKY

Certified mail;
personal receipt requested


Dr. Kerr replied with the following letter:

## UNIVERSITY OF CALIFORNIA

BERKELEY · DAVIS · IRVINE · LOS ANGELES · RIVERSIDE · SAN DIEGO · SAN FRANCISCO    SANTA BARBARA · SANTA CRUZ

CLARK KERR
*President of the University*

BERKELEY, CALIFORNIA   94720

February 18 , 1966

Mr. Morris Kominsky
400 East Franklin Street
Elsinore, California 92330

Dear Mr. Kominsky:

This will acknowledge your letter of February 4. As you are undoubtedly aware, the first years of communist power in China were marked by great social turmoil. The dispossession of the landlords was carried on with the same excessive zeal as has marked subsequent political and economic campaigns, particularly the Great Leap Forward. The communist press contained many accounts of public trials in the villages, and no attempt was made to hide the executions that followed the voice verdicts of the massed villagers.

No one really knows, probably not even the Chinese government itself, how many people lost their lives during this terrible period. All sorts of estimates appeared in the contemporary press, but none of them can be confirmed, for obvious reasons. You may recall that similar charges were levied against Stalin, and indignantly denied by Western liberals, only to be confirmed by Krushev -- though never quantitatively. I append several statements by scholars who have been working on the problem. If you are able to come up with a firmer estimate than has hitherto been possible, we shall all be in your debt. I might add that the book by Liu and Yeh, which I cite, is regarded by all Western scholars as a landmark in the objective analysis of the postwar Chinese scene.

Sincerely,

Clark Kerr

Clark Kerr

Enclosure

On March 2, 1966, we sent the following letter:

Dr. Clark Kerr, President
University of California
Berkeley, Calif.

400 East Franklin St.
Elsinore, Calif. 92330
March 2, 1966

Dear Dr. Kerr:

Thank you very much for your letter of Feb. 18, 1966. While I am deeply appreciative of the cordial and restrained tone of your letter and while I am also appreciative of the research memorandum that you sent along with your letter, I find your letter unresponsive to my questions. Perhaps I am partially responsible too, because of the brevity of my questions. So, I will start all over again.

In your speech at Pomona College, Feb. 12, 1959, you said: "Perhaps 2 or even 20 million people have been killed in China by the new regime; in India none. China knows the rigid discipline of the anthill—blue-clad ants toiling ceaselessly at their alloted tasks. India is a free country."

My first question was: "Do you have any proof or valid documentation in support of this statement?" While I did not formulate my question precisely, I really meant to ask you what proof you had on Feb. 12, 1959 for the statement you made on that date. It seems to me that all the studies you have relied upon for your documentation were available to you on or before Feb. 12, 1959, unless I am willing to attribute to you the possession of some clairvoyant powers. So, the question still remains: Upon what dependable source did you rely in making such a serious public pronouncement? Lest you think I am quibbling with you, I am constrained to inform you that your speech is being quoted *today* by such Ultra-Rightists as the American Intelligence Research of Des Moines, Iowa, Harding College of Searcy, Askansas (the "West Point" of Ultra-Rightist propaganda), and Christian Crusade.

Overlooking for the nonce the tenuous basis for your reliance upon books you have quoted in your research memorandum, I think that a fair examination of the quotations you sent me offer you small consolation for your position. You say that the book by Liu and Yeh "is regarded by all Western scholars as a landmark in the objective analysis of the postwar Chinese scene." Alright, I accept your judgment. The first two sentences of your quotation from these scholars are most germane to our discussion: "In sharp contrast to the *moderate policies pursued in the urban areas,* the land redistribution was carried out with full force and violence. *An unknown number of people were liquidated through mob trials and mass executions.*" (The italics are mine.—M.K.) Even if this scholarly report had been available to you on or before Feb. 12, 1959, pray tell me, Dr. Kerr, how could you magically transform these words into "perhaps 2 or even 20 million"?

The book by T.J. Hughes and D.E.T. Luard summarizes by saying that "frequently landlords were murdered." Surely you cannot stretch this into 2 or 20 million.

Cheng Chu-Yuan's book says: "About twenty million peasants were sentenced to execution, imprisonment or exile." I am sure that you can discern the vagueness of this sentence and that you will agree with me that it offers no basis for your "2 or 20 million" statement.

A. Doak Barnett's book does say something definite: "Several millions of landloards and their families were killed in the process." Without any knowledge of Barnett's reputation as an honest and objective scholar and without any knowledge of source of his information, I am reluctant to place too much credence on his omnibus charges. In any case, by the criteria of historical research, this does not give you a firm basis for your ex cathedra "2 or 20 million" statement.

Your admonition about the mistake many people made in refusing to believe the reports of Stalinist atrocities has validity only in the context of urging one to be cautious and open-minded, but cannot be used to prove your "2 or 20 million" statement, unless you wish to rely upon a non-sequitur argument. I have no intention of coming up with a firmer estimate, because I do not have the research facilities to do so. This does not, in my opinion, foreclose my right to challenge anyone who makes a statement without adequate evidence of a probative nature.

My next question to you was: "How do you explain the disparity between the figures of 2 million and 20 million"? With a full realization of some of the pitfalls of reasoning by analogy, I am wondering how you would judge a person who estimates the age of a passerby on the street as being "perhaps 2 or even 20 years old." Or what would you think of a physician who tells you to take "perhaps 2 or even twenty teaspoonsful of a remedy"? This could go on ad infinitum, but I think this should suffice to make my point. In a serious and responsible discussion one would say "2 or 3 million" or "2-4 million," but *never* "2 or 20 million." I think, Dr. Kerr, that this was a most unfortunate slip of the tongue at a time that lambasting of Communists was most fashionable.

Finally, I will quote, in refutation of your "2 or 20 million" statement, a well-known scholar, whose veracity you will not question: "No one really knows, probably not even the Chinese government itself, how many people lost their lives during this terrible period. All sorts of estimates appeared in the contemporary press, but none of them can be confirmed, for obvious reasons." I am quoting one, Dr. Clark Kerr—his letter to me of February 18, 1966. If none of the estimates can be confirmed, why did you presume to take some figures out of thin air on February 12, 1959? That is the $64 question.

While I abhor bloodshed and violence, no matter by whom perpetrated, and while I do not consider that two wrongs add up to a right, I think it most appropriate to remind you of the White Christian record of atrocities in conquering this continent, in Africa, in old-dynasty China, and in India. In a recent essay on this subject, the Rev. C. P. Bradley of Australia estimates that, over the years, the White men have slaughtered 100 million Africans. And I am also wondering when you will join Dr. Robert Hutchins and Dr. Linus Pauling in denouncing U.S.A. aggression and atrocities in Vietnam, including Napalm and poison-gas bombing.

Your further comments are earnestly requested. Meanwhile, please be assured of my esteem for you.

Respectfully yours,

Certified mail;
return receipt.

MORRIS KOMINSKY

*P.S.:* A story in *Los Angeles Times* of Feb. 18, 1966 tells us that in the "free country" of India it is estimated that 10 to 15 million people will die of starvation this year. Another story in the same issue of the *Times* quotes Dr. Joseph W. Goldzieher, of the Southwest Foundation for Research and Education in San Antonio: "It is predicted that 30 million Indians will starve to death by 1970. In Calcutta, garbage collectors pick up the bodies each morning of persons who died during the night."

Question: When people revolt against a social order that allows such atrocities, who is qualified to sit in judgment of the ensuing violence?—M. K.

Dr. Kerr replied with the following letter:

## UNIVERSITY OF CALIFORNIA

BERKELEY · DAVIS · IRVINE · LOS ANGELES · RIVERSIDE · SAN DIEGO · SAN FRANCISCO          SANTA BARBARA · SANTA CRUZ

CLARK KERR
*President of the University*

BERKELEY, CALIFORNIA  94720

March 21, 1966

Mr. Morris Kominsky
400 East Franklin Street
Elsinore, California 92330

Dear Mr. Kominsky:

I am sorry that my reply was unclear to you.

The basis for my statement on February 12, 1959, was a number of reports from China circulating at the time among scholars who followed Far Eastern affairs. They probably also appeared in the press. I cannot recall now precisely what these sources were. Nevertheless, I was satisfied at the time that they were reliable. That they were reliable is supported by assertions made subsequently in print by scholars, and this is what I intended to convey when I quoted them to you.

The phrase, "two or even twenty million", indicates that casualties were very substantial, probably running into the millions, that an estimate as high as twenty million had been made, but that an exact figure could not be fixed except with a very wide margin of error. Again, the scholarly sources confirm this in substance.

Sincerely yours,

*Clark Kerr*

Clark Kerr

361

Dr. Kerr's final letter is, of course, very vague and unresponsive. With the research facilities available to him as the President of this country's largest university, he should have been able to come up with something more substantial than "a number of reports from China circulating among scholars who followed Far Eastern affairs." One of these scholars, upon whom Dr. Kerr relied, was Dr. A. Doak Barnett, whom we have discussed and who was shown to have been spreading misleading stories about Mao Tse-tung and China. For the rest, it is clear that Dr. Kerr was relying upon the unreliable press reports when he made that speech in Pomona College. When challenged to prove his statements, Dr. Kerr made a very poor showing.

It is fitting to conclude our examination of Dr. Kerr's speech by quoting the first and last paragraphs of a letter of his which appeared in *Ramparts* magazine, August 1966:

Your April 1966 issue contains serious distortions of my views of the modern American university.

*Ramparts,* in its attempt to be provocative and stimulating, ought not to neglect the other journalistic virtues of accuracy and responsibility. Both the references to views I am said to hold are totally inaccurate and irresponsible.

We submit that the same criticism applies to Dr. Kerr's speech about 2 or 20 million Chinese people allegedly murdered by the Chinese Communists! We submit that scholars who wish to retain a reputation for integrity should not spread stories which they cannot prove.

When the Rev. Dr. James Bales relied on Dr. Clark Kerr's speech, he must have suspected that he was leaning on a very weak reed, because he immediately adds this argument:

Mao, himself, admitted that 800,000 people had been liquidated by his security forces from October 1949 until the beginning of 1954. This I take from an AP dispatch in the Searcy, Arkansas *Daily Citizen,* June 13, 1957, page 1.

It needs no extended discussion to show that the liquidation of 800,000 people cannot be used as the basis for proving the murder of "37 million good Chinese citizens." But even the 800,000 figure is a distortion of the truth.

In a dispatch to the *New York Times* from Warsaw, June

13, 1957, Sydney Gruson *quotes* a summary of speeches delivered by Mao Tse-tung, on February 27 and March 12, to Communist leaders in Peking:

As for Stalin, his opinions can be considered negatively. The experience of the Soviet Union in this respect shows that Stalin made the mistake of substituting internal differences for external antagonism, which resulted in a rule of terror and the liquidation of thousands of Communists.

In dealing with enemies it is necessary to use force. We in China have also used force to deal with the enemies of the people. The total number of those who were liquidated by our security forces numbers 800,000. This is the figure up to 1954.

(The 800,000 are believed to include mainly opponents of the regime killed in civil warfare after 1949, as well as persons executed on charges of spying and counter-revolution.)[26]

Since then we are no longer using methods of terror. Instead we have substituted persuasion and education.[27]

We believe that this speech by Mao has the ring of truth, and while the loss of lives is deplorable, it must be pointed out that people die in all revolutions and civil wars. In the Civil War 1861-1865 in the U.S.A., 880,213 people perished. Considering that China had some 650,000,000 people in 1949 and the U.S.A. had 31,443,000 in 1860, it is obvious that the Chinese Civil War was less bloody than ours.

Dr. Bales' final proof is the phoney story about Mao being willing to destroy hundreds of millions in an atomic war. In his anxiety to prove the unprovable, Dr. Bales "piles it on" with whatever argument or weapon comes to hand. But the truth will out!

The Rev. David A. Noebel, first lieutenant of Rev. Billy James Hargis, is the author of *Rhythm, Riots and Revolution,* a sequel to a previous opus entitled *Communism, Hypnotism and the Beatles.* On page 230 of "Rhythm, Riots and Revolution" we are told: "Red China has murdered and butchered twenty to 40,000,000 human beings in cold blood over the past fifteen years." Suddenly there is a change from 2-20 million to 20-40 million. The Reverend also makes the point that these

26 The parenthetical explanation was made by Mr. Gruson.
27 The story in the Searcy, Arkansas *Daily Citizen,* which Dr. Bales cited, quotes Mr. Gruson's *New York Times* dispatch faithfully. In quoting from the *Daily Citizen,* Dr. Bales conveniently omitted any mention of the last two paragraphs, which contradict his charges.

people were "murdered and butchered." That word "butchered" makes one wonder if the Rev. Noebel is trying to subliminally accuse the Communists of cannibalism!

Dr. Robert Morris, former counsel of the Senate Internal Security Subcommittee, in his column in the Catholic Ultra-Rightist weekly, *The Wanderer*, December 3, 1964, says:

Red China has cruelly executed more than thirty million human beings. It imposes the worst kind of bondage on its six hundred million people.

Dr. Howard Kershner, who operates the Ultra-Rightist Christian Freedoms Foundation, said in a speech at Harding College, April 17, 1961:

Who were responsible for the death sentence passed on 30 million Chinese people? That number was given to me by a friend who returned from Hong Kong recently telling me that a Communist propagandist from the mainland had assured him that at least 30 million Chinese had been liquidated.

One can only wonder how Dr. Kershner would feel if someone gave him some of his own "medicine," and spread a malicious lie about him that was obtained from an anonymous source, which, in turn obtained it from another anonymous source.

In his monthly newsletter, *Documentation*, February 1965, the Rev. W. S. McBirnie, Jr. reproduced an undated column by Eston McMahon in the Los Angeles *Herald-Examiner*. The opening paragraph reads:

Chinese Red soldiers have executed about 60 million of their countrymen on the mainland since the Communist conquest, a Catholic medical missionary and one-time prisoner of the Reds, estimated yesterday.

Referring to the period, 1950-1953, when China was involved in the Korean War, Dr. Medford Evans writes in the October 1967 *American Opinion:*

It was during these three years that the peace-loving agrarian reformers executed all the landlords and other "unreliable" elements of the population—50 million is the estimated kill.

According to this version, nothing happened in the atrocity business in 1949 and from 1954 to 1967. Dr. Evans does not explain why 50 million were killed in 1950-1953 and apparently none during the other periods. There you have it. Take your choice: 2 million, 20 million, 30 million, 37 million, 40 million, 50 million, and 60 million. All honorable Christian gentlemen these atrocity-reporters be!

This, by no means, exhausts the list of stories about the disappearing Chinese millions. It has been circulated and is being circulated in thousands of Ultra-Rightist books, pamphlets, brochures, tape recordings, leaflets, and lectures. In addition, thousands of columns and editorials, as well as broadcasts, have repeated variations of this theme.

The Ultra-Rightist Education Information, Inc., which has operated sometimes out of Amarillo, Texas and at other times out of Fullerton, California, has issued a leaflet entitled *Progressive Education Undermined China*. It carries the subheading:

> "Progressive Education
> is Undermining America"

It goes to such lengths, in order to carry out an assault against our schools and educational procedures, that it refutes the story of the 2-to-60 million allegedly murdered by the Chinese Communists. We give the reader our sacred word of honor that we did not invent the following, that it is actually the first sentence of the leaflet:

Millions of people have refrained from becoming acquainted or familiar with the Communist technique of infiltration and subjugation, yet they are amazed how a country like the Republic of China could be conquered by the Communists without firing a single shot.

Speaking of prestidigitators, is it not quite a feat to murder 60 million "good Chinese citizens," without firing a single shot?

During the period of armed struggle to oust the regime of Chiang Kai-shek from the mainland of China, Mao Tse-tung and Chou En-lai issued these instructions to the Eighth Route Army:

a.  Take nothing from the people, not even a single needle or thread.

b. Turn in everything you capture.
c. Speak politely at all times.
d. Return everything you borrow.
e. Pay for anything you damage.
f. Do not hit anyone, and do not swear.
g. Do not damage any crops.
h. Do not take liberties with women.
i. Do not ill-treat captives.

After quoting these instructions, the Rev. C. P. Bradley of Merewether, Australia, comments in the October 1966 issue of his newsletter, *United People*:

Those were Mao's instructions during the war against Chiang. When Mao's army reached Shanghai, they slept on the footpaths rather than disturb the people!

"No army in history behaved as did Mao's Communists." This was grudgingly admitted by western writers.

Further corroboration of the excellent behavior of the famous Eighth Route Army is given by Jack Belden in his authoritative book, *China Shakes the World*:[28]

Incessantly, the army dinned into the soldier's head that he could not molest the people, that he had to pay for everything he bought, that he could not loot, that he had to clean up rooms that he had used, that above all he must not make the people feel that the army was crushing their privileges. Naturally, this was of extreme importance, as the people of China have commonly hated all soldiers.

The success of the Communists in this type of political training was amazing to anyone who knew anything about China. . . I have never seen an army quite like the 8th Route Army led by the Chinese Communists. In many ways, it was absolutely unique among the armies of the world.

Belden relates a remarkable story of how the Red Army went about the task of winning the loyalty of soldiers captured from Chiang's army. The procedure resembles to some extent a group psychotherapy session. Belden then adds this comment:

While the Communists welcomed any soldier of Chiang's into the 8th Route Army, at the same time they also released any prisoner who wanted to go back to Chiang's side. As a matter of fact, they even gave prisoners traveling expenses to get home.

[28] Published by Harper & Brothers, New York, 1949.

There are too many witnesses to this Communist policy, both Chinese and foreign, to doubt its authenticity. An American Army officer who was captured by the Communists in Manchuria tells how six thousand men of Chiang's 88th Division were brought to a mass meeting and treated as honored guests. An American girl in Shantung tells how she visited a camp for fifty captured Kuomintang generals and saw them getting far better food and living under better conditions than 8th Route officers. Finally, I myself, when in Kuomintang areas have seen hundreds of prisoners released by the Communists pouring across the lines.

By way of contrast, it is fitting to tell about conditions in *Chiang's army* and about the terroristic tactics used in conscripting soldiers. Theodore H. White and Annalee Jacoby, in *Thunder Out of China*,[29] tell us:

Conditions in combat units were horrible, but by comparison to conditions in induction centers they were idyllic. Recruits ate even less than the starving soldiers; sometimes they got no water. Many of them were stripped naked and left to sleep on bare floors. They were whipped. Dead bodies were allowed to lie for days. In some areas less than 20 per cent lived to reach the front. The week that the stories of Belsen and Buchenwald broke in Europe coincided with the height of the conscription drive in China; the doctors who dealt with the recruit camp about Chengtu refused to be excited about German horrors, for descriptions of Nazi camps, they said, read almost exactly like the recruit center in which they were working.

Is it not clear why Cold War propagandists invent and purvey atrocity stories about the Chinese Communists? Is it not clear that the shock value of such stories is that it gives Chiang Kai-shek a "face-lifting" and makes the American people impervious to the acceptance of the truth about Communist China?

In the November 2, 1965 *Look* article, which we have previously quoted, we are told:

In Shanghai alone, about 90,000 former owners of businesses and factories draw an income from their old holdings, but only for their lifetimes.

The *Los Angeles Times*, February 14, 1966, carreis a Reuters dispatch from Shanghai which corroborates the *Look* story. The headline reads:

Ex-Capitalists Live in Luxury in Red China

[29] Published by William Sloane Associates, Inc., New York, 1946.

The story begins with the experience of the Yung family, which has drawn an income equivalent to $10,080,000 during the last 10 years. It goes on to tell of the 90,000 "reformed" capitalists from Shanghai "who draw regular, and often sizable, dividends from the state on their former shares and property."

During the Communist take-overs in all the other countries, the wealth-producing property of capitalists and big landowners was expropriated without any compensation. Those who were lucky enough to survive either fled from their native lands or were forced to do some useful work in order to earn a living. Contrary to the procedures followed in the other Communist-controlled countries, the Chinese Communists provided an opportunity for capitalists and big landowners to "integrate" with the new social order and to derive an income, *during their own lifetimes,* from their former properties. It is enough for any thinking person to realize how humane this procedure is when one considers that the emancipation of chattel slaves in this country during our Civil War was not accompanied by any compensation to the slave owners.

We have now arrived at a point in our examination of the facts where we can ask three questions:

1. If the Chinese Communists exterminated between 2 million and 60 million "good Chinese citizens," where are the Chinese counterparts of the Nazi murder camps, such as Belsen, Buchenwald, Dachau, Treblinka, Maidenek, Auschwitz, and the rest? (As a corollary to this question, one may ask why the figures vary from 2 to 60 million in the case of the Chinese, while there are fairly firm figures in the case of the Nazi atrocities.)

2. If the Chinese did indeed exterminate millions of "good Chinese citizens," why have they spared the lives of thousands of capitalists and big landowners? Why didn't they take the easy way out and save the yearly cost of millions of dollars in compensation to these former members of the ruling classes?

3. Why has there been no "Nuremberg" trial of the perpetrators of these alleged atrocities? Even if the accused were tried "in absentia," world public opinion could be meaningful if evidence of *probative value* were produced.

In the article previously quoted from *New World Review,*

March 1961, Anna Louise Strong tells about the origin of this monstrous slander:

The tale of the alleged fifteen to twenty million people "executed" by the present Chinese Government in consolidating its power seems to have been started by *Time* magazine some years ago. When it first appeared, Edgar Snow challenged Henry Luce about it, and was told by the *Time* editor that the figures came from a bureau of the United Nations. Snow persevered and learned from the UN bureau that they had made some estimates of the human cost of World War II, and had estimated for China figures of losses occurring from the war with Japan, the civil war and the various floods and famines of those years. These were the figures *Time* used as "executions by the Communists"!

## Will the Real China Please Step Forward?

Like the popular television skit which employs two impostors, as well as the *real* person, it is time to have the *real* China step forward and identify itself. At the risk of being accused of selective presentation of data, the items which follow are quoted with a full realization that there is a seamy side to life in China. The justification for this presentation is that it serves as an antidote to the many malicious and mendacious stories, and it illustrates how the truth becomes drowned out by a steady barrage of untruth. It is a fair estimate that, for every truthful story that our media of communication tell about China, there are 25 untruthful or misleading stories.

The March 7, 1952 issue of *U.S. News & World Report* (which must be considered a "hostile witness"), says:

China for the first time in modern history is ruled by a central Government with the power to impose its will. War lords are gone. Civil war is ended.

This is consistent with Mao Tse-tung's speech, which Sidney Gruson reported in the *New York Times*, June 13, 1957, in which Mao stated that force was no longer used against internal enemies after 1954.

Professor V. K. R. Rao, head of the Department of Economics at the University of Delhi, India and a scholar of international repute, gave his impressions of China, after touring the country, in two articles that appeared in *The Nation*, April 5 and 12, 1952. The following are some excerpts from his report:

Admittedly the government functions as a dictatorship, but the only groups conscious of repression are those with vested feudal interests and persons who, having lost their special positions of privilege or power, would like to bring back the old regime. I cannot help feeling that part of the emphasis one finds in China on the suppression of these classes is due to the fact that Chiang Kai-shek's rule in Formosa constitutes a standing threat to the Peking government, especially since it is supported by the United States.

The system has brought people into close contact with the government and given them the opportunity to ventilate their needs and express their criticisms.

The Chinese leaders are essentially Chinese patriots; the program by which they are consolidating their hold is essentially a domestic program designed to solve the many economic, social, and cultural problems that confront the Chinese people.

Mr. Clement Attlee, the leader of the British Labor Party who later became Britain's prime minister, made a tour of China in 1954, and delivered a speech at a parliamentary luncheon in Canberra, Australia on September 9, 1954.[30] These are some of the highlights of his report:

> I think it is the first Government China has ever had that set out to deal with corruption. This Government is based on peasants and at least 90 per cent of Chinese people are peasants.
> I've been told—and I believe it—that it is the first time the peasants have had a square deal. This is a pretty solid basis for Government.

Ross Terrill, a member of the faculty of the Political Science Department of Melbourne University, Australia, reported in the January 2, 1965 issue of *The New Republic* on his visit to China. Among the points Mr. Terrill made were:

1. Whenever he tried to tip a restaurant or hotel employee, it was refused. On at least one occasion he was given a lecture about the "absurdity of tipping."

2. He found that honesty was so prevalent that it is customary for tourists to leave their room keys in the door and to leave the door unlocked when one steps out. One evening, while he was dining in a hotel, a bartender came in and handed him his wallet which he had lost two hours earlier. When he examined the wallet later, he found everything intact. Mr. Terrill

---

[30] Reported in *U.S. News & World Report*, Sept. 17, 1954.

concludes his comment on this episode with these words: "Anyone, incidentally, who has been to Hong Kong will appreciate that the honesty of New China is a social, not a racial phenomenon." This is a most important observation, because Mr. Terrill is here comparing the behavior patterns of Chinese people of Hong Kong (part of the "free world") with that of the people of Communist China.

3. On his visit to the Peking Library, he found that it carried 6 million books and copies of 9 thousand periodicals, among which were many foreign ones. As a test, he looked up the name of the American sociologist, the late Professor C. Wright Mills, and he found four of his books in English.

In an article written specially for the Associated Press, John Haylock reported:[31]

Shanghai, "known once as the center of gangsterism and a city of beggars and prostitutes" (Encyclopaedia Britannica 1962) is today the most moral of cities. Shanghai, where people starved to death on the streets and about whose thoroughfares fathers carried babies to whose backs "for sale" notices were fixed, is now without beggars; no one is in rags and everyone has enough to eat.

A photograph, which accompanied the article, shows the smiling faces of Chinese children and has a caption which includes this statement: "Everyone, and especially the children, looks well fed, healthy and full of energy."

Among other things that Mr. Haylock reported were:

1. Bookshops are full of readers.

2. One gets the feeling that the standard of living is improving.

3. There is no income tax. (This probably will surprise some of the Ultra-Rightist groups who want the income tax abolished in this country.)

4. Rent is never more than ten per cent of one's salary.

5. As a result of a nationwide campaign, the common house fly has been virtually eliminated in China.

6. China has made great strides in industry.

Mr. Haylock winds up his report by solemnly stating that, with all these improvements in the quality of life, there is no

31 Riverside, Calif. *Daily Enterprise,* June 13, 1965.

fun in China! It is typical of the grudging manner in which so many reporters have written about China!

William C. White is one of those American soldiers who defected to Red China during the Korean War. After 11 years of voluntary exile in China, he returned to this country. The Associated Press reported an interview with him, of which the following is the concluding paragraph:

He said the Chinese government "is doing wonders to improve the standard of living of the Chinese people. They're now producing just about everything that can be produced, with no outside aid."[32]

Lisa Hobbs visited China in 1965, and upon her return wrote a series of articles for the Hearst Headline Service. The Hearst papers stated that she is "the first staff reporter to visit Red China in nearly a decade. . . ." In the fourth instalment, she states categorically that nowhere in China could she find any evidence of the food shortage that hostile propagandists had described. She really became an investigator. She carefully examined the scalps of babies, the fingernails of young and old, and the walking habits of growing children. She caused people to smile so that she could take note of the condition of their teeth. As hard as she tried, she could not discover a single case of rickets or malnutrition. She traveled in many rural areas, as well as in the cities of Canton, Peking, Shanghai, Wushi, Soochow, and Hangchow. During three weeks of travel, she visited many food markets in many areas and watched what the homemakers were bringing home. She found a plentiful supply of eggs, fish, potatoes, pork, and fresh green vegetables.[33]

In the seventh instalment, Miss Hobbs reports that the greatest surprise, "even shock," that she received upon visiting Peking was to see the number of people from all nations who come and go freely. Presumably, she was shocked because she could not find the Bamboo Curtain and the secret police under every bed and every table. On the outskirts of every principal city that she visited there were large housing projects, eight and ten stories high, going up at a rapid pace. Contrary to the "think pieces" written by many of the Cold War propagandists, Miss Hobbs was pleasantly surprised by "the people's general

32 *Los Angeles Times,* June 5, 1966.
33 *Los Angeles Herald-Examiner,* June 23, 1965.

demeanor of dignity and self-confidence." She reports further that everyone seemed to have something to do and somewhere to go, that "there was an air of buoyancy and business."[34] This hardly squares with Dr. Clark Kerr's description of the Chinese as being subjected to "the rigid discipline of the anthill—blue-clad ants toiling ceaselessly at their allotted tasks."

Peter Dalhoff is the foreign affairs commentator of Denmark's national television center. He spent four weeks in China assembling material for Danish programs. In an article that he wrote for the Associated Press, Mr. Dalhoff reported that "the slums are gradually giving way to new houses" and that most people live better in China than the people of Bangkok or Bombay. He stated that the food shortage had been overcome: "In the shops and food stores there is an abundance of food— meat, vegetables, fruit and bread. Today only rice and cotton cloth are rationed, but you can have a large bowl of rice without giving up ration cards in any restaurant or canteen for only 0.15 yuan."[35] (0.15 yuan is approximately 6 cents—M. K.)

So much for the general living conditions of the people of China. It is in the fields of education and science that the Chinese can very properly boast of spectacular achievements. Richard Harrington, a Canadian freelance writer and photographer, first visited China in 1964. In 1966 he spent 11 weeks traveling throughout that vast country, and wrote about his experiences in *Parade* magazine, June 5, 1966. He brought back an estimate that, not counting part-time students, there are 150 million Chinese attending school at various levels. In the primary schools, the students spend a 6-hour day, 6 days a week. They study mathematics, grammar, music, history, geography, and nature studies. After six years of primary school, there are three years of lower middle school, three years of middle school, and the university. Foreign language teaching begins in the middle school, and English is the most popular foreign language being taught at present.

Like many foreign observers, Mr. Harrington found some things of which he was sharply critical, but what we find in his report of deepest significance is his description of the intrinsic democratic content of the educational program:

34 *Los Angeles Herald-Examiner*, June 26, 1965.
35 Riverside, Calif. *Daily Enterprise*, Oct. 1, 1965.

Throughout their education, the young are lectured about the joy and value of work. At least an hour of labor weekly is required of students, and every schoolyard has its own carefully-tended vegetable patch. Near Changchun I even visited a school where students, in their work period, had built classrooms.

The stress on work is part of a calculated plan. China's leaders are determined that young intellectuals shall not feel superior to workers and peasants.

In the middle of 1952—three years after the Communists had assumed power in China—Premier Chou En-lai issued a decree calling for the establishment of technical and trade schools throughout the nation and for greater emphasis in technical training at all the existing schools. The goal which the decree envisioned was the training of 500,000 technicians within a few years, in order to expedite the program for industrialization of China.

At the annual meeting of the American Association for the Advancement of Science held in New York City on December 26, 1960, a discussion was held on China's technological development. A dozen experts, who participated in the discussion, found China's scientific progress in the 10 years since the Communists came to power very impressive. Some of the experts said that in another 10 years Chinese scientists in several fields could equal the best in the Western nations.

A specialist of the U.S. Bureau of Mines said that China had expanded coal production approximately seven-fold and was approaching U.S.A. production. Iron and steel production had increased six-fold, and the opinion was expressed that China may become the third largest producer in the world by 1970.

An expert of the U.S. Geological Survey in Washington told of reports from China that, while in 1950 there were 200 geologists, now (in 1960) there were 21,000; and many new mineral discoveries had been made.

A scientist from the staff of Thiokol Chemical Corporation, Trenton, New Jersey, reported that Chinese biochemists are studying human food needs and life processes at high altitudes. There was speculation on the possibility that this meant the Chinese were planning to put a man in a rocket for a journey into outer space.

Dr. Robert T. Beyer of Brown University presented data which had been gathered by a scientist of the National Research Council at Ottawa, Canada. In this report it was shown that Chinese physicists were doing theoretical work in nuclear physics. This led to speculation among the scientists that China might soon develop atomic weapons. It was also pointed out that most of the research in solid state physics was being applied to the development of steel production and heavy industry.

In the field of chemistry, it was reported that China had made tremendous strides, that a whole new generation of bright, well-trained young men were digging the channels of progress through chemistry.

Dr. William Y. Chen of the U.S. National Institutes of Health told the conference China is using "human wave" tactics in a war against vermin. Millions of people were mobilized in a patriotic campaign, *not to war on other human beings, but to war on enemies of human beings—mosquitoes, flies, and grain-eating sparrows.* The campaign resulted in eliminating a billion sparrows, 1½ billion rats, and many trillions of flies and mosquitoes. For the first time in the long history of the Chinese people, a government took decisive steps to eliminate these pests that prey on human beings. This campaign has brought such a spectacular reduction of communicable diseases, that it was the subject of a report to the 77th annual meeting in San Francisco of the Association of American Colleges, October 22, 1966, by Dr. Ronald V. Christie, dean of the medical faculty at McGill University, Montreal. Dr. Christie and five other faculty members visited China on exchange professorships with China Medical College at Peking, and he pointed out that the emphasis in China today is on medical research.

Dr. Christie's report confirms a *Chicago Daily News* Service dispatch from Hong Kong three years earlier.[36] This dispatch tells of the attendance of China's leading physicians and physicians from 11 foreign countries at the eighth national congress on surgery held in Peking. Reports that emerged from this congress "highlight surprising advances Communist China is making in public health and some other fields of medicine." The dispatch explains also:

1. During the 14 years of their rule, the Communists have ex-

36 *San Antonio News,* October 2, 1963.

tended modern medicine of sorts to almost every "hsien" (county) in China proper.

2. The Communists built vaccine laboratories in Chungking, Shanghai, Wuhan, Dairen, and Peking. China is now making most of her own antibiotics.

3. Advanced heart surgery is now done on a scale that surprises some Western specialists.

It hardly needs to be pointed out that in the light of the tremendous improvements in the quality of life in China, it requires a special kind of mental gymnastics to accept the stories about the murdering of 2-60 million "good Chinese citizens" or the equally meretricious story about Mao Tse-tung's willingness to "accept" the loss of 300 million Chinese in an atomic war.

Dr. Klaus Hofman, director of the Protein Research Laboratory at the University of Pennsylvania, told a meeting of the American Chemical Society, held in New York City on September 11, 1966, that the Chinese biochemists have performed a major feat by the full synthesis of insulin. He described it as "the most complex synthesis of a biologically active natural product accomplished to date." This constitutes a scientific breakthrough that had baffled German and American researchers for many years.

A British scientist, Dr. Kurt Mendelsohn of Oxford University, traveled thousands of miles through China. As a result, he expressed the opinion that China will eventually create "by far the largest scientific and technological force in the world." In a conversation with Mao Tse-tung he was told that scientific advance was being given priority treatment. Professor Mendelsohn added: "The Chinese make their own electron microscopes and Chinese-built hydrogen and helium liquifiers have been operating for several years."[37]

In an excellent article that appeared on July 23, 1967, the Los Angeles Times science editor, Dr. Irving S. Bengelsdorf, writes about "Red China's Incredible Technological Revolution." Dr. Bengelsdorf points out:

Now, in three short years, from 1964 to 1967, the "underdeveloped" Red Chinese have test-exploded both nuclear and thermonuclear weapons—a technological feat that thus far has eluded France, a highly developed nation.

37 UPI dispatch from New York, Los Angeles Times, Sept. 14, 1966.

Summarizing an article by Professor Mendelsohn in *Nature,* an international journal of science published in Britain, Dr. Bengelsdorf says:

The stage has now been reached when Chinese industry can manufacture practically anything that the West can produce.

Furthermore, explains Dr. Bengelsdorf, China is producing standard industrial products such as ocean-going ships, diesel-driven trains, cars, buses, trucks, electric generators, gas turbines, computers, and a variety of precision instruments. They are making artificial industrial diamonds of a high quality and are conducting a high quality research program in photosynthesis, the process by which green plants convert the energy of sunlight into food. The city of Shanghai is now one of the largest manufacturing centers in the world.

Now that China has refused to disappear and now that the real China has stepped forward, we conclude with another portion of a speech we have previously quoted. General David M. Shoup, retired Commandant of the U.S. Marine Corps, who served on the Joint Chiefs of Staff under three presidents, said on May 14, 1966:

From my experiences over parts of five years in China and what I know of conditions there today, I'm sure that more Chinese know where tomorrow's food is coming from, than ever in the history of living man. And to what must go the credit? The system they're serving under.

The alienation of the friendship of the great and wonderful Chinese people will surely vie for decades to come as the greatest blunder this country ever made in her relations with other nations, unless the final results from our Vietnam commitment overshadow it.

You say, what about the Republic of China vis-a-vis Red China? I reply time is on the side of the one with the bigger hunk of earth. And that's not Taiwan.

# CHAPTER VI

## The Narcotics Hoax

Don Keller, the District Attorney for San Diego County, California, told a reporter for the now-defunct Los Angeles *Daily News*, on January 28, 1953, that Communist money may be backing the blossoming narcotics industry in Mexico. With a complete disregard for the rules of evidence he would have to follow when prosecuting a case in court and with a full realization that no one would sue him for libel, Mr. Keller said:

> We know that more heroin is being produced south of the border than ever before and we are beginning to hear stories of financial backing by big shot Communists operating out of Mexico City.

In the course of the interview, Keller expatiated on the subject and spoke of a world-wide narcotics ring backed by the Soviet Union and the countries allied with her. Keller gave as the source for these grave charges the December, 1952, issue of *Intelligence Digest*, which was described as "a British information magazine edited by Kenneth De Courcy." The *Digest* charged that more than 4500 tons of illegal opium were produced in China and the Soviet Union during 1952, and that the Soviet Union has two purposes in mind: 1. To obtain American dollars for trade purposes. 2. To demoralize the democracies.

De Courcy did not explain how opium could be produced in any country with government approval and still be illegal. But that is one of the pitfalls one must expect when concocting tall stories.

Kenneth De Courcy is an Ultra-Rightist propagandist, who disseminates a philosophy quite similar to that of the John Birch Society. In the March 1964 issue of *American Opinion*, Professor Revilo P. Oliver pays tribute to De Courcy for his contribution to the expounding of the "Force X" doctrine, a thinly

378

disguised version of the fraudulent "Protocols of the Learned Elders of Zion." Oliver explains that "Mr. De Courcy's private intelligence organization, which largely consists of *former members of British Military Intelligence* now stationed throughout the world *as representatives of British industries*[1] or in similar capacities," has brought the theory of "Force X" into prominence.

The former State Controller of California, Mr. Alan Cranston, described *Intelligence Digest* as "one of the vilest, gutter-level, anti-Semitic hate sheets in the world" and that it "is one of the most popular in all the world's sewers, where demented souls worship swastikas and long for the grand old days of the storm troopers." Mr. Cranston is uniquely qualified to recognize and expose Fascist and Neo-Fascist elements, because as a former journalist he was among the first to recognize and warn the world of the Nazi menace, at a time when so many laughed it off as just a movement of "kooks."

One of De Courcy's issues "exposed" the number of people of Jewish heritage who worked in the late President Kennedy's administration, and according to *Los Angeles Times* columnist, Paul Coates, De Courcy's "exposé" appeared to be a plagiarism of Gerald L. K. Smith's hate pamphlet, *Jews in Position of Great Power.*

In July of 1967, *Intelligence Digest* sent out a promotion letter for its companion publication, *The Weekly Review.* It advised the reader that forthcoming issues will expose *"The Attack on America."* This consists of a Communist plot "to create a vast revolutionary force inside the United States by employing 20 million Negroes." A second part of the "plot" is a plan to pack the United Nations with Black African states. The third element is to decrease American influence in Europe by using De Gaulle as the front man for that part of the operation.

De Courcy is the son of an evangelist preacher. In some mysterious manner, he acquired considerable wealth and was able to throw lavish parties in his $200,000 mansion. In 1963 he was convicted in London's Old Bailey court of 11 charges of fraud, forgery, perjury, and financial manipulations. The prosecution charged him with responsibility for an ingenious

1 Emphasis has been added.

379

multi-million-dollar real estate swindle. He was sentenced to seven years in prison. Without success, he has appealed his sentence several times. During one of these appeals, when he was allowed to go to his lawyer's office accompanied by guards, he tried to escape. He was captured the next day, after a nationwide police bulletin had been sent out. That "educational" magazine, *American Opinion*, forgot to mention De Courcy's qualifications to be a member of the Birchers' "hall of fame." Anyway, he is anti-Communist and that makes him acceptable.

Another expert on Communist plots is the syndicated columnist, Victor Riesel. In the same week that District Attorney Keller "exposed" the Communist narcotics plot, Riesel assured his readers that "Operation Opium" was well known to Army officials here and in the Orient. Riesel claimed that an eastern Congressman documented a story about dope addiction among American servicemen in Japan and Korea, but that the Defense Department took no action.

The following month, on February 25, 1963, Republican Congressman Norris Poulson announced his candidacy for Mayor of Los Angeles. At the same time he called for an investigation of a possible Communist plot to supply narcotics to addicts in this country. He went on to suggest that the dope habit is "the real secret weapon of the Kremlin" and that the House Un-American Activities Committee should investigate. Poulson warned:

The slaves of Stalin swore to break the resistance in China by killing one out of every four Chinese. They failed. What was the alternative? To destroy minds and souls, where they had failed to destroy bodies, by forcing or beguiling millions of Chinese into becoming narcotics addicts.

Congressman Poulson was no piker. While other dragon-slayers accused the Communists of slaying between 2 and 60 million "good Chinese citizens," Poulson charged that they had murdered one-fourth of the then population of 600,000,000— making it the murder of 150 million! It is not clear whether Poulson was accusing the Russian Communists or the Chinese Communists when he attributed this gigantic atrocity to the "slaves of Stalin." After this oratorical flight of fancy, Poulson ventured the warning that drug smuggling may be a Soviet plan to weaken America just as the Russians had (according to Poulson) forced the Chinese to become dope addicts.

In December of 1953, Mrs. Lois Higgins, director of the Chicago Crime Prevention Bureau, told a meeting of the American Association for the Advancement of Science at Boston, Mass., that the Communists were using narcotics as a weapon against the West. The two top narcotics officers in Los Angeles, Walter Creighton, Chief of the State Bureau of Narcotics and George T. Davis, agent in charge of the local office of the Federal Bureau of Narcotics, told reporters that there was no concrete evidence to support Mrs. Higgins' charge.

On July 17, 1958, an editorial in the now defunct *Los Angeles Mirror* summarized a speech delivered at a Town Hall luncheon during that week by prominent attorney Robert Neeb, Jr. According to the *Mirror*, among Neeb's points were:

1. Drug addiction in the U.S.A. had been practically wiped out in 1948, and then Russia started to flood the world with heroin from Red China. Also that Russia is actively "pushing" the narcotics traffic in the non-Communist world.

2. U.S. aid should be denied to any nation that declines to cooperate in a world narcotics control program. Among those who had thus far refused to cooperate were Britain, France, Belgium, and Italy.

3. The great bulk of illicit drugs is smuggled into the United States through Mexico, which refuses to cooperate in stamping out the drug traffic.

On November 5, 1958 we sent attorney Neeb a courteous letter, asking where we could find the proof that drug addiction had been wiped out in the U.S.A. in 1948, that Russia is actively "pushing" the narcotics traffic, and that Russia began to flood the world with heroin from Red China. No reply was received. Had Mr. Neeb replied, we were prepared to fire a series of questions to the eminent counselor-at-law. Among them would have been: *How could Russia begin to flood the world with heroin from Red China in 1948, when Red China did not come into existence until 1949?*

On May 5, 1960, commentator George Putnam said on Station KTTV that the Communists were behind the sale of habit-forming drugs in order to weaken us. When we challenged him to prove this statement, he wrote to us on May 13, 1960, that we should ask for documentation from H. J. Anslinger, Chief of the Federal Bureau of Narcotics, Washington, D.C. A letter to Mr. Anslinger was sent on May 23, 1960, with a polite request for documentation. No reply was received.

On October 3, 1960, Federal narcotics agents in New York City arrested the Guatemalan Ambassador to Belgium and three accomplices on charges of smuggling $4 million in heroin into the United States. Guatemala is ruled by a Fascist military dictatorship, so it is not likely that the ambassador is a Chinese or Russian Communist or any other kind of Communist. Two of his accomplices were Frenchmen and the third one was a Greek. The heroin, according to the Federal agents, came from France, not Russia and not China. On October 3, 1960, Attorney Robert Neeb, Jr. appeared on George Putnam's television program. He could only have heard about the arrest of the ambassador and his accomplices on the radio or television, but Mr. Neeb knew enough about it to make some important disclosures. On October 7, 1960, we sent a letter to Mr. Neeb, advising him that we understood him to say on George Putnam's telecast of October 3 that there is some link-up between international Communism and the $4 million smuggling. We politely asked where we could obtain proof and documentation of this charge. We even enclosed a stamped, self-addressed envelope. No reply was received.

On March 22, 1960, Governor Edmund G. Brown of California created by Executive Order the Special Study Commission on Narcotics. On June 2, 1961, the Commission transmitted its Special Interim Report to the Governor. The following is part of the Commission's letter of transmittal:

The Commission was informed that, in a twenty-three day period, one million units of dangerous drugs of the stimulant variety were shipped from American drug manufacturers to Tijuana at the apparently regular wholesale price of 76¢ per 1,000 units. More recently, six hundred thousand units were shipped to a Mexican border town in three days. These drugs were in turn sold openly and without prescription to Americans, including teenagers, who brought them back into California.

Under present California laws, the illegal possession and sale of dangerous drugs are misdemeanors. Since the dangerous drugs are potentially as harmful to the mind and body as is the use of narcotics, the punishment for illegal trafficking in such drugs should be the same as for an equivalent violation of the State Narcotic Act.

382

Among the interesting items in the Report itself, we found the following shocking story:

In 1958, a Los Angeles doctor was convicted by a jury in the federal court on 20 counts for illegally dispensing dangerous drugs. Investigation into the doctor's conduct was commenced in 1955 by the United States Food and Drug Administration, the Bureau of Narcotics Enforcement, and local police agencies. Over 100 purchases of dangerous drugs were made by federal, state, and county officers working undercover. This doctor conducted a cursory physical examination of those who came to him for drugs. The "patient" was then asked if he wanted "reducers" (drugs for reducing purposes) or "sleepers" (barbiturates). The doctor's nurse testified that 8,000 pills were sold weekly at 10 cents a pill. Undercover agents who were extremely thin, asked for and received reducing pills. One Sheriff's deputy who received "reducers" was 5′ 11½″ and weighed 136 pounds. A staff member was on duty at the office on holidays and weekends, dispensing pills up to 10:30 P.M. to anyone who was a "patient." Some of the regular "patients" received an average of 12 pills daily for several months without any medical examination, discussion of symptoms, or other checks of his need for medication. The doctor was given a $100 fine for each of the 20 counts for which he was convicted; however, the imposition of these fines was suspended. The doctor was placed on probation, and the court expressly stated that no moral turpitude was involved in these crimes. This doctor is practicing medicine in Los Angeles at the present time.

One of the members of this Special Study Commission on Narcotics was *Mr. Robert Neeb, Jr.* One of the strangest things about this Report is that there is not a single word about Communists or Russia or China—not a single word about the plot to make big money and demoralize the people of the "free world." Having declaimed so eloquently about the Communist "plot," one wonders why Mr. Neeb did not grasp this golden opportunity, while clothed with official powers and with a staff at his disposal, to produce some evidence of probative value to back up his speeches of July, 1958 and May 5, 1960. When he made the latter speech on George Putnam's television program, he was already a member of the Special Study Commission on Narcotics. Indeed, in the first Interim Report of his Commission, dated December 3, 1960, we find Mr. Neeb and his associates *refuting Mr. Neeb's previous pronouncements.* In one portion of this Report we read :

Over ninety percent of the marijuana found in this state is illegally smuggled across the border. Over seventy percent of the heroin which reaches our state is raised and processed from opium poppy fields in Mexico. Mexico is also the source of almost all of our marijuana.

Strangely enough, we have not been able to find any record of Mr. Neeb making thunderous speeches about the Republicans, Democrats, Catholics, Protestants, Jews, Americans, Mexicans, and others who are not Communists, but who produce and distribute marijuana and heroin. Nor have we found any record of Mr. Neeb denouncing the American drug manufacturers who ship millions of dangerous drug pills to Mexico with the full knowledge that they will be peddled to American teenagers. Surely Mr. Neeb knows that these drug manufacturers are good Republicans and Democrats; probably members of the Chamber of Commerce, the Rotary Club, the Lions Club, the American Legion, and other respectable groups. One wonders also why Mr. Neeb did not mention the political affiliation of that physician who peddled dangerous drug pills. Why did not Mr. Neeb mention the physician's name? Can it be that Mr. Neeb does not care to expose the fact that behind the illicit drug and narcotics traffic there is the driving force of *greed for profits*, not ideological considerations?[2] It is so much easier to blame everything on the Communists! And no one is likely to sue you for libel!

In the December 1961 issue of *The Cross and The Flag*, the Rev. Gerald L. K. Smith had an article which caused us to write a letter on April 5, 1967 to Senator Thomas J. Dodd of Connecticut. We explained that, in the course of our research, we ran across this article which quoted a speech by him, and then we said:

In what purports to be a speech of yours at Carnegie Hall, New York, under the auspices of the Committee of One Million, you are quoted as saying that the Peking regime of China is "a government which has made a State industry out of producing opium and other narcotics and peddling these drugs to criminal elements all around the world at an annual profit of several hundred million dollars."

2 The Reports of the Special Study Commission on Narcotics will be found in Part 12 of Hearings before the Subcommittee to Investigate Juvenile Delinquency of the Senate Judiciary Committee, August 6 and 7, 1962. It appears as Exhibit No. 17 on pp. 2863-2980.

We asked for proof and documentation not only of this statement, but also of another statement that the article attributed to him: that the "Red regime has succeeded in murdering 30 million of its own people." No reply was received from the Senator.

One of the witnesses who testified before the Senate Subcommittee to Investigate Juvenile Delinquency was Joel Fort, M.D., an outstanding expert on the narcotics problem, a special adviser to the President's Committee on Juvenile Delinquency and Youth Crime, and a lecturer at the School of Criminology at the University of California. Dr. Fort is also a psychiatrist of great repute and has had two years of full-time experience at the Federal narcotics treatment hospital at Lexington, Kentucky. He has been a consultant on illicit drug traffic to the United Nations headquarters at Geneva, Switzerland and was the head of a 16-nation survey of the illicit drug traffic under the auspices of the United Nations. Many people consider him the world's foremost authority on the illicit drug traffic.

After defining drug addiction in scientific terms, Dr. Fort stated:

To put the problem in its perspective, *the most serious type of drug addiction in the United States is alcoholism, which affects some 6 million*[3] people of the 80 million who drink alcoholic beverages, with the greatest number, 600,000, in California, and the total number in the United States increasing by some 200,000 per year, and having tremendous social, economic, health, and criminal consequences.

In a paper he presented to the Third World Congress of Psychiatry, Dr. Fort said:

Narcotics addiction, although it receives much more attention in the mass media and legislatures of the United States, is a far smaller problem, affecting somewhere between 50,000 and 100,000 Americans.[4]

The Federal Bureau of Narcotics reported that for the year ending December 31, 1961, there were 46,798 active narcotic addicts in the entire country. This, of course, does not include

[3] Emphasis has been added.—M. K.
[4] This Report is listed as Exhibit No. 39 in Part 12 of the Hearings Before the U.S. Senate Subcommittee to Investigate Juvenile Delinquency, 1962.

the people who are "hooked" on the dangerous drugs mentioned by the California Special Study Commission on Narcotics. When the total number of narcotic addicts is compared to the number who are "hooked" on the non-narcotic dangerous drugs and the 6,000,000 that are "hooked" on alcohol, one has a right to ask why Mr. Neeb and others have not directed their fire against the profit-greedy drug manufacturers and liquor manufacturers who poison 100 times as many as the Russian and Chinese Communists could possibly poison, even if the charges against them were true—which they are not!

Dr. Charles S. Poling is a retired Presbyterian minister, who makes speeches in which he paints the National Council of Churches with the Red "paint brush" and is not too retired when it comes to lending support to Ultra-Rightist causes. On August 4, 1963, he was one of the speakers at the annual convention in Oklahoma City of Billy James Hargis' Ultra-Rightist *Christian Crusade*. Among the other luminaries on the same platform were Rev. Billy James Hargis, former General Edwin A. Walker, the late Fulton Lewis, Jr. and number one Bircher, Robert Welch. On August 15, 1965, the Rev. Dr. Charles S. Poling delivered a sermon entitled "How a Republic Died." It pleased the Ultra-Rightist Congressman from Orange County, California so well that the Hon. James B. Utt placed it in the Congressional Record on October 1, 1965. The *Minutemen* leader, Robert De Pugh, liked it so well that he copied it from the Congressional Record and printed it in the *Minutemen* organ, *On Target*, April 1, 1966, once again proving that the Ultra-Rightist Congressmen "feed" the Ultra-Rightist propaganda machine via items planted in the Congressional Record. A letterhead received in April, 1966, from the Ultra-Rightist *We, the People* lists the Rev. Poling as its treasurer.

In "An Expanded Statement," issued by the National Committee of Christian Laymen of Phoenix, Arizona, and circulated also by the Committee of Christian Laymen of Woodland Hills, California, during July of 1963, the Rev. Dr. Poling uses the Red "paint brush" pretty liberally on the National Council of Churches. He chides this group especially for advocating recognition of Red China and her admission to the United Nations. The Rev. Poling points the finger of accusation against the National Council of Churches for committing these "crimes" and then adds:

386

And knowing well that this nation slaughtered over thirty-million of her own people, gives millions of acres to the culture of opium poppy with which to corrupt her own and the peoples of the world, rather than convert this land to the raising of grain that her starving millions may be fed.

There are at least three false statements in that one single paragraph! China did not slaughter thirty million of her own people. The consumption of opium is illegal in China, and the sale of opium, except upon a physician's prescription for legitimate purposes, is punishable by death. There are no starving millions to be fed. Indeed about two weeks after Dr. Poling's brochure was mailed out, an Associated Press dispatch from Ottawa, Canada told of an agreement signed on August 1, 1963, for the purchase of between 112,000,000 and 186,700,000 bushels of Canadian wheat by the Peking Government of China. This was done to offset the results of a prolonged drought and was the first time in history that a Chinese government took such a step to *prevent* hunger. In previous eras, Chinese died like flies from famine. A fourth departure from truth—the alleged growing of opium—we shall deal with a little later.

On July 18, 1963, we sent a letter to Dr. Poling challenging the veracity of the statement that China "gives millions of acres to the culture of opium poppy with which to corrupt her own and the peoples of the world. . . ." On July 22, 1963, Dr. Poling replied that the only answer he would give is that one who challenges this statement "should read more and perhaps visit the editor of an accredited newspaper." Dr. Poling then adds this comment:

Even the Chinese government does not deny that the opium traffic is one of their major sources of income. As you know we have many well read and informed church leaders who oppose us and are constantly looking for one mistaken or undocumented statement. The publication you handed your neighbor has gone forth by hundreds of thousands.[5] In not one instance have our charges been challenged nor proven false.

May God lead and keep you always.

If the Rev. Poling had taken his own advice and read the newspapers, he would not have compounded his misstatements

[5] This is a reference to a statement in our letter to Dr. Poling that we had shown his brochure to a neighbor, who challenged its veracity.

of fact by another one, contained in his letter. The Chinese government has definitely denied any participation in the illicit opium traffic.

On July 29, 1963, we wrote a letter to the Rev. Poling, in which we told him:

1. That we are deeply disappointed in the fact that he failed to supply any evidence of probative value.

2. That even if China did not reply to the charges it would not support the validity of the charges. We pointed out that neither General Eisenhower nor Allen W. Dulles replied to the fantastic charges against them by Bircher Robert Welch.

3. That as a believer in the Commandment, "Thou Shalt Not Bear False Witness Against Thy Neighbor," it was incumbent upon him to give better proof of his charges. We asked him to give any citation from reputable sources, to prove his charges.

4. That he did not prove his case by claiming that no one had challenged him previously.

5. That we were prepared to furnish overwhelming documentation to refute his charges.

6. That there is a fundamental question of morality involved.

No reply was received from the Rev. Dr. Poling, who proclaims that *every* Communist has "rape and slaughter in his heart"! Such is the standard of truth and morality of an Ultra-Rightist preacher, who professes to be a disciple of Christ!

Probably the most influential, of those who have attributed the illicit narcotics traffic to China, is Harry J. Anslinger. In his position as Commissioner of the Federal Bureau of Narcotics for some thirty years, he has hurled the charge with an air of infallibility. Despite the fact that he is a most formidable opponent, we propose to challenge the veracity of his charge. There are ample precedent and proof that Federal officials do sometimes tell lies as part of the Cold War propaganda struggle. It was not so long ago that Arthur Sylvester, Assistant Secretary of Defense, publicly justified the use of falsehoods in the interest of national security. The Central Intelligence Agency has been caught in so many lies that it would take many pages to catalogue them.

In 1950, Mr. Anslinger made the headlines when he appeared

before an American Legion narcotics conference and stated that the narcotics traffic was a "Red" conspiracy. He made the same charge a little later when he appeared before a Committee of the U.S. Senate, which was conducting an investigation of organized crime in interstate commerce. His testimony before the Committee, following this blanket charge, put Anslinger in the position of refuting himself. He told the Committee that during the 1930's a world-wide narcotics smuggling ring was headed by the late mass murderer, Louis "Lepke" Buchalter, who obtained one-fifth of all the illicit heroin supply reaching this country from a factory operating in the Japanese concession in Tientsin. He tells the same story in his book, *The Murderers,* published in 1961, and adds:

The full truth behind Lepke's role in crime has been kept from the public, for his power reached to the highest pedestals of authority and held some of our most honored citizens in servitude.

Anslinger relates that Lepke's plan of operation "revolved around the bribery of two Customs officers in New York," who received $1,000 each time a Lepke courier brought in a shipment of heroin in travelers' trunks. In another part of his book he tells of a "syndicated narcotic underworld that came into being in the 1920's and 1930's." He tells of the Mafia involvement in the narcotics traffic and names the gangster, Lucky Luciano, as the one who "put together a super-syndicate that would dominate international crime, particularly the traffic in dope."

All this, of course, is taking place some 20 years *before* Red China came into existence, and we find an international narcotics smuggling ring getting its heroin from a city in China that was under Japanese domination. We find corruption of Customs officers, and we find "some of our most honored citizens" involved! One thing is absolutely certain: every single one of these precious characters was staunchly anti-Communist and 100% American!

After Anslinger had told the Senate Committee about the China drug traffic in the 1930's and the role of Lepke and other gangsters, Senator Kefauver asked him what are the sources of the illicit narcotics of the present period. Anslinger replied:

389

The present main source of supply for heroin in this country is Istanbul, Turkey; for opium, it is Iran. There is a considerable amount of heroin coming in from Italian ports. I think that is a transit point for the heroin from Istanbul. The same thing can be said about French ports, Marseilles, and so forth. These countries are the main sources of supply.

How does one explain Mr. Anslinger's behavior? We are inclined to believe that he is essentially an honest man, but the Cold War has lowered our standards of morality and it has become "patriotic" to blame the Communists for every evil in the world. A zealous Cold War propagandist has no difficulty in finding rationalizations for telling falsehoods about Communists. It "helps our national security," it "strengthens the free world," and it is no longer falsehood, but "patriotism." In his book, Mr. Anslinger speaks of "Red China's longe range dope-and-dialectic assault on America and its leaders." That is a Cold War propaganda formulation which confirms what we suspect is the real explanation for Anslinger's holy crusade against Red China.

It is interesting to note that Anslinger refutes two of the statements made by the Rev. Dr. Charles Poling:

Poling says that Red China "gives millions of acres to the culture of opium poppy with which to *corrupt her own people and the peoples of the world. . ."* (Emphasis added—M. K.)

Anslinger says in his book: "The standard policy employed in Red China is to *suppress addiction among the Chinese* while encouraging the cultivation, manufacture, export, distribution and sale of morphine and heroin to other countries and other peoples."

Poling says that Red China has never denied involvement in illicit narcotics traffic.

Anslinger reports that when he made these charges against Red China at the United Nations Commission on Narcotics, China could not deny them because she had no delegate there, not having been admitted to membership in the U.N. However, the Soviet delegate did vehemently deny the charges on behalf of China.

A few months after Anslinger's 1950 testimony, another U.S. Senate Committee was conducting an investigation of organized crime in interstate commerce. This Committee was not interested in using its mandate as a springboard for anti-Communist propaganda. In a Report dated May 1, 1951, we read:

> Presently, a large flow of heroin is coming from Turkey where it is manufactured from excess opium production in that country and Iran. Also, a large amount of heroin has been coming from Italy lately as the result of diversion from medical stocks available by reason of allotments of heroin obviously excessive for alleged medical purposes.

It is most significant that the Committee's information came from Harry Anslinger's Bureau of Narcotics:

> Testimony before this committee of one representative of the Bureau of Narcotics is to the effect that the influx of heroin from Italy coincided with activity there of Salvatore Luciano ("Lucky" Luciano) who was deported to Italy in February, 1946.

Mr. Anslinger also testified, on July 17, 1954, at a hearing before the U.S. Senate Subcommittee of the Foreign Relations Committee. As on the previous occasion, Anslinger's anti-Communist zeal caused him to testify in a contradictory fashion. At one point he said:

> There are countries like China, Burma, Thailand, and Mexico, where opium is grown illegally, and those governments must take firm measures to cope with this illegal production.

He preceded this statement by remarking that the U.S. Government had been trying for some 40 years to get a limitation of opium production.

A few minutes later in the Senate hearing, the following dialogue took place:

*The Chairman.* I understand that at every meeting of the UN Commission on Narcotic Drugs there has been an effort to try to seat Red China on the Commission. Would you tell us briefly a word about the history of the Communist effort in that regard?
*Mr. Anslinger.* Mr. Chairman, beginning with the first meeting of the United Nations Commission in 1946, Communist China attempted to unseat Nationalist China. Their efforts were defeated year after year. Our vote is getting a little slimmer, but nevertheless we have been able to keep them out of the commission.
I do not believe they have any place in the commission, because

they are the worst offender. Red China represents the major source of the illicit traffic for the entire world. . .

It is obvious from this testimony that Anslinger is more than a fighter against the narcotics traffic. He is also a zealous anti-Communist crusader. If Communist China is really the biggest offender in the illicit narcotics traffic, why does it want a seat on the United Nations Commission on Narcotics Drugs, whose function is to control and try to suppress this traffic? Why does Anslinger oppose its membership on the Commission? Would not its presence give him an opportunity to tell the Chinese Communists directly to their faces about the crimes of which he accuses them? Could it be possible that Anslinger prefers to make charges in a forum where he will not be challenged to prove his statements?

There is a propaganda sleight-of-hand involved in the charges against Communist China. It is embodied in this sentence from Anslinger's further testimony:

Southeast Asia is flooded with opium from Yunnan.

We will come back to this, but it is important to remember that the key to this mystery is Yunnan.

Continuing with Mr. Anslinger's testimony:

The amount of heroin that is flowing out of China is used for several purposes: to obtain foreign exchange (it is a very good means of obtaining foreign exchange, since they cannot export other commodities) and also the demoralization of people who use this deadly drug in many countries. That is certainly one of the objectives—you cannot get away from that—a poison being spread from Red China.

We have brought this matter up before the Commission on Narcotic Drugs in the United Nations repeatedly. We have had one note from the Communist government which was submitted through the Soviet delegation. Their only answer to many, many charges, well documented, was that *they prohibited the production of opium.* (Emphasis added.—M. K.)

Who is telling the truth? First of all, it is absolutely untrue that Communist China "cannot export other commodities." This is an Anslinger invention, which by itself serves to discredit all his charges against Communist China. If Anslinger had been more careful with the truth, he could have ascertained from the Department of Commerce, only a short distance from his office, that Communist China does indeed export many industrial products, as well as raw materials, and enjoys commercial relations with many countries including England, Canada, and Japan. Secondly, the facts we have presented from reliable sources show that more people in the U.S.A. are poisoned by dangerous drugs, including alcohol, that are manufactured in the U.S.A., than could possibly be poisoned by all the narcotics coming into the country. Thirdly, even if Communist China were engaged in the illicit narcotics traffic—and we shall prove this is untrue—there are other *major* sources of narcotics, and we present as a witness against Anslinger's charge, that "Red China represents the major source of illicit traffic for the entire world," the testimony of one, Harry J. Anslinger, a few minutes after that charge was made:

Lebanon has become the center of the illicit traffic in the Middle East. Most of the hashish is grown in Lebanon. But the illicit production of opium out of Turkey and the illicit manufacture of heroin from opium is going by way of Lebanon to Italy, France, and the United States.

Mr. Anslinger's obsession with the need to prove his charges against Communist China assumed ludicrous proportions when he testified about Mexico:

Mr. Chairman, opium is grown illicitly in the states of Chihuahua, Sonora, and Sinaloa, way back in the recesses of the mountains.
While they have a terrific cannabis problem—and we get most of our cannabis from Mexico—nevertheless the opium and heroin in the West comes from China, *I think*,[6] for the most part. Some comes from Lebanon and Turkey in through New York, and is flown out to California. But the Mexican narcotics found illicitly in the West and in other parts, maybe Texas, I would say, would not amount to more than 25 percent of the total.

There was good reason for Anslinger's equivocal statement about the amount of opium and heroin coming into the West from Mexico. In order to place a charge against Communist China, it was necessary to reduce the percentage of opium and heroin coming in from Mexico. As we shall show a little later,

---

6 Emphasis added.—M. K. Apparently Anslinger was getting a little wobbly, and had to qualify his statement with "I think."

Anslinger's figures are not dependable. For the present it is enough to recall that the California Special Study Commission on Narcotics reported:

Over seventy percent of the heroin which reaches our state is raised and processed from opium poppy fields in Mexico. Mexico is also the source of almost all our marijuana.

It is time to play a little game of comparisons again:

1. Attorney Robert Neeb, Jr. has stated that Russia is behind the illicit narcotics traffic.

2. San Diego County District Attorney Don Keller quoted Kenneth De Courcy's *Intelligence Digest* that Communist China and Russia are in a conspiracy to peddle narcotics.

3. Congressman Norris Poulson said that the Russians forced the Chinese to become narcotic addicts.

Along comes Commissioner Harry J. Anslinger and spoils the little game for these gentry, testifying at the Senate Subcommittee Hearing:[7]

The Soviet orbit, that is Russia, Bulgaria, Hungary, Poland, and Czechoslovakia, do carry out their obligations. We do not find any leakage from that Soviet orbit.

It is only Communist China that Anslinger is gunning for. It is worthy of note that Anslinger's efforts coincide with the Cold War propaganda needs of the State Department, the House Un-American Activities Committee, the Senate Internal Security Subcommittee and Chiang Kai-shek's propaganda lobby in this country.

Not satisfied with the damage done by the propaganda that was made a part of the record in the 1954 Hearing before the Subcommittee of the Senate Foreign Relations Committee, the Cold War propaganda machine staged another propaganda soiree under the aegis of the Senate Internal Security Subcommittee of the Committee on the Judiciary, March 8, 18, 19 and May 13, 1955. In the foreword, the Ultra-Rightist and Racist Senator from Mississippi, James O. Eastland, stated that the purpose of the hearings was "to determine whether the Chinese Communists are using narcotics to weaken the morale of the

[7] Hearing Before a Subcommittee of the Committee on Foreign Relations, United States Senate on The International Opium Protocol, July 17, 1954.

free nations of the western world and, collaterally, to obtain the huge amounts of hard money needed to build and sustain their war machine."

Before examining the highlights of this hearing, we cannot resist the temptation to play another little game of comparisons. The star witness of this Hearing was Richard L. G. Deverall, "representative in Asia of the free trade union committee of the AFL." He testified that he was in MacArthur's Headquarters as Chief of Labor Education in Tokyo until late in 1948, when he returned to the United States. He returned to Japan for the AFL in 1952 and has been there since. Now we can begin our little game of comparisons:

| Harry Anslinger<br>July 17, 1954 | Richard L. G. Deverall<br>March 18, 1955 |
|---|---|
| There is a terrific amount of consumption in China itself. The amount of heroin and opium used there would probably take as much as 80 percent of the total produced. (This would leave only 20 per cent with which to undermine the "free world."—M. K.) | I might say I have interviewed Japanese who have returned from Red China within the last year and they have verified that the Red Chinese regime has been very vigorous in stamping out the use of opium in China. Missionaries who have been expelled from China through Hong Kong have also verified that from 1951 forward, the Chinese regime has been very active in stamping out the use of opium inside Red China, and third, Chinese official sources themselves indicate the passage of two opium-use-suppression laws in 1950. |

The 1955 Hearings were obviously held to make propaganda against Communist China, by preparing a document that could be quoted and copied endlessly by the Ultra-Right. Harry Anslinger was the first witness. One of the exchanges we found interesting was:

*Senator Welker.* Do you know of any organized syndicate in the United States, organized to receive narcotics heretofore mentioned from couriers bringing them these narcotics into this country from Red China?

*Mr. Anslinger.* Well, no really organized syndicate.

In his 1950 testimony before the Kefauver Committee and in his book published in 1961, Anslinger told of huge gangster syndicates who obtained heroin from China for distribution in the U.S.A. during the 1930's. Now Mr. Anslinger is admitting that the gangster syndicates no longer obtain their supplies from China, which is now under Communist leadership. One of the nice things about Mr. Anslinger is that he makes such a good witness against himself!

The phoney nature of the Hearing was exposed by the final question that was asked of Mr. Anslinger. The Committee was going far afield at the very outset. when it started to investigate alleged illicit narcotic traffic from Communist China, because the Committee's mandate is "To Investigate the Administration of the Internal Security Act and Other Internal Security Laws." This mandate was stretched beyond recognition with the pretext that it was "to determine whether the Chinese Communists are using narcotics to weaken the morale of the free nations." Now Senator Jenner asked Anslinger his opinion as to U.S.A. recognition of Red China and her admission into the United Nations. The Senator conceded that "maybe it is not a proper question." In his reply, Anslinger was very coy, insisting that this was a question of policy for a higher echelon than himself. In the end, he did give his opinion, and anyone can guess what it was.

The next witness before the Subcommittee was Mr. "Nameless," whose identity was not disclosed.

The excuse given was that he is an undercover agent for the Bureau of Narcotics, with assignments in the Far East. He began his testimony with:

The flow of heroin into Japan from Communist China began in 1947 at the same time it did into South Korea. By 1948 there was considerable traffic, and by 1949 great numbers of the smugglers from Communist China were being arrested.

The next time that the chief counsel of Senate Internal Security Subcommittee, Mr. Julian Sourwine, prepares a mystery witness for the spinning of a yarn, he should be more careful of his dates. Red China did not come into existence until 1949! Witness may now step down!

Following Mr. "Nameless," Richard Deverall testified. Throughout his testimony, Mr. Richard Arens, Associate

Counsel to the Committee, asked him leading questions, leading him along to deliver the predetermined results the Committee was seeking.

Bearing in mind that this is a Committee to Investigate the Administration of the Internal Security Act and Other Internal Security Laws, what is the relevance and purpose of these questions, which were among those asked by Mr. Arens?

Now, Mr. Deverall, what in your judgment is the importance of Japan to the security of the United States from the standpoint of our own internal security?

. . . would you give us your overall appraisal of the degree to which Japan is under the shadow of the Soviet regime or the Red Chinese threat? How serious is the threat to Japan from Communists?

What is the potency of the Communists within the trade-union movement in Japan since independence?

Is the teachers union, in your judgment, under Communist control and domination?

What would be your best appraisal as an overall judgment of the Communist influence and control in Japan?

We could go on and on, but the point is clear that the hearing was a farce. None of these questions had any relation to the *internal security* of the U.S.A. and none of them had anything to do with the administration of the Internal Security Act. The Committee was bent on providing some *ideological ammunition* for the Ultra-Rightists. There is no other explanation for this Committee getting into the jurisdiction of the Foreign Relations Committee.

Deverall was, of course, a friendly witness for the Committee's aim, which was to pin the illicit narcotics label on Communist China. At one point Mr. Arens asked him to estimate how much Red China was receiving per year from the alleged sale of narcotics. Mr. Deverall gave an estimate of $70 million. This caught Mr. Arens in a very embarrassing—almost ludicrous—position. For a nation of some 700 million people, $70 million is only a miniscule portion of its income. Especially was this so when Deverall stated that some of the $70 million from the alleged narcotics sales remained with the Communist Parties of the respective countries where the narcotics were allegedly sold. It began to look as if this propaganda ploy would fizzle out, but Arens is a resourceful Red-hunter. By the use of a series of questions, he blew up the $70 million to $700 million! Arens developed the point, that narcotics go through many hands from the opium grower to the pusher in the streets of New York and Los Angeles, and that $70 million grows to $700 million in the process. After all, if you can make it look as if Communist China gets $700 million per year, it sounds more plausible as a policy for obtaining needed foreign exchange. After a series of questions which brought unsatisfactory results for Arens, and realizing that the witness, Deverall, was not "catching on," Arens became blunt:

*Mr. Arens.* What I am trying to interrogate you on is this: The end user pays much more than is received by the producer of narcotics, does he not?
*Mr. Deverall.* Yes, sir.
*Mr. Arens.* Could you give us some indication as to the multiplication which is involved by the time the end user makes his payment for the shot or dosage of narcotics? That is, when it is cut?
*Mr. Deverall.* That is rather difficult because for one thing, I do not think there are any statistics on it, but from what I have learned in Japan from the Japanese narcotics people, the markup is from 5 to 10 times by the time it reaches the pusher who is pushing the stuff out in the field.
*Mr. Arens.* Then instead of $70 million, there would be involved then 10 times $70 million?
*Mr. Deverall.* An enormous traffic.
*Mr. Arens.* Is that right, in the aggregate?
*Mr. Deverall.* Yes.
*Mr. Arens.* It would be about $700 million then, involved, right?
*Mr. Deverall.* I would say it is a large amount. I would not want to say definite figures.
*Mr. Arens.* I understand. I just wanted to get a general appraisal of how significant this traffic is from a monetary standpoint.
*Mr. Deverall.* It is an enormous amount of money. I might add that.

There is little need to comment on the essential dishonesty of this line of interrogation, excepting to point out that this kind of testimony would be inadmissible in a court of law and it hardly confirms a statement in the speech attributed to Senator Thomas Dodd, that China makes an annual profit of several hundred million dollars on narcotics. Even Arens' friendly witness would not go beyond $70 million, and was very equivocal about Arens' attempt to blow it up to $700 million.

As we have previously mentioned, the Senate Subcommittee

to Investigate the Administration of the Internal Security Act and Other Internal Security Laws went far afield when it undertook to prepare this tendentious document, entitled "Communist China and Illicit Narcotic Traffic." Supposing, that just for the sake of a discussion, we grant the propriety of the Committee's little safari into narcotics-land. But how can we justify the following line of interrogation, and what relationship does it bear to the illicit narcotics traffic?

*Mr. Arens.* Do you have any information respecting the recent tour of Madam Li Te-Chuan, Minister of Health in Red China, in Japan?
*Mr. Deverall.* Well, Madam Li Te-Chuan is Minister of Health of the Red Chinese regime—she is now a rather militant Communist, I might add. She arrived in Tokyo last October . . . her tour of Japan was a remarkable triumph for the Red Chinese . . . She toured the major cities of Japan and wherever she went there were guards of honor . . . I think I might characterize her tour by saying when she left Japan, thousands of Japanese gathered to sing and wave her good-by and to see her off from the hotel and airport, almost at the same time the then premier of Japan, Mr. Yoshida, had arrived back from his world tour.

Very few people met the man at the airport, and [at] his first press conference—the first question the poor man was asked was, "When do you intend to resign?" And here you had a picture of the Japanese leftwingers fawning before the Minister of Health of Red China and their own premier returning to the country, unhonored, unsung, and being asked, "When are you going to resign?"

*I think that answers your question as to the effectiveness of Red China propaganda in Japan.*[8]

That last sentence lets the cat out of the bag! The illicit narcotics charge is a smoke screen behind which Cold War propaganda is carried out. It is one of the weapons of the Plain Liars, the Fancy Liars, and the Damned Liars!

It appears that Richard Arens was not completely satisfied with Richard Deverall's performance at the hearing on March 18, 1955. The next day—Saturday, March 19, 1955—he questioned Deverall in an *informal* session and under oath. As one reads the questions and answers of this session, it is difficult to avoid the conclusion that Deverall had been induced to "beef up" the previous day's testimony, to "pile it on." He regaled Arens and his staff assistants with stories which a capable

8 Emphasis has been added.—M. K.

neophyte lawyer could have demolished by skillful cross-examination. Again a few kittens were let out of the bag, to wit:

*Mr. Arens.* How successful is Red China at the present time in shaping public opinion in Japan through its propaganda efforts?

*Mr. Deverall.* Well first I should point out that in the Far East, because of the role of educated young men, the youth movement is very important, politically. I say that because the success of Red China in Japan, in shaping public opinion to accept its view, can be seen very easily in both the youth movement and in the labor movement. From what I have observed over a 10-year period in the Far East, of which 6 years have been in Japan, Red Chinese propaganda has been significantly—and I would say somewhat dangerously successful, in orientating the minds of many of the leaders of organized labor, and the youth and students of Japan, in favor of Red China, and against the United States of America.

*Mr. Arens.* Now, how would you on the basis of your background and experience, appraise this situation from the standpoint of the security interests of the West, particularly the United States?

*Mr. Deverall.* I would say it is very dangerous.

Would it be impolite to suggest that Mr. Arens and the Senate Internal Security Subcommittee are more interested in "dangerous ideas" than in dangerous drugs?

On March 3, 1955, the Chairman of the Senate Subcommittee sent a letter to the Department of the Army, asking about the extent of narcotics addiction in the armed forces and whether the source of the narcotics is Communist China. On March 31, 1955, Brigadier General C. C. Fenn replied to Senator James O. Eastland, enclosing with his letter a number of expertly prepared memoranda on various aspects of the narcotics problem within the armed forces. Pertinent to our study is item #4 of Memorandum A:

Reference Senator Eastland's inquiry concerning information on the sources of production and avenues of distribution of narcotics from Communist China, Air Force investigative agencies have not developed any evidence to prove that Communist China is promoting drug distribution or usage. Some reports containing such expressions of opinion have been received. However, the reliability of the informants cannot be proved and the reports cannot be declassified.[9]

9 The letter and documents from the Army are included in the Subcommittee's Report, dated March, 1955.

Will the Department of the Army be labeled "subversive" because it does not swallow the propaganda of Eastland and Arens?

Less than four months after the Guatemalan Ambassador to Belgium and three accomplices had been arrested in New York on charges of smuggling $4 million in heroin into the United States, Lee Mortimer wrote the following in the *Los Angeles Herald-Express*, February 23, 1961:

Harry J. Anslinger, the dedicated U.S. Narcotics Commissioner who's sitting in N.Y. this week as a member of the U.N.'s international Narcotics Conference, told me he has long been disturbed by the knowledge that large amounts of junk are smuggled "legally" into the U.S. in the diplomatic pouches of some U.N. personnel (especially from behind the Curtain) as well as by certain envoys to Washington. Nothing can be done about it, even if the money remains behind for subversive purposes.

Someone is lying, and we don't know whether it is Mortimer or Anslinger. In exhaustive research, we have not been able to find one single authenticated case of a Communist diplomatic official being arrested and charged with using the diplomatic pouch for smuggling narcotics. There have been other cases besides the Guatemalan Ambassador, but they are all diplomats from non-Communist countries. In his column of September 13, 1961 (seven months after that Lee Mortimer story), Drew Pearson tells of a meeting with Nikita Khrushchev, in which there was some discussion of a number of projects in which the governments of the U.S.A. and U.S.S.R. are cooperating. At one point Pearson reminded Khrushchev:

Then in the prevention of opium smuggling, Harry Anslinger, our commissioner of narcotics, tells me that he gets his best support from the Russians. The United States and the Soviet work together in preventing opium smuggling and the Russians even proposed him as chairman of the international commission.

Henry L. Giordano is Harry Anslinger's successor as Commissioner of the Bureau of Narcotics. An interview given to Pete Martin for the *American Legion Magazine*, January, 1964, shows that the new Commissioner is carrying out the Cold War policies of his predecessor, albeit not so vehemently:

*Martin:* I've been told that the communists are trying to flood our

401

country with narcotics to weaken our moral and physical stamina. Is that true?

*Giordano:* As far as the drugs are concerned, it's true. There's a terrific flow of drugs coming out of Yunnan Province of China. That's one of the reasons we put an office in Bangkok. There's no question that in that particular area this is the aim of the Red Chinese. It should be apparent that if you could addict a population you would degrade a nation's moral fiber. Also, if they're able to sell drugs to us, they're going to get dollars back, and that kind of drain can weaken us financially, too.

It should be noted that Mr. Giordano has also specified *Yunnan Province* as the source of illicit narcotics emanating from China. Not one word is said about any other part of China as a source of narcotics. After giving the big build-up on *Yunnan Province*, the dialogue that ensued put the problem in different focus:

*Martin:* What is the source of most of our illegal narcotics?

*Giordano:* I've mentioned that heroin is derived from opium. It comes into the United States from three sources: two major ones and a third that isn't of much consequence except in the southwest. *Most of our narcotics come from Europe and the Near East. Opium comes out of Turkey.*[10] Turkey is one of the world's legitimate producers, but in that area there's a certain amount of illegal diversion going on, so that instead of selling it to the Turkish government, the producer sells it to the trafficker. The opium that is diverted then usually moves on into France. Along the way it's processed from raw opium and a morphine base of heroin. Then it comes into the United States.

*Martin:* It sounds almost as if the drug supply flows through a regular channel or funnel.

*Giordano:* The problem is that the channel or funnel shifts constantly. One year it's in Syria, another time in France. Sometimes it comes here directly, or it may come via Mexico or Canada. . . .

*Martin:* It seems as if dope is being routed by some pretty slippery characters.

*Giordano:* It is. We also have dope coming in from the Far East out of the Yunnan Province by way of Burma, Thailand, or down into Singapore and Hong Kong, each of which has a bad addiction problem of its own. To add to our troubles, some cultivation of opium is done in Mexico. Heroin from this crop appears generally in our southwest, but it's only a small portion of the total. However, most of the marijuana used in the United States comes from Mexico.

10 Emphasis has been added.—M. K.

The conclusion that emerges from all the testimony produced so far is that the illicit narcotics traffic is a well-organized business in the hands of international gangsters. Furthermore, the overwhelming portion of the narcotics, if not all of it, comes from countries other than China. Are these countries trying to weaken us and destroy our moral fibre? Why would this be true only of narcotics that come from China? Finally, whatever semblance of truth there may be about narcotics coming from China, it seems to be blamed only on *Yunnan Province*. And thereby hangs a tale!

The test of any theory is: Does it correspond with or does it clash with reality? Using this criterion as our point of departure, we can examine the actual phenomena of illicit narcotics traffic as distinguished from the Cold War propaganda diatribes which have been launched under American Legion auspices by both Commissioners of Narcotics.

On December 20, 1965, Federal narcotics officers arrested 6 persons in New York City, who had in their possession 209 pounds of heroin, with ultimate sales value of $18.5 million. Among those arrested was a U.S. Army chief warrant officer stationed at Fort Benning, Georgia, who reportedly brought the heroin to this country from France. The New York district supervisor for the Federal Bureau of Narcotics said that there were links between sources in France and a smuggling ring which "definitely has contacts in the United States with the Mafia." Of the six people arrested, four were Frenchmen, one was Brazilian, and one was American. On the following day French police arrested a retired United States Army major near Orleans, France in connection with the six members of the narcotics ring apprehended in New York City.

On June 16, 1967, the Associated Press reported that a three-judge tribunal from Italy had concluded hearings in New York in preparation "for the trial in Italy of 32 persons accused of taking part in a $150 million heroin smuggling operation, said to have been run by the Mafia between 1950 and 1960 in France, Italy, Canada and the United States."

On September 13, 1963, New York State Supreme Court Justice Samuel Leibowitz handed out a three to six years prison sentence to Jacques Angelvin, a popular star of French television. He had concealed $3.5 million in heroin, in an automobile which he shipped here aboard the liner *United*

403

*States.* Judge Leibowitz stated that Angelvin was the courier for a Parisian narcotics ring which was to have paid him $10,000 for bringing the heroin into this country.

On July 26, 1962, a Federal grand jury indicted 38 persons, of whom 34 were employees of the main post office in Chicago. They were part of a narcotics ring that sold marijuana, heroin, and cocaine in the post office or the post office garage. They operated in the post office that is situated one floor above the Federal Narcotics Bureau Office!

In his column of September 8, 1966,[11] syndicated columnist Joseph Alsop charged that there was a "highly profitable participation of the French secret service in the Laos opium traffic. . ."

A *London Sunday Times* dispatch in the *Los Angeles Times* of November 19, 1964, told of raids conducted in West Germany by nearly 1,000 West German police and U.S. narcotic agents in an unsuccessful effort to apprehend the leaders of an international smuggling ring that was selling marijuana to U.S. soldiers. The German police did discover that the marijuana was being imported in vast quantities from Morocco. The cost of the marijuana at wholesale in Morocco was 48 cents an ounce and was sold in West Germany at retail for $60 an ounce.

On February 21, 1964, Federal officers arrested three men in New York City with $13.5 million in heroin, in their possession. It was the largest seizure since the arrest, (and subsequent conviction) October 3, 1960, on similar charges of the Guatemalan Ambassador to Belgium. In the 1964 arrest, one was a Frenchman, one was an employee of the Uruguayan foreign ministry in Montevideo, and the third one was *the Mexican Ambassador to Bolivia.* On July 22, 1964, the Mexican Ambassador was sentenced to fifteen years in prison by the U.S. District Court. His accomplices were each given 10 years. All three were also fined $40,000 each.

On December 5, 1964, Federal officers arrested a woman at Kennedy International Airport as she tried to smuggle in $5 million worth of cocaine from Chile in the false bottom of three suitcases. One week later Federal authorities arrested 4 more people and identified 4 additional suspects, thus crack-

---

11 *Los Angeles Times.*

ing an international dope smuggling ring that had brought more than $25 million worth of cocaine from Chile into the United States.

In a Copley News Service dispatch from Mexico City,[12] August 28, 1965, we read that the U.S. Bureau of Narcotics said that "Mexico is the second largest (after France) supplier of heroin in the United States." The report states further "that most of the opium seized in the U.S. came from Singapore, Malaysia and Mexico," that "drug traffickers use Mexico as a crossroads to get to the United States from other South American countries, Europe and Asia," and that Peru is "the biggest supplier of cocaine to the United States."

Testing Anslinger's theory against the hard facts of life, the reports we have quoted do not show a jot or tittle of evidence about a Chinese Communist conspiracy to flood the U.S.A. with narcotics. Moreover, our charge that the story is phoney rests on much stronger evidence. On March 2, 1961, Dr. Joel Fort was interviewed in Los Angeles on KTTV by Paul Coates. He stated categorically that his interviews with Interpol Officials[13] and Hong Kong Police indicated that Communist China is not a significant factor in the dissemination of narcotic drugs for illegal purposes and that most of the narcotic drugs used on the Asian mainland comes from Thailand. In the course of the interview, it was disclosed that Dr. Fort had been the director of a 16-nation study of narcotics traffic. Three years later we wrote to Dr. Fort in his capacity as the Social Affairs Officer, United Nations Division of Narcotics Drugs, Geneva, Switzerland. We received three documents from Dr. Fort's office on November 24, 1964. They are all official documents of the United Nations Economic and Social Council.

One report, dated November 16, 1959, is entitled "Middle East Narcotics Mission." The gist of the report is contained in two short paragraphs:

As to the sources of the large supplies of illicit drugs in the region, firstly all evidence points to Lebanon as the main source of hashish production in the region.

With regard to opium, there is much evidence to show that substantial quantities of opium have up to now been coming from

12 Riverside, Calif. *Daily Enterprise.*
13 Interpol is an International Police Organization.

Turkey. Small quantities of opium may be produced illicitly in other parts of the region, and a flow of some significance from Afghanistan was noticed. There is also some evidence of distribution from Iran.

A second report, dated May 26, 1964, is entitled "Commission on Narcotic Drugs, Report of the Nineteenth Session." The *Far East* is summarized in this single sentence:

The Commission noticed that the traffic in opium and opiates in the Far East was being supplied mainly by illicit opium production in the Burma-China-Laos-Thailand border regions, and in the Middle East from opium production in Turkey.

The key words in this report, with respect to China, are "border regions," which refers to *Yunnan Province.*

A third report, dated March 18, 1964, is entitled "Illicit Traffic, Memorandum by the International Criminal Police Organization, Interpol, for 1963." Some highlights of this elaborate report should suffice:

The main sources of raw opium supplies are Turkey, Burma (Shan States) and the district situated over the northern border of Thailand.
The main source of prepared opium seems to be Burma.
The main sources of morphine supply are Turkey and the district situated over the northern border of Thailand.

With respect to diacetylmorphine, the report said:

Eight clandestine laboratories were discovered: 4 in Iran, 1 in Lebanon, 1 in Hong Kong, and 2 in Thailand.

With respect to cocaine, the report said:

Three clandestine laboratories wer discovered: 1 at Cochabamba, Bolivia and 2 at Lima, Peru.

With respect to Cannabis, the report said Lebanon was the source of 38.3% of the amount of this drug seized, and Thailand was the source of 28.2%.

These reports are the result, as previously mentioned, of a survey in which the narcotics agencies and police agencies of 16 nations cooperated, under the direction of Dr. Joel Fort

406

and under the sponsorship of the United Nations Economic and Social Council.

Of utmost significance in this 16-nation survey is that the only mention of China, as a source of illicit narcotics, is in the reference to "the frontiers of China, Burma, Thailand and Laos." Again it must be noted that "frontiers of China" is consistent with previous allusions to *Yunnan Province*. Despite the participation of Harry Anslinger and the U.S. Bureau of Narcotics in this 16-nation project, the Cold War line about China being a principal source of illicit narcotics was not included in the reports. Anslinger tried hard, but the police agencies of other countries laughed at his charges.

One of the best studies of the question of responsibility for illicit narcotics traffic was done by a New York newspaper man, John O'Kearney, who had spent some time as a correspondent in the Far East. His article, entitled "Opium Trade, Is China Responsible?," appeared in *The Nation*, October 15, 1955.

Mr. O'Kearney begins by pointing out that charges that have been hurled by Harry Anslinger have helped "to keep the American public in a state of hypnotized conviction that the Peking government is too barbarous to be permitted to assume China's seat in the United Nations." After study of a report issued by an International Criminal Police (Interpol) Commission to the United Nations in 1954 and another U.N. report, O'Kearney concludes:

A close reader of the statistics is led to conclude that the opium traffic has become a useful weapon in the hands of the anti-communist propaganda warriors of the cold war.

O'Kearney reports that narcotics officers in British Hong Kong and Singapore dismiss Anslinger's charges against Red China as "political exaggerations." Another veteran correspondent who has spent many years in Southeast Asia is David E. Walker, author of a study entitled *The Modern Smuggler*, published in London by Secker and Warburg. In an article from London, which was published in *The Nation*, July 15, 1961, Mr. Walker discusses Anslinger's charges about the illicit narcotics traffic and reports that British officialdom "stubbornly rejects the Anslinger theory about its being a deliberate political weapon used by Red China." Mr. Walker gives additional evidence that the U.S. Bureau of Narcotics under Anslinger became a Cold War propaganda agency. He tells of a committee report to the Federal Bureau of Narcotics in 1958, which contains this gem: "The unfortunate narcotics situation in the United Kingdom is a reflection of the free National Health Service, otherwise known as socialized medicine." Here we have proof again that Anslinger fights narcotics and Socialism as twin evils.

John O'Kearney exposes one of Anslinger's propaganda tricks. He points out that narcotics traffic has been traditional for hundreds of years in the Orient, that it is no surprise that many Chinese individuals are narcotic smugglers, and that when a Chinese is caught smuggling narcotics, Anslinger uses this as evidence against the Peking government. O'Kearney argues that Anslinger's charge "is no more justified than to blame the United States for crimes committed by private American citizens in Africa." He correctly points out that, what is of importance, is *the source* of the narcotics. He tells of a map in the Narcotics Bureau of Singapore, which shows the main opium-producing areas of Burma, Thailand, Laos, and Cambodia, as of January, 1955. The map shows the origin of the opium and opium products which pass through Singapore: 37% from Thailand, 43% from the Persian Gulf area, 16% from India and Burma, *4% from Yunnan Province of China.* In corroboration of these figures, O'Kearney refers to a 1954 report of the International Crime Police Organization to the United Nations, giving the source of the raw opium seized by police and narcotics officers: *97% was identified as of Indian, Iranian, and Lebanese origin.*[14] O'Kearney comments wryly: "Perhaps the three per cent came from China. Perhaps."

Repeatedly, Yunnan Province has been referred to by many of the experts as a source of illicit narcotics. The "mystery" is cleared up in David Walker's article in *The Nation:*

When the fighting that preceded Chiang Kai-shek's defeat was virtually over, 125,000 of the Generalissimo's men were cut off and stranded in the southernmost tip of Yunnan Province. They straggled south into north Burma's Kachin states. This is natural opium country. These men, and their women camp-followers, have had to survive. They knew how to grow opium and the facilities were at hand.

14 Emphasis added.—M. K.

Mr. Walker goes on to comment that, if there is a plot to "undermine American youth" with heroin, it is a cruel irony that it comes from these former anti-communist soldiers who belong to a regime on Taiwan *which is supported by the U.S.A.*

Another description of the activities of Chiang Kai-shek's former soldiers is contained in a dispatch from Fang, Thailand by Seth S. King of the *New York Times* News Service.[15]

Up against the mountain sides, within sight of Fang's wrinkled main street, are the bright green patches that mark the Kuomintang refugee camps.

Here the remnants of Chinese Nationalist army units, squeezed out of eastern Burma seven years ago, grow their vegetables and rice and trade for opium with the hill tribes scattered along the border.

Further on in the dispatch, Mr. King tells of 800 Chinese refugees from Burma who had filtered quietly into these Kuomintang camps.

With the Chinese refugees came reports of new pressures against the Kuomintang remnants still in Burma. According to these reports the Burmese army, cooperating with Chinese Communist forces, have been cutting the opium traffic that the Kuomintang groups have conducted into and out of Yunnan Province and across Burma and Laos.

Here we have the evidence that Chiang's former soldiers are opium growers in some areas and opium runners in other areas. The Chinese Communists, who have been accused by Harry Anslinger and Henry Giordano as traffickers in narcotics, are here shown to be using their armed forces *to suppress* the opium business of Chiang Kai-shek's men. The irony of this story is that Chiang Kai-shek's propaganda machine has fed phoney statistics and phoney documents to the U.S. Bureau of Narcotics, whose leadership has avidly seized upon this misinformation as a weapon in the Cold War.

In order to understand the role of Yunnan Province in the narcotics traffic, one should take a look at the map. It will be seen that Yunnan Province is the southernmost section of the vast China mainland. It juts out like a peninsula against Burma and Laos, which are met at the opposite side by a "peninsula"

15 Riverside, Calif., *Press-Enterprise*, August 1, 1965.

protruding from Thailand. Thus is formed the famous Yunnan area quadrangle, from which comes a small portion of the world's opium. Insofar as the Communist Chinese government is concerned, both the production and the sale of non-medicinal narcotics are illegal. This does not rule out the possibility of a small amount of clandestine growing of illicit opium in remote and rugged mountain areas, just as moonshiners in the hills of Kentucky manage to elude Federal agents.

In a *New York Times* News Service dispatch[16] from Vientiane, Laos, Harrison E. Salisbury describes the opium business in the Yunnan area quadrangle:

> In the center of the whole trade is a hardy band of Chinese Nationalist troops who were flown to China's Yunnan Province border years ago in one of the more spectacular early CIA operations and then, after being abandoned officially by both the U.S. and Taiwan, have dug themselves in in the heart of the opium area with their own barracks, defense lines, airstrips and helicopter landing spots. They have managed to turn a pretty penny in poppies.

Mark Gayn, in a *Chicago Daily News* dispatch from Thailand,[17] reports that the world's largest poppy fields are within a few minutes' distance from the palace of the King, in the city of Chieng Mai:

> One can journey west from here, to Burma; or north, as far as China's Yunnan province; or northeast, to Laos, and never leave the opium country.

Mr. Gayn explains that no matter where the poppy is grown, most of the opium travels over the rugged mountains in caravans, sometimes as many as 400 horses. These caravans are protected against hijackers, whom Mr. Gayn identifies:

> The toughest, the wiliest and the best organized are Gen. Chiang Kai-shek's former soldiers, who for the last 17 years, have been operating in Burma and Thailand. There are 2,700 or 2,800 of them available as opium train guards, and when they are on the job, the drug is not easily hijacked.

The Central Intelligence Agency is not the only division of

16 Riverside, Calif., *Daily Enterprise*, June 13, 1966.
17 *Los Angeles Times*, August 18, 1966.

the U.S.A. Government that has made it possible for narcotics traffickers to operate. In an article written for *Le Monde* (Paris),[18] May 24-25, 1964, the well-known French writer on military and Asian affairs, G. Penchenier, tells of the assorted rackets in which the army generals of Laos are engaged:

> Finally, the latest monopoly of the military in Vientiane: an opium den. It is the only one in the whole world which exists legally. Since its opening, it has always been full.
> To forestall the expected criticism from their American allies, the Vientiane military hit upon a wonderfully clever idea. They put a placard over the doorway of the opium den: "Clinic for The Cure of Addicts."

Nowhere have we read any thunderous denunciations of our allies, the Laotian generals, for their operation of an opium den. You see, they are anti-communist, and that makes the difference in the Cold War morality!

Another "free world" ally of ours is the Shah of Iran. Of him, Michael Parrish says in an article published in *The Minority of One*, December, 1962:

> Two years ago, the Swiss police arrested the Shah's sister, Princess Ashraf, for having several suitcases full of heroin. The FBI and the U.S. Customs Department know that Iran is the greatest source of narcotics smuggled into this country; but the Shah is an ally and we cannot afford to antagonize him.

And why can we not afford to antagonize him? The answer is our Cold War morality: that anything goes, if it helps to fight Communism or what we imagine to be Communism!

The final and *incontrovertible* proof, that the charges against Communist China are indeed The Narcotics Hoax, is contained in a document entitled "Mainland China in the World Economy," Hearings before the Joint Economic Committee, Congress of the United States, April 5, 10, 11, and 12, 1967. In the course of the testimony of Robert Dernberger, Professor of Economics, University of Chicago, the following dialogue took place:

*Senator Javits.* Would any one of the witnesses have any idea whether traffic in illicit drugs, opium, et cetera, represented a way

---

18 Quoted in *I. F. Stone's Weekly*, June 8, 1964.

which Communist China has managed to pile up this $300 million in foreign exchange—in U.S. dollars?

*Professor Dernberger.* Unfortunately, I am not an expert in the drug traffic, but Harry J. Anslinger, a U.S. Commissioner of Narcotics, once testified that these efforts—smuggling of opium and heroin—were significant. I have seen no evidence that this trade is large or is sponsored by the Communist government, with the exception of his testimony. I would find it very hard to believe that with their possibility of earning the given amount of foreign exchange from other sources that we know exist, they would engage in this traffic merely for the purpose of earning foreign exchange.

*Senator Javits.* Can you account for the $300 million otherwise?

*Professor Dernberger.* Yes, sir.

*Senator Javits.* In other words, the $300 million can be accounted for without a resort to drug traffic?

*Professor Dernberger.* Yes, sir.

Further on, Professor Dernberger testified:

In the trade with Japan which is based on barter, Chinese exports consist of inputs for Japanese industrial production: iron ore, pig iron, coal, and soybeans. . . . In 1964, 1965 and the first half of 1966, China's exports to Western Europe increased by approximately 20 percent annually, but China's imports from Western Europe increased even more rapidly.

In order to currently finance the approximately U.S. $50 million import surplus in trade with Western Europe and the large-scale imports of grain from Canada, Australia, and Argentina, Communist China has earned sterling in trade with Hong Kong, Malaya, and Singapore. Communist China's earnings of sterling in trade with these three areas have increased steadily since 1961, reaching almost U.S. $500 million in 1965. . . . In addition, Communist China's technical ability to produce some of the required commodities and factories domestically has increased significantly during the past 17 years.

Finally, Communist China has earned an excellent credit rating during the last 17 years and many firms in the non-Communist countries desire to increase exports, including complete plants and technicians, to China on credit. Communist China has not yet sought long-term credit from the non-Communist countries, but should be able to obtain these imports on credit if and when they are desired.

Professor John G. Gurley of Stanford University Department of Economics corroborated Professor Dernberger's testimony about China's economic progress, thus laying to rest Anslinger's canard about China's desperate need for foreign exchange as the reason for alleged trafficking in illicit narcotics.

412

The Bureau of Narcotics is a division of the Treasury Department, and accordingly the Secretary of the Treasury is boss of the Bureau of Narcotics and its Commissioner. The exchange of correspondence between Senator William Proxmire, the Chairman of the Joint Economic Committee, and Secretary of the Treasury Henry H. Fowler, gives the final proof of our thesis of The Narcotics Hoax.

## Appendix V

### ILLICIT DRUG TRAFFIC AS A POTENTIAL SOURCE OF FOREIGN EXCHANGE EARNINGS FOR MAINLAND CHINA*

(The following letter was sent by Chairman Proxmire to the Secretary of the Treasury:)

APRIL 12, 1967.

Hon. HENRY H. FOWLER,
*Secretary of the Treasury,*
*Washington, D.C.*

MY DEAR MR. SECRETARY: At hearings which the Joint Economic Committee has been conducting on the economy of Mainland China, it was reported to us that, in spite of serious weaknesses in the available statistical information, there is unanimous agreement among experts that the Chinese Communists have been able to build up and maintain at least $300 million (valued in U.S. dollars) in foreign exchange reserves. We were informed that this figure is probably low and that the amount might run as high as twice that figure.

The question was raised at the hearings as to the possibilities that Communist China had been able to add significantly to its foreign exchange earnings through illicit drug traffic via Hong Kong or otherwise.

I wonder if we could have a statement from the Treasury Department for inclusion in our record (1) indicating what your Department feels may be the facts with respect to the foreign exchange reserves of Mainland China, and (2) any comments which the Department or the Bureau of Narcotics may have on the extent to which illegal drug traffic may be contributed or continue to contribute to its foreign exchange earnings.

Sincerely,

WILLIAM PROXMIRE, *Chairman.*

* See colloquy, pp. 145, 146.

(The reply received from the Secretary of the Treasury follows:)

THE SECRETARY OF THE TREASURY,
*Washington, D.C., May 11, 1967.*

Hon. WILLIAM PROXMIRE,
*Chairman, Joint Economic Committee,*
*Congress of the United States, Washington, D.C.*

DEAR MR. CHAIRMAN: The data brought out on Mainland China in the hearings of the Joint Economic Committee were most interesting, and I wish in response to your letter of April 12 I could add something substantial to the information which you have already collected respecting foreign exchange reserves.

Unfortunately such information is not exchanged on an official basis, and what little we do have should be viewed as subject to a wide margin of error. I have no basis for suggesting that some of the estimates which have been made are not the best possible under the circumstances.

Your letter also asks this Department to comment on the extent to which trade in illicit narcotics might be contributing to the foreign exchange earnings of Mainland China. At present the Far East is not thought to be a major source of the illicit narcotics being smuggled into the United States. The drug chiefly implicated in smuggling from abroad is heroin. The Bureau of Narcotics has estimated that some 80 percent of the heroin reaching the United States is manufactured in France from opium diverted from legitimate cultivation in Turkey. Approximately 15 percent is thought to originate in Mexico. The remaining 5 percent might be attributable to sources in the Far East, but here it must be recognized that Mainland China, specifically the Yunnan Province, is only one of several active opium growing areas. This crop is also cultivated in India, Thailand, Laos, and Burma. The small quantity of opium which may be coming out of Mainland China and entering the United States in the form of heroin does not represent any significant sum in United States dollars.

There is, of course, considerable local consumption of opium produced in the Far East. Hong Kong and Singapore, for example, have serious addiction problems. It is not reliably known whether the high rate of addiction in these areas generates foreign currency earnings in Mainland China.

Sincerely yours,

HENRY H. FOWLER.

It took considerable courage for Secretary Fowler to announce the truth and contradict the statements made by the present Narcotics Commissioner, Henry L. Giordano, and his predecessor, Harry J. Anslinger. It is regrettable that Secretary

414

Fowler did not add to his statement about the situation "at present" the equivalent truth that Communist China *never* engaged in the illicit narcotics traffic.

The sad part about this retraction is that it received only scanty notice in the media of communication. Despite the fact that in our research we monitor quite a number of publications and even though the story came over the Associated Press wire service, we saw it in only one newspaper, the Riverside, Calif. *Daily Enterprise,* May 28, 1967. There were probably others that carried it, but not enough to begin to serve as an effective antidote to the "poison" spread over a period of many years.

With 95% of the heroin smuggled into the U.S.A. attributed to Turkey, France, and Mexico, there is only 5% that could possibly come from Communist China. This 5%, however, is the total that comes from India, Thailand, Laos, Burma, and the Yunnan province of China. It is very obvious that Communist China is not flooding the U.S.A. in particular and the "free world" in general with narcotic drugs. It will be argued by some that Communist China is the source of the opium from which heroin is manufactured. The answer to this possible charge is given in the yearly reports of the Bureau of Narcotics for the two years in which Harry Anslinger was bandying his charges. In the 1954 report, we read:

The principal sources of raw opium were Mexico, India, Pakistan, and Iran. (Page 8.)

The principal sources of prepared opium were Mexico, Kuwait, and Hong Kong. (Page 9.)

In the 1955 report, we read:

The principal sources of raw opium were Lebanon, Hong Kong, Turkey, and Mexico. (Page 15.)

The principal sources of prepared opium were Mexico and Hong Kong. (Page 16.)

The principal source of morphine seized during 1955 was Mexico. (Page 19.)

The principal source of cocaine seized during 1955 was Bolivia. (Page 19.)

These yearly reports were signed by Harry Anslinger. It should

415

be added that he did include in these and other reports the unfounded and unproven charge that Communist China was one of the sources of heroin. One of the strange aspects of this whole Cold War propaganda campaign is that no one has located a single laboratory in Communist China where heroin could be manufactured!

Harry Anslinger's charges were incorporated in many documents that we have not attempted to quote, because of space limitations. However, it is worthwhile examining how his propaganda spread.

In an article that appeared in the Ultra-Rightist weekly, *Human Events*, January 2, 1965, syndicated columnist Irene Kuhn warns American mothers to be concerned about "the clear and present danger of Red China's cold-blooded pushing of narcotics for propaganda and profit." And she continues:

> According to data released by police organizations all over the world, about 90 percent of the illicit narcotics on sale in the free world come from the Red Chinese mainland. Peking's income from this "black merchandise" amounts to about $5 million annually. . . .
> Mao has always been a believer in the gospel preached by Lenin: "When you have no pure principled weapons, then seize the dirty ones."
> One of Mao's "dirty weapons" is narcotics. . . .
> Red China has intensified the traffic and the Chinese Communist drug ring, operating around the world, is using such rim areas as Hong Kong, Macao, Vientiane, Phnom and Bangkok as main transshipment centers. . .
> Most of the seizures of the narcotics agencies in the free world can be traced to the origin, which is Peking.

We have quoted only a small portion of Miss Kuhn's article. The reader can easily detect the misstatements of fact and can imagine how much there is of the same quality in the rest of her diatribe. Two things, however, should be noted. The *quotation* attributed to Lenin cannot be found in any of the known writings and speeches of Lenin. Miss Kuhn says that Peking's income, from all the world-wide narcotics traffic amounts to $5 million annually. This is a far cry from Richard Arens $700,000,000, but in any case, the figure of $5 million for world-wide operations is so ridiculously low that it immediately discredits her entire article.

416

The Rev. W. S. Mc Birnie has written a pamphlet, entitled *Why We Must Not Recognize China.* Along with his other specious arguments, the Rev. Mc Birnie says:

One of the goals of communism is the demoralization of American youth. That they have succeeded all too well is evident from the numbers of students they have influenced on Berkeley campus and in other universities. Very extensive inroads upon the physical and moral well being of American youth have also been made by means of the illicit drug traffic.

How does the Rev. Mc Birnie prove his charge of demoralization of American youth by way of China's alleged illicit drug traffic? He relies solely on Irene Kuhn's article, which he introduces as documenting his charge "admirably." Rev. Mc Birnie prides himself upon being quite a scholar and researcher. Consequently, we must hold him guilty of gross irresponsibility in committing the following "sins" against good scholarship: 1. He should not depend on one columnist's essay to make such a grave charge against a government of one-fourth of the human race. 2. With a small amount of research he could have ascertained the truth. 3. The inner evidence of the article itself should warn any perceptive scholar of its tendentious and unreliable nature.

Perhaps this is expecting too much of a man who writes:

The U.S. could go to war with Red China to help the Nationalists without a formal declaration of war, since the U.S. does not recognize Red China.

This professed disciple of the Prince of Peace can write such shocking statements and at the same time write about "the gangster-like government of the Communist Chinese." Immediately after quoting Irene Kuhn's entire article, Mc Birnie says: "It is impossible to overestimate the danger of recognizing Red China." This, of course, is Mc Birnie's real reason for purveying the narcotics hoax.

The Committee of One Million is one of many Ultra-Rightist propaganda front-groups operated by public relations specialist and renegade Communist, Marvin Liebman of New York City. One of the first things that can be said about the Committee of One Million is that it is not a committee of one

417

million members. In a brochure issued by the Committee of One Million we are told:

To counteract much of the propaganda intimating that Communist China was a "responsible" government, the Committee of One Million published full page advertisements throughout the country citing Red China's leading role in the international drug traffic. The advertisement *was based on information supplied by Commissioner Harry J. Anslinger,*[19] U.S. Representative to the UN Commission on Narcotic Drugs, which proved conclusively that Red China was officially promoting the infamous international traffic in narcotics to provide the foreign exchange necessary to carry out world-wide activities of Communist infiltration and subversion.

Little did the millions of readers of those full-page advertisements realize that they were the victims of a gigantic Cold War propaganda hoax!

Another of Marvin Liebman's Cold War propaganda operations is the American Afro-Asian Educational Exchange. In 1962 it received a contribution of $25,000 from The Lilly Endowment, a trust fund established by members of the family which owns Eli Lilly Co., pharmaceuticals manufacturer. The Vice-Chairman of American Afro-Asian Educational Exchange is Senator Thomas J. Dodd, former FBI Agent, member of the steering committee of the Committee of One Million, radio commentator for the Ultra-Rightist American Security Council, and Vice-Chairman of the Senate Internal Security Subcommittee. Among Dodd's other achievements are his acting as agent for the Guatemalan government for a yearly fee of $50,000; and on June 23, 1967, the U.S. Senate censured Dodd for conduct "which is contrary to accepted morals, derogates from the public trust expected of a senator, and tends to bring the Senate into dishonor and disrepute." The resolution of censure was based upon the findings of the Senate Ethics Committee that Dodd had converted at least $116,083.00 of campaign and testimonial funds to his personal benefit.

Mme. Suzanne Labin is an Ultra-Rightist French author, who has been cheered and employed by various Ultra-Rightists and by Dodd's Senate Internal Security Subcommittee. Indeed, this Subcommittee published her pamphlet, *The Techniques*

19 Emphasis has been added.—M. K.

418

*of Soviet Propaganda,* which was subsequently reprinted by the American Afro-Asian Educational Exchange. Its total circulation up to February, 1965 was around 350,000 copies. Mme. Labin and a group of Ultra-Rightists from the U.S.A. attended a symposium on anti-communism in that bastion of the "free world," Pretoria, South Africa, in the Fall of 1966. The Ultra-Rightist Constitutional Alliance advertised her in *Human Events,* January 21, 1967, as one of the scheduled speakers at an Ultra-Rightist pow-wow in Washington, D.C., in March, 1967. Among the other participants scheduled were the racist Senator Strom Thurmond of South Carolina; Steve Shadegg, former ghost writer for Barry Goldwater; and Kenneth W. Ingwalson, former publisher of *Human Events.*

Infuriated because the French Government granted diplomatic recognition to Communist China, Mme. Labin "retaliated" by writing a pamphlet, entitled *Embassies of Subversion,* which was published, in English translation, by the American Afro-Asian Educational Exchange. The Vice-Chairman of A.A.A.E.E., Senator Thomas J. Dodd, wrote a glowing introduction, dated at Washington, D.C., February 1965. Mme. Labin avers that recognition of Peking "must be considered a very dangerous move, although the majority of French people approved more or less in principle."

As one reads this vitriolic essay, one gets the feeling that the lady is progressively raising her blood pressure. She says of Chiang's rump regime: "Taiwan represents the authentic and respected China, not only from a juridical viewpoint, but also from the human perspective." She decries her "foolish world" which does not fully appreciate the glories of Chiang Kai-shek's Fascist regime. Then she moves to a higher pitch of denunciation of Communist China, with the shopworn lie: "Thirty million human beings, slaughtered amidst the cruelest terror, implemented by the most horrible tortures!"

Mme. Labin's pamphlet consists of 45 pages of vituperation. She finally reaches her crescendo on page 43:

Late in 1960 the United States narcotics commissioner, Harry S. Anslinger,[20] published a report which was discussed by the Competent Commission of the United Nations. . .

20 The correct name is Harry J. Anslinger.

It is Peking, the high Areopagist, which cultivates the poppy, extracts the drug, arranges its transportation, opens the opium dens, consummates the illicit sales and controls the global drug market. Its goals are threefold: to acquire funds, to enslave agents, and to deprave the Free World. For the first time in the history of mankind, the chief magistrates of a major State have become patrons of the vilest of underworld activities. After all, isn't it easier to transport drugs in diplomatic pouches?

It is certain that Mme. Labin has achieved some sort of a world's record in being able to compress so many misstatements of fact in two paragraphs.

Rev. Kenneth Goff says in his *Pilgrim Torch* of February— March 1965:

Lenin once said: "Demoralize the youth of the land, and the revolution is already won."

This is one of many Goff inventions. Lenin never said it. At least, it does not appear in any of his writings.

Goff entertains his followers with these fairy tales:

Dope has become the Communist secret weapon to destroy our youth and to fill their revolutionary coffers.

About 1960, after Fidel Castro had sent to the United States 14,000 trained agents and spies, the real silent war began.

Cuban Dictator, Fidel Castro, has lined up with the United States underworld to form a smuggling syndicate which today is flooding this country with heroin, cocaine, and other deadly drugs, pumping the stuff in from Cuba over the biggest and busiest dope pipe-line in the long history of illicit narcotic traffic.

There is only one thing wrong with the Rev. Goff's statement: it is a most flagrant violation of the Commandment: Thou Shalt Not Bear False Witness Againt Thy Neighbor. Goff adds another whopper: He claims Castro has a *three-billion dollar* business in dope!

In his May 5, 1965 newsletter, Goff has a new approach:

In the drive to undermine our youth the [Communist] Party has been aided by finances from the Cuban and Red Chinese sale of dope in the U.S.A. This last year, Cuba obtained from the UN one million dollars for the establishing of 13 agricultural experimental stations. 400,000 dollars of these funds came from the United States taxpayers. These stations are being run by Red Chinese, who are teaching Cubans in the art of raising poppies for the manufacturing of dope. Let us not think for a minute that our enemy is asleep and is not interested in the capturing of our youth.

The inventive genius of Kenneth Goff has no bounds, and his fanatical followers readily accept his false statements, wrapped up in religious garb. For sheer reckless abandon, hardly anything can equal his performance in the Fall, 1966 issue of *Pilgrim Torch*:

If the trend continues across the nation, fluoridation within ten years may become a lost issue and the people may have won a definite victory of a drive to make them human guinea pigs and to subvert them to a phase of the Soviet plot.

With this nonsense about a Soviet plot to fluoridate water supplies, Goff was only warming up for the task of hitting the "enemy" with a real blockbuster:

Narcotic experts claim that over five million acres in starving China are now devoted to extensive cultivation of narcotic poppies; that Chinese Communist leaders have forcibly kidnapped Chinese youths and shipped them off to sea on a dope fleet. They tie their hands and feet and forcibly give them injections until they manifest a craving for narcotics. They soon become confirmed addicts. This is the young army of slaves produced by Chinese dope monsters who are now willing and eager to undertake any criminal assignments in exchange for daily narcotic requirements. Many of these are now stalking the streets of every major city in America. Around the world the reports are the same.

Communists are spending much time and money in enslaving unsuspecting teen-agers everywhere. They are cultivating new drugs daily.

It may tax the reader's credulity that there are people who are willing to believe these fantastic lies, but unfortunately such is the case. We have attended some of Kenneth Goff's rallies and we have made tape recordings of his harangues, as well as the response of his fanatical dupes. We consider him one of the most dangerous Ultra-Rightist propagandists in the country. One thing is certain; Kenneth Goff learned well his lessons from Harry J. Anslinger's narcotics hoax.

William C. Douglas is a Sarasota, Florida, physician who operates a propaganda network called Let Freedom Ring. An

421

admitted member of the John Birch Society, Dr. Douglas sends out tape-recorded messages with charges as fantastic as those in Robert Welch's "The Politician." His associates in communities across the country advertise a phone number for people to dial. When the number is reached, Dr. Douglas' message is played back to the listener automatically. In January, 1967, Douglas and his collaborators were broadcasting a story that the hallucinatory drug, LSD, was being smuggled into the United States from the world-renowned Weizman Institute of Science in Israel. When apprised of this, a spokesman for the Institute said "there is not a scintilla of truth in the outrageous broadcast." The same Douglas message suggested that there is some kind of link between LSD and Communism, and then suggested that, if a sufficient quantity of LSD were to be dropped into a central water supply, "a metropolis could suddenly become a city of fools totally incapable of reason as to invasion or sabotage and not really caring." There is, of course, a scientific and practicable basis for what Dr. Douglas is suggesting, but to any *rational* person or organization desiring to effect social change, it would appear to be egregiously immoral and self-defeating. The danger, however, is that constant repetition of these kinds of suggestions will one day "trigger" a response in some person who is emotionally unstable and he will perform such a diabolical act. Reports have already come in about discussions, among the Fascist stormtroopers of the Minutemen, of proposals to introduce lethal substances in the air-conditioning ducts at United Nations headquarters in New York.

Frank A. Capell, alias Francis A. Capelle, has made a career of Red-Baiting for quite a number of years. He edits and publishes a bi-weekly newsletter called *The Herald of Freedom*. A companion newsletter is called *The Religious News Edition of The Herald of Freedom*. Among Frank's claims to fame is his conviction in Los Angeles Superior Court on July 20, 1965, for his part in a conspiracy to libel U.S. Senator Thomas H. Kuchel. He was fined $500, sentenced to 180 days in jail (which was suspended), and placed on probation for three years. One of the conditions of probation was that for the 3-year period he must submit his writings to the Los Angeles County District Attorney. The record also shows that, while working as an investigator for the compliance division of the War Production

Board during World War II, he was indicted on three counts of conspiring to ask, accept, and receive bribes from two manufacturers. The second and third counts of the indictment specifically mentioned bribes of $1000 and $400. *Capell pleaded guilty* to all three counts, and on May 29, 1945, he was sentenced to pay a fine of $2,000 and to serve a year and a day in prison. The prison sentence was suspended and he was put on probation for two years. Capell has circulated his own ingenious explanation of that episode. He says that, while working for the War Production Board, he "narrowly missed getting jailed while working in a Communist-infested war agency and acting under orders." Who ordered him to solicit and receive bribes is not made clear. Nor does he explain why he pleaded guilty on all three counts of the indictment.

In *The Herald of Freedom,* August 12, 1966, Capell warns:

> The International Communist Conspiracy has long manifested its interest in the use of drugs and has conducted extensive experiments on human beings. . .
> Concerning the Communist use of drugs, the Senate Internal Security Sub-Committee took sworn testimony from Richard L.G. Deverall who was a Far East representative for the AFL-CIO and formerly had been on the staff of General Douglas MacArthur.

He quotes Kenneth Goff as authority for the claim that the Communists are preparing to poison public water supplies and that fluoridation of water supplies is a Communist plot. Capell concludes with his final judgment of LSD:

> It is truly a weapon of destruction, more dangerous than the atom bomb and the nuclear "holocaust" that worries (?) the left-wingers and peaceniks.

The gross exaggeration, the sneers, the innuendoes, and the distortions of truth in that final sentence are typical of Capell's writings. A case in point is his book, *The Strange Death of Marilyn Monroe,* a witches' brew of sly innuendo that the Communists and former Attorney-General Robert Kennedy were responsible for Marilyn Monroe's death!

The Rev. Walter Huss runs the Ultra-Rightist propaganda Freedom Center in Portland, Oregon. In his publication, *The National Eagle,* September 15, 1966, Huss has an article entitled "Opium, Peiping Regime's Primary 'Weapon Against Free World Defense.' " It is based upon a dispatch from Taipei that was distributed by the North American Newspaper Alliance (NANA). The reporter, Jeff Endrst, is described as "an American free lance writer who visited Taiwan recently." We are told further: "This is a documented finding of Nationalist China's counter-intelligence, corroborated by narcotics agents elsewhere in Asia." Properly translated, that last sentence means that Jeff Endrst used the lying propaganda of Chiang Kai-shek's Fascist regime as the raw material for an article, which is made to appear as if it is based upon authentic evidence. Zealots like Walter Huss are willing to seize upon anything, no matter how ridiculous, to carry on their "holy crusade."

In line with the Cold War propaganda policy of the Federal Bureau of Narcotics, Patrick P. O'Carroll, director of the Bureau's Narcotics School in Washington, told the annual convention of the International Association of Chiefs of Police in Miami, Florida on October 2, 1965:

> Cuba has become a problem in this respect, and because of the smuggling of this drug by Cuban nationals some of whom have been determined to be Castro sympathizers, we now find considerable quantities of cocaine in the United States, particularly in Miami and New York City.

This little speech made it certain that the false information of the Narcotics Hoax would filter down to practically every police department in the nation. It was an assurance that every policeman would "catch on" that it is his "patriotic" duty to spread the story that Communist countries are responsible for the illicit narcotics traffic.

Strangely enough, the Bureau of Narcotics report for the year ending December 31, 1965, gives not one bit of evidence to support Mr. O'Carroll's charge. The report, entitled *Traffic in Opium and Other Dangerous Drugs*, gives the sources of the various narcotic drugs that are smuggled into this country, *but makes no mention of Cuba*. It does give the details of the seizure by Mexican Police of a large shipment of cocaine paste that arrived in Mexico City via airplane from Lima, Peru. The Mexican national to whom it was consigned was working in league with an Ecuadorian chemist, whose illicit cocaine labo-

424

ratory was seized by the Mexican Police. The entire investigation was carried out with the assistance of agents of the U.S. Bureau of Narcotics. Perhaps there is no significance to the fact that the illicit cocaine laboratory was located near the U.S. Embassy.

As in the case of Communist China, the Cold War propagandists of the Federal Bureau of Narcotics, took all the proof that illicit drugs were being smuggled by Cuban anti-Communists and fastened it onto the Cuban Communists. In March, 1966, Anselo Barrios was arrested in New York City for engaging in the illegal numbers racket. Arrested with him was a narcotics pusher, Jose Fernandez, who was being sought by police on previous narcotics charges. Who is Anselo Barrios? He is the fellow who was the Minister of Transportation in Cuba *under Batista.* On December 19, 1964, Federal narcotics agents seized two Cuban refugees[21] in Miami, Florida, in connection with what the officers called one of the largest narcotics rings to operate in the United States in recent years. The culprits were apprehended pursuant to warrants that had been issued by Federal Courts in New York and New Jersey.

On March 27, 1964, Los Angeles Police seized 6 suitcases crammed with *unrefined marijuana plant,* at the baggage stand of the Los Angeles International Airport. The *Los Angeles Times,* March 28, 1964, reported that this was part of the operation of an international drug-smuggling ring:

Two suspected Cuban couriers for the ring stepped on a New York bound jet minutes before police arrived. They surrendered docilely on arrival at Kennedy International Airport in New York City.

The *Times* story also reported that the police acted in response to an underworld informant, who had told the police that "two of the suspects, a man and a woman, had crossed the border at Tijuana and were headed for the airport here."

The two Los Angeles policemen, who participated in the seizure of the marijuana at the International Airport, were Sergeant Duwayne Beckman and Lieutenant W. A. Stephenson of the narcotics squad.

21 Cuban refugees are usually anti-Castro and anti-Communist.

425

Sergeant Beckman told the press:

This whole deal is Communist-inspired and designed to raise American dollars for Castro. Smuggling narcotics helps Castro two ways. It bolsters his economy, and it corrupts morals of the American public.

Beckman stated further that four other batches of marijuana, that were seized in the last year, had been traced to the same international drug-smuggling ring which allegedly had sent in the present shipment. Beckman added that Cuban courier teams have contacts in "virtually every town in Southern California."

Before proceeding with any further investigation of Sergeant Beckman's charges, there are some questions that need to be answered:

1. Why would an international drug-smuggling ring do such an inept job as to smuggle *unrefined* marijuana plant, when the refined product would bring much more money and not be so bulky?

2. Why would any drug-smuggling ring fill up six suitcases with any kind of marijuana, when one suitcase full of heroin or cocaine would run into more money and be less conspicuous?

3. Why would anyone need to transport marijuana to Mexico and thence to the United States, when Mexico is the source of all the marijuana smuggled into this country, according to all reports of the Federal Bureau of Narcotics?

4. Why did Sergeant Beckman issue the statement to the press, instead of his superior, Lieutenant Stephenson?

5. Is it not outside the purview of police work to issue an obviously political statement?

6. If Castro is smuggling narcotics to this country in order to raise money, why would he bother with marijuana, when heroin and cocaine are more lucrative items?

7. How does one explain that none of the reports of the Federal Bureau of Narcotics or the speeches of Anslinger and Giordano mention Cuba as a source of the marijuana that comes into this country?

The two suspects of the alleged international drug-smuggling ring, Clara Vasquez-Alvarez and Augusto Lazaro Millares, were

426

extradited to California. Although they were arrested on March 27, 1964, there was no record in the files of the Los Angeles Municipal Court or the files of the Los Angeles County Superior Court of any felony complaint against these two people. The files were searched for us by one of our attorneys, and that was the situation up to November 23, 1965. In response to our inquiry, John A. Childress, Clerk of the United States Court for the District of Southern Calfiornia, advised us in a letter dated December 7, 1965, that the indictments against both suspects on charge of concealment and transportation of marijuana after illegal importation had been dismissed.

Thus did the blatant statement of Sergeant Duwayne Beckman collapse; but with the exception of the readers of this book, no one knows about it. Sergeant Beckman played Anslinger's "phonograph record," but no one has given the *Times* readers the true facts as they developed.[22]

Almost nine months after Sergeant Beckman's grandstand declaration, the late Fulton Lewis, Jr. wrote a column,[23] which started off by saying:

Narcotics of Cuban origin—marijuana, cocaine, opium, and heroin—are now peddled in big cities and tiny hamlets throughout this country.

For his proof, Lewis quoted Sergeant Beckman's statement of March 27, 1964. In addition, Lewis said:

Several Cubans arrested by the Los Angeles police have boasted they are Communists.

This sentence was placed in such juxtaposition that the clear implication was that Cuban dope smugglers have boasted they are Communists. The sheer improbabiltiy of a dope smuggler compounding his troubles with the police by such boasting, is

22 In the interest of truth, it should be pointed out that, after the charge against her had been dismissed, Clara Vasquez-Alvarez was indicted on a separate charge of illegal acquisition of marijuana, and was given a sentence of 1 year. This sentence was suspended, and she was placed upon probation, so that she might return to New York State. However, this development gives no comfort to Sergeant Beckman's story. Illegal acquisition can be a charge against anyone, without any connection to an international ring or to Fidel Castro.
23 *Los Angeles Herald-Examiner*, January 21, 1965.

something that didn't bother Lewis when he told that tale. It takes utter contempt for the intelligence of one's readers to expect them to believe that kind of nonsense, regardless of who originated it.

After we read the Lewis' column, we decided that an investigation of the investigator was in order. Accordingly, on March 11, 1965, we visited the office of the Los Angeles Police Narcotics Squad twice. Each time we were told that Sergeant Beckman was expected momentarily, and each time, after a long wait, we did not see Beckman. On April 15, 1965, we sent Beckman a letter, for which we hold a postal return receipt, showing that it was delivered to the headquarters of the Los Angeles Police Department. At the time we sent this letter, we had completely forgotten about Sergeant Beckman's statement that had appeared in the *Los Angeles Times* on March 28, 1964. After all, almost a year had elapsed, and in that space of time we had poured over millions of words in newspapers, magazines, books, documents, and recordings.

We explained in our letter that we were working on a book, which was aimed at exposing fabrications and distortions of truth. We asked Sergeant Beckman if Fulton Lewis, Jr. had quoted him correctly, and, if so, we wanted the proof of his statements that Lewis had quoted, and also we wanted the proof that Cuban narcotics smugglers, when apprehended by Los Angeles Police, had boasted they are Communists. No reply was received from Sergeant Beckman.

On June 5, 1965, we sent a letter to the late Chief of Police William H. Parker, enclosing a copy of the letter we had sent to Sergeant Beckman. We explained to Chief Parker that, since writing to Sergeant Beckman, we had ascertained that Sergeant Beckman's statements were originally carried in the *Los Angeles Times,* nine months before Fulton Lewis' column had appeared in the *Los Angeles Herald-Examiner.* We pointed out that what was now at issue was the veracity of Sergeant Beckman's remarks. Then we asked:

Would you be good enough to inform me whether or not this represents an official position of L.A.P.D. or is it just an unfortunate off-the-cuff remark of a lower-echelon officer?

If it is the official position, would you be good enough to inform me whether or not you have any proof of probative value?

The letter of reply, dated June 11, 1965, follows:

## CITY OF LOS ANGELES
### CALIFORNIA

OFFICE OF THE
CHIEF OF POLICE
W. H. PARKER

SAMUEL WM. YORTY
MAYOR

DEPARTMENT OF
**POLICE**
150 N. LOS ANGELES ST
LOS ANGELES CALIF 90012
PHONE 624-5211

IN REPLYING PLEASE GIVE
OUR REF NO  **2.1**

June 11, 1965

Mr. Morris Kominsky
400 East Franklin Street
Elsinore, California  92330

In your letter of June 5, 1965, you allude to a statement
attributed to a member of this Department which appeared in
a local paper something over a year ago, and ask whether
this represents the official policy of the Los Angeles
Police Department.  You also included a copy of a letter
which you wrote earlier this year to the officer to whom
the statement was attributed.  In that letter you made
reference to the hearings before the Subcommittee to
Investigate Juvenile Delinquency, headed up by Senator
Thomas J. Dodd.  In that same document and in the preceding
one, part 11, are statements made by the Chief of Police
of the City of Los Angeles as well as several other members
of this Department.  These statements are contemporary with
those of Dr. Joel Fort and represent the official position
of the Los Angeles Police Department.

It might be worthy to note that following that portion of
Dr. Fort's testimony quoted by you in your earlier letter
is a statement in which he says that we don't know the full
extent of the (narcotics) traffic.

I hope this information will satisfactorily fulfill your
needs.

W. H. PARKER
CHIEF OF POLICE

R. F. ROCK, CAPTAIN
COMMANDER, PUBLIC INFORMATION DIVISION

We replied to Captain Rock on June 24, 1965:

Capt. R.F. Rock
Commander, Public Information Division
Los Angeles Police Department
150 No. Los Angeles Street
Los Angeles, Calif. 90012

Re: Your file number 2.1

Dear Captain Rock:

Thank you very much for your letter of June 11th. I enjoyed your cooperative spirit and the forthright tone of your remarks.

I had previously read the entire testimony before Senator Dodd's Subcommittee and was thoroughly familiar with the testimony of Chief Parker, Lieut. Kennedy, Capt. Colwell, and Capt. Collins. The only testimony that relates to our present discussion is Lieut. Kennedy's conjectural remarks about an alleged "posture of Red China as a major power in the illicit international narcotic traffic." I think that it is fairly indicative of the lack of substantial evidence of probative value that Lieutenant Kennedy very frankly stated: "Indicia, however, force the conclusion that our southern border is infested by dope peddlers of Mexican extraction. The heralded specter of the East commands less attention than the ever-present dealer scurrying across the border."

In summary, there is nothing in the testimony of members of the L.A.P.D., Dr. Joel Fort, or anyone else to support Sergeant Duwayne Beckman's ex-cathedra statement to the *Los Angeles Times* on March 28, 1964, which was subsequently quoted (without attribution to the *Times*) by Fulton Lewis Jr. in his column, which appeared in the *Los Angeles Herald-Examiner* of January 21, 1965. As you will probably recall, the story begins with the seizure of six suitcases containing $100,000 worth of marijuana at Los Angeles International Airport, on March 27, 1964. Simultaneously, the New York Police, after being alerted by your Department, arrested Clara V. Alvarez and Augusto Lazaro Millares. And Lieut. W.A. Stephenson announced that extradition proceedings would be started.

The *Times* of March 28, 1964, quoted your Sergeant Duwayne Beckman as saying: "This whole deal is Communist-inspired and designed to raise American dollars for Castro. Smuggling narcotics helps Castro two ways. It bolsters his economy, and it corrupts morals of the American public." Further on the *Times* quotes Beckman as saying that Cuban courier teams have contacts "in virtually every town in Southern California."

Fulton Lewis, Jr. quotes all this and then adds another item: "Several Cubans arrested by the Los Angeles police have boasted they are Communists." Now, with all due respect to your honorable intentions, which I do not question, the fact remains that your letter of June 11, 1965, does not answer my questions or my needs. My questions are:

430

1. Are the above-quoted remarks of Sergeant Beckman part of the official position of the L.A.P.D.?

2. And if the answer is yes, where may I obtain proof of the validity of these statements?

3. Were the two arrested persons brought to trial, and is there anything in the trial record to substantiate Sergeant Beckman's public pronouncements?

4. Do you have any evidence to substantiate Fulton Lewis' supplementary statement alluded to above?

I agree wholeheartedly with your concluding remark, that it is noteworthy that Dr. Joel Fort has pointed out that we don't know the full extent of the narcotics traffic. This, to me, underscores the importance of avoiding sensational and unsupported statements, especially of a time-serving nature.

I want to appeal to you, Capt. Rock, for an adequate answer to my questions. I am going to deal with this question of narcotics charges being bandied about, and I want to be as fair as you will allow me to be with the L.A.P.D. I am frank in telling you that I intend to vigorously assail Sergeant Beckman's statements, and if they do not represent your official position, I will say so. If you furnish me any proof of the authenticity of Sergeant Beckman's statements, I will present it in my forthcoming book. Can I be more fair with your Department?

I would like to add one more thought, which I hope you will not consider boastful. I have researched this subject very thoroughly, and my research and investigation are continuing. I intend to *prove* any statement that I make in my book.

Thank you for your cooperation.

Respectfully yours,
MORRIS KOMINSKY

No reply was received from Captain Rock.

On August 13, 1965, we sent Chief Parker the following letter, and we hold a postal return receipt showing it was received at police headquarters and signed for by Edward Howard:

William H. Parker
Chief of Police
150 No. Los Angeles St.
Los Angeles, Calif.

Dear Chief Parker:

On June 5, 1965, I sent you a letter, together with which I enclosed a copy of a letter I had sent on April 15, 1965 to Sergeant Duwayne Beckman of the narcotics squad.

431

On June 11, 1965, Captain R.F. Rock sent me a letter, acknowledging my letter of June 5, 1965 addressed to you.

On June 24, 1965, I sent a letter to Captain Rock, a copy of which I enclose herewith.

I am calling this to your attention, because the evidence seems to point to false statements with political overtones being issued by members of your department, and I do not wish to be reproached for not calling this to your attention before my findings are published.

Very truly yours,

MORRIS KOMINSKY

No reply was received from Chief of Police Parker; nor were we surprised. We knew the reason: The Los Angeles Police Department was and is permeated with Ultra-Rightist philosophy, and has its own official and unofficial Cold War propaganda policy. As we shall prove in volume II, the Los Angeles Police Department is moving towards the concept of a Fascist U.S.A.

It is time to play a little game called:

## FULTON LEWIS, JR.
### vs
## FULTON LEWIS, JR.

*Excerpts from his column, January 21, 1965*[24]

Narcotics of *Cuban* origin —marijuana, cocaine, opium, and heroin—are now peddled in big cities and tiny hamlets *throughout this country*.

Several Cubans arrested by the Los Angeles police have boasted they are Communists.

*Excerpts from his column, April 18, 1966*[24]

The dogged agents of the Federal Narcotics Bureau last year seized more than 15,000 pounds of heroin and marijuana brought into this country from *Mexico*. But Bureau spokesmen are the first to admit they confiscate but a minute percentage of the *Mexican* drugs.

The dopelords of the *Cosa Nostra* control distribution *throughout most of the nation*.

In order to win this game, you have to guess when Fulton Lewis, Jr. was telling the truth.

[24] Emphasis throughout has been added.—M. K.

It would be asking too much for Dr. Howard Kershner and his Christian Freedom Foundation to refrain from using the Narcotics Hoax. It was therefore no surprise to find this editorial in the April 6, 1965 issue of *Christian Economics*:

### Castro's Dope Pushers

Dope pushing is a little known but important aspect of the Cold War. It is said to be the principal source of dollar income for Communist China. Recent arrests indicate that narcotics is an important source of dollars for Castro's Cuba. Former Senator Kenneth Keating said:

"Fidel Castro's narcotic trafficking, like his ransom notes and firing squads, is a lesson in Communist methodology. The Communists will stop at nothing in their attempt to undermine and demoralize people who live in freedom. They have now joined crime in an unholy alliance with subversion to advance their diabolical aims."

Numerous arrests of Communists in possession of very large quantities of dope have been made in New York and Los Angeles recently. One batch alone was said to be sufficient to supply all the dope users in our country for a period of two months. Most of these persons are Cuban Communists, sent here for the purpose of earning dollars for Castro.

---

If Dr. Howard Kershner had the slightest interest in telling the truth about Communists, he could easily have checked with police and court records, as well as the yearly reports of the Federal Bureau of Narcotics, and have learned that there were no "numerous arrests of Communists in possession of very large quantities of dope." On May 17, 1965, one of our research assistants sent Dr. Kershner a letter, inquiring about his editorial, "Castro's Dope Pushers." The final paragraph in the letter said:

Now, what surprises me is that I have apparently missed this item of news, in spite of the fact that I read carefully both major Los Angeles newspapers. So I ask you to kindly tell me the source of this report.

A letter, dated May 25, 1965, from H. Edward Rowe, Executive Vice-President of the Christian Freedom Foundation, informed our research assistant that the source of information in that editorial was *Human Events* of April 6, 1965. A careful comparison of the *Human Events* article with Kershner's editorial leaves no other conclusion than the obvious one, that Kershner plagiarized the *Human Events* article without attribution. This is hardly a legitimate journalistic procedure.

The article in *Human Events* is a syndicated column by Bill Schulz, entitled "Cuban Dope-Peddling Increases." It is based partly on the remarks of Sergeant Duwayne Beckman, which Fulton Lewis, Jr. relied upon. The sequence of events is as follows: The *Los Angeles Times* carried Beckman's remarks on March 28, 1964. Bill Schulz relied, in part, upon Beckman's story for his column in *Human Events* of November 28, 1964. Fulton Lewis, Jr. used the same alleged facts in his column of January 21, 1965. Besides using Beckman's "facts," Schulz tells a fantastic story, which impelled us to send him a letter on August 13, 1965, for which we hold a postal receipt showing it was delivered to his office at King Features Syndicate, New York City, on August 17, 1965. We asked for proof or his sources of information on 7 items in his column. No reply was received. Schulz makes statements for which he gives neither proof nor the source of his information. For instance, among others, he tells this story:

> While cocaine is a major export, Castro agents will sell anything for which there is a market. Government files tell the story of Jose Francisco Zavala, a Peruvian national active in the Miami narcotics trade.

First of all, it is positively untrue that cocaine is a major export of Castro's Cuba. Secondly, it is only a wild figure-of-speech to assert that "Castro agents will sell anything for which there is a market." In fact, it is just Cold War propaganda. It is interesting how ingenious Schulz is in transforming a Peruvian narcotics peddler into a Castro agent:

> Zavala obtained his narcotics from a Cuban-based Chinese who has traveled around the hemisphere setting up a network of Castro-supplied pushers.

Schulz' column contains several more items just as preposterous as this last one. Unfortunately, the readers of his syndicated column are not aware of what makes Schulz indulge in such flights of fancy.

Schulz was trained by James Wick in the school of journalism run by the Ultra-Rightist *Human Events*. Later he became an assistant to Fulton Lewis, Jr., and substituted for him at times when Lewis could not produce his regular column. He was a co-author, with Allan Ryskind and M. Stanton Evans, of a book, *The Fringe on Top*. From 1960 to 1963 he was a director of the Ultra-Rightist *Young Americans for Freedom*. It is easy to understand Dr. Howard Kershner's eagerness to repeat Bill Schulz' contribution to the Narcotics Hoax, but it is not so easy to understand an earlier performance. On June 1, 1964, Dr. Howard Kershner delivered a speech at Friends University, Wichita, Kansas. It is distributed in pamphlet form[25] by the Ultra-Rightist *Constructive Action, Inc*. At one point in his lengthy speech, Kershner said:

A principal source of dollar income in Communist China . . . is the systematic pushing of the sale of dope in many parts of the world, but especially in our country. Young foreigners in China have been forcibly injected with dope until they become addicts, and then are sent to other parts of the world to push the traffic as the only means of satisfying their own craving. The number of addicts in our country is increasing alarmingly. While Communist China pushes this nefarious trade abroad, death is the penalty for those who use heroin or morphine in China.

It is time to play our little game of comparisons again:

*Kenneth Goff says:*

Chinese Communist leaders have forcibly kidnapped *Chinese youths*[26] and forcibly given them injections. . . . This is the young army of slaves produced by Chinese monsters who are now willing and eager to undertake any criminal assignments in exchange for daily narcotic requirements.

*Howard Kershner says:*

*Young foreigners*[26] in China have been forcibly injected with dope until they become addicts and then are sent to other parts of the world to push the traffic as the only means of satisfying their own craving.

25 Title of the speech is "The Hangman's Rope."
26 Emphasis has been added.—M. K.

435

*Dr. Charles S. Poling says:*

This nation gives millions of acres to the culture of the opium poppy with which to corrupt her own and the peoples of the world. . . . (Dr. Poling means Communist China when he speaks of "this nation.")

*Dr. Howard Kershner says:*

While Communist China pushes this nefarious trade abroad, death is the penalty for those who use heroin or morphine in China.

The John Birch Society has a most unique stable of creators-of-fantasy. Among the ablest of them is a young Los Angeles journalist, Gary Allen. This fellow can find a Communist angle in any problem or any situation. His ingenuity and resourcefulness are superb. In an essay, entitled "On L.S.D." and subtitled "Harvard, Hallucinations, and Hippies,"[27] Allen concedes that opium smoking was "early encouraged in China by Europeans to foster acquiescence to their imperial interests." In a rambling and irresponsible manner, Allen discusses narcotics and hallucinogens, arriving at the inevitable conclusion of the Cold War propagandists:

What role if any do the Communists play in the skyrocketing popularity of narcotics? For many years they have engaged in a cynical alliance with Organized Crime to pump funds into the coffers of Communism while at the same time working to destroy the character and morality of our citizenry. The *Philadelphia Inquirer* of January 23, 1966, reported that "a new survey reveals the shocking fact that in 1964, the Peking warlords collected $800,000,000 for the treasury of Red China in spewing into the world more than 10,000 tons of heroin." While Mao deals in "H," his crony in Cuba merchandises "snow" (cocaine).

Mr. Allen adds to this statement, as further "proof," the same quotation from former Senator Kenneth Keating that was used by Bill Schulz in his *Human Events* column of April 6, 1965. In a footnote to his own statement, Allen refers to an item in a magazine of the "psychedelic crowd," which reports that in Seattle the *Mafia* has taken over the distribution of LSD.

It is a safe assumption that Allen knows that the Communists have no "cynical alliance with Organized Crime to pump funds into the coffers of Communism to destroy the character and

[27] *American Opinion*, June, 1967.

morality of our citizenry." At any rate, he produces no evidence of probative value and quotes no official documents. He quotes the *Philadelphia Inquirer,* without telling his readers that it is *not* the *Philadelphia Inquirer* that made those remarks, but rather a Right-Wing syndicated columnist, Pierre J. Huss. In fact, the *Inquirer* carried a box, 1½" x 7⅝", above Mr. Huss' column, and in that box there was a heading in big, bold letters: "AS OUR COLUMNISTS SEE IT." Mr. Allen also took the liberty of *changing* what Pierre Huss wrote. In the column, as it appeared in the *Philadelphia Inquirer* of January 23, 1966, Pierre Huss actually wrote, "more than 10,000 tons of the stuff," and it was in reference to cocaine, heroin, and morphine. The Birch Society "researcher" plays fast and loose, in his quoting Huss, by changing "stuff" to "heroin." Honest writers do *not* change the words in a quotation. Huss' column really contains nothing of probative value. He quotes an anonymous "survey" and makes a series of unproved statements; but this is the kind of stuff that Gary Allen needed for the Birch Society magazine. The main point, however, is that the statements made by Gary Allen are completely disproven by every responsible agency, and especially by the latest statement of the Bureau of Narcotics, which was contained in that letter received by Senator William Proxmire.

While we have found no record of a President of the United States helping to spread the Narcotics Hoax, it is extremely disquieting to learn that the man who nearly became President has helped to spread this monstrous lie. In his column, which appeared in the *Los Angeles Times* on December 1, 1965, General Barry Goldwater[28] wrote:

The United Nations itself, even with Red China not a member, daily feels the sting of Red Chinese activity as it studies ways to stamp out the world-wide trade in opium. Red China is the virtual master of that trade, using narcotics as a routine item of ammunition in its war against the rest of the world.

It is perhaps fitting to once again recall that Secretary of the Treasury Henry H. Fowler has disclosed:

1. That 80% of the heroin reaching this country is made in France from opium raised in Turkey.

2. That another 15% of the heroin comes in from Mexico.

28 Goldwater holds a commission as Major-General in the Air Force Reserve.

437

3. That opium is also cultivated in India, Thailand, Laos, and Burma.

4. That the small quantity of opium that *may be* coming out of mainland China and entering the United States in the form of heroin "does not represent any significant sum in U.S. dollars."

Once again, it should be noted that Secretary Fowler has jurisdiction over the Federal Bureau of Narcotics.

There are political desperadoes who are willing to gamble the future of the human race in a third world war. It is for these reasons that we deemed it necessary to painstakingly expose and demolish the Narcotics Hoax, because, in our judgment, it has been a powerful and insidious weapon in the campaign to transform the Cold War into a hot war.

## Postscript to Chapter VI

Since the completion of this chapter, the Federal Bureau of Narcotics has been merged into the newly-created Bureau of Narcotics and Dangerous Drugs within the Department of Justice. In its Fact Sheet 3, the Bureau moves away from the position of Harry J. Anslinger:

The North American continent is the principal target of illicit heroin traffic. The bulk of this drug is produced from opium poppies grown in Turkey. The raw opium is converted into morphine base in clandestine laboratories close to the growing areas and then shipped through Istanbul and Beirut and smuggled into France to be processed into heroin. At this point, the heroin may be smuggled directly into the United States or transported through Italy, Canada or Mexico. It is, nevertheless, destined for the United States Market.

The final proof of the thesis of this chapter is contained in a UPI dispatch from Washington on January 7, 1970:

A White House source said yesterday that high-level talks with France, Turkey, and Mexico—begun at the direction of President Nixon—have raised hopes that most heroin shipments can be dried up within one to three years. . .

The source said that about 80 per cent of the heroin entering this country is made from poppies grown in Turkey and is processed in plants in and around Marseille, France. Another 15 per cent comes from Mexico and *the remaining 5 per cent dribbles in from several Asian countries.* (Emphasis has been added.—M.K.)

438

# CHAPTER VII
## The Manuilsky Hoax

If this planet should ever suffer the horrifying devastation of a third world war, substantial credit for immobilizing the forces of peace would have to be given to a renegade Communist, Joseph Zack Kornfeder, and an ex-liberal journalist, Richard L. Stokes. These gentlemen invented the Manuilsky Hoax, a scarecrow device to convince gullible readers that peaceful coexistence with the Soviet Union is impossible and, as a corollary, that war is inevitable. One would think that rational and decent people would recoil with horror at the prospects of a thermonuclear holocaust, and would struggle to avert such an occurrence. That there are individuals who would use deliberate falsehood to generate a war psychosis and help pave the way for the possible annihilation of the human species—this is something that taxes the credulity of honest and rational people. Yet, the evidence shows that some human beings can descend to the level of justifying anything in the "holy crusade" against Communism. Stated in its simplest terms, these people are willing to destroy mankind in order to "save" us from Communism.

Our story begins with an article in the Ultra-Rightist *Human Events* of August 12, 1953. This essay, entitled "The War of Peace" by Richard L. Stokes, starts with these exact words:

War to the hilt, between Communism and Capitalism, is inevitable. Today, of course, we are not strong enough to attack. Our time will come in about 20 or 30 years. To win we shall need the element of surprise. The bourgeoisie will have to be put to sleep. So we shall begin by launching the most spectacular peace movement on record. There will be electrifying overtures and unheard of concessions. The capitalist countries, stupid and decadent, will rejoice to cooperate in their own destruction. They will leap at another chance to be friends. As soon as their guard is down, we shall smash them with our clenched fist!

There are quotation marks at the beginning and at the end

439

of that opening paragraph, and this can denote only one thing: it is presented as *the exact words* of someone. Immediately following, Richard Stokes explains;

The lecturer, at the Lenin School of Political Warfare in Moscow, was Stalin's deputy to the Comintern, Dimitri Z. Manuilsky. The year was 1930. He advanced later to the rubber-stamp post of Foreign Minister of the Ukrainian Soviet Socialist Republic. In 1948-49 he was chief Ukrainian member of the Security Council of the United Nations. Under its rotation system, he acted as president of the Security Council during July, 1949.

His pupil 23 years ago was a bright-eyed little Jewish tailor, Joseph Zach Kornfeder, who was born in Slovakia and became an American citizen. He was one of the founders of the Communist Party USA and a member of its National Committee. In 1927 he was assigned to the Lenin School and finished its three-year course with such credit that he was rewarded with postgraduate indoctrination under Comrade Manuilsky.

Stokes goes on and on with his rambling story, making wild statements and giving no proof of anything that he says. At no point does he state explicitly and categorically that Manuilsky made that statement, but rather he insinuates it strongly enough so that the reader knows he is quoting Manuilsky. This, of course, is Stokes' intent, but in the light of the evidence that it is a fabrication, one can only wonder if Stokes chose this style of writing because he felt it would be too brazen to come out and say: "Manuilsky said the following."

Any student of political science, and especially one who is familiar with the writings and speeches of Manuilsky, would reject this quotation immediately, because it is completely inconsistent with the style of his writings and speeches. In fact, the style is neither Communist nor Russian. It is a thinly disguised American hoodlum style of speech. It is the language of the stoolpigeon or the agent-provocateur. It so happens that Manuilsky was a prolific writer of pamphlets and political tracts, and nowhere in any of his writings and published speeches is there any hint of such an attitude. In fact, the alleged quotation is in diametrical opposition to his known philosophical posture.

Manuilsky was one of the participants in the founding conference of the United Nations at San Francisco in 1945, at which time he publicly declared that "there is no place on

440

earth where the interests of American people run counter to those of the Soviet peoples." An examination of all his subsequent speeches at the United Nations shows Manuilsky to be a most zealous devotee of world peace. As an example, in a strongly worded speech to the Political and Security Committee of the United Nations in October, 1948, Manuilsky called for the outlawing of the atomic bomb and the setting up of international controls. In view of the fact that the nuclear test ban treaty of 1963 was the first step in that direction, history may yet record Manuilsky as a prophet of peace rather than having essayed the role attributed to him by Kornfeder and Stokes.

Manuilsky had an excellent command of the French language and he spoke English fluently. He was a member of the Academy of Sciences of the U.S.S.R., and was a professor of historical science. We are asked to believe that a person of this calibre would issue such a fantastically stupid and ignorant statement. In 1930, when he allegedly made that statement, the Soviet Union was so weak industrially and militarily that any Soviet leader who would utter such a statement would ipso facto be a candidate for entry to a psychiatric hospital.

Additional internal evidence of the unreliability of Richard Stokes' article is that even Kornfeder's middle name of ZACK is incorrectly spelled ZACH. Perhaps Stokes would say this is a typographical error, but how does he explain his reference to Kornfeder as "bright-eyed little Jewish tailor" in the light of this testimony before the Dies Committee (the Special House Committee on Un-American Activities), September 30, 1939?

*Dies.* There is one other question that we always ask for the record: Are you a Jew?
*Kornfeder.* No, sir; I am by breeding a Catholic.

At this same Dies Committee hearing, Kornfeder testified that his wife and son were being held as hostages in the U.S.S.R.; that all efforts over the years to effect their return were of no avail. Then, in a show of bravado, Kornfeder asserted that he would tell the truth about the Communists, because it would make no difference either way in the treatment of his family. A letter, dated June 18, 1963, from the sister of Mrs. Joseph Zack Kornfeder, reads:

In reply to your letter, seeking information about Joseph Zack Kornfeder, all I can tell you is that he was married to my sister Chave. (I don't know whether this was his first marriage.) They had a boy named Spartac. Zack went to Soviet Union in 1927 and Chave with the child followed him in 1928. Zack is *not* Jewish; he is Slovak. After coming back to the U.S.A. he had an affair with another woman and Chave refused to go back to him to the U.S.A. She died later in Moscow and what happened to Spartac we don't know. This is about all I can tell you about this matter.

On June 13, 1964, we interviewed Kornfeder's sister-in-law at her daughter's home in Santa Rosa, California. She reaffirmed the statements in her letter, and added that she remembered her sister telling her that she was leaving Zack because he was a stool pigeon. We spent considerable time at this interview in a probing type of interrogation, but could not shake the lady's story. The lady's daughter and son-in-law corroborated her story on the basis of it having become a matter of common knowledge within the family unit.

The *New York Times,* May 4, 1963, in a story reporting Kornfeder's death, told of his frequent testimony before Congressional Committees regarding Communist activities:

At one appearance, he testified that his birthplace was Scranton, Pa.; at another he said he was born in what is now Czechoslovakia.
Later he explained that he had been taken to Europe by his father at an early age, that his father died during this trip, and that on returning he was unable to prove he was born in the United States. He was naturalized in 1948 in a Michigan Federal Court.

The trouble with Kornfeder's ingenious explanation is that his wife's sister stated he was a Slovak and that, if he were in fact born in Scranton, Pa., there would be a record in the City Hall. Scranton, Pa. keeps vital statistics and is not in the same category as some of the benighted villages under the Czarist regimes of Russia, where records of birth and deaths were kept only by the village priest. In addition, when he testified before the Dies Committee on September 30, 1939, he told the Committee of the existence of a birth certificate. If this were so, he should have been able to prove his place of birth.

In the *New York Post* of June 4, 1957, Murray Kempton relates the story of how the Department of Justice obtained a denaturalization verdict against James Matles. One of the star witnesses for the prosecution was Kornfeder, who, for a fee of $740.42 testified:

1. That Matles was a Communist in New York in 1925, when it was proven that Matles was a 15 year old schoolboy in Rumania at the time!

2. Although Kornfeder was in Russia at the time of the Communist Party convention in New York, in 1930, Kornfeder testified he saw Matles at that convention.

Kornfeder's reliability as a witness was put to the test at a hearing on October 27, 1948 of charges against some professors at the University of Washington at Seattle. Kornfeder branded a number of organizations as Communist fronts and had included the prestigious *Consumers Union*. One of the defense attorneys, upon cross examination, pointed out that he had been a member of Consumers Union for a number of years and demanded that Kornfeder furnish proof that it was a Communist front. Just a few items from the cross examination will show the measure of Kornfeder:

Q. Can you name any person who is a director or officer of the Consumers Union who is a member of the Communist Party?

A. Well, if you will give me the letterhead of their national board I may be able to do so.

Q. What kind of local activities does the Consumers Union carry on?

A. From the literature that I have seen of theirs, they carry on activities against the high cost of living.

Q. They are opposed to the high cost of living?

A. Yes, sir.

Q. And what else are they opposed to?

A. Well, they have passed resolutions on various occasions in conformity with the Communist Party line.

Q. In what manner have they passed resolutions?

A. Well, they have passed resolutions generally favored by the Party, on issues of public or civil liberties.

Q. Let me ask you this, Mr. Kornfeder, have you ever been a member of the Consumers Union?

A. No.

Q. Do you know what you are talking about when you say that the Consumers Union is a Communist front organization?

A. Yes.

Q. All right. Now you name one resolution that the Consumers Union has passed that you claim is a Communist resolution.

A. Well, I will tell you, if you give me the resolutions that they have passed and the literature that they issue—if you will give me those I will tell you exactly where it corresponds with the Party line.

Q. I want to know upon what basis you have formed that conclusion.

A. I have formed that conclusion on the basis of their type of agitation.

Q. What type of agitation?

A. That I have seen off and on in the past years.

Q. Now, let us be specific, Mr. Kornfeder. Just cite one type of agitation that you claim causes you to arrive at that conclusion. You say that they are against the high cost of living. Now what else?

A. That happens to be one activity that I am in favor of.

Q. All right. Now what else?

A. Well, I say that they throughout conform in a diluted form to the Party line with all its changes.

Q. Just a minute, Mr. Kornfeder. I asked you for a specific example. You are giving us general statements now. Let me ask you a question. Are you familiar with the publication issued and published by the Consumers Union? Do you know what it is called?

A. I think it is called *The Consumer*.

Q. You are an expert, now. What is it called?

A. Now, I never claimed to be an expert on the Consumers Union.

Q. Well, you testified as an expert that the Consumers Union was a Communist Front organization. Do you want to change your testimony on that?

A. I will say right now that the Communist Party has so many fronts, and I am not familiar with the detailed activities of each of them. I am more familiar with some than with others.

Q. Do you want to change your testimony, then, and say that in your opinion you do not know that the Consumers Union is a Communist Front organization?

A. No. I will not. My impression is, from what I have seen of their activities.

Q. Now . . . will you name the things that they sponsor or do that makes them a Communist Front organization?

A. I will not tell you any more unless I see their letterhead to refresh my memory on.[1]

On March 7, 1957, Kornfeder appeared as an expert witness on racial unrest at a Hearing of the Joint Legislative Committee of the State of Louisiana. These are portions of his testimony under oath:

Q. Mr. Kornfeder, are you a citizen of the United States?
A. I am.

---

[1] Some portions of the dialogue have been omitted for the sake of brevity. The entire cross examination of Kornfeder with respect to Consumers Union will be found in Professor Vern Countryman's book, *Un-American Activities in the State of Washington*.

Q. Born or naturalized?
A. Naturalized.
Q. Where were you born, Mr. Kornfeder?
A. I was born in Slovakia, at the present time part of Czechoslovakia.
Q. How old are you at this time, Mr. Kornfeder?
A. I am sixty years.
Q. What is your trade or profession that you follow for your livelihood, Mr. Kornfeder?
A. For the last ten years—I have been occupied in writing and speaking against Communism. I have been a lecturer and a writer.
Q. To go back, when did you arrive in the United States? When did you come to this country, Mr. Kornfeder?
A. I came to this country in 1917.

Inasmuch as Kornfeder testified at other hearings that he was born in Scranton, Pa., it is clear that he was a liar and a perjurer. At this very Hearing, it was another FBI stool pigeon that proved him to be a perjurer in another respect. Two days after his appearance, Mrs. Martha Nichols Edmiston, who had been planted in the Communist Party by the FBI testified; and our little game of comparisons is now in order:

| *Joseph Zack Kornfeder* | *Martha Nichols Edmiston* |
|---|---|
| Moscow controls the Communist Party here in so many different ways. Of course, Moscow spends quite a bit of money on the American Communist Party. The Party has a standing subsidy. Its principal newspapers are subsidized from Moscow. | There has been a lot of misconception about money pouring into the party from Soviet Russia. As a matter of fact, in our day, and I assume it is still true, we paid international dues, subtracted a fourth out of every dollar, and the money was all shoveled over to New York, to party headquarters there. A fourth was deducted and sent to the Soviet to support the party there or any other party—which means, of course, that the Soviets had this immense spy system here which not only didn't pay its way, but we paid them dividends. In our case, unfortunately, we had to pay our dues occasionally from our FBI expense money. That was quite a "joke." |

It becomes very obvious when one reads the 350 book-size pages of the Louisiana Legislative Committee's Report, entitled "Subversion in Racial Unrest," that it was a project contrived to sweep racial injustices under the rug and to make it appear that all would be sweetness and light were it not for the machinations of the Communists, whose diabolical schemes are supposedly directed from Moscow. This neat little formula makes it unnecessary to cope with problems of poverty, unemployment, discrimination, lynchings, and police brutality. When repeated often enough, the bible-quoting, tub-thumping racists begin to believe this departure from reality. Who would be more fit to give the Southern racists the ideological and psychological ammunition they were seeking than Joseph Zack Kornfeder? After all, he stated in his initial testimony that he was a professional anti-Communist, who was earning his living telling stories, with the full knowledge that no one would sue him for libel in the climate of opinion existing at the time. So, we find some 73 printed pages of testimony devoted to Kornfeder's slanderous fairy tales, with just enough truth thrown in to give his lies a semblance of credibility. The way Kornfeder tells it, the National Association for the Advancement of Colored People and every other organization or committee that strives for improvement of the Negro's condition are dupes of a Moscow-controlled conspiracy. Among the people at whom Kornfeder aimed his billingsgate were Dr. Channing H. Tobias, the eminent Negro educator, whom he credited with links to 42 Communist Fronts; Eleanor Roosevelt, 33 Fronts; the distinguished Negro jurist, Judge Hubert T. Delaney, 14 Fronts; and the accomplished musician and composer, Oscar Hammerstein II, 25 Fronts. Apparently to forestall criticism of a weakness in Kornfeder's performance, Mr. W. M. Shaw, counsel of the Committee took steps to remedy the defect:

Q. Mr. Kornfeder, we have been talking here about a period from 1935 to 1939. Now, you were no longer in the party at that time. Is that correct?
A. That's correct, but I am very familiar with their operations.

In response to the next question, asking how he could keep informed of current developments in the Communist Party, Kornfeder added an aura of mystery by explaining that, when a party member drops out, he and "others" manage to interview him and ferret out the latest inside information.

446

Kornfeder did not identify the "others," but his ingenious explanation is sheer twaddle. With the large number of FBI stool pigeons operating within the Communist Party, there were no "secrets" for Kornfeder to investigate. To add further melodramatic effect, Kornfeder confessed to having committed a felony, viz.: that he carried a gun for several years after his expulsion from the Communist Party, without a permit and with full knowledge that he was in violation of New York State's Sullivan Law. His explanation was that he was in fear of assassination, although in the next breath he conceded that the danger of such an occurrence "is not very big."

There can be no question that, in testifying before this Committee, Kornfeder accomplished his mission: to give the Southern racists the propaganda basis for their built-in verdict. The Chairman of the Committee, State Senator W. M. Rainich, gave his "benediction" at the conclusion of Kornfeder's performance in very frank terms:

Mr. Kornfeder, on behalf of the committee, the Chair would like to express our official appreciation to you for coming here from Detroit to present this interesting history of the conspiracy that, from your testimony, we feel originated in the offices of Stalin himself and which has resulted in the acceptance of the Communist doctrine of racial nationalism by a serious percentage of the Negro population of this country—which acceptance is posing a threat in the form of a move toward eventual Communist control of this nation and the overthrow of our Government as we now know it.

Well may the Committee have been grateful to Kornfeder, for his "testimony" became the cornerstone of a gigantic racist campaign to drown the aspirations of the Negro people with a witches' brew of prejudice, lies, and hate. The Committee's Report has been widely circulated, widely quoted, and widely emulated. It has set the tone and the pace for the Ultra-Rightists in general and the overt peddlers of hate in particular. The Committee got what it wanted. It ignored the fact that Kornfeder was such an unreliable witness that, after he testified before the Subversive Activities Control Board, a Federal judge commented that the Board had unwisely relied upon Kornfeder "whose demeanor led the Board to examine his testimony with . . . caution."

The case against the Manuilsky Hoax could very well rest at this point, because the evidence is clear that Kornfeder was a liar, a perjurer, an opportunist, and a person of elastic morality. It is also clear that Richard Stokes departed from the established norms of journalistic integrity. However, in view of the enormous damage done to the cause of peace by the persistent use of this fabrication, the evidence that follows is presented in order to completely demolish this hoax for all time.

*Three weeks* before the Manuilsky Hoax appeared in *Human Events,* Joseph Zack Kornfeder testified before the House Committee on Un-American Activities. The date was July 7, 1953. His testimony can be found in the Committee's Report of that date, entitled "Communist Activities in the New York Area." He testified that he had been sent to the Lenin School in Moscow for a three-year course, and he spelled out all the procedures or alleged procedures in minute detail. He gave the Committee a copy of the Curriculum, Lenin University, Moscow, U.S.S.R. It was placed in the record of the Hearing on pages 2039-2043, and was signed by Kornfeder, who attested its authenticity. In the section on textbooks used in the various courses, the names of the authors of the textbooks are given. Not once does the name of Dimitri Manuilsky appear. In the section on teachers staff, a list of prominent Communist officials is given, but not once is Dimitri Maniulsky mentioned as an instructor. The question that must be honestly answered is: How can Richard Stokes explain that his "bright-eyed little Jewish tailor" left Manuilsky's name out of a document he presented to the House Committee on Un-American Activities, in view of the fact that he was testifying at the approximate time that Stokes was interviewing him for an article revolving around Manuilsky? There is, of course, only one answer. Stokes needed a sensational story for the readers of the Ultra-Rightist *Human Events,* so that he could collect a fee. Kornfeder furnished the raw material for that story—also for a fee! The proof of this conclusion will soon be presented in a form that no one can challenge.

On September 24, 1962, a member of our staff, whose name must remain confidential for the present, wrote a letter to Joseph Zack Kornfeder at the address given as his residence by the Library of Congress: 3210 Book Tower, Detroit, Michigan. We asked Kornfeder to tell us under what circumstances Manuilsky had made that statement, if there were any other witnesses who could confirm the authenticity of the statement, and if the statement was published anywhere.

In a friendly, but cocky, letter dated September 28, 1962, Kornfeder explained:

Dimitri Manuilsky's statement was made at a meeting of Senior students of the Lenin School (March 1930) in response to a question. It was a group assigned to him for final coaching. They were from different lands, and I was one of them. No, you won't find it in print, but you can find equivalent statements by the top leaders during the early years or the so-called 3rd. period of the Comintern. As to those who were present I don't know their whereabouts, some of them may have quitted. One, Smith, whom they claim has repudiated it, was from Canada but he was a Junior and was not present.

After telling us about a few irrelevant matters, Kornfeder gave his new address as: 7343 Senator Street, Detroit.

There are a number of things that need explaining in his explanation. First, he states that Manuilsky made that statement in his presence during March of 1930. In his testimony before the Dies Committee on September 30, 1939, Kornfeder testified that he was in South America as a delegate of the Communist International (Comintern) during 1930 and until the end of 1931; that he was arrested and imprisoned in Venezuela during that period; and having testified that he was in South America until the *end of 1931,* he stated a few minutes later that he returned to the U.S.A. in the *fall of 1931.* Secondly, there is no clue in his letter as to why Manuilsky's name did not appear on the document which listed the instructors. The document did list Molotov, Losovsky, Ercoli, and Marshal Simeon Budyenny, all names that were equally as prominent, if not more so, in the Russian Communist leadership. Thirdly, Kornfeder *enclosed with his letter* a mimeographed leaflet in which he reproduced a letter sent on March 7, 1961, to Dr. James D. Bales of Harding College, Searcy, Arkansas. He reproduced also an essay that he claimed he wrote in 1955, entitled "Dimitri Manuilski, Pacifist or Bolshevik?" The entire essay later appeared in the Ultra-Rightist *American Mercury* of July 1963, nine months after Kornfeder sent us the mimeographed version. Both are identical in wording. In quoting some pertinent excerpts, it should be noted how it contradicts his letter:

449

Sometime in the summer of 1953, I gave Richard L. Stokes, a writer, an interview. The article appeared a month or so later in *Human Events...*

Thus, Kornfeder confirms our conclusion that he gave Stokes the interview at about the same time he was testifying before the Dies Committee, in July, 1953. The *Human Events* article appeared in August, 1953. So, the mystery still remains of why such a "juicy" item as the alleged Manuilsky statement was not given in his testimony before the Dies Committee and why Manuilsky's name does not appear in Kornfeder's own document of instructors, books, and curriculum at the Lenin School where he claims the statement was made. Kornfeder continues:

Manuilsky had been my special coach at the end of the Lenin School term and hence I did some reminiscing about him, one quote of which *was summarized*[2] by Richard L. Stokes as follows:

Then the Manuilsky Hoax is quoted in full, and Kornfeder adds:

I did not see the quotation until I saw it out in print, but I did consider it *an able summation of Manuilsky's views*[3] on the subject as stated by me.

As we have seen previously, Kornfeder was a resourceful fellow. When cornered in a lie, he could shift positions with remarkable agility. And because there had appeared numerous challenges for documentation that Manulisky had made that statement or that he ever wrote or spoke in that style, Kornfeder was finally forced to admit that what Stokes wrote was not a direct quotation from Manuilsky, but a summation of Kornfeder's reminiscences 23 years later. Even if Kornfeder were an honest reporter, such reminiscences, after such a lapse of time, would have to be considered of doubtful dependability. But a story from a proven liar and perjurer must be summarily rejected, especially when the second-hand source, Richard L. Stokes, perpetrated a shocking act of dishonesty: putting quotation marks around a summary or paraphrasing of another

2 Emphasis has been added.—M. K.
3 Emphasis has been added.—M. K.

person's version of someone's views, whom he had not met personally!

After Kornfeder makes that "confession" in his essay, he mounts a "rear guard" attack against the Communists and their newspaper, the *Daily Worker*. From the volume and intensity of the insults and intemperate remarks, it is apparent that Kornfeder was stung to the quick. He berates the Communists for being too "particular" about quotation marks. He avers that there is nothing in the Marquis de Queensberry rules "which says that one cannot quote a speaker if one has heard him, or that only authorized printed speeches can be quoted." He adds that criticism about the use of quotation marks around something that is not a direct and accurate quotation is only a "smoke screen." We are reasonably certain that every reader will understand the danger and downright immorality of using quotation marks in a careless or flippant manner, that only a person's actual words may be placed in quotation marks, and that a summery or paraphrase must be so labeled or identified. A single true story that graphically illustrates this point is the traumatic experience of the late Senator Robert La Follette, Sr. In the course of a speech on the Senate floor opposing our entry into World War I, La Follette said:

We had grievances against Imperial Germany.

Then he went on to argue that these grievances were not sufficient to warrant our entry into a war. The wire service and the newspapers quoted him as saying:

We had no grievances against Imperial Germany.

This was shortly after the sinking of the Lusitania by a German submarine. The addition of that little "no" resulted in lynch mobs threatening La Follette's life and an unprecedented campaign of calumny against him.

After delivering his moral strictures against the Communists, Kornfeder proceeds in his essay:

According to Lenin, "Everything is moral which serves the Cause and immoral if it does not." I could look up the very exact words of Lenin for the diseased minds of the *Daily Worker*, but they could

451

get no comfort out of that because the essence of it is as quoted above. *The same could be said about the Manuilsky quotation under dispute.*[4] Yes, let anyone look up the works and speeches—even the printed ones—of Lenin, Stalin & Co. and see whether what Manuilsky said was not in line not only with their speeches but even more so with their practices, and the same holds good for their "Understudy" Manuilsky and his speeches. *No, you won't find the exact words of Stokes' quotation, via me, but you will find plenty which connotes the same.*[4]

Kornfeder is here using a very prevalent gambit of Ultra-Rightist propagandists. When confronted with proof that they have used a phoney quotation, they counter with the argument that the phoney quotation is justified because, forsooth, it expresses the meaning of something else the quoted person has said. The shabbiness of this type of alibi needs no comment—it is deception, pure and simple. Kornfeder's brazen challenge to his readers, that they look up "the works and speeches of Lenin, Stalin & Co." for statements similar to the alleged Manuilsky quotation—this is another Kornfeder swindle, because no such quotation can be found in any of the writings of Lenin, Stalin and other leading Communist leaders.

On October 5, 1962, we replied to Kornfeder's letter of September 28, 1962. We asked him where in Lenin's writings we could find the quotation: "Everything is moral which serves the Cause and immoral if it does not." On October 14, 1962, Kornfeder replied, and we quote some excerpts:

What now appears as the Manuilsky quote originally was part of a lengthy article on Communism by the late Richard L. Stokes based on an interview with me. Cardinal Spellman picked it out as a quote for one of his speeches (1953) and it has been rolling ever since, making the rounds of all the continents and 10 years after it is still rolling.

Concerning the Lenin quote you asked, you can find it in Lenin's *Left Wing Communism-An Infantile Disorder,* but I have not got it handy to give you the page number.

On October 16, 1962, we wrote to Kornfeder again, pointing out that, after carefully reading Lenin's essay to which he had ascribed that quotation about morals, we could not find it. On October 20, 1962, he replied:

4 Emphasis has been added.—M. K.

452

You are quite right about the Lenin quote on morals. It is in Lenin's booklet on *Religion*, page 47 and 48—part of the *Little Lenin Library* series, volume 7, published by International Publishers, New York.

As luck would have it a friend of mine from Flint, Mich. (Catholic) was visiting me and he had it with him. *The words are different but the substance is the same.*[5]

That last sentence is the real clue to Kornfeder's amoral position, and the reader can well understand how dangerous it is for people to think that it is proper for them to decide what constitutes another person's thinking, write it up to suit their own fancy, and then put quotation marks around it. It can and does result in misrepresentation, deception, and fraud. It lays the basis for frame-ups.

On December 31, 1962, we sent Kornfeder another letter, in which we advised him that, at his behest, we had carefully read and studied Lenin's pamphlet on *Religion*, and that we could find neither the quotation nor anything that could possibly be equated with the quotation. We also asked him if his testimony about being a Catholic, during the Dies Committee Hearing, was correct. No reply was received, so on February 3, 1963, we sent a follow-up letter. He replied on February 9, 1963. We quote some pertinent excerpts:

I can't account for your assertion that the quote you are seeking is not in Lenin's booklet on "Religion" as stated by me. Under Stalin however it was not rare to tamper even with Lenin's writings by omission or commission, if it served the purpose. Hence I am not challenging what you say and if you send me a photostat of the pages in question I will compare it.

No, I'm not Jewish, converted or otherwise. My parents were Catholic and hence I came up that way. At present I am an agnostic.

Here again we see Kornfeder's capacity for resourcefulness and shifting of position, when trapped in his own lies. In the first place, he had previously written that those exact words are not found in Lenin's pamphlet, but only words that mean the same as the quotation he had used. Now his excuse is that Stalin may have tampered with Lenin's writings, but this idea occurred to him only after we wrote to him. The *Little Lenin Library* pamphlet on *Religion* was issued in this country in

5 Emphasis has been added.—M. K.

453

1933, and it took Kornfeder until 1963 to find a reason for questioning its authenticity.

On February 25, 1963, we replied to Kornfeder's letter; a portion of our reply follows:

I am enclosing photocopies of pages 47 and 48 of Lenin's pamphlet on *Religion,* and I have underlined the portion that seems to contradict your summary of Lenin's views. Furthermore, I cannot agree that I or you or anyone has the moral right to put a summary of someone else's views in quotation marks, which are reserved strictly for *exact* quotations. I am a firm believer in the Commandment: "Thou Shalt Not Bear False Witness."

Kornfeder did not reply to this letter; the following telegram, received by our research assistant, gives the reason.

LLZ 9 Rx Pd Detroit Mich NFT May 3 1963
400 East Franklin St
Elsinore
The Freedom Defender Joseph Zack Kornfeder has passed away in Washington D C. Funeral Services will be held in the Sawyer Funeral Home 2125 Twelve mile Road Berkley Mich Phone Lincoln 10711 at 2PM Sunday May 5th Respectfully
ROSALINE MARTIN

It should be apparent that the correspondence with Kornfeder was a painstaking task, in order to establish rapport and in order to elicit the information that was forthcoming. We have in our possession every letter from Kornfeder that we have quoted. Every one of them is hand written and signed by him. In order to dispel any possible doubts, we are presenting here a photocopy of his letter of October 20, 1962, so that any of his followers can check the authenticity of his handwriting and signature. We have obliterated the name of our research assistant from the photocopies of both the telegram and the letter, because, as previously mentioned, his identity must remain confidential for the present. (See page 455.)

There can be no doubt that Manuilsky never uttered the words attributed to him or any words that could be interpreted to mean the same, as Kornfeder claimed. The question of why Kornfeder did not include the Manuilsky Hoax in his testimony before the Dies Committee is something that has always intrigued us. A possible explanation may lie in a claim made

454

Dear Mr.

*You are quite right about the Lenin quote on Morals. It is in Lenins booklet on "Religion" page 47 and 48 —. part of the "Little Lenin library series" Volume 7. published by International Publishers, New-York. —*

As luck would have it a friend of mine from Flint, Mich. (Catholic). was visiting me and he had it with him. — . *The words are different but the substance is the same. —*

As to Smith, I am afraid that is all I can do for you. I do not have the clipping and hence cannot give the exact wording or the date. —

Thanks for your comments on my polit-warfare piece. The commies of course are old hands at this, but as to counter-warfare, it is as yet a novelty. Over the Years a brilliant French Woman (Su. Labin) myself, and Possony, wrote more on it than anyone else. It could be the thing to decisively weaken Bolshevism without a war! Its a rich subject. —

Cordially Yours;

Joseph Z. Kornfeder

by Mr. Pat Walsh of the Ultra-Rightist *Canadian Intelligence Service* (not a governmental agency). In the October, 1958, issue of their newsletter, a Mr. Ian W. McTavish quotes Lenin as saying: "It does not matter one whit whether three-quarters of the world perish. What matters is that the quarter which remain are Communists." This, of course, is another variation of the Mao's Expendable Millions Hoax, which we have previously discussed. When we wrote them a letter, asking for authentication of that Lenin quotation, Mr. Pat Walsh sent us a letter on November 11, 1964, advising us that he would get in touch with Mr. McTavish to ascertain his source of the phoney Lenin quotation. In a delightfully frank vein, Walsh added:

Personally I may add that I have studied Lenin's works for years (mostly in the French texts) but I do not recall such an exact quote as Mr. Mc Tavish claims Lenin made.

I was instrumental in tracking down a quote by Dimitri Manuilsky along the same lines and finally found out that John Lautner was the source of this mis-quote. Lautner (a former high Commie official) admitted that Manuilsky had not said these exact words as quoted but *meant* them in a much larger text. It is possible that we will find the same thing happening in the Lenin quote.

He went on to say that he would write to us as soon as he had ascertained the facts, but that was the last we ever heard from him.

There is, of course, the possibility that Pat Walsh was honestly confused when he wrote that letter, and that he meant Kornfeder instead of John Lautner. On the other hand, if his story is correct—Kornfeder is not easily confused with Lautner—it could mean that Kornfeder sold Richard L. Stokes a "gold brick," that he planted a story on him which he had picked up from Lautner. The latter was also a renegade Communist, who made a career as a paid professional witness. Professor Herbert L. Packer says of Lautner: "The most important source for the impeachment of Lautner was Lautner himself."[6] Professor Packer shows from actual transcripts of court proceedings that Lautner, like Kornfeder, was quite adept at "remembering" things that never happened and remarkably proficient in discovering the "true" meaning in the words of others.

Rev. Gerald L. K. Smith's magazine of hate, *The Cross and The Flag*, in its April 1967 issue, carries an essay by the Ultra-Rightist novelist, Taylor Caldwell, in which the lady mounts

---

6 "Ex-Communist Witnesses," Herbert L. Packer, Stanford University Press, 1962.

a furious assault against her favorite target, the Liberals. She claims that forty years ago *Lenin*—not Manuilsky—wrote "that the Communists would make 'amazing' peace overtures to the free world, so that they will eagerly embrace all offers—and 'then we will smite them with our clenched fist'—we are warned and we are, in a way, faced by an enemy who makes no bones that he hates us and intends to destroy us and enslave us and rob us." The lady got so excited, when she wrote that essay, she forgot to tell us how you can enslave anyone *after* you destroy him!

There is another important question that has never been answered regarding Kornfeder's story. Why did he wait from 1930 to 1953 before telling the Manuilsky story?

Kornfeder was not the only one with a convenient memory that serves the Cold War propaganda machine. The Ultra-Rightist *American Committee to Free Cuba, Inc.,* in a Special Report sent out in February of 1964, gives a "word for word translation from a Russian, now residing in this country, of a letter directed to a U.S. Government Agency."

The mysterious, anonymous "Russian" tells a tale of being arrested by the Soviet secret police on April 8, 1935, and of striking up a conversation with a Communist official on the train that was taking him to prison. The Communist official, he claims, told him of Moscow's plan to seize Cuba and to direct the struggle of the Negroes in the U.S.A. With the same extraordinary capacity for remembering verbatim that Kornfeder had shown, the "Russian" is able to *quote* from the Communist official, 29 years later, the detailed plans of Moscow. The Communist official supposedly concluded with these words:

Then it will be easy to overpower all America, without using any kind of armed force, and taking advantage of its liberal structure, which is opening for us wide opportunities of propaganda and diplomatic leverages, by which her political officers and circles will be confused.

If one is willing to believe this version of Moscow's alleged diabolical plans, what becomes of Manuilsky's plan to "smash them with our clenched fist!"? Obviously, one cancels out the other. Consistency, however, is not one of the attributes of the

457

Cold War propagandists. Thus we find the Rev. I. E. Howard writing in *Christian Economics,* May 12, 1964:

The Communist conspiracy is bent on destroying Western civilization, not by war, but by the easier method of subversion.

On August 1, 1967, Lawrence Sullivan writes in *Christian Economics*:

Communism declared all-out war on American capitalism in 1917, and reaffirmed the policy in 1931, when Dimitri Manuilsky declared before the Lenin School of Political Warfare, in Moscow:

Then he quotes in its entirety Kornfeder's Manuilsky Hoax with the "smash-them-with-our-clenched-fist" nonsense. This was probably not the only time that *Christian Economics* quoted the Manuilsky Hoax, nor is it likely to be the last.

Another interesting aspect of the Cold War propaganda orgy is the ability of its participants to use mutually contradictory anti-Communist fabrications. It may be hard to believe, but we have seen both the Manuilsky Hoax and Lenin Fabrication, No. 2 used in the same issue of more than one Ultra-Rightist publication, including those of the Coast Federal Savings and Loan Association. The two fabrications, as is easily seen, contradict each other:

| *The Manuilsky Hoax* | *Lenin Fabrication, No. 2.* |
|---|---|
| War to the hilt, between Communism and Capitalism, is inevitable. Today, of course, we are not strong enough to attack. Our time will come in 20 or 30 years. To win we shall need the element of surprise. The bourgeoisie will have to be put to sleep. So we shall begin by launching the most spectacular peace movement on record. There be electrifying overtures and unheard of concessions. The capitalist countries, stupid and decadent, will rejoice to co-operate in their own destruction. They will leap at another chance to be friends. As soon as their guard is down, we shall smash them with our clenched fist! | First, we will take Eastern Europe, then we will encircle the United States, which will be the last bastion of capitalism. We will not have to attack. It will fall like an overripe fruit into our hands. |

458

The Ultra-Rightist *Fire and Police Research Association of Los Angeles,* in its June, 1963, *FIPO News,* quotes the Manuilsky Hoax on one page, and three pages later, Paul Jackson intones:

> . . . for communists there is NO ETERNITY and for this reason they will NEVER VOLUNTARILY START a nuclear war of annihilation. To do so, would terminate communism FOREVER.

While Kornfeder did not launch his Manuilsky Hoax at the Hearing, on July 7, 1953, of the House Committee on Un-American Activities, he did succeed in launching a companion hoax. Being an expert in changing quoted statements, he changed the name of the Lenin Institute (sometimes called Lenin University) to the Lenin School of Political Warfare. All throughout his testimony, both he and his interrogators used the name of *Lenin School* or *Lenin University,* but at one point Kornfeder testified: "In 1927, I was sent to Moscow for additional training, and I attended the Lenin School in Moscow, U.S.S.R., which is a political warfare-training college. . . ." The following month, Richard L. Stokes used the name, *Lenin School of Political Warfare in Moscow.* It was immediately picked up by Ultra-Rightists, including Mr. Richard Arens, while he was staff director for the House Committee on Un-American Activities. In his article that appeared in the *American Mercury,* July 1963, there appears this description of Kornfeder under his by-line:

> Graduate of the Lenin School of Political Warfare in Moscow and a former pupil of Manuilsky.

Lest the reader think we are doing some quibbling here, we hasten to point out that there is a crucial difference between the name, *Lenin School,* and *Lenin School of Political Warfare.* The big difference is in the sinister connotation in the latter name. It is no doubt true that political warfare is part of the curriculum of the Lenin School, but many other subjects are taught in addition. Kornfeder would, no doubt, argue the justification for changing the name on the ground that political warfare is taught there. Supposing Kornfeder's hair were red, would we be justified in stating that his name is Joseph Red-Head Kornfeder? Biology is taught at the Uni-

459

versity of California. No one would conclude from this fact that it would be proper to call it the University of California for Biology. No, Mr. Kornfeder, a name—a proper noun—cannot be changed at anyone's whim.

The list of names of Ultra-Rightist tracts, books, leaflets, and pamphlets that have used this deceptive name would fill several pages. Some of the Ultra-Rightists have not been willing to go along with this Kornfeder deception, and in the interest of truth and fair play, we are happy to point out those that have come to our attention:

1. In his book, *Masters of Deceit,* John E. Hoover refers 11 times to the *Lenin School.*

2. In his book, *Brainwashing,* Rev. Kenneth Goff refers to the *Lenin University.*

3. In his testimony before the House Committee on Un-American Activities, FBI informer Karl Prussion refers to the *Lenin School in Moscow.*

4. Frank Capell, in *Herald of Freedom,* July 2, 1965, refers to the *Lenin Institute.*

5. In Report No. 629, July 20, 1965, Congressman Edwin E. Willis, Chairman of the House Committee on Un-American Activities, refers 5 times to the *Lenin Institute.*

6. The anti-Communist monthly of the American Legion, *Firing Line,* November, 1966, refers to the *Lenin School.*

Apparently, some Ultra-Rightists who accepted the Manuilsky Hoax realized that Kornfeder's fabrication of a new name for the *Lenin School* is too easily exposed. One Ultra-Rightist, Mr. Edward Scannel Butler, Director of the Ultra-Rightist Information Council of the Americas, has his own little variation of Kornfeder's invention. In Part II of a brochure, entitled *Conflict Management,* Butler refers to the *Lenin School of Strategic Studies in Moscow.*

The most persistent in the use of the fabricated name, *Lenin School of Political Warfare,* was the staff director of the House Committee on Un-American Activities, Mr. Richard Arens (now promoted to Commissioner of the Court of Claims, Washington, D.C.). It seems that the multimillionaire, Cyrus S. Eaton, had made some pretty salty remarks about John E. Hoover and the FBI on a television network program. Mr. Arens came to Hoover's defense on the American Broadcasting Company's network, May 19, 1958. In the course of his remarks, Arens referred to the *Lenin School of Political Warfare*. We verified this by obtaining from Mr. Arens a copy of his script.

On July 10, 1958, we wrote to Mr. Arens and told him that we had never heard of the *Lenin School of Political Warfare*. Then we deliberately gave him an opportunity to extricate himself from a tight situation, by asking: "Are you sure this is the correct name or is it your way of describing it?" On July 15, 1958, Mr. Arens replied:

> In answer to the specific questions contained in your letter of July 10, 1958, the Lenin school of political warfare is the Lenin University. It should not have been capitalized since I was only referring to it in this manner. As you state, it was my way of describing it.

Seven months after writing that letter, the House Committee on Un-American Activities issued a document prepared under Mr. Arens' supervision, entitled "Patterns of Communist Espionage," January 1959. On page 3, we found the Manuilsky Hoax. On May 29, 1959, we wrote Mr. Arens, asking for verification of the Manuilsky Hoax, and we added:

> I note that Manuilsky is alleged to have delivered these remarks at the Lenin School of Political Warfare in Moscow, 1930. In a letter that you sent me on July 15, 1958 you informed me that there is no Lenin School of Political Warfare.

On June 2, 1959, Mr. Arens replied; and we quote the three pertinent paragraphs:

> There appears to be no one proper name for the Communist training institution in Moscow named after Lenin. It is variously referred to as "The Lenin School," "Lenin University" and "Lenin Institute." For this reason the Committee's cumulative index for the years 1938-1954 lists this institution as follows: "Lenin Institute (School or University) (Moscow)."
>
> Technically, the words "Political Warfare" in the source notation after Manuilsky's statement should not have had the initial letters capitalized.
>
> I hope that this information satisfactorily answers your questions.

No, Judge Arens your information does not satisfactorily answer these questions:

1. After admitting in your letter of July 15, 1958, that using

the name *Lenin School of Political Warfare* was improper usage, why did you repeat it in the document you released in January of 1959?

2. Inasmuch as the cumulative index of your Committee for years 1938-1954 does not list the Lenin School with the improper name, why did you refer to the *Lenin School of Political Warfare* (your script shows it capitalized) in your network speech on May 19, 1958? Didn't you know that you were disseminating false information?

3. Isn't it a fact that the proper name is the *Lenin School* and that Lenin Institute and Lenin University are just vernacular substitutes?

On a number of occasions a research assistant has written letters to Mr. Tom Anderson, member of the National Council of the John Birch Society, associate editor of *American Opinion,* syndicated columnist, and editor-publisher of several farm magazines of wide circulation. We have challenged a number of quotations he has used, and we shall deal with this in volume II. In our letter of November 4, 1963, we referred to an article of his, entitled "Message to the Constitutional Underground," which the Ultra-Rightist Congressman James B. Utt placed in the Congressional Record of October 15, 1963. We challenged Anderson to publish a letter that we would draft, with the proof that the Manuilsky quotation was fraudulent. In his reply of December 16, 1963, Mr. Anderson said:

> When I published the quotation attributed to Manuilsky, I did not realize that prevailing evidence indicates he never made the statement.

After assuring us of his good intentions, he offered to publish our letter, if we would send him one that was suitable for the letters-to-the-editor columns of his magazines. On January 7, 1964, we sent him a letter with the proofs that we had at hand at the time. In the June 1964 issue of *South Carolina Farm and Ranch,* Anderson did publish a condensed version of our letter. However, immediately under the letter there was printed in bold-face type:

> Whether Manuilski wrote it or not, I believe it accurately describes the Comrat's diabolical plans.
>
> —Tom Anderson

This is typical of Anderson's intemperate and vitriolic style, and is representative of the style of many Ultra-Rightist scribes. Oh, yes, we forgot to mention that Anderson put this heading in enlarged and bold-face type over our letter:

## MAYBE A HOAX; BUT TRUE

On September 18, 1963, U.S. Senator Carl T. Curtis of Nebraska delivered a speech on the floor of the Senate, telling why he would vote against the nuclear test-ban treaty. We quote a portion of his speech from page 16515 of the Congressional Record of that day:

Mr. President, I must be guided by the lamp of experience and I cannot turn my back on history. Neither can I ignore the warnings that have come from the Communists themselves.

I hold in my hand a little devotional book written by Father James Keller, founder of the Christophers. It is entitled, *3 Minutes a Day*. I want to read about the boast made some 20 years ago. In reading it I want to point out that time is running against us:

"War is inevitable," were the strong words used by Dimitri Manuilsky, when he addressed the students of the Lenin School of Political Warfare in 1930.

His dire forecast continued:

"Today, of course, we are not strong enough to attack. Our time will come in 20 or 30 years.

"In order to win we shall need the element of surprise. The bourgeoisie will have to be put to sleep, so we shall begin by launching the most spectacular peace movement on record.

"There will be electrifying overtures and unheard of concessions. The capitalistic countries—stupid and decadent—will rejoice to cooperate in their own destruction. They will leap at another chance to be friends.

"As soon as their guard is down, we shall smash them with our clenched fists."

After reading this phoney quotation, Senator Curtis thundered away with his reasons for voting against the nuclear test-ban treaty. All throughout the months of debate before the treaty was finally ratified by the Senate, the Manuilsky Hoax was incorporated in many speeches made both on the floor of the Senate and the House of Representatives, even though the latter body has no voice in the ratification of treaties. In the case of Senator Curtis, his lack of responsibility is shown by his willingness to accept a quotation from a second-hand source, Father Keller's book. Senator Curtis and the others had at their call the facilities of one of the world's greatest research organizations, the Library of Congress. A phone call would have resulted in a research report advising them that the Manuilsky quotation cannot be authenticated. Furthermore, a little checking with the State Department would have brought the additional information that the State Department did *not* include the alleged Manuilsky quotation in its comprehensive volume, entitled *Soviet World Outlook, Handbook of Communist Statements,* which has significant quotations, beginning with Karl Marx and ending with Nikita Khrushchev. It was prepared by the Bureau of Intelligence and Research of the State Department. The Cold War morality, of course, inhibited all of these statesmen from seeking the truth.

After several exchanges of correspondence with Senator Curtis and Father Keller, we obtained a copy of *3 Minutes a Day,* in which the Manuilsky Hoax was contained. It was no easy job to find the correct volume, because Father Keller had issued some 12 volumes under the same title and without any index. Finally, on May 14, 1964 we wrote Father Keller that, inasmuch as he had used the Manuilsky "quotation," it was incumbent upon him to supply the proof of its authenticity. We concluded our letter with these remarks:

I am sure that you adhere to the Commandment: Thou Shalt Not Bear False Witness Against Thy Neighbor. In the absence of any authentication of the Manuilsky quotation, you should publicly retract it, and make your retraction as well known as the original use made of the alleged quotation. However, in spite of this maxim of justice and fair play, I am prepared to furnish you overwhelming documentation that Manuilsky did not make that statement. I am willing to prepare this documentation for you, if you will promise to publish a retraction.

Will you accept this challenge in the interest of Truth and in compliance with the Commandment?

On May 19, 1964, Father Keller replied:

. . . Our source material for this quote is long since gone as you can understand since the book was published many years ago. There would be no way for us to locate it now. But since the publication we have learned that there are two schools of thought on this. Because of this, we haven't used the quote in any subsequent Christopher publications. . . .

464

Thanks again for taking the time to write, Mr. Kominsky.
Blessings to you!

Sincerely in Christ,
JAMES KELLER

We quote our letter of June 8, 1964:

Dear Father Keller:

Your letter of May 19th was received, and I do appreciate the friendly tone. Also I received your complimentary copy of Volume 6 of *Three Minutes A Day*, for which I thank you.

Regretfully, I am constrained to tell you, my dear Father Keller, that your letter does not meet the moral challenge of my letter. You have helped in the dissemination of a falsehood, perhaps unwittingly.

You tell me that you do not know where you picked up that Manuilsky fabrication, but how can you possibly have forgotten the role played by Cardinal Spellman, in spreading this phoney quotation? Then you tell me there are now two schools of thought on this phoney quotation, and that you are not using it in any subsequent Christopher publications. This does not meet the moral challenge to make amends and to make an effort to have the Truth overtake falsehood. Furthermore, you are still selling Volume 2 of *Three Minutes A Day*, with the Manuilsky fabrication on page 131. You sent me a copy of Volume 2 in April of this year.

In spite of the fact that the burden of proof should be on you, in spite of the fact that you cannot prove the authenticity of that Manuilsky quotation—I again offer to send you overwhelming documentation that the Manuilsky quotation is a fraud, if you will make a public announcement that proof of its fraudulent character has reached you and that you disavow it.

Otherwise, I must consider all your Moral exhortations in your voluminous publicity materials and broadcasts to be disingenuous.

One concluding thought about your advice that there are two schools of thought about this Manuilsky quotation. There are also two schools of thought in every murder trial. There are many situations where there are two schools of thought, but men of integrity and good will strive to ascertain the truth. The Manuilsky quotation is true or false. Those are the two schools of thought. Now, I offer you the Truth, with overwhelming proof. That is my challenge: Thou Shalt Not Bear False Witness Against Thy Neighbor.

Cordially yours,
MORRIS KOMINSKY

Certified Mail
Return Receipt

The return postal receipt shows that the letter was delivered in Father Keller's office on June 11, 1964. No reply has been received from Father Keller.

It would fill a large volume if one would undertake to chronicle all the known instances of the use of the Manuilsky Hoax, but we will confine it to only a small portion of those that we have seen. When we interviewed Colonel Fred S. Stevers, U.S. Air Force Retired, he told us on December 10, 1964 that he heard the Manuilsky quotation over 15 years ago from General Partridge of the Air Defense Command. If Colonel Stevers is not mistaken in saying "over 15 years ago," this would mean that the Manuilsky Hoax was in use in the indoctrination courses of the Armed Forces four years before Kornfeder and Stokes publicized it in *Human Events* of August 12, 1953. This would also be consistent with the claim of Pat Walsh of Canadian Intelligence Service that the hoax originated with John Lautner.

The Manuilsky Hoax is used in a brochure issued by the Ultra-Rightist *Altadena Study and Research Group* (California), which quotes it from a document of the House Committee on Un-American Activities. The hoax is quoted in the *Freedom Club Bulletin,* May 11, 1965, of the Ultra-Rightist *Freedom Club,* which is run as an adjunct to Rev. James W. Fifield's First Congregational Church of Los Angeles. It is also quoted in Rev. Gerald L. K. Smith's hate sheet, *The Cross and The Flag,* October 1955. It is used in an editorial in the November 30, 1965 issue of the Ultra-Rightist *Independent American.* The Ultra-Rightist Rev. C. W. Burpo quotes the hoax in the February 1966 issue of his *Bible Institute News.* In the August, 1966, issue, the Rev. Burpo prints an interview with Dr. Y. C. Yang, the South Korean Ambassador to the United States, and the Manuilsky Hoax is contained in Dr. Yang's remarks. Yes indeed, Kornfeder was correct when he boasted that the "quotation" was traveling around the world! The Manuilsky Hoax was also quoted in Rev. Kenneth Goff's Ultra-Rightist magazine, *Pilgrim Torch,* January 1964, and also in a leaflet issued in May 1964.

On October 28, 1960, there appeared in the now-defunct *Los Angeles Mirror* a letter from Mrs. H. Scotty Wolfe, which began with:

I read an article in the *Mirror* headed, "Eaton Risks Scorn in Fight for Peace." I agree with Cyrus Eaton that war is folly. However, I wonder if Mr. Eaton has read this. . .

466

The "this" was the entire Manuilsky Hoax, following which Mrs. Wolfe concluded:

The quote is from Dimitri Z. Manuilsky, Lenin School of Political Warfare, 1931.

The next day we wrote a letter to Mrs. Wolfe, asking her where she had obtained that Manuilsky quotation. She replied:

I refer you to the Coast Federal Savings and Loan, who sent out the quote to its customers.

We wrote to Coast Federal Savings and Loan Association on November 7, 1960, asking for a copy of the item to which Mrs. Wolfe had alluded. By return mail we received several copies of a pink 3″ × 5″ leaflet with the heading:

### A REMINDER

The entire Manuilsky Hoax is directly under this heading, and we are told that it is a statement of Dimitri Z. Manuilsky of the Lenin School of Political Warfare, in Moscow, 1930. At the bottom of this leaflet we are told that it is "distributed as a public service" by Coast Federal Savings.

On November 28, 1960, we wrote Mr. Joe Crail, President of Coast Federal Savings, giving him some proof that the Manuilsky quotation is fraudulent, and demanding proof of its authenticity. Mr. Crail replied on November 30, 1960, that Coast Federal was unaware of the charges of inaccuracy and would check with the Ultra-Rightist writer and lecturer, former FBI agent, W. Cleon Skousen. He promised to pass along to us any further information that he could obtain, and assured us of Coast Federal's desire to "back up the truth with facts." On December 11, 1960, we sent Mr. Crail another letter, with additional proof of the phoney nature of the Manuilsky quotation. On May 5, 1961, we sent another letter to Mr. Crail. We called attention to our previous letters and his promise to investigate further and advise us. We concluded with:

Not having heard from you, should I interpret your silence as meaning that you were somewhat disingenuous when you wrote me that the truth "is the only way we can effectively combat Communism"?

The postal receipt shows that our letter was delivered to Coast Federal Savings on May 6, 1961. No reply was received from Mr. Crail.

On June 23, 1964, we received in the mail, pursuant to an inquiry, a good-sized book from an Ultra-Rightist project called Freedom University of the Air, which was run by American Forum, Inc., Los Angeles. It is entitled *The Truth About Communism, A Manual for Study Groups.* It is issued by Coast Federal Savings and Loan Association. Among the numerous fabrications and distortions of truth contained in this manual, there appears again the Manuilsky Hoax. This time, Coast Federal took some precautions, apparently in the light of our correspondence in 1960-1961. The source given of the Manuilsky quotation is a pamphlet entitled "How the Reds Won" by Rosalie M. Gordon of the Ultra-Rightist propaganda outfit, *America's Future.* Three months later we picked up at the main office of Coast Federal the latest version of that pink 3" × 5" leaflet. After quoting the Manuilsky Hoax, they placed below it in *very fine print* which taxes one's eyesight:

The above quotation is a summation of Manuilsky's views as cited by Joseph Z. Kornfeder, a former communist and a student of the Lenin School of Political Warfare in 1930, under Manuilsky's coaching (American Mercury, July, 1963).

Thus, Coast Federal can continue to peddle the Manuilsky Hoax and fall back on *American Mercury* and *America's Future.* The evidence to support the proposition that Coast Federal does not easily back down is shown by the fact that, on March 20, 1961, which was *after* we had sent Mr. Crail two letters of proof that the Manuilsky quote is phoney, Coast Federal issued a large booklet, entitled *The Ideological War, Communist Myths & American Truths.* On page 6, the question is raised whether the U.S. should believe the Communists are sincere in wanting peace. The "truth," that is given as an answer, is: the Manuilsky Hoax! One thing is quite apparent, that Coast Federal has done a job of massive dissemination of the Manuilsky Hoax.

The hoax was quoted in a radio editorial on February 16, 1962 by station KRUX, Phoenix, Arizona. Congressman James B. Utt of Orange County, California, quoted the hoax at a U.S. Day Rally at Evanston, Illinois on October 24, 1963, and then he placed this speech in the Congressional Record of October 14, 1966.

Some of the gems in the Congressman's "Patriotic" oration are excerpted:

Government is the natural enemy of man, and the tendency of all governments is to extend control and dominion over the life of the individual.

We have shifted our reliance from God to man and from spiritual values to material values.

The worst entangling alliance, ever entered into by a free country, was the United Nations Treaty, designed and promulgated to reduce this country to the lowest common denominator among the nations of the world. It is the vehicle by which this Nation surrenders its sovereignty to an alien government and will subject every American citizen to the oppressive will of evil men. I would like to quote from 2 Corinthians 6:14: "Be ye not unequally yoked together with unbelievers: for what fellowship hath righteousness with unrighteousness? And what communion hath light with darkness?"

We have not only failed to give heed to the admonitions of our Founding Fathers, but also to the admonition of the Lord which I have just quoted.

Many years before the United Nations Charter was signed, Dimitri Manuilsky, speaking at the Lenin School of Political Warfare in 1919 said:

Mr. Utt then recited the entire Manuilsky Hoax, after which he quoted the phoney story about Khrushchev threatening to bury us and said:

By means of peaceful coexistence Soviet Russia and the international Communist conspiracy have been able to subvert the mental and moral integrity of a great portion of our globe, and the march continues unabated.

The President of the United States has either forgotten his oath of office, or fails to understand the pledge of allegiance to this country ... Unless Congress puts a halter on him, President John F. Kennedy will commit the lives, the fortunes, and the sacred honor of the citizens of the United States to the formation of a world government in which we will be outnumbered, outgunned, and outvoted.

Following this, Mr. Utt quoted something *out of context* that had been written by Presidential Assistant, Professor Walt W. Rostow, and then exclaimed:

That, ladies and gentlemen, is nothing short of treason, and should be dealt with accordingly.

*Newsweek* magazine, September 5, 1955, ran an editorial to combat the growing feeling of good-will towards the Russians. It used as its "heavy artillery" the Manuilsky Hoax, which it placed in a separate box at the top center of the editorial.

The Honorable Edward J. Gurney, Congressman from Florida, delivered a speech on the floor of the House of Representatives, August 14, 1963, in opposition to the pending nuclear test-ban treaty. He too quoted the Manuilsky Hoax. Letters addressed to him on September 6 and November 21, 1963, inquiring as to his source of the quotation, brought no reply.

The Ultra-Rightist magazine, *American Mercury,* never tires of using the Manuilsky Hoax. In its issue of November 1954, it carried an essay by the professional anti-Communist, Eugene Lyons, entitled "Coexistence, Formula for Surrender." Like all the Ultra-Rightist essays of this type, it doesn't openly call for a third world war, but you are supposed to "catch on." In order to drive home the point, the editors quoted the Manuilsky Hoax at the conclusion of Eugene Lyons' essay, and gave it this heading:

## MEMO TO MR. ATTLEE

Presumably this was meant to warn Prime Minister Attlee of the perils of co-existence. And we are told authoritatively that the statement is "From a speech by Dimitri Z. Manuilsky to the International Students of the Lenin School of Political Warfare, Moscow." To make sure that the Lyons-Kornfeder message would be more widely read, the *American Mercury* advertised for sale reprints of the article.

The *Washington Daily News* of November 30, 1954 picked up the Manuilsky Hoax from the *American Mercury,* and the late, unlamented Senator Joseph McCarthy picked it up from the *Daily News* and placed it in the Congressional Record on May 31, 1955, pages A 3763-3764. From there the Ultra-Rightists picked it up and issued millions of leaflets, quoting the *Congressional Record* as their authority for this scarecrow story.

In its July, 1958, issue, the *American Mercury* carried an article by the Ultra-Rightist Rev. Bob Shuler, entitled "The Price of Peace at Any Price." This man of the cloth obliquely calls for an anti-Soviet war, basing his thesis largely on the

Manuilsky Hoax. He says of this alleged quotation: "No Russian leader has arisen to deny it. It is in the books for all who read to see." The journalistic sleight-of-hand in this charge is, of course, obvious to any rational and informed person. The Soviet leaders have long ago given up the job of answering all the purveyors of lies. You just can't keep up with the number of falsehoods that are regularly put into circulation by gentlemen of elastic morality.

On April 2, 1964, the *Los Angeles Times* published a letter to the editor from a Mr. Miles Andrews of New York City. It runs to 11 column inches and argues that disarmament conferences are just "Bosh" and "Russian make-believe." He begins his letter by telling us that "In 1931, a top Communist by the name of Dimitri Manuilsky made a speech before the Lenin School of Political Warfare, saying. . ." And then he quotes the entire phoney statement. We immediately composed a letter to the editor of the *Times,* in reply to Mr. Andrews. Feeling very dubious about the chances that the *Times* would publish our letter, we made a 150-mile round trip to the *Times* office on May 6, 1964, and conferred with an assistant to the editor. After a 2-hour discussion, during which we came to a mutual agreement on a condensed version of our letter, the *Times* promised to publish our letter. The *Times* did publish it in the center of the page on May 9, 1964.

We were prepared for a barrage of nasty and insulting responses from the Ultra-Rightist network that specializes in pouncing upon the writers of that kind of letter. To our utter surprise, there was only one such letter. It appeared in the *Times* on May 21, 1964 and was signed "L. F. B." Its arguments have already been disposed of in this chapter, so we need not pause for discussion, excepting to observe that it was a pathetic example of the indoctrination of so many people with the Ultra-Rightist tampering with the truth.

On September 30, 1959, Congressman Edward J. Derwinski of Chicago "celebrated" Khrushchev's visit to the U.S.A. by placing in the Congressional Record "one of the most thought provoking editorials that I have ever seen regarding this question." The editorial which sent the Congressman into such ecstasy was from an obscure community newspaper, the *Chicago Daily Calumet.* It contained at least six of the fabrications attributed to Lenin and Stalin that we have debunked, and, of

471

course, it contained the big weapon, the Manuilsky Hoax. Congressman Derwinski could have ascertained the truth about these phoney quotations by the simple procedure of making an inquiry at the Library of Congress.

On October 6, 1959, we saw the syndicated column of the late Eleanor Roosevelt in the *Los Angeles Mirror*. A photocopy is here presented. The underlining is ours. (See page 473.)

On October 7, 1959, we sent a letter to Mrs. Roosevelt, asking for source of her quotation from Manuilsky and for information about his alleged role as "one of the Soviet founders of the United Nations." The following is her reply:


MRS. FRANKLIN D. ROOSEVELT
202 FIFTY-SIXTH STREET WEST
NEW YORK 19, N. Y.

October 14, 1959


Dear Mr. Kominsky:

Thank you for your letter and your interest. I got the Manuilski statement from an advertisement which was sent out by a reputable organization but I do not remenber which organization. If you wrote to the New York Times, they could give you the exact quote and the circumstances of it. I only know it was made 25 years ago.

Mr. Manuilski was not a founder of the UN. I said he was a delegate to the UN.

Very sincerely yours,

*Eleanor Roosevelt*

# Eleanor Roosevelt

### ——————— NIKITA A PEACE ENVOY?

NEW YORK — As one reads Soviet Premier Khrushchev's report to the Communist Chinese and the praise given him by Chinese Premier Chou En-lai at a dinner for more than 5,000 Chinese the other night in Hong Kong, one cannot help but smile a little at the picture of Mr. Khrushchev as "an envoy of peace."

There is so much more to making the peace than just coming to the United States and announcing you want peace in the world and speaking at the United Nations on disarmament. Mr. Khrushchev carefully avoided mentioning a few of the difficult problems that must be faced before disarmament can be achieved.

**ELEANOR**

I am delighted that President Eisenhower feels there is a lessening of tension and that the Berlin question is no longer a threat. Now, it is felt, it is one of the problems that can be negotiated.

We must never forget, however, the statement made some years ago by Dmitri Manuilski, one of the Soviet founders of the United Nations. The gist of that statement was that we would be lulled to sleep by the peaceful offers of the Communists and that then the Soviets would strike when our wishful thinking had made us weak.

**Must Be Staunch**

Of course, he knew nothing of the atomic age, and so the situation has changed.

But it is well to remember that our defenses, moral and spiritual, economic and military, must never let down.

We must never use them for aggression; we must never use them to threaten our neighbors. But we must be as staunch in our beliefs and in our purposes as are the Communists.

The kind of world the Communists want we do not want; and we can be sure that the majority of peoples in the world must be in opposition to communism. And since we do not intend to bring about our kind of world with military strength, it will take constant and unremitting work to bring it about and keep it, with the balance on the non-Communist side.

**Will Not Compromise**

This does not mean that I do not expect to see changes in our world, both in our economic and cultural situations, but it does mean that we must never lose sight of the fact that our political system was designed to give people the maximum freedom possible, both of choice and of opportunity, and that we will never compromise our right to freedom of religious beliefs.

Eleanor Roosevelt was a gracious lady and a person of great attainments, for whom we had the profoundest respect and admiration. It is with the deepest regret that we have to say that she too became a Cold War propagandist and found justification for the use of such a shabby device as the Manuilsky Hoax, and when challenged, fell back on "an advertisement sent out by a reputable organization" that she could not remember. Inasmuch as we wrote to her the next day after her column appeared, the question arises: Was she writing from memory when she quoted Manuilsky? If not, why would her source-material be inaccessible so soon after sending her manuscript to the syndicate? And why did she see fit to deny something which is in her column, viz.: Dimitri Manuilsky is referred to as "one of the Soviet founders of the United Nations."

General Thomas S. Power was Chief of the Strategic Air Command of the United States Air Force. In a speech that the General delivered before the Economic Club of New York City on January 19, 1960, he quoted the Manuilsky Hoax in order to make a point. Senator Stuart Symington placed the speech in the Congressional Record on March 2, 1960, thus making more ammunition available to Cold War propagandists.

On April 18, 1964, General Power told 300 members of the Rotary Club at a luncheon in the Riviera Hotel at Palm Springs, California:

A nuclear war would prove that mankind will have reached his highest level of stupidity.
If you get in one (war) there will be no winners. Just losers of varying degrees.

On October 19, 1964, we sent a letter to General Power c/o the Strategic Air Command headquarters at Omaha, Nebraska. We explained to the General that we had just run across his 1960 speech and that we were doing research for a book that would expose the use of fabrications. We asked the General for the source from which he had obtained the Manuilsky quotation, and after giving him some proof that it is a fraudulent quotation, we concluded with the following:

Don't you think that, when the opportunity presents itself, you should somewhere along the line publicly retract the Manuilsky

474

Hoax? Even though some time has elapsed, I submit, General Power, that it is never too late to utter truth in refutation of falsehood.

In conclusion, I want you to know that I do not believe that you would knowingly use a fabrication to prove a point. In the interest of world peace that you and I both desire, you can add to your previous excellent pronouncements by sending a letter to the *New York Times* or some other reputable newspaper, pointing out that you have just learned that this hoax, which has been so widely used, is completely false, and that its use and constant repetition can only serve to exacerbate U.S.A.—U.S.S.R. relations.

With kindest personal regards, I am, sir,

Respectfully yours,
MORRIS KOMINSKY

No reply was received. Meanwhile, we learned of his retirement from the Armed Forces. On January 14, 1965, we sent the General a short letter, to his home in Rancho Mirage, California. We enclosed a copy of our letter of October 19, 1964, and asked for a reply. We offered to pay him a personal visit, if that would be his preference. The postal receipt shows that this letter was delivered to his home on January 15, 1965. No reply was received.

On November 28, 1962, the *Los Angeles Herald-Examiner* carried a letter from a reader, which starts off with:

In the light of recent events in Cuba where Mr. Khrushchev so graciously bowed before President Kennedy's ultimatum (?), I think the following words spoken before the Lenin School of Political Warfare by Dimitri Z. Manuilsky are quite interesting:

This was followed by the entire Manuilsky Hoax, with the final words capitalized for emphasis: ". . . . . we shall SMASH THEM WITH OUR CLENCHED FIST." The letter concludes with:

Well, we now have the electrifying overtures and concessions and any idiot can see we are being put to sleep—so watch out folks! The next step is the BIG FIST!

On December 4, 1962, we sent a letter to the *Los Angeles Herald-Examiner,* in which we referred to the letter containing the Manuilsky Hoax, and we offered a $500.00 reward to anyone who could prove to the satisfaction of a committee of three attorneys that the Manuilsky quotation was authentic. We stipulated that the claimant of the reward could choose one attorney, we would choose a second one, and these two would choose the third one. The postal receipt shows that our letter was delivered to the *Herald-Examiner* on December 5, 1962. The *Herald-Examiner* did not publish our letter. On December 24, 1962, we sent the *Herald-Examiner* another letter giving reasons why our previous letter should be published. No reply was received and our letter was not published. On January 21, 1963, we called at the editorial offices of the *Herald-Examiner* and talked to the editor of the Letters-to-the-Editor column. After considerable discussion, he promised to publish a condensed version of our letter of December 4, 1962, which was still in his files. We checked every issue from that day until February 22, 1963, but we did not find our letter. However, we did find a letter on January 31, 1963, from the paid propagandist of the Fascist forces of Katanga province in the Congo!

There are throughout the country hundreds of little weekly and semi-weekly newspapers that "hang on by their eyelashes," in an attempt to exist in the face of the competition from radio, television, and the big-city newspapers. Quite often these papers are edited and published by a person with little or no journalistic training, usually a printer by trade. Not to be outdone by the *Herald-Examiner*, the *Lake Elsinore Valley Sun*, whose editor at the time was a printer by the name of Jerry Gilbertson, ran an editorial in its issue of November 29, 1962, in which the Manuilsky Hoax is featured. This is done after admonishing his readers to believe the propaganda of some anti-Castro Cubans who claimed that the Russian missiles were not withdrawn from Cuba. Gilbertson uses the Manuilsky scarecrow to bolster the credibility of the anti-Castro faction. The performance of Gilbertson was duplicated, with variations, by many small-town sheets which take their cue from the big-city newspapers, the Chamber of Commerce, the American Legion, John E. Hoover, and the House Committee of Un-American Activities.

John G. Tower, U.S. Senator from Texas, is one of the darlings of the Ultra-Right. In a speech on the floor of the Senate, in opposition to the pending nuclear test-ban treaty, the Senator made a big issue out of a letter he allegedly received from a 17-year old graduate of the Pasadena, Texas High School. The letter quotes the Manuilsky Hoax and repeats the usual Ultra-Rightist clichès. Our suspicions aroused, we decided to contact the student. In response to our inquiry, the Senator declined to reveal the student's address, but promised to forward our letter to him, if we cared to write to him. On November 21, 1963, we sent a letter to the student c/o Senator Tower, with a request that the address be placed on the envelope and that it be posted. No reply was received. We finally located the student's address through other sources, and on June 23, 1964, we sent him a courteous letter, inquiring of his source for the Manuilsky quotation. No reply was received. We are still suspicious that someone other than the student wrote that letter. If the 17-year old student did write that letter, it is a sad commentary on the ethos of our country that, at such a young age, a person is already indoctrinated by the fabrications of the warmongers. In any case, when the Senator made that speech and placed the letter in the Congressional Record, the Ultra-Rightists had one more item that they could quote as "official," from the Congressional Record.

It is safe to assert that hardly a day passes without someone sending a letter to an editor, issuing a leaflet, or writing a column, in which the Manuilsky Hoax is quoted with that ex cathedra assurance of the Ultra-Rightist mentality. Typical of these is a letter in the Ultra-Rightist *Santa Ana Register,* April 4, 1967. The writer of this letter got so excited that she couldn't copy Manuilsky's name correctly:

Let us look again at the words of Dimitri Manuelsik, one time presiding officer of the U.N. Security Council.

Then follows the entire Manuilsky Hoax, with the parenthetical explanation. "(From Moscow, 1931)." (The lady got the date wrong, too.—M. K.). Mrs. Margaret Mullins concludes her letter with this clarion call to action:

The truth of this seems more and more obvious. All kinds of Peace overtures and concessions are being made, as Manuelski predicted. The "Lame-brains" in Washington are making overtures and concessions every day, crying "Peace, peace!" and apparently believing every word of the enemy. It's like a snowball going downhill, gathering momentum and getting larger and larger with every foot, readying to smash this country and its people. The vote put many of these men in Washington. Get them out! The pen is mightier than the sword. Look at the handwriting on the wall.

477

The Manuilsky Hoax is quoted in a little Ultra-Rightist newsletter, *Fact Finder*, November 15, 1965, published by Harry Everingham; it is also quoted in a leaflet issued by Everingham in March 1967.

Professor Anthony T. Bouscaren, member of the Strategy Staff of the Ultra-Rightist *American Security Council*, member of Board of Trustees of the Ultra-Rightist *Americans for Constitutional Action*, and speaker for and sponsor of many other Ultra-Rightist projects, quotes the Manuilsky Hoax in his book, *A Guide to Anti-Communist Action*. We find it difficult to believe that a professor of political science would be so naïve as to accept the authenticity of the Manuilsky Hoax.

Professor Lev Dobriansky, who teaches economics at Georgetown University, is on the editorial staff of *Washington Report*, the weekly newsletter of the Ultra-Rightist *American Security Council*. In a magazine article, which Congressman Edward J. Derwinski obligingly placed in the Congressional Record of April 26, 1966, Professor Dobriansky refers to: "The famous Lenin school, the Lenin Institute of Political Warfare." The correct name is Lenin School, with the first letter of *school* capitalized. The other name is a flagrant deception. Again, we find it hard to believe that Professor Dobriansky does not know that the correct name is the Lenin School (or Lenin Institute or Lenin University). No one authorized him to name it the Lenin Institute of Political Warfare. Similarly no one has the right to change the professor's name to Professor Lev Political Economy; his teaching of political economy does not change his name.

John Stormer, in his book, *None Dare Call It Treason*, quotes the Lenin Fabrication #2 on page 26 and the Manuilsky Hoax on page 88, in spite of the fact that one cancels out the other.

The Manuilsky Hoax is quoted in *Common Sense*, August, 1967, one of the many times that *Common Sense* repeated the hoax since Kornfeder launched it.

A letter in the *Progressive* magazine, March, 1960, reveals that *Reader's Digest* has apparently created a "successor" to the Manuilsky Hoax:

Dear Sirs:

"Reverend" Gerald L. K. Smith recently sent me a form letter soliciting funds for his "Christian Nationalist Crusade," enclosing

478

slips of paper on which the unverifiable Manuilsky "quotation" was reproduced with the sketch of a clenched fist. In the text of the letter he quoted Khrushchev as vowing revenge on Americans who opposed his visit to their country and saying, "The day will come when we will fry these men like little devils on a skillet."

I wrote to Harrison E. Salisbury, the *New York Times* expert on the Soviet Union about this, and he replied: "Of course Mr. K. never said such a thing! It is just those little devils making up fresh and lively misquotes again."

A Bostonian wrote me that an article in the *Reader's Digest* reported that children working in Soviet candy factories were given the death penalty for stealing one single piece of candy. This was carefully documented from a certain issue and page of *Pravda*.

Being able to read Russian, she went to the Boston Public Library, got that issue of *Pravda* and read it carefully. It contained nothing about children or candy factories. She wrote to the *Reader's Digest* editors, informing them of this. They replied with a curt note, merely changing the documentation to an issue of *Pravda* which came out before the United States recognized the USSR and before the Boston Public Library started subscribing to *Pravda*.

Despite a considerable amount of research on the subject, we have been unable to determine whom to give credit for originating one of the shabbiest and dishonest propaganda devices. This, as we have previously mentioned, consists of justifying the use of a phoney quotation on the ground that it represents the views of the person to whom the phoney quotation is attributed. It is certain that among the earliest to use this deception were the Cold Warriors of the State Department, Joseph Zack Kornfeder, the House Committee on Un-American Activities, and the Senate Internal Security Subcommittee. Later they were joined by Rev. Kenneth Goff, Rev. Gerald L. K. Smith, and various writers for the John Birch Society, including Tom Anderson. It has now become so fashionable that even "respectable" Ultra-Rightist columnists consider it appropriate to use this device. The argument appears somewhat plausible, even to people of intelligence and integrity. It is for this reason that we have decided to meet this argument headon and confront it with the facts that will destroy any basis for the belief that the Manuilsky Hoax in any way represents the thinking of responsible Soviet leaders and officials. We consider this of utmost importance in the struggle to avoid a third world war.

On November 8, 1917, one day after the Communists assumed state power in Russia, the All-Russian Congress of Soviets listened to a report made by Lenin and voted to approve a Decree on Peace. This was an appeal to all peoples and all governments to forthwith end World War I, to conclude an armistice, and commence immediate negotiations for peace. The message was sent out to the entire world by wireless telegraphy. The Decree said that the Soviet Government considered it "the greatest of crimes against humanity" to keep on fighting a war that was essentially a struggle to determine "how to divide among the strong and rich nations the weak nationalities they have conquered." Two years later, in a speech at St. Louis, Missouri, on September 5, 1919, President Woodrow Wilson admitted the essential accuracy of the Soviet analysis of the nature of the war, when he told his audience:

This war, in its inception, was a commercial and industrial war.

Thus did he concede that all the talk about "The War to Make the World Safe for Democracy" was a cruel hoax.

Beginning in December of 1917 and continuing into the first few months of 1918, the fledgling Soviet Government published, for the entire world to see, more than *one hundred secret treaties and documents* entered into by both the Czarist regime and the short-lived Kerensky regime. The publication of these treaties and documents exposed the imperialist nature of World War I, and may have been a factor in Woodrow Wilson's subsequent admission of the truth about that war. For the first time in history millions of people throughout the world were given a clear view of the behind-the-scenes manipulations of the merchants of death.

Over the years, the American people have been deluged with propaganda about the dangers of Soviet "aggression." Still, on March 8, 1949, John Foster Dulles, who later became Secretary of State in Eisenhower's administration, stated:

So far as it is humanly possible to judge, the Soviet Government under conditions now prevailing does not contemplate the use of war as an instrument of its national policy. I do not know any responsible high official, military or civilian, in this Government or any Government, who believes that the Soviet Government now plans conquest by open military aggression.

What this means is that the combined intelligence services of all the non-Communist countries of the world could not discover the slightest bit of evidence to support the diabolical plans embodied in that alleged Manuilsky quotation, supposedly uttered in 1930! This means that, nineteen years after Manuilsky allegedly confided in Kornfeder, no evidence had come to hand to support the Kornfeder-Stokes thesis.

George F. Kennan, who served for many years as an aide in the U.S. Embassy at Moscow and later become U.S. Ambassador to the U.S.S.R., wrote in *Harper's* magazine, August, 1956:

> The image of a Stalinist Russia poised and yearning to attack the West, and deterred only by our possession of atomic weapons, *was largely a creation of the Western imagination,* against which some of us who were familiar with Russian matters tried in vain, over the years, to make our voices heard. (Emphasis added.)

Ambassador Kennan is using the polite language of diplomacy when he describes fabrications and hoaxes as "creation of the Western imagination."

In the September, 1960, issue of *Kommunist,* the theoretical journal of the Communist Party of the Soviet Union, there is an article entitled "The Leninist Theory of Socialist Revolution and Our Times." It states that:

> . . . the working class cannot conceive of the creation of a Communist civilization on the ruins of world centers of culture, on desolated land contaminated with thermonuclear fallout, which would be an inevitable consequence of such a war. For some peoples the question of socialism would in general cease to exist: they would physically vanish from the planet. It is thus clear that *a present-day nuclear war in itself can in no way be a factor that would accelerate revolution and bring the victory of socialism closer.* On the contrary, it would hurl mankind, the world revolutionary workers' movement and the cause of the building of socialism and Communism back by many decades.[7] (The emphasis appeared in the original.)

The statement in *Kommunist* is one that the peddlers of the Manuilsky Hoax would not dare place side by side with the hoax quotation, because it demonstrates the sheer insanity, in the era of the thermonuclear bomb, of entertaining such notions as smashing them "with our clenched fist." Even if some of the Cold Warriors believe that Manuilsky ever made that

7 Quoted in *Reporter* magazine, December 12, 1960, by Professor Zbigniew Brzezinski.

statement, they know, or should know, that repeating it now, out of historical context, is downright dishonest and is damaging to the cause of world peace.

In November of 1960, there was assembled in Moscow the representatives of Communist Parties from 81 countries. After extended debate and discussions, these Parties unanimously adopted a statement of principles, which brings their theoretical position up to date, and from which the following are excerpts:

> The Communists of all the world uphold peaceful coexistence unanimously and consistently, and battle resolutely for the prevention of war.
> The Communist Parties regard the fight for peace as their prime task.
> The Communists regard it as their historical mission not only to abolish exploitation and poverty on a world scale and rule out for all time the possibility of any kind of war in the life of human society, but also to deliver mankind from the nightmare of a new world war already in our time. The Communist Parties will devote all their strength and energy to this great historical mission.
> . . . ideological and political disputes between states must not be settled through war.

In a companion statement, the conference issued a document, entitled "Appeal to the Peoples of the World," from which the following is excerpted:

> Socialism does not need war. The historic debate between the old and the new system, between socialism and capitalism, should be settled, not by a world war, but in peaceful competition, in a competition as to which social system achieves the higher level of economy, technology and culture, and provides the people with the best living conditions.
> We Communists consider it our sacred duty to do everything in our power to deliver mankind from the horrors of a modern war.
> In our epoch the peoples and states have but one choice: peaceful coexistence and competition of socialism and capitalism, or nuclear war of extermination. There is no other way.[8]

In October, 1961, the Twenty-Second Congress of the Communist Party of the Soviet Union adopted its new program, from which the following is quoted:

---

[8] Both statements of the 81 Communist Parties are published in *Political Affairs*, January 1961.

The C.P.S.U. considers that the chief aim of its foreign policy is to provide peaceful conditions for the building of a communist society in the U.S.S.R. and developing the world socialist system, and together with the other peace-loving peoples to deliver mankind from a world war of extermination.

When confronted with these Communist pronouncements, the Ultra-Rightists and other Cold War zealots counter with the argument that the Communists don't mean what they say, that the Communists are using Aesopian language. This, of course, is the central motif of the Manuilsky Hoax. In fact, it was concocted to serve exactly that purpose, to poison the atmosphere, to paralyze attempts of people of goodwill to keep open the channels of communication. One of the most important studies in this area of conflict is a volume published in 1961, entitled *Arms Control, Disarmament, and National Security*.[9] It brings together 23 essays by experts in every phase of the subject, and is edited by Professor Donald G. Brennan of the Massachusetts Institute of Technology. In his own essay, Professor Brennan says:

An extreme view sometimes encountered is that the Soviets will strike us at the first moment they see a reasonable chance of escaping overwhelming retaliation. Does this "preventive war" outlook really represent the Soviet doctrine that guides their actions?
The evidence seems overwhelming that it does not. To begin with, the Soviets for many years have been conducting among their own people an intensive propaganda for peace, by means of films, radio and television broadcasts, and newspapers. . . . In addition to their overt campaign, the Soviets are surrounded by many reminders of World War II, which hurt them very badly; to the present day, many of their cities still show scars.
Official Marxist-Leninist doctrine has never suggested a preventive war.

It is worth digressing a bit, in order to consider the question of who really threatens the peace of the world. (This will be discussed in great detail in volume II.) Former President Harry S. Truman has admitted that his administration at one time seriously considered using the atomic bomb in the Korean War. Former President Dwight D. Eisenhower has disclosed that in 1953 he quietly let word get out that, unless a satisfactory armistice could be arranged in Korea, he would use the

9 Published by George Braziller, Inc. and copyrighted.

483

atomic bomb. In 1954, the year of the French debacle at Dien Bien Phu, John Foster Dulles, Secretary of State, twice proposed to French Premier Bidault that atomic bombs should be dropped on Vietnam and southern China. On February 16, 1962, Mr. Frank Corley, Republican national committeeman for Missouri, called for "detonation of a clean weapon just off the three-mile limit," as a means of getting our "message" to the Russians in connection with the harassment of allied aircraft over the Berlin corridor. Corley added: "Certainly this would shock the world. Right now, I think the world needs a shock."

On September 21, 1961, U.S. Senator Margaret Chase Smith, Republican from the State of Maine, made a speech on the floor of the Senate, in which she sharply criticized the administration for not showing greater determination to use nuclear weapons in the dispute with the Soviet Union over the West Berlin problem. Expressing the usual pious disclaimers of being guilty of war-mongering, Senator Smith called for greater nuclear power, and exclaimed:

Until the Soviets change their ways and join the society of respectable nations, I see no hope of deterring them by making the risks they must face less fearful for them. . .

The greatness of this country was not won by people who were afraid of risks. It was won for us by men and women with little physical power at their command who nevertheless were willing to submit to risks. Could it not be lost for us by people with great physical power at their command but nevertheless willing to risk submitting? I believe it could.

Premier Nikita Khrushchev responded, in a message to the Labor Party members of the British House of Commons, which was made public on October 13, 1961:

Who can remain calm and indifferent to such provocative statements, made in the U.S. Senate by this woman, blinded by savage hatred toward the community of socialist countries?

It is hard to believe how a woman, if she is not the devil in a disguise of a woman, can make such a malicious man-hating call.

I don't know whether she has children and how many, but she should understand that in the fire of nuclear war millions of people would perish, including her own children, if she has any.

Even the wildest of animals, a tigress even, worries about her

484

cubs, licks and pities them. Margaret Smith, in her hatred of everything new and progressive, has decided to beat all records of savagery.

The distinctive feature of Khrushchev's remarks—its extraordinary characteristic—is its moral tone, its humanitarian posture. He does not resort to threats or to sabre rattling. He appeals to one's reason, to one's sense of justice and compassion. In this respect, it is unusual in the annals of political pronouncements.

While attending a conference in Rome, Frol R. Kozlov, a Soviet official, said on December 3, 1962 that the chief problem of our times is "that of defending peace, of preventing a world war." He explained the problem in these simple terms:

There is a Russian saying that in peacetime the young bury the old and in wartime the old bury the young.
But if thermonuclear war broke out, in many countries there would be no young or old left.

Perhaps the Cold War zealots will not believe any of the evidence presented thus far of the peaceful posture of the Soviet Union, but surely they will believe their Presidential candidate of 1964, General Barry Goldwater. Don Irwin, in a dispatch from Washington to the *Los Angeles Times,* August 22, 1964, quoted Congressman Albert H. Quie, chairman of a Republican Party task force on NATO, who said that Goldwater emphasized in a speech that the Reds have "sworn to defeat the West without firing a shot." This does not sit well with the theory of a sneak attack to "smash them with our clenched fist."

On October 16, 1964, shortly after Nikita Krushchev was deposed as Premier of the U.S.S.R., Ambassador Anatoly Dobrynin called at the White House to assure President Lyndon Johnson that the Soviet foreign policy of "strengthening peace, peaceful coexistence among countries with different social systems, and further relaxations of tensions" would remain unchanged. On October 27, 1964, President Johnson disclosed that he was pleased with a note he had received, through U.S. Ambassador Foy Kohler, from the new Soviet Premier, Alexei Kosygin. In this message, Kosygin reiterated that peaceful coexistence would continue to be the basis of Soviet foreign policy.

The American people have been so thoroughly drenched with propaganda based on fear that many of them blithely ignore the *actions* of our own militarists and continually raise the bogey of Communist "aggression." On August 6, 1965, President Nasser of Egypt and President Toure of Guinea urged the United States to stop its air attacks on North Vietnam. Repeat: they urged *the United States*, not the Soviet Union, to stop bombing a very small country whom we were attacking without a declaration of war, contrary to our Constitution and in violation of international law.

It has become fashionable these past few years for Cold War propagandists to claim that China threatens the peace of the world. These gentlemen must provide an answer to a statement made by the Chinese Ambassador, Wong Kuo-chang, in an interview at the British Embassy in Warsaw on June 11, 1965:

If China wanted war with the United States, it could have had it long ago.

It should be obvious that Peking does not want war, otherwise we could have retaliated for repeated violations of our territory about which we have issued more than 380 serious warnings in the past few years.

On October 20, 1964, shortly after exploding its first atomic bomb, Chinese Premier Chou En-lai called for a world summit conference on nuclear disarmament. He suggested that the proposed summit conference should bring together leaders "of all the countries of the world to discuss the question of the complete prohibition and the thorough destruction of nuclear weapons."

A real test of the Soviet Union's peaceful policy occurred in 1965. Hostilities broke out between India and Pakistan. On September 10, 1965, Soviet Communist Party Chairman Leonid I. Brezhnev declared:

We appeal to the governments of Pakistan and India to display realism, restraint and reasonableness, to dampen the fires of war and to withdraw troops of both nations to the territories they held before the conflict started. We are willing to offer our help.

The next day Premier Alexei Kosygin warned that the Indo-Pakistan border conflict could erupt into general war. In identical messages to the Prime Minister of India and the

486

President of Pakistan, Kosygin appealed to both sides to "stop the tanks and silence the guns." He urged them to enter negotiations at once, and said:

As for the U.S.S.R., both sides can count on its good cooperation or, as it is said, good offices in this. We are ready for this if both sides would consider it useful.

Two days later the Soviet Government issued its third appeal in a week for an end to hostilities, and again offered help in mediation of the differences. The next day Brezhnev renewed his plea to both sides for a cessation of hostilities.

On September 19, 1965, the Soviet Government invited India and Pakistan to meet on Soviet soil and negotiate a peace settlement. On the very same day, the *Los Angeles Times* correspondent, Ruben Salazar, sent a dispatch from Saigon, Vietnam, which began as follows:

American officials admitted Sunday after two days of hedging that U.S. planes bombed both the Communist and the South Vietnamese sides of a demilitarized zone which separates North and South Vietnam.

On September 23, 1965, Soviet Premier Alexei Kosygin congratulated the Prime Minister of India and the President of Pakistan for having achieved a cease-fire agreement. Kosygin said:

In this decision we see above all a display by Indian and Pakistani statesmen of realism, restraint and understanding of the grave consequences that further development of the armed conflict would have had.

The cease-fire is an important step to general settlement of the disagreements existing between Pakistan and India.

The Kornfeder-Stokes formula, for creating an image of Soviet aggressive intentions, was unwittingly refuted by one of the most prominent of the Cold War scribes, Professor Stefan T. Possony, Strategy and Military Affairs Editor of *Washington Report*, the weekly newsletter of the Ultra-Rightist *American Security Council*. In the January 27, 1966 issue, Dr. Possony wrote: "Traditionally, Soviet Military planners have favored defensive weapons." The key word here is *defensive*.

487

Vincent J. Burke reported from Moscow[10] that, in response to proposals voiced by President Johnson, Soviet Communist Party leader Leonid I. Brezhnev said that, in order to achieve better relations with the Soviet Union, the United States must first stop bombing North Vietnam and stop its "aggressive war" in South Vietnam. Once again, the Soviet Union gave evidence of its desire for world peace and its understanding that peace is indivisible. That is why Brezhnev stated at the dedication of a huge monument in Volgograd on October 16, 1967: "There are still madmen who threaten to plunge mankind into a new war."

Throughout the period in which he served as Premier of the Soviet Union, Cold War propagandists accused Nikita Khrushchev of harboring aggressive intentions and of endangering the peace of the world. Senator Margaret Chase Smith's speech of September 21, 1961 was replete with shrill accusations that Khrushchev was, in effect, the world's public enemy number one. David Lawrence and other syndicated columnists wrote truculent denunciations of Khrushchev. Publications of the John Birch Society and other Ultra-Rightist groups published so many accusations against Khrushchev that it made one wonder whether he were a man or a monster. In this respect, they followed the lead of the phoney documents produced by the House Committee on Un-American Activities and the stories planted by the Central Intelligence Agency. But life itself has a way of sometimes catching up with the truth.

On April 13, 1964, a rumor got started that Khrushchev was dead. The next day, Robert Sullivan, the assistant financial editor of the *Los Angeles Times* described the reaction of the financial community:

The report that Premier Khrushchev was dead produced a wave of exciting trading on the Pacific Coast Stock Exchange Monday. . .
Selling pressure was intense for a time in some major stocks in late activity on the PCSE. Trading subsided and prices recovered when the reports of Khrushchev's death were denied in Moscow.

The *Wall Street Journal* reported on April 14, 1964:

The rumor reached the U.S. in the afternoon after most stock exchanges had closed. On the Pacific Coast Exchange, which was still

10 *Los Angeles Times,* October 16, 1966.

open, volume expanded and prices dropped. Trading "simmered right down" when the rumor was labeled as unconfirmed and vague, a spokesman said.

Louis B. Fleming, the United Nations correspondent of the *Los Angeles Times,* summarized it very well on the next day:

> The shock, anguish and fear which greeted false reports Monday of Premier Nikita S. Khrushchev's death dramatized the general feeling that the cause of peace will best be served by his survival.

Thus, to the tune of millions of dollars, hardheaded business men demonstrated that Khrushchev was a pillar of world peace and that they did not believe he would "smash them with our clenched fist!" Some of them may have been supporters of Ultra-Rightist groups that peddled the Manuilsky Hoax, but at the crucial moment they decided to abandon the concept of that hoax as a basis for manipulating their investments.

Having demonstrated that reports of his demise were, as Mark Twain said about himself in a similar situation, "greatly exaggerated," Khrushchev wrote a statement, which was reported by United Press International,[11] from which the following seems pertinent:

> That system will triumph which in its development would help to strengthen peace, to meet more and more fully the needs and interests of the popular masses.
>
> This is our credo, and we propose to all political parties: Let us compete in this field.

There may be those who would consider the behavior of the stock market, when the false reports of Khrushchev's death were circulated, as just a fluke, and of no real significance. These people would have to reconsider such a conclusion, in the light of the stock market's reaction to Khrushchev's removal as Premier, some six months later. The Associated Press[12] reported that trading was heavy and that the stock market experienced "the worst wave of selling since the Kennedy Assassination." The dispatch explained that frantic selling was triggered by the report of Khrushchev's removal from leadership of the Soviet Government. A paid advertisement by

11 *Los Angeles Times,* May 6, 1964.
12 *Los Angeles Times,* October 16, 1964.

Scantlin Electronics, Inc. in the *Wall Street Journal* of October 26, 1964, has this heading in bold-faced type:

MR. KHRUSHCHEV'S RESIGNATION CAUSED A 50% CHANGE IN THE "TEN MOST UP" STOCKS WITHIN 20 MINUTES . . . during the market break on October 15th.

As we conclude our exploration in the "never, never-land" of delusions inspired by the Manuilsky Hoax, we can only express the fond hope and earnest wish that people of goodwill can make use of the data in a vigorous campaign to clear the air of false information and paranoidal assumptions. World peace is a goal worth striving for by all people.

# CHAPTER VIII

## The Blackout Spree

The electric power blackout, at 5:16 p.m. on November 9, 1965, threw some thirty million persons into darkness and suddenly brought to a halt all activities dependent upon electrical energy in eight states of the northeastern portion of the United States and the province of Ontario in Canada. It also presented an excellent opportunity to study the behavior of the Ultra-Rightists.

On October 30, 1965, nine days *before* the blackout, the Right-Wing semi-monthly *Freedom Press* of Los Angeles carried a story which came from a Right-Wing outfit, *Citizens Information Center* of Phoenix, Arizona. It told of a report which originated with Mrs. Mary Mundt, the wife of Senator Karl Mundt. In this story Mrs. Mundt told of a visit to Hoover Dam, where she found out how easily the mere pushing of a button at the Hoover Dam generating plant could play havoc with the entire West coast area. Mrs. Mundt tied the story of her visit at Hoover Dam to an alleged Communist Party club meeting that she and the Senator had supposedly infiltrated in 1934! As Mrs. Mundt told it, there was a professor from the University of Colorado speaking, and she quoted him as saying, inter alia: "What we want is to get our members planted in vital spots where at a given signal by merely pushing a button or pulling a lever they can plunge the country into darkness and disaster."

An exchange of correspondence, in March of 1966, which this writer had with Senator Karl Mundt about this alleged Communist meeting (which the Senator and his wife claim to have attended) has raised some serious doubts about the whole story. It has, however, furnished much grist for the mills of Right-Wing propaganda groups.

The *U.S. News & World Report* of November 22, 1965, pointed out: "In fact, there have been brief regional power failures in the past, but none that inconvenienced so many

491

people." It quoted Charles Hoppin of New York's Consolidated Edison Company as saying: "If you ask me whether it could happen again, I'd have to say yes."

The *Los Angeles Times* of December 7, 1965, quoted the Federal Power Commission's report to President Johnson, giving the results of the engineers' investigation. It gave the reasons for the blackout in terms of a series of mechanical failures, resulting from poor planning and poor coordination by the respective power companies.

By far the best technical explanation of the cause of the blackout and an outline of what is needed to prevent similar interruptions of power, appeared in *Consumer Reports* of March 1966. The article also points out that "power engineers have long known that electrical systems in many parts of the country are vulnerable. *There have been other extensive blackouts, both before and since.*" (Emphasis is mine.—M. K.)

One could hope that all this testimony and evidence would convince sensible people that there was no conspiracy, Leftist or Rightist, involved. But that is not the way the Right-Wing operates. It has the need to sow confusion and obscurantism. It has the need to titillate the fancy of its followers. It has the need to keep its dupes on a perpetual emotional jag of paranoidal assumptions. As the evidence will show, they took their faithful ones on a Blackout Spree, depending in large measure for "proof" on the fact that a Mr. Vernel Olsen, an apparent Communist sympathizer, works as a technician in a laboratory of the Ontario, Canada Hydro-Electric Power Commission.

Victor Riesel, in his column, *Shreveport Journal*, November 13, 1965 (4 days after the blackout), said:

It makes no difference whether the mechanism, just outside Syracuse, New York was sabotaged. Fact is that just a handful of Communist saboteurs *could have* accomplished what would take armadas of manned enemy aircraft." (Emphasis added.—M. K.)

This, of course, is a new doctrine in jurisprudence. According to Riesel, a person is guilty or probably guilty of a crime, if it can be shown that he could have done it.

On the same day that Riesel's column appeared, the *Shreveport Times* carried a column by David Lawrence. He starts off with the blackout, hints about secret agents knowing the location of our vulnerable spots, and arrives at this conclusion:

The two major Communist countries—Russia and China—continue to assert their right to go into other countries and establish secret agencies for the purpose of performing acts of sabotage at critical moments.

This November 13 column seems to clash with the item we have quoted from the *U.S. News and World Report* of November 22. Mr. Lawrence is the editor-in-chief of *U.S. News and World Report.*

Enters on the scene an ex-FBI agent, Dan Smoot, who tells us in the November 29, 1965, issue of *Dan Smoot Report* that the blackout could have been caused by mechanical failure or human error, but:

Hidden somewhere in some inconspicuous job could be a communist agent who sabotaged the CANUSE power grid on November 9 to serve a twofold communist purpose:

1. to test the effectiveness of communist sabotage plans; and
2. to create a national mood which will let the government move faster and further toward a tight nationwide power grid which would enable a saboteur to blackout and paralyze the whole nation when the critical time arrives.

In the November-December 1965 issue of *Independent American,* Right-Wing ideologist Kent Courtney, speculates at length about the possibility that the blackout was caused by a flying saucer.

Harry Everingham, president of *We, the People,* quotes the Mary Mundt story in the November 30 issue of *Fact Finder,* and then writes about the Communists, the KKK, the Nazis, etc., all under the big headline:

TOTAL BLACKOUTS PLANNED BY OUR ENEMY

A little Right-Wing propaganda group called Keep America Committee, operated by a Mrs. Helen Courtois of Los Angeles, got into the act by issuing a leaflet with this heading:

Blackout November 9, 1965
Was the wrong button pushed?
If so, by whom and why?

The leaflet then goes on to report the entire Mary Mundt statement, as issued by Johnny Johnson of Citizens Information Center, Phoenix, Arizona.

In the December 3, 1965 issue of *Herald of Freedom,* Ultra-Rightist Frank Capell quotes the Mary Mundt story, which he found in the February 18, 1965 issue of a Right-Wing publication called *Action in Kentucky.* Capell then regales his readers with stories about Communist infiltration of TVA. From this he moves on to use the Red paint brush against the chairman of the Federal Power Commission, Joseph C. Swidler. Finally, he winds up with a call to have "these enemies" prosecuted for *treason.*

The December 1965 circular letter of *The Network of Patriotic Letter Writers* asks: "Did Sabotage Trigger the Eastern Blackout?" Again the Mary Mundt story is told and the reader is referred to the issues of *Dan Smoot Report* and *Freedom Press,* which we have quoted.

Kenneth Goff, former associate of the notorious Gerald L. K. Smith, operates a Right-Wing group called *Soldiers of the Cross.* He is listed as a member of the Board of Policy for 1966 of *Liberty Lobby.* Goff was prominently associated with Robert DePugh, Der Fuehrer of the *Minutemen,* in the launching of the *Patriotic Party* at Kansas City on July 3. Goff's newsletter, circulated during the first week of December 1965, is headed:

BLACK OUT
Dress Rehearsal for the Revolution

Our next exhibit comes from the "Alert," which is issued by the *Defenders of the American Constitution,* which is run by retired military Brass Hats. It says:

Calling all patriots
Alert No. 26
December 24, 1965
Those Unsolved "Blackouts"—Beware Americans!

The "Alert" also quotes the Mary Mundt story, giving credit to Frank Capell's *Herald of Freedom* and *Action in Kentucky.* Kenneth Goff is quoted as an authority on the rules of revolution, and Chairman Swidler of Federal Power Commission is smeared liberally.

Former Communist and former FBI informer, Karl Prussion,

in his little monthly sheet, *Heads Up,* December 1965, solemnly asserts: "Because of the training I had received, while a communist, I can flatly state that communist sabotage has been (and will continue to be) the reason for most all of the catastrophes." Being a modest fellow, Prussion not only explains the past, but also predicts the future.

Harding College at Searcy, Arkansas, is considered by some experts to be the "West Point" of the Anti-Communist crusade. The December 1965 issue of its news letter praises Victor Riesel's column, which we have quoted, and asks: "What if some Communist agent should jam another electronic relay at some strategic moment in the future?"

The February 21, 1966 issue of *Freedom Club Bulletin,* First Congregational Church of Los Angeles, contains this:

Do you remember what confessed Soviet Spy Robert G. Thompson said in March last year? He said that the Communists were interested in information on water reservoirs, gas lines and *power systems* affecting the New York area. (How much later was the "couldn't happen" power failure?)

The February 1966 issue of *Task Force,* the monthly newsletter of the *Defenders of the American Constitution,* reproduced its "Alert No. 26." In addition, it had a column entitled "Those Unsolved Blackouts." It claimed a circulation of over 100,000 copies of "Alert No. 26." With evident relish, *Task Force* quotes from a letter of approval received from *Canadian Intelligence Service,* a privately operated Right-Wing project, whose name misleads some people into believing that it has some official status. (Several years ago a Los Angeles County Supervisor naively swallowed this bait, and made a spectacle of himself.) *Canadian Intelligence Service* "solves" the mystery of the alleged Communist saboteur.

During the month of March *Delaware Defenders of the Republic* circulated a leaflet. On one side there was a reproduction of the Mary Mundt story from the *Action in Kentucky* newsletter of February 18, 1965. On the other side was an essay entitled "Blueprint for a Blackout." It begins by quoting from December 16-22, 1965, *Review of the News,* a Birch Society publication:

Is it not possible that a small group of saboteurs who have penetrated our major power facilities have studied the grid system with sufficient thoroughness to know exactly where the controlling links are? Is it too far-fetched to imagine that our enemies have studied the vulnerabilities of our industrial civilization and are learning how to paralyze us at a push of a button?

Billy James Hargis, in the March 1966 issue of *Christian Crusader*, gives a capsule version of the Vernel Olsen story, after assuring the readers that the realists in America are not to be taken in with such trivia as the Liberal view that the Red Scare is an exaggeration. After explaining that Olsen is a technician at the Canadian power station where the breakdown occurred, *Christian Crusader* asks: "Is this simply coincidental or is it proof that one man in the right place at the right time can betray a nation?"

The Birch Society's *American Opinion* of April 1966 has a ten-page article by Jim Lucier of the editorial staff of the *Richmond News Leader*. Lucier is no stranger to readers of *American Opinion*. Title of his essay is "Mr. Blackout"; subtitle is "Power, Sabotage, And The Communists." It seems to be a roundup of all the arguments and documentation we have encountered so far. He Red-baits Mr. Swidler. He tells us that the Canadian Broadcasting Corporation "acts like it were an arm of the W.E.B. DuBois Clubs." He tells of anarchists, dynamite, the Cuban Embassy, Robert Williams, Vernel Olsen —a real witches' brew—saying little and proving nothing.

Our final item is from Gerald L. K. Smith's *The Cross and The Flag* of June 1966. A column is headed:

### A SENSATIONAL LETTER

We are indebted to a little bulletin entitled "Action in Kentucky," published in Louisville, for the following revealing statement. . .

The "sensational" and "revealing" letter is that Mary Mundt story again.

On March 18, 1966 we sent a letter to Mr. Ross Strike, Chairman of the Ontario Hydropower Commission. Two excerpts from his reply of March 22, 1966 should suffice:

Mr. Olsen is employed at our research laboratory as a meter technician. We employ about two hundred and seventy-five people in our laboratory which is located in the city of Toronto about

100 miles from Niagara Falls. Mr. Olsen's job has nothing to do with relays and I would be surprised if he has ever been in one of our sixty-seven hydraulic plants.

We have known of Mr. Olsen's sympathy for the communist cause for some years. However, his activities in this regard are strictly confined to his leisure hours and we have no fault to find with the way he performs his job as a minor technician. I might add that certainly his overt communistic slanted activities have tapered off in the last two years.

The Associated Press carried a story (*Santa Ana Register*, November 3, 1966), which reveals that, since the November 1965 power blackout, the Ontario Hydro-Electric Power Commission and the 21 other utilities involved in the Canada—U.S. Eastern Power Grid have completed a detailed study of the blackout at a cost of several million dollars. In reporting an interview with Harold Smith, chief engineer of Ontario Hydro, the A.P. story said: "Smith said that as a result of studies by the Northeast Power Coordinating Council established last January, additional relays have been built into the power grid and their settings have been adjusted."

Apparently the hard-headed business men and the top-flight electrical engineers did not buy the Communist-plot-explanation of the Ultra-Rightists.

On June 5, 1967, another electric power blackout occurred in the Northeast. This time some 13 million persons in a 15,000 square-mile area of Eastern Pennsylvania, New Jersey, Delaware, and Maryland were affected. The Federal Power Commission attributed the blackout to human error and uneven distribution of power. This time the Ultra-Rightists did not give a repeat performance.

A lengthy article in the *Wall Street Journal*, November 8, 1968, reports from Washington, D.C. that "the danger of electric power breakdowns is just about as high now as it was in 1965. The reason is the continuing possibility of overloaded circuits." The article points out further that major power failures have been increasing during the recent years and that they occur at the rate of 100 to 110 per year. The Federal Power Commission concluded its study of the problem with the observation that a lack of automatic load-shedding devices and a shortage of power transmission lines are the main causes of the blackouts. "Load-shedding devices," says the article, "are like giant fuses;

when too much power is being drawn, they cut off the current to customers on the overheated line, keeping the whole network from blowing. At the time of the 1965 Northeast blackout, most utilities in that region had none of these devices." The Federal Power Commission stated that the power companies do not build transmission lines far enough in advance, and as a result they often lack enough reserve transmission lines for periods when their regular lines are operating to full capacity. This results in overloading the regular lines, and in the absence of load-shedding devices, a whole area will suffer a blackout. It has nothing to do with Communist "conspirators."

This study does not exhaust the list of all the Right-Wing outfits that spread the phoney Communist conspiracy story about the blackout. We have presented only a cross section of its production in order to show, in microcosm, the harm being done by the hundreds of Right-Wing groups of various sizes, who keep up a steady barrage of falsehoods, distortions of truth, and hysteria—all of which augurs ill for the future of our country, unless more people of courage and goodwill take positive action to expose and defeat the Ultra-Right propaganda network.

498

# CHAPTER IX
## The Stalin Fabrication

Another weapon, used by the Cold War propagandists against proposals for peaceful coexistence, is a *garbled* version of something Joseph Stalin wrote some 40 or more years ago. Like the Manuilsky Hoax, it is used to silence socially-conscious people who strive for peace. A typical example of its use is a letter in the now-defunct *Los Angeles Mirror*, October 4, 1960:

**Elizabeth P.** Steiner writes: "What about working for universal disarmament and beginning to encourage our people to make it come true? As a Christian nation it will be forever to our disgrace if we leave any stone unturned in determined efforts for understanding and disarmament. Do we, like Russia, put all our trust in the power of violence?"

For her information, Stalin once said, commenting on diplomatic relations and statements, "Words must have no relation to actions— otherwise what kind of diplomacy is it? Words are one thing, actions are another. Good words are a mask for concealment of bad deeds. Sincere diplomacy is no more possible than dry water or wooden iron."

Miss Steiner as a "Christian" may be ready for martyrdom, but the majority of free-thinking Americans will, I think, speak a trifle softly on this disarmament, and in the interest of the ultimate welfare of the world—keep our powder dry.

That is the way to be among the ultimate survivors.

JAY GUREY

If it were true that Stalin ever wrote such a statement, it would still be dishonest, immoral, and dangerous for the future of mankind, for anyone to use it as an argument against efforts to prevent a third world war. The fanaticism and desperation of the Cold War propagandists are of sufficient intensity to cause them to justify almost anything—including possible nuclear incineration—in order to "save" us from Communism. It so happens that Stalin did not write what the liars attribute to him.

The following appears on pages 285-286 of volumn 2, *J. V.*

*Stalin Works*, Moscow, 1953, Foreign Languages Publishing House. It is catalogued in the Library of Congress as DK 268.S 75A 267:

When bourgeous diplomats prepare for war they begin to shout very loudly about "peace" and "friendly relations." When a Minister of Foreign Affairs begins to wax eloquent in favour of a "peace conference," you can take it for granted that "his government" has already issued contracts for the construction of new dreadnoughts and monoplanes. A diplomat's words *must* contradict his deeds— otherwise, what sort of a diplomat is he? Words are one thing— deeds something entirely different. Fine words are a mask to cover shady deeds. A sincere diplomat is like dry water or wooden iron.

The same must be said about the Liquidators and their mendacious clamour about unity. Recently, Comrade Plekhanov, who is in favour of unity in the Party, wrote concerning the resolutions passed by the Liquidators' conference that "they smell of diplomacy ten versts away." And the same Comrade Plekhanov went on to describe their conference as a "splitters' conference." To put it more bluntly, the Liquidators are deceiving the workers by their diplomatic clamour about unity, for while they talk about unity they are engineering a split. Indeed, the Liquidators are diplomats in the Social-Democratic movement; with fine words about unity they cover up their shady deeds in engineering a split. When a Liquidator waxes eloquent in favour of unity, you can take it for granted that he has trampled upon unity for the sake of a split.

The quoted remarks of Stalin date back to Czarist times, and must be considered in *that* historical context. Far from advocating duplicity, Stalin was pouring forth irony, scorn, and bitter sarcasm at lying diplomats and crooked politicians. He was comparing some of his political adversaries to the lying diplomats. Little did Stalin dream that 50 or 55 years later the House Committee on Un-American Activities and other Ultra-Rightist propaganda agencies and individuals would take his remarks out of historical context, and use them to impede the struggle for peace.

In a speech delivered to the Ninth All-Russian Congress of Soviets on December 23, 1921, Lenin seems to have prophesied the attitude that enables the Cold War propagandists to concoct such scarecrows as the Manuilsky Hoax and the Stalin Fabrication:

This old world has its old diplomacy, which cannot believe that it is possible to speak frankly and straightforwardly. This old diplomacy thinks to itself—there must be a trap of some sort here.[1]

The American Bar Association has its own little Cold War propaganda apparatus, which calls itself the Special Committee on Communist Tactics, Strategy, and Objectives. In both its Reports of August 1958 and February 1959, this Special Committee took special pains to pick up as many of the anti-Soviet fabrications as it could locate, and, of course, the Stalin fabrication was included. The Report provided itself with an escape hatch, by quoting the Stalin fabrication from a 1956 document of the House Committee on Un-American Activities. If these lawyers had been apprehensive of a libel suit, they would have done just a bit of research to attempt verification of that alleged Stalin quotation. It is as simple as sending a letter of inquiry to the Library of Congress or to the political science department of any large university. In the Cold War climate that obtains at present, a pursuit of the truth on such an item is not "patriotic." Consequently, the lawyers, who know the rules of evidence, decided to ignore these rules.

The 1958 Report was placed in the Congressional Record by Senator Everett Mc Kinley Dirksen on March 1, 1962, and the 1959 Report was placed in the Congressional Record by Congressman Gordon H. Scherer on February 25, 1959. Scherer was a member of the House Committee on Un-American Activities, a member of the Board of Trustees of the Ultra-Rightist *Americans for Constitutional Government*, and was listed in 1961 as an endorser of the John Birch Society. The insidious nature of this procedure may be summarized as follows: The Reports have brought together dozens of fabrications and distortions of truth. Both Reports were placed, in their entirety, in the Congressional Record. Ultra-Rightists have reprinted them by the millions as a Report of the American Bar Association *and* the Congressional Record, thus giving official "sanction" to falsehoods.

The Honorable William G. Bray, Congressman from Indiana, placed a speech in the Congressional Record on November 15, 1965. His thesis is that the Chinese Communists and the Vietnamese Communists plan to defeat the United States by

1 Quoted in Lenin, Collected Works, volume 33, 4th Russian edition, p. 124.

501

use of the U.S. peace movement in a psychological warfare offensive. In addition to quoting a phoney statement attributed to Lenin, the gentleman clobbered the Communists with a quotation from Sun Tzu, a Chinese military writer and general of 2500 years ago! After this, Congressman Bray declared:

Deceit and duplicity are considered with pride by the Communists, as suggested in statements from Stalin:
"Words must have no relation to action—otherwise what kind of diplomacy is it? Words are one thing, actions are another. Good words are a mask of concealment of bad deeds."

On November 24, 1965, we sent a perfectly courteous letter to Congressman Bray. The postal receipt shows that it was delivered to his office on November 26, 1965. Together with our letter, we enclosed a research memorandum, showing that his quotation from Stalin was garbled and taken out of context, so that it was made to convey a meaning quite different than was intended. Our letter concluded with:

Inasmuch as your use of this inaccurate quotation will be mentioned in my book, I am showing you the courtesy of advising you about it, and in order to give you the benefit of any doubt, I would like to pose two questions:
1.   Where did you obtain this alleged Stalin quotation?
2.   Would you consider it a matter of personal integrity to place a correction in the Congressional Record when Congress next convenes? All you would need to do is place my memorandum in the Record. You can easily check the accuracy of it with the Library of Congress.

No reply was received from the Honorable William G. Bray.

Henry J. Taylor is a syndicated columnist. He is the former U.S. Ambassador to Switzerland, and the recipient of a medal from the Ultra-Rightist *Freedoms Foundation at Valley Forge*, as well as from the Wall Street Post of the American Legion. His column is carried in many newspapers, including the Ultra-Rightist weekly, *Human Events*. In a column entitled "Reds and Broken Promises,"[2] Mr. Taylor said:

Stalin spelled out the principle, and while men change, the system does not: "Words must have no relation to actions—otherwise

2 *Los Angeles Times*, July 21, 1967.

what kind of diplomacy is it? Words are one thing, actions another."

Until President Johnson can make the Reds reliable, which he cannot do, it is utterly impossible to think there will be a solution to the Vietnam war by next year's Presidential election—or even, I would say, by 1972.

It is very plain. The killings, the maimings, the destruction must go on and on—because Stalin said something or is alleged to have said something. Little did Mr. Taylor's readers suspect, when he struck that charismatic pose, that his discourse was based upon a falsehood.

On July 21, 1967 we sent Mr. Taylor a letter, and we enclosed a research memorandum to prove to him that his quotation from Stalin had no foundation-in-fact. We added:

It may be that you have unwittingly accepted this, because you read it elsewhere. This is sometimes the explanation.

If you care to publish a retraction in an early column, I shall be happy to include your retraction in my manuscript as an example of journalistic integrity.

After a follow-up letter, Mr. Taylor replied on September 25, 1967. After apologizing for the delay, he said:

I appreciate the background of the quotation but my reference is an accurate one and describes Stalin equally when in power. I simply fail to see how journalistic integrity is involved but appreciate your helpful letter.

On September 27, 1967, we wrote to Mr. Taylor:

While I appreciated the friendly tone of your letter of the 25th Instant, I am terribly disappointed in its lack of candor.

You quoted Stalin. You used quotation marks around his alleged remarks. I sent you documentary proof that you used a garbled and distorted version of his remarks, the effect of which is downright false. No amount of extrapolation or rationalization can justify phoney quotations.

I repeat that journalistic integrity is involved, and I regret that you did not see fit to meet the challenge.

On September 30, 1967, Mr. Taylor replied:

I am sure you intend to be reasonable when you declare your definition of "journalistic integrity."

You must, at the same time, accept my good faith in questioning your verdict as a journalist who has some pride in his own through about 30 practicing years. Mr. Kominsky, I dislike disappointing you but why this defense of Stalin's equivalently documented intentions and opinions even as you submit them?

We must confess that we find this reply so incoherent that we are not sure what he is trying to say. Is he, perchance, using the language of the diplomat, as Stalin described it? Or is he brazenly arguing that he did quote Stalin accurately? Perhaps we can find a clue by examining some more of Mr. Taylor's columns.

His column in *Human Events* of September 16, 1967 minimizes the danger of the late George Lincoln Rockwell and his indigenous native Nazi followers. In his column of September 2, 1967, written in Madrid, Spain, he sings the praises of the Fascist dictator of Spain, General Francisco Franco:

I interviewed Franco for the first time 24 years ago. Contrary to foreign impressions, he stood high then and, believe it or not, he obviously stands higher now.

Using Henry J. Taylor's criteria, one could prove anything about anyone. All the rules of evidence would go down the drain, and the methodology of science, as well as jurisprudence, would be destroyed.

Together with the Manuilsky Hoax, the Stalin Fabrication is used to badger, browbeat, and ridicule attempts to make a start at universal disarmament. The danger that inheres in the use of all these fabrications and falsehoods was well stated by Mr. Harry Porter in a letter to the *Los Angeles Times*, September 21, 1966:

I submit that "truth pollution" is a greater threat to contemporary society than air and water pollution. Truth pollution invades our feelings and values as well as our ideas, and ultimately deprives us of our humanity. Eventually we will be turned into a mass of zombies, alienated from real human experience and striving, unable to cope with the very real and desperate problems we face.

# CHAPTER X

# The Many Disguises of Khrushchev

## Khrushchev—The Mortician

In a dispatch from Moscow that appeared in the *New York Times*, November 20, 1956, Welles Hangen reported:

> . . . in commenting on coexistence last night Mr. Khrushchev said *communism did not have to resort to war to defeat capitalism.* "Whether you like it or not, history is on our side," he said. "We will bury you."[1]

Any intelligent and fair-minded person who reads that entire statement would quickly realize that, having disavowed the use of armed force to defeat capitalism, the allusion to burying is metaphorical, only a figure of speech. However, trouble arose because the sentence, "We will bury you," was quoted out of context in thousands of stories in editorials, columns, speeches, leaflets, booklets, tracts, sermons, and books. The American people were subjected to a saturation campaign by the Cold War propagandists. Dr. Carl McIntire, the Ultra-Rightist preacher, ran a Faith and Freedom Rally in Pasadena's (California) Rose Bowl on September 18, 1959. It was advertised in the *Los Angeles Mirror* in this fashion:

KHRUSHCHEV
Comes Selling Communist "Peaceful Coexistence"
While Vowing to "Bury Us"!

The *Mirror* reported the next day that more than 1,000 people —many of them carrying Bibles and wearing black armbands— gathered to protest Khrushchev's first visit to the U.S.A., which was in response to an invitation from President Eisenhower. The crowd was smaller than the organizers of the affair had expected, but they made up for it by loud applause and shrill cries of "Amen" when a speaker called the President's personal

---

1 Emphasis added.—M. K.

guest "the biggest murderer the world has ever known." Thus, by comparison, Hitler becomes a gentleman!

The following evening there was a civic dinner given in honor of Khrushchev at the Los Angeles Ambassador Hotel. The affair was shown on television, so that millions of people saw the disgraceful performance of Mayor Norris Poulson. (This is the same Poulson, who as a Congressman, had helped spread the Narcotics Hoax.) At one point in his speech of "welcome," Poulson remarked:

We do not agree with your widely quoted phrase, "We shall bury you." You shall not bury us and we shall not bury you. We are happy with our way of life. We recognize its shortcomings and are always trying to improve it. But if challenged, we shall fight to preserve it.

It was plainly evident to television viewers that consternation spread over most of the guests at that banquet, because of Mayor Poulson's egregious show of discourtesy and belligerence. When Khrushchev's turn came to speak as the guest of honor, he temporarily pushed aside his prepared speech, and turning to Mayor Poulson, he said:

My dear host, I am deeply concerned over these, I believe to be conscious distortions of my thoughts, which can lead to nothing but the aggravation of the Cold War. But choose for yourselves the language you prefer to use. . .

The unpleasant thought sometimes creeps up on me: what if Khrushchev had not been invited here for you to rub him in your sauce, show him your might, make him shaky at the knees.

It took us only about 12 hours to get here. Perhaps it would take us only about 10¼ hours to get back.

Poulson had a glum look on his face while Khrushchev delivered these remarks, which were followed by Khrushchev's well-reasoned and conciliatory speech. Most of the audience seemed to enjoy Khrushchev's speech, and the stories in the press were mostly critical of Poulson's behavior. Indeed, the episode had international repercussions. On the train, heading towards San Francisco, Khrushchev remarked that Poulson "does not shine by his intelligence." For many days after the banquet, the Los Angeles newspapers were deluged by letters from all points of the compass, in condemnation of Mayor Poulson. Only a fraction of them could be published, but they showed definitely that most of the American people want peace. One newspaper stated that its mail was running 35 to 1 against Poulson.

The U.S. Ambassador to the United Nations, Henry Cabot Lodge, had been assigned by the State Department to accompany Khrushchev on his cross-country trip. He had talked with Poulson, as "an old Congressional buddy," and had asked that Khrushchev be handled in a dignified manner. A State Department attaché, who was also part of the Khrushchev entourage and who preferred to remain anonymous told the press:

If he runs into any more mayors like that one, he really is likely to pack up his bags and fly home.
He's running into one attack after another about old dead issues. If these mayors want votes, they should do it some other time.

Some evidence that Poulson made those remarks with malice aforethought came to light in a story told by Pat Michaels, KTLA news commentator. After he filmed an interview with Poulson on the day before the banquet, Michaels reported that Poulson said:

Everybody else has been nice to him (Khrushchev), but I'm not going to be. You should see my speech. I'm having 200 copies printed up.
I'm going to have my fist out there, but it's going to be covered with brocade. And under the brocade, I'm going to have a long, sharp knife. And I am going to ram it all the way into that son-of-a . . .

At San Francisco, two days after the banquet, the U.S. officials accompanying Premier Khrushchev made it plain that they would like to see no more needling of Khrushchev, and in Washington, White House press secretary James Hagerty released an appeal from President Eisenhower for courteous treatment to Khrushchev. In London, the *Daily Sketch* remarked that disarmament "won't get far if America's small-time politicians continue to needle him (Mr. K.) with loaded questions." The London *Daily Mail* commented: "It would be a tragedy if Khrushchev were to go home in a huff. We think he has had a rough ride in the U.S. and some people treated him offensively." The staid *London Times* said Khrushchev had shown remarkable restraint while subjected to heckling "which has been blunt to the point of outright rudeness."

With the possible exception of the Manuilsky Hoax, the "We will bury you" distortion is the most widely exploited by the warmongers and the other Cold War propagandists. In a not too inspired apologia for some of the peccadilloes of the "dirty tricks" department of the Central Intelligence Agency, the *U.S. News and World Report* said on March 13, 1967:

> In carrying out that mission, the CIA must face enemies of many kinds—enemies masked as "do-gooders" as well as enemies trained in the dark arts of subversion, espionage, blackmail and assassination—all dedicated to the Communist aim once stated bluntly by Nikita Khrushchev and never denied by his successors: to "bury" the U.S.

Aside from the shabby use of the distortion of Khrushchev's remarks, the last statement is an outright lie. The *U.S.N. & W.R.* was well aware of the repeated denials and explanations by Khrushchev and others. One example, which was made public three years before the *U.S.N. & W.R.* made that statement, is an article written by Khrushchev's son-in-law, Alexei Adzhubei, in the Encyclopedia Britannica's 1964 edition of "The Great Ideas Today," he quotes Khrushchev as saying:

> Communists realizing the inevitability of the downfall of capitalism, and rejoicing that such an hour will come, are all the same not guided in their actions by naïve feelings and notions and are not preparing to bury each capitalist individually; they understand that capitalism is digging its own grave.

The Cold Warriors, who so avidly search for out-of-context quotations in Lenin's writings that they can distort, might have found this statement of Lenin's, which contains the concept expressed in Khruschev's pronouncement:

> Capitalism can be utterly vanquished, and will be utterly vanquished, by the fact that Socialism creates a new and much higher productivity of labor.[2]

The editors of the *U.S. News & World Report* and all the

2 Lenin, *Selected Works*, volume IX, page 438; International Publishers, New York.

508

rest of the journalistic fraternity are well aware of the fact that Khrushchev himself had earlier explained the "We will bury you" statement in terms that should have terminated the use of it by all persons for all time. In the course of a press conference at the National Press Club in Washington, D.C., on September 16, 1959 (three days before Mayor Poulson made his not so brilliant remarks), the following exchange took place:

QUESTION: It is frequently attributed to you, Mr. Khrushchev, that at a diplomatic reception you said that you would bury us. If you didn't say it, you could deny it; and if you did say it, could you please explain what you meant?

KHRUSHCHEV: There is only a small section of the American people in this hall. My life would be too short to bury every one of you if this were to occur to me. (Laughter.) I did speak about it, but my statement has been deliberately misconstrued. It was not a question of any physical burial of anyone at any time but of how the social system changes in the course of the historical progress of society. Every educated person knows that there is now more than one social system in the world. The various states, the various peoples have different systems. The social system changes as society develops. There was the feudal system. It was superseded by capitalism. Capitalism was more progressive than feudalism. Capitalism created better conditions than feudalism for the development of the productive forces. But capitalism engendered irreconcilable contradictions. As it outlives itself, every system gives birth to its successors. Capitalism, as Marx, Engels and Lenin have proved, will be succeeded by communism. We believe in that. Many of you do not. But among you, too, there are people who believe in that.

At the reception concerned, I said that in the course of historical progress and in the historical sense, capitalism would be buried and communism would come to replace capitalism. You will say that this is out of the question. But then the feudal lords burned at the stake those who fought against feudalism and yet capitalism won out. Capitalism fights against communism. I am convinced that the winner will be communism, a social system which creates better conditions for the development of a country's productive forces, enables every individual to prove his worth and guarantees complete freedom for society, for every member of society. You may disagree with me. I disagree with you. What are we to do, then? We must coexist. Live on under capitalism, and we will build communism. The new and progressive will win; and the old and moribund will die. You believe that the capitalist system is more productive, that it creates better conditions for social progress, that it will win. But the brief history of our Soviet state does not speak in favor of capitalism. What place did Russia hold for economic development before the Revolution? She was backward and illit-

509

erate. And now we have a powerful economy, our science and culture are highly developed.

I don't recall just how many engineers we graduate annually—

V. P. YELUTIN, Minister of Higher Education of the USSR: Last year 94,000 engineers were graduated and 106,000 this year, or three times as many as in the United States.

KHRUSHCHEV: Some say in your country that if the USA will have more scientists, we will perish. We are willing to "perish" in that sense, we are seeing to it that there are more scientists in our country, that all our people are educated, because communism cannot be built unless we do so. Communism is a science.

Thank you. (Stormy, prolonged applause.)

The Ultra-Rightists have been circulating something which is humorous, in a perverse sort of way. It is a small advertisement, printed in a block, that has appeared in some Ultra-Rightist publications, as well as on $3'' \times 5''$ handouts. This is it:

Main office
Moscow

Branch offices in
principal cities
of the world

### N. KHRUSHCHEV & CO.
### MORTICIANS
"We bury you so gently,
    you never know you're dead."

Another factor in the explanation of why this distortion of truth was so widely exploited in this country is that most Americans are not linguists. In their ignorance of other languages, they do not realize the dangers of *literal translations of an idiom* from one language to another. For instance, it is common in the use of German, Yiddish, and other languages for one to describe an argument by saying: "I buried him good and deep." That is the way it translates *literally* into English. The meaning of that idiom in the other languages is simply that one person gave the other a pretty severe tongue-lashing or bested him in the argument. This is something that the ignoramuses failed to understand when they called upon Khrushchev to withdraw or retract his "threat." Actually, Khrushchev had nothing to retract, unless he wanted to descend to the level of the ignoramuses. Some examples of American idiom will make this point clear.

A foreign language correspondent would be ignorant or dishonest if he translated literally into the language of his country our idiom, "cut throat competition." Using the same shabby method that was used against Khrushchev, he could paint a picture of business men running amuck with stilettoes and machetes, and slitting each other's throats from ear to ear. Consider the literal translation into a foreign language of the idiomatic expression contained in a Los Angeles newspaper story that referred to County Fire Chief Klinger as "throwing two hundred men into the fire." Shades of Dachau and Buchenwald! The Rev. James W. Fifield, Jr., in his March 1, 1962, column in the *Los Angeles Times,* refers to a man "whose mother I buried and whose daughter I married." This, of course, when translated literally into another language, can have some sinister connotations.

A dishonest person could translate the term *vice-president* to mean that this country has a special official to preside over vice. The term *criminal lawyer* could be translated to mean a lawyer with a criminal record. The term *desert rat,* translated literally, means a desert rodent, but we use it as an idiomatic term to denote a lover of, or habitué, of the desert. It is used in a respectful and jocular vein. A newspaper headline reads:

## L.A. POLICE CHIEF HIT FOR SUSPENDING OFFICER

This does not mean that someone physically assaulted the chief of police, but if that idiom is translated literally, it can be made to mean it. Jim Lucier, in *American Opinion,* January 1965, says: "I am in favor of sin. . ." That sounds as bad as "We will bury you," but when you read it *in its proper context,* it is only a satirical literary device. A magazine reports about two Catholic nuns who "have discarded their religious habits." If this is translated literally, it can mean they have renounced their religious principles or left the convent. Actually, it means they have discarded the traditional garb of the convent in favor of conventional clothes. The term "political machine," translated literally, can have some very weird implications.

A headline on the sports page of the *Los Angeles Times,* March 18, 1967, reads:

## BRUINS MASSACRE COWBOYS, 109-60

Supposing the Tass reporter sent a dispatch to a Moscow paper and reported it literally, so that Russian readers would conclude that murder is committed by our football players? Tass reporters have not done this, because journalistic integrity requires that a reporter refrain from *literally* translating idioms from one language to another.

A special dispatch from New Orleans to the *Los Angeles Times*, March 12, 1967, includes this item:

> Few are willing to bet against him now. As Gov. John J. McKeithen observed last week, "Garrison has 'buried' past political foes, and I don't want to be among the deceased."

Here was the Governor using "buried" in a metaphorical sense, but nobody reproached him and no one started a campaign of malicious slander and ridicule against the Governor.

Americans need not be proud of the attempts to portray Nikita Khrushchev in the role of the mortician.

A little postscript to our study of this hoax will illustrate the irresponsibility and the disregard of truth that are characteristic of the Cold War dialogue. In a speech delivered on the floor of the Senate, September 10, 1962, Senator Alexander Wiley made the usual dragon-slaying speech about Communism, and declared:

> Stalin said that he "would bury" us.

With all the experts on Khrushchevian demonology attributing that remark to Nikita, it startled us to see the Senator's sensational discovery. We wrote to him on September 17, 1962. We sent a follow-up letter on February 3, 1963. We sent a final letter on January 27, 1964. The postal receipt shows that it was delivered to his office on February 5, 1964. No reply was ever received to our repeated question of the source of his quotation and our suggestion that, as a matter of integrity, a retraction would be in order.

## Khrushchev—The Medicine Man

In his campaign to defend General Edwin Walker and others in the Armed Forces who were using Ultra-Rightist material to indoctrinate the soldiers and sailors, Senator Strom Thurmond of South Carolina made an impassioned speech on the floor of the U.S. Senate, on July 26, 1961, in which he quoted Nikita Khrushchev as saying:

We cannot expect the Americans to jump from capitalism to communism, but we can assist their elected leaders in giving Americans small doses of socialism, until they suddenly awake to find they have communism.

Thus did the Honorable gentleman cast Khrushchev in the role of a medicine man. With their usual alacrity, Cold War propagandists and Ultra-Rightists picked it up as coming "from the Congressional Record," and gave it massive circulation. The story was best told by one of the most enlightened members of the Senate, the Honorable Lee Metcalf of Montana, in a speech on the floor of the Senate, March 8, 1962:

> Mr. METCALF. Mr. President, a basic maxim of law is "falsus in uno, falsus in omnibus." A witness' testimony, if false as to any material part, generally should be discarded as a whole and cannot be relied on for any purpose, unless strongly corroborated.
> One of the statements thrown at Members of Congress many times in recent months reads as follows:

> > We cannot expect the Americans to jump from capitalism to communism, but we can assist their elected leaders in giving Americans small doses of socialism, until they suddenly awake to find they have communism.

> The quotation is attributed to Nikita Khrushchev, and is said, by the people who use it, to have been made some 3½ months before his visit to the United States in September 1959.
> I have seen this statement in letters to editors. It is sometimes attached to letters I receive. Sometimes it is printed, against a red background, on post cards distributed as a public service by Coast Federal Savings of Los Angeles, which has circulated thousands of copies of literature endorsing the John Birch Society.
> Sometimes it appears on post cards bearing the imprint of Poor Richard's Book Shop of Los Angeles, which disseminates rightwing material. Sometimes, in mail I receive, this quotation is followed by statements like the following:

> > Your socialistic voting record leads me to believe that you are one of the elected leaders upon whom Nikita Khrushchev depends to carry out his plan.

> I asked the Library of Congress to find the origin of the statement. I received the following reply:

> > We have searched the Legislative Reference Service files, checked all the standard reference works on quotations by Khrushchev, and consulted with the Slavic Division of the Library of Congress, the Department of State, and the U.S. Information

513

Agency, in an attempt to determine the authenticity of this quotation. From none of these sources were we able to produce evidence that Khrushchev actually made such a statement.

I asked the Senate Internal Security Subcommittee if its files showed any documentation for the quotation. Chairman James O. Eastland, on February 26, advised me that:

Inquiry to the Slavic Division of the Library of Congress discloses no authentic source for the quotation.

A similar inquiry to the House Committee on Un-American Activities brought the following response, dated March 2, from Chairman Francis E. Walter:

The research section of our committee as well as the Legislative Reference Service of the Library of Congress have been unable to find the origin of the quotation referred to above.

I queried Director J. Edgar Hoover of the Federal Bureau of Investigation. On March 1 he advised me that:

I have had the files and reference material available to us reviewed; however, it has not been possible to verify the authenticity of the statement.

I asked the Central Intelligence Agency. On February 13, 1962, Director John A. McCone advised me as follows:

The quotation . . . does not appear in any of Khrushchev's speeches, interviews, articles, or off-the-cuff remarks which have come to our attention. To the best of our knowledge, we believe the quotation to be spurious.

Mr. President, this fabrication, attributed to the leader of the Communist Party, arouses Americans against their elected officials. Readers and listeners are led, by the mischievous persons who authored and use the false quotation, to believe that their President, their Senators, their Representatives, their judges and local officials are Communist stooges. Thus a lie is used to perpetrate a greater lie.

30 March 1962

Mr. Morris Kominsky
400 East Franklin St.
Elsinore, California

Dear Mr. Kominsky:

I have your communication about the origin of a quotation widely attributed to Premier Khrushchev. A copy of my speech is enclosed. Before I was elected to any office, I was a practicing lawyer, later I was an Assistant Attorney General of the State of Montana. In both capacities, I prepared briefs for argument before the Montana

Supreme Court. The procedure there is similar to that of every court. Previous court decisions are found and appropriate citations are presented to the court. Later, for six years, I was an Associate Justice of the Montana Supreme Court. I would have never had the temerity to cite a false quotation to the court in my capacity as a lawyer and officer of that court. I would know that such an action would lose my case, make me subject to discipline of the court and destroy an opportunity for future effectiveness in arguing cases before that court.

Similarly, as a member of that court, if I learned that any lawyer had fabricated a citation or quotation to strengthen his case, I would have immediately demanded that he be cited for contempt.

Yet, the American people are being subjected to this sort of thing by such false quotations as the one which I discussed in my recent speech on the Senate floor. The people who base their whole case upon such falsity are destroying their credibility before the American people and are defeating their own cause and, at the same time, perpetuating a false premise.

Very truly yours,<br>LEE METCALF

Enclosure:

On the surface of it, the quotation is an obvious fraud. Anyone familiar with Communist ideology would recognize that it is a vulgarization. For some reason which is not apparent, Congressman Clyde Doyle, a vigorous Ultra-Rightist, spoke on the floor of the House of Representatives on October 3, 1962 in condemnation of the use of this phoney quotation. He quoted an item from the *Christian Science Monitor*, which contained a brief resumé of Senator Metcalf's data (without giving credit to the Senator), and he remarked:

Mr. Speaker, it is regretted that so many folks believe all which appears in some publications which habitually emphasize attacks upon the United States of America and the free world *without first ascertaining the actual facts before printing them.* (Emphasis added. —M. K.)

The euphemisms that Congressman Doyle used to describe Ultra-Rightist publications are quite typical of Ultra-Rightist orators and scribes: "publications which habitually emphasize attacks upon the United States of America and the free world." Congressman Doyle, who was a member of the House Committee on Un-American Activities for 14 of the 15 years he served in Congress, could have performed an important service for the American people by exposing the extent to which the dissemination of fabrications and hoaxes has been done continually by that Committee. He might also have explained what he was doing as one of the main speakers at a rally of the virulent Ultra-Rightist *Project Alert*, in the Shrine Auditorium, Los Angeles, on December 14, 1961. At that meeting attorney Loyd Wright said: "I'm in favor of a preventive war." He made it very plain that he was in favor of attacking the Soviet Union. Supplementing the remarks of John Rousselot of the John Birch Society, ex-Congressman Donald Jackson, a former Member of the House Committee on Un-American Activities, heaped lavish praise on the John Birch Society, and a retired colonel of the Marine Corps, Mitchell Paige, declared that Chief Justice Earl Warren should be hanged! Congressman Doyle did not call upon his Committee to investigate any of these gentlemen. Both he and the Committee do not consider these people "Un-American."

In an excellent essay that he wrote for *New Republic* magazine, May 7, 1962, Congressman Morris K. Udall of Arizona tells of his own experiences in tracking down the phoney Khrushchev quotation. When he wrote to the late Conde Mc Ginley, editor of the hate sheet, *Common Sense*, inquiring as to his source of the Khrushchev quotation in his January 1962 issue, Mc Ginley replied:

As I remember, we took this from a very reliable publication, but I do not remember that it gave the date that Khrushchev stated this. Ordinarily, we like to have the date, *but this was so good, that we were tempted to run it*.[3]

The Congressman then relates that he received some plasticized cards that came to his office from Coast Federal Savings of Los Angeles, with the phoney Khrushchev quotation and the comment that these cards are being "distributed as a public service." A letter of inquiry brought a reply from Mr. S. A. Adair, "acting director, economics and education" of Coast Federal Savings. It consisted of a vague explanation of its possible origin and a promise to let the Congressman know when they succeed in tracking down the date of the alleged speech of Khrushchev. Adair explained that Coast Federal Savings picked it up from

3 The emphasis was added by Congressman Udall.

516

Senator Strom Thurmond's Speech, in the Congressional Record of July 26, 1961, and enclosed a copy of an article from *Time* magazine, "which contains a very similar statement by the Communist leader." Congressman Udall comments wryly: "Mr. Adair's sense of comparison seems a little liberal."

The Congressman then wrote a letter of inquiry to Senator Strom Thurmond, asking him for the source of the Khrushchev quotation. Up to the date of writing this essay for *New Republic*, no reply was received from the Senator. In a speech on the floor of Congress, February 11, 1963, Congressman Udall said:

Of late I have noticed in certain publications, and even in the Congress, an eagerness to quote famous personages in support of one's arguments without a corresponding eagerness to establish the accuracy of such quotations.

Last year, for example, I discovered that the Congressional Record carried a widely printed but spurious quotation attributed to Nikita Khrushchev. Even after the fictional nature of this quotation was brought to light there was no attempt on the part of those parties having circulated this false quotation to correct the record.

Apparently stung by the exposures and constant criticisms, Coast Federal Savings issued an 8½" × 11" leaflet, printed on both sides, which came to our attention in June of 1963. The title is:

THE MYSTERY OF THE "K QUOTE"!

We quote the opening paragraphs:

The Free Enterprise Department of Coast Federal Savings and Loan Association is searching for the authentication of the following statement made by Nikita Khrushchev sometime shortly before his visit to the United States in September of 1959:

"We cannot expect the Americans to jump from capitalism to communism, but we can assist their elected leaders in giving Americans small doses of socialism, until they suddenly awake to find they have communism."

Mr. K. has made other statements similar to this one, which are listed below, so that although the words are different, the thought is still the same.

As for the original quote, the Free Enterprise Department obtained the statement from Mr. William Aldrich of Anaheim. Mr.

Aldrich, who copied the quote verbatim from a magazine, was unable to locate the original magazine when we asked him for his verification of the quote several months after it had been printed in August of 1960.

In attempting to verify the complete quote, we wrote to many groups and organizations. The Library of Congress informed us that, although they could not find the quote, they did not have that quote on their list of fabricated quotes either.

Senator Strom Thurmond entered the quote into the "Congressional Record" for July 26, 1961, but he too is unable to produce the necessary documentation as to where he obtained the quote.

It seems that Coast Federal Savings simply compounded their "crime" when they issued THE MYSTERY OF THE "K QUOTE"! They start by saying they are searching for authentication of "the following statement made by Nikita Khrushchev." Honesty would dictate that they should have said "an alleged statement made by Nikita Khrushchev" or "a statement attributed to Nikita Khrushchev." The point is that, in the absence of authentication, it is dishonest to make the ex cathedra statement that the remarks *were made* by Khrushchev. They give the date of the alleged Khrushchev statement, but give no source of that date. Neither do they explain why they could find no wire service or newspaper story of that approximate time to verify the Khrushchev statement. They give as their source a Mr. Aldrich, but in the letter they had written to Congressman Udall they apparently gave Strom Thurmond's speech of July 26, 1961 as their source. With their admission of having printed the phoney Khrushchev statement in August of 1960, the possibility arises that Strom Thurmond got it from Coast Federal, and not vice versa. Furthermore, Coast Federal Savings admits that it printed the phoney statement and then went looking for authentication about 3 years later! Instead of graciously admitting error, Coast Federal further compounds its "crime" by giving out-of-context quotations (and alleged quotations), in which they claim "the thought is the same." It happens that the thought is not the same. Perhaps the best way to cure the Coast Federal Savings is for several people to start making their loan payments to some other bank, on the theory that "the thought is the same." What difference does it make if payments due to Coast Federal are paid to some other

518

bank? Isn't the thought the same, the thought that *some* bank should receive the money?

It would be nice to be able to say that this Khrushchev fabrication, having been thorougly exposed, is no longer being used. Unfortunately this is not the case, because we find it cropping up regularly. Typical was a leaflet issued around March 1967 by Harry Everingham, editor of the Ultra-Rightist *Fact Finder* and President of the Ultra-Rightist *We, the People*. As the late Conde Mc Ginley admitted, the Ultra-Rightists find it "too good" to pass up. Who cares about the truth? We're fighting Communism, aren't we? No one should express surprise if it is found that *we ourselves* are quoted some time in the future as having said:

"Who cares about the truth?"

## Khrushchev—The Diplomat

A pamphlet published by the Fascistic *Minutemen*, entitled *Principles of Guerrilla Warfare*, quotes Nikita Khrushchev as having said at the Leipzig, Germany Fair in March of 1959:

You should not take too seriously the treaties made with the imperialists. Lenin, too, signed a peace treaty after World War I that remained valid only so long as it proved necessary.

A little reflection by any intelligent person would lead one to the conclusion that, if Khrushchev had really made such a statement *in public*, he would be a first-class imbecile. Notwithstanding such considerations, Mr. Richard Arens, staff director of the House Committee on Un-American Activities, used that alleged quotation in a speech he made to the Daughters of the American Revolution on April 19, 1960. The alleged Khrushchev quotation was also used in a pamphlet written by Rosalie M. Gordon, entitled *How The Reds Won*, which is published by the Ultra-Rightist *America's Future*. When we queried Rosalie Gordon about the source of her quotation, she did not refer to any wire service dispatch or to any newspaper account of such a speech. Instead, she referred us to a book, *Prosperity Through Freedom*, by Lawrence Fertig. The index of the book lists Khrushchev as being mentioned on pages 19,

20, 27, 28, and 37. The quotation does not appear on any of these pages. However on page 35 we find:

"We value trade least for economic and most for political purposes," said Khrushchev in 1955, and Soviet theoreticians have further emphasized the point.

This does not correspond with the alleged quotation and, in any case, it refers to 1955, not 1959.

We checked the *New York Times Index* for the entire month of March, 1959. The *Times* reported in detail all of Khrushchev's speeches at the Leipzig Fair in its issues of March 5, 6, 7, and 8. A careful perusal of the microfilm record of those issues disclosed no speech or statement even remotely resembling the alleged Khrushchev quotation. A *New York Herald Tribune News Service*[4] dispatch from Leipzig by the veteran correspondent, Gaston Coblentz, quoted Khrushchev as publicly stating to a group of Eastern and Western businessmen at the Leipzig Fair:

Peaceful economy is the source of life, not rearmament. We must banish war. We are near to this goal.

Nowhere in the lengthy dispatch is there the slightest hint of the phoney quotation.

Khrushchev went directly from Leipzig to Berlin, where he made a speech the day after he left Leipzig. *The New York Times*, March 9, 1959, carried an Associated Press dispatch from Berlin, which reported Khrushchev as saying that a peace treaty must be concluded with Germany, and quoting him as saying:

We hope these peaceful suggestions will find acceptance in the Western world. We will undertake everything to eliminate the cold war and reduce international tension and misunderstanding between peoples. We will try to bring about peaceful coexistence.

We are asked to believe that, one day prior to making that public statement, Khrushchev made a statement advising his listeners that he does not take a serious view of treaties. Inasmuch as no one has ever accused Khrushchev of being an idiot, the quotation used by the *Minutemen, America's Future,* and

4 Riverside, Calif. *Daily Enterprise*, March 7, 1959.

Richard Arens of the House Committee on Un-American Activities must be considered a fabrication. Like the other fabrications, it has traveled from one Ultra-Rightist group to another. *Christian Economics* carried it in an editorial on September 11, 1965. *Fact Finder* picked it up for its issue of November 11, 1965.

In assessing the responsibility for initiating this alleged Khrushchev quotation, we find that *America's Future* published Rosalie Gordon's pamphlet on September 10, 1959; Richard Arens made his speech to the Daughters of the American Revolution on April 19, 1960; and the Minutemen published their booklet in 1961.

## Khrushchev—The Speech Magician

Any man who can influence people by a speech that he prepared and did not deliver—such a man has earned the title of speech magician. The *San Diego Union* carried a *New York Times News Service* dispatch in its issue of April 5, 1964, with this headline:

### NIKITA'S "SPEECH"
### ROCKS RED WORLD

Now, that is real powerful stuff! So, bracing ourselves for something new and sensational, we rubbed our eyes in amazement when we read the opening paragraph of this dispatch from Budapest:

Soviet Premier Nikita Khrushchev went boating on the Danube River yesterday while reverberations of a speech he never made echoed around the world.

The reporter goes on to speculate what would have been in that phantom speech, and tells us Khrushchev would undoubtedly have excoriated the Chinese Communists. This excursion into Alice-in-Wonderland journalism goes on for three paragraphs beyond the one we have quoted, and is followed by this:

Although Khrushchev did not make the speech, there appeared little reason to doubt that it had been prepared for him to deliver Friday night at a gala in Budapest's national opera house marking the start of the 19th anniversary of the World War II liberation of Hungary from the Nazis.

Then, putting on his best Sherlock Holmes gumshoes, our journalistic sleuth discovers that, at the last minute, Khrushchev substituted a speech with a milder version than the phantom speech. No source or authority is given for all these revelations, so it is anyone's guess what inspired this reporter to concoct a story out of nothing. This proves once again that any kind of story can be sold if it is an attack against the Soviet Union and the Communists.

On another occasion, Khrushchev said, in the course of one of his public speeches:

In this program (chemistry) the Soviet Union relies, from billions of rubles down to the last kopek, *on its own resources, its own potentialities,* and on cooperation with the fraternal socialist countries. As for our going to capitalist firms who wish to trade with us and make money from Soviet orders, *this is an additional factor* in the development of our chemistry.

The *U.S. News & World Report,* January 6, 1964, found this meaning in Khrushchev's pronouncements:

You can guess how desperate Khrushchev is when he had to ask the West to bail him out.

This leaves us wondering just who the magician is in this instance!

We were hardly prepared for our next experience with the Cold War propagandists. In October of 1966, we received a booklet from the Rev. Bob Wells, an Ultra-Rightist radio and pulpit preacher in that stronghold of Birchism, Orange County, California. The booklet is entitled *The Murderous Communist Conspiracy,* and is distributed by Anchor Bay Evangelistic Association, New Baltimore, Michigan. An inquiry brought us the information that it was written by the Rev. Marion Dye, 19600 Appleton Street, Detroit, Michigan. In the next to the last paragraph of the booklet, it states:

From reliable sources we learn that the Communist planned conquest of America calls for the LIQUIDATION OF 50 MILLION AMERICANS!!! Surely every thoughtful person will agree that the
TIME FOR ACTION IS NOW!

On the front cover, the foreword reads:

The compiler of these pages noted in the Detroit Free Press (1-18-61, city edition) the following statement spoken to Communist leaders, gathered in Moscow: "There will be war, if the capitalist nations try to resist the Communist (worldwide) victory. And war will mean the killing of 500 million to 750 million people within sixty days." The writer believes that any system which has as its top leader a character WICKED ENOUGH to launch a war that would kill 500 million within sixty days should be viewed with intense alarm by every decent man, woman, and child on earth. A system led by such WICKED LEADERS should be vigorously opposed and thoroughly exposed by every one who is capable of lending any help in its exposure. Indeed, it may be a matter of life and death to every lover of freedom to help expose this murderous conspiracy.

On October 28, 1966, we sent the Rev. Marion L. Dye the following letter:

Dear Rev. Dye:

I am currently working on a book, which is the culmination of almost 5 years of research and investigation. A portion of my book is being devoted to an exposé of the use of fabrications, distortions of truth, and out-of-context quotations. I find that your pamphlet, *The Murderous Communist Conspiracy*, contains a number of fabrications and distortions of truth, and I am writing to you as a matter of courtesy and fair play. In other words, I believe that you are entitled to state your defense to any charges that I make.

The outside cover of your booklet purports to have a quotation from Khrushchev, based on a story in the *Detroit Free Press* of January 18, 1961. I have before me a photocopy of the story in that issue of the *Detroit Free Press*. Your "quotation" has two sentences: The first consists of the *Newspaper's* words, which you have put in Khrushchev's mouth, and you have placed quotation marks around them. This is falsification, Rev. Dye, because quotation marks are permissible only for exact words of a person, not someone's paraphrasing. The second sentence that you attribute to Khrushchev is *not* in the *Free Press* story, and in any case, it was never uttered by Khrushchev. I have seen the same statement attributed to Mao Tse-tung, but he also never said it.

On page 3 you have a garbled and distorted quotation from the Communist Manifesto.

On page 4 you quote Marx as saying: "The end justifies the means." Marx never said it.

On page 7 you have two quotations attributed to Lenin. He never said these things.

On page 8 you quote Lunacharsky. It is a fabrication.

On page 8 you have another garbled quotation from the Communist Manifesto.

On page 8 you have a phoney Stalin quotation, three phoney Lenin quotations, and two phoney Besbozhnik quotations.

On page 8 you refer to something called *ABC of Communism,* but you do not mention who issued it. Can you tell me?

On page 9 you have a phoney Marx quotation.

On page 9 you have two phoney Lenin quotations.

On page 9 you have a garbled quotation from the Communist Manifesto.

On page 9 you have two phoney Zinoviev quotations.

On page 9 you have a phoney Kollontay quotation.

On page 11 you have a phoney Lenin quotation.

If you can document any of these items, I earnestly bespeak your cooperation in sending me the proof. If you cannot document them, please tell me where you obtained them.

Please let me hear from you at your earliest convenience.

Thank you.

> *Faithfully yours,*
> MORRIS KOMINSKY

The postal receipt shows that the Rev. M. L. Dye signed for the letter upon its arrival on November 1, 1966. No reply was received. On December 27, 1966, we sent a follow-up letter via certified mail. It was returned to us unopened and stamped "REFUSED."

The Rev. Marion L. Dye not only can read things in Khrushchev's speeches that are not there, but he can also dream up "reliable sources" to prove that Khrushchev wants to bury 50 million Americans.

# CHAPTER XI

## Stalin's Great Secret

*Life* magazine of April 23, 1956, carried a lengthy article by Isaac Don Levine, entitled "A Document on Stalin as Czarist Spy." A companion article of even greater length was included in the same issue, in support of Levine's thesis. The latter essay is written by Alexander Orlov, who purports to be a former Soviet intelligence officer.

An excellent analysis of the Levine-Orlov story was presented in the form of a paper, by Mr. Martin K. Tytell, to the New York Meeting of the American Association for the Advancement of Science on December 29, 1956. Mr. Tytell is one of this country's outstanding experts in his field. He is a Lecturer on Questioned Documents at New York University's Institute of Criminology; a Lecturer on Police Science at Brooklyn College; a Lane Scholar at New York University; and the author of numerous magazine articles. With his kind permission, his scientific paper follows:

On April 23, 1956, *Life Magazine,* one of the most influential mass-circulation media in the United States, published an article by the prominent journalist, Isaac Don Levine, entitled "Stalin's Great Secret." The substance of the article was that the late dictator of the Soviet Union, Joseph Stalin, had been a Czarist spy in pre-revolutionary days, working for the government against his revolutionary comrades. In support of this contention was produced a typewritten document purportedly signed by a Colonel Yeremin in St. Petersburg on July 12, 1913.

To substantiate the authenticity of this document, which identified Stalin as a Czarist spy, another letter, an official communication from the Russian Acting Director of the Department of Police dated November 5, 1912, was presented as a "standard," in document examiners' parlance. The *Life* article asserted that the Stalin-Yeremin document and the standard were both typed on the "same model and same make" of typewriter. Mr. Levine cited a noted document examiner, Mr. Albert D. Osborn, in support of this finding. Mr. Levine's article was later expanded into a book published earlier this year by Coward-McCann.

The *Life* article was of great interest to me, and I read it carefully. Having devoted a lifetime to the study of type and typewriters, and having engaged in document examination for many years, I was especially attracted by the comparison of the Stalin-Yeremin letter and the standard, as presented in photographs accompanying the article. Even working from the photographs reprinted in the magazine, it was obvious to me that these documents were *not* typed on the same model typewriter, and in that respect at least the *Life* article was inaccurate.

The next day, I obtained from *Life* a number of reprints of the article. These reprints were distributed by me to my classes in Police Science at Brooklyn College for examination. The students in my classes easily detected twenty-five differences in type design between the two documents, and none of the students in the group was of the opinion that the Stalin-Yeremin letter and the standard could have been typed on the same model or make of machine.

My interest in questioned documents led me to request an examination of the originals of both letters. I communicated regarding the Stalin-Yeremin letter with Mr. Levine, the author, and with Leland Stanford University Library concerning the standard. I could obtain the original of neither; the Stalin-Yeremin letter is in a vault of the Tolstoy Foundation, while the Leland Stanford people could not locate the standard. However, I did secure a good photostat copy of the Stalin-Yeremin letter from the Tolstoy Foundation, and a good photostat copy of the standard from Mr. Levine.

But my investigation of the Stalin-Yeremin letter, which eventually involved my traveling through several European countries, interviewing people who might have knowledge of this matter, and examining several thousand documents, has convinced me that the letter is a fraud.

Now, I would like to make clear that my investigation concerns the authenticity of the Stalin-Yeremin letter only as a problem in document examination. I say this because I understand that in some circles the letter has led to political controversy in which I have no interest whatsoever. In addition my findings are not to be construed as impugning the motives of *Life,* Mr. Levine or Mr. Osborn. As a document examiner, however, I am concerned with exposing fraudulent documents, and the Stalin-Yeremin letter is a fraud.

Because it seems the most logical way in which to tell the story, I should like to relate the course of my investigation chronologically, from that day when my classes at Brooklyn College and I examined the questioned document and the standard.

The Levine book and article identify the typewriter used to produce the documents as a Russian machine made by Remington and exported to Russia in pre-revolutionary days. An investigation at the Remington Plant in Elmira and at the offices of the company in this city established that the standard was indeed produced by a Remington machine. However, the questioned document, as I shall refer to the Stalin-Yeremin letter, was not written on a Remington at all.

My investigation led me abroad, to Germany, in July of this year. In Frankfurt, I found that the questioned document was in fact written on an Adler—a machine manufactured in Germany. The Adler factory was demolished by bombing, and therefore a determination of the date of the machine used for the questioned document was impossible. However, company employees who had been manufacturing typewriters for many years, stated that Russian type which produced the questioned document was first manufactured in the year 1912. But the questioned document could not have been typed in 1912 or even 1913, but much later since the type is worn and battered. The questioned document must have been written many years after the manufacture of the machine used. I have samples of type taken from the 1912 Adler, which may be compared with the questioned document in support of my identification.

While in Germany, I retraced some of the steps described by Mr. Levine in his book. On page 107 of the book, STALIN'S GREAT SECRET, Mr. Levine tells of his search for a Dobroliubov, who had been an officer of the Okhrana, or Czarist Secret Police. The author related how he visited the Greek Orthodox Church on Nachodstrasse in Charlottenburg, Berlin, where the priest "responded instantly" to the name of Dobroliubov, and he dates this incident some time in March 1950. I visited the same church and spoke to the priest, who had held his office for many years. He knew nothing about Dobroliubov, and did not recollect meeting any American or anyone else who had mentioned that name. In fact, there was a second priest who assisted at the church whom I interviewed, who likewise knew nothing about Dobroliubov and did not recollect any inquiry about such a person.

Mr. Igor Fromke, a man of thirty-nine, who serves as a ministrant, or mass servant, who had been a prisoner of war of the Americans and speaks fluent English as well as Russian and German, offered to assist me in my research. In brief summary, let Fromke tell his own part of the story:

"On Sunday, July 15, I was called out of the altar to meet an American who introduced himself as Martin K. Tytell. He asked could I speak English and what time the church service would be over. After the last sermon, Mr. Tytell again approached me and Father Sergius and put the following questions to us: Could Father Sergius remember an American writer, Isaac Don Levine, coming to Berlin in March, 1950, asking about a sexton who should work at our church for a long period before the last war by the name of Dobroliubov? Father Sergius said that such a sexton was never at our church and he can't remember Mr. Don Levine. But since our church has always had two priests, he said we also should contact Father Michael. On July 16th at 9:30 A.M., me and Mr. Tytell met again at the entrance to the church, went at once inside and saw Father Michael preparing for his duty. We asked him the same questions. Father Michael denied them even more strictly and assured me that he doesn't know any such man."

In the Levine book, also on page 107, it is stated: "The search for Dobroliubov brought me to Wiesbaden and ended there, in the adjoining cemetery. The good local priest had taken me to his grave. He had recently died, and with him lay buried many secrets of the Okhrana."

The next day I left Berlin for Wiesbaden, taking Fromke with me to act as an intrepreter for a visit to the German Crime Laboratory, still in search of clues to the typewritten Stalin-Yeremin letter. A short distance away lay the beautiful chapel referred to by Mr. Levine on page 107, and I spoke to the local priest mentioned there. This priest too knew nothing of Dobroliubov, and had never heard the name in his tenure at the church dating back to 1908, and again let Fromke tell it:

"Near to that office (the crime laboratories) on a hill called Nevoberg is erected a beautiful Russian Orthodox Church in honor to a dead grand duchess of Russia and for her sepulchre. We were led to see the old Russian priest in an adjoining small cottage. This still lively and erect old patriarch of eighty-four years, who performs his duties in Wiesbaden now for fifty-five years, this priest whose memory is functioning well in spite of his age, never saw a Mr. Levine at all, and in 1950 especially, never talked to him about a man named Dobroliubov, and never showed him the grave of such a person. The same thing was confirmed by his daughter, who is speaking English fluently. We also checked the books about all the funerals since 1945 up to now, and couldn't find any trace of a Dobroliubov. There is also no grave in the Russian cemetery with such a name. I for myself, can only say that, belonging since my early childhood to the church in Berlin Nachodstrasse, I don't know any sexton with such a name. The same applies to my mother who is also an old member of this church. Our long time sexton and church warden cannot be that man. He has quite another name. Living in the Russian-occupied zone of Eastern Germany, his name cannot be quoted for reasons of safety. But no other sexton was employed during all that time (25 years)."

I went through the adjoining cemetery; there was no tombstone for Dobroliubov. There was no record in the church registry of deaths, going back to 1945, of a burial of such an individual or anyone bearing a name similar to Dobroliubov.

The "lively and erect old patriarch," Levine's "good local priest," who led him to see Dobroliubov's grave, himself gave me, voluntarily, the following affidavit:

"Wiesbaden, 17-VII-1956. I, the signer of this, am on duty at the Russian Orthodox Church in Wiesbaden since September 1906, till today, except the time of the First World War (1914-1919). With me there was not at our church on no kind of job any person with the name Dobroliubov. Similarly on our Russian cemetery (sic) is no grave with the same name. About my encounter with an Amer-

528

ican journalist Mister Don Levine I don't remember anything."
Signed: Dean of the Orthodox Russian Church in Wiesbaden, Archpriest Paul Adamantov.

I then went to Hamburg, where I consulted Professors Tange and Johansen, heads of the Slavonic and Finnish departments of the Hamburg University. They examined my copy of the Yeremin-Stalin document and labeled it a fraud. They referred me to the archives in Helsinki, Finland, for documentary proof.

From Hamburg, I made a side-tour to Varel, near Bremen, where I was able to interview two men who had worked in government offices in St. Petersburg in Czarist days. Col. Feodor Yurieff of the Russian army worked as a government prosecutor from 1904 to 1917, while Stepan Rusanow worked from 1908 to 1918 as a typist in various offices in St. Petersburg. They had seen many Remington machines in the course of their work, while the Adler was a stranger to them. I have affidavits from both these individuals.

Later in Helsinki, I found that a tremendous quantity of documentary evidence dating back to Czarist days is available. In fact, there is a question as to why Mr. Levine chose an obscure document from Leland Stanford University Library as a standard, when thousands of authentic official communications of Czarist days are available in Finland.

Finland before World War I, was a province of Russia, and the same Yeremin who supposedly signed the questioned document identifying Stalin as a spy, served as chief of the gendarmerie of the province. I examined more than 3,000 documents, including 85 signed by Yeremin. None of the documents was typed on an Adler machine; as for the signatures, the difference is so obvious that no further comment is needed.

I was assisted in my research in the Helsinki archives by a trained librarian. In extract, here is her statement:

"I, Maria Widnas, Ph.D., University of Helsinki-Helsingfors, elder assistant librarian at the University Library, was asked by the University Rector's secretary on July 25 to meet Mr. Martin Tytell, Examiner of Disputed Documents, and go with him to the state Archives in search for documents dated from July, 1913, and issued by the Russian Ministry of Internal Affairs, Police Department, Special Section, to compare them with the document brought to Finland by Mr. Tytell, issued by the Ministry of Internal Affairs, head of the Department of the Special Section of the Police Department on 12th July 1913 (Nr. 2898), and signed by Eremin (Yeremin). We went through three thousand documents issued by the Police Department, but we did not find even one bearing the name Director of Special Section of the Police Department (Zavedujuscij Osobym Otedelom Departamenta Policii). The opinion of the archivists who have spent their lifetime in filing Russian documents, and especially those of the Governor General's Office's Chancellery, which is the only place where documents sent by Russian authorities can be found in Finland, is that the document shown by Mr. Tytell must be a photograph of a forgery.

"We spent the first day of research assisted by Archivist Salmelma, M.A., and Archivist Valoniemi, M.A., who was kind enough to have photostats (of genuine Yeremin letters) arranged for us. In the next few days, we looked with the help of Archivist Salmelma through all the documents even of 1914 from the Chancellery of the Governor General of Finland. We found some more documents signed by Eremin. The handwriting of all of these signatures of Eremin, the first of them dated 19th July, 1913, is different from the signature of the document belonging in photostat to Mr. Tytell, which is the second reason why the archivists, Seitkari, Salmelma, Valoniemi, and also the elder Archivist Blomstedt, considered that the document brought from America could not be authentic. On July 27th we went with Mr. Tytell to the Central Police to make sure that there were no Russian documents preserved elsewhere in the archives of Helsinki."

Certified and Signed: Maria Widnas, Dr. Phil., Elder Assistant Librarian.

As further corroborative evidence, among the Helsinki documents I found a government order appointing Yeremin to his post in Finland, dated June 21, 1913. A piece of correspondence indicating that Yeremin was in the midst of his business in Helsinki dated July 19, 1913, was also uncovered. Mr. Levine is aware that the questioned document, dated July 12, 1913 from St. Petersburg is inconsistent with the time of his appointment in Helsinki, but has said that it is possible that Yeremin did not report to his new post immediately upon assignment. But the document dated July 19, which indicates that Yeremin was fully in charge of his post in Finland and apparently working there for some time, makes it most unlikely that he could have been in St. Petersburg just a week before.

The Finnish authorities were most cooperative, and I have photostats and microfilm of numerous documents which have been offered to Mr. Levine and *Life* for their inspection.

All of the circumstances surrounding the Stalin-Yeremin letter, therefore, support the finding that this document is fraudulent.

I might add, as a postscript, that I have offered my findings to *Life,* and to Mr. Levine. But truth usually has a difficult time catching up with falsehood, so that it is unlikely that this bit of research will ever gain the circulation given the fraudulent document. (See pages 531-533.—M. K.)

Miss Millie Salwen, who attended the meeting of scientists at which Mr. Tytell read his paper, sent a lengthy description of what took place to the West Coast Communist newspaper, the *Daily People's World*. From its January 8, 1957 issue, we quote the final one-third of Miss Salwen's report:

All these facts, and more, were gathered into a report, backed by

# COMPARISON CHART of
# QUESTIONED DOCUMENT and
# TYPE of AMERICAN MANUFACTURE

| Questioned Document | М | И | Л | О | С | Т | В | Ы | Й | Г | У | Д | а | р | Ь |
|---|---|---|---|---|---|---|---|---|---|---|---|---|---|---|---|
| Remington No 30 | М | к | л | о | с | т | в | ы | й | Г | у | д | а | р | ь |
| Remington No 32 | М | к | л | о | с | т | в | ы | й | Г | у | д | а | р | ь |
| Remington No 33 | М | И | Л | О | С | Т | В | Ы | Й | Г | у. | д | а | р | ь |
| Remington No 35 | М | И | Л | О | С | Т | В | Ы | Й | Г | У | Д | а | р | Ь |
| Remington No 49 | М | И | Л | О | С | Т | Ь | Ы | Й | Г | у | Д | а | р | Ь |
| Underwood No 506 | М | И | Л | О | С | Т | В | Ы | Й | Г | У | Д | а | р | Ь |
| Smith-Corona No 51 | М | И | Л | О | С | Т | В | Ы | Й | Г | У | Д | а | р | Ь |
| Royal Russian Key. | М | И | Л | О | С | Т | В | Ы | Й | Г | У | Д | а | р | Ь |
| Underwood No 1055 | М | И | Л | О | С | Т | В | Ы | Й | Г | У | Д | а | р | Ь |

photographic proof, and made available to the press last weekend. Tytell read it in open session when the 300 scientists met.

Levine was there. He had been invited to speak in rebuttal. When his turn came, he turned to introduce a woman he brought with him, Mme. Elizaveta Lermolo, who wrote a book last year, one of the covey of people whose careers were built on exposing communism. She rose to applause and informed the scientists that she knew, through the grapevine, that Stalin had been a Czarist spy.

Then, Levine spoke, for 48 minutes. For 40 minutes of that time he spoke of corroborative evidence that keeps coming to his attention, but which he cannot divulge. Whenever history has called someone a spy, he said, it's eventually shown to be true. When there's smoke, there is fire.

He said the State Department has proof of the validity of the documents, but that it won't be released for ten years. Then, at the end, he tackled the evidence against him.

The name of that Czarist officer wasn't Dobroliubov, as it had

531

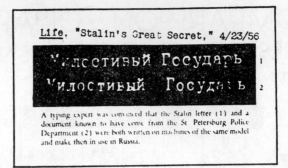

COMPARISON OF TYPE DESIGN CHARACTERISTICS BETWEEN THE QUESTIONED AND STANDARD

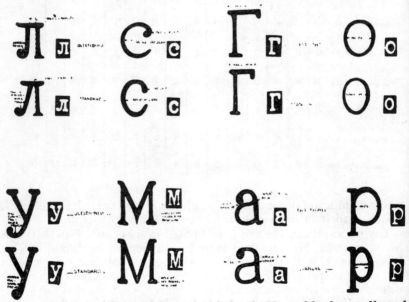

been printed in *Life,* and later, in his book. He suddenly recollected that it was really Dubrolovski. In an insinuating aside, he said he would go to Europe to prove it if he had the money that Mr. Tytell seemed to have at his disposal.

As for the age of the typewriter, he had just come across proof that it was really made in 1909. But he didn't have the evidence with him.

And he had an explanation for the visible contrast between Yeremin's actual signature on 85 documents on file in the Helsinki library, and the scrawl at the bottom of his "Stalin" letter.

# QUESTIONED DOCUMENT

Милостввыйгдударь

Милоствѣйй Гудар ь

# THE ADLER TYPEWRITER

# COMPARISON CHART

## Questioned Document Signature
## With
## Known Standard Signatures

QUESTIONED
SIGNATURE
'STALIN - YEREMIN' Document

STANDARD SIGNATURES
of YEREMIN selected at
random from 85 photographed
at the Helsinki, Finland
Government Archive.

**Martin K. Tytell   Document Analyst**
**123 Fulton Street, New York 38, NY.**

It was probable, he guessed, that Yeremin actually had two signatures, one for ordinary documents, and another, secret handwriting, for letters like this.

But handwriting analysts who examined them say that Yeremin could never have written both. The signatures differ in too many ways—even if a man tried to disguise his writing, he could only change it superficially. They were definite: Yeremin never signed the letter that Levine produced.

Levine turned back to Tytell. His voice rising in tones of the victim of persecution he demanded, "Who in Washington put you up to this? Who in Washington wants to destroy me?"

It was apparent that, face to face with Tytell's report, Levine felt he was destroyed.

In addition to the results of Mr. Tytell's superb research and investigation, other evidence was presented to prove the dubious nature of Isaac Don Levine's "discovery." *Life*, in its issue of May 14, 1956, carried some letters critical of the Levine-Orlov thesis. Madame Nina Spiridovich complained that Don Levine's article of April 23, 1956, showed a picture of her husband, General Alexander Spiridovich, which was *not* his picture. W. J. Walter expressed the opinion that: "The circulation of these facts would give an immense momentum to the revolutionary forces gaining more foothold there."[1] A professional anti-Communist writer, Bertram D. Wolfe, expressed general approval of the Don Levine-Orlov articles, but pointed out that some of Don Levine's evidence is dubious. He wrote: "In 1952 I was consulted by an official of the State Department, expert on Russia, concerning a document which seems to be the one you have now published. We came to the conclusion that the charge was plausible but difficult to prove, and that the results of publication at that time were incalculable." It would seem from Bertram Wolfe's story that Don Levine's "documents" were reject merchandise. At one point in his article, Don Levine quotes some alleged proof from a book by Leon Trotsky. Wolfe points out that another person completed that particular Trotsky book after his death. Wolfe also states that Don Levine had claimed, in a newspaper story, that Stalin was arrested in a Czarist police raid on April 15, 1906. Wolfe adds that this could not be possible, because Stalin was known to have been in Stockholm, Sweden at the time.

The best letter printed by *Life* in the same issue came from David Dallin, a lecturer and writer, with 10 books on Russia to his credit. He made the following points:

1. In 1917, after the revolution, the police official, Vissarionov, to whom Stalin was supposed to have been reporting, was interrogated by a special investigation commission. He was very

---

[1] The letter writer was alluding to possible attempts to overthrow the Soviet Government.

cooperative, giving names, dates, and places. He did *not* mention Stalin, although there was nothing to inhibit him from doing so.

2. Stepan Beletsky, Vissarionov's superior, was also interrogated and made no mention of Stalin.

3. After 1917, the archives of the Czarist police were made public in the Russian newspapers, and if Stalin had in fact been a Czarist spy, he would have fled. Instead he continued to live in Petrograd and carried out his functions as a member of the Bolshevik Central Committee.

4. Orlov, in his article, had quoted from a document that he had not seen, but relied on what a brother-in-law told him was in that document.

5. The alleged police records that Don Levine relied upon contained usage of language that was not the standard way in which Czarist police records were kept.

6. "..... careful analysis leads me to the conclusion that the document of the Russian police department which he presents cannot be accepted as genuine, and that it was fabricated, probably after the last war, somewhere in the Far East."

7. The question must be answered, where was the Don Levine "document" from 1913 to 1947? If it were genuine, it would have to be smuggled out of Russia between 1918 and 1921, because after 1921 all the Siberian Okhrana archives were in Bolshevik hands. If it had been smuggled out, both the Japanese and the German governments would have paid a fabulous sum for such a document.

8. Finally, "the facts do not confirm the specific accusations made by Mr. Orlov and Mr. Levine."

*Life* gave Don Levine access to these letters from its readers, so that he had an opportunity to respond in the same issue in which they appeared. His response was pitifully inadequate, relying mainly on advice that his forthcoming book on the subject should be consulted!

Isaac Don Levine's book, "Stalin's Great Secret", from which his *Life* article was excerpted, was reviewed in *Saturday Review*, September 15, 1956, by Professor Michael T. Florinsky of Columbia University. Professor Florinsky is the author of *Russia: A History and an Interpretation* and other books. The professor points out that, when Don Levine was writing a

535

Stalin biography 25 years earlier, he had rejected the Czarist spy theory as unfounded. Examining some of the alleged evidence that Don Levine claims to have since uncovered, Professor Florinsky asks:

Why did Mr. Levine, a journalist with a flair for sensational revelations, keep quiet about his discovery for over five years? "Because," he writes, "I felt that it would have fallen on deaf ears before Moscow itself shocked the whole world out of the Stalinst mythology." This is a surprising statement. Since 1947, especially following the outbreak of the Korean War in 1950, the popularity of the U.S.S.R. and Stalin declined markedly and there is nothing to indicate that the revelation of his betrayal of the Revolution, supported by adequate evidence would have been ineffective.

The Professor concludes that Levine's "documentary evidence" "is totally unconvincing."

Unlike some of the other hoaxes, the Levine-Orlov yarn seems to have fallen flat on its face. Perhaps the reason is that it taxes human credulity just a little too much!

# CHAPTER XII

## The Great Crusade: The Psychopolitics Hoax

Almost from its inception on November 7, 1917, a Great Crusade commenced against the Soviet Union. No epoch in history has produced the quantity and unique characteristics of the hoaxes that have been invented about the Soviet Union during the past fifty years. One can only marvel at the ingenuity and resourcefulness of some of these liars. Not the least of these is the Rev. Kenneth Goff of Englewood, Colorado, with his hoax booklet, entitled *Brain-Washing, A Synthesis of the Russian Textbook on Psychopolitics*.

The title itself, when carefully analyzed, reveals the basic deception of the entire booklet. One speaks of a condensation of a book or a synopsis of a book, but whoever heard of a *synthesis* of a book? Webster's New International Dictionary, Second Edition, Unabridged, 1949, defines synthesis: "Composition or combination of parts, elements, etc., so as to form a whole." Accordingly, it is clear that Goff has *concocted* something. This is further borne out by the fact that the word *psychopolitics* is not listed in the 1949 Webster dictionary; it is not listed in the American College Dictionary, published in 1963; and it is not listed in Webster's Seventh New Collegiate Dictionary published in 1963. One can also brand his booklet a fraud by citing the fact that psychopolitics has no equivalent word in the Russian language. Consequently, there is not and could not have been a Russian Textbook on Psychopolitics! Perhaps that is the reason that Goff gives his own definition of psychopolitics on the front cover, underneath the title:

### Psychopolitics

the art and science of asserting and maintaining dominion over the thoughts and loyalties of individuals, officers, bureaus, and masses, and the effecting of the conquest of enemy nations through "mental healing."

Goff's definition gives us the hint of some things that become clear from a careful study of his booklet:

1. It is a crude parody on the fraudulent "Protocols of the Learned Elders of Zion."

2. It is a vicious attack against the sciences and professions of psychology and psychiatry, as well as against the entire legitimate mental health movement.

3. It raises the Red Scare hysteria to new paranoidal heights.

On the first page, Goff has his own introduction. Among other things, he tells us that an example of the psychopolitical warfare being waged against us by the Communists is:

> ... the attempt to establish a mental Siberia in Alaska, which was called for in the Alaskan Mental Health Bill. A careful study of this Bill will make you see at once that the land set aside under the allotment could not be for that small territory, and the Bill within itself establishes such authority that it could be turned into a prison camp under the guise of mental health for everyone who raises their voice against Communism and the hidden government operating in our nation.

At this point, it would be well for the reader to go back to the final segment of chapter 1, and read again our discussion of The Alaska Mental Health Hoax. Without any further evidence, his remarks about the Alaska Mental Health Bill prove that Goff is a mountebank.

In the next to the last paragraph, Goff tells us that the book was used in underground schools and contains a speech delivered by Lavrenti Beria, the head of Stalin's secret police, "to the American students in the Lenin University prior to 1936." Goff does not explain why he can only give "prior to 1936" as the date of the alleged speech. It is obvious that this gives him great maneuverability, but as we shall soon see, he outsmarted himself on the date. While he tells us on the front cover that this book is a synthesis of the *Russian Textbook on Psychopolitics,* he claims on the introductory page that his material comes from another source. In his typically obscurantist style, Goff says:

> The text in the book in general is from the Communist Manual of Instructions of Psychopolitical Warfare, and was used in America for the training of Communist cadre. The only revision in this book is the summary, which was added by the Communists after the

538

atomic bomb came into being. In its contents you can see the diabolical plot of the enemies of Christ and America, as they seek to conquer our nation by subjecting the minds of our people to their will by various sinister means.

There are some strange facts in connection with Goff's claims. First of all, no one has ever produced a copy of that *Russian Textbook on Psychopolitics*. Secondly, no one but Goff has ever seen that "Communist Manual of Instructions of Psychopolitical Warfare." None of the stool pigeons planted in the Communist Party by John E. Hoover has ever been able to pick up a copy of that "Manual." Thirdly, neither the House Committee on Un-American Activities nor the Senate Internal Security Subcommittee has been willing to accept Goff's "documents." They have stooped pretty low at times, but Goff's concoction is too fraudulent even for these Committees. Fourthly, Goff does not explain how he obtained "the summary, which was added by the Communists after the atomic bomb came into being." The atomic bomb came into being some 6 years after Goff had left the Communist Party, and he no longer had access to secret "documents," real or imaginary.

The alleged speech by Beria, which follows on the next page and one-half of Goff's opus, is enough to cause decent people to feel very distressed. Only a depraved person would utter or write such anti-social statements. There is ample proof, however, that Beria did not make that speech. On July 29, 1963, we sent Goff's booklet to Senator Thomas Kuchel's office, with a request that it be evaluated by the various intelligence and research agencies, to which a member of Congress has access. On January 6, 1964, Mr. Ewing Hass, the Senator's administrative assistant, sent us the results of what appears to have been an exhaustive investigation. Enclosed with his letter was a photocopy of a report from the Department of State, which we quote in full:

Thank you for your communication of October 14, forwarding a booklet entitled *Brain Washing, A Synthesis of the Russian Text Book on Psychopolitics*. You asked for any information the Department might have to enable you to assess the authenticity of the text of an address, printed in the booklet, which was allegedly made by former U.S.S.R. Minister for Internal Affairs, Lavrenti P. Beria, to a class of American students at Lenin University.

The Department is unable to find any indications that this

speech was ever made or that Minister Beria ever addressed a group of American students on any subject.

I am returning the booklet, as requested. If the Department can be of further assistance, please do not hesitate to let me know.

Sincerely yours,
FREDERICK G. DUTTON
*Assistant Secretary*

If we are to believe Kenneth Goff's version of the alleged Beria speech, we have to believe that he has better intelligence sources than the Department of State's Bureau of External Research and Intelligence, which in turn has access to the data of the Central Intelligence Agency:

Mr. Ewing Hass wrote to us:

Additionally, through discussion with various people here in Washington, it has been pointed out to us that Beria was not in Moscow until 1937, and the speech in question was allegedly given prior to that time. Also, psychopolitics is not a word found in the Soviet jargon, and we have not been advised of any instance where it has been used. Also, we gather, it would not have been normal for Beria to have given this type of speech at the particular time indicated.

In an excellent essay entitled "The Far Right's Fight Against Mental Health," which appeared in *Look* magazine, January 26, 1965, Donald Robinson discusses briefly Goff's pamphlet and the alleged Beria speech. He concludes his examination of the evidence with these remarks:

Absolutely no evidence has been produced to support the assertion that Beria ever made such a speech. Benjamin Mandel, research director of the Senate Internal Security Subcommittee, has officially stated: "We have no grounds to believe that this document is genuine."

The alleged Beria speech itself has ample internal evidence of its fraudulent nature. It begins with:

American students at the Lenin University, I welcome your attendance at these classes on Psychopolitics.

Thus does the opening sentence establish that he is talking to *Americans only.* Seven paragraphs later, in that same speech,

540

Beria is addressing them as if they are *foreigners* living in the U.S.A. There can be no other interpretation of these exhortations:

> You must dominate as respected men the fields of psychiatry and psychology. You must dominate the hospitals and universities. You must carry forward the myth that only a European doctor is competent in the field of insanity and thus excuse amongst you the high incidence of foreign birth and training. If and when we seize Vienna you shall have then a common ground of meeting and can come and take your instructions as worshippers of Freud along with other psychiatrists.

In addition to the contradiction of addressing American students as if they are not Americans, the clear implication of the Beria remarks is that he is talking to a group of psychiatrists. There is no evidence that the Lenin University conducted classes for American psychiatrists, and no one has ever located an American psychiatrist who attended Lenin University.

"Beria" concludes his speech with these remarks:

> By psychopolitics create chaos. Leave a nation leaderless. Kill our enemies. And bring to Earth, through Communism, the greatest peace Man has ever known.

There are two things to be said about these alleged remarks. First, that nowhere in the published speeches or writings of Communist leaders can one find anything which parallels these remarks. Secondly, the remarks are so idiotic that only a feeling of revulsion could have arisen from a group of psychiatrists, and Beria would have to be an imbecile to be making remarks that would antagonize the students.

Two paragraphs, which are typical of the entire booklet, should be sufficient for the reader to grasp the true nature of the Rev. Kenneth Goff's production:

> Exercises in sexual attack on patients should be practiced by the psychopolitical operative to demonstrate the inability of the patient under pain-drug hypnosis to recall the attack, while indoctrinating a lust for further sexual activity on the part of the patient. Sex, in all animals, is a powerful motivator, and is no less so in the animal Man, and the occasioning of sexual liaison between females of a target family and indicated males, under the control of the psychopolitical operative, must be demonstrated to be possible with

complete security for the psychopolitical operative, thus giving into his hands an excellent weapon for the breaking down of familial relations and consequent public disgraces for the psychopolitical target.

Just as a dog can be trained, so can a man be trained. Just as a horse can be trained, so can a man be trained. Sexual lust, masochism, and any other desirable perversion can be induced by pain-drug hypnosis and the benefit of Psychopolitics.

The evidence adduced up to this point would seem to be adequate to prove that Kenneth Goff's booklet is an unmitigated fraud. Realizing however, that Ultra-Rightist zealots will find it hard to accept factual data that disturbs their prejudices and misconceptions, we have left no stone unturned in our research and investigation.

On July 23, 1963, we addressed a letter of inquiry to the Research Director of the Senate Subcommittee on Internal Security. On July 29, 1963, the Research Director, Mr. Benjamin Mandel, wrote us:

I would have to see the *Russian Text Book on Psychopolitics* to which you refer to judge its authenticity. I do know that there is considerable phoney material floating around on this subject.

On September 3, 1963, we sent another letter to Mr. Mandel, together with a copy of Kenneth Goff's booklet. We asked a series of questions regarding Goff's booklet and the alleged *Russian Text Book on Psychopolitics* and the alleged Beria speech. On September 12, 1963, Mr. Mandel sent us a short letter, to which was attached a carbon copy of a report he received from Dr. Sergius Yakobson, Senior Specialist for Russian Affairs of the Library of Congress. We quote its entire contents:

With reference to your telephone inquiry of September 9:

Upon a number of occasions, the Library of Congress has been asked for information about the availability of a Russian textbook or manual on psychopolitics and of a speech by L. P. Beria on this subject in the Library's collections. Since these requests have not been accompanied by an indication of the original Russian title or of the place and date of publication of such a book, it has not been possible to provide any answer to these inquiries. A general examination of speeches and other writings by L. P. Beria which are available in the Library of Congress has not revealed any reference to such a topic.

542

One can sympathize with Dr. Yakobson's complaint, but the fact remains that Kenneth Goff's pamphlet gives no information about the original Russian title, the place of publication, and the date of publication—and for obvious reasons.

In addition to the Report from the Library of Congress, Mr. Mandel enclosed a fact sheet; we quote verbatim:

## KENNETH GOFF

Kenneth Goff was a member of the Communist Party and the Young Communist League from May 2, 1936 to October 9, 1939. He used the alias of John Keats. (Vol. 9 of the Report of the Committee on Un-American Activities for 1939)

For many years Goff was an assistant to Gerald L. K. Smith in his Christian Nationalist Crusade. In 1948 Goff left Smith, complaining that he was being exploited by Smith in that he was forced to put up at third rate hotels while the leader (Smith) and his wife invariably stopped at the best hotels. (*A Measure of Freedom*, Arnold Forster, p. 40.)

In 1946, Goff received a suspended sentence for passing fraudulent checks; and in 1948 was fined $100 in Washington, D.C., for illegal picketing. (*The Plotters*, John Carlson, p. 96.)

The Mayor's Committee on Human Relations branded Goff as a professional "agitator" and named him in "hate groups." (*Denver Post*, November 23, 1947.)

The *Denver Post*, in an editorial, July 31, 1953, praised the civic leaders of Englewood for "their prompt denunciation of the Rev. Kenneth O. Goff." "As long as they are alert to the menace of bigotry as personified by Goff, he can do no real harm there." "Long a disciple of Gerald L. K. Smith, Kenneth Goff is one of the minor menaces among American hate merchants."

Kenneth Goff is the author of a pamphlet entitled *Brainwashing, A Synthesis of the Russian Textbook on Psychopolitics,* which includes an alleged speech by Beria at the Lenin University. No responsible source is given for this speech, the authenticity of which is therefore highly questionable.

On July 23, 1963, we also addressed a letter of inquiry to the Bureau of Intelligence and Research of the Department of State. The reply, dated August 13, 1963, said:

Your letter of July 23, 1963, addressed to the Department's Bureau of Intelligence and Research, asking for information relating to a Russian textbook on psychopolitics, is acknowledged. Considerable searching was done in an effort to identify this title, but without success. I regret, therefore, that we are unable to pass on any information as to its authenticity.

FRED W. SHIPMAN
*Librarian*

Earlier in our investigation—before we had written to Senator Kuchel—we asked Senator Lee Metcalf of Montana to get a report on Goff's booklet from the Library of Congress. We quote from the Report, dated February 15, 1963:

To: Senator Lee Metcalf
From: Sergius Yakobson, Senior Specialist for Russian Affairs
Subject: *Brain-Washing. A Synthesis of the Russian Textbook on Psychopolitics*

On the basis of the title given in the editorial note, *The Communist Manual of Instructions of Psychopolitical Warfare,* an effort was made to locate in the Library's collections the original Russian text from which the pamphlet *Brain-Washing. A Synthesis of the Russian Textbook on Psychopolitics* was said to be derived, but no such text was found in the Library's catalogs. Therefore, no examination of the authenticity of this pamphlet, as suggested by Mr. Kominsky, could be undertaken. In case additional bibliographic data could be supplied, a further search will be undertaken.

The pamphlet in question includes on pp. 3-4 an "Address" by Lavrenti P. Beria, stated in the editorial note to have been delivered "to the American students in the Lenin University prior to 1936." Therefore, works by Beria published before the end of 1936 which are in the Library of Congress collections were examined; none of them contained such an "Address."

On January 24, 1964, we wrote a letter to Richard Arens, who for many years was Research Director of the House Committee on Un-American Activities and who now sits on the U.S. Court of Claims in Washington, D.C. In response to our series of questions about Goff's booklet, he replied on January 28, 1964 that "I do not consider myself competent as an expert in the field of psychopolitics." This statement would seem to have considerable significance, because it really means that, in all of his years of investigating Communist activities, the Kenneth Goff thesis had not made any impact upon his thinking. And Richard Arens is one who would never shrink from an opportunity to hit the Communists with any charge that would have some semblance of credibility. He suggested that I contact two professional anti-Communist writers, Edward Hunter and Duane Thorin.

In response to our letter of inquiry, Edward Hunter wrote on March 22, 1964, regarding Goff's booklet:

The "book" is a hoax, and what it has mostly achieved is to fool people who think they are getting my "Brain-Washing in Red China", which was based on first-hand sources, and put the word into the language. A fake always reacts this damaging way. The hoax was written with my book as a basis, in England.

In a letter dated March 20, 1964, Duane Thorin wrote that he had never seen a copy of the *Russian Text Book on Psychopolitics*. This statement has significance, because a reading of Duane Thorin's writings, as well as Edward Hunter's, indicates that both gentlemen have looked far and wide for any material they could use against the Communists. It would seem strange that such a "juicy" item would elude both of them. Regarding Kenneth Goff's booklet itself, Thorin wrote:

Because there is a question as to its authenticity, in the absence of the original document it is claimed to represent, it is not material upon which any responsible researcher, writer or analyst can safely base a thesis or use in support of an argument or debate.

Mr. Thorin concludes his letter with:

I regret that I cannot give you any more specific information—proof or disproof—with regard to the document in question. The best I can do is tell you my own decision on it, as far as my own works are concerned; it being of no value to me either as research material or as something to aid in promoting understanding on the part of others whom I might be trying to reach, I relegated my copy to the evergrowing heap of similarly questionable or useless material, and I set myself to searching out and developing more practical things.

One of the scholars, who was involved in the research work to which we have had access up to this point in the investigation, suggested that we contact another scholar. This resulted in our obtaining the most conclusive and damning evidence against Kenneth Goff's booklet. Unfortunately, this other scholar, for reasons that we can understand, has asked to remain anonymous. This we regret exceedingly, but we are honor-bound to comply with his request. This scholar is considered the top man, or at least among the top men, in his field of specialization. He is a psychologist who has a fluent command of the Russian language and has quite an impressive number of attainments to his credit. We give the reader our word of honor that we are reporting accurately the findings of this scholar.

545

Let us call him "Scientist X," in order to facilitate our reporting. We should add further that he is an honest scholar, who is definitely anti-Communist in his philosophical posture.

In our first letter to Scientist X we asked if he had ever seen or heard of the *Russian Text Book on Psychopolitics* and if he had ever seen books or booklets that were based upon the Russian book. In a letter dated September 9, 1963, he said that he had never seen nor heard of any books or booklets that were based on the Russian book. With respect to the *Russian Text Book on Psychopolitics,* he wrote:

It is hard to believe that there is such a book. The title is very strange, hardly reflecting Soviet usage of the Russian language. But the title may be merely an adapted one in English translation. More important is the simple fact that psychology, as a discipline, is very weakly developed in the Soviet Union and such a sophisticated subject as *psikhopolitika* would be beyond its competence. As a matter of fact, social psychology (which would ordinarily include political psychology) has only recently been recognized as a proper subdivision of psychology. I have never seen any Soviet work on political psychology reported in scientific journals or technical books and doubt whether there is or ever was a systematic treatment of this subject in the Soviet Union. If such may be thought, as existing, it could only be as a strictly classified document for limited circulation and could hardly be empirically based.

Scientist X then expressed a desire to see Goff's booklet and other material of similar nature, and offered to be helpful to us in evaluating the material.

On September 16, 1963, we sent him the booklets and a long letter, giving him additional information. On October 31, 1963, Scientist X wrote to us as follows:

Thank you for the materials which you have sent me to date. They make most curious reading.

Let me tell you my impression and considered opinion of them. First of all, I must say that it has been a long time since I've read such dull and unimaginative drivel. I can't even get myself to read the stuff without a constant impatience. Secondly, it's all a hoax. My reasons for this judgment are as follows essentially:

1. There is not a trace of the original Russian that one should sense behind the English.

2. The expressions and development of ideas and arguments are neither Russian nor Soviet, but are a caricature of someone's notion about Soviet policies and procedures, some of which are certainly correct but simplistically stated.

3. There appear contemporary American ideas and expressions which do not have past or present Soviet counterparts. For example, in the document the expression "psychiatry and psychology" appears. This is from America, not from the Soviet Union. Psychiatry in the latter country is considered as strictly within medicine, as is frequently the case here; but psychology has been excluded from the healing processes covered by the term psychotherapy which is assigned instead to psychiatry. It has only been recently that psychotherapy has been considered something that perhaps should be of essential interest to psychologists. In other words, psychiatry and psychology have not been considered as partners until only recently, and even now it's all very tentative. One does not ordinarily couple the words "psychiatry" and "psychology" when talking about psychotherapy in the Soviet literature.

4. There never has been developed a subject called "psychopolitics" in the Soviet Union. The semantics of it alone would damn it in advance as idealist, however it might in actuality be practiced in unsystematized form.

On May 12, 1964, the Rev. Kenneth Goff held one of his rallies at the Embassy Auditorium in Los Angeles, California. At the conclusion of his harangue, which we tape-recorded, we walked over to the podium and invited Goff to step down, so that we could talk to him. In order that the reader may thoroughly understand the interview, it is necessary to point out that there is another version of *Brain-Washing, A Synthesis of the Russian Text Book on Psychopolitics,* which is published by the Ultra-Rightist women of the Burbank, California area, who call themselves American Public Relations Forum, Inc. It contains the identical material as Goff's booklet, but carries additionally two items that were placed in the Congressional Record by the late Congressman Usher L. Burdick of North Dakota. The introduction, which is quite lengthy, is by one, Charles Stickley, who claims to be a professor living in New York City. He claims that he compiled the booklet, a claim which is contradicted by Goff. Our interview with Goff, which was recorded, follows:

*Kominsky.* Say, Dr. Goff, may I trouble you for a couple of minutes to answer a couple of questions about this. (Showing him his pamphlet entitled: *Brainwashing—A Synthesis of the Russian Textbook on Psychopolitics.*) When you say: "A Synthesis of the Russian Textbook on Psychopolitics", do you have that Russian Textbook?

*Goff.* No, we don't have it. We have only . . . .

547

*K.* Did you ever have it?

*G.* I've seen it, but we only have this part of it. This part of it we have from the papers of the Communist Party. You see, in the orientation classes of the Communist Party, if you read this. . .

*K.* Yeh.

*G.* From the orientation classes we have this much.

*K.* Well, do I understand then. . . . ?

*G.* That this is only part of the whole book.

*K.* That you have compiled this pamphlet from these orientation sheets? Is that the idea?

*G.* From the Communist Party.

*K.* Yes, but, you haven't taken this from the Russian Textbook.

*G.* It was taken by the Party from the Russian Textbook.

*K.* But, where is that Russian Textbook?

*G.* That Textbook is in Russia, in the Communist Party headquarters.

*K.* Yes, but how could it have been taken in this country?

*G.* How could it have been taken in this country?

*K.* Yes.

*G.* Because the Communist Party—This question continually comes up from some one in California that wants to challenge this book—I have said that I will go in court with the Communist Party material any time they want me to go into court.

*K.* Nobody is going to go into court over this.

*G.* A year ago I offered to go into court with *Mad Magazine,* if they wanted me.

*K.* Yes, but this is only a matter of settling some questions.

*G.* This thing came right out of the Communist Party headquarters.

*K.* Where?

*G.* The Communist Party headquarters in New York. If you read this here, it tells you where it is used, and everything—at 113 East 12th Street, New York.

*K.* Yes, but you see, I'm not clear about what is meant by a "Synthesis" of a textbook. Now, you see, here is another one, and this guy here claims to be the author of it, a Charles Stickley. Now, who *is* the author of it?

*G.* I don't know Charles Stickley. I don't know who he is author of, or anything else.

*K.* And he claims to be a university professor.

*G.* Well, do you know where he is at?

*K.* No. It says "Charles Stickley, New York City, 1955."

*G.* This thing (pointing to his own pamphlet) was not put out in 1955. If you look back at the date there, it mentions the date when this came out. It came out by us in mimeographed form, in which the first edition was 1000.

*K.* You're the originator of it.

*G.* I was the first one to publish it. This was taken from the Communist Party Manual, the orientation Manual.

*K.* Apparently then (pointing to a copy of the American Public

Relations Forum version of the pamphlet), these people have plagiarized your . . .

G. That's right. Not only them, but another one in this state came out with it, and when I told him that he had no right to circulate it, he said: "Why, you can't sue me, because you can't copyright Communist Party material."

K. Yes, there's a fellow down there in. . .

G. In the southern part of the state.

K. Yes, in the southern part of the state. And he makes it look as if he is the fellow who brought it out.

G. But, the thing is that it is Communist Party documentation. That's what it tells you right here in the beginning, that this was the orientation sheet. Orientation sheets were used on chauvinism, all these other subjects.

K. But there is no copy of this *Russian Textbook on Psychopolitics* available in this country?

G. We've been trying to get one from France. There are some in France, but we have never been able to get one. I tried on this trip to get one through a fellow in Brussels who thought he had his hands on one. I've seen one that was used in the Communist Party headquarters in which this orientation sheet was taken from. But the Party translators in New York at the time that Earl Browder was the head of the Communist Party, Alexander Bittelman and these fellows, did the translation from the Russian in these parts that they wanted to teach in the schools, in the Workers Schools in this country. Uh, prior to that, prior to '36, all the students were trained in Moscow. You went to Moscow. There was no need for any of this in this country, but when they began establishing schools and training institutes here, then there was the need to have certain manuals on hand. But these other two, the only reason that we haven't done anything about it is because we wanted this material out. Stickley didn't write it.

K. But, I haven't found anyone who knows who this Stickley is.

G. No, I haven't found out who this Stickley is, and I have put up a reward for him, trying to find out who this Stickley is.

K. How much of a reward will you put up. Maybe I will go looking for him myself.

G. I think it was $500. that the office offered to find Charles Stickley.

K. He's a mysterious character.

At this point the interview was abruptly interrupted by members of Goff's entourage and some of the religious fanatics who support Goff.

Another scientist whose findings confirm those of Scientist X is Robert C. Tucker, who had ample opportunity to study the Soviet scene, while serving as an attaché of the American Embassy in Moscow. Beginning in 1954, Mr. Tucker has been engaged in research for the Social Science Division of the Rand Corporation, a research organization which analyzes problems for the U.S. Government, especially for the Defense Department.

In the July 1956 issue of *World Politics,* Mr. Tucker has an article entitled "Stalin and the Uses of Psychology." Mr. Tucker, having lived in the Soviet Union and having research facilities at his disposal which Goff could not possibly have, does not make a single reference to psychopolitics. He has studied and researched the subject for the period during which Goff claims the program of psychopolitics was developed. Far from having developed a diabolical scheme based upon manipulating people's minds, Tucker argues that the Stalin regime's attempts to apply psychological principles *within* the country were a colossal failure.

One of the most exhaustive studies of the subject of Brainwashing is contained in The *Journal of Social Issues,* Vol. XIII, No. 3: 1957. It is published quarterly by The Society for the Psychological Study of Social Issues, a Division of the American Psychological Association. The entire issue is devoted to the subject in its various aspects. Most pertinent to our investigation is the essay by Dr. Raymond A. Bauer, entitled "Brainwashing: Psychology or Demonology." Dr. Bauer's qualifications to deal with this subject are that he is a highly respected psychologist, who has been for many years a student of Soviet affairs, and especially the role of psychology in the Soviet Union. He explains in his essay that he has been "continually interested in finding any direct evidence of the systematic employment of psychiatry or psychology as an instrument of social policy, for either propaganda or eliciting confessions."

Dr. Bauer's first and most trenchant observation is:

It has been particularly disturbing to find a number of otherwise responsible citizens accepting the thesis that "brainwashing" is based on psychiatric principles developed from Pavlovian psychology. Without exception the evidence is inferential.

Dr. Bauer points out also that you can find some application of any meritorious psychiatric or psychological theory in any series of human events. This point can be stated in another fashion: that some people pounce upon a small kernel of truth, elaborate upon it, ignore all contrary evidence, and expand

550

the small kernel of truth to grotesque proportions. Dr. Bauer illustrates the point by relating that he had once read a document which actually stated that Stalin created the famine of 1931 in order that his weakened subjects might be more susceptible to Communist propaganda! This, as can readily be seen, is another variation on the theme of Kenneth Goff's hoax.

Dr. Bauer reviews the attempts to apply psychological techniques in the Soviet Union, and makes these observations:

1. The last reference, as far as I am aware, to the possibility of using psychology (as a formal discipline) in propaganda work took place in 1931; and this article consisted of a bitter complaint that nothing useful had been offered to political workers by psychologists.
2. . . . with reasonable diligence and a considerable sense of curiosity I have found no single piece of direct positive evidence—since the early thirties—that would link Soviet psychologists and/or psychiatrists with work on political indoctrination or the eliciting of confessions.

Dr. Alfred Auerback, Associate Clinical Professor of Psychiatry, University of California School of Medicine at San Francisco, took notice of Kenneth Goff's booklet in an excellent essay entitled "The Anti-Mental Health Movement," which appeared in *The American Journal of Psychiatry*, August, 1963. Referring to Goff's booklet by name, Professor Auerback says:

It contained some of the most bald-faced lies ever directed against the psychiatric profession. The book has had a tremendous circulation and has been cited at great length. Quotes crop up in publications of the Daughters of the American Revolution and in various other brochures such as "Lifelines," "Common Sense," "Freedom Builders of America," "Freedom Forum," etc. In each it is stated unequivocally that under the "False name of 'mental health'" a communist master plan is being put into operation in hundreds of American cities and that mental health groups are being used to further the goal of communist conquest of the mind. A sampling of this treatise on "brainwashing" must be quoted to indicate the source of phraseology now in frequent use:
"Psychopolitics is a branch of geopolitics concerned with mental healing. It is used to produce chaos in the fields of mental healing. It is designed to have every doctor and psychiatrist act as an unwitting agent of the communist doctrine. Through it you achieve dominion over the minds and bodies of the nation. Institutions for the insane provide the means of holding a million persons without any civil rights or any hope of freedom. By use of electric shock or brain surgery you can keep these people so

they will never again draw a sane breath. By making readily available drugs of all kinds, by giving the teenager alcohol, by praising his wildness, by stimulating him with sex literature, the psychopolitical operator (psychiatrist) can create the necessary attitudes of chaos, idleness and worthlessness in the teenager. The psychiatrist has no interest in cures, hence the greater the number of insane in hospital, the greater the number of people under his domination and the greater will become the size of his hospitals. Exercises in sexual attack on patients can be practiced by the psychiatrist to demonstrate the inability of the patient to withstand him while indoctrinating the lust for further sexual activities on the part of the patient. If a psychiatric ward could be established in every general hospital in every city in the nation, it is certain that at one time or another leading citizens of the nation could come under the ministrations of the psychopolitical operator. The attraction of the field of mental healing to many people is that it provides unlimited sexual opportunities and the possibility of complete dominion over the minds and bodies of patients, the possibility of complete lawlessness without detection."

While these statements are ludicrous, the fact remains that millions of Americans are being exposed to them over and over again. In addition to thousands of pamphlets and brochures repeating them there are many radio and television stations across the United States which routinely broadcast this philosophy, although in a more subtle manner. The attack on mental health is coupled with attacks on our educational system, churches, minority groups, and governmental institutions amongst others. It must be recognized that this is part of a well organized and well financed campaign against our democratic institutions carried out by groups and individuals making resounding statements about their "patriotism" and "Americanism."

Dr. Auerback's last remark is a most astute observation. The evidence is overwhelming that Goff's booklet has become one of the most formidable and insidious weapons in the ideological armamentarium of the Ultra-Rightists. The extent to which this booklet has been quoted, reprinted, and distributed is frightening. In addition to Goff's own version, there is, as we have pointed out before, the one issued by the American Public Relations Forum, Inc. of Burbank, California. There are also exact duplicates of Goff's version that have been issued by the Ultra-Rightist *Counter Insurgency Council* of Collinsville, Illinois; *Freedom Builders of America*, a subsidiary of Dr. Merle Parker's *Foundation for Divine Meditation*, formerly located at Valley Center, California and now at Cedar Heart of the

Ozarks, Thornfield, Missouri; and *The Lutheran Research Society, Inc.,* Lowell, Arizona.

Mr. Eric Butler is the Director of the Ultra-Rightist and racist *Victorian League of Rights,* Melbourne, Australia. He has written articles a number of times for the John Birch Society monthly, *American Opinion,* and for the Ultra-Rightist *Canadian Intelligence Service* (a private organization). A newsletter, issued by the virulently anti-Semitic *Western Front* of Los Angeles, advertises Butler as a speaker at its monthly meeting of March 24, 1967. In 1956, *The Victorian League of Rights* issued *Brain Washing, A Synthesis of the Russian Text Book on Psychopolitics.* In the introduction, Butler says:

> The material on psychopolitics was first published in America last year by a Charles Stickley, who said that he could not reveal the sources of his material without endangering individuals who had assisted him. Early this year Kenneth Goff, former American Communist, also issued the material in booklet form. His material is exactly the same as Stickley's with the minor exception of a change of several words in Beria's address. We are using Stickley's text.
>
> A former American military intelligence officer has stated in a letter to the League of Rights that although he has been unable to find a copy of the original Communist textbook on brain-washing, there was "no question that he (Goff) has read literature which he would not now be able to get hold of. Furthermore, the internal evidence of the book is most convincing to anyone thoroughly familiar with the Communist machine, its techniques and objectives." There is no argument that the techniques for brain-washing outlined in this material are being applied in various forms throughout the whole world.

We have quoted Butler's remarks, because they illustrate graphically the essentially dishonest and casuistic methods used by Ultra-Rightist propagandists. There are at least 6 untenable planks in Butler's forensic structure:

1. He relies upon "a Charles Stickley" whom he cannot otherwise identify and whom no one has been able to locate, as far as we can ascertain.

2. This phantom Charles Stickley "could not reveal his sources." Why he could not do so, at a time when anti-Communist scribes were riding the crest of popularity and prosperity, is not explained. Secret sources of information are usually a device of those who present fabricated documents.

3. Butler reports blithely about "the minor exception of a

change of several words in Beria's address." Apparently he sees nothing wrong in changing the report of what one has said or is alleged to have said.

4. He does not identify his mysterious "former American military intelligence officer," who so conveniently has written him exactly what he needed in order to help spread a hoax. This intelligence officer may very well be a phantom of Butler's imagination.

5. Far from being convincing, as Butler's "intelligence officer" claims, the internal evidence of the booklet is that it is a fraudulent document.

6. Butler gives no proof of his own statement that the techniques outlined in the booklet are being applied throughout the world, because his statement is completely untrue and is not susceptible of proof.

Among the first to promote the psychopolitics hoax was the Ultra-Rightist *Defenders of the American Constitution, Inc.* In the Aug.-Sept. 1956 issue of *Task Force,* its President, Pedro A. Del Valle, a retired U.S. Marine Corps General, writes:

*Task Force* has sounded repeated warnings of the real purpose behind the plethora of "Mental Health" bills in the state legislatures and in the Congress, with especial emphasis on the "Alaskan-Siberia" bill introduced by Representative Green.

We are proud, therefore, to recommend to our readers, the booklet: "BRAIN WASHING," a Synthesis of the Soviet textbook on psychopolitics published by *TRUTH, Inc.,* P.O. Box 10188, Fort Worth 14, Texas, with an introduction by a former communist, Kenneth Goff.

This book contains in its sixty-four pages all proof one needs of the sinister purpose behind these innocent-appearing mental health bills. It is gruesome reading, beginning with a speech of welcome to American students by the late head of the M V D, Beria. The "American" students obviously were there to learn the techniques of becoming "psychopolitical operators," which apparently means the use of insanity, real, induced, or just imaginary, as a political weapon of the first order, in the conquest of this country from within.

You will gasp when you read how persons of power and influence are bent to the will of the psychopolitical operator; how wide publicity for juvenile delinquency makes this a factor in our planned downfall; how religion is undermined and used against us; how the degradation of the populace works to the communists' advantage.

. Any red-blooded American patriot who, having read this booklet, does not explode into action in defense of his country does not deserve its blessings. This is a book which will turn the tide against the enemy within and lead to a breach of relations with those who work so cynically to destroy our Republic. Price is one dollar for a single copy, fifty dollars for one hundred. It is priceless.

The surprising element in the General's editorial is the authoritative tone of his statements, leaving no room for doubt or for questioning the authenticity of the hoax booklet. More damaging, however, was the planting of this propaganda in the Congressional Record.

On June 13, 1957, the late Congressman Usher L. Burdick of North Dakota placed a horrendous story in the Congressional Record. He related a yarn about 10 million people in Russia being subjected forcibly to a delicate brain operation called frontal lobotomy. The operation consists essentially of severing the nerves of the frontal lobes of the brain from the rest of it. This surgical technique, which originated in the non-Communist world, was used in the U.S.A. and other countries largely to control violent patients. Since the advent of the tranquilizer drugs, it has been virtually abandoned as a procedure by the psychiatrists. The only "proof" that Congressman Burdick gave of his charge against the Stalin regime was—you guessed it—some quotations from the phoney Beria speech and this alleged statement from former Soviet Premier, Georgi Malenkov:

There will be no more lobotomies while I am dictator of Russia.

No source for this alleged statement is given. The internal evidence brands it as fraudulent, because no record exists of any Soviet leader referring to himself as *dictator of Russia*. The general tone of the Congressman's presentation can be deduced from the heading: "Beware of Psychiatrists."

On the same day, Congressman Burdick placed another item in the Congressional Record. This one carries the heading: "Communist Brainwashing for Americans." Mr. Burdick told his colleagues:

Mr. Speaker, to apprise the people of this country just what the Communist practice was and probably still is in regard to the treatment of so-called mentally sick persons, I have decided to

555

reprint the entire speech made by Communist Beria to a class of American students at Lenin University.

The is the same Beria who was at the head of the police system in Russia, and who caused the execution of millions of Russians, and who finally was himself executed by the Malenkov dictatorship.

With these opening remarks, Congressman Burdick then placed the Beria "speech" in the Record. Mr. Burdick's reckless disregard of the facts is also shown by his statement that Beria was executed under Malenkov's administration. It actually occurred later, under the Khrushchev administration.

The next Congressman to publicize Goff's psychopolitics hoax was Congressman Edgar W. Hiestand of California, an admitted member of the John Birch Society. Among his other activities, Hiestand has served as a trustee of the First Congregational Church of Los Angeles, whose *Freedom Club* is a bastion of Ultra-Rightism. He was listed in 1966 as the Pacific Coast States Regional Vice-President of the Ultra-Rightist *We, the People,* and is a founder of an ominous-sounding Ultra-Rightist group called *"The 1976 Committee,"* which, in 1966, announced a "ten year plan." On August 14, 1958, Mr. Hiestand placed in the Congressional Record two columns by George Todt, an Ultra-Rightist scribe of the Hearst papers. Both columns are vicious attacks against the mental health programs and the profession of psychiatry. Goff's hoax booklet is strongly recommended, and the address where it may be obtained is given. As usual, the phoney Beria speech is quoted in full. On August 15, 1958, Mr. Hiestand placed in the Congressional Record two more columns by George Todt, which deal with psychopolitics and use copious quotations from Goff's hoax booklet. On August 21, 1958, Mr. Hiestand placed in the Congressional Record George Todt's final two columns in his series on psychopolitics.

On October 12, 1962, Congressman Bruce Alger of Texas placed in the Congressional Record the entire contents of a brochure issued by an Ultra-Rightist group in California, which calls itself *Liberty League, Inc.* It contains a sly attack upon mental health programs. In addition, Mr. Alger reprinted the remarks on "Brainwashing for Americans" made by Congressman Usher L. Burdick in the Congressional Record of June 13, 1957. This Usher presentation consisted mainly of the entire Beria "speech."

The dishonest and/or reckless nature of placing this kind of material in the Congressional Record is easily understood when one realizes that none of these gentlemen, whom we have to address as Honorable by virtue of their election to Congress, took the trouble to inquire of the Library of Congress about the authenticity of Goff's booklet and the Beria speech. It is also a sad commentary on the deterioration of the political morality of our elected officials that no member of Congress, as far as we know, has ever challenged the authenticity of these items or the morality of placing them in the Congressional Record.

The Ultra-Rightist ladies of California, who operate American Public Relations Forum, Inc., issued a booklet, entitled *Facts on "Mental Health" Movement*. It is sickening to read this compendium of lies, garbled quotations, and distortions of truth. It quotes in full the Beria "speech," but instead of quoting it from their own edition of the hoax booklet on "Brain-Washing," they tell their readers about a group of American students who attended an international seminar on education that was held in Moscow. Then they add:

We do have the opening address given these students by the head of the dreaded Secret Police of Russia at that time, BERIA. This was placed in the Congressional Record for the first time on June 13, 1957, by Congressman Usher L. Burdick, and again on August 13, 1958 by Congressman Edgar Hiestand. It follows:

The entire Beria "speech" is then given.

It so happens that the publication of the Charles Stickley version of the hoax booklet on psychopolitics antedated their publication of the booklet on "Mental Health." The ladies published both of them, so they should know. It also happens that Congressman Burdick obtained the Beria "speech" from either Goff's version of the booklet or the ladies' version. Consequently, when they quote the Congressional Record as the source of the Beria "speech," it is a dishonest and misleading device to give the Beria "speech" a sort of Congressional imprimatur. The proof is overwhelming that Ultra-Rightist groups and individuals have an understanding with Ultra-Rightist members of Congress, that this procedure is to be followed. This is especially true of members of the House Committee on Un-American Activities and the Senate Internal

Security Subcommittee. (Ample evidence to substantiate this charge will be presented in volume II of this study.)

It is almost axiomatic that lies travel faster than truth, and no lie of recent years has done more damage to the cause of world peace than the psychopolitics hoax. An example is this letter in the Riverside, Calif. *Daily Enterprise* of September 10, 1960:

Here is a statement from the Russian textbook used in training their agents to take over the world:

"By making readily available drugs of various kinds; by giving the teenager alcohol; by praising his wildness; by stimulating him with sex literature and advertising to him or her practices as taught in "Sexpol," the psychological operator can create the necessary attitude of chaos, idleness and worthlessness into which can then be cast the solution, which will give the teenager complete freedom everywhere. If we can effectively kill the national pride and patriotism of just one generation, we will have won that country."

. . . Parents awake! It is later than you think. Already we are reaping the rewards of a secular—without God—education. Already the lives of peace-loving citizens are in jeopardy, as well as the destruction of property at the hands of mere children. Secular education is producing a generation that ignores or denies God. . . It is interesting to note that the only two nations in the world where it is forbidden by law to teach the Bible in the schools are the United States and Russia. Remember, Godless education is the root of communism. Dr. C. C. Morrison, former editor of "Christian Century" made this observation over ten years ago. "The Public Schools are creating secular mentality faster than the church can Christianize it."

Are we going to allow this to be true of our own beloved Riverside? Are there enough awakened citizens in this city to attack this situation? . . .

Mrs. Matilda B. Randall

In response to our letter of inquiry, Mrs. Matilda B. Randall wrote to us on September 23, 1960:

In reply to your letter I wish to say that the news items I quoted appeared in the November issue of *American Mercury* under the heading of "Planned Delinquency." It was released by the Canadian Intelligence Service, excerpts from "Brainwashing" a synthesis of a Russian textbook on psychopolitics used in training Red agents. This was brought to public attention locally by George Putnam, who read it on all of his television news reports during the week of March 7, 1960.

I do not have this Russian textbook, nor do I know where you could find one.

On February 24, 1960, the Los Angeles *Herald-Examiner* carried the following letter:

Stalin's dreaded chief of secret police, Beria, once said: "If we can effectively kill the national pride and patriotism of just one generation, we will have won that country. Therefore we must continue propaganda abroad to undermine the loyalty of citizens in general and of teen-agers in particular."

If anyone wants to obey Kremlin orders, just keep right on knocking patriots and patriotism, calling it "nationalism."

The freedom you destroy, the country you destroy, the humane civilization you destroy, may be your own.

ROBERT WASSMAN

On March 2, 1964, we sent the following letter to the editor of the *Herald-Examiner,* whose interest in truth did *not* impel him to publish it:

Robert Wassman's letter, in your issue of Feb. 24th, quotes from an alleged speech supposedly made by the late, unlamented Soviet secret police chief, Lavrenti Beria, in Moscow.

This alleged speech has been widely circulated, and those who peddle it should be advised that it is a fabrication.

The research director of the U.S. Senate Subcommittee on Internal Security has definitely stated that the speech cannot be authenticated.

The administrative assistant of a well known U.S. Senator has written to me that Beria actually did not arrive in Moscow until one year after he was supposed to have made that alleged speech; and that all the intelligence agencies consider the alleged speech to be a hoax.

The Caxton Printers, Ltd., of Caldwell, Idaho, are the publishers of many Ultra-Rightist books. In the June, 1963, issue of the Birch Society magazine, *American Opinion,* they advertise a book entitled *Youth On A Pendulum,* by Sue Vance. The advertisement begins with:

"IF WE COULD EFFECTIVELY KILL THE NATIONAL PRIDE AND PATRIOTISM OF JUST ONE GENERATION WE WILL HAVE WON THAT COUNTRY"—Russian Textbook on Psychopolitics.

559

In response to our inquiry, Caxton Printers wrote us on August 23, 1963: "This particular quote was picked up from the author's own material—background material supplied for her book, *Youth On A Pendulum.*" On September 3, 1963, we wrote Mrs. Sue Vance, inquiring where we could obtain a copy of that *Russian Text Book on Psychopolitics.* On January 27, 1964, we wrote her again, calling to her attention our previous letter which was unanswered, and repeating our question. In her reply of February 2, 1964, which was quite peevish in tone, she wrote:

I enclose the pamphlet from which I took the quotation that you question. As you can see, it has been placed in the Congressional Record. The exact quote is on page 38. My quote has also been used on the air by George Putnam several times.

I paid one dollar for this pamphlet and I think it would be only fair if you reimbursed me.

We quote the following from our letter of February 10, 1964 to Mrs. Vance:

Your letter proves the following:

1. You quoted from a non-existent "Russian Text Book on Psychopolitics," which you had never seen, because you were careless or indifferent to the necessity of proper verification of facts.

2. The fact that something is placed in the Congressional Record is not proof of its authenticity. There are all kinds of politicians. Some are honest; some are dishonest. Some are bright; some are stupid. Some are cultured; others are vulgar. Some are educated; others are ignorant. And some combine two or more of these attributes.

3. Many of George Putnam's "facts" can be challenged. I do not consider him infallible and/or a paragon of virtue.

Our letter stated further that, although we had about seven copies of that booklet on hand, we were enclosing $1.20 to reimburse her for the booklet and the postage. We suggested that a personal meeting, with a full and frank exchange of views, would be mutually beneficial, and asked for an appointment. The lady replied on February 17, 1964, sarcastically suggesting that, because of our concern for the origin of the quotation she had used, we should contact the author or the publisher of the booklet she had sent us. She refused an appointment, and stated that this must terminate our correspondence. She informed us that before submitting her own book to the publisher, she had asked a number of people to check it over. Among these, she informed us, was "a person from the FBI" and "a Congressman from the House Committee on Un-American Activities."

The Daughters of the American Revolution, through its so-called National Defense Committee, has issued a leaflet which quotes from the Congressional Record of June 13, 1957, the speech of Congressman Usher L. Burdick, in which he quoted the entire phoney Beria speech. This particular leaflet was a companion piece to a number of others which contained shameful attacks upon the mental health program, psychiatrists, and psychologists. In the leaflet that quotes Burdick and Beria, the *Daughters* cautioned:

As you read this release, remember the recent visit of American students to Russia and Red China, the Supreme Court decision regarding the Communists, mental health legislation, and the increased use of drugs. All agree that the United States is losing the cold war. We know that all facets of our national and community life are being infiltrated with those who would destroy us. By any chance could Beria's address be a description of the system being used by the proponents of Mental Health?

It is obvious that these ladies see a Communist under every bed.

The Ultra-Rightist magazines have for many years indulged in a veritable orgy of hate-peddling, with the psychopolitics hoax as one of its main weapons. In the November, 1959, issue, the Ultra-Rightist *American Mercury* carries a quotation from the "Brain-Washing" booklet, but quotes it by way of a propaganda release from the Ultra-Rightist *Canadian Intelligence Service* (a private organization). The psychopolitics motif is expressed by former FBI stoolpigeon, Matt Cvetic, in an article that was carried in the November 1961 *Christian Crusade,* which is published by Rev. Billy James Hargis:

This "phony" concern about our so-called declining "mental health" has been planted by Communist agents, fronters and sympathizers for the purpose of demoralizing the American people and spreading defeatism. As a part of the Kremlin's psychological warfare, this negative propaganda is calculated to destroy our morale, thereby rendering us ineffective, and making us easy prey for the Red vultures.

The irony of all this is that we, the intended victims, are being

561

asked to pay for this "destruction of our morale" through excessive spending by our government's social, health and welfare agencies, and through professional fund-raising campaigns.

The Communists' psychological warfare is a typical Communist technique of demoralization devised by Lenin and Stalin. This systematic and diabolic scheme to destroy the moral fibre of people and nations is being carried on right now in this country by highly trained and disciplined secret Soviet and American Red agents. Through the "professional cells" of the Communist Party, Reds are funneling their conspirators into our Social, Health, Welfare, Church and Educational fields.

Lest anyone be tempted to question the sanity of the late Matt Cvetic when he wrote those vitriolic remarks, we hasten to point out that he was just a fellow who followed an easy way to make a fast dollar in the period of the Cold War. He sold the kind of merchandise for which there was a ready and lucrative market: fantastic lies about the Communists!

*California Liberty Bell,* a small propaganda magazine issued by the Ultra-Rightist *San Diego (Calif.) Patriotic Society,* in its issue of May 1963, quotes from the phoney Beria speech. It gives as its source the Ultra-Rightist biweekly sheet, *Christian Economics. Liberty Bell* concludes:

Beria has laid bare the means by which the Communists are taking us over. Now that we know their objectives and procedures, surely there are enough people who can think straight and who have courage to thwart the Communist plan for our destruction.

The former stalwart of the John Birch Society, Professor Revilo P. Oliver, has an essay on "Brainwashing" in *American Opinion,* November, 1964. Dr. Oliver leans on other Ultra-Rightist books in the writing of this essay, but he succeeds in arriving at the same conclusion as Kenneth Goff:

But "mental health" prisons are being increasingly used for the kidnapping and mental, if not physical, murder of patriotic Americans...
The Conspiracy's increasingly frequent and increasingly open use of madhouses for the purpose of jailing its enemies forms a revolting narrative...

Five years earlier, on April 9, 1959, Professor Oliver delivered a long speech at the 8th Annual Congress of Freedom, held at Colorado Springs, Colorado. It was the type of speech that was calculated to send this convention of Ultra-Rightists into orbit. Oliver refers to "that great Communist department of our government, the Department of Health, Education, and Welfare." Then Oliver tells us:

And it is becoming increasingly clear that the only purpose of "mental health" is to provide quasi-legal means of kidnapping and torturing Americans who oppose the Communist conspiracy.

There is no question about the inspiration for these profound conclusions, because Dr. Oliver proceeds to quote part of Beria's "speech" from Kenneth Goff's hoax booklet, *Brain-Washing, A Synthesis of the Russian Text Book on Psychopolitics*. He concludes this portion of his harangue with this warning:

The ghastly question that we must ask ourselves is, How far have the conspirators advanced toward this goal in the past quarter of a century?

He is referring to the fantastic program outlined in the phoney Beria speech. It may tax one's credulity, but Professor Oliver and huge numbers of Ultra-Rightists believe such fairy tales.

Dr. Oliver is not the only Birchite theoretician to embrace the psychopolitics theory. The novelist, Miss Taylor Caldwell, who writes regularly for *American Opinion,* has an essay in the March, 1965, issue, entitled "The Insane." She rambles and rants, and "reveals":

The Communists use psychiatrists to destroy the minds of dissenters.

Another Birchite scholar, Dr. Medford Evans, reviews a sleazy book, that is based on Goff's hoax booklet, in *American Opinion,* May, 1967. The book is entitled "The Soviet Inferno," and is written by Louis Zoul. Evans is very skillful in not quite endorsing Zoul, but he manages to support the psychopolitics thesis by telling the readers they can find independent confirmation of Zoul's rantings in the writings of more "moderate" authors. Evans reprints "an excerpt from Beria as quoted by Zoul" and assures us: "It is worth quoting as an example of

563

power thinking," whatever that may mean. He also assures us that "the bomb was produced by psychopolitical means, and Beria was top man in that field." This must come as a great surprise to nuclear physicists, this revelation according to Saint Medford Evans!

The Rev. Kenneth Goff continues his exploitation of the psychopolitics hoax, preying upon the ignorance and superstitions of his followers. In numerous leaflets, newsletters, and magazine articles, he attacks the United Nations, mental health programs, psychiatrists, and the public school system. Typical of these attacks is a newsletter he sent out in April of 1966, entitled "The Battle for Your Mind," in which he outlines the "plot" that the Ultra-Rightists insist is in existence:

Throughout the twentieth century, we have seen great improvement in our mental institutions and in the care given to patients. Yet, today, the hoppers of our State legislatures and our Congress have been filled with mental health bills not intending to improve the condition of the patients, but designed to place complete power in the hands of a group of atheistic psychiatrists, and to turn our mental institutions into concentration camps. The contemporary attitude of leading liberals is that American patriots who stand for a restoration of constitutional government in the United States, and a return to traditional foreign policy, are mentally ill and should be removed from society because they are dangerous. The propaganda mills of these liberal groups have filled the press, radio and television with the smear words of "paranoic," "lunatic fringe," "extremist" and "sick people."

The fountainhead for most of the propaganda about the need for mental health programs is the U.N.; principally, these three subagencies: UNESCO, World Health Organization, and The World Federation of Mental Health. The propaganda is filtered to the American public through a large number of volunteer and governmental agencies. Among the volunteer agencies is the National Association of Mental Health with some forty State branches and nearly three hundred local branches. Among the governmental agencies are the Department of Health, Education and Welfare; the U.S. Public Health Service; The National Institution of Mental Health; and State departments of mental health. It is true that many of these civic-minded and humanitarian citizens know nothing about *the hidden hand* nor the purpose of this speeded up drive for mental health legislation. Many of them have never read the bills which they are helping to promote. (Emphasis has been added. —M. K.)

After explaining about an alleged visit he received several

years ago "when twelve psychiatrists called upon me to discuss the Russian textbook on Brainwashing which I was circulating,"[1] Goff explains:

The instrumentality of psychopolitics is a major weapon in the Soviet drive for total world control. In their own country through lobotomy, shock treatment, hypnosis, and other means, they have been able for half a century to keep hundreds of millions of people under their rigid police state control. Through these same methods, they have subjected one-third of the world to a population of weak and vacillating puppets unable to think for themselves or to throw off the yoke of tyranny. Yet they know that total world power cannot be theirs until America falls, and it is for this reason they have entered into an all-out drive to subjugate our minds to their materialistic ideologies.

Today in our schoolrooms a massive brainwashing program is being carried out to educate our young people with the idea of evolution; that they are mere species of a higher animal kingdom; that all of our thinking comes from some psychological reasoning; and that our crime is not a product of Satan or evil, but a problem of the mind.

In his magazine, *Pilgrim Torch,* issued in the Fall of 1966, Goff returns to the same theme with an article entitled "Conquerors of the Mind." Side by side with his title at the top of the first page, he reprints *in Russian* the title of a magazine article, which, in translation, reads "The Naked Human Brain." It is largely a rehash of the previous article, but with some pictures of psychological experiments, reprinted from the Russian publication. With his usual flair for discovering sinister purpose in everything done by the Soviet peoples, Goff gives a garbled and distorted version of the experimental work. He concludes his tirade with his typical anti-Semitic and conspiratorial line:

Our leader, Christ, the Captain of our Hosts, does not intend to, nor will not, surrender this world to the International Bankers, the Political Zionists, the One-Worlders, the Illuminati, nor the Communist Conspiracy.

He finally assures his dupes:

1 This is a sample of Goff's reckless disregard for the truth. By his own admission, he has never seen a copy of the *Russian Textbook,* but has been circulating a booklet which purports to be a "synthesis" of the imaginary Russian book.

The fact of the matter is, we are the only ones with sound minds and a sure hope. The enemy is the one that is in derision.

Congressman Edward J. Derwinski of Illinois placed in the Congressional Record of July 18, 1966, the entire contents of a pamphlet by Professor Lev Dobriansky, who is on the staff of the Ultra-Rightist *American Security Council* (a private organization). The professor is the leader of an Ultra-Rightist propaganda operation called National Captive Nations Committee, which specializes in heating up the Cold War. In this pamphlet, the professor repeatedly accuses the Soviet Union of carrying on *psychopolitical warfare,* without giving Kenneth Goff any credit for his inspiration. There is an aura of mystery generated by the constant repetition of this exotic term, which creates an impression in the minds of the readers of something sinister. Little does the reader suspect that the professor's arguments are based upon extremely tenuous grounds and that our own government conducts propaganda throughout the world on as large, or possibly larger, scale as the Soviet Union. By emphasizing Soviet propaganda and soft-pedaling U.S.A. propaganda, the professor creates the impression desired by the American Security Council.

The Rev. David A. Noebel, first lieutenant of the Rev. Billy James Hargis, is the author of a fantastic pamphlet, entitled *Communism, Hypnotism and the Beatles.* Among his many charges, he states that "communist scientists and psycho-politicians" have devised "a means of combining the use of hypnotism and music to nerve-jam the children of a nation without our leaders, teachers or parents being aware of its implications." After some garbled references to the scientific work of Pavlov, Luria, and other Soviet researchers, the Rev. Noebel tells us:

Following the laboratory experiments, the communists contacted educators and procured entertainers to convert this devilish scheme into a program scientifically designed to destroy American youth—mentally and emotionally! The intermediary between the scientists, educators and entertainers was a man by the name of Norman Corwin. This psycho-political plot was hatched in the United States of America in the year 1946.

Rev. Noebel leaves no doubt about his inspiration for these remarks, because he has a footnote at this point, which tells us

566

how psychopolitics is defined in *Brainwashing: A Synthesis of the Russian Textbook on Psychopolitics.*

The late Dr. L. A. Alesen served as President of the Los Angeles County Medical Association; at another time he was President of the California Medical Association; and he was Chief of Staff of the huge Los Angeles County General Hospital. Unfortunately, his medical training did not prevent him from adopting an Ultra-Rightist philosophy in sociological matters. He was a Director of the Ultra-Rightist *Freedom Club,* an adjunct of the First Congregational Church of Los Angeles; he was a member of the Executive Council of the Ultra-Rightist *Defenders of the American Constitution;* and he was listed in the 1963 Report of the California Un-American Activities Committee as a member of the National Committee of Endorsers of the John Birch Society. Dr. Alesen joined in the Ultra-Rightist campaign which saw a Communist plot behind the mental health movement. One of his pamphlets is entitled *Who Owns Your Mind?* Among his shocking statements, we find this one:

Please note that no one has been called a Communist. Such a designation is unnecessary. It is however quite obvious that in this so-called mental health program many of the techniques, the methods of operation and many of the goals of the Communist Party for America have been wittingly or unwittingly embraced. This is well-substantiated in the book entitled BRAINWASHING, a synthesis of the Russian textbook on psychopolitics.

In a footnote Dr. Alesen says:

BRAINWASHING, a Synthesis of the Russian Text Book on Psychopolitics, Including an Address by Beria, formerly Head of the Russian Secret Police. This was made a part of the Congressional Record on Thursday, June 13, 1957, by Congressman Usher L. Burdick of North Dakota.

Isn't there something pathetic about a man of Dr. Alesen's stature being misled by such an obvious hoax as Kenneth Goff's booklet? Even more tragic is his insistence that the educators, psychiatrists, legislators, and prominent civic-minded citizens, who support a program for better mental health facilities, are witting or unwitting tools of a Communist conspiracy. Any person with the slightest amount of scientific training

567

should be able to detect the fraudulent nature of Goff's booklet *by simply reading it.* In addition, if a person is not anxious to seize upon anything to bolster his prejudices, one could easily do a small amount of research, which would develop the proof that it is just as fraudulent as the "Protocols of the Learned Elders of Zion." Unfortunately, in the Cold War era people are prone to believe what they want to believe, and therein lies one of the great dangers of our time.

The Rev. Paul C. R. Peterson is the pastor of the First Baptist Church of Burbank, California, a city whose economy rests squarely on the "fools gold" of war industry. Rev. Peterson is the leader of an Ultra-Rightist operation called *Awake America for Christ,* which seems to imitate the Rev. Billy James Hargis' *Christian Crusade.* Mr. Peterson is also in the psychopolitics act by virtue of a pamphlet entitled *Mental Health, Facts You Must Know.* After expressing his belief that "all normal people could avoid nervous, emotional or mental breakdowns if they knew how to completely trust in the Lord," he says:

There are sinister forces at work within the mental health program. Many years ago the communists conceived the idea that they could subvert and capture a nation through the mental health program. How successful have they been? We shall seek to objectively present the facts.

He presents the "facts" by quoting the "speech" that Beria did *not* deliver and by copious quotations from Kenneth Goff's hoax booklet. Repeatedly, in his attacks on psychiatrists and religious leaders who support the mental health program, Rev. Peterson places a quotation from the person under attack in juxtaposition with a quotation from the Beria "speech" or from some other portion of Goff's booklet. It is a shabby and deceptive performance, but we would not doubt that, in his anti-Communist zeal, the Rev. Peterson has succeeded in deluding himself into believing such claptrap.

The number of people that have written books, columns, and speeches based upon the alleged facts of the Goff booklet is simply amazing. We are inclined to believe that a contributing factor in the explanation of this phenomenon is a psychological one. We believe that some of these people are carried away by a compulsion to indulge in some "make-believe," that they enjoy fairy tales. Thus, the psychopolitics

568

hoax serves both the propaganda and the emotional needs of some of the Cold War zealots.

One of the full-sized books based upon the Goff booklet is *The Soviet Inferno* by Louis Zoul. It has been advertised in *American Opinion, Free Enterprise, The Councilor,* and *Human Events.* Zoul was listed as a contributing editor in the now-defunct racist magazine, *Western Destiny.* His book is published by *Public Opinion,* Long Island City, New York. Nowhere and at no time have we ever seen anything to match the vituperation and the vitriolic content of this book, which is described on its title page as "A validation of the Soviet Manual of Materialistic Bestiality known in communist jargon as The Manual of Instructions on Psychopolitical Warfare." A careful reading of this book seems to indicate that the author (and probably a group of Birchite supporters) realized that Goff's booklet is not based on any evidence of probative value; and that if it could be "beefed up," it would be more effective in the anti-Communist crusade of the Cold War. Zoul blithely assumes the accuracy of the Goff booklet, and proceeds to "validate" twenty-nine excerpts from the booklet. It is done in a very cunning and fallacious manner, which is transparent to a person with some scientific training, but it will convince anyone who *wants to believe* its unfounded claims.

A few examples should suffice for an evaluation of Zoul's book.

1. Even though the Federal Income Tax was enacted long before the Soviet Union came into existence, he finds the enactment of the Income Tax to be a validation of the item that he lists as the twenty-eighth excerpt from the "Manual" (Goff's booklet).

2. He finds the Vietnam war an implementation of the twenty-ninth excerpt.

3. He expresses the Robert Welch thesis in his references to "Moscow's control of Washington," "the almost unbelievable control Moscow exercises over it," and "its subtle control of this nation" (page 112). Further on, he speaks of "the enormous control Moscow already has over this nation" (page 130) and that "the United States is itself so dominated by Moscow collaborating criminals and their dupes" that they made it "possible for Moscow to capture Cuba."

4. He charges that there are Communists masquerading as

Priests, Ministers, and Rabbis. After this, he says: "The whole of the National Council of Churches is infested with this vermin." Regarding Dorothy Day, editor of the *Catholic Worker* for many years, his comment is that she is "a very unsavory female wretch who has done her best to befoul Catholics by masquerading as a Catholic."

5. He makes a spirited defense of the John Birch Society, hurling his imprecations against the mildest of its critics.

It is indeed fitting to conclude this necessarily short examination of "The Soviet Inferno" by quoting something pleasant from Louis Zoul's labors:

Some people's idea of advancing the truth consists of trying to validate their prejudices. . .

It is just too bad that Louis Zoul did not take a good look in the mirror when he wrote that bit of truth.

Clifford Schrammeck is an anti-Communist crusader who holds forth in the Seattle-Tacoma, Washington area. He has conducted his own radio program and has done considerable pamphleteering. His style is more restrained than that of Louis Zoul, but he aggressively challenges opponents to debate and he offers cash rewards to anyone who can disprove some of his claims. Our impressions of his challenges and his offers of reward are that he makes sure there will be no takers, by hedging his challenges and offers with conditions that will not be met or cannot be met.

His book, *Secret Weapons of Communism,* published in 1962, contains a lie in its very title. Inasmuch as it is based upon the Charles Stickley version of *Brain-Washing, A Synthesis of the Russian Text Book on Psychopolitics,* which was published around 1956 by the ladies of American Public Relations Forum, Inc., all his "secret weapons" had become known and were no longer secret. His most egregious deception is his repeated quoting from the *Russian Text Book on Psychopolitics* by chapter number, despite he fact that he makes no claim to his having a copy of the alleged Russian book in his possession; and no one else has produced a copy. The quotations that he gives by chapter number correspond to the chapters in the Charles Stickley version of the *Synthesis* of the alleged Russian Text Book, and on page 37 of his book Schrammeck quotes from "Charles Stickley, Brain-Washing." His disregard for the accepted rules of evidence, which civilized men follow, is shown by these facts:

1. On pages 39, 51, 60, and 78, he refers to *"the purported,*[2] Russian Text Book on Psychopolitics.".

2. On page 61, he refers to *"the alleged*[2] Russian Text Book on Psychopolitics."

3. In spite of these explicit admissions that he cannot prove the existence of the Russian Text Book, he compounds his deceptions by proceeding to "prove" the authenticity of the non-existent Text Book by selective presentation of data. It is as if one were to undertake to prove that all red-headed persons are criminals. Using the techniques employed by Schrammeck, all one has to do is to publicize all the crimes committed by red-heads and make no mention of crimes committed by others.

His book can best be described as a rambling collection of quotations from professional anti-Communists, FBI stool pigeons, Congressman Usher L. Burdick, and Professor Revilo P. Oliver. Whenever it suits his purpose, Schrammek produces a quotation from the non-existent Russian Text Book to "prove" anything he wants to prove. A few examples will illustrate his technique:

"At the very same time that my wife got her divorce the Communists were extending a hand of friendship to me and working for my conversion. They were very nice to me. Would that not be consistent with the 'clever' Communist psychopolitical warfare?"
"Later we got evidence that in 1947 a whispering campaign was going on among Adventists alleging that my wife had become a patient in a mental institution. Thus psychopolitics continued to operate, and the story was passed on by Adventists who could easily have learned the truth. . . There was no basis whatever for such a story. . . Thus to the letter the *Russian Text Book on Psychopolitics* was fulfilled over and over. . .
"Should not even Adventists welcome an opportunity to blame such conduct upon Communists rather than have to believe that their own people, unmanipulated, could be guilty of such methods as this story reveals?"

At this point Schrammeck bolsters his argument by quoting parenthetically from the Bible: ". . . certain men crept in unawares"—Jude 4.

2 Emphasis has been added.—M. K.

*Page 26.* On this page he tells a story about his daughter being committed to the State Hospital in Pendleton, Oregon. He quotes from the non-existent Russian Text Book to "prove" that this committal followed the pattern of the Russian Text Book!

*Pages 27-29.* Schrammeck tells us that in 1936 one of his brothers "became a target of psychopolitics." His brother was committed to a psychiatric hospital. When he visited him, he (Schrammeck) could tell just by looking at him that his brother was sane! That's when he started to read books on the subject, and he seriously states that no psychiatrist can be found who will debate with him. His principal conclusion from all this is: "I affirm that it is reasonable to conclude from the evidence that 'Psychopolitics' is the biggest and most dangerous racket in the world, and that the science, psychiatry, and the legal machinery of America have been moulded to serve Communist psychopolitics—and are misused by others."

*Pages 36-37.* Schrammeck tells a story of an eighteen-year-old niece, who was seduced by an Adventist minister. Once again Schrammeck displays his peculiar concept of morality by asking: "Isn't it the most charitable thing one can do for that religious group, to insist that Communist infiltration is the best explanation for such debauchery?" Then he produces a quotation from the non-existent Russian Text Book to "prove" that this is the kind of conduct advocated by the practitioners of psychopolitics!

*Page 60.* "All over America we see laws being passed—bills in every state—fulfilling to the letter the instructions of the Text Book. The internal and external evidence is irrefutable.

We suggest that the evidence is irrefutable that Clifford Schrammeck is a very capable student of the Kenneth Goff school of hoaxes!

There will be a tendency on the part of some readers to minimize the danger of the psychopolitics hoax. Therefore, it must be pointed out that the books we have discussed have received tremendous distribution and are still being distributed all over the country by American Opinion Book Stores, Ultra-Rightist religious groups, and Ultra-Rightist organizations and individuals of every sort. We found them on sale at the bookstore of the Freedom Club, the adjunct of the First Congregational Church of Los Angeles. In order to make sure they could not deny selling the Goff hoax booklet, we sent a letter of inquiry, received a reply, and ordered it by letter with an enclosed postal money order. The Freedom Club cannot plead innocence, because their Bulletin of June 1, 1966 says: "Authorized literature is available only after review by the Freedom

Club committee and then sold through the office or at our booktables. No other material is sponsored."

A leaflet mailed out in the latter part of September, 1965, by the Ultra-Rightist *Liberty Lobby* advertises Goff's booklet on "Brain-Washing." Their *Liberty Letter*, No. 61, of February 1966, gives Goff's booklet a very strong recommendation.

Education Information, Inc., an Ultra-Rightist propaganda group, whose headquarters have been variously listed as Fullerton, Calif., Amarillo, Texas, and Omaha, Nebraska, issues an imposing-looking brochure, entitled *Secret Files For Secret Purposes*. It is a sly attack against the public school system in general and against school-employed psychologists and psychiatrists in general. The garbled quotations are the familiar ones that can be found in the various tracts issued by other Ultra-Rightists. It warns that Federal Aid to education will play into the hands of "home-grown psycho-politicians." In discussing tranquilizer drugs and other psychotherapeutic drugs, the brochure says:

One cannot help but wonder if some of these drugs are being given to travelers in Soviet Russia, judging from the glowing tales they bring back from that Slave State.

One of the big points the brochure raises, by way of proving a sinister conspiracy in the public school system, is that the files of questionnaires and psychological testing are kept confidential. The brochure insinuates that it is "the educational psycho-politicians" who want these files to be kept confidential. After charging that the public schools have abandoned concepts of morality, the brochure says:

Basing their philosophy of character education on Pavlov, Hall, and assorted mental hygienists and psychopoliticians, the professional educationists proceeded to sully the minds of America's children with tests, questionnaires, and analyses. . . .

At another point in this brochure, it correctly states that in certain cases parents are *requested* to take a child to a school-approved psychiatrist. The brochure then asks:

Who can say that the recommended psychiatrists are not "psycho-politicians" . . . mind-changers under the Pavlovian system . . .

who, if the child's record shows a consistent tendency toward aggressiveness, leadership, or competition, would prefer, for the sake of social change, to incarcerate him where he can be "changed" under more drastic methods?

Thus we can see that the psychopolitics hoax is being used to heat up the Cold War, to attack the mental health programs, and to undermine the public school system. In the context of the present social and political conditions, the exploitation of the psychopolitics hoax can only strengthen the forces of incipient American Fascism.

The State of California has on its statute books a law called the Short-Doyle Act. Its essential feature is to allocate a certain percentage of State funds to any county that agrees to participate in setting up *local* mental health clinics and to provide counterpart financing. The main purpose is to provide out-patient service to emotionally disturbed patients and to *reduce* the number of commitments to psychiatric hospitals. In county after county, the Ultra-Rightists have conducted a vicious smear campaign against the Short-Doyle program. Disregarding the wholesale evidence of its *proven* benefits, the Ultra-Rightists mount a campaign of fear and smear whenever the program is proposed. Typical was the campaign against the Short-Doyle program in Butte County, California during the summer of 1965. The Ultra-Rightists brought in Mr. Tom Sullivan, who was formerly on the speakers bureau of the so-called Free Enterprise Department of Coast Federal Savings & Loan Association. Sullivan has made a specialty of fighting mental health programs, but significantly, when we interviewed him in his home on June 25, 1965, he stated categorically that Kenneth Goff's *Brain-Washing, a Synthesis of the Russian Text Book on Psychopolitics "cannot be documented."* The story of this Ultra-Rightist campaign in Butte County will be told in volume II, but for the present a letter, which appeared in the weekly *Feather River Times* of Paradise, California on July 28, 1965, will illustrate how the poison of the psychopolitics hoax spreads.

Dear Editor:

In the summer of 1935, hundreds of American educators were sent to Russia for indoctrination of COMMUNISM at the Lenin University; they were chosen by the Institute of International Edu-

574

cation, Inc., cited by Congressional documents as a tax-exempt, left-leaning organization.

Instructions to American Communists, students and educators at the Lenin University were introduced, as evidence, in the Congressional Record. Excerpts therefrom as follows: "Propaganda should continue and stress the rising incidence of insanity in the country. The entire field of human behavior . . . can be broadened into abnormal behavior. . . . Thus, anyone . . . could be silenced. . . . Disable him or swerve his loyalties.

"The psychiatrist is aptly suited to his role, for his brutalities are committed in the name of science and are inexplicably complex and entirely out of view of the human understanding. Cloaked in authority, he can continue a campaign of propaganda . . . describing various treatments which are administered to the insane.

"In a capitalistic state you are aided on all sides by the corruption. Use the courts, use the judges, use the Constitution . . . medical societies and the laws to further our ends. . . . You can effect your legislation at will. . . . Make your own legislators, by their own appropriations, finance the quiet Communist conquest of the nation.

"With the institutions for the insane . . . your prisons can hold a million persons . . . without civil rights or any hope of freedom . . . upon these people can be practiced shock and surgery so that never again will they draw a sane breath. You must carry forth the myth that only a European doctor is competent in the field of insanity."

These Soviet instructions have been carried out. Thousands of European doctors, trained in Communist psychiatry, have been brought into the United States by the early years of the Roosevelt regime. President Lyndon B. Johnson stated that 10,000 more psychiatrists are needed for proposed nationwide community mental health clinics.

Psychopoliticians, psychologists and psychiatrists for years have been in all Federal Agencies, guiding the managed news propaganda, brainwashing the public into acceptance of liberalism and humanitarianism which is prohibited in the Soviet.

To name a few instances that are aiding their conquest, under the guise of Foreign Aid, finances are greatly helping the Communist conquest of our country.

Many Supreme Court decisions are pro-Communist and unconstitutional.

Alaska Mental Health Act, H.R. 6376, an act passed in 1956 where a million acres were set aside in Alaska to provide for the hospitalization and care of the mentally ill, and for other purposes. This is a very dangerous bill and every loyal American should read and understand this Act, protest this "Mental Health" propaganda, that we are receiving through channels such as radio, T.V., schools, etc.

All loyal citizens are in favor of setting up the best possible care

575

for those mentally ill but it must be insisted in so doing that the individual is entitled to the maximum protection allowed us under the Constitution.

DOROTHY THRESHER

Needless to add, Dorothy Thresher's letter is based upon misinformation and garbled quotations. She is probably honest and sincere, but a victim of the psychopolitics and other hoaxes.

Perhaps the best evidence of the organized nature of Ultra-Rightist attacks upon the mental health program was a full-page advertisement in the August 11, 1965, issue of *Feather River Times*. It was placed by the Ultra-Rightist *Poor Richard's Book Shop* of Hollywood, California, some 500 miles away. (Poor Richard's Book Shop has since moved to Hamilton, Montana.) The heading of the advertisement is:

### WHAT DOES MENTAL HEALTH REALLY MEAN?
### WHAT IS PLANNED FOR YOU?

It begins with a "quotation" from the speech that Lavrenti Beria did *not* deliver, quotes from Goff's introduction to his "Brain-Washing" booklet, and then quotes excerpts from each of the 15 chapters of Goff's booklet. As "documentation" of the items quoted from Goff's booklet, Poor Richard's Book Shop quotes smear items from various Reports of the California Un-American Activities Committee, the House Committee on Un-American Activities, the Senate Internal Security Subcommittee, and other sources. The Red paint brush is used liberally to impugn the motives and assassinate the character of a respected former California Superior Court Judge and others who are active in mental health work. This episode proves once more that the witch-hunting Committees, that operate under the guise of exposing "Un-American Activities," furnish the ideological ammunition for the Ultra-Rightists. The advertisement concludes with:

### DEMAND REPEAL
### OF
### UNCONSTITUTIONAL MENTAL
### HEALTH LEGISLATION

The final item is a blatant lie. The mental health legislation has not been adjudicated as unconstitutional. Arbitrarily calling laws, which displease them, unconstitutional, is a common propaganda device of many Ultra-Rightist zealots.

The *Los Angeles Times* of May 2, 1964 carried an advertisement, 16 inches long and 9 inches wide, by evangelist A. A. Allen. For many years, Allen has claimed the ability to effect cures of every conceivable ailment, including those that defy medical and/or surgical intervention. In this particular advertisement, Allen shows "before and after" pictures of victims of crippling diseases, who could discard their crutches, wheel chairs, and steel braces after praying with Allen. The advertisement is headed by:

COMING YOUR WAY!  FOLLOW THE CROWDS!
GOD'S LAST CALL TO AMERICA!
GREAT SPIRITUAL
AWAKENING!
A.A. ALLEN
GOD'S MAN OF FAITH AND POWER
WITH THE WORLD'S GREATEST MIRACLE
REVIVAL EVANGELISTIC PARTY!

Under these headlines, this "man of God," admonishes his readers:

DON'T BE DECEIVED BY PROPAGANDA!
DON'T BE MISLED BY "POISON PEN" WRITERS!
DON'T LET RUSSIA BRAINWASH YOU
IN A CHURCH WASH PAN!

This is followed by some more warnings and the following:

Here are partial quotes from Brainwashing, a book with part of Russia's instructions for destroying the Church in America! "Ridicule and Defame the Preachers; if they Advertise a Healing Campaign, call it a hoax; the Church, especially the Healing Campaign, must be destroyed, even if you have to resort to wild lies, personal defamations, false evidences, and constant (bad) propaganda!"

HAVE YOU BEEN BRAINWASHED
BY THESE METHODS?

Strange as it may seem, his quotation from the "Brainwashing" booklet cannot be found in that booklet! When liars lie about liars, they are pretty desperate for material with which to influence people!

In thousands of letters-to-the-editor from coast to coast, one can find recurring examples of the influence of the psycho-politics hoax. Typical of these is a letter in the Ultra-Rightist *Santa Ana Register,* November 6, 1967, in which we are told that "our high schools and colleges . . . are disgorging brain-washed robots", that psychologists "corrupt our children even in elementary school," and that priests and ministers are "caught up in this civil rights madness." Perhaps the most ludicrous example of the influence of the psychopolitics hoax involved Dr. C. C. Trillingham, who retired on June 30, 1967, after serving as Los Angeles County Superintendent of Schools for 25 years.

Our story begins with a little item, headlined "PLANNED DELINQUENCY," in the November 1959 issue of the Ultra-Rightist *American Mercury:*

By making readily available drugs of various kinds, by giving the teen-ager alcohol, by praising his wildness, by stimulating him with sex literature and advertising to him or her practices as taught at the Sexpol, the psychopolitical operator can create the necessary attitude of chaos, idleness and worthlessness into which can then be cast the solution which will give the teen-ager complete freedom everywhere. . .

If we could effectively kill the national pride and patriotism of just one generation we will have won that country. Therefore there must be continual propaganda abroad to undermine the loyalty of the citizens in general and the teen-ager in particular. (Brainwashing, A Synthesis of the Russian Textbook on Psychopolitics used in training Red agents, p. 23.)

—CANADIAN INTELLIGENCE SERVICE

Television newscaster, George Putnam, one of the darlings of the Ultra-Rightists, seems to have gotten all steamed up over this item, because he featured it in a most dramatic fashion. In response to our inquiry, Putnam sent us a memorandum on August 25, 1964, which he had apparently circulated at the time he telecast the "Brainwashing" item:

The following was printed in the November 1959 issue of American Mercury under the heading "Planned Delinquency," and is an excerpt from "Brainwashing, a Synthesis of the Russian Textbook on Psychopolitics" used in training Red agents.

George Putnam considers it so important, that he read it on all ten of his television news reports for the week of March 7th, 1960. He thinks that it should be circulated in every school in America.

578

Following this he quotes the entire item from *American Mercury* exactly as it appeared. Very obligingly, Putnam has a footnote to advise that the "Brainwashing" booklet may be purchased for $1.00 by writing to American Public Relations Forum, Inc. It is not clear whether Putnam read the November issue of *American Mercury* in March, just prior to his telecasts, or whether he read it in November and took four months to work up a "head of steam."

One of the listeners to Putnam's telecasts of March 7, 1960, was Kenneth Hahn, a member of the Los Angeles County Board of Supervisors. Three days later, he introduced a resolution, instructing the County Superintendent of Schools to bring the message of George Putnam's telecast to all the students in the County school system. Kenneth Hahn was once known as a liberal of sorts, but the impact of many years of witch-hunting by governmental committees has affected the thinking of millions of Americans, including Mr. Hahn. As late as July 12, 1965, Supervisor Hahn was telling an audience in San Diego, California that he is advocating underground fallout shelters for all of the 7 million inhabitants of Los Angeles County. Mr. Hahn seems to be oblivious to the fact that a thermonuclear explosion over the Los Angeles area would start a "fire storm," which would consume all the available oxygen, and the 7 million people would suffocate in their underground shelters.

On March 11, 1960, Gordon T. Nesvig, Clerk of the Board of Supervisors, sent this message to Dr. C. C. Trillingham, Los Angeles County Superintendent of Schools:

At the meeting of the Board of Supervisors on March 10, 1960, on motion of Supervisor Hahn, the attached bulletin from Television Channel KTTV was referred to you with instructions to bring it to the attention of all students in Los Angeles County.

In an interview on July 28, 1964, in his office, Dr. Tillingham told us that, after much soul-searching and some conferences with his staff. he wrote an editorial, in order to "cover" the mandate of the Supervisor's resolution. This is how it appeared in the Monthly Bulletin sent out of Dr. Trillingham's office in April, 1960:

ARE WE AWARE . . .
By C. C. Trillingham

The Canadian Intelligence Service has recently released some dramatic excerpts from *Brainwashing,* a synthesis of a Russian text-

579

book on psychopolitics used in training Red agents. These paragraphs appeared in the November issue of *American Mercury* under the heading "Planned Delinquency." They were brought to public attention locally by George Putnam who read them on all of his television news reports during the week of March 7, 1960.

The Los Angeles County Board of Supervisors has urged the County Superintendent of Schools Office to bring this message to the attention of all students in the schools of Los Angeles County. It is hoped that school district administrators and boards will cooperate by alerting their youngsters to this danger.

Here is the statement from the Russian textbook used in training their agents to take over the world.

"By making readily available drugs of various kinds, by giving the teen-ager alcohol, by praising his wildness, by stimulating him with sex literature and advertising to him or her practices as taught at 'Sexpol,' the psychopolitical operator can create the necessary attitude of chaos, idleness and worthlessness into which can then be cast the solution which will give the teen-ager complete freedom everywhere."

"If we could effectively kill the national pride and patriotism of just one generation we will have won that country. Therefore, there must be continual propaganda abroad to undermine the loyalty of the citizens in general and the teen-ager in particular."

This is one way the Communists are doing their part to soften the younger generation. They seem to have considerable help inside our own country. Wittingly or unwittingly, they seem to have plenty of assistance in preparing our young people for the "moral decay" that has preceded the fall of all previous civilizations, according to historian Toynbee. With alcohol, narcotics, and pornographic materials available to our youth and with much of our movie and TV fare featuring crime, violence, and loose morality, it is time that our homes, churches, schools and government combine forces to convince youth that honest and decent living represent the highest type of intelligence and patriotism.

Too many unscrupulous individuals are permitted to ply their nefarious trade for the dollars in it and do so under the guise of freedom and democracy. Without regard for the common welfare, freedom becomes license.

The high summit meeting of Communist leaders and representatives of the West is just ahead of us. Millions of people everywhere have great hope in the outcome. American visitors to the U.S.S.R. are impressed with the smiles, the handshakes, and the talk about peace and friendship.

But the declared purposes, the avowed time tables, and past records show that trained agents of the Soviet Union are working like termites everywhere, probing for our weaknesses and attempting to take us over without a fight.

Let's inform our youngsters what the Communists are trying to do to them. Then, let's review with them our many freedoms and opportunities, our comforts and conveniences that are too often taken for granted. Let's try to build a new loyalty and dedication to our Bill of Rights, our free enterprise system, our universal education, and our Judeo-Christian religion. Let's begin living up to the best promises of these great foundation stones. Let's help the youngsters see that we're in a battle of ideologies for keeps.

Under further pressure, Dr. Trillingham delivered a speech at a rally organized by Dr. Fred Schwarz' Christian Anti-Communism Crusade, August, 29, 1961, at the Los Angeles Sports Arena. This rally was run under the deceptive title of the Southern California School of Anti-Communism. We say that Dr. Trillingham did this under pressure, because we are convinced that he had to knuckle under or run the risk of becoming the target of abuse by the peddlers of hysteria, and possibly losing his job and his pension rights. In other words, his loyalty would be questioned by the assorted Red-hunters. In his speech, he quoted from the editorial on "Brainwashing" which he had written, and even misquoted his own editorial at one point. We are willing to attribute this to error rather than lack of integrity, but the sad part is that educators are "bludgeoned" into conformity with reactionary ideologies.

It doesn't take long for falsehood to travel, whether it is uttered wittingly or unwittingly. Less than 4 months after Dr. Trillingham delivered his speech, Dr. Drummond J. Mc Cunn, Superintendent of the Contra Costa Junior College District, delivered a speech on December 6, 1961 before the California Association of School Administrators. Among his remarks was this item:

The Communist Party has stated "If we could effectively kill the national pride and patriotism of just one generation we will have won that country. Therefore, there must be continual propaganda abroad to undermine the loyalty of the citizens in general and the teen-ager in particular."

Dr. Mc Cunn gives the source of his quotation, in this footnote to the script of his speech:

Quoted from Russian Textbook on Psychopolitics in a speech "The Communist Challenge to Education" by Dr. C. C. Trillingham, Los Angeles County Superintendent, Los Angeles County, California.

581

The Communist Party, of course, did not say what Dr. Mc Cunn attributed to it. The item which he attributed, in quotation marks, comes directly from the "Brainwashing" booklet. When Dr. Trillingham placed that quotation in the mouth of the Communists, during his speech at the Fred Schwarz rally, the stage was set for others to use this erroneous quotation, and Dr. Mc Cunn was one of those who picked it up.

After several exchanges of correspondence, Dr. Trillingham agreed that we could interview him in his office on July 28, 1964. We found him to be a pleasant, soft-spoken, and even-tempered gentleman. He made it very clear that he was not particularly proud about his role in spreading the psycho-politics hoax. Some of the statements he made are here summarized, accurately and faithfully:

1. Dr. Trillingham began by saying that he is not so sure that Kenneth Goff knows what he is talking about.

2. Dr. Trillingham said that he thought the Los Angeles County Board of Supervisors was misled by the official sounding name of Canadian Intelligence Service. Dr. Trillingham confessed that he too was very much misled by the official sounding name of Canadian Intelligence Service. It was only after a member of his own staff made inquiry at the office of the Canadian consul in Los Angeles that he learned the truth: the Canadian Intelligence Service is a *private* organization.

3. Dr. Trillingham had once served on the so-called Committee for Observance of Bill of Rights Week, but resigned when Joe Crail, president of Coast Federal Savings and Loan Association, who was head of it, began to use it as a vehicle of Ultra-Rightist Propaganda.

4. Dr. Trillingham said that educators were under tremendous pressure from the propaganda films, "Operation Abolition" (produced by the House Committee on Un-American Activities) and "Communism on the Map" (produced by the Ultra-Rightist Harding College); and from the John Birch Society and television commentator George Putnam.

5. Dr. Trillingham said that after much discussion with his staff, and largely as a "defensive" measure, a program was started in the Los Angeles County Schools under the title of "Our American Heritage"; the idea being *to seize the initiative* from the Ultra-Rightists. The program was discussed in advance with William Wheeler, the West Coast investigator of the

House Committee on Un-American Activities, who is a former FBI Special Agent. In the course of a luncheon meeting, Wheeler offered some suggestions for the program. Dr. Trillingham's dream of appeasing the Ultra-Rightists was shattered by the attacks upon the program almost immediately after it got under way. It became necessary to work closely with the local FBI Office, Dr. Trillingham said, on account of the threatening phone calls received by members of his staff.

6. Dr. Trillingham said that he accepted the invitation to speak at the Fred Schwarz rally of the Christian Anti-Communism Crusade on the theory of *seizing the initiative* from the Ultra-Rightists.

7. As the conversation proceeded, Dr. Trillingham appeared to become more uncomfortable because of the questions we asked him. He said that he once attended a dinner where Dr. Robert Morris, former counsel of the Senate Internal Security Subcommittee, spoke. He thought that Dr. Morris' speech was "objective," but that Dr. Morris has since changed for the worse. At one time he counted 24 major Ultra-Rightist organizations operating in Los Angeles County. He reached into his desk and brought out a copy of John Stormer's Ultra-Rightist tract, *None Dare Call It Treason,* and a copy of the now-defunct Ultra-Rightist propaganda weekly, *Tocsin.*

8. In a moment of refreshing candor, Dr. Trillingham exclaimed: "Where do people like Clarence Manion get all their malarkey?" (Dr. Clarence Manion, a member of the National Council of the John Birch Society, operates a radio network program and issues newsletters and other propaganda of the Ultra-Rightist slant.)

9. Dr. Trillingham's most astute observation, which is borne out by the extensive research of a number of social psychologists, was that constant reading of Ultra-Rightist material produces disorientation, and that once a person stops reading the stuff, he can return to being rational. He added that constant immersion in the stuff is harmful.

10. Having reached the point where we had established better rapport with Dr. Trillingham, he agreed that a complete exposé of the Ultra-Right is needed, and requested that he be notified when this book is published.

Little do most Americans realize the extent to which the psychopolitics hoax has been used to intimidate educators into retreating from sound educational procedures and into appeasing the forces of incipient American Fascism. Little do most Americans realize that the House Committee on Un-American Activities and the Senate Internal Security Subcommittee exert a subtle (and sometimes not so subtle) pressure against our educational system.

Another possible result of the psychopolitics hoax came to light during the 1960 trial in Moscow of U-2 pilot Gary Powers on charges of espionage. Oliver Powers, his father, told *Life* magazine that he believed his son had undergone "some sort of brain-baking." He said that both he and his wife noted that their son's forehead was peeling, as if from sunburn! Upon his release and return to the U.S.A., Gary Powers repeatedly stated that he was treated humanely, and did not make that "brain-baking" charge. However, these facts never caught up with the original falsehood.

It is an interesting commentary on the lack of interest in the truth that *a real program* for manipulation of the human mind is underway by the military of this country, and the Ultra-Rightists are silent about it. One does not need the phoney *Russian Text Book on Psychopolitics* (or anything of like nature) to prove this charge. Drew Pearson reported in his column, *Los Angeles Times,* August 27, 1965:

> Our laboratories have developed germs that could incapacitate a whole nation without killing a soul. The population would be too weak to resist an invasion, later would recover without any harmful effects.

In addition to the germ warfare agents being developed by the military at a number of research laboratories, there have been developed a deadly nerve gas and a number of *psychochemical* agents. In a document entitled "Research in CBR, Report No. 23 of the Committee on Science and Astronautics of the House of Representatives, August 10, 1959," we read:

> Introduced into a command center, there is no telling what psychochemicals would do, except that the results would be disastrous.
> The incapacitating agents suggest employments where military necessity requires control of a situation, but where there is good reason for not harming either the surrounding population or even the intended target troops.
> They also suggest covert uses either to confuse defenses or retalia-

tory forces, or *to affect the rationality of important leadership groups at some particular crucial point in history*.[3] (Emphasis has been added.—M. K.)

In the *Bulletin of Atomic Scientists*, January 1962, Mr. E. James Lieberman comments on the possible consequences of perfecting psychochemicals as instruments of coercion and control:

We can envision grave political consequences apart from war. Virtually complete control of the individual may come to rest with governments, or with whoever possesses the weapons. Under such circumstances a government could outwardly uphold the noblest statutes of political freedom, while subtly extinguishing the actual expression of individual liberty. Since self-control is essential for nonviolent resistance, Gandhian methods could be rendered ineffectual by mood-altering drugs. Brainwashing may become a specialty of chemists, and other crude techniques of totalitarian systems may be superseded by mass tranquilization.

Mr. Lieberman's fears have been realized. Not only are police increasingly using tear gas as an answer to the cry for justice in America, but a new and dangerous chemical agent called MACE is being used, which nauseates the victim, causes prolonged irritation and watering of the eyes, and produces a burning sensation on the skin. Even more ominous for the future are suggestions made public on November 11, 1967 by the Institute for Defense Analysis:

1. Sticky strings, bands of adhesives, explosively or mechanically spread, that might slow the movement of the crowd "by linking people together or to themselves."

2. A hand-held net which could sweep out a portion of a crowd, or a net that could be dropped by Helicopters.

3. Plastic confetti spread on the ground to make walking difficult.

4. A foam generator to block streets or spray the crowd. The claim for this diabolical device is that people immersed in foam "are psychologically distressed by the loss of contact with the environment. There is also the feeling of being stifled."

5. The super water pistol. One model shoots water to a distance of some 35 feet and uses *a pepper-based solution.*

3 The House Committee's Report is quoted in the article by E. James Lieberman in *Bulletin of Atomic Scientists*, January 1962.

6. Metal darts, tipped with tranquilizing drugs, to be shot from a special pistol. These have been successfully used on wild animals.

7. Itching powder to be used to break up sit-in demonstrations.

One can only wonder whether or not it would be in order for a Russian counterpart of Kenneth Goff to write a booklet, entitled *Brain-Washing, A Synthesis of the American Text Book on Psychochemical Politics!* Of one thing we can be sure. In the Great Crusade of lying about the Soviet Union, the psychopolitics hoax has been a formidable and treacherous weapon.

# CHAPTER XIII

## The Great Crusade: Fifty Years of Hate

### The Liars' Potpourri

It is questionable whether there is any historical parallel to the fifty years of hate-peddling that has been the principal ingredient of the Great Crusade of propaganda to discredit the Soviet Union. It has been conducted on such a massive scale that we found it necessary to spread the proven data over a number of chapters. In addition to the many fabrications and distortions of truth that we have discussed up to this point, there are a few more that need the spotlight shone on them, because they are still being circulated.

One of the canards that has been discarded was the "Moscow Gold" hoax. For a period of at least twenty years after the Bolshevik Revolution in 1917, a standard device for smearing any effort to achieve social reforms or to organize labor unions was to charge that the activity was being financed by "Moscow Gold," which was being mysteriously distributed by secret agents. Moreover, it was charged that activities in almost every corner of the globe were being financed by "Moscow Gold." News stories, editorials, speeches, sermons, lectures, and propaganda tracts were replete with "authoritative" stories about the use of "Moscow Gold" to bribe and corrupt the entire world. It did not dawn on some of these dimwits that there was a tremendous contradiction in telling people that the Soviet system was a colossal failure and simultaneously crediting it with distributing enough gold to systematically buy up so many people in country after country. This hoax finally died a natural death, because people became tired of it and realized it was without foundation. Some of the latter-day Crusaders have, however, concocted a yarn resembling the old hoax. It consists of giving a figure, of the amount of dollars the Soviet Union allegedly spends on foreign propaganda, that is of astronomical proportions and for which no proof is given, excepting its constant reiteration by the Cold Warriors.

587

One of the early anti-Soviet Crusaders was the late Senator Arthur Robinson of Indiana. In a speech, which can be found on pages 1538-1543 of the Congressional Record, April 12, 1933, Senator Robinson used a number of fabricated quotations. Whether he was deliberately lying or merely the unwitting dupe of some anti-Soviet propagandists, it is difficult to say, but he deserved criticism for not doing some research before spreading the yarns. The Senator was campaigning against diplomatic recognition of the Soviet Union. So he trotted out this fabrication, which he attributed to Menjinsky, the head of the secret police:

As long as there are idiots to take our signature seriously, and put their trust in it, we must promise everything that is being asked, and as much as one likes, if we can only get something tangible in exchange.

This statement contains some elements of the pie-crust fabrication that we exposed as Lenin Fabrication No. 1 and some elements of the Manuilsky Hoax.

The Senator quoted Lenin as saying in 1923:

We must hate—hatred is the basis of communism. Children must be taught to hate their parents if they are not Communists. If they are, then the child need not respect them; need no longer worry about them.

The Senator quoted Anatole Lunacharsky, the Commissar of Education, as saying:

We hate Christianity and Christians; even the best of them must be regarded as our worst enemies. They preach love of one's neighbor and mercy, which is contrary to our principles.

Christian love is an obstacle to the development of the revolution. Down with the love of one's neighbors. What we need is hatred. We must know how to hate; only thus shall we conquer the universe.

Following these "quotations," the Senator told his colleagues that in the Soviet Union:

The family as an institution has all but disappeared. Children are separated from parents; wives are separated from husbands; marriage is debauched and divorce is worse than a travesty.

The statement by the Senator was a variation on the theme of that obscene canard, the nationalization of women. There was not a word of truth in the Senator's statement. The same is true for the "quotations" that he used. First of all, he gave no sources for documentation of his "quotations." Secondly, no such statements appear in the speeches and writing of the three men he "quoted." Thirdly, the sentiments expressed in those "quotations" clash with the philosophical posture in the known writings and speeches of all three men. Nowhere can one find anything that remotely resembles these alleged quotations.

In the debate on the floor of the Senate, the late Senator William E. Borah politely gave the lie to Senator Robinson's propaganda, when he stated:

I am aware, Mr. President, of the supposed statements referred to by the Senator from Indiana. . . In my opinion, the charge that the Soviet Government is seeking to undermine or destroy our Government is an exploded and absurd proposition.

Later in the debate Senator Borah said:

I have no fear of their landing an army, even if their ambassador were here. And I have no fear of their propaganda though it come in carload lots.

At this point Senator Long asked:

Is there not more danger of this country being destroyed by 1 percent of the people owning 80 percent of the wealth than there is of a Russian army destroying it?

There is very convincing internal evidence in another portion of Senator Robinson's speech, which supports the conclusion that his "quotations" came from one of the propaganda mills that specialized in fabricating Communist quotations. The Senator "quoted" from the Communist *Daily Worker* of September 18, 1918. The first issue of the *Daily Worker* came off the press on Sunday, January 13, 1924, and is shown on the front page to be Vol. 1, No. 1. It is quite a feat to quote a newspaper 5 years and 4 months before it is born! The alleged story in the *Daily Worker* contains two misstatements of historical fact. It alludes to the Union of Soviet Socialist Republics and to the Third Internationale. The political merger of Russia

589

and a number of other political entities, to form the Union of Soviet Socialist Republics, did not take place until 1922, which was 4 years after the phoney newspaper story referred to it as already in existence! Similarly, the Third Internationale did not come into existence until one year after the phoney newspaper story told all about its activities!

Senator Robinson's work lives on after him. We found the Lunacharsky fabrication being quoted by the Rev. Paul Neipp of Ridgecrest, California, who conducts an anti-Communist crusade via radio, pamphlets, and a monthly paper. It was quoted by Hal Hunt in *National Chronicle* of March 11, 1965; in a circular sent out in January 1966 by *Americans for Freedom,* Santa Barbara, California; in *Life Line* Freedom Talk, October 20, 1966; and by Tom Anderson, in his syndicated column, *Santa Ana Register,* December 19, 1966.

The Menjinsky fabrication is quoted in the September-October 1964 issue of *Golden Sphinx,* the official publication of the National Counter Intelligence Corps Association, a worldwide group of former Counter Intelligence Corps agents. Its bimonthly newsletter carries on a persistent anti-Communist campaign, with the usual disregard for facts. The same issue, for good measure, carried Lenin Fabrication No. 1 and Stalin Fabrication No. 1. In response to a letter requesting authentication of these three quotations, the Board Chairman wrote to us on October 28, 1964:

Our quotations were taken from Page 9 of the Friday, May 25, 1962 issue of the University of Washington Daily. All quotes are authentic.

The item upon which the Board Chairman of *Golden Sphinx* relied was a paid advertisement, signed *U. of W. New Conservatives,* and is distributed in reprint by an Ultra-Rightist group in Seattle, Americans for America. It consists of fabrications, as well as out-of-context quotations. As a former Counter Intelligence agent, the Board Chairman knows, or should know, that he cannot rely upon this propaganda advertisement for authentication of quotations.

Typical of the fantastic stories that are invented, as part of the Great Crusade, was a hoax story that was debunked, as a by-product of a campaign to make gas and chemical warfare more palatable. The story was told succinctly by California Assemblyman Charles J. Conrad in a statement that was placed in the Congressional Record, April 5, 1965, by Congressman Don H. Clausen. It should be noted that Assemblyman Conrad is a vigorous Ultra-Rightist, and is not inclined to furnish any support to the Communists. Mr. Conrad said:

> While U.S. officials regard honest discussion of chemical and biological warfare "rather delicate," fantastic yarns make headlines several times a year.
>
> A prime example was the report of an anti-espionage expert in the West German Embassy in Moscow being drenched with mustard gas in a monastery. The U.S. medical official mentioned in the story is not known and no Soviet agent would think of using mustard because of its strong odor and comparatively slow action.
>
> Reports from Cuba have been equally inaccurate.

Ultra-Rightist journalistic pundits wrote many indignant columns and editorials about this Soviet "atrocity," but nowhere have we seen a retraction or correction. We are sure that many of these gentlemen monitor the Congressional Record and had access to Assemblyman Conrad's exposure of this hoax story.

One of the features of the Great Crusade is the tendency to forget the revolutionary heritage of the U.S.A. As a result, revolution has, in effect, become a "dirty" word in our language. As a corollary to this position, the Cold War propagandists continually assert that the oppressed and impoverished peoples in the so-called underdeveloped countries would accept their lot in life, were it not for instigation by foreign agitators. Every revolt is labeled as Moscow-inspired or Peking-inspired or Castro-inspired. This monstrous lie then furnishes the "moral" justification for such acts as the recent U.S.A. aggression against the people of the Dominican Republic and our genocidal war against the people of Vietnam. The gentlemen who inspire this falsehood are fully aware of its true nature. Among the principal purveyors of this fairy tale is, of course, the Central Intelligence Agency. But sometimes they make a slip, and in an unguarded moment the truth emerges. This happened in 1964, when the CIA Board of National Estimates had a so-called position paper drawn up by Willard Matthias. It dealt with a possible neutral solution to the Vietnam problem, and it was "leaked" to the *Chicago Tribune*. As far as we know, only *I.F. Stone's Weekly* of September 7, 1964, publicized this portion of the CIA paper:

Despite any disinclination to get involved in crises or any interest in a detente which may exist, the situation in most of the under-developed world is so disorderly that many situations are likely to develop from which the great powers will have difficulty remaining aloof or which they will have difficulty controlling if they get involved. Individuals or groups calling themselves Castroites or Communists might stage revolutionary attempts or initiate guerilla movements *not on the orders of Moscow, Peiping or Havana* but in the hope of gaining their support. Similarly individuals or groups may organize or execute plots simply to gain U.S. support. (Emphasis has been added.—M. K.)

## Ask Me Anything

It would take many volumes to deal with all the hate-the-Soviets items that have been carried by the Hearst press. One of these stories first appeared in a book entitled *Ask Me Anything,* written jointly by William Randolph Hearst, Jr., Bob Considine, and Frank Conniff, the latter two being Hearst columnists. In their discussion of the execution of former secret police chief, Beria, the Hearst trio say:

No official report of the events surrounding Beria's liquidation has ever been released, but Khrushchev himself is reputed to have given a pungent description of it to Pierre Commins, member of a French Socialist delegation which visited Moscow in May, 1956. This account appeared two months afterward in a Socialist publication:

These remarks are followed by 28 lines of printed words, allegedly quoting the article in "a Socialist publication," whose name is strangely omitted.

On February 10, 1964, we sent a letter to both Mr. Hearst and to Mr. Conniff, asking the name, the date, and the address of that "Socialist publication." On April 16, 1965, we sent a letter to Mr. Hearst, with which we enclosed a photocopy of our previous letter to him and a photocopy of our previous letter to Mr. Conniff. We quote the most important portion of our letter:

Neither you nor Mr. Conniff showed me the elementary courtesy of replying to my letter, which was written in a most courteous style.

My suspicions aroused, I engaged the services of a scholar who teaches French, has lived in France, and has studied in France.

Enclosed is photocopy of a letter, dated March 4, 1965, which this scholar received from M. Georges Brutelle, Deputy Secretary General of the Unified Socialist Party of France. I have snipped out the scholar's name and address, because he need not be involved in this matter and his identity is irrelevant.

Enclosed also is a photocopy of this scholar's translation of the letter from Paris, France.

It would appear from all this that you have deliberately concocted this story and perpetrated a hoax upon your readers. This hoax was further compounded by the fact that it was quoted in *Look* of Nov. 19, 1963 and *Christian Economics* of Jan. 7, 1964.

I urge you to publish a retraction of this story, and will await with keen anticipation your reply to this letter. Incidentally, the name of the man you "quoted" is Commin, not Commins.

The postal receipt shows that our letter was received in the Hearst office, 959 Eighth Ave., New York City on April 20, 1965. No reply was received from Mr. Hearst.

The letter, in the original French, from M. Georges Brutelle, dated March 4, 1965, is in our possession. We present a translation which was done by our French scholar:

Dear Sir:

Mr. Edouard Depreux, Secretary General of the Unified Socialist Party, informs me of a communication that you addressed to him on January 18 and which concerns the Socialist Party (S.F.I.O.).

Here is my response to your questions:

1. A Socialist delegation did in fact visit Moscow in May, 1956;
2. M. Pierre Commin, Deputy Secretary General of the S.F.I.O., did lead this delegation;
3. There was no official report of this visit published.

May I inform you that, on several occasions, I have been questioned by American citizens about a report that Pierre Commin supposedly made of our interviews, precisely regarding the death of Beria. Now, for one thing, Pierre Commin never wrote a single line on that subject; for another, the intent of the questions that have generally been asked of me, indicate that a totally erroneous report of our conversations has circulated in the United States. I have already had the opportunity to clarify this subject in an interview that I gave to a U.S. television network.

Having myself been a member of this delegation, having personally negotiated in Moscow even the program of our visit and directed the part of the delegation that went to Kiev, Odessa, and Kharkov, I am at your service for any further information that I may be able to furnish you.

Only I must tell you that the death of Pierre Commin has made it impossible for us to get possession of the dossier relative to this delegation. It is therefore only through my own recollections and the notes that any of the other members of the delegation kept personally that I can be of any assistance to you in the future.

> Sincerely,
> (signed)
> GEORGES BRUTELLE
> *Deputy Secretary General*

If Pierre Commin "never wrote a single line on that subject" (the Beria execution), how did the Hearst trio quote from an article by him? That is the question that must be raised continually when one examines the writings and speeches of the participants in the Great Crusade.

Some time after July 5, 1962, M. Georges Brutelle was interviewed in Paris by Morris Calden of the Rome, Italy office of the National Broadcasting System. The interview was recorded on video tape, which was presented as a part of an NBC White Paper, "The Death of Stalin," on a nationwide telecast, narrated by Chet Huntley, Sunday, January 27, 1963. It should be remembered that M. Georges Brutelle was on that delegation that visited Moscow. We present, for comparison, Brutelle's version of Beria's execution, as told to him by Khrushchev, and the version that the Hearst trio "quoted" from Pierre Commin:[1]

| *Hearst version, Commin allegedly quoting Khrushchev* | *Brutelle's version on NBC program* |
| --- | --- |
| "We came to the conclusion that the only correct measure for the defense of the Revolution was to shoot him immediately. This decision was adopted by us and carried out on the spot." | Khrushchev then added that Beria was allowed to go out of the room. He was arrested in the antechamber and taken to Lubianka prison. |

In the course of the telecast, several other people tell versions of the Beria incident, but they are definitely hearsay, because

1 We are grateful to the National Broadcasting System for sending us a copy of the entire script of the telecast.

none of them is based upon conversation with Khrushchev, as is the case with M. Georges Brutelle. Chet Huntley summarized it very well towards the close of the program:

How did Beria die? Officially he is tried December 16, 1953, executed December 24th. Only the men in the Kremlin know beyond doubt when and how Beria died. We can only be certain that he did die, that with his death the domination of the Secret Police in the Soviet power struggle is broken, that the breaking of this domination marks the real death of Stalin, who for a quarter of a century ruled Russia with this weapon of terror.

On November 19, 1963, *Look* magazine carried an article by Richard Harrity & Ralph G. Martin, the gentlemen who "did a job" on Lenin in *Look* of May 22, 1962.[2] In the 1963 article, Messrs. Harrity & Martin discourse on "Khrushchev: The Red Riddle." The "scholarship" of these gentlemen is epitomized in the opening sentence:

Long before he got around to befuddling the West, Nikita Khrushchev built a career on confusion, conniving and subterfuge.

Whatever merit or demerit there may be in that estimate of Khrushchev, it is an obviously unfair procedure to begin a story about anyone with a pejorative remark of such devastating nature. Fair play and good taste would dictate that some proof be presented first.

While telling the usual "atrocity" tales about Khrushchev, they say:

His first victim was the wily Beria.
Pierre Commins, a French Socialist, who visited Moscow in 1956, learned how this was accomplished. Here is the account, as reported in the McGraw-Hill book *Ask Me Anything:*

This is followed by the entire "quotation" given by the Hearst trio from that alleged "Socialist publication." One of the strange things about this is their reference to *the publisher* rather than *the authors* of *Ask Me Anything.*

On April 16, 1965, we sent a letter to the managing editor of *Look.* We enclosed photocopies of all the pertinent documents of our investigation, and then we told *Look:*

2 See discussion of this article in Chapter IV, "The Anti-Soviet Liars."

I think you will agree that this throws an entirely different light on the matter, and I hope that *Look* is sufficiently dedicated to the truth to make this information available to its readers.

In a reply, dated May 11, 1965, Miss Anne Celli, Assistant to the Editors, told us:

Your new book sounds quite worthwhile, and your recent research has certainly disclosed some interesting data on Commin. Unfortunately, however, we are unable to carry an article on the subject at the present time.

In a letter we sent Miss Celli on May 24, 1965, we asked:

Does this mean that there is no way of getting the truth on this matter presented to your readers? If you do not wish to carry an article, would you publish a letter-to-the-editor, which I would write? If you agree to this, please advise what is the outside limit of the size that would be acceptable.

No reply was received from *Look.*

On April 16, 1965, we wrote to the editor of *Christian Economics,* and we enclosed photocopies of all the pertinent documents. We said to the editor:

In the light of the information herewith adduced, I trust that you are sufficiently dedicated to truth to apprise your readers of the facts.

In a letter dated April 21, 1965, Mr. H. Edward Rowe, Assistant to the President wrote:

We are in receipt of your letter of April 16, which we have read with care. We have also noted the documents which you enclosed with it.

We do not feel that we are responsible for any errors contained in the quotation from LOOK magazine of November 19, 1963. Our editorial does not claim to be based on any original source. It cites LOOK magazine as the source of this information. One reason why an editor refers to his source is that he wishes to absolve himself from any responsibility for error in reporting which may have rendered the source defective in some way.

Has LOOK magazine issued any clarification or retraction of its quotation of this item? If not, why not? It may well be that LOOK magazine has not been able to obtain sufficient factual information to merit a retraction. Further, the fact that you did not receive a reply from Mr. Hearst or Mr. Conniff may be indicative of their feeling that the information as given was well founded.

Beyond these considerations, I call your attention to the vague attitude of the letter from Mr. Georges Brutelle, dated March 4, 1965. Mr. Brutelle admits in the last paragraph of his letter that the dossier relative to the delegation in question has not thus far been obtainable. He admits his complete dependence upon his memory and on the notes of other members of the delegation for any information on this case.

At the same time, I note Brutelle's statement that he has clarified this matter in an interview given to a United States television network. It would seem that a transcript of the television interview to which Brutelle refers would be an important document for you to see. I am wondering whether you have attempted to procure it.

With regard to the final paragraph of your letter, may I remind you that our editorial did not mention Mr. Commin by name, even though LOOK magazine did mention him and misspelled his name.

Under the circumstances it does not seem to be incumbent upon us to go to print with any further information on this case at the present time.

We assure you that we would not print or reprint from another periodical a quotation which we knew to be spurious. In this case, if the quotation to which you refer is spurious, it devolves upon those who are responsible for the original reporting of it to issue some sort of retraction or qualification.

Thank you for taking the trouble to call this whole matter to our attention. It would be interesting to hear from you if your further researches should turn up anything new on this case.

On July 12, 1965, we wrote *Christian Economics* the following letter:

With further reference to my letter of April 16th and yours of April 21, 1965.

First of all, I want to thank you for taking the time to write to me. I wish to comment on some of the points raised in your letter.

I am well aware of the legal aspects of quoting from other sources, but I am raising the moral issue. My position is that, regardless of what others may do, it devolves upon you to publish a correction when it is proven that you have unwittingly contributed to the dissemination of falsehood. It seems to me that this is a corollary to the precept: Thou Shalt Not Bear False Witness Against Thy Neighbor. And I am sure that the Christian Freedom Foundation considers this a part of its principles.

LOOK magazine answered with a cordial letter of praise for my research and pleaded inability to run an article on the subject at present. Hearst and Conniff did not reply. But I cannot accept your non-sequitur arguments as to their reasons.

597

I am amazed at your effort to discount my proof of falsehood by quoting from the last paragraph of Monsieur Brutelle's letter. Those remarks are clearly aimed at the prospect of trying to furnish any supplementary information and in no way do they vitiate his remarks, two paragraphs above the one that you selected to try to prove a point. Brutelle said: ". . . Pierre Commin never wrote a single line on that subject. . . ." That is definite, explicit, and categorical; and is not subject to any twist.

In the next paragraph Brutelle explains that he was a member of the delegation in a leadership capacity.

Yes, I did finally obtain the entire script of the TV program alluded to by Brutelle. That is why I waited to write this letter. Brutelle's version of what Khrushchev told the delegation about the Beria execution directly contradicts the Hearst version.

In view of the fact that Brutelle was there in person at that interview with Khrushchev, in view of the fact that Hearst and Conniff apparently quoted from a non-existent article by Pierre Commin, in view of the fact that Hearst and Conniff have not met my challenge to name the magazine and the date in which Pierre Commin's article allegedly appeared, it would seem to me that the proof is adequate that the story is a fraud.

Incidentally, that same NBC program contained another version of the Beria incident, which was related to NBC by a renegade Italian Communist, who, in turn, got the story second hand from another Communist, who is now deceased. But Chet Huntley follows up this story by adding that the story is denied by the two Italian Communist delegates who accompanied the deceased one.

I might add one more consideration. Brutelle is an official of a political party that is not very friendly with the Communists.

Now the matter rests with your conscience and your dedication to truth.

P.S.: If you decide to run a story of disavowal of the Hearst-*Look* item, I can send you a photocopy of the pertinent pages of the NBC script on the matter.

In a letter of reply dated July 22, 1965, Mr. Rowe makes a spirited defense of the Hearst trio, who he says "are widely recognized for their objective reporting. They are not given to the fabrication of stories out of thin air." He expresses regret that neither Mr. Hearst nor Mr. Conniff saw fit to reply to our letter of February 10, 1964, and says: "Your inquiry should have merited a reply." Then he asks why we do not try writing a similar letter to Bob Considine. The reason we did not write to Considine is that his office is the same as Conniff's, and we assumed that Conniff would inform Considine about our letter. Preparing photocopies of all the pertinent documents was expensive in time and money. That is another reason. The main thrust of Mr. Rowe's letter is in this paragraph:

By no means desiring to reflect upon the reputation of Mr. Brutelle, we wonder how he can be so certain that Mr. Commin never wrote a single line about the death of Beria. We do not know Mr. Brutelle, and apparently you are not acquainted with him either. Why should we accept his word as against that of Hearst, Conniff and Considine? After all, if Brutelle had some reason for denying the Commin report which was alleged to have been published in "a Socialist publication," it would be easy to succeed with the denial because Mr. Commin is no longer present to speak up on the subject.

Mr. Rowe's syllogistic arguments impress us as straining at a gnat and swallowing a camel. The answers to Mr. Rowe are:

1. The Hearst trio did not name "the Socialist publication" in their book. Why?
2. They did not respond to two letters challenging them to name the publication, the address of the publication, and the date of the issue containing the alleged article. Mr. Rowe must answer the question: "Why?"
3. Mr. Brutelle could be certain that Commin never wrote a single line about the death of Beria, because both he and Commin were Deputy Secretary-Generals of the Socialist Party of France.
4. Mr. Brutelle would not dare to falsely claim that Commin never wrote a magazine article about the death of Beria, because he could easily be exposed and discredited. When we sent Hearst a photocopy of Mr. Brutelle's letter to our French scholar and a translation of the letter, Hearst was in a splendid position, due to his world-wide connections, to easily prove Brutelle a liar, if his statement were not true. It is not too hard to investigate and research an item like this. If Hearst chose to let this matter go by default, after we had advised him that our inquiry is related to a book that we are writing, the conclusion is almost inevitable that Brutelle was telling the truth.
5. The restrained style shown in Brutelle's letter and in his statement on television is the hallmark of an honest scholar.
6. We can think of nothing that Mr. Brutelle would gain by denying that Commin wrote such an article, if it had been written.

The alleged Khrushchev quotation from the alleged article by Pierre Commin in that alleged "Socialist publication" has been picked up by Alfred J. Reiber and Robert C. Nelson, who have included it in "The USSR and Communism: Source Readings and Interpretations," published in 1964 and being used as a high school textbook. The Ultra-Rightist Professor Anthony T. Bouscaren "strongly recommends" this book for everyone. His review[3] illustrates how dubious items of Cold War propaganda get fastened onto the consciousness of an unsuspecting public. Dr. Bouscaren introduces the alleged quotation with these remarks: "There is a grimly amusing selection from Khrushchev, describing the liquidation of Beria." Thus the professorial authority is added as a stamp of approval. Professor Bouscaren's qualifications as an expert include the fact that he quotes the Manuilsky Hoax in his own book, *A Guide to Anti-Communist Action.* Abraham Brumberg, in his excellent article in the *New Republic,* August 29, 1960, refers to Bouscaren's book as "a dreary little book." Professor Bouscaren has a long list of Ultra-Rightist affiliations and accomplishments to his credit, which we will discuss in volume II.

We conclude that we were not successful in our efforts to "Ask Me Anything" of Hearst, Conniff, and Considine!

## Communist Rules for Revolution

In the May 1964 issue of the Rev. Billy James Hargis' monthly magazine, *Christian Crusade,* there is a full page devoted to a sensational story. The upper half of the page is sky-blue and has a map of the United States outlined in white. Superimposed in heavy, black letters is:

### COMMUNIST "BLUEPRINT FOR WORLD CONQUEST"

Underneath there appears:

COMMUNIST RULES FOR REVOLUTION
(Captured in Dusseldorf May 1919 by the Allied Forces)

[3] Professor Bouscaren's review appeared in Textbook Evaluation Report No. 387, received in August 1967 from the Ultra-Rightist *America's Future, Inc.*

A. Corrupt the young, get them away from religion. Get them interested in sex. Make them superficial, destroy their ruggedness.

B. Get control of all means of publicity and thereby:

1. Get people's minds off their government by focusing their attention on athletics, sexy books and plays and other trivialities.

2. Divide the people into hostile groups by constantly harping on controversial matters of no importance.

3. Destroy the people's faith in their natural leaders by holding the latter up to contempt, ridicule and obloquy.

4. Always preach true democracy, but seize power as fast and as ruthlessly as possible.

5. By encouraging government extravagance, destroy its credit, produce fear of inflation with rising prices and general discontent.

6. Foment unnecessary strikes in vital industries, encourage civil disorders and foster a lenient and soft attitude on the part of government toward such disorders.

7. By specious argument cause the breakdown of the old moral virtues, honesty, sobriety, continence, faith in the pledged word, ruggedness.

C. Cause the registration of all firearms on some pretext, with a view of confiscating them and leaving the population helpless.

"NOTE: The above 'Rules for Revolution' were secured by the State Attorney's Office from a known member of the Communist Party, who acknowledged it to be still a part of the Communist program for overthrowing our Government."

GEORGE A. BRAUTIGAM
(Signed)
*State Attorney, State of Florida*

At first glance, anyone familiar with the mad ravings of the "Protocols of the Learned Elders of Zion" or the hoax pamphlet, *Brainwashing, a Synthesis of the Russian Text Book on Psychopolitics,* would recognize the same motif and the same style of writing. Unfortunately, most of the people who are misled by this type of propaganda have neither the time nor the facilities to do research on such matters, even if they possessed the capability. The second item of internal evidence of fraud is the vague phrase "Captured in Dusseldorf May 1919 by the Allied Forces." It does not specify *which* governmental entity might have possession of the alleged document, thus creating a built-in barrier in investigation of its authenticity. Thirdly, the terminology and the subject matter are consistent only with the conclusion that this "document" was concocted many years after the date of alleged capture. For instance, the question of

601

legislation for registration of firearms did not come up for discussion until some 40 years later! Finally, neither the State Department nor the Defense Department has a copy of this "document." That explains why Mr. Brautigam ascribes the document to an anonymous member of the Communist Party. It would be reasonable to expect that, if the "document" actually existed and were authentic, the original or photocopies would have been made available to the State Department, the Defense Department, the CIA, and the FBI. In fact, they would in all probability have demanded it.

On May 16, 1964, we sent a letter of inquiry to Florida State Attorney George A. Brautigam. A letter of June 8, 1964 from State Attorney Richard E. Gerstein informed us that Mr. Brautigam has not been State Attorney since 1956 and passed away in May of 1959. Mr. Gerstein acknowledged that Brautigam *originally distributed* the "Communist Rules for Revolution", and very significantly added: "I am not familiar with this statement issued by Mr. Brautigam nor do I know its source." This would seem to indicate that this project was an unofficial and extra-curricular activity on the part of Mr. Brautigam. This would also seem to be the only explanation for the apparent lack of anything about this "document" in the permanent files of the State Attorney's office.

On June 24, 1965, we sent a letter of inquiry to the Department of Defense. A letter from the office of Colonel Glines, Chief of the Magazine and Book Branch of the Directorate for Information Services, dated July 9, 1965, said:

I am unable to locate a document carrying the title of "Communist Rules for Revolution." However, since the document may exist under another title, if you will provide me a copy of the reprint you spoke of in your letter, I will make a further effort to trace the original.

As a result of his further search, Colonel Glines referred the matter to the office of the National Archives and Records Service, a division of the General Services Administration. On November 30, 1965, a letter from the Army and Navy Branch of the National Archives and Records Service informed us that, after a search in the voluminous postwar records, no such document was located in the War Department records. (The name was later changed to Department of Defense.) They promised to keep on searching. A few months later, we asked Senator Kuchel's office to prod the National Archives and Records Service into more intensive search, on the theory that they would respond better to a Senator's request.

On April 21, 1966, Mr. Robert Bahmer, Archivist of the National Archives and Records Service, wrote to Senator Kuchel:

Your letter of April 13 to Mr. East of my staff, in behalf of Mr. Morris Kominsky, concerned a document titled "Communist Rules for Revolution," alleged to have been captured by Allied Forces in Dusseldorf in May 1919.

This alleged document first came to our attention last summer when the Office of Assistant Secretary of Defense for Public Affairs asked us to search for it in War Department records for the post World War I period. Later, in November of 1965, as a result of an inquiry from Mr. Kominsky, we made another effort to determine the origin of the so-called "Communist Rules for Revolution." All of these searches in the records, including even more intensive efforts recently as a result of your interest in the matter, have been without success.

The enclosed copy of a 1920 report on Bolshevist Propaganda, may be of interest to you. It would appear that both the phraseology and the aims of the postwar propaganda efforts of the Bolshevists, as represented in this 1920 report, are quite different from the overall tone of the so-called "Communist Rules for Revolution," as quoted in the Billy James Hargis publication of May 1964.

That final sentence in Mr. Bahmer's letter gives additional proof that the "document" was a concoction of one of the anti-Communist propaganda mills. Furthermore, the 1920 report on Bolshevist Propaganda is a document entitled "AMERICAN FORCES IN GERMANY, Second Section General Staff." In the upper right-hand corner, it bears the stamp of "Office Chief of Staff, Military Intelligence Division." Similarly, if the "Communist Rules for Revolution" were a genuine document, captured in 1919, it would have been in the hands of the military, unless the Ultra-Rightists wish to uphold the thesis that a document, "captured in 1919 by the Allied Forces," was turned over to a "known Communist" in the U.S.A., whose name was never disclosed.

In further pursuit of the elusive document, we found it quoted by the Ultra-Rightist former FBI Agent, Dan Smoot, in *Dan Smoot Report* of April 26, 1965. As a participant in the Ultra-Rightist crusade to prove that legislation regulating the sale of firearms is either a Communist plot or will redound to the benefit of the Communists, Smoot quotes Lenin *out of historical context* and then says:

In May, 1919, a group of allied intelligence officers raided the headquarters of a revolutionary group in Dusseldorf, Germany. One document seized was entitled "Rules for Bringing About a Revolution." Three basic rules were set out. The first involved corruption of the young by instilling in them contempt for religion and traditional morality. The second involved capturing means of communication so that revolutionists could control the thinking of the people and the programs of government. The third rule read:
*"Cause the registration of all firearms on some pretext, with a view to confiscating them and leaving the population helpless."*

One could expect that Smoot's ex cathedra tone would imply his possession of some solid documentation. He gives a footnote, indicating his source to be *The American Rifleman,* August 1946. This publication, however, quotes it, in turn, from *New World News* of February, 1946, which was a news bulletin of Moral Re-Armament, an Ultra-Rightist outfit that spreads obscurantist propaganda with religious overtones. This is the way an editorial, entitled "Rules for Revolution," introduced the "document":[4]

On a dark night in May 1919 two lorries rumbled across a bridge and on into the town of Dusseldorf. Among the dozen rowdy, singing "Tommies" apparently headed for a gay evening were two representatives of the Allied military intelligence. These men had traced a wave of indiscipline, mutiny and murder among the troops to the local headquarters of a revolutionary organization established in the town.
Pretending to be drunk, they brushed by the sentries and surprised the ringleaders—a group of thirteen men and women seated at a long table. They arrested them and took them behind the lines where they were dealt with according to military law.
In the course of the raid the Allied officers emptied the contents of the safe. One of the documents found in it contained a specific outline of "Rules for Bringing About a Revolution." It is reprinted here to show the strategy of materialistic revolution, and how personal attitudes and habits of living affect the affairs of nations:

Following this introduction, there was given the entire "Com-

---

4 *The American Rifleman* quoted the entire editorial from this issue of *New World News,* which included the "Communist Rules for Revolution."

munist Rules for Revolution," exactly as we quoted it from *Christian Crusade*.

In response to two letters of inquiry, Mr. H. Mead Twitchell, Jr., of Moral Re-Armament, wrote to us on October 7, 1966:

"Rules for Revolution" goes back a long ways—it is a story of 1919. *It appeared in German in a German paper during the twenties or thirties, was translated into English in Britain.* I believe it was first used in the U.S. in *Rising Tide,* a magazine published about 1937. But I cannot find a copy to check this, and do not know the name of the German newspaper. (Emphasis has been added.—M. K.)

The most plausible explanation, on the basis of what Mr. Twitchell has reported, is that "Communist Rules for Revolution" is a product of the Nazi propaganda machine, and was picked up by the British and American Ultra-Rightists as a weapon in the Cold War.

*The Rising Tide,* to which Mr. Twitchell alluded in his letter, was a periodical for boys and girls of the Presbyterian Church of England. A file of this publication is kept in the Yale University Divinity School. The reference librarian, Miss Jane E. McFarland, wrote to us on November 10, 1966 that she searched all the 1936 and 1937 issues and could not locate any mention of the "Communist Rules for Revolution." The magazine suspended publication at the end of 1937.

The Rev. Billy James Hargis was not satisfied with his use of the fraudulent "Communist Rules for Revolution" in the May, 1964, issue of *Christian Crusade.* The following month he gave additional shock treatment to his followers with this announcement:

COMMUNISM'S SECRET PLANS FOR 1964

Open admissions by international Communism that Assassination is a favorite weapon in the war against Freedom. 10 separate revelations, documented, photostated, with introductory interpretation by Billy James Hargis. 24 pages.

It would seem to reasonable people that documents of authentic nature and probative value would require no "introductory interpretation." The gimmick employed by Hargis makes it possible to sell a ten-cent pamphlet for two dollars! The advertisement tells us that this breath-taking document is:

"Sent free with a contribution of $2 or more."

605

No, we did not make this up. The Reverend gentleman does send out "free" documents if you send him hard cash! We have been waiting breathlessly since 1964 for our Billy to give us a report on how these "Secret Plans" were carried out in 1964. But alas and alack, 1968 is almost gone, and we have waited in vain!

As a sequel to his *Communism, Hypnotism and the Beatles,* Billy James Hargis' first lieutenant, the Rev. David A. Noebel, wrote a larger volume, entitled *Rhythm, Riots and Revolution.* This larger compendium of fear and smear gives further circulation to the fraudulent "Communist Rules for Revolution." Noebel adds a dangerous element of authoritativeness, because he seductively creates the impression of being a careful and objective researcher. The truth of the matter is that he researches for material that he can present *selectively,* to prove a preconceived and predetermined thesis. In *Rhythm, Riots and Revolution,* Noebel says:

> George A. Brautigam, State Attorney for the State of Florida, secured a copy of the Communist Rules for Revolution from a known member of the Communist Party, who acknowledged it to be still a part of the Communist program for overthrowing our Government. It seems the rules were originally captured by the Allied Forces in Dusseldorf in May of 1919. Among the rules were, "Corrupt the young, get them away from religion. Get them interested in sex. Make them superficial, destroy their ruggedness."

How does the Reverend Noebel know that George A. Brautigam obtained this "document"? In a footnote, he tells us that *Christian Crusade,* in its issue of May, 1964, "reprinted Mr. Brautigam's findings." Sounds so authentic, doesn't it? And hasn't a good Christian minister told us we can believe this document? On the basis of some elementary concepts of honesty, it would be in order to put Mr. Noebel on the witness stand and cross-examine him:

1. Mr. Noebel, as a Christian minister, do you not believe in the Commandment: Thou Shalt Not Bear False Witness Against Thy Neighbor?

2. Is it not incumbent upon you to practice what you preach?

3. As a researcher, did it not occur to you that the internal evidence of that "document" called for some caution on your

part before publicizing it? And as a corollary to this question, did it not call for some research and investigation, to ascertain its authenticity, before using it against people, who are not in a position to reply, because of the hysterical climate of opinion?

4. Did it not occur to you that "captured by Allied Forces" is a vague and suspicious explanation?

5. Did it not occur to you that there is something irregular about such a document being in the hands of an anonymous Communist, instead of the Defense Department, the CIA, and the FBI?

6. Do you really believe that Communists are so stupid that they issue directives to "Get them interested in sex"? Do young people have to be *urged* to get interested in something which is a fundamental instinct? As a researcher, have you never heard of the "biological urge"?

These and other questions, which the Rev. Noebel should have answered to himself before quoting the fraudulent document, are usually ignored by the zealots of the Cold War propaganda machine. Untruth becomes truth when these people fight Communism. What is the reason that they must utilize so much falsehood?

A typical example of how the fraudulent document affects many unsuspecting people is a letter by Mrs. Henry Schneider in the Riverside, Calif. *Daily Enterprise,* October 11, 1960. After considerable rambling on the question of pornographic literature and after quoting John E. Hoover, Mrs. Schneider delivers the knockout punch:

> I would like to quote from the Communist manifesto of 1919 under "Rules for Bringing About Revolution": "Corrupt the young, get them away from religion, get them interested in sex, make them superficial, destroy their ruggedness," etc. . .

On October 14, 1960, we wrote Mrs. Schneider, pointing out that the *Communist Manifesto* is an historical document, issued in 1848; that we had not heard of one issued in 1919. We asked where we might obtain a copy of the alleged 1919 manifesto or whatever source she had quoted from. No reply was received.

One of the most violent and hysterical of the Ultra-Rightist groups is *Paul Revere Associated Yeoman, Inc.,* called PRAY for convenience. Its headquarters is in New Orleans, Louisiana, and it is operated by a cabinet manufacturer, Henry S. Riecke, Jr. In March of 1965, PRAY circulated a leaflet that was originally issued by Mr. George Edward Hiscott, IV, of Highland Park, Illinois. Mr. Hiscott is an automobile dealer, a former operative of the Office of Naval Intelligence, and a member of the so-called Counter-Subversive Committee of the American Legion Post 738, Deerfield, Illinois. Mr. Hiscott's leaflet, which PRAY circulated, is actually in the form of an open letter to all members of Congress. It is an hysterical appeal against the passage of any legislation to control the sale of firearms in interstate commerce. He concludes his diatribe with this argument:

Should you be curious to read in its entirety, you will see the communist plot for USA 1965, written 46 years ago. The entire enemy plan for us is now operational except the capstone—anti-gun legislation.

This is followed by a reproduction of the entire fraudulent document, the "Communist Rules for Revolution." As a companion piece, PRAY sent out at the same time another leaflet, which has a number of items excerpted from the fraudulent "Protocols of the Learned Elders of Zion." Then the leaflet says:

All sectors of organized Christianity have capitulated to the Enemy—have become part of the conspiracy to destroy Christianity. First, the big Protestant denominations went under and today the Catholic Church is falling into the orbit of a satellite to the International Plan to communize the entire globe under the vicious leadership of the International Jews.

On June 9, 1965, the *Feather River Times*, Paradise, California, carried a long letter from E. L. Barthelemy of New Orleans, Louisiana. It begins by quoting the "Communist Rules for Revolution" in its entirety. Then it says that the entire "plan" has been carried out up to date, with the exception of the registration and confiscation of all firearms. Then Mr. Barthelemy warns:

The scheme of the firearms bill is to have you register all arms as was done in Germany, and then disarm you by confiscating said weapons at a later date—even to your kitchen knives. Once we are disarmed, the "takeover" is complete.

Slavery is on the horizon. Act now and quick. Write your Congressman to vote against all anti-firearms bills.

The irony of the Red Scare campaign of the Ultra-Rightists is, that the principal sponsor of the legislation to regulate the sale of firearms in interstate commerce is Senator Thomas J. Dodd, who is vice-chairman of the Senate Internal Security Subcommittee, and a vigorous Red-hunter in his own right. In addition, he is a spokesman for the Ultra-Rightist *American Security Council* (a private organization) and has affiliations with a number of other Ultra-Rightist groups and committees. The nature of the witch-hunt is that it eventually engulfs all, and the Red-Baiters themselves get Red-Baited!

On November 17, 1965, the publisher of the *Feather River Times* decided to render a "public service." He printed the entire fraudulent "Communist Rules for Revolution" in a space 3¾" × 8½", completely surrounded by a heavy black border, as if it were a message of mourning. A few weeks later he carried a long article warning the readers of alleged Communist infiltration in folk singing, and, by some strange twists of logic, he connected this music with the Viet-Cong and the war in Vietnam. In all fairness, it should be noted that a new owner took over the *Feather River Times* in January of 1966, and has transformed it into a newspaper instead of a vehicle for Ultra-Rightist gobbledegook.

On July 16, 1965, Defenders of the American Constitution sent out "Alert No. 22, Calling All Patriots," over the signature of its president, General Pedro A. del Valle, United States Marine Corps, Retired. The General warns us solemnly:

One of the rules for bringing about a successful revolution according to a document captured by Allied Intelligence Officers at Dusseldorf, Germany, in May, 1919 states: "Cause the registration of fire arms on some pretext with a view of confiscating them and leaving the population helpless."

After presenting additional "evidence" of the perils facing us in the proposed gun legislation of Senator Dodd, the General concludes:

Whether they know it or not, members of Congress who advocate

609

these and other similar bills are guilty of preparing the way for the fall of the U.S.A. to Communism. They are likewise guilty of attempting to amend the Constitution by statute, whereas the Constitution provides that amendments must be ratified by ¾ of the States. Thus we would have malfeasance in office followed by treason.

One of the occupational risks in the witch-hunting business is that, when you run around calling other people un-American and subversive and traitor, you create a climate of opinion that makes it possible to be called traitor yourself. We submit that the General comes pretty close to calling Senator Dodd a traitor, which, of course, he is *not*!

The Freedom Center, operated by the Rev. Walter Huss in Portland, Oregon, sent out an urgent warning in October of 1965:

### "Don't Let Them Take Your Guns Away!"

It quotes Article Two of the Constitution, and shows a U.S. Citizen sitting asleep, with a rifle in one hand. The rifle is labeled "Bill of Rights". A long hand, labeled "Threat of Tyranny", is shown in a menacing position, ready to grasp the "Bill of Rights rifle". Underneath, there is reproduced the fraudulent "Communist Rules for Revolution."

The Rev. Paul Peterson reprinted the "Communist Rules for Revolution" in his March, 1966 newsletter, entitled "Awake America for Christ." He copied the "Rules" from *Christian Crusade* magazine of May, 1964. "Dear Friend of Freedom: It is time to weep for America," Rev. Peterson begins. Indeed, we must weep, when falsehood and fraud are used in the name of Christ!

Dr. T. Jeff Toma is a dentist in Bell, California, who carries on an anti-Communist crusade, sending out literature at his own expense and writing letters to newspapers. The June 25, 1966 issue of the *Santa Ana Register* has a letter from Dr. Toma, in which he quotes the Second Amendment of the Constitution and a paraphrase of "The Rules For Bringing About a Revolution." He urges the readers to write letters to Congress to stop "the harassment of the legitimate gun owner." The good doctor was taken in by the story in the *Dan Smoot Report* of April 26, 1965; and others will be taken in by his "authoritative" repetition of the phoney story.

610

That relentless foe of Communism and Satan, Frank Capell, devotes the September 9, 1966, issue of *Herald of Freedom* to a discussion of "Firearms Controls—A Danger Signal." Frank has an inimitable style of quoting God or other authority to prove a hoax story. He begins by quoting part of the "Rules For Revolution": "Cause the registration of all firearms on some pretext with a view to confiscating them and leaving the population helpless." Frank puts his proof in "affidavit" form by telling us: "The above statement has been certified by George A. Brautigam, State Attorney, State of Florida." Then comes the usual Ultra-Rightist verbal artillery shell:

Well informed people agree that firearms control is but a step toward disarming the people and such disarming is a necessary measure before the communist takeover of a country.

There can be no question of the fact that the "Communist Rules for Revolution" or "Rules For Bringing About a Revolution" is a fraudulent concoction. To well-informed people, it is a hoax on its very surface, because revolutions have never been brought about by the rules outlined. The authors and peddlers of this hoax are simply pandering to the fears, the ignorance, and the prejudices of their dupes. We have cited only a small portion of the actual examples of its use, but it clearly shows that the modern witch-hunt, under the guise of fighting Communism, poisons the thinking of people sufficiently to cause irrational behavior patterns. This is the great danger America faces, a danger which must be energetically combatted by all people of good will. The fifty years of hate peddling against the Soviet Union (and nineteen years of the same against Communist China) has brought the world to a very dangerous impasse.

# CHAPTER XIV

## The Great Crusade: The Treaty Breaking Hoax

As part of the campaign to heat up the Cold War, the propagandists of the Great Crusade have made continual use of The Treaty Breaking Hoax. Stated in its simplest terms, the position of these gentlemen is that we cannot have peaceful coexistence with the Soviet Union, because it *always* breaks its agreements and we, who *always* keep our agreements, are at a dangerous disadvantage in trusting them. Even if this argument were valid, sane men and women of good will would still be constrained to struggle for peace and the prevention of a third world war. Fortunately, there is little or no validity to the argument, and once we can dispel this delusion, one more obstacle to world peace can be removed.

Chief among the protagonists of The Treaty Breaking Hoax is the Standing Committee on Education Against Communism of the American Bar Association. Its predecessor, the Special Committee on Communist Tactics, Strategy, and Objectives, presented a report to the A.B.A. house of delegates in August of 1958, in which the claim is made that, during the previous 25 years, the Soviet Union had broken 50 out of 52 agreements with the United States. Preceding this statement, the gentlemen of the legal profession quote the Lenin Fabrication No. 2. Further on, they quote the Manuilsky Hoax, completely ignoring the fact that one cancels out the other! In between, they quote Lenin Fabrication, No. 1, No. 9, and No. 8; also Stalin Fabrication, No. 1, the Khrushchev "We Will Bury You" Hoax, and a fabricated Dimitrov quotation. Senator Everett Dirksen, a member of the Senate Internal Security Subcommittee, placed the entire report of the Bar Association committee in the Congressional Record, March 1, 1962. This carried out one of the purposes of the Senate Committee—to feed defamatory material, which is protected by Congressional immunity, to Ultra-Rightist groups, who reprint it as gospel truth by authority of the Congressional Record. Under this neat little arrangement, persons libeled or smeared have no legal redress and no opportunity to cross-examine their detractors.

On February 24, 1959, the Bar Association committee presented another report to the house of delegates of the Association. In this report, the committee says:

Never forget that international communism—particularly the Soviet—has the worst record for broken treaties in all history.

Congressman Gordon H. Scherer, a member of the House Committee on Un-American Activities, placed the entire report in the Congressional Record of February 25, 1959. Inasmuch as this report had been made to the house of delegates of the American Bar Association at its meeting in Chicago *the previous day,* it would appear that there was some liaison between the Bar Association committee and the Congressional committee. In any case, the House Committee's purpose was carried out—the Congressional Record once again became the source of Ultra-Rightist propaganda.

The American Bar Association hierarchy side-steps responsibility for the productions of its special committee by *accepting* its reports at the meetings of the house of delegates, but not officially *adopting* or *endorsing* them. This legal fiction was ignored by Congressman Scherer when he told his colleagues that the report had been "overwhelmingly adopted" by the A.B.A. house of delegates.

In a steady barrage of Cold War propaganda emanating from the State Department, the Senate Internal Security Subcommittee, the House Committee on Un-American Activities, the American Legion, John E. Hoover, the John Birch Society, and many others, the Treaty Breaking Hoax has been drummed into the consciousness of the American people. One of the principal architects of this campaign is the professional anti-Communist, Eugene Lyons, who claimed in a *Reader's Digest* article, April, 1958, that the Soviet Union had "cynically violated" 37 out of 40 promises in the 15 years since the World War II conference at Teheran.

An interesting sidelight to the workings of the Cold War propaganda zealots is an article written by attorney G. A. Sheppard, a leader in the Freedom Club of the First Congregational

Church of Los Angeles. This article, entitled "Grim Record of Soviet Broken Promises," appeared in the Ultra-Rightist publication *Freedom Press* of February 15, 1967, edited and published in Los Angeles by wealthy attorney, William Hocker Drake and his wife, Lillian. The article was reprinted and circulated by the Ultra-Rightist *Americans for Freedom* of Santa Barbara, which claims to have obtained permission on February 13, 1967, two days before publication. That is quite a feat, unless you have some arrangements made in advance. There is, of course, an Ultra-Rightist network functioning in this country, and it is more powerful and ominous than most Americans suspect.

The deception that is at the heart of The Treaty Breaking Hoax consists of telling the truth (or part of the truth) in such a manner as to constitute a lie. It is the device of *selective* presentation of evidence. This practice is bad enough when indulged in by ordinary mortals, but when lawyers (who are trained in the rules of evidence) perpetrate this kind of deception, the crime is compounded.

It can readily be conceded that the Soviet Union has abrogated many treaties it has signed and has withdrawn some promises it has made, but it is an unmitigated lie to say that it breaks all treaties and all promises. Two cases of Soviet treaty "breaking" are usually soft-pedaled or totally ignored. Under the Yalta agreement of 1945, the Soviet Union won control of Port Arthur, won the right to participate in joint control, with China, of the Chinese Eastern and South Manchurian railroads, and was successful in getting the port of Dairen internationalized. Several years later the Soviet Union "broke" these agreements, returned the ports of Dairen and Port Arthur to the Chinese, and relinquished its share of control of the railroads. In March of 1950, the Soviet Union made an agreement with China for joint exploitation of the oil and mineral resources of Sinkiang province. A few years later, the Soviet Union "broke" that agreement and relinquished its share of the project to the Chinese.

Many of the propaganda tracts that promote the Treaty Breaking Hoax use a "quotation" to prove that Lenin taught that treaty breaking is a Communist virtue:

But to tie one's hands with something permanent, with an agree-

614

ment, that will hamper Social Democracy, with anybody, it would be madness and criminal.[1]

The sentence structure gives one the clue that, when it is read in proper context, it has no relationship to treaty breaking. So, the Ultra-Rightists solve that problem by quoting a garbled version of that sentence, making it read something like this:

To tie one's hands in a permanent treaty with anyone is criminal, and sheer madness.

The actual fact is that the quotation given first, above, is a translation from the Russian of some polemics conducted by Lenin in 1907, which dealt with political alliances and groupings in the struggle against the Czarist tyranny. It has nothing to do with treaties between nations; and it is a gross deception to quote it out of historical and literary context.

A frequent charge made by the Cold Warriors of the Great Crusade is that the Soviet Union broke some of the agreements made at the time that Franklin D. Roosevelt granted diplomatic recognition to the Soviet Union. Regarding this question, the diplomatic correspondent of the Associated Press, John M. Hightower, said in a lengthy feature story:[2]

It seems a debatable question whether Roosevelt actually thought that the Soviet government would fulfill the deal, which he made with Foreign Commissar Maxim Litvinov on Nov. 16, 1933, the day of recognition.
Experts with first-hand knowledge suggest that Roosevelt was essentially cynical in his attitude toward the promises he exacted,
Ambassador George F. Kennan in his 1960 book, "Russia and the West Under Lenin and Stalin," asserts that Roosevelt "was interested only in their momentary psychological effect on the American public, not on their effectiveness in practice."

In an excellent booklet, entitled *But—You Can't Trust the Russians,* written by Professor A. Glenn Mower, Jr. and published in 1960 by the American Friends Service Committee, it is pointed out that "under international law it is impossible to attach conditions to the act of recognition." Professor Mower adds this observation:

[1] This quotation will be found in an essay, in the original Russian, in *Sochineniya,* Lenin, 3rd. Edition, volume 10, pages 380 and 381. On file in Library of Congress.
[2] Riverside, Calif. *Press-Enterprise,* November 10, 1963.

To express "shock" at behavior that could be anticipated, and against which there is no sanction in international law, is either an act of woeful ignorance of international legal and political realities or unpardonable hypocrisy. At best one can only conclude that Americans seeking such assurances were optimistic, or maneuvering the Soviets into a position from which the West could later make propaganda capital; at worst, that they were stupid.

A very sensible summary of the problem is made in a 1951 booklet, entitled *Steps to Peace*, issued by the American Friends Service Committee:

Much has been written about the faithlessness of the Soviet Union in living up to its agreements, but the Soviets have just as vigorously accused the United States of the same transgression. Part of the vituperation on both sides is traceable to different meanings being assigned to the same words by the two parties, but beyond that, the fact remains that in an ungoverned world *all sovereign states have tended to abridge agreements when it was to their self-interest to do so,* and this makes the element of self-interest all-important in negotiation at the present time. This conclusion is supported by existing evidence in commercial fields, *where Russia has in general lived up to her obligations.* (Emphasis has been added.—M. K.)

Not only has the Soviet Union lived up to its commercial obligations in good faith, but it has been a trustworthy wartime ally, as witness this statement delivered to the British Parliament by Sir Winston Churchill, shortly after his return from the Yalta Conference of February, 1945:

I know of no Government that stands on its obligations more solidly than the Russian Government. Sombre indeed would be the fortunes of mankind if some awful schism arose between the Western democracies and the Russian people.

In 1959, twelve nations, including the U.S.A. and the U.S.S.R., signed a treaty banning military activities or nuclear explosions from the Antarctic continent. After giving notice of intent on September 13, 1963, the U.S. Government invoked its rights under the treaty and sent an inspection team to the Russians' scientific station approximately 900 miles from the South Pole. The American observers reported to Washington that they were given a most cordial reception at the station and were allowed to inspect both the station and the scientific base on the Antarctic coast. Their report stated that the Soviet

616

Union was living up to both the letter and the spirit of the treaty.

In the Southeast Asia situation, Joseph Alsop reported regarding the Laotian truce agreement, of which the Soviet Union is one of the guarantors:[3]

From the day the truce agreement was signed, it must be said in fairness to Nikita S. Khrushchev, the Soviets in Laos seem to have done their best to secure observation of the truce terms.

One could go on and on, citing treaties and agreements by the hundreds, with which the Soviet Union has complied both in letter and spirit. Using the *selective* presentation of data device, one could "prove" that the Soviet Union *always* keeps its agreement; but this would be just as dishonest and misleading as the Ultra-Rightists' campaign to prove that the Soviet Union breaks *all* agreements and treaties. It is necessary for people to understand that treaty breaking is indulged in by *all* nations. In order to present this fact of life, it becomes necessary to risk the accusation of being unpatriotic and un-American, and tell the story of U.S. violations of treaties and agreements.

In 1778, after France had helped us in our war of the Revolution, we signed a treaty which called for our support of France in her struggle with England. When France and England went to war, President George Washington proclaimed our neutrality, thereby breaking our agreement with France. It was justified by our leaders, at the time, on the grounds that compliance with the treaty *was not in our national interest.*

It is extremely doubtful if any country has broken as many treaties as we have broken with the tribes of natives we have chosen to call Indians. It is a shameful story that is still being enacted. Congresswoman Frances P. Bolton stated on the floor of Congress, February 7, 1964:

Mr. Speaker, when the Congress of the United States voted to build the Kinzua Dam within the Allegheny Indian Reservation in New York and Pennsylvania it tore into shreds the first treaty this country ever made. It was a treaty made between the Seneca Nation and the United States, signed on behalf of George Washington November 11, 1794. This action was reexamined by Thomas Jeffer-

---

[3] Riverside, Calif. *Daily Enterprise*, Feb. 25, 1964.

son March 17, 1802, when he stated that these lands shall remain the property of the Seneca and Onondago Nations forever unless they shall voluntarily relinquish or dispose of them. But the treaty was broken and some two-thirds or 20,000 acres of their best land was taken to be flooded by this dam.

An article regarding this matter by Robert Trumbull, in the *New York Times,* March 1, 1964, points out that *the United States Supreme Court has ruled more than once that the U.S. Government has the right to break treaties*! Is it not strange that the committee of the American Bar Association has been so quiet about the numerous treaties with the Indians that we have broken? Nor have we heard about them appearing before the Supreme Court with an amicus curiae brief, in opposition to the doctrine that the U.S. Government has a right to break treaties. This criticism is reserved for the Soviet Union.

The ruthless breaking of the treaty was accompanied by another piece of shabby business. This is the way Senator J. William Fulbright told it on the floor of the Senate, March 18, 1964:

I am very sorry that our Government found it necessary to break the treaty with the Senecas. I am even more distressed that, having broken the treaty under the power of eminent domain, the compensation which was agreed to—while not final, it is at least in the initial stages of planning—apparently has been drastically reduced. I believe that constitutes a further breach of faith with the Senecas. To me, that is distressing. I feel ashamed of our Government, first, for having broken the treaty, and then, in a sense, for having reneged on the compensation which had been promised.

The specifics of this episode are:

1. The House of Representatives had passed a bill providing $20,150,000 for reparation, relocation, and rehabilitation for the Senecas. The Indians considered this an inadequate amount, but agreed reluctantly to back the bill.

2. When the bill reached the Senate during the week of March 9, 1964, the Senate Interior Subcommittee cut the bill by 64 percent, allowing the Senecas only $9 million.

3. Three years earlier the Government gave the Pennsylvania railroad $20 million for a 28-mile right of way *to reach the 20,000 acres being taken away from the Senecas.*

One month later, the Senate was still haggling over the lives of these "foreigners." Senator Paul Douglas told his colleagues on April 22, 1964, that the Senate proposal "does not provide adequate financing for the rehabilitation of the Seneca Indians, and, moreover, is immoral to the extent *it provides for abrogation of the remaining treaty guarantees from the United States to the Seneca Indians.* (Emphasis has been added—M. K.)

The Congress finally passed a compromise measure in August, 1964, giving the Senecas $15 million, in spite of the fact that the Interior Department had recommended a minimum of $29 million. The dilatory tactics of our lawmakers, when confronted with a problem of justice and human welfare, and their parsimonious attitude are in sharp contrast with the lightning speed in appropriating billions for war making purposes.

The Indian tribes who reside in the State of Washington thought they enjoyed certain fishing rights, off the reservations, on the Puyallup River. The State of Washington banned the off-reservation fishing, and the state supreme court held the law to be constitutional, thus breaking the Medicine Creek Treaty of 1854. Movie actor Marlon Brando and the Rev. John Yaryan of Grace Episcopal Church in San Francisco were arrested on March 4, 1964, when they went fishing with a Puyallup Indian, in order to dramatize the injustice against the original 100% Americans.

The *Santa Ana Register,* February 24, 1966, carried a letter which should have been sent to the committee of the American Bar Association. We quote a portion of that letter:

As an American citizen, and as an American Indian, I am writing this letter in the hopes that it may call attention to the great injustice that has been done to me and my people.

It is a fact that over one hundred years ago my ancestors signed a peace treaty with the United States government, with the understanding that we were, as peaceable Indians of California, entitled to receive a monetary settlement for our lands, which at the time comprised about three-fourths of the State of California. . .

I and many other Indians of California are still waiting to see if the federal government is ever going to pay its debt to us and right this long overdue bill.

In attempting to justify American intervention in the Vietnam civil war, Secretary of State Dean Rusk said: "We must make it clear that the United States keeps its word whenever

619

it is pledged." In a letter to the *Nation* magazine, March 28, 1966, Richard B. Gregg observes:

> The American Indians would have some harsh comments on that statement. In the case of the Iroquois tribe, most of whose land has recently been taken from them, the treaty guaranteeing their possession was, I understand, signed on behalf of the U.S. Government by George Washington.

This by no means exhausts the list of broken treaties with the Indians, but it is enough to illustrate the point that treaty breaking is a 100% American custom, not an exclusive Soviet procedure. But we need not rest our case with the outrageous treatment meted out to the Indians.

In the setting up of the Republic of Panama, there is a story that we Americans need not be proud of. Dan Smoot told it succinctly in his *Report* of January 4, 1965:

> Prior to 1903, the Isthmus of Panama was a province of Colombia. The revolution which separated Panama from Colombia was fabricated by a New York lawyer and five ambitious men in Panama, three of whom were United States citizens. These private Americans, backed by the United States government, created the nation of Panama in 1903.

Besides the violations of international law involved in this act of subversion, which our experts in subversion like to overlook, the U.S. Government signed a "treaty" with its illegitimate child. This can hardly be called bona fide observance of the sanctity of treaties.

In April of 1941 Japan and the Soviet Union signed a treaty which provide that, if either one got involved in hostilities with another nation, they would "undertake to maintain peaceful relations between them." Before the year was ended, General Douglas MacArthur proposed that our government obtain permission from the Soviet Union to use Siberian bases for air strikes against Japan. Secretary of State Cordell Hull tried to get Soviet permission, but to no avail. He also kept up pressure to get the Soviet Union to go to war with Japan. Thus, we had the spectacle of the United States Government urging the Soviet Union to break its treaty with Japan—the very thing we have the brazen effrontery to accuse the Soviet Union of doing exclusively. It is a matter of historical record that the

Soviet Union maintained that treaty with Japan until the very last days of World War II, entering only when Japan's debacle was a foregone conclusion.

In the Cairo Conference of World War II, attended by Roosevelt, Churchill, and Chiang Kai-shek, in November, 1943, it was agreed that territories seized by Japan would be returned to China. This included the island of Formosa. The United States has, by military force, prevented the real government of China from assuming control of this area and continues to maintain the ridiculous fiction that Chiang's rump regime is China!

This country's intervention in the Korean War was carried out by illegal means under the fiction of it being a United Nations project, but actually it was brought about by U.S. violation of the United Nations Charter, which it had signed as a treaty. The charter clearly provides that action by the Security Council must be approved by all five of the permanent members. In the absence of the Soviet delegate, the U.S. brought the matter up, but before action could be taken, the Soviet delegate vetoed the action. Whereupon, the U.S. succeeded in railroading through the General Assembly a resolution authorizing military action against North Korea and designating General MacArthur the United Nations' commander. This was a flagrant violation of the United Nations Charter, under which the General Assembly is *not* authorized to initiate any military action and is *not* authorized to amend the charter. In a moment of astonishing candor, the Ultra-Rightist *Washington Report,* June 13, 1966, said:

The U.S. Government has been grossly inconsistent and hypocritical in its use of international law and the UN Charter to oppose or justify actions by itself or others. . . But these kinds of hypocrisies are a built-in feature of a world where power remains the predominant element in international affairs.

This is quite an admission from the Ultra-Rightist *American Security Council* (a private organization). One of its most stalwart supporters, Congressman Craig Hosmer, wrote in the September 11, 1967 issue of *Washington Report*:

When nations believe survival is at stake they tend to ignore treaties and do what they must to stay alive.

621

As one of the harshest critics of the Soviet Union, Congressman Hosmer is reluctant to concede the Soviet Union's right to operate according to the same rules followed by other nations.

A favorite pastime of Cold War propagandists is to claim that the Cold War was brought on by the Soviet Union breaking its war time agreements and the provisions of the Potsdam agreements. We shall discuss this in greater detail in volume II, but for the present, the testimony of a man who had an inside look at many of the diplomatic conferences will shed some light on the question of who *first* broke the treaties. Elliott Roosevelt writes in *As He Saw It*:

In my effort to get back to first and underlying causes for our critical present, I note only that it was the United States and Great Britain who first shook the mailed fist, who first abrogated the collective decisions.

The *Washington Star,* June 26, 1963, carried an Associated Press dispatch from Berlin relating an incident of President Kennedy's visit:

Facing him [the President] from the Communist side of the wall was an East German sign which said:
"In the agreement at Potsdam, United States Presidents Roosevelt and Truman undertook:
To uproot German Militarism and Nazism.
To arrest war criminals and bring them to judgment.
To prevent rebirth of German Militarism.
To ban all Militarist and Nazi propaganda.
To ensure that Germany never again menaces her neighbors and world peace.
These pledges have been fulfilled in the (East) German Democratic Republic. When will these pledges be fulfilled in West Germany and West Berlin, Mr. Kennedy?"

Mr. Kennedy read the sign but showed no reaction.[4]

The ugliness and the duplicity of our violation of the Potsdam agreement, in the rearming of West Germany, is a story that has been almost drowned out by the propaganda of the

---

[4] The *Los Angeles Times* Moscow correspondent, December 9, 1967, reported that for the second time this year the Soviet Union had sent a note accusing the West German government of violating the Allies' 1945 Potsdam agreement which called for German demilitarization.

Great Crusade. The *Kiplinger Washington Letter* of December 10, 1949 stated very frankly: "West Germany is to be rearmed, despite denials from the top men."

*U.S. News & World Report,* September 8, 1950, carried a revealing interview with Hitler's former Chief of the Army General Staff, General Heinz Guderian. While he was a prisoner of war, Guderian wrote a plan for future wars which seems to have fascinated the American militarists. Some of the questions asked of him by *U.S. News & World Report* were:

> General Guderian, what would Germany do as a fighting force against Russia if war started?
> How would you deploy the German divisions, and how would you arm them?
> Under what sort of command should German divisions operate?

In the course of answering the final question of the interview, the Nazi said:

> My manuscript was submitted to Washington as a top secret paper, though without my ever obtaining a translation of it. General Bradley, who like many other American generals agreed with my ideas, showed President Truman the manuscript, who, I understand, also shared his opinion . . . a U.S. Senator, full of annoyance, said my report seems to constitute a sort of Bible for the majority of American officers.

And this, only shortly after being allied with Russia in a war to defeat the Nazis! Is it any wonder that the East German Communists taunted President Kennedy with that sign containing some embarrassing questions, which he chose not to answer?

An article entitled "Germany: We Are Playing With Fire," which appeared in *Look* magazine, March 27, 1951, accuses Russia of some violations of the Potsdam agreement, but observes that "The rearmament of Germany is as provocative an act as can be imagined. A strong, warlike Germany is a gun leveled at the Russian heart." *Look's* European Editor, Stephen White, correctly draws this conclusion:

> A general peace settlement with Russia, honestly adhered to by all concerned, could turn back the clock to the Potsdam Agreement and make the future a little less of a gamble.

Fourteen years later, it was cautiously disclosed that the United States had not only rearmed the Nazis, who are in control of West Germany, with a variety of conventional weapons, but had violated the Potsdam agreement, as well as our own McMahon Act, by surreptitiously equipping West German planes and missiles with *nuclear warheads. The New York Times,* November 23, 1965, quoted presidential press secretary Bill Moyers as saying that the "custody of all such warheads remains with the United States." In order to get the people's acquiescence in this dangerous and treacherous move, the Defense Department issued assurances that all the nuclear warheads are guarded by American sentries. The assumption, that two or three U.S. soldiers at each warplane hanger is ample protection against any attempt of the Germans to use the nuclear warheads, is too idiotic for words, and betrays the militarists' contempt for civilians.

Under the terms of the Kellogg-Briand Pact of 1928, which the United States helped create, the United States Government *renounced war as an instrument of national policy.* It would be interesting to see the committee of the American Bar Association prepare a disquisition on U.S. violations of that agreement.

The United Nations Charter, of which the United States Government is a signatory, in addition to being the principal initiator of, commits each signatory power to settle its international disputes by peaceful means.

The United States is also signatory to a regional pact, the Charter of the Organization of American States. One of its prime articles is that interference in the internal affairs of any other country of Central and South America is strictly forbidden, unless approved by a resolution of that Organization.

On April 28, 1965, the United States Government violated the Kellogg-Briand Pact, the United Nations Charter, and the Charter of the Organization of American States by invading the tiny Dominican Republic with 32,000 troops and an armada, which included a flotilla of warships, an aircraft carrier, and 275 warplanes. This action was condemned by Mexico, Uruguay, Chile, Ecuador, and Peru.

In a press conference on May 26, 1965, Secretary of State Dean Rusk openly conceded that President Johnson had intervened unilaterally with U.S. forces, without laying the matter before the Organization of American States. Former Senator Barry M. Goldwater said in his column of May 14, 1965,[5] that our policy is naked imperialism and gunboat diplomacy. United Nations Secretary General U Thant pointed out on May 27, 1965[6] that, under Article 53 of the United Nations Charter, even an O.A.S. decision to intervene militarily must be authorized by the U.N. Security Council. The Chairman of the Senate Foreign Relations Committee, J. William Fulbright, bitterly castigated our treaty-breaking intervention, in a long speech on the floor of the Senate, September 15, 1965. The Senator said: "Throughout the whole affair, it has also been characterized by a lack of candor." He presented massive documentation to prove that every reason given the American people for our aggression against the Dominican people was an outright falsehood. Senator Fulbright quoted these pertinent items from the Charter of the Organization of American States:

*Article 15.* No state or group of states has the right to intervene, directly or indirectly, for any reason whatever, in the internal or external affairs of any other state.
*Article 17.* The territory of a state is inviolable; it may not be the object, even temporarily, of military occupation or of other measures of force taken by another state, directly or indirectly, on any grounds whatever.

Senator Fulbright pointed out:

The sole exception to the prohibitions of articles 15 and 17 is spelled out in article 19 of the OAS Charter, which states that "measures adopted for the maintenance of peace and security in accordance with existing treaties do not constitute a violation of the principles set forth in articles 15 and 17."

Then the Senator quoted Article 6 of the Rio Treaty, which provides for *collective decision* before proceeding with any military action against another state.

On October 15, 1965, the following dialogue took place between Senator Joseph Clark of Pennsylvania and Senator Wayne Morse of Oregon:

5 *Los Angeles Times.*
6 *Los Angeles Times,* May 28, 1965.

*Mr. Clark.* Is it the Senator's view, as it is mine and that of the Chairman of the Foreign Relations Committee, that our intervention in the Dominician Republic, once we got past the stage of sending in a battalion or two of marines to protect American rights and aid in the evacuation of Americans and other nationals whose lives may have been in jeopardy, was in complete violation of our treaty commitments?

*Mr. Morse.* Complete violation of Rio, complete violation of the Organization of American States Charter, complete violation of Punta del Este, complete violation of Bogota, and complete violation of our understanding at the Foreign Ministers' Conference in Washington, D.C., in 1964.

The breaking of all these treaties brought not a ripple of condemnation from the committee of the American Bar Association or any of the other purveyors of The Treaty Breaking Hoax. The opinions expressed by Senator Morse should be considered in light of the fact that he is a leading member of the Senate Foreign Relations Committttee and is a lawyer who is a specialist in international law.

Another example of treaty breaking in U.S. relations with smaller countries was the suspension of our aid program to the Republic of Panama on January 20, 1964. The State Department issued a "cover" story, claiming that Panama had forced the departure of our aid personnel. The facts are that Panama had demanded the recall of our *diplomats only,* and had specifically requested that Alliance for Progress and Peace Corps officials remain and that the aid programs be continued. The cutting of our aid program was a move calculated to discourage the Panama Republic from demanding renegotiation of the Panama Canal Treaty and was a violation of the Treaty signed in 1948 at Bogota, Columbia, which established the Organization of American States. That Treaty specifically prohibits any signatory from taking any unilateral economic reprisals against another country that is a member of the Organization of American States.

The invasion of Vietnam by American armed forces was in violation of our own Constitution, which gives only the Congress the power to declare war. The illegal nature of this war has been partially obscured by the passage of the so-called Tonkin Bay Resolution of August 6, 1964. While the pretext for this Resolution—an alleged unprovoked attack against our naval vessels—has all the earmarks of a frame-up, the fact remains that reprisals in peacetime[7] *are prohibited* under the Kellogg-Briand Pact and the United Nations Charter. When confronted with this argument, the apologists for U.S. aggression in Vietnam fall back on the South East Asia Treaty (SEATO). This offers no legal consolation to the proponents of aggression, because the treaty clearly states that any country taking military measures *must consult with its treaty allies and obtain agreement beforehand.* This was not done, thus adding one more treaty broken by the U.S.A. in the prosecution of this illegal military adventure.

One of the best summaries of U.S. treaty breaking, in the war against Vietnam, was presented by Senator Wayne Morse on the floor of the Senate, September 23, 1965:

. . . No nation was more deeply involved in the creation of the United Nations than was the United States; and no nation in the world has preached to others more than we have that peaceful settlement of disputes among nations must be practiced, preferably under United Nations auspices.

In Vietnam, we have flouted the rule of law, and we have flouted the United Nations Charter. . .

Ever since our first violations of the Geneva Accords, starting with the imposition of our first puppet regime in South Vietnam, the Diem regime, we have violated one tenet after another of international law and one treaty obligation after another, and the world knows it. For more than 10 years, we have written on the pages of history with the indelible ink of U.S. violations of the Geneva Accords of 1954, as well as article after article of the United Nations Charter and even Article I, section 8 of the Constitution of the United States, a sad and shocking chronicle of our repudiation of the rule of law in our foreign policy practices.[8]

There is strange silence in Ultra-Rightist circles about U.S. treaty violations in the Vietnam aggression.

One of the byproducts of the aggression against Vietnam has been the U.S. violation of the 1962 Accords, which were signed by the United States, Communist China, North Vietnam, and 11 other countries. This agreement specifically prohibited the introduction of foreign troops in Laos. On January

7 In the absence of a formal declaration of war, it is illegal, under international law, to claim wartime privileges.

8 Following his speech, Senator Morse placed in the Congressional Record of that same day a brilliant Memorandum of Law, prepared by the Lawyers Committee on American Policy Toward Vietnam. This Memorandum deserves a careful study by all thoughtful and serious people.

19, 1965, Senator Wayne Morse characterized U.S. air strikes against Laos as a "shocking" substitution of "jungle law" for the rule of law. Senator Morse told his colleagues:

Our unilateral interpretation and our unilateral action of that interpretation means that Red China, North Vietnam, the Pathet Lao and all other signatories are also free to interpret the accord as they please and to act on those interpretations.

Commenting on the State Department's argument that the Communists had violated the accords and therefore we had the right to do so, Senator Morse said:

What we ought to do is live up to our obligations under the United Nations treaty. We ought to call on the U.N. to enforce the treaty in Vietnam and Laos.

The Soviet Union issued a statement on February 6, 1965, accusing the United States of "barbarous" bombing of Laos and charged that the U.S. was planning to enlarge the Vietnam war. The statement said that the United States was flagrantly violating the Geneva agreements of 1954 and 1962.

In 1911, the United States agreed to submit to arbitration a dispute with Mexico about a small piece of land called Chamizal, in the Rio Grande River between Mexico and El Paso, Texas. When the verdict of the French arbitrator went against us, the United States refused to abide by the verdict, which involved some 400 acres of land. This flouting of our agreement was finally rectified in October, 1967, when the United States finally ceded the land to Mexico.

The attempt of the Cold Warriors, to make it appear that the Soviet Union is the only government that abrogates treaties from time to time, would be ludicrous if it were not so tragically misleading. An alternate gambit of these gentlemen is to concede that others break treaties, but that the Soviet Union is the worst offender. A brief review of some diplomatic history should put the subject in proper perspective.

Great Britain's diplomacy for several centuries has been of such a nature that she has frequently been referred to as "perfidious Albion." Whatever truth there may or may not be in this characterization, it can be shown that Great Britain, like other countries, has broken many agreements, promises, and treaties. A United Press International dispatch from Buenos Aires in *The New York Times*, November 16, 1963, begins with:

President Arthuro Illia annulled tonight all foreign oil concessions, including eight American-held contracts, in the first step toward nationalization of the petroleum industry.

An Associated Press dispatch from Damascus in the *Los Angeles Times*, April 29, 1964, begins with:

Syria abrogated the military union treaty with neighboring Iraq Tuesday in a sign of mounting tension between the two countries.

An Associated Press dispatch in the *Los Angeles Herald-Examiner*, October 7, 1964, begins with:

The Nicaraguan Congress has repudiated the 1914 Bryan-Chamorro treaty granting the United States perpetual rights to build an interocean canal through this Central American country.

On August 12, 1964, the Soviet Union challenged the sanctions against Cuba, that were imposed in July by the Organization of American States with the inspiration of the United States Government. The Soviet statement was circulated as a United Nations Security Council document. It pointed out that the OAS sanctions were in violation of Article 53 of the UN Charter, which provides that such regional action requires the authorization of the UN Security Council. The statement also said that, since the October, 1962 missile crisis, there had been "some 2,000 acts of provocation against the Republic of Cuba in the form of fire on Cuban guard posts from the U.S. base at Guantanamo, violation of Cuban air space by U.S. military aircraft, and direct connivance in piratical raids by sea and air on industrial installations, ports and inhabited localities in that country." Regrettably, these charges were substantially correct and showed that the United States Government had repeatedly violated international law and agreements.

The spurious nature of The Treaty Breaking Hoax was proven by the experience with the Nuclear Test Ban Treaty. After extensive hearings, the Senate Foreign Relations Committee voted 16 to 1 that the Senate should consent to its ratification. The significance of this is that the vote came after peddlers of The Treaty Breaking Hoax had carried on a campaign, in which all the familiar arguments were marshalled against ratification. The nature of the opposition campaign was described vividly by Senator George D. Aiken, Republican, of Vermont, on the floor of the U.S. Senate, September 18, 1963:

At no time in my recollection has the mail on any issue before Congress contained so many threats and vituperations as that of the last few weeks. . .

The country is being flooded by circulars purportedly issued by organizations with highly respectable sounding names, but which are unknown to official Government agencies. These circulars contain inflammatory statements intended to make the reader hate the word "peace" and all those who dare to advocate it. They even go so far as to imply that the Senator from Illinois [Everett Dirksen] is opposed to the treaty and that those who do not help him kill it are either blind or disloyal. . .

I do believe, Mr. President, that fear is at the bottom of most of the opposition to the treaty—not alone the fear of losing one's life through enemy instruments of destruction, but the fear that from this very small first step there may emerge a changing pattern in the world, a pattern from which may be molded a world of universal law rather than universal war and preparation for such war.

If we should find ourselves in a position of not having to be constantly preparing for war, it would indeed change the pattern of our national economy. A substantial part of our gross national product is generated directly and indirectly from arms production and preparation for possible war. This business has always been profitable in many countries.

I can well understand the fears of management, investors and employees that their business, their incomes, and their jobs might be curtailed if the seed planted by the treaty should grow to greater proportions. . .

We have been living on borrowed money and borrowed time for many years. The danger to our political system today is probably greater from monetary disaster or internal disturbances or a continued deterioration of governmental processes than it is from an enemy attack from the outside.

*It is clear from Senator Aiken's remarks that people who have a stake in the armaments race furnish much of the inspiration and financial support for the campaign to keep alive The Treaty Breaking Hoax.*

The urgency of getting ratification of the Nuclear Test Ban

Treaty animated a campaign to debunk The Treaty Breaking Hoax. Even some of the Cold Warriors of the State Department had to either take a back seat or come forward with some grudging admissions of the truth about Soviet treaties, Thus when Secretary of State Dean Rusk was testifying before the Senate Foreign Relations Committee on August 12, 1963, the following dialogue ensued:

*Senator Lausche.* I understood you to say this morning that in discussing article IV of the agreement concerning how it might be terminated that the Russian representatives took the position that renunciation is a matter of sovereign right and, therefore, required no delineation in the treaty; is that correct?
*Secretary Rusk.* Yes, sir, and that has been a rather general approach of theirs to this problem.
*Senator Lausche.* That is Red Russia takes the position that when it makes a treaty, in the absence of specifying a particular period of time that it is to endure, it has the inherent and sovereign right to terminate it whenever it pleases. [It should be remembered that the U.S. Supreme Court has ruled on several ocasions that the U.S. Government has the right to break a treaty.—M. K.]
*Secretary Rusk.* That is a general point of view, sir. I would not want to say that that is flat and comprehensive over every issue. I would have to be advised on that point.

Following this dialogue, Senator Lausche recited a list of treaties and/or agreements that the Soviet Union had allegedly abrogated. Then the discussion was resumed:

*Senator Lausche.* Now, may I ask, Mr. Secretary, which is the last agreement that Red Russia has violated? I have in mind the Cuban commitment that we would have the right to inspect and ascertain whether the missiles were removed. Am I correct in that or not?
*Secretary Rusk.* That was a basis of the exchange between the President and Khrushchev during the week beginning October 22.
*Senator Lausche.* That promise was not kept.
*Secretary Rusk.* That is correct, sir. As you recall, *Castro would not accede to that.* [Emphasis added.—M. K.]
*Senator Lausche.* Yes. That is, the commitment was made that neutral nations would be permitted to go in and see whether the missiles were removed. That commitment was not executed, is that correct?
*Secretary Rusk.* That is correct, sir; but there were certain alternative arrangements that were made, as you remember.

The explanation given by Secretary Rusk, which happens to be a truthful and accurate one, is a far cry from the charge of the Ultra-Rightist propagandists that the Soviet Union broke its agreements regarding missile inspection after the Cuban crisis.

During his appearance on the *Meet the Press* television program, August 4, 1963, Under Secretary of State Averell Harriman was asked by Lawrence E. Spivak:

Governor,[9] why do we enter agreements with the Soviet Union at all when there are so many old agreements that they have yet to live up to? Yalta, for example, is one of them. Don't you think we ought to ask them to live up to some of the old agreements before we make new agreements that might trick us again, as you yourself suggested we might be tricked?

To this, Secretary Harriman replied:

No, I don't think so. I think we have the present day situation, and the past is the past. As a matter of fact, part of the trouble at that time was the misunderstanding as to what the words of the agreement meant. He has maintained the Austrian agreement. There are other agreements he has made that have been maintained. This idea that you can't trust the Soviet Union as a reason why we should go to nuclear war, I just don't understand.

Professor George F. Kennan, former Ambassador to the Soviet Union, former Ambassador to Yugoslavia, and the author of many books, offered some interesting and incisive comment during his appearance on *Meet the Press*, August 18, 1963:

I think the trouble with the wartime agreements was that they used general language which meant one thing to them and another thing to us. I think if you stick to specific language, if the agreement does not try to describe what people's motives are or what their philosophy is, but merely says, "We will do this if you will do this," I think then such agreements can be useful.

At another point in the discussion, Ambassador Kennan gave some cogent reasons why the Nuclear Test Ban Treaty in particular and disarmament agreements in general are feasible and desirable:

The disaster of an atomic war is just as serious a prospect for the Russians as it is to us. They too are made out of flesh and blood,

9 Harriman also has served as Governor of New York State.—M. K.

they too can be killed just as we can be killed. They have children that they worry about just as we do. I think he is very well aware that a war fought with nuclear weapons would be a calamity from which none of us would have anything but horror.

The crowning achievement in the debunking of The Treaty Breaking Hoax was accomplished by Senator J. William Fulbright. In a speech on the floor of the U.S. Senate, September 24, 1963, the Senator said, in part:

A list, prepared by the Assistant Legal Adviser for Treaty Affairs, of the U.S. Department of State, includes 128 treaties and other international agreements now in force between the United States and the U.S.S.R.

Of this list, 70 are treaties—that is, formal instruments which have have been entered into by the United States, with the advice and consent of the U.S. Senate.

The significant fact that emerges from an examination *of the 70 treaties* to which the United States and the Soviet Union are parties is that *only 6 of them* are viewed as having been violated by the Soviet Union. And of the six violated by the Soviet Union, one is the Kellogg-Briand Pact of 1928, which was a renunciation of war as an instrument of national policy. Another is the Charter of the United Nations,[10] which, according to the Department of State, the Soviet Union has violated in various of its terms. Three of the other treaties are treaties of peace with Hungary, Rumania, and Bulgaria. The final one is the Convention on Prisoners of War of 1949.

Fifty-eight other, less formal, international agreements to which the United States and the Soviet Union are parties are included in the list. *Of these 58 other agreements,* the Department of State views the Soviet Union as in violation of 21. Included among the other international agreements the Soviet has violated are the Roosevelt-Litvinov agreements establishing diplomatic relations with the Soviet Union, certain lend-lease agreements, the Yalta agreements relating to prisoners of war and civilians, the Atlantic Charter, a series of armistice agreements, the Potsdam agreements, and various others. It should be noted that *none of the agreements in the latter category was a treaty* in the formal sense of having to be approved by the Senate. Perhaps they should have been, but they were not. [Emphasis throughout has been added.—M. K.]

Some of these alleged violations have been vehemently denied by the Soviet Government, and some of them are abrogations of agreements on matters of less than world-shaking

10 Both of these treaties have been repeatedly violated by the United States and other signatories.

importance. In any case, the thesis of the Special Committee of the American Bar Association and others—that the Soviet Union has violated 50 out of 52 "major agreements"—is an out-of-context buildup, which is accomplished by *selective* presentation of data. It is something less than an honest and forthright statement.

The exigencies of the problem, in piloting the Test Ban Treaty through the Senate, caused the State Department to mildly slap down the purveyors of The Treaty Breaking Hoax. In a Memorandum, dated August 22, 1963, which is included in the appendix of the hearings before the Senate Foreign Relations Committee, the State Department spoke up as it had never done previously:

It has been said that the Soviet Union has violated 50 out of the last 52 or 53 treaties that it entered into. This statistic appeared in the July 29, 1963 issue of *U.S. News and World Report,* and in a 1959 report of a special committee of the American Bar Association on Communist tactics, strategies, and objectives. (This report has not been endorsed by the American Bar Association.) . . .
Despite their repeated violation of treaty obligations, the Soviet Union is party to a number of multilateral and bilateral agreements that, so far as we know, it generally has satisfactorily observed, presumably because it continues to find it in its interests to do so.

This statement is followed by a list of "such agreements."

Someone has said that facts are stubborn things that refuse to go away. This became apparent in the debate on the floor of the Senate, when such stalwart conservatives as Senator Stuart Symington and Senator Everett Dirksen made presentations in favor of ratification of the Nuclear Test Ban Treaty. The more virulent of the Ultra-Rightist propagandists were especially taken aback at Dirksen's vigorous campaign in support of the Treaty, because he is a member of the Red-hunting Senate Internal Security Subcommittee. But Dirksen was facing reality with his sober senses, and he could not go along with those who were willing to bury their heads in the sand and gamble on the future of humanity. Not only was the Treaty recommended by a vote of 16 to 1 in the Senate Foreign Relations Committee, but it was finally ratified on September 24, 1963 by a Senate vote of 80 to 19. Of the 80 who voted for ratification, 25 were members of the Republican Party. President Kennedy signed the Treaty on October 7, 1963, and it became effective on October 10, 1963. One of the byproducts of the negotiations which culminated in the Treaty was the Hot Line teletype communications system between Moscow and Washington, which became operational on August 31, 1963. This is an important step towards eliminating the possibility of a nuclear war through mishaps. It provides for dependable, constant, and instantaneous communication between Washington and Moscow. Since then, over 100 other countries have joined in the treaty and have agreed not to conduct nuclear tests in the atmosphere.

It is a cardinal precept of The Great Crusade that the Soviet Union and the other Communist countries can do nothing that is praise-worthy. Such "experts" as John E. Hoover, Fred Schwarz, Carl McIntire, Billy James Hargis, Barry Goldwater, Robert Welch, William F. Buckley, Jr., Congressman John M. Ashbrook of the House Committee on Un-American Activities, and Senator Thomas J. Dodd of the Senate Internal Security Subcommittee perennially assure us that whatever these countries do is, ipso facto, horrible. A case in point is the story of the Soviet struggle to bring an end to nuclear testing; and the falsehoods that have been told about this effort.

On December 10, 1957, the Soviet Union proposed to the United States and Great Britain that all three countries discontinue nuclear testing as of January 1, 1958. Meeting with no favorable response, the Supreme Soviet issued a unilateral decree, ending Soviet testing in the atmosphere of atomic and thermonuclear weapons. It must be clearly noted that this was *not* a treaty, *not* an agreement, and *not* a promise. It was *a decree* of the Soviet Government, designed to set an example to other nations. On August 22, 1958, President Eisenhower announced that the United States would discontinue nuclear testing in the atmosphere for a period of one year from the beginning of negotiations with the Soviet Union for an agreement on this problem, unless the Soviet Union resumed testing. On August 26, 1959, the United States *extended its unilateral suspension* to the end of the year. The following day Great Britain pledged not to resume testing while the negotiations, currently taking place in Geneva, were in progress. The next day the Soviet Union pledged not to resume testing unless the other countries did so. On December 29, 1959, the *United States Government announced that it was free to resume testing* beginning January 1, 1960, but would give notice before any resumption.

On March 21, 1961, the Geneva Conference on Discontinuance of Nuclear Weapons Tests held its first meeting since the advent of the John F. Kennedy administration. At this session, the Soviet delegation presented its so-called "troika" proposal. Its essential feature called for a treaty to ban all nuclear testing, and supervision and control by equal representatives of three groups: the Communist states, the Capitalist states, and the neutral states. On August 30, 1961, the Soviet Union announced plans to resume testing. The reasons given were the Western powers' rejection of the "troika" proposal, the nuclear testing France had done since February 13, 1960, and the tensions arising from the Berlin situation.

From September 1 to November 4, 1961, the Soviet Union conducted a series of nuclear tests in the atmosphere, which were massive in scope and included the detonation of a bomb, on October 31, 1961, of unprecedented size: 55-60 megatons. On September 5, 1961, President Kennedy announced that the United States would resume atmospheric nuclear testing. On March 2, 1962, President Kennedy announced that he had ordered resumption of atmospheric nuclear testing in late April, unless the Soviet Union agrees before that time to an "ironclad" treaty banning all tests. On April 25, 1962, the United States resumed nuclear testing in the atmosphere. On August 5, 1962, the Soviet Union detonated in the atmosphere a 30-megaton nuclear device. This was the first of a scheduled series to run until December 25, 1962.

On August 29, 1962, President Kennedy announced his approval of a Soviet proposal to end all nuclear testing by January 1, 1963, but he insisted that a treaty with inspection provisions be signed first. On November 2, 1962, President Kennedy announced the end of the current series of atmospheric nuclear tests, but said that underground testing would be continued. On February 8, 1963, a series of underground tests were begun in Nevada.

On August 5, 1963, the limited Nuclear Test Ban Treaty was signed in Moscow, and, as previously mentioned, was ratified by the United States Senate, and was signed by President Kennedy on October 7, 1963.

All these moves and counter-moves are reduced to a simplistic formula by the Ultra-Rightists. As they tell it, it is made to sound as if the Soviet Union *broke an agreement* regarding nuclear testing. This argument was heavily exploited in an attempt to block ratification of the Treaty of Moscow.

The Ultra-Rightists do not give up easily, as can be seen from some of the propaganda that charges the Soviet Union with violations of the Nuclear Test Ban Treaty (the Moscow Treaty). As usual, the Cold Warriors pick on some incident which they can distort and magnify. During January, 1965, the Soviet Union was conducting some underground nuclear tests, which are permissible under the terms of the Test Ban Treaty. A small amount of radioactivity was "vented" from these tests, and was detected outside Soviet territory by the Atomic Energy Commission. After several discussions with Soviet officials, the State Department was satisfied that it resulted from miscalculation and was not an intentional violation. This, however, did not satisfy many of the Ultra-Rightists, who conducted an "I told you so" campaign to resurrect The Treaty Breaking Hoax. The practitioners of the Great Crusade were strangely silent about some of the officially admitted "venting" from our own underground tests in Nevada. In one case, the fallout was reported to have crossed into Mexico. Neither Russia nor Mexico saw fit to protest this incident or to use it as a basis for propaganda attacks.

In January, 1966, an American B-52 nuclear bomber crashed along the coast of Spain, dropping a thermonuclear bomb. The Soviet Union protested that the United States was violating the Nuclear Test Ban Treaty by actions that threatened to contaminate the high seas. It asserted that the United States was endangering foreign lands and peoples with its B-52 practice flights. It stated also that the flights carried a risk of war by accident or miscalculation, and it called on the United States to end "without delay the flights of aircraft carrying nuclear or thermonuclear weapons beyond national frontiers." As far as could be ascertained, the Special Committee of the American Bar Association has made no protest of this incident.

On October 10, 1966, the Soviet embassy at Washington made some inquiries about the repeated "ventings" from the Nevada underground tests. The State Department replied on October 28, 1966 that only "a very small amount" of radioactivity had leaked into the atmosphere and that the United

637

States did not consider itself in violation of the Test Ban Treaty.

One of the most vehement in opposition to ratification of the Test Ban Treaty was Congressman Craig Hosmer of California. As a member of the House of Representatives, Mr. Hosmer could have no voice on the question of ratification, which is the sole province of the Senate. Nevertheless, over a period of weeks, he filled page after page of the Congressional Record with arguments, articles, editorials, and anything else he could use. In addition, he wrote an article for the September 7, 1963 issue of the *Saturday Evening Post,* entitled "Beware the Test Ban!." Despite the fact that he has always taken an anti-Soviet position, it would appear that Congressman Hosmer is beginning to face the realities of the world in a most sober fashion. His remarks on the floor of the House of Representatives, March 2, 1967, deserve serious study by all who think it impossible to move in the direction of progressive universal disarmament:

Mr. Speaker, frequently I have been severely critical of far-out Johnson administration arms control and disarmament schemes. However, I want to indicate approval of plans just announced by the President for discussions with the U.S.S.R. on simultaneously limiting the build-up of both offensive and defensive nuclear missiles.

Each country now has a sufficient strategic nuclear offensive capability to deter the other from starting a war. Piling additional offensive capability on top of the existing deterrent is a waste of money for both sides.

As to defensive ABM systems, although the Soviet Union has started a deployment, it is only in an early stage and insufficient to blunt the U.S. deterrent by substantial damage limitation. At this point it is not much better off than the United States, which possesses only the early rudiments of an ABM system.

If one of the two goes ahead with a full system, the other is required to do so to maintain its deterrent capability. Further, and for the same purpose, both are compelled to factor costly sophistications into their offensive systems in order to overcome ABM defenses. After massive outlays in the magnitude of billions of dollars and rubles, the net result is that each is no better off vis-a-vis the other than before.

Mutual restraint in expenditures for offensive and defensive systems thus do not involve risks to the national security of either power. It is advantageous to each in that the resources otherwise consumed may be diverted to more productive channels.

All this would not be true except for the fact the existing intelligence systems of both countries are fully capable of detecting cheating on the restraints by the other. *A properly drafted agreement* in this area would not be subject to a charge that undetectable cheating might lead to a nuclear Pearl Harbor. This cannot be said of most other Johnson arms control and disarmament proposals. (Emphasis has been added.—M. K.)

It should be noted that Congressman Hosmer, as a member of the Joint Congressional Committee on Atomic Energy, is privy to considerable strategic military data. This makes his present position most significant.

Further proof that Congressman Craig Hosmer has abandoned the thesis of The Treaty Breaking Hoax is in a speech he delivered on the floor of the House of Representatives, in support of the Consular Treaty, on April 27, 1967:

Mr. Speaker, some 23 bilateral treaties and other international agreements are in force between the United States and the Union of Soviet Socialist Republics. These range in date from 1825 to 1967. A 24th will go into effect when ratified by the U.S.S.R. It is the consular convention recently ratified by the Senate. The big year for such agreements was 1945 in which three went into effect. Two were effected in each of the years 1955 and 1966. The most recent agreement actually entered into force was on February 13 of this year. It concerned certain fishery problems in the northeastern part of the Pacific Ocean.

Following these remarks, Congressman Hosmer listed the 23 agreements according to subject and other details.

Despite the dolorous predictions of the Cold Warriors, our nation's experience with the functioning of the Nuclear Test Ban Treaty has resulted in another step—the treaty banning military bases and nuclear weapons from outer space, the moon, or the planets. Sponsored and initiated by the United States, Great Britain, and the Soviet Union, the outer space treaty had been signed by 84 countries, when a tally was made on October 10, 1967. For some strange reason, the Ultra-Rightists did not unlimber their heavy artillery for attacks against this treaty.

Before leaving the story of the Ultra-Rightist opposition to the Nuclear Test Ban Treaty, it is worthy of note that the man who aspired to the Presidency of the United States, Gen-

639

eral Barry Goldwater, called for the breaking of that Treaty.[11] We have looked in vain in the writings of the Ultra-Rightist literary pundits for some word of rebuke to the General for his advocacy of treaty breaking.

The classic example of The Treaty Breaking Hoax *in action* occurred during the debate on the Consular Treaty in 1967. This treaty was first signed by the United States and the Soviet Union in June, 1964. It was designed to encourage trade and tourist travel by establishing rules and procedures for consulates and consular relations. At the request of the administration in Washington, the Senate Foreign Relations Committee did not hold any hearings in 1964. In March, 1965, while testifying before a House Appropriations Subcommittee, FBI Director John E. Hoover voiced opposition to the Treaty on the ground that the opening of Soviet consulates in the U.S.A. would facilitate Soviet intelligence activities. This argument was immediately picked up by the Ultra-Rightist *Liberty Lobby,* which deluged the Senate with letters and telegrams of protest. At the core of this massive propaganda campaign was a quotation from John E. Hoover. The Liberty Lobby and other Ultra-Rightist groups carried on their campaign of opposition in 1965, 1966, and 1967.

As is usual in Ultra-Rightist campaigns, the true facts were obscured. First of all, the new treaty was not needed in order to legalize Soviet consulates in the U.S.A. That right already existed. In fact, it was the Soviet Union which *closed* its consulates in New York, San Francisco, and Los Angeles during 1948. If the espionage theory of John E. Hoover and the Liberty Lobby were valid, it would be necessary to conclude that in 1948 the Soviet Union decided to curtail its intelligence operations in the U.S.A. But the record shows that in that year, as in many other years, John E. Hoover, the American Legion, and others were issuing thunderous pronunciamentos about Soviet espionage. The second fact that was obscured is that all U.S. Embassies and Consulates have CIA operatives and other spies, disguised as diplomatic personnel. The third fact hidden by the Ultra-Rightist clamor was that the treaty was more to U.S. advantage than to the Soviet Union; the reason being, that more Americans visit the Soviet than vice versa. In 1964,

---

11 *Los Angeles Times,* February 27, 1967.

for instance, 12,000 American tourists visited the Soviet Union and only 204 Russian tourists visited the U.S.A. The fourth concealed fact was that the new Treaty was drawn up upon U.S. initiative, in order to give greater protection to American tourists.

Among the leaders of the campaign against ratification of the Consular Treaty was Professor Lev Dobriansky, one of the functionaries of the Ultra-Rightist *American Security Council* (a private organization). Not only did the professor write a frantic letter to Senator J. William Fulbright, Chairman of the Senate Foreign Relations Committee, but he wrote an essay, whose main thrust is:

Finally, and worse still, as an additional step toward peaceful coexistence, the Convention deprives us of a cold war advantage with no parallel sacrifice by the Russians.

It is plain for all to see that Professor Dobriansky is opposed to peaceful coexistence, but at the same time he claims to be against a Third World War. In addition, the professor presented a long-winded argument by which he "proved" that the Soviet Union is not a nation! Both the letter and the essay were placed in the Congressional Record, August 9, 1965, by Congressman Edward J. Derwinski of Illinois, who is usually most cooperative with Dobriansky and the American Security Council.

The professor is a prolific letter writer, never tiring of devising new arguments against the Soviet Union. On August 6, 1965, his letter in the *Washington Post* berated the editor for an editorial favorable to the Treaty. Dobriansky called it an "ill-written and Moscow-oriented pact" and said that "its very language contradicts even the U.S.S.R. Constitution and the most advanced knowledge on the Soviet Union." The most "advanced knowledge," of course, is Dobriansky's viewpoint. At least he gives no other explanation. Nor is it clear why he is so anxious to defend the Constitution of the U.S.S.R.! This letter and another one Dobriansky wrote to the *Post* were placed in the Congressional Record, August 19, 1965, by Congressman Derwinski. On February 8, 1966, Congressman Harold R. Collier of Illinois placed in the Congressional Record a long essay by Dobriansky. This time the professor was introduced as the chairman of one of his pet propaganda projects, the so-called National Captive Nations Committee. The professor's main argument is that the Treaty acknowledges that the U.S.S.R. is a nation! He brazenly ignores the fact of diplomatic recognition since 1933! On January 24, 1967, Congressman Derwinski had the professor in the Congressional Record again, with a long essay, entitled "Ten Reasons Against the United States—U.S.S.R. Consular Treaty." This essay was also featured in the Ultra-Rightist *Human Events,* February 11, 1967. On February 23, 1967, Congressman Derwinski placed in the Congressional Record a speech delivered by Professor Dobriansky before the Senate Foreign Relations Committee. It was a desperate plea to block ratification of the Consular Treaty.

Syndicated columnists Robert S. Allen and Paul Scott reported[12] in matter-of-fact fashion that John E. Hoover's disapproval "has been largely responsible for the Senate's failure to consider this pact." The shocking fact, that the head of a secret police agency is dictating foreign policy, is something which our commentators have seen fit to ignore. In a dispatch from Washington to the *Los Angeles Times,* January 24, 1967, John H. Averill confirmed the Allen-Scott story about Hoover's opposition to the Treaty, and he reported that Senator Everett Dirksen was also opposed to ratification. In the meantime, Secretary of State Rusk explained that President Johnson possessed the power under our Constitution to permit the opening of Soviet consulates in this country, but that the Treaty was needed to grant U.S. diplomats the right to render prompt assistance to Americans who got into trouble in the U.S.S.R. The reports out of Washington seemed to indicate that Senator Dirksen and others had been influenced by John E. Hoover's warning that the opening of Soviet consulates in a number of cities would result in spies swarming all over this country. In an excellent editorial, the Riverside, California *Daily Enterprise,* January 26, 1967, pointed out John E. Hoover's inconsistency. He had sent a letter to Senator Fulbright, in which he said that the potential spy problem was manageable. "But, in a letter to the historically Red-baiting Sen. Karl Mundt, he switched the emphasis back to the magnitude of

12 *Santa Ana (Calif.) Register,* November 30, 1966.

the problems." The editorial concluded: "For the Senate to let a warmed over spy scare turn it aside from the consular treaty would be an exercise in folly."

On January 26, 1967, Congressman John M. Ashbrook, one of the most vociferous members of the House Committee on Un-American Activities, went into battle against ratification of the Treaty, despite the fact that only the Senate has jurisdiction over treaties:

Mr. Speaker, one of the most dangerous proposals which will come before the 90th Congress is the so-called Consular Treaty. . .

It borders on idiocy to appease Communist overlords in Moscow who are directly and indirectly responsible for aggression, subversion, and atrocities, while at the same time 400,000 Americans in Vietnam are trying to stem the tide of Communist conquest in Southeast Asia.

It will be recalled that a statement by Director J. Edgar Hoover of the FBI provided the impetus for much opposition to the consular agreement and was undoubtedly a major reason why the measure was never brought to the Senate floor for action.

As Congressman Ashbrook warmed up to his job, he painted a picture of the perils of espionage that would ensue from the opening of Soviet consulates. Of course, our spies in the Soviet Union would not be objectionable to Mr. Ashbrook. He went to such lengths as quoting from Litvinoff's letter to Roosevelt in 1933! He waved the Red flag by quoting from a statement on January 4, 1967, of the Central Committee of the Communist Party in the Soviet Union, entitled "On Preparations for the 50th Anniversary of the Great October Socialist Revolution." Mr. Ashbrook concluded his oration by inserting in the Congressional Record a letter of Senator Karl Mundt to FBI Director John E. Hoover and Hoover's reply to Mundt.

On February 3, 1967, Warren H. McDonald, research director of the American Legion, spent almost three hours testifying against ratification. He told the Senate Foreign Relations Committee that he hadn't "given thought" to the provision in the Treaty giving immunity from arrest to U.S. Consular personnel in the Soviet Union. McDonald was sure that the treaty would open the floodgates of Soviet espionage and that the entire treaty would be "too costly" to the U.S.

The high point in Red Scare hysteria was reached by Congressman John R. Rarick of Louisiana. Rarick is a former

643

Louisiana district judge and was a member of the board of directors of the Louisiana group which founded *The Councilor,* the semi-monthly hate sheet of the Louisiana (White) Citizens Councils. Although ratification of the Treaty was none of his business, Rarick placed a speech in the Congressional Record, February 13, 1967, attacking what he called "the controversial Communist Consular Treaty." Congressman Rarick began his speech by telling his colleagues that "lobbying in our Congress by Communist agents of the Soviet Union is a shocker." It is amusing to note what constituted a shocker to Mr. Rarick. It seems that a newly-arrived Soviet diplomat was making the rounds in get-acquainted visits to Congressional leaders. Senator Everett Dirksen was one of them. He chose to interpret a conversation of a general nature as a lobbying call to spread propaganda for East-West cooperation. Dirksen is known for his flair for dramatics, and it came as no surprise that he issued a statement which sent Congressman Rarick's blood pressure into a high climb. Rarick called upon his colleagues to "study this revolting invasion" and gave them real, hard intelligence information by reading from the Washington, D.C. telephone book the listings of the Soviet Embassy and its several departmental offices. Thus did the great patriot from Louisiana expose a dark, deep Soviet plot, in order to prove that the Consular Treaty should not be ratified.

It seems that, at some point in the "great debate," President Lyndon Johnson had a heart-to-heart talk with FBI Director John E. Hoover. On February 2, 1967, Mr. Johnson held a press conference, at which he made these disclosures:

1. The Treaty would protect some 18,000 Americans who travel annually to the Soviet Union, because U.S. authorities would have to be notified when Americans are arrested and U.S. officials would have the right to visit them.

2. There are 452 Soviet officials in the United States who now enjoy diplomatic immunity from arrest. The addition of 10 to 15 more, which could result from the opening of 3 Soviet consulates, would not add an undue burden to the FBI.

3. John E. Hoover had assured the President that no insurmountable problem would result from ratification of the Treaty.

The hypothesis about a Johnson-Hoover tête-à-tête is borne

out by the report of columnists Rowland Evans and Robert Novak.[13] The sequence of events in the J. E. Hoover foreign policy safari, as told by Evans and Novak, is as follows:

1. In the fall of 1966, Hoover wrote a letter to Secretary of State Dean Rusk, in which he said he was not in "opposition" to the Consular Treaty.

2. On January 23, 1967, Hoover wrote a letter to Senator Karl Mundt, in which he raised the spy scare by the double-entendre route.

3. "Now comes the third letter, which is secretly circulating among key Senate friends of the new treaty. In it, Hoover states that the FBI can definitely handle the extra 'responsibilities' of a new Soviet consulate." The letter, we are told by Evans and Novak, is "a highly confidential one to President Johnson himself" and gives the President and the State Department "powerful ammunition to kill off the effect of Hoover's earlier epistles."

There were rumblings of the secret Johnson-Hoover conference some two weeks before the President's press conference of February 2, 1967. In a Washington dispatch to the *Los Angeles Times,* January 21, 1967, Tom Lambert wrote:

The Johnson administration made a long-delayed move Friday to quash congressional misgivings about an American-Soviet consular treaty which stem from the belief that FBI Director J. Edgar Hoover opposes it.

The tragic aspect of this story about Hoover's role in the Treaty dialogue is that so few Americans understand this elementary political truism: participation by secret police in the formulation of governmental policy, domestic or foreign, is the stuff of which a Fascist police state is made. Hoover's pretensions cause one to ask, as did Cassius in Shakespeare's *Julius Caesar:*

> Upon what meat doth this our Caesar feed,
> That he is grown so great?

Among the prominent Republicans who carried forward the

[13] *Los Angeles Times,* February 21, 1967.

fight for ratification was Senator Thruston B. Morton of Kentucky. As a former Assistant Secretary of State, Senator Morton was in a position to wield considerable influence with his colleagues. In a speech on the floor of the Senate, January 31, 1967, Senator Morton said, in part:

The sound and fury of the unenlightened have distorted the substance of the proposed consular convention.

By any realistic yardstick, the advantages to be gained by ratification of the consular convention favor the United States.

After explaining the provisions of the Treaty, which give U.S. officials the right to see and advise American citizens arrested in the Soviet Union, Senator Morton added:

But the real issue here is not a meaningless number game involving tourists and spies. The real issue is whether the government of the United States will be authorized by the Senate to explore a dim light at the end of the dark tunnel that is the "cold war."

The task before the Senate and the administration is clear. We must educate, not placate. Let us not placate those who would creep out from darkness to bomb embassies and legations. Let us not placate those who would use patriotism as a shield for twisted conspiracy.

Senator Morton finally was successful in converting Senator Everett Dirksen, who left a hospital bed to deliver the principal speech in favor of ratification, on March 16, 1967. On a roll-call vote that day, the Treaty was ratified by a vote of 66-28. There were 44 Democrats and 22 Republicans who voted for ratification; 15 Democrats and 13 Republicans voted against ratification.

More than a year elapsed after the U.S. Senate ratified the treaty, but the Supreme Soviet had delayed its ratification. Strange behavior, indeed, for those wily Communists who are supposed to be so anxious to get more secret agents into the U.S.A. Ironically enough, a story by Willard Edwards of the *Chicago Tribune—New York News Syndicate*[14] suggests that the Soviet Government is apprehensive about the CIA wanting to plant its agents in a new consulate at Leningrad, in order to

14 *Human Events*, October 28, 1967.

ferret out information about Russian's anti-ballistic missile system. Is it possible that the shoe fits on the other foot?[15]

A letter in the Riverside, California *Daily Enterprise*, May 25, 1967, expresses beautifully some thoughts on the subject:

Editor, the Press and Enterprise:
In his letter to the Open Forum of May 19, Mr. G. L. Hills ended with the question, "Would you want a Russian consulate in your neighborhood?" I certainly would not, but my reasons may not be those Mr. Hills would anticipate.

I would not want a Russian consulate in my neighborhood because I could not explain to my new Soviet neighbors why a man could not buy a house in my neighborhood if his skin were black. I would be at a loss to tell him why a woman, doing the same work as a man, is paid less wages in this democracy. How could I justify in this most wealthy of nations that to relieve the poverty amongst the plenty is considered against the finest American traditions?

I couldn't begin to explain the American theology which bolsters and promotes a degenerative materialism, but utters nothing more than "Well, that's war," at the thought of thousands of non-combatants being killed and maimed weekly in Vietnam.

Nor could I explain why students are treated like children, but expected to behave like adults, or why the arts are treated as non-productive frills in our educational system. I could not inform him of the delicate reasons why a man who can die or kill for his country may be considered too young to have a say in why he should die or in whom he should kill . . .

I wouldn't want a Russian consulate in my neighborhood not because of the harm it might do, but because I wouldn't want any other nation to know how deeply ashamed I am of my nation's abject moral poverty.

PHIL HOLMER

In a very real sense, the survival of the human race depends upon a period of peaceful coexistence with the Soviet Union and the initiation of a series of steps leading to universal disarmament. It will undoubtedly be a painful struggle, but one which humanity must go through in order to survive and progress. Consequently, it is essential that people of good will energetically combat The Treaty Breaking Hoax. Furthermore, the message must go forward that we can and must find areas of agreement with and conclude disarmament treaties with the Soviet Union and China.

A man whose experience should be helpful is former United

15 The U.S.A. and the U.S.S.R. formally concluded the treaty on June 13, 1968.

States Ambassador to the U.N., James J. Wadsworth. During a dinner speech in New York on November 15, 1962, Ambassador Wadsworth said:

So we must give more thought and attention to what I call the "Three A's": the *Attitude* which can help create the *Atmosphere* in which we can take the *Action* which will lead us and our adversaries away from the brink together. Neither of us really wants to jump off. You can be sure of that. It would mean destruction for both. Why not put as much thought and energy into creating and developing such a progression as we do in creating and developing ever new and more devastating weapons? Which is more likely to be our salvation in the long run? Which makes more sense? Let's try being adult.

The former Governor of Pennsylvania, Harold E. Stassen, served as special assistant on disarmament to President Eisenhower and has served on many negotiating missions. From his vast experience in negotiating with the Russians, this, in part, is what he told the Air Force Academy American Assembly:

A gentleman at a dinner party in Pittsburgh said to me a while ago, "It would be a better world if Russia weren't in it!" Well, Russia is in it! It is a part of the world in which we live! We must think of the situation as it will exist in the years ahead with the Russian scientific advances.

I remember the negotiations over Austria after the Second World War. There were those who said it is no use negotiating over Austria. The U.S.S.R. will never pull the Red Army out of Austria. You are wasting time. You are in a foolish posture. But first President Truman and then President Eisenhower sustained the other view that from the whole tradition of America and for the sake of Austria, we must continue to negotiate. Those negotiations went on, and on. I remember it was the 367th negotiating session, when suddenly the Soviet Union said, "We agree." Nobody knows for certain why they agreed. But they did. The Austrian treaty was worked out very carefully, very carefully. We did not provide that the U.S. would pull out one day and the Soviet Union would pull out a year later. We established that treaty precisely so that each condition was arranged such that both sides moved at the same time. No one could take advantage. And the U.S.S.R. respected that treaty. Now the opera is heard again in Vienna, and Austria today is independent and sovereign, and there's a little brighter hope for the future of peace in Europe. All because of that persistent negotiating with the U.S.S.R. over Austria.

I talked to the president of Finland after the war when he finally arranged for the withdrawal of the Red Army from Finland. He said it was a tough negotiation, but they kept at it. Finland is still under somewhat of a threat, but the agreements over Finland have been respected and even their naval bases have been returned to them. It was a tough situation, but the Finns stood up, and they also negotiated. Finland today has made considerable progress since World War II, as a result of negotiations with the U.S.S.R.

Iran was another tough situation after World War II. The negotiations worked out and the Red Army finally pulled back. Today Iran has its oil flowing, and the lands that once were the "Garden of Eden" are being irrigated and developed.

The United Nations Charter itself, with all its limitations, holds, as I see it, the best hope of the future of peace. And that Charter was the result of long, tough negotiation with the Russians. But it was worked out with certain minimum provisions as we persistently negotiated at San Francisco in 1945. . . . It is not a perfect document. But it is the beginning in mankind's struggle for finding a way to resolve differences and live together on this earth without turning to wars and violent destruction. It is an agreement reached with the U.S.S.R. and with the others.

It is difficult to negotiate with the Soviet Union. But those who say that it never can be done are in error. . . .[16]

Some very sound advice regarding treaties with the Soviet Union comes from the pen of former Ambassador to the Soviet Union, Professor George F. Kennan. In an article entitled "Can We Deal With Moscow?" which appeared in the *Saturday Evening Post,* October 5, 1963, he said:

Our greatest hope for the future lies in the possibility that as time goes on, more and more things which seem to us to be in our interests will also seem to various Communist leaders to be in theirs. This is something we can influence, to some extent, by the way we conduct our diplomacy. We can use our imaginations to devise proposals compatible with our own security which will hold some advantage for them as well.

In these few words, Ambassador Kennan has brilliantly summarized the procedures and attitudes that are necessary for peaceful coexistence. His sharp criticism should be pondered by all, when he refers to "a diseased suspiciousness which rejects every possibility of agreement because of the ever-present possibility that the other fellow may violate it."

The Chairman of the Joint Chiefs of Staff of the U.S. Department of Defense is without question a man who is in-

---

[16] Quoted in *War/Peace Report,* April 1963.

formed on the realities of a possible thermonuclear holocaust. He is charged with the responsibility of protecting this country from attacks, from any possible source. For these reasons, the testimony of General Earle E. Wheeler on *Meet the Press,* February 26, 1967, is of utmost significance. In response to a question from the distinguished journalist, Marquis Childs, on the possibility of getting an agreement with the Soviet Union, to forestall another arms race for installations of Anti-Ballistic Missile Systems, General Wheeler replied:

I think it is very wise and it is very proper for us to explore with the Soviets any manner of a reduction in the nuclear threat to world peace. I certainly think that these possibilities should be explored, Mr. Childs.

It is also worthy of note that, during the discussion of the Nuclear Test Ban Treaty, General Wheeler was among those who favored ratification.

From all the data available, two inescapable conclusions clearly emerge. The Treaty Breaking Hoax must be thoroughly exposed and discredited and the philosophy of peaceful co-existence must become an integral part of Americanism.

# CHAPTER XV

## Alice in Birchland

(With apologies to the late Lewis Carroll, whose *Alice in Wonderland* still brings joy to millions of people.)

An examination of the falsehoods and distortions of truth, that form the phantasmagoria of the John Birch Society, has led some observers to conclude that its founder and leader, Robert Welch, is a psychotic. We rise to the defense of Mr. Welch, and hereby depose that he is perfectly sane. Welch is a shrewd salesman, a clever propagandist, an astute public relations expert, and a skillful advertising specialist—all rolled into one—who has devised a plan for harnessing dissent, discontent, and frustration in support of a goal. That goal is to stabilize Capitalism by enhancing the power of Big Business and its military allies. Advertising in general contains so much deception, that it comes "natural" for an advertising specialist to use it in the promotion of political aims. When Welch's outrageous statements are exposed, he resorts to the strategy so successfully employed by Hitler, Goebbels, Mussolini, Franco, and other Fascists—blaming it onto the Communists.

In the April, 1961 Bulletin of the John Birch Society, Robert Welch discussed the "present all-out attack on the John Birch Society." He attributed it to "the signal given" by an article in the West Coast Communist paper, the *People's World,* on February 25, 1961. It seems that Welch had some help, in arriving at this conclusion, from another Ultra-Rightist, Bryton Barron, a former State Department official. Welch reported with approval the remarks made by Bryton Barron on a Washington, D.C., radio station, in which Barron charged that the *People's World* article furnished the "line" for articles in many non-Communist publications. Welch charged, in effect, that an article in the March 10, 1961 issue of *Time* magazine is the offspring of "the mother article" in the Communist *People's World.*

651

Welch's charge against *Time* magazine was made, while informing his readers that *Time* had sent a reporter to interview him in his office. Welch said that the interview lasted about 3 hours. He also admitted that *Time* reporters were engaged in interviewing Birchers all over the country during the week before the article's appearance. Welch would have his readers believe that *Time* discarded all the data assembled by its own reporters, at great cost, and simply did a re-write job of the *People's World* article. Welch "proved" this thesis to his own satisfaction and that of his followers by stressing some similarities between the two articles and conveniently ignoring the dissimilarities. This was followed by the charge that the same type of article—with the same "line"—was carried in almost every other newspaper and magazine that published an article critical of the Birch Society. Welch claimed that the *Time* article was followed by attacks against the Birch Society in more than 100 newspapers all over the United States in about 2 weeks' time. He let his readers forget two things:

1. That newspapers get much news from press wire services, resulting in similar stories in hundreds of publications.

2. When a subject is "hot," everyone gets into the act.

Welch's principal "proof" is interesting, because it illustrates the sophistry that is used continually in Birchite and other Ultra-Rightist circles. The *People's World* article said, in part:

On Welch's council are such veterans of democratic rights as Dean Clarence Manion; T. Coleman Andrews, former income tax collector; Spruille Braden, former Latin-American "expert" of the U.S. State Department; and Adolphe Menjou, unsavory relic of the "House Un-American" raid on Hollywood.

In the *Time* article, Manion, Braden, and Menjou were discussed; Andrews was omitted. In other articles, according to Welch, all four names that appeared in the *People's World* article were mentioned. This, then, was Welch's main proof. Welch was using the non-sequitur line of reasoning, because he ignored another possible explanation, which could be that these names were used because of their prominence. In fact, when Welch made this charge, he was indulging in a most brozen and reckless gamble, because in *the previous month's Bulletin* he had photostatically reproduced an article critical of the John Birch Society from the February 19, 1961, Louisville *Courier-Journal*. This was two days before the *People's World* article, and lo and behold, we find in the *Courier-Journal* article the names of Andrews, Manion, and Menjou! By using Welch's logic, it could be "proven" that the *People's World* followed the lead of the *Courier-Journal*.

The best witness against Robert Welch, in the matter of this reckless charge, is Robert Welch himself. In the February, 1961 Bulletin, which is dated January 31, 1961—twenty-one days before the *People's World* "signal"—Welch was complaining that "we have given up all hope of avoiding publicity, either good or bad." Even more damaging to his thesis are his remarks in the August 1, 1960, issue of the Society's Bulletin, in which Welch refers to "the series of newspaper attacks on myself and on the Society that has already started." Would Welch, perchance, argue that these newspaper writers were clairvoyant and got their "signal" from the *People's World* 6 months before the "signal" was published? Welch specifically complained in his August 1, 1960, Bulletin that the *Chicago Daily News* had carried two anti-Birchite articles in July, 1960. Welch added this comment: "And we have reason to believe that the same attack will be picked up and repeated in other 'liberal' newspapers." Here he attributed the "signal" to the *Chicago Daily News*. Could it be possible that the *People's World* copied from the Chicago paper?

In a postscript to his August, 1960 Bulletin, Welch stated that the *Milwaukee Journal* had just published an exposé of the Birch Society "even more vicious than that which had appeared in the *Chicago Daily News*." He concluded his discussion of newspaper articles by asserting that articles in other papers about the Birchers had appeared "in papers having a total circulation many times that of the *Chicago Daily News* and the *Milwaukee Journal* combined."

Other newspapers which carried articles critical of the Birchers, *prior to* the *People's World* February 21, 1961, article were:

| | |
|---|---|
| *July 26, 1960* | *Chicago American.* |
| *July 30, 1960* | Racine (Wisc.) |
| | *Journal Times & Sunday Bulletin.* |
| *August 1960* | Boston (Mass.) *Herald.* |
| *January 1961* | Santa Barbara *News-Press.* |

653

The *Los Angeles Times* ran a five-part series from March 5 to 9, 1961, which Welch admitted was researched independently several weeks prior to the *People's World* article.

Welch does indeed refute Welch!

An "unofficial" and supplementary explanation of the newspaper and magazine articles about the Birch Society was furnished by the professional anti-Communist, W. Cleon Skousen. This gentleman is a former FBI Agent, former chief of police of Salt Lake City, former employee of the American Security Council, editorial director of the policeman's magazine, *Law and Order,* and author of *The Naked Communist.* In a pamphlet, entitled *The Communist Attack on the John Birch Society,* Skousen assures us that he is not a member of the John Birch Society. If he is telling the truth, one cannot help wondering why he doesn't become a "card-carrying" member. In addition to serving as a member of the Advisory Council of the Ultra-Rightist *Americanism Education League,* Skousen has appeared around the country as a speaker for the Birch Society's American Opinion Speakers Bureau.

Skousen begins his explanation by conceding that there was a critical article by Jack Mabley in the *Chicago American* on July 26, 1960, but that he did not see any further public criticism of the Birch Society "until the Communist Party ordered the annihilation of the John Birchers six months later." Skousen quotes from a Moscow manifesto against anti-Communism in December, 1960 and a speech by Nikita Khrushchev on January 6, 1961. "A short time later," Skousen avers, "the opening blast against all anti-Communists in the United States was initiated by a concentrated attack on the John Birch Society." The opening blast, Skousen tells us, was the article in the *People's World* on February 25, 1961. Then, Skousen says, "the transmission belt began to function so that this story was planted in one major news medium after another until finally even some of the more conservative papers had taken up the hue and cry." He follows this with the same argument that Welch used about *Time* magazine, and he adds a spirited defense of Robert Welch and the Birch Society.

Skousen's "evidence" consists of using a sequence of events as a non-sequitur argument, to prove a preconceived notion. This is typical of Ultra-Rightist propagandists. The best cure for these gentlemen would be to give them some heavy doses of their own medicine. For instance, if a compilation should be made of all the murders, robberies, burglaries, rapings, and embezzlements committed in each city *after Skousen has lectured there,* that would be as much proof of Skousen's responsibility for inspiring these crimes as the proof he adduces of Communist inspiration of hundreds of newspaper stories that were critical of the Birchers.

It is not known whether Welch got the "brilliant" thesis from Skousen or vice versa. Perhaps, as sometimes happens, two great minds made simultaneous discoveries. One thing is certain, that regardless of overwhelming proof that the Welch-Skousen theory is completely erroneous, Welch clings to it tenaciously. Thus, on the *Meet the Press* television program, September 6, 1964, Welch complained:

We have been subjected to more smear, probably, than any other organization in American history. We have certainly had the Moscow press devote more space and more attention to laying down the line for the smears of us, and the rest of the press elsewhere in the world, than they have ever given to any other non-governmental opposition.

True to its secret role as a part of the ideological fountainhead of the Ultra-Rightist drive for power, the California Senate Factfinding Committee on Un-American Activities gave an "official" boost to the Welch-Skousen thesis. In its 1963 Report, we read:

The attack against the John Birch Society commenced with an article in the *People's World,* California Communist paper, in February 1961, although the Chicago *Daily News* had attacked statements made in *The Politician* and the *Blue Book* several months previously.

The small-town lawyer, Richard Combs, who writes these yearly "reports" for the Committee has an inimitable style of giving himself an "out" when he does an outrageous smear job. Immediately after claiming that the attacks on the Birch Society commenced with the *People's World*—a statement which is an unmitigated falsehood—Mr. Combs explained the results of the Chicago *Daily News* articles:

655

This was sensational news, and as the John Birch Society started to grow rapidly in California, several newspapers took up the attack. Naturally, these articles varied with the basic editorial policies of the papers.

Thus, Combs admits that the sensational news, which newspapers are always eager to publish, was the basic reason for so many newspapers publishing stories critical of the Birchers. Of course it was sensational "news" that Dwight D. Eisenhower was a tool of the alleged Communist conspiracy and that so many others were crypto-Communists. Even though some truth emerged from Mr. Combs' "report," which is palmed off as the findings of a committee investigation, the Birchers and their supporters can and do quote the "California *Senate* Report," as stating that newspaper attacks on the Birch Society were inspired by the *People's World*.

On September 27, 1964, the Birch Society had a 16-page Sunday supplement in principal newspapers across the country. Almost two pages are devoted to exploiting the California Report's boost to the Skousen-Welch thesis about the *People's World* article as the inspiration for newspaper criticism of Birchland. An additional feature of the Birch newspaper supplement was a picture of Dwight Eisenhower and an alleged endorsement of the Birch Society, taken from a column by the Ultra-Rightist George Todt, in the Los Angeles *Herald-Examiner* of March 23, 1964. It takes a special kind of brazenness to smear a man as part of a Communist conspiracy, and then use his photograph and an alleged endorsement of a professed anti-Communist organization. On October 1, 1964, *Los Angeles Times* columnist, Paul Coates, published the results of his communication with General Eisenhower. Not only did Eisenhower *repudiate* the alleged endorsement, but he expressed resentment at the *unauthorized* use of his photograph.

In Birchland, as Alice would soon find out, no newspapers would criticize the Birch Society without a "signal" from the *People's World*. Nay more, in Birchland the other newspapers and magazines would know nothing about the Birch Society, were it not for the *People's World,* the Moscow manifesto, and Khrushchev's speech. If all this makes the reader feel groggy, it should be understood that this is the intent of the Birch Society and the California Senate Factfinding Committee on Un-American Activities.

The late, unlamented Senator Joseph McCarthy is one of the heroes of Welch and Skousen. It would be interesting to find out if the Welch-Skousen thesis had been plagiarized from a speech by McCarthy, that was carried on television and radio networks from New York on November 24, 1953. During the course of his speech, McCarthy said:

The other night, Truman defined what he calls "McCarthyism." The definition was identical, word for word, comma for comma, with the definition adopted by the Communist *Daily Worker,* which originated the term, "McCarthyism."

Historically, Fascists have always used the Red Scare as an ideological and psychological battering ram to destroy democratic rights, as a prelude to a Fascist coup d'etat.

The second adventure of Alice in Birchland left poor Alice in a state of shock. You see, Alice was not prepared for so much skulduggery. It seems that the John Birch Society was pleased with the 1963 Report of the California Senate Factfinding Committee on Un-American Activities, because it reprinted it as one of its American Opinion booklet series, at a dollar per copy, and gave it nation-wide distribution. However, the Birchers decided to "improve" the Report. Consequently, in the Birch reprint, the following items from the Report were *OMITTED:*

1. *From page 5. ". . . The possibility of Dr. Eisenhower's having been a member of this ephemeral movement in 1924 is far too remote to warrant serious consideration."*

2. *From page 10.* On this page the original Report comments on Robert Welch's charge that the novel, *Dr. Zhivago,* was sponsored by the Soviet Secret Police, and the Report quotes Eugene Lyons as saying: *"Only someone bereft of his senses could conceivably be converted to Marxism by* Dr. Zhivago."

3. *From page 61. "The accusations he made in 'The Politician' in 1954 are shared by few of his followers, but he has since made other declarations that are as irresponsible and insusceptible of proof."*

The three items, in quotation marks and italicized, were *omitted* not only in the Birchers' reprint of the 1963 California Report, but also from the 16-page Sunday newspaper supplement of September 27, 1964. These omissions did not go unnoticed, so the Birch Society issued another edition of the 1963 Report, which restored the previously deleted items, and which contained some added Birch commentaries. The later edition, however, did not get the massive circulation which the first edition attained, with the result that the first edition, with its distortions of the truth, is the most widely quoted by Birchers and Birchsymps.

As Alice wandered further into the labyrinthian reaches of Birchland, she came upon another wonder of Birchism. On October 17, 1965, the newspapers carried another 16-page Birch Society Sunday supplement. One of its features was the quoting of some favorable remarks by Ultra-Rightist William F. Buckley, Jr., taken from something Buckley had written in his magazine, *National Review,* several years earlier. The quotation was accurate enough, but the bible-quoting Birchers "forgot" that, two months before the supplement was published, William Buckley had written three syndicated newspaper columns, *sharply critical of Welch and the John Birch Society.* These later remarks by Buckley were not quoted by the Birchers. Another feature of this supplement was its use of a full page of *favorable* quotations from the *1963 Report* of the California Senate Factfinding Committee on Un-American Activities, but nary a word about some of the *unfavorable* items in the *1965 Report* by that same Committee. The latter Report was distributed in the middle of the summer of 1965, which gave ample time for the Birchers to learn about its contents. (Lest the reader assume that Richard Combs and the Committee had suddenly been converted to democracy and truth, we hasten to point out that they were forced to make some grudging admissions about the Birchers, because the facts had become public knowledge. The Committee could not afford to be completely discredited, so it had to make a strategic ideological retreat.)

Not the least of the wonders in Birchland that Alice discovered was Professor Revilo P. Oliver. In addition to the fun Alice derived from spelling both his first and last names backwards, she was thrilled, beyond the power of words to describe, by the professor's tale of Appendix IX. Fortunately for all of us, the tale was related by Dr. Oliver in the Birchite *American Opinion,* April 1965, p. 43.

It seems that the House Committee on Un-American Activities (or, more accurately, its predecessor, the Dies Committee), had compiled a document, in 1944, of some 1900 pages, which was published as Appendix IX to the Committee's Hearings. It was the most disgraceful collection of malicious gossip, witch-hunting smears, and libelous statements ever published by a Congressional Committee. As Oliver tells it, upon publication of this document, "the Conspiracy went into action." Who this "Conspiracy" might be, Oliver doesn't tell us, but we gather from the article and from other writings of his that all anti-Fascists are members of the "Conspiracy."

The first thing that happened after Appendix IX was published, according to Oliver, is that the Chairman of the Committee, Congressman Martin Dies, "was immobilized by a mysterious illness." Oliver doesn't come out with a direct accusation, but he leaves the clear implication that the illness was caused, or could have been caused, by the "Conspiracy." He refers the reader to an article by Martin Dies in *American Opinion*, May 1964, page 67. Dies explains the "mysterious illness" in this manner:

In 1944, I developed a strange and general weakness. Never had I experienced anything like it before or since. A sore appeared on my larynx which a Galveston physician thought might be cancerous. I have never known for sure the cause of that strange and unprecedented illness but it compelled me to quit public life.

There is, of course, nothing strange or unprecedented about a person becoming ill with symptoms he never experienced previously. As the old saying goes, there is always a first time. Even the best of medical diagnosticians are frequently baffled about the etiology of a disease. Throughout his article, Dies insinuates so many things, that it is little wonder that a person with Professor Oliver's imaginative powers would see his illness as somehow related to the "Conspiracy" and its machinations.

Dr. Oliver explains the next episode of this story in his inimitable style:

The Conspiracy, through its control of venal Congressmen, procured the burning of all unsold copies of Appendix IX. The copies in the Library of Congress were removed. Communist agents systematically stole the copies that were in other libraries throughout the country.

659

No source is given by Dr. Oliver for these sensational "disclosures," but he does conclude that his alleged facts attest to "the frantic efforts of our domestic enemies to conceal it from the American people."

Pursuant to our request, Congressman John V. Tunney asked the Library of Congress to research the charges made by Professor Oliver (and many other Ultra-Rightists). A number of months elapsed, and finally Congressman Tunney was sent a report on August 9, 1965, signed by Adoreen M. McCormick, Special Assistant in the Library of Congress:

Your letter in behalf of a constituent has been referred to this office for a reply.

We have made an exhaustive search to determine whether or not the Library of Congress has or has ever had a copy of Appendix IX, a publication of the House Un-American Activities Committee, in its collections. Our records do not indicate that a copy was ever accessioned for our collections. I understand that the publication was a committee print and was not issued as a regular government publication. This would explain why we did not receive a copy for the collections.

We have checked the *National Union Catalog*, which contains entries for books and pamphlets in other libraries in the United States, and find that no library has reported having a copy.

This simple, honest, and forthright explanation will, of course, not be acceptable to the Birchers and other Ultra-Rightists, who dote on tales of Communist conspiracies. For the rest, it is a well-known fact that many committees of Congress issue reports that are printed for use of the respective committees only, and are not sold to the public by the Government Printing Office. While the supply lasts, a citizen can usually obtain a copy of such a report by writing to his Senator or Congressman, or by writing to a member of the committee that issued the report. (We have obtained a variety of such little-publicized reports, and have never suspected that the "Conspiracy" prevents the Government Printing Office from selling them.)

It is strange that the "Conspiracy," with the help of venal Congressmen, could burn non-existing, unsold copies of Appendix IX and could remove non-existent copies from the Library of Congress; and that Communist agents could steal a document from libraries that never received the document.

Anyway, the tale helps the Birchers sell a reprint of Appendix IX for $30.00!

Alice finally returned from Birchland with a greater appreciation of the world of reality.

# CHAPTER XVI

# The Red Scare

It is a foregone conclusion that the author will be attacked and condemned by bigots and Ultra-Rightists for having allegedly written a book in defense of Communists. There is little one can do to change the mind of a bigot, because the bigot's mind is closed to facts. Rational people will understand that it is a dangerous state of affairs when truth is concealed by intimidation and defamation, that the challenge of Communism must be met by truth, and that lies are not a proper instrument of dialogue on any subject. The author is not to blame for the fact that so much lying propaganda against the Communists has created a climate of opinion that paves the way for Fascism and a third world war. This study is concerned only with dispelling of fear, with opening the channels of communication, and with reversing the dangerous trend in the U.S.A. towards Fascism and a third world war. Critics should meet the challenge of the factual data presented and not muddy the waters with speculation about motives. It is to be hoped that many people will consider the search for truth a virtue to be cherished, not only as an end in itself, but as a guide to intelligent action in a dangerous world. With these thoughts in mind, we can examine the smokescreen of lies that obscures the real problems of this country.

## The Gus Hall Fabrication

In the April 1961 issue of Rev. Kenneth Goff's *Pilgrim Torch,* and also in *Citizen's Intelligence Digest,* issued by an Ultra-Rightist group in Bakersfield, California, at about the same time, the Communist leader, Gus Hall, is quoted as saying:

I dream of the hour when the last Congressman is strangled to death on the guts of the last preacher. Why not give them a little of it [the blood about which Christians sing!] Slit the throats of their children and drag them over the mourner's bench and the pulpit, and allow them to drown in their own blood; and then see whether they enjoy singing these hymns.

In the context of the editorial that embodied this alleged quotation, the implication is conveyed that Gus Hall made these remarks at the funeral of Communist Party National Chairman, Eugene Dennis, in January, 1961.

The *Citizen's Intelligence Digest,* edited by retired Army Colonel, Robert E. Grigsby, said of Gus Hall:

Here is his revolting statement made at the funeral of Eugene Dennis, National Chairman of the Communist Party: "I dream of the hour when the last Congressman is strangled to death on the guts of the last preacher—and since Christians seem to love to sing about the blood, why not give them a little of it? Slit the throats of their children and drag them over the mourner's bench and the pulpit, and allow them to drown in their own blood; and then see whether they enjoy singing these hymns."

In a footnote, Colonel Grigsby gives *Pilgrim Torch* of April, 1961, as his source for the alleged quotation.

The first thing that has to be said about such a statement is, that any person uttering such remarks places himself outside the pale of civilization and needs to be confined in a psychiatric hospital. The second observation that can be made about these alleged remarks is that nowhere, in any of Gus Hall's known writings and speeches, can one find anything remotely resembling these words. The third observation that can be made is that, if Hall or any other leader of the Communist Party or any other party had made such remarks, he would have been summarily removed from leadership, if for no other reason than the one of discrediting his party and inviting criminal prosecution. The final observation is that the Rev. Kenneth Goff is notorious for concocting atrocity stories and eerie documents, such as his "Brainwashing—A Synthesis of the Russian Textbook on Psychopolitics."

*The New York Times* carried a story on February 1, 1961, telling of the death of Eugene Dennis. On February 2, 1961, it told of the funeral plans. Thus, the funeral was a public event, and no secret speeches could have been made at the funeral. Reporters from a number of papers were present, and

663

typical of the reports was the story in *The New York Times* of February 6, 1961. The headline said:

1,000 Attend Rites for Eugene Dennis

In the body of the story, the only mention of Gus Hall was the following:

> Gus Hall, general secretary of the Communist Party here, paid tribute to Mr. Dennis as "a seasoned Marxist-Leninist" by whose death "our nation lost an illustrious son."

On November 21, 1962, we wrote a letter to the Rev. Kenneth Goff, in which we referred to the alleged Gus Hall remarks, and we asked:

> Can you tell me what wire services or other news media carried the following remarks, which you attributed to one, Gus Hall?
> The reason I am asking what news media carried this story is that I would like to inquire why any man that makes such a statement has not been indicted for inciting to riot.

On February 2, 1963, a letter "From the Desk of Kenneth Goff" was sent to us:

Dear Brother in Christ:
Please excuse this belated reply to your kind letter. I have been out of the city on a speaking tour for over a month.
The statement by Gus Hall was not carried by any press service, but obtained through our agents working in the party.
I trust this is a satisfactory answer to your inquiry.
Sincerely yours, for Christ and America.
                                    KENNETH GOFF
                                    (Signed)

Goff is asking us to believe that the reporters at the funeral did not tell about those bloodcurdling remarks. No informed person can believe that the newspapers would be willing to forego the opportunity to publish such a sensational story, which, with appropriately screaming headlines, would have sold many additional newspapers.

As happens frequently with fabrications, the Rev. Gerald L. K. Smith has another explanation for the alleged Gus Hall remarks. In *The Cross and The Flag*, January, 1964, Smith quotes the remarks exactly as did Colonel Grigsby, and says that Gus Hall made the alleged remarks "at the Eighth National Convention of the Young Communist League." Some additional snippets of wisdom in the same issue are an explanation of inflation, by quoting from the fraudulent "Protocols of the Learned Elders of Zion" to prove the Jews are responsible, and an endorsement of John E. Hoover for President of the United States. It is worthy of note that, just as Goff is the only one that knows about Gus Hall's alleged remarks at the Eugene Dennis funeral, Smith is the only one who knows about his alleged performance at the convention of the Young Communist League!

We have never met Gus Hall and we have never heard him speak, but when we read a newspaper story that told of a meeting where he would speak in Los Angeles, we wrote one of our research assistants to interview Hall about the alleged remarks attributed to him. The report, dated May 15, 1965, said: "I saw Gus Hall on Sunday, May 2, 1965. He said that type of slanderous misquote 'goes back to the Middle Ages. There's nothing we can do about it now because of peculiarities in the McCarran-Walter Laws. If I sued these people for libel, their defense attorney could put me on the witness stand and put questions to me, the answers to which would then be subject to government prosecution.'" Americans may well ponder the fact that there are laws on our statute books that destroy the constitutional rights of people holding minority views.

An article in the March 21, 1962, issue of *Christian Century* tells the story of the Ultra-Rightist campaign to prevent Gus Hall from speaking on campus of the University of Oregon. As part of this unsuccessful campaign, the so-called Freedom Center of Portland, Oregon, operated by the Rev. Walter Huss, issued leaflets with the phoney Gus Hall remarks. When this leaflet was shown to Hall by a reporter, he said that it was so vile that he wouldn't bother denying it, that "Only a degenerate would put out material like this."

The hate sheet, *Common Sense,* ran a picture of Gus Hall in its issue of October 15, 1963. Above the picture is this caption:

MOSCOW ORDERED TOP COMMUNIST
TO GET THE RIGHT WING IN U.S.

Under the picture, it reads:

*"I dream of the hour when the last Congressman is strangled to death on the guts of the last preacher."*
(This statement first given before the 8th National Convention of the Young Communist League in New York during May 1937; repeated early in 1961 at the funeral of Eugene Dennis.)

The June 1964 issue of *The Liberty Bell,* published by the Ultra-Rightist *San Diego Patriotic Society,* quotes the Gus Hall Fabrication and explains:

Speech of Gus Hall, head of Communist Party in USA on January 25, 1962, on occasion of the funeral for Eugene Dennis.

The funeral was actually held on February 5, 1961, but facts don't matter when Ultra-Rightists tell stories about Communists. In this case, the gentlemen gave a Communist almost a year more of life, and they ran the risk of being charged with "treason"!

On March 11, 1965, Hal Hunt's little hate sheet, *The National Chronicle,* ran the Gus Hall Fabrication on the front page, referring to Hall as "the ex-convict Jew." Hunt's anti-Semitism is so overpowering that he makes Jews out of Gentiles with great facility. It so happens that Gus Hall is not a Jew.

The May 11, 1965 *Freedom Club Bulletin,* of the Rev. James W. Fifield's First Congregational Church in Los Angeles, shows a picture of and advertises a speech by the Rev. Billy James Hargis. It begins with: "In words taken from the 1961 Congressional Record, the following commendation was given. . ." Following this introduction, there is quite a eulogy of Hargis. It is downright misleading to credit it to the Congressional Record. Simple honesty dictates that one specify *who* placed it in the Congressional Record and credit it to *that person,* not to the Congressional Record. Attorney G. A. Sheppard, who has an article in the same issue, is well aware of the misleading nature of quoting in that manner from the Congressional Record.

The article by Sheppard is entitled "United Nations Web Spins Tighter." He uses the Manuilsky Hoax, the Treaty Breaking Hoax, and the *Gus Hall Fabrication.* As an attorney, Mr. Sheppard should have known better than to quote the Gus Hall Fabrication, but he also knows that no one will sue him for libel.

In June of 1965, the Americans for Freedom of Santa Barbara, California, mailed out large quantities of a leaflet issued by Rev. Walter Huss' Freedom Center of Portland, Oregon. The title of the leaflet is *How The Communists Plan to Conquer the U.S.* In accordance with the pattern of at least 75% of Ultra-Rightist propaganda, it starts with a quotation from John E. Hoover. This is followed by a discourse, which is obviously plagiarized from the propaganda material of Dr. Fred Schwarz and his Christian Anti-Communism Crusade. In the center of the leaflet we read:

Communists have convinced a considerable segment of the intelligentsia that they have renounced violence and thus are a normal political party. *The truth is that Communists intend to come to power without violence,*[1] but then will follow a systematic program of human extermination that will dwarf anything the world has seen. The victims will be you and your family.

The one and only proof adduced by Rev. Huss, to prove this predicted reign of terror, is the Gus Hall Fabrication, which he states was uttered at the funeral of Eugene Dennis in February, 1961; and he gives Rev. Goff's April 1961 *Pilgram Torch* as his source. The millionaire, Frank Ketcham, who operates Americans for Freedom, is convinced of the danger of a Communist take-over. For this reason, the Gus Hall Fabrication provides a convenient scarecrow story to enlist the support of the "lower classes."

In September of 1965, the Ultra-Rightist *Paul Revere Associated Yeomen* of New Orleans circulated a 4-page leaflet issued by Rev. Walter Huss' Freedom Center of Portland, Oregon. This opus is entitled "Revolution—It Can Happen Here!" In the upper left-hand corner of the first page is a small picture of Kenneth Goff, taken when he was probably 20 years younger. Under the picture is the caption: "Dr. Kenneth Goff." In spite of the fact that Rev. Walter Huss said in the previous leaflet that the Communists plan to take over in a peaceful manner, he quotes with approval from Goff's book, "Confessions of Stalin's Agent," to prove that the Communists

---

[1] Emphasis has been added. It should be noted that Communists have been prosecuted and jailed on the charge that they plan to overthrow the U.S. Government by force and violence. The Rev. Huss is, in effect, saying that these charges were framed.

plan a violent and bloody revolution. The leaflet gives as part of its proof the phoney Lunacharsky quotation:

We hate Christians. Even the best of them must be regarded as our worst enemies. All religions are poison. A fight to the death must be declared upon all religions.

As we have previously shown, Lunacharsky never uttered such insane drivel. Huss quotes it from Goff, and Goff quotes it from the late Senator Arthur Robinson of Indiana. Rev. Huss gives as final "proof":

Gus Hall, the man who heads the illegal revolutionary conspiracy within America to turn this country over to the Communist Soviet Union, expresses his contempt of America as follows:
"I dream of the hour when the last Congressman is strangled on the guts of the last preacher—and since the Christians seem to love to sing about the blood, why not give them a little of it? Slit the throats of their children and drag them over the mourners' bench and the pulpit and allow them to drown in their own blood; and then see whether they enjoy singing these hymns."

In October of 1965, Rev. Walter Huss was still circulating the Gus Hall Fabrication. This time it went out on a throw-away card.

Mr. Houston Myers is an automobile repairman in Alhambra, California, who spends considerable time and money sending out Ultra-Rightist alarms, to arouse people about the alleged imminent danger of a Communist take-over. Included in his material are propaganda of the Greater Los Angeles (White) Citizens Council and publicity for meetings of Jim Clark, former sheriff of Selma, Alabama. In February, 1967, Mr. Myers sent out a mimeographed leaflet, entitled:

### FELLOW AMERICANS
#### What Are You Doing to Save Our Nation?

The entire leaflet revolves around the Gus Hall Fabrication, which is quoted in full and followed by the information that it was part of a speech in February, 1961 at the funeral of Eugene Dennis. The leaflet concludes:

Fellow Americans, it is up to you and me to stop these Socialist and Communist Traitors. Write your Government Representative and demand that they pass a law at once to outlaw the Socialist and Communist Party in the United States forever. Fellow Americans, with the help of Almighty God, I know we can defeat this tyranny that is upon us here in America. May God give us the courage and strength.

About ten days after issuing his own leaflet, Mr. Myers started a distribution of the Rev. Walter Huss' leaflet, *Revolution— It Can Happen Here!,* which, as we have noted, also contains the Gus Hall Fabrication. In April of 1967, Mr. Myers again sent out his "Fellow Americans" leaflet. Apparently Mr. Myers intends to get the last bit of "mileage" out of the Gus Hall Fabrication.

This does not exhaust the list of the users of the Gus Hall Fabrication, but it does show the fear-and-smear technique being used by a section of the Ultra-Right to mislead the American people. Another interesting example of distortion of Gus Hall's views was contained in an election campaign brochure, issued by the Republican Party of Texas, 330 Littlefield Bldg., Austin, Texas. The brochure contains this item:

"Our people (U.S. Communists) have made it clear that they will give full support to the Johnson administration, as they did to the Kennedy administration, if its policies continue in the same direction."
Gus Hall, secretary and number 1 spokesman for the Communist Party of America, The Worker, Dec. 1, 1963.

An examination of Gus Hall's article in *The Worker* of December 1, 1963 shows that the words, "U.S. Communists," which the Republican Party brochure quoted, are *not* there. Moreover, when the quotation is read *in context,* it is perfectly clear that Gus Hall is referring to *the American people in general* when he uses the term "our people." In fact, three paragraphs below the one from which the quotation is excerpted, Hall begins a paragraph with "The American people. . ." This is part of a continuing discussion, and there can be no question that the Republican Party's scribe perpetrated a deception, in order to use the Red Scare against Lyndon Johnson in the 1964 election campaign.

## The Force and Violence Hoax

The basis for a good deal of the anti-Communist hysteria in this country has been the repeated charge that the Communist

669

Party is desirous of and is planning a violent revolution. As previously noted, Communists have been prosecuted and jailed on this charge. This has been accomplished by quoting out-of-context statements from Communist documents and literature, and especially by quoting Lenin out of both literary and historical context. As we have previously stated, our interest is not in defending the Communists. Our interest is in demonstrating the need for approaching problems with facts instead of falsehoods, and rationally instead of hysterically. If it can be demonstrated that the charge is false, the basis for much of the Red Scare would become untenable.

At the very outset, one can agree that any individual or organization, that advocates force and violence for the sake of force and violence or advocates such a policy without compelling reason, deserves condemnation in the strongest terms. Contrariwise, one cannot deny that this country came into existence as a nation through the force and violence of the Revolutionary War. The Civil War of 1861-1865 eliminated the system of chattel slavery and established the supremacy of the capitalistic economic system. With the exception of some die-hard Southerners, no one condemns the force and violence that was used under the leadership of Abraham Lincoln. It is generally accepted that the force and violence used against Hitler and his allies were necessary to destroy the military might of Fascism. From these few historical examples, it should be clear that the question of force and violence should be approached *concretely* instead of *abstractly*. It is interesting to note how often people, who vociferously proclaim their opposition to the use of force and violence, will argue that "circumstances alter cases," when they find it advantageous. Such people find nothing wrong in the force and violence that was used by the bible-quoting white settlers to wrest the land and resources of this continent from the native Indians. They are strangely silent, for the most part, about the lynchings and other violence used against Negroes, Mexican-Americans, Puerto Ricans, and other minority groups throughout our history. These facts must be borne in mind, in order to approach the problem with clarity and proper perspective.

A careful and honest examination of the literature and programs issued by the Communist Party of the U.S.A. shows that the "line" or policy has been and is: that every avenue of democratic procedure should be utilized to effect social change, but, when opportunity for peaceful change is denied, it is the right and duty of the people to use force and violence. This is saying no more and no less than the world-famous American Declaration of Independence. For instance, if a Fascist dictatorship were established in this country, the belief in the possibility of effecting peaceful social change would become academic. As we shall soon see, the charge against the Communist Party has been "proven" by *the selective presentation of data,* by phoney quotations, and by constant repetition of the charge.

We can begin our examination of the question with some remarks of the co-founder of the world Communist movement. In his address to the First Communist International at Amsterdam, Holland, in 1873, Karl Marx said:

> We do not assert that the way to reach this goal is the same everywhere. We know that the institutions, manners and customs of the various countries must be considered; and we do not deny that there are countries like England and America . . . where the worker may attain his object by peaceful means.

The late Dr. J. B. Matthews was a professional anti-Communist of long standing. He was the chief counsel for the Dies Committee and was on the staff of the House Committee on Un-American Activities. He was later on the staff of the Birch Society's *American Opinion* and was director of research, for several years, in the office of the Ultra-Rightist *Church League of America.* Upon his death, his personal files and anti-Communist data were sold to the Church League. A brochure of the Church League, issued in February, 1966, said that Matthews' files "are valued in excess of $150,000." With these credentials, there is no chance of his saying a kind word about the Communist Party.

In an Ultra-Rightist publication, *Facts,* issued in September 1958 by Facts in Education, Inc., Pasadena, Calif., there is a long essay by Dr. Matthews. At one point Matthews makes this grudging admission:

> The Kremlin long ago realized the futility of conquering nations by force and violence. With jets, guided missiles and H-bombs, a country reduced to rubble would be of little value, and the Communist mind is not one to calculate in terms of negative values.

In 1954, the Communist Party issued a Draft Program entitled *The American Way to Jobs, Peace, Democracy*. This *entire* pamphlet was reprinted by the Church League of America, with this declaration:

The Church League of America is reprinting this draft program of the Communist Party for only one reason: So that you and other Americans can see how this insidious atheistic movement plans to conquer us. We do not believe in helping the Reds to spread their propaganda; therefore, we want it understood clearly that we are not in sympathy with what is contained in this pamphlet. *We know of no better way to inform you as to their tactics than to let you read their plan.*

Note that this was first published in 1954. Note also how much has been accomplished since that year. *Those who declare that the Reds are advocating force and violence for our defeat are in for a surprise when they read this Draft Program. The "peaceful path to Socialism" is their strategy—just what many of us have been saying for years; but WHO would listen!*[2]

In 1967, the Church League was still distributing that pamphlet, apparently convinced that its original evaluation of the Communist Party's program was correct.

The hard-hitting, Ultra-Rightist *America's Future* distributes a pamphlet entitled *The Methods of the Enemy*. It consists of a series of articles by Reuben Maury in the New York *Daily News,* and is reprinted with apparent endorsement. Written in a hostile and tendentious style, it nevertheless refers to the Communist Party's program in a manner that challenges the force-and-violence charge:

The objective of all these campaigns, which have gone on in this country, since about 1920, is to condition most Americans' minds for an eventual peaceable Communist take-over in the United States.

If what Mr. Maury says is true, how can he explain the fact that American Communists have been jailed for allegedly advocating force and violence? The only explanation is the use of falsehood and frame-up.

There can be no mistaking of Mr. Maury's thesis, because on the next page he states that the Communists carry on what he calls "psy-war" against the American people, and he adds:

2 Emphasis has been added.—M. K.

672

That objective is to soften up Americans for an eventual peaceable take-over by the Communists.

That is a far cry from a conspiracy to use force and violence.

In the violent polemics, that have taken place between the Soviet Communist Party and the Chinese Communist Party during the past few years, much discussion has taken place about Communist tactics and strategy. In answer to the charges against it by the Chinese Communists, the Soviet Communists issued an "Open Letter" on July 14, 1963, in which the following appears:

In its letter of March 1963 the CPSU Central Committee again outlined its position in this connection: "The working class and its vanguard, the Marxist-Leninist parties, endeavor to carry out socialist revolutions in a peaceful way, without civil war. The realization of such a possibility is in keeping with the interests of the working class and all the people, and with the national interests of the country. At the same time the choice of the means of developing the revolution depends not only on the working class. If the exploiting classes resort to violence against the people, the working class will be forced to use nonpeaceful means of seizing power. Everything depends on the particular conditions and on the distribution of class forces within the country and in the world arena."

Perhaps the reader will conclude that this is so much Communist "eyewash," but the professional anti-Communist, Dr. Fred Schwarz, is certainly one who will not concede anything favorable to the Communists, and he does concede that the Communists do not plan to use force and violence in order to achieve political power. In his March, 1964 *News Letter,* Schwarz says:

To reveal the Communist plan clearly, we must clear the ground of some general misconceptions concerning possible methods of Communist conquest. The Communists do not propose any of the following:

1. The defeat of the United States in thermonuclear war.
2. The seizure of power by a violent revolutionary coup under Communist leadership.

To this, Schwarz adds that the Chinese Communists do advocate a violent program.

673

In his April, 1964 *News Letter,* Dr. Schwarz comments about Chile:

The Communists in that country are seeking to come to power this year and to do so without violence or bloodshed.

In his July, 1964, *News Letter,* Schwarz again concedes that the Communist Party does not advocate force and violence as a means of achieving political power, although he clothes the admission in cynical language.

The Ultra-Rightist *Christian Economics,* in its issue of May 12, 1964, joins the chorus with Dr. Schwarz, in stating that the Communists intend to take us over, "not by war, but by the easier method of subversion."

The general trend in Communist thinking about procedures was illustrated again by a Paris, France dispatch to *The New York Times,* January 16, 1964. The correspondent, Henry Giniger, reported on a draft resolution of the French Communist Party, which rejected "the idea that the existence of a single party was a necessary condition for the passage to Socialism." Mr. Giniger also reported:

The party also said it was now possible to foresee a peaceful way to Socialism. It noted that 50 years ago Marxists considered peaceful means "a possible but rare eventuality", but that a new balance of power in the world in favor of Socialism had created new conditions.

Peaceful change to Socialism is possible, the party declared, thanks to a mobilization of forces "capable of making the great monopolist bourgeoisie yield after having isolated it."

It is perfectly clear that the charge of force and violence depends upon a *misrepresentation of views previously held,* and a complete *disregard* of present views and programs. Obviously it is dishonest to criticize and prosecute anybody for a *discarded program.* The correctness of this estimate is also attested by the number of anti-Communist leaders and groups that are willing to admit that the force and violence charge is untenable. The crux of the problem, in meeting the challenge of Communism, was stated very clearly in the January 1965 issue of *Freedom's Facts,* the monthly bulletin of the All-American Conference to Combat Communism. In discussing Communist political strategy, the article said:

A realistic, if general, survey of the present situation indicates that Communists will fail in this endeavor during the foreseeable future, if representatives of the major parties can provide practical solutions to outstanding problems facing the majority of the American people.

If we do experience an economic depression, a sharp rise in unemployment, or serious overseas reverses, the Communist strategy might have much improved chances of success. This is what they are counting on, and are contributing toward.

Strange as it may seem, these remarks closely parallel some remarks made by Premier Nikita Khrushchev, when he was interviewed by William Randolph Hearst, Jr., as reported in the official Soviet Communist organ, *Pravda*, November 29, 1957:

Challenging the United States to competition to produce more meat, butter, clothes, and footwear, to build more good housing, to manufacture more television and radio sets, vacuum cleaners, and other goods and articles necessary to man, the Soviet people are confident in their victory. You are not being threatened with intercontinental ballistic missiles. *You are threatened with a peaceful offensive, peaceful competition* in the manufacture of consumer goods and articles that serve to improve the culture and life of people. In this we will be relentless. *This competition will show which system is better.*[3]

The article in *Freedom's Facts* concludes:

Communists are campaigning hard to win popular elections in West European countries. Many expect to win, simply by doing more political home-work and by out-campaigning their non-communist and anti-communist opponents.

One of the most vitriolic opponents of the Communist Party is Karl Prussion, a former Communist Party member who became an FBI informer within the ranks of the party and was the principal witness in the 1960 hearings at San Francisco of the House Committee on Un-American Activities. Graphically illustrating the principle, that much of the anti-Communist drive is directed against whatever semblance of democracy still remains in this country, is an article in the February-March, 1965 issue of his now-defunct monthly bulletin, *Heads Up*. The title of this article is:

3 Emphasis has been added.—M. K.

675

Discussing the alternatives of insurrection or legislative methods, Prussion says of the Communists that they have chosen the path of political action. As he tells it, Lyndon Johnson and almost everybody, except the Ultra-Rightists, are cooperating in preparing the path to Communism!

*Task Force,* the monthly bulletin of the Ultra-Rightist *Defenders of the American Constitution,* in its issue of February, 1965, quotes with approval from a bulletin of another Ultra-Rightist group, *The Truth About Cuba Committee:*

The Communists, who realize fully that the real weapon in the world today is not the hydrogen bomb, but PUBLIC OPINION, are succeeding spectacularly in selling their ideas and in winning public opinion over to their side.

Publication No. 122, issued February, 1965, by the Ultra-Rightist *Committee of Christian Laymen of Woodland Hills, California,* quotes Jan Kozak, historian of the Communist Party of Czechoslovakia, as saying: ". . . it is in the interests of the working class, of the masses, that the revolution be carried out in a peaceful way."

Students of Communist tactics and strategy are aware of the fact that one of the most authoritative sources is the monthly *World Marxist Review.* The December, 1963 issue carries an article by Luis Corvalan, a Chilean Communist leader, entitled: "The Peaceful Way—a Form of Revolution." It is a long and well-researched article, of which the following are representative quotations:

In our time situations may arise in some countries when election campaigns can be a means of winning political power.

The Communist parties are opposed as a matter of principle to military coups, of which there have been so many in Latin America. They hold that seizure of power without the backing of the masses is adventurism.

In upholding the peaceful way our Party aims at solving the tasks of the revolution without civil war or armed uprising.

The thesis of Luis Corvalan is consonant with the position of the Italian Communist Party, as described by James S. Allen in the June, 1965 issue of *Political Affairs,* the theoretical monthly of the Communist Party U.S.A.:

The Italian Communists in particular say flatly that direct transfer of power to the working class, under the complex conditions of the modern monopoly state, is no longer applicable. They hold forth the perspective of working class and democratic forces, in coalition, taking over commanding sectors of government, as a consequence of parliamentary and mass-struggle victories, thus opening the way to the elimination of monopoly from its position of power in the economy and the state, and going to socialism by peaceful transition.

The oil tycoon, H. L. Hunt, who is reputed to be the richest man in the world, said in his syndicated newspaper column: "Communists hope to control the United States without firing a shot."[4]

The April, 1966, Newsletter of the Fascist *Minutemen* says: "The communists have no intention of a violent internal revolution." It should have added that the Minutemen are using violence and terror, and are definitely planning to increase the tempo of their violent and terroristic tactics.

A clue to where the real danger of force and violence lies was made clear by the Ultra-Rightist intellectual, Dr. Russell Kirk. Discussing the election campaign of the Communist leader, Dr. Herbert Aptheker, Dr. Kirk said in his syndicated column:

Were Aptheker elected to Congress, the House of Representatives promptly would refuse to seat him.

Dr. Kirk could have added that, in the present climate of opinion, the majority of the American people would acquiesce in the refusal to seat Aptheker. This was clearly illustrated in the lack of substantial protest against the unseating of the Negro Congressman, Adam Clayton Powell, while Senator Thomas J. Dodd was allowed to retain his seat in the face of more serious charges against him.

The conclusion is inescapable that the force and violence charge is a scarecrow device to distract attention of unsuspecting citizens from the real, pressing problems of the day. Fear

4 *Santa Ana (Calif.) Register,* September 27, 1966.

of imaginary problems should not be a substitute for a courageous approach to real problems, however difficult and complex they may be. It is the tendency of so many people to seek simplistic answers to complex problems that makes it easy for the falsifiers of history and the Ultra-Rightist propagandists to paralyze the thinking of so many good people.

## Schools for Riots

Contradictory as it may sound, the Ultra-Rightists accuse the Communists of operating schools to teach rioting, at the same time that they disavow the force and violence charge. If the reader has followed carefully the various fabrications we have discussed, it will be recalled that this is not the only instance of their making *mutually contradictory charges* against the Communists.

As one could expect, the chief architect of this hoax is the originator of The Psychopolitics Hoax and the Gus Hall Fabrication, the Rev. Kenneth Goff. His newsletter of August, 1965 is entitled:

**BLOOD ON THEIR HANDS**
**AND**
**BLOOD ON THE EARTH!**

The first page of this 3-page letter reads as follows:

Dear Christian Friends:

Over twenty-five years ago, when I left the Communist Party and became one of the first to give testimony against it; I exposed their blueprint for the revolution. I told that when the zero hour arrived they would seize 70 of our largest cities by the following plan:

"At that hour, two large race riots are supposed to take place in every city of any size. Leaders of these mobs are to be carefully chosen and trained in advance. The disturbances are to be of such extent as to require sending large forces of police to those areas. While the authorities are trying to quell these riots, picked bands of Reds are to seize the radio stations and telephone exchanges. With the aid of their comrades who are employed inside, all communication systems are to be instantly crippled.

"Flying squads of Communists are to seize control of the water supply and shut it off; also the electrical power and gas. This means that no elevators or street cars are to be running. Homes would be without water, fuel, or light. It would be impossible to communicate with friends or loved ones, even in another part of the city.

"Goon squads of professional murderers are to round up the people in business districts. Men are to be held as hostages in some of the larger buildings. Women are to be turned over to the sex-crazed mobs to be ravished and raped."

These are exactly the methods that were used in Russia, Spain and other places where the Communist Party has been allowed to organize and come to fruition. They firmly expect to do the same thing in the United States.

"Bridges, subways and street car stations are to be blown up. Downtown areas are to be isolated from the rest of the city. Sharp-shooters and snipers are to be detailed in taxicabs and vehicles, which are to be taken over, to wipe out the police, soldiers, uni-formed persons and known vigilantes. Smoke bombs properly lo-cated in subways, buildings and large stores are to add to the terror of the people."

This is the day—the big day toward which every Communist in America is looking. . . and for which he is preparing his entire training.

"When night comes, the city is to be in pitch darkness. Murder-ous bands of reds will roam the streets, plundering shops and start-ing fires in old buildings. This will increase the panic and facilitate the surrender of women, children and old people, who will be held as hostages to hasten the surrender of unarmed men.

"When as the morning sun casts her first rays on the community, one will be able to see blood flowing in the streets. This is no idle dream. The Communist Party is working methodically and with deadly precision toward this objective. It is now happening in Bul-garia, Roumania, Hungary, etc. It can happen here. Unless we de-stroy the Red menace in America, the day is at hand when we shall suffer the same fate as our Christian brethren in Europe."

For years many good people attacked me, for trying to scare the public. They said this was an untruth; that the negroes loved our nation and had no animosity toward the whites.

On the next page, Goff says:

Today the nation stands astonished and shocked, as the Commu-nists, through the negroes are carrying on the rehearsal for the revolution.

(His anti-Negro bias is shown even by such a petty device as

679

refusing to capitalize the word, Negro.) Goff devotes the second and third pages to a diatribe, in which he attempts to prove that the Negro revolt against the oppressive conditions of poverty, unemployment, and constant humiliations is part of a Communist plot. The absence of any evidence to prove this thesis does not disturb Goff. In his December 1965 bulletin, he comes back with the plans-for-riots hoax, this time quoting it as part of an article, entitled:

## BLACK OUT
## DRESS REHEARSAL FOR THE REVOLUTION

In this essay, he ties his phoney story of Communist plans-for-riots to the electric power blackout in November, 1965, which we have discussed in Chapter VIII, "The Blackout Spree." Goff has used this hoax story on many occasions; and it has been quoted by other Ultra-Rightists, among them Mr. Frank Capell.

Apparently inspired by Goff's hoax, Capell ran a 3-part series, entitled "Rehearsal for Revolution," in his biweekly *The Herald of Freedom,* September 10, December 3, and December 31, 1965. Capell begins his first installment by reminding the reader of the essay, "Revolution U.S.A., 1964," in his May 8, 1964 issue. Capell's reliability, for giving us any worthwhile and dependable information, can be determined by reading some excerpts from the May 8, 1964 issue:

Possible resistance to the International Communist Conspiracy is dealt with by the C.I.A. which has turned over names of underground leaders in Cuba, Panama, and the Balkan countries to Soviet Intelligence, which has resulted in their torture and death. In one American Embassy the C.I.A. man in charge of security was caught in a homosexual act in the embassy itself.

It is not surprising, once a person accepts as factual the non-existent International Communist Conspiracy, that he can also believe that the Central Intelligence Agency is part and parcel of that phantom conspiracy, and is giving information to Soviet Intelligence. One gathers from another section of this essay that there are only four dependable anti-Communists in the U.S.A., namely: Frank Capell, John E. Hoover, Robert Morris, and Jay Sourwine. (Robert Morris is the former counsel and Jay Sourwine is the present counsel to the Senate Internal Security Subcommittee.) This is the way Capell explains it:

Bobby Kennedy should be removed from office and replaced by a competent American such as J. Edgar Hoover, Robert Morris, Jay Sourwine, each of whom knows who the enemies of our country are, and would not be afraid to do what needs to be done.

Throughout Capell's writings there runs the thread of two obsessions: Communism and sexual perversion. He seems to delight in labeling a person either as a Communist or a sexual pervert. Nowhere in his essay does Capell give any source or any documentation for his remarks about the C.I.A.

Having disposed of both the C.I.A. and Soviet Intelligence, Capell takes on the Communists:

> To complete the take-over of the United States it is necessary that the people become frightened by some terror or violence which justifies establishing martial law to supercede state and local laws, police or militia units, which could cope with the violence if left on their own. To bring this about the Communist Conspiracy has been working for many years on plans to create chaos, violence and terror through the use of Negro extremists.

The only "proof" Capell gives to support his charges is a series of smear attacks against a number of citizens, with information about as reliable as his charges against the Central Intelligence Agency.

As one can easily understand, writing the May 8, 1964 article prepared Capell for expanding on Goff's hoax, which was first published in August of 1965. Capell's September 10, 1965 issue was only a "warming-up" process. In this essay he brings together a number of unrelated items, and agrees with a Southern racist Congressman that Dr. Martin Luther King is the "MOST DANGEROUS MAN IN U.S." In the December 3, 1965 issue, Capell quotes the unsupported yarn told by Mary Mundt, the wife of Senator Karl Mundt (which we referred to in Chapter VIII), moves on to find a conspiracy in the electric power blackout of November, 1965, and arrives at the Goff hoax:

> In the Nov.-Dec. 1965 issue of "Soul," a Catholic magazine of the Blue Army of Our Lady, they quote from Kenneth Goff who left the ranks of the Communist Party in the 1940's and since then has conducted a Christian ministry and militant anti-Communist educational program.

This is followed by quoting the entire Goff hoax, word for word as it appeared in Goff's newsletter of August, 1965.

681

The concluding segment of Capell's series, in the December 31, 1965 issue, is entitled "Revolution USA, 1966." (Remember his "Revolution, USA, 1964.") In this essay, he quotes from the Ultra-Rightist book, "Strike From Space," which tries to prove that we are almost disarmed militarily; from former FBI informer, Marion Miller; and from the reports of the Senate Internal Security Subcommittee and the House Committee on Un-American Activities. His conclusion, after assembling all this hodgepodge, is an interesting test of his reliability as a political prognosticator:

1966 may well be the crucial year in our history, the year the atheistic Communist Conspiracy will try to make its final moves. It must, therefore, be the year that an alert American public is prepared to defeat it.

Someone has said that a prophet is usually without honor in his own country. It would seem that such is the case with Frank Capell, because nowhere have we read about alert Americans rushing to mount the ramparts after Capell sounded the tocsin.

The story that Goff tells about the Communist plans for riot and revolution can be disposed of without much research. First of all, no one but Goff has heard of these plans, just as no one else has seen his phantom "Russian Textbook on Psychopolitics," and just as no one but Goff's "secret agents" have heard Gus Hall make that alleged speech. Secondly, only a degenerate would concoct such a set of plans. Thirdly, only a madman would think such plans could be carried out. It is perfectly obvious that no one could achieve and hold political power by such methods. The only results would be chaos and the common ruin of all concerned. But there are stupid people, fanatical people, and neurotic people who are willing to believe Kenneth Goff's tall yarns; and there are unscrupulous people who are ready and willing to spread such poisonous falsehoods.

Karl Prussion devoted the front page of the September, 1964 issue of his *Heads Up* to an article entitled:

SHOCKING EXPOSE OF RED PLOT
TO INCITE CIVIL WAR

Prussion's "sensational" disclosure consists of quoting from a little newsletter published by a Negro, Robert Williams, who

682

had become disenchanted with American democracy and sees insurrection as the only road to freedom for the American Negro. While disagreeing with Robert Williams and his proposals, one can understand how he arrived at his present frame of mind. It seems that Williams fled to Havana, Cuba, after escaping from a Southern lynch mob and Ku Klux Klan-minded police. In Cuba, Williams had been issuing a newsletter, called *The Crusader,* and had been broadcasting on a radio program. Little would be known or heard of Williams and his doctrines, had it not been for Prussion and other Ultra-Rightists who quoted Williams' material, thus giving it coverage that Williams could never have dreamt of achieving. In typical "whodunit" style, Prussion tells of obtaining a copy of Williams' newsletter through a "plant" who "procured it in a communist book store in Los Angeles." Inasmuch as Williams' newsletter was sold and circulated openly, one fails to appreciate the necessity for a "plant" to buy a copy. Prussion sent out a reprint of the May-June 1964 issue of *The Crusader* with the September, 1964 issue of his *Heads Up*. At the conclusion of his "sensational" exposé, Prussion says:

*Heads Up* feels that every family in America must have a copy of this communist document of strategy for civil war. If every American would read it, the fight would soon be won. Barry [Goldwater] would win hands down. Each pamphlet (8 pages) has been stamped "communist propaganda" and an explanatory editorial affixed to the last page. An initial 100,000 have been printed. Order now. There is no time to waste.

The Ultra-Rightists, ever eager for something to arouse their followers to a high pitch of frenzy, quoted from or reproduced Williams' essays on how to make cheap fire bombs, hand grenades, and other lethal weapons. The effect that this might have upon emotionally unstable persons was something that the Ultra-Rightist propagandists were willing to ignore. Thus *Councilor,* the organ of Louisiana (White) Citizens Councils reproduced 4 pages of Williams' *The Crusader* of May-June, 1964, the same issue that Karl Prussion reprinted in full. The Canadian Intelligence Service (a private organization), in its newsletter of October, 1964, reproduced the front page of *The Crusader.* And so it went in Ultra-Rightist publications throughout the United States and Canada.

One of the most scandalous examples of the use of the plans-for-riots hoax is the article by Eugene Methvin in *Reader's Digest,* January 1965, entitled "How the Reds Make a Riot." (We have dealt with this article in Chapter I, in the discussion of Lenin Fabrication No. 6.) The amount of damage to rational thinking that resulted from this essay is beyond calculation. In a paid advertisement carried in the February 11, 1964 issue of the *Wall Street Journal, Reader's Digest* boasted of $14\frac{1}{2}$ million *paid* circulation in the United States and $10\frac{1}{2}$ million overseas. It stated further that *Reader's Digest* covers households in 3,078 U.S. counties; and in 1,562 counties, the *Digest* reaches 25% or more of the households. Thus the hoax of Communist schools-for-riots could conceivably have reached some 29 million people in this country, if we assume that the $14\frac{1}{2}$ million copies sold in this country were read by an average of 2 people per copy. In addition to this huge coverage, *Reader's Digest* issued reprints, which were widely distributed by Ultra-Rightists and others, who thought they were participating in a righteous crusade. Among those was the Ultra-Rightist *Fire and Police Research Association* of Los Angeles, which mailed out copies with its January, 1965 issue of *FIPO News.* Senator Karl Mundt referred to the *Digest* article in a speech on the floor of the Senate, May 14, 1965, and stated that Methvin's alleged facts were sufficient justification for one of the pet projects that the Ultra-Rightists are trying to get passed in Congress: the establishment of a so-called Freedom Academy, which would really be a "West Point" academy for Cold War propaganda. The Methvin-*Digest* essay also inspired a spate of newspaper editorials and columns, some of which Senator Mundt placed in the Congressional Record, thus again making possible Ultra-Rightist use of *the authority* of the Congressional Record to "prove" the schools-for-riots hoax.

The anti-Communist propaganda monthly of the American Legion, *Front Line,* in its February, 1965 issue, recommended distribution of the Methvin-*Digest* essay, and announced that the Legion's so-called Counter-Subversive Activities Committee had already distributed about 10,000 reprints.

The Senate Internal Security Subcommittee reprinted the Methvin-*Digest* article in the Report of a hearing it held on May 17, 1965.[5] Once again this Committee showed its role as a

5 The document is entitled "Communist Youth Program", Part 1.

part of the ideological fountainhead of the Ultra-Rightist propaganda network.

Kent and Phoebe Courtney's *Independent American* issued one of its Tax Fax series of pamphlets in November, 1965, entitled "Treason on the Campus." It contains 5 quotations from John E. Hoover, 1 from *Washington Report* of the Ultra-Rightist *American Security Council* (a private organization), 3 from a Report of the California Senate Fact-Finding Committee on Un-American Activities, 1 from the *Life Lines Newsletter* of oil tycoon H. L. Hunt, 1 from the Allen-Scott Report, 1 from Edgar Ansel Mowrer, and a quotation from the Methvin-*Digest* article *which it quoted from the Report of the Senate Internal Security Subcommittee.*

The Ultra-Rightist *Cardinal Mindszenty Foundation* published an editorial entitled "Our Weakest Link?," which advised its readers:

> See "How the Reds Make a Riot" in the Jan. 1965
> READER'S DIGEST.

The Rev. Paul Neipp reprinted the Mindszenty essay in his Ultra-Rightist monthly, *Through to Victory,* April 1965.

The Ultra-Rightist *National Program Letter,* issued at Harding College, Searcy, Arkansas, devoted a full page in its April, 1965 issue to extravagant panegyrics for the Methvin-*Digest* essay.

There is no mistaking of the fact that the Methvin-*Digest* essay was greatly appreciated by the Ultra-Rightists. One of these groups, the Information Council of the Americas, with headquarters in New Orleans, rewarded Methvin for his services almost immediately after the essay appeared. At a banquet held in the Roosevelt Hotel, INCA presented Methvin its Golden Microphone Award. There can be no doubt about the reason for the award, because the March 3, 1965, issue of INCA's newsletter, *Victory,* reports the event as follows:

> Edward Scannell Butler, INCA Executive Vice-President, introduced another Golden Mike winner, Eugene H. Methvin, with the *Reader's Digest* in Washington, D.C. Mr. Methvin's article, "How the Reds Make a Riot," in which the INCA was featured, appeared in the January 1965 issue of *Reader's Digest.*

Methvin responded by stating:

For a number of years I have pondered the problem of the Cold War and bothered the bureaucrats in Washington and experts around the country.

It was shortly after these remarks that Methvin recited to the audience the Lenin Fabrication #15, which we have already discussed.

Another gentleman who spreads the schools-for-riots hoax is a Negro, Leonard Patterson. This former bootblack and renegade Communist was a paid informer for the Immigration and Naturalization Service of the Department of Justice. During a period of two years he was receiving about $160 per month for his "fingering" services. This professional stool pigeon testified against the Negro scholar and Nobel Prize winner, Dr. Ralph Bunche. The Loyalty Board cleared Dr. Bunche *unanimously* and requested that the Justice Department review Patterson's testimony for the possibility of prosecuting him for perjury. Patterson has another distinction. He testified before those sterling "friends" of the Negro people, the Joint Legislative Committee of the State of Louisiana, on March 8, 1957. The title of the Hearing Report is "Subversion in Racial Unrest." In his testimony before the Committee, Patterson gave as part of his qualifications as an expert, the fact that he had already testified before the House Committee on Un-American Activities and the Senate Internal Security Subcommittee. Patterson, of course, gave the Committee exactly what they were paying for: that everything would be just heavenly in this country, were it not for Communist agitators who subvert Negroes into believing they are unemployed, poverty-stricken, discriminated against, humiliated, and segregated. Patterson's testimony furnished the ammunition for racists and other bigots, and has been reprinted, or quoted from, in many racist and Ultra-Rightist tracts and publications.

With this background and these experiences, Patterson was eminently qualified to become a Birch Society functionary. In 1965 and 1966, Patterson was on the lecture circuit of a Birch front called TACT (Truth About Civil Turmoil). The title of one of Patterson's lectures was "My Moscow Training in Civil Riots." The quality of Patterson's "information" can best be judged by his concluding remarks, while being interviewed

686

by Louis Lomax on station KTTV, Los Angeles, January 27, 1966. Patterson charged that the violence in the Watts rebellion of the summer of 1965 *was inspired by the civil rights movement on orders of the Communist Party!*

Speaking under the auspices of the John Birch Society in Attleboro, Massachusetts, Patterson told his audience on February 28, 1966 that the civil rights movement is part of a conspiracy that he learned of in *the 1930's,* that the revolts in Watts and Harlem were "a pattern, just a continuation down the line." He advocated civil rights negotiations with reason "in a Christian way." He didn't explain how you could negotiate in sweet reasonableness with the Ku Klux Klan, the (White) Citizens Councils, the National States Rights Party, the American Nazi Party, the Rev. Kenneth Goff, the Rev. Gerald L. K. Smith, the Rev. Oren F. Potito, and other bigots—open and concealed—who consider Negroes to be sub-human creatures. Patterson revealed the real purpose of the Birch campaign, when he cried out:

We've got to say "no rotten liberalism toward Communism."

That is the key to what the Birch Society has in mind: block all efforts to improve the Negro's position in our society by branding all such efforts as a scheme to move us toward Communism. Lest there be any doubt about this, Patterson told his audience that the National Association for the Advancement of Colored People, the Congress of Racial Equality, and the Rev. Martin Luther King are all "under the leadership of the American Communist Party." In none of the speeches and writings of the Negro Birchers can one find the name of a single Negro civil rights organization that is not Communist-controlled. The implication is clear: do not struggle for improvement of conditions or we will brand you a Communist!

Patterson concluded his lecture by urging his listeners to support their local police department. He charged that proposals for civilian review boards to handle complaints about police malpractice are part of a Communist plot to destroy law and order. The Communists, Patterson opined, would gain control of the review boards.

One can best evaluate the dastardly nature of Patterson's role as a Birch Society lecturer, if one contrasts his statements with the remarks made by a millionaire white man, who chose to face the Negro revolt with some semblance of honesty and integrity:

After all, we are very proud of the fact that we had a revolution and overthrew a government because we were taxed without representation.

I think there is no doubt that if Washington or Jefferson or Adams were Negroes in a northern city today, they would be in the forefront of the effort to change the conditions under which Negroes live in our society.

These remarks were made by Senator Robert F. Kennedy in a speech delivered before the New York State Convention of the Independent Order of Odd Fellows, Spring Valley, New York, August 18, 1965.[6]

A leaflet distributed by the Rev. Gerald L. K. Smith in November of 1967 begins with:

In 1940 the House Committee on Un-American Activities, headed by Martin Dies, released the following statement concerning the threat of a Black Revolution. For this, Mr. Dies was ridiculed and abused by Eleanor Roosevelt and her fraternity of Moscow sympathizers.

Following this, Smith quotes word for word the Goff school-for-riots hoax, but leaves the impression that the words are those of Martin Dies. It is bad enough that a Committee of the United States Congress got down into the gutter with Kenneth Goff and quoted his hoax statements, but the crime is compounded by the Rev. Smith when he makes the false claim that it is an *original* statement released by the House Committee. Let no one underestimate Kenneth Goff's capacity to do harm to the American people. It is all the more insidious, because he does it under the guise of preaching the doctrines of Jesus Christ! The same is true of the Rev. Gerald L. K. Smith!

Karl Prussion was back in the business of finding Communist plots, in the August, 1965, issue of *Heads Up,* which he designated as a "Special Edition." Prussion's headline this time is:

---

6 Senator Kennedy was assassinated in Los Angeles, California, on June 5, 1968.

# WATTS INSURRECTION—RESULT OF
# COMMUNIST CIVIL RIGHTS MOVEMENT

The "unfettered truth," Prussion tells us from his "twenty-six years of bitter and frightening experience within the Communist conspiracy," is that the Watts rebellion "was born in Moscow" more than 30 years ago and was actually planned by the Los Angeles Communists for many years.

The Ultra-Rightist *Liberty Lobby*, on whose Board of Policy Prussion serves, said in its September, 1965 *Liberty Letters*:

> Any student of Communism knows that the Reds plan for a repeat of Los Angeles in every major city. *Of what need has the Kremlin for missiles to knock out our major cities if Communist driven mobs will do it, on order, for them?*[7] It's much safer that way —for the Kremlin.

While Prussion is telling the "unfettered truth," it never becomes clear why he remained 26 years in the Communist Party, to endure a "bitter and frightening experience." After all, according to John E. Hoover, Prussion was a paid informer within the ranks of the Communist Party for about 9 years. But why did he endure the "bitter and frightening experience" during the preceding 17 years?

Shortly after the Watts rebellion, Governor Edmund G. Brown appointed a blue ribbon commission to investigate, and report to him, the underlying causes of the Watts rebellion. Prussion knew, of course, that no honest investigation would corroborate his own explanation of the causes. Prussion therefore goes on the offensive and refers to the commission as "an array of top flight leftist-liberals headed by none other than John McCone, former head of the Central Intelligence Agency." After a few stabs at the CIA, Prussion warns of the Governor's appointment of McCone: "This appointment appears to be very sinister and bears close surveillance."[8] In true gladiator fashion, Prussion then takes on the Governor:

> The opinion of the Governor, that the uprising was without leadership and formless is a malicious lie bordering on treason.

---

7 Emphasis is in the original.

8 It is not generally known that the McCone Commission had on its staff two ex-FBI Agents. Would Karl Prussion consider it necessary to exercise his "close surveillance" over these two alumni of the Federal Bureau of Investigation?

Either the Governor is mentally immature on the subject or he is wittingly cooperating and helping the enemy. I do not think he is naïve. The uprising from top to bottom is rigidly controlled by the Communist international which includes both Red Russia and Red China. Both red powers are spending hundreds of millions of dollars for propaganda which is flooding our land, agitating the Negro people to rise up against "their brutal oppressors."

There is, of course, no communist international in existence at the present time, and Red Russia and Red China are at loggerheads, but these facts mean nothing to Prussion. His insulting remarks about the Governor and his hurling of the charge of treason completely eliminate him as a dependable witness.

After the outburst against Governor Brown, Prussion advises us that President Lyndon B. Johnson is a revolutionary. He quotes a statement Johnson made on a national television hook-up one week before the Watts rebellion, and he finds a causal relationship between Johnson's remarks and the Watts rebellion. Next he goes after the distinguished Negro Congressman, Augustus Hawkins. He quotes the California Senate Factfinding Committee on Un-American Activities 1947 Report to prove that, when Hawkins was a State Assemblyman, he "consistently followed the Communist Party line." Another of Hawkins' "crimes", according to Prussion, is that he was "one of a handful of legislators in the Assembly who consistently voted against the Senate Committee investigating Un-American Activities." Prussion does not explain how a member of the Assembly can vote regarding a Committee of the Senate! His coup de grace follows:

Congressman Hawkins has been identified as a member of the communist party by counter-spy Paul Crouch at the H.C.U.A. hearing held in Beaumont, Texas in July, 1940.

Paul Crouch was never a counterspy. There is no such category in the FBI apparatus. He was just a plain FBI stool pigeon. Prussion knows very well that Paul Crouch was proven to be a perjurer on several occasions. In fact, his testimony was ordered stricken from the record in one case by the U.S. Supreme Court, because of its perjurious nature.

Not to be outdone by Robert Welch, Prussion summarizes his discussion with:

690

What conclusions can be made about the critical situation we find ourselves in today? Most important is the fact that the entire Civil Rights Movement of which President Johnson and Governor Brown are a part, is a major communist instrumentality through which they aim to win.

If the reader finds Prussion's statements outrageous, it should be noted that the inspiration for much of Prussion's ranting comes from the California Senate Factfinding Committee on Un-American Activities and the House Committee on Un-American Activities, which, together with the Senate Internal Security Subcommittee, furnish the libelous and defamatory material, used by Ultra-Rightist propagandists to smear decent people and intimidate those who challenge the inequities and iniquities of our society.

Kent and Phoebe Courtney's *Independent American* issued *Tax Fax* No. 66 in October, 1966, entitled:

### COMMUNIST INFLUENCE
### IN THE
### LOS ANGELES RIOTS
### BY KARL PRUSSION

It is a rehash of Prussion's articles in *Heads Up* of September, 1964 and August, 1965. It is copyrighted by *Independent American*. In addition to Prussion's material, it quotes John E. Hoover three times. It admonishes the reader to BEWARE OF DEMONSTRATORS and to SUPPORT YOUR LOCAL POLICE. It urges the reader to:

Send copies of this pamphlet to your friends, neighbors, your Congressman and Senators, civic and political leaders, patriotic and study groups, doctors, employees, and police officers.

Regrettably, this pamphlet did get widespread circulation by the Birchers and other Ultra-Rightists. We picked one up at the Freedom Club of Rev. James W. Fifield's First Congregational Church in Los Angeles, we received one in the mail, and a friend sent us one from Jacksonville, Florida, after picking it up in a Birch Society bookstore.

Prussion began "tooling up" for his role as a bitter adversary of the civil rights movement, in 1963. On September 28, Prussion swore to an affidavit before a notary public. The

691

affidavit and two letters received from John E. Hoover by interested individuals are reproduced on pages 692-694. We have covered up the names of the individuals who received the letters, in order to protect their privacy. We have also covered up the non-essential portions of Mr. Hoover's letters, in order not to distract from the essential point of the letters.

A comparison of the first sentence in Prussion's affidavit with Mr. Hoover's letter, shows that either Prussion has com-

### AFFIDAVIT

I, Karl Prussion, a former counterspy for the Federal Bureau of Investigation from 1947 to 1960, do hereby swear under oath and under penalty of perjury, that from the years 1954 through 1958 I attended five county committee meetings of the Communist Party of Santa Clara County, California. (A county committee meeting of the Communist Party consists of one delegate representing each Communist cell in a county.) The meetings were held during the aforementioned period in the following locations:

The residence of Robert Lindsay, Communist, in San Jose, California, 1954; the residence of Mary Field, Communist section organizer, Palo Alto, California, 1955; the residence of Isobel and Edwin Cerney, both Communists, Menlo Park, California, 1956; the residence of Gertrude Adler, Communist, Palo Alto, California, 1957; the residence of Karl Prussion, counterspy for the F.B.I., Los Altos, California, 1958; the residence of Myra White, Communist, Mountain View, California, 1959.

I hereby further solemnly state that at each and every meeting as set forth above, one Ed Beck, Communist, who is presently secretary of the National Association for the Advancement of Colored People of San Mateo County, California, and a member of the Congress on Racial Equality (CORE), presented the directive from the district office of the Communist Party in San Francisco to the effect that:

"All Communists working within the framework of the NAACP are instructed to work for a change of the passive attitude of the NAACP toward a more militant, demonstrative, class struggle policy to be expressed by sit-ins, demonstrations, marches and protests, for the purpose of transforming the NAACP into an organization for the achievement of Communist objectives."

I further swear and attest that at each and every one of the aforementioned meetings, one Reverend Martin Luther King was always set forth as the individual to whom Communists should look and rally around in the Communist struggle on the many racial issues.

I hereby also state that Martin Luther King has either been a member of, or wittingly has accepted support from, over 60 Communist fronts, individuals, and/or organizations, which give aid to or espouse Communist causes.

*Karl Prussion*

Subscribed and sworn to before me, this
_28_ day of _Sept_ , 19_65_.

*George F. Pensler*
Notary Public
My Commission Expires Sept. 17, 1966.

UNITED STATES DEPARTMENT OF JUSTICE

FEDERAL BUREAU OF INVESTIGATION

WASHINGTON, D.C. 20535

December 1, 1964

     With respect to Karl Prussion, he assisted this Bureau by furnishing information on subversive activities from November, 1949, to July, 1958, during which time he was compensated; however, he was not a Special Agent. His personal ventures and his opinions and comments are strictly his own and the FBI is not in a position to comment on these in any way whatsoever.

     Enclosed is some literature which includes suggestions all of us can use in combating the evil of communism. Perhaps you may also wish to read my books, "Masters of Deceit" and "A Study of Communism." These were written in order to help readers gain an insight into the strategy and tactics of communists, both in this country and abroad. Copies may be available in your local library.

Sincerely yours,

*J. Edgar Hoover*

Enclosures (5)

mitted perjury or Hoover is not telling the truth. We are inclined to believe Hoover this time, because there is no such category in the FBI as a "counterspy." There are Special Agents, supervisors, clerks, crime laboratory technicians, etc.,

UNITED STATES DEPARTMENT OF JUSTICE

FEDERAL BUREAU OF INVESTIGATION

WASHINGTON, D.C. 20535

February 17, 1965

With respect to your inquiry, I would like
to point out Karl Prussion assisted this Bureau by furnishing
information on subversive activities from November, 1949,
to July, 1958, during which time he was compensated; however,
he was not a Special Agent. His personal ventures and his
opinions and comments are strictly his own and the FBI is not
in a position to comment on these in any way whatsoever.

Enclosed is some literature I trust will be of
interest.

Sincerely yours,

J. Edgar Hoover

Enclosures (5)

but no counterspies. Prussion knows very well that he has no
right to allow publicity in which he is referred to as former
counterspy for the Federal Bureau of Investigation, former FBI
undercover agent, former Federal Bureau of Investigation agent,
or FBI undercover operative. All these designations mislead
people into believing that Prussion was *a Special Agent of the
FBI,* whereas he was just a paid informer, with no special
training in investigative techniques.

Prussion claims that he worked as a "counterspy" for the FBI
from 1947 to 1960. Hoover says that Prussion was a paid in-

former from November, 1949 to July, 1958. If Prussion's memory is so poor, how can anyone depend upon his other alleged "facts"?

The final paragraph of the affidavit violates accepted legal procedure, because it lumps together "Communist fronts, individuals, and/or organizations", so that we have no way of knowing whether he means 58 individuals and 1 each of the other categories, or any other breakdown of his total of 60. There is no way of knowing whether he is including such "Communists" as President Lyndon B. Johnson, Governor Edmund G. Brown, Dr. Ralph Bunche, and General Dwight D. Eisenhower. The affidavit has been circulated as a special leaflet and has been reprinted widely by racist and Ultra-Rightist publications.

In April of 1965, Prussion used another device to capitalize on FBI prestige. He issued and circulated a 4-page, 8½″ × 11″ brochure. Pages 2, 3, and 4 consist of a reproduction of an essay by John E. Hoover *on FBI stationery*. In reproducing it, the impression one gets is that Prussion still has some official status in the FBI. In any case, it served Prussion's purpose very well, because it was a glorification of ex-Communists who have become stool pigeons. On the front page of the brochure, there is an essay by Prussion. It is entitled:

## LYING, A COMMUNIST POLICY

As is quite common in Prussion's writings, the essay contains a number of shocking errors of spelling and syntax. He begins by bragging about his anti-Communist exploits, and he asserts that all the statements of the FBI and the California Attorney General, which show *him* to be a liar, are just so many Communist lies:

The communists feel that if they can make these labels stick they can destroy all of my effectiveness in my fight against them. All of their charges are lies. Lying is their policy.
Regrettably many honest liberals have been duped into accepting lies as fact, therefore many of my principal tormentors are members of our educational system, clergymen and politicians.
I am courageously fighting back by taking the offensive. I am thoroughly ashamed that I had been a communist for four years and repent and ask all Americans to forgive this great criminal mistake I had made in the early 30's. However, I am proud to have

contributed in this titanic battle against communism by serving God and Country as an undercover agent for the F.B.I. for 12 years (1947 through 1959), having testified before the House Committee on the Un-American Activities and other governmental agencies and for lecturing, writing and encouraging Americans to organize against the greatest threat of these master barbarians of the 20th century who repudiate God's civilization, who have reincarnated the Law of the Jungle: "Might makes Right." They have elevated lying to a status of policy, brutality to a status of virtue, and enslavement of men to a science.

Once again, Prussion tells a story of having been an informer for a period of twelve or thirteen years, while FBI Director Hoover says he served less than nine years. There is also a discrepancy in the number of years Prussion claims to have been a member of the Communist Party. In statements issued during the same year, 1965, Prussion said that he had been a member of the Communist Party for twenty-six years; now he says that he "had been a communist for four years."

The Chico (California) *Enterprise-Record,* May 8, 1964, told a story of Prussion's activities in that area:

Karl Prussion, former Communist Party member and a counter-spy for the FBI during the 1950's, will not be permitted to speak to high school students in this area.

High school officials in Paradise, Gridley and Oroville told the *Enterprise-Record* today that they had cancelled meetings at which Prussion had been scheduled to address their students.

Officials at Live Oak High School, where Prussion is scheduled to speak Monday afternoon, indicated that his meeting there will probably be cancelled.

The former FBI undercover agent was, however, permitted to keep an engagement to address Chico State College students here this afternoon at 3:30 o'clock.

And his public address at 8:15 o'clock tonight in the Chico State College Auditorium also will go on as scheduled.

In setting forth their reasons for cancelling the programs of the nationally-famed anti-Communist, high school officials placed primary stress on the opinion that Prussion and his sponsors had "misrepresented" his identity and his affiliation with the FBI.

For example, Doran Tregarthen, Paradise school superintendent, said the cancellation there was based on "a lack of understanding" due to the fact that the sponsors had indicated to him initially that Prussion was currently "associated with the FBI."

Paradise High School Principal Glen Russell concurred with his superintendent and added that he (Russell) was fearful that Paradise students might be "taken in" by Prussion.

696

Gridley High School Supt. Robert Vaughn said he had cancelled Prussion's appearance there "after I received a call from a person asking me to check into Prussion's background."

Vaughn declined to identify the telephone caller, declaring that the call had been "just given in confidence as a tip to investigate."

Vaughn said he subsequently checked with the FBI and learned that Prussion is not associated with them and never was an actual employed FBI agent.

During the same period, a professor of political science on the Chico campus of California State College, Dr. Ben Franklin, inquired of the California Attorney General about some of the statements made by Prussion. A telegram, dated May 8, 1964, signed by Howard H. Jewell, Assistant Attorney General, says, in part:

This office feels that public statements and publications of Prussion on Communism are so bizarre as to destroy his credibility.

A photocopy of this telegram was presented in the May 15, 1964 issue of a student newsletter issued on campus, *The Furious Fly*.

In an open letter to Prussion, the editor of *The Furious Fly*, Clyde H. Echols, pointed out some of Prussion's inconsistencies. Echols said, in part:

On 8 May, Friday, when asked about your book, *California Dynasty of Communism*, you stated it was not available, out-of-print, and that you had no copies of it. You also said that you were going to put out another printing of it. You sold this same book in Paradise on May 11, 1964.

On Friday, May 8, you blamed the Communist Party for your persecution following the HUAC hearings; on Monday the ACLU was blamed. Do you identify the ACLU with the Communist Party?[9]

On Friday you stated that you "guessed" there might be Communist activity in Chico. When crowded by a member of the audience, you quickly stated that you had no proof.

On Saturday, May 9, in Oroville, after two young ladies distributed our material in front of your "school", your press release blared out the news that "the Chico State College faculty is the most thoroughly influenced by Communists in the country." You gave no evidence to support your charge.

---

[9] *HUAC* stands for House Un-American Activities Committee; *ACLU* stands for American Civil Liberties Union.—M. K.

On July 25, 1963, Prussion spoke before an audience of more than 350 persons in the Continental Room of Hotel San Diego, in San Diego, California. Sharing the platform with Prussion was a Negro woman, Mrs. Julia C. Brown, who also served as an FBI informer within the ranks of the Communist Party. Like Leonard Patterson, she travels the Birch Society lecture circuit, explaining the civil rights movement and the Negro rebellion as a Communist plot. The San Diego *Union* report of the meeting referred to both Prussion and Brown as FBI undercover agents. The *Union* referred to Prussion also as one who had spent 14 years as a member of the Communist Party and had been "a counterspy for 12 years." The willingness of the news media to constantly repeat distortions of truth creates the impression that paid informers have been Special Agents of the FBI or have been counterspies. Consider the latter item. When has a spy been prosecuted and convicted in a court of law as a result of the efforts of "counterspy" Prussion or the likes of him? The answer to this question should reveal the fraudulent nature of the claim to the title of counterspy. In any case, Prussion's claim to service as a "counterspy" for 12 years clashes with Mr. Hoover's statement that he was a paid informer for less than 9 years.

According to the newspaper report, Prussion charged that known Communists "are taking a leading part" in the National Association for the Advancement of Colored People. He charged that Dr. Martin Luther King is surrounded by Communists, and he said that the Communists are "trying to throw the nation into civil strife" by provoking demonstrations under the guise of supporting civil rights.

Prussion did not get very far, because, just about the time he was regaling his audience with fantastic yarns, the Justice Department was issuing a statement that gave the lie to the charges made by both Prussion and Julia Brown. It should have been a source of great embarrassment to Prussion that the San Diego *Union* carried the report of his lecture on page 18, and carried the story about the Justice Department's report on page 2. The story from Washington, D.C., reads in part:

The Justice Department has no evidence that any top leaders of major civil rights groups are Communist or Communist controlled, Atty. Gen. Robert F. Kennedy said yesterday.

698

He said his statement was based on "all available information" from the Federal Bureau of Investigation and other sources.

Inasmuch as both Prussion and Brown were no longer informing from within the ranks of the Communist Party and inasmuch as Kennedy's information was based upon the reports of *hundreds of informers* within the Communist Party *at that time,* it is clear that Kennedy's information is factual and the Prussion-Brown charges are fictional.

The correctness of this conclusion was attested to by two FBI informers, Howard Thompson and his wife, who posed as Communist Party members for 14 and 9 years, respectively. Testifying at a hearing of the House Committee on Un-American Activities, held in San Francisco on July 12, 1964, Thompson said that the Communist Party had not been successful in attempts at infiltrating the National Association for the Advancement of Colored People. One thing is certain: Thompson has disqualified himself as a lecturer for the Birch Society's front group, TACT. He also runs the risk of being called a traitor by the Birch purveyors of the Communist schools-for-riots hoax.

The many years of using the Red Scare against all attempts to improve the conditions of the Negro people, came to fruition during the revolts of desperate, frustrated, and oppressed people in the 1965, 1966, and 1967 revolts in the cities. The bigots and the Ultra-Rightists met the challenge, not by an honest appraisal of the true conditions, but by an intensification of the Red Scare and an increase in the use of vituperation. With a pretense of not being racist in philosophical posture, the John Birch Society set up its front group, Truth About Civil Turmoil (TACT). This operation consists of sending out on the lecture circuit both white and black racist agitators, who have been well trained in wielding the Red paint brush. In addition, TACT shows films, specially designed to inflame the passions and divert attention from the real problems of the Negro people: unemployment, poverty, sub-standard housing, discrimination, humiliation, and segregation. All these problems are "solved" quickly and simply by blaming them onto the Communists. This Birch Society campaign is graphically illustrated in an article entitled:

# THE PLAN
## To Burn Los Angeles

The article is in the May, 1967 issue of the Birch monthly, *American Opinion*. It is written by Gary Allen, one of the more fanciful of the Birch Society's "fiction" writers. Allen is the son and grandson of policemen, and a wag has suggested that his employment by the Birch Society is an implementation of the "Support Your Local Police" slogan.

Allen begins his essay with the cleverly disarming remark, that he is telling the story about the Watts rebellion, as a result of the urging by a Negro policeman, whom he does not identify. He claims that his information comes from this Negro policeman and other "Los Angeles law enforcement officers." In summarizing his article, we are placing our own comments in parentheses. Allen makes these points:

1. That police experts believe, that riots which last more than a few hours are always planned in advance. (This is a dubious and unprovable assumption.)

2. That a "board of revolutionary strategy" consisting of 40-50 Negroes, who had been sent into Los Angeles by the Communists, planned and instigated the Watts revolt. (Neither the investigators of the Los Angeles Police Department nor the investigators of the District Attorney's office were able to find any evidence to support this theory. With the Birchers and racists of *every* strife-torn city blaming the Negro rebellion onto outside agitators, one wonders whether or not these agitators could possibly be from some other planet.) (Allen may very well have been spoon-fed this yarn by some Birchite policemen, of whom there are a goodly number in the Los Angeles Police Department.)

3. That this "board of revolutionary strategy" is referred to in the Watts area and by the Intelligence Division of the Los Angeles Police Department as "The Organization." (The L.A.P.D. found no evidence of "The Organization.")

4. That the Los Angeles Negroes "have access to virtually any job for which they are qualified." (Aside from the fact that many employers and some labor unions *do discriminate* against qualified Negroes, Allen blithely ignores the plight of the un-skilled Negro workers, especially those whom automation has displaced.)

700

5. That Negroes in Los Angeles can travel where they please and take advantage of almost unlimited free education. (Allen ignores the continual rousting of Negroes by racist-minded policemen, the lack of a mass transportation system, and the crushing of the spirit by poverty and unemployment, as well as by segregation.)

6. That 90% of the world "would give a left ear to live in such misery" as do the Negroes of Los Angeles. (Both in the previous item and this one, Allen uses the sleight-of-hand device of referring to Los Angeles instead of *the Watts section* of Los Angeles. The figure of 90% is a gross exaggeration, because more than 10% of the world's population lives better than do the Negroes of Watts. Furthermore, it is an insult to ask people to enjoy miserable conditions of life because people of other countries may be more miserable.)

7. That "The Organization" created and popularized the "myth" of police brutality. (Both the American Civil Liberties Union and the NAACP have published overwhelming documentation of police brutality and/or malpractice against the Negro population of Los Angeles, especially in the Watts area.)

From this point on, the article quotes information about "The Organization" from police sources or law enforcement sources, in a manner calculated to convey the impression that Allen has been privy to the confidential files of the Los Angeles Police Department's higher echelons. (This, as we shall soon see, is something less than the truth.)

Allen quotes from an alleged pamphlet or leaflet of the *Communist Party of the United States (Marxist-Leninist)*, without informing his readers that this group has no relationship to the Communist Party, but is really a handful of individuals who issue fire-eating pronunciamentoes, which make for sensational headlines. There are some observers who consider this group to be composed of agents-provocateurs in the employ of either the FBI or the CIA.

Allen quotes from other anonymous splinter groups, giving no proof of the veracity of his alleged quotations. We have no way of ascertaining whether he is actually quoting from documents or from a lurid imagination.

It is unfortunate for the Birch Society theory of the Watts

rebellion that not all Right-Wingers agree with Gary Allen's revelations. Los Angeles Mayor Yorty, whom no one will accuse of sympathy for the Communists, is one who does not buy Allen's merchandise. In a press conference while visiting New York City, Yorty said on April 26, 1967 that *the sensational television reporting was partially responsible for rioting* in the Watts section of Los Angeles in 1965 and 1966. He quoted the late Chief of Police Parker as citing one example in March of 1966, when, according to Parker, a Negro youth grabbed a television microphone and yelled: "We're going to burn, baby, burn." If the Parker-Yorty theory has any validity, it puts Gary Allen in the position of having to accept the thesis that the television stations of Los Angeles are under the control of Allen's mythical "The Organization."

Another facet to the problem of rioting, that Allen and the other Birchers conveniently overlook, is the agent-provocateur role in the Watts area (and other places) of the Minutemen, (White) Citizens Councils, Ku Klux Klan, and American Nazi Party. We shall deal with this in volume II, but for the present it can be stated that there is definite evidence that agents-provocateurs have been planted in many areas, in order to discredit the Negro struggles. There is a bit of irony in the fact that, alongside the newspaper story telling of Mayor Yorty's press conference, there was a story of the seizure by federal agents in San Francisco of an arsenal of weapons and ammunition in the home of William Thoresen III, son of the president of Great Western Steel Corporation, of Chicago. The seizure included automatic weapons, machine guns, an anti-tank gun, and some 55,000 pounds of guns and ammunition. This, and an abundance of other stories that have been published, show that a considerable number of Ultra-Rightists are arming for "Der Tag," as the German used to say. Yes indeed, a Fascist coup d'etat is being planned by certain elements of our society. Strangely enough, not one word of criticism or protest or comment of any kind about this clear and present danger have we been able to discover in the publications of any of the anti-Communist crusaders. Dr. Fred Schwarz, Robert Welch, William F. Buckley, Jr., Barry Goldwater, Billy James Hargis, Clarence Manion, Dr. George S. Benson, Dr. Robert Morris, and similar personalities have not conducted any crusades against the formation of a number of para-military

702

organizations and their infiltration of the military and police. This is the "acid test" of the sincerity of all those noisy Ultra-Rightists who constantly proclaim their intention to defend the Constitution of the United States! Why are they silent in this matter?

The best analysis of Gary Allen's essay was a 2-column article that appeared in the *Los Angeles Times,* April 28, 1967. The staff writer, Mr. Gene Blake, is without question one of the most skillful and responsible of investigative journalists. His 5-part series of articles on the John Birch Society, which appeared in the *Los Angeles Times* the early part of March, 1961, are still worth reading by anyone desiring to understand the John Birch Society, its philosophy and its program. With the kind permission of the *Los Angeles Times,* we present Mr. Blake's entire article:

Police Chief Tom Reddin has disputed a John Birch Society magazine article citing unnamed police as authority that the 1965 Watts riot was a rehearsal for a nationwide Communist revolution to be touched off by total burning of Los Angeles.

"The facts as stated in the article are not based on information in our files," Reddin said. "We do not reach the same conclusions the writer does. We do not make the same reading."

The article in the May issue of *American Opinion* is entitled "The Plan to Burn Los Angeles." It was written by Gary Allen, identified as a Los Angeles journalist and Stanford graduate.

Allen writes that his information came from Los Angeles police officers, and particularly the intelligence division of the Police Department.

"We have investigated to determine whom he may have talked to," Reddin said. "It was nobody in a position of authority—not I, the intelligence captain nor the former police chief (the late William H. Parker)."

Reddin conceded the writer may have talked to "someone at the working level." But Capt. Harold E. Yarnell, Jr., head of the intelligence division, said an investigation failed to turn up any officer to whom the writer had talked.

"If we had such information, we wouldn't talk to a writer," Yarnell pointed out.

Yarnell said the article "attempts to recite some history we believe is not based on fact," and then attempts to recite a major plot in the making.

"It is not our position that the August, 1965, riot was Communist-inspired," he said. "We have never been able to isolate any group as being motivating forces or manipulators."

Nevertheless, the article says it was a team of "highly trained

703

Communists" known to the intelligence division as "The Organization" that planned and directed what happened in Watts.

The article claims the board of revolutionary strategy was composed of 40 to 50 Negroes sent by the Communists into the Los Angeles area from all over the United States.

It said they included Black Muslims, Black Nationalists, representatives from the paramilitary Deacons for Defense, the Communist Revolutionary Action Movement (R.A.M.) and professionals from other such "militant and Marxist groups."

Said Yarnell:

"We haven't been able to establish that any organization had anything to do with it. Three or four groups wanted to take credit. But when someone seriously became interested in talking to them about it, they backed down.

"I'm sure the Communist Party is gleefully watching every bit of dissension. But they haven't gone out in front."

The article specifically mentions reports that during the rioting, men wearing red armbands and speaking through bullhorns gave directions to the mobs. Yarnell said thorough investigation has failed to substantiate such reports.

The article also claims the rioters used stolen loot to build up an arsenal of weapons to be employed in the forthcoming major Communist revolution.

"The only arsenals we've found have been those of paramilitary right-wing groups," Yarnell said.

The article says that when the signal for the revolution is given, hundreds of officers will be lured into the Watts area by calls for police help, but will be assassinated.

Then "the plan" calls for destruction of the Central and Valley Services Divisions, the two main sources of police communications, possibly with rocket launchers or dynamite. Off-duty policemen would be assassinated in their homes.

Next, the torch would be put to Los Angeles, first in the surrounding oil fields and foothills, then the Civic Center and Wilshire area. Mobs would shoot all white men and children on sight, with the women being utilized as "rewards for the insurrectionists."

Finally, the revolution would spread to other urban areas across the country, the article claims.

Yarnell said the purported plot is reminiscent of weekly rumors which poured in after the 1965 riot and reached a peak last July.

"We maintain a rumor board," he said. "Everything we hear, we log and investigate. We've never been able to substantiate anything.

"We would certainly be foolish to say it can't happen. But we don't know of any organized plot.

"We've heard many rumors and we would be interested in any information Mr. Allen has to substantiate them."

Yarnell said Allen even missed one of the best rumors—that gasoline tanker trucks would be used to spray gasoline on Civic Center buildings to set them afire.

"I don't know why they print such stuff," Yarnell said. "All it does is give some of these 'kooks' ideas."

One of the things that stands out in a careful reading of Allen's essay is the similarity to the motif of Kenneth Goff's school-for-riots hoax. Is it possible that Allen's source of information is Goff rather than law enforcement agencies?

This concludes the prosecution's evidence in the case of the People of the United States of America vs. Gary Allen and the John Birch Society.

## The Conspiracy That Never Was![10]

One of the pillars, upon which the Red Scare hysteria is based, is the theory of an international Communist conspiracy. Indeed, a law still on the statute books of this country, the McCarran Act, begins by a "Congressional finding" of the existence of such a conspiracy. So well ingrained is this belief, that any attempt to refute it is usually met with the charge that one is defending the Communists. Nevertheless, this risk must be assumed by those who wish to restore rational political dialogue as a basis for coping with the pressing problems of our era. Any other course is fraught with danger to the very existence of the human race. Our study, of necessity, must begin with a definition of conspiracy and by the establishment of some criteria.

Webster's New International Dictionary, Second Edition, 1949, defines conspiracy as:

1. "Act of conspiring; combination of men for evil purpose; an agreement between two or more persons to commit a crime in concert, as treason; a plot."

2. "Combination of men for a single end; a concurrence, or general tendency, as of circumstances, to one event; harmonious action."

3. "*Law*. An agreement, manifesting itself in words or deeds, by which two or more persons confederate to do an unlawful act, or to use unlawful means to do an act which is lawful; confederacy."

10 The inspiration for this title came from the now-defunct satirical television program, "That was the week that was."

705

The American College Dictionary, 1963 edition, gives substantially the same definitions, although in more concise form. It points out, however, that the concept expressed in the Webster definition number 2 is now obsolete. This must be conceded, unless one is willing to call conspiracies the concurrences of action in the Roman Catholic Church, the World Council of Churches, the United Nations, and a huge number of international societies, businesses, and groups.

Reduced to its simplest terms, the use of the word "conspiracy" usually denotes a secret combine to do something evil and/or illegal. That, in essence, is the image that the users of the term international Communist conspiracy intend to convey. In our examination of the question, we have to consider the two essential elements of our definition: secrecy in methods of achieving a goal; a chosen goal that is evil.

The question of whether the goal of a Communist society is intrinsically evil is, of course, beyond the purview of this study. We need only point out that it depends upon one's point of view, upon one's frame of reference. To the British ruling class of the 18th century, the American revolutionists were conspirators with an evil goal in mind. In the early years of the labor movement, reactionary employers looked upon union organizers as unspeakable conspirators, and many working people were jailed on charges of conspiracy, only because they were organizing themselves into unions. Anti-Catholic bigots consider the Roman Catholic church as a vast conspiracy to control the world, just as the anti-Semites use the fraudulent "Protocols of the Learned Elders of Zion" to "prove" that the Jews are plotting for control of the entire world. In fact, they have invented the term, "the International Jew," to signify that concept. Furthermore, along with many of the evil deeds perpetrated by some Communists in countries where they have assumed control, it is conceded even by zealous anti-Communists that the general conditions of life have improved. (There are a few die-hard scribes who attempt to prove that living conditions have worsened in the Communist countries, in comparison with pre-Communist standards. This is accomplished by juggling facts and figures to conceal the truth.) Inasmuch as the question of evil is a debatable one, we can now examine the question of secrecy.

One of the strangest things about the proponents of the

secrecy charge is their simultaneous support of laws to make the Communist Party illegal and to drive it underground. It would seem to be fair to ask: Why not allow it to operate openly, where it is easier to watch it? Another fact that militates against the secrecy theory is the relative ease with which the FBI plants its informers in the Communist Party and the relative ease with which some of these informers have risen to top leadership. This hardly conforms with the concept of tight secrecy for any purpose, good or evil. The memories of some people are short, so it is necessary to remind them that before the hysteria of the McCarthyite period and before the repressive laws were enacted, the Communist Party operated openly, and conducted forums, public meetings, election campaigns, and May Day parades, in which Communist Party members marched without concealing their identity. In the light of these facts, the secrecy charge would appear to be one that partakes of the nature of self-fulfilling prophecy. It seems to be sheer hypocrisy to force people to go underground and then taunt them with the charge of operating in secret. The easiest way to eliminate the "secrecy" of the Communists is to allow them to operate openly and to compete in *the marketplace of ideas,* where they can be confronted with rational arguments in open debate. Who is afraid of open debate and why?

The concept of an international Communist conspiracy had gripped the Ultra-Rightists so severely that for a long time they refused to accept the facts of life, that each Communist country is pursuing an independent policy and that, whatever degree of collaboration exists between them, is no more and no less than U.S.-British or U.S.-Canada or U.S.-Australia collaboration, which no one in his right mind would call an international conspiracy. Believers in the theory of a monolithic bloc of Communist countries—an essential ingredient of the conspiracy theory—found it hard to believe that hostility had developed between the Soviet Union and Communist China. Some of the more desperate of the Ultra-Rightist scribes and orators have resolved this question by an increase in the use of slander and vituperation.

Closely related to the conspiracy thesis, and forming almost an intergral part of it, is the oft-repeated charge that Communism is a foreign importation. When one stops to think that the charge is made in *every country*, then it refutes itself by the sheer absurdity of it. With the advent of investigations of flying saucers, one can soon expect to hear that Communism was introduced by strange beings from another planet. Anyone who might consider this to be idle raillery should consider this item from the October 30, 1966 issue of the (White) Citizens Councils paper, *The Councilor:*

Los Angeles—According to the highly reliable *Cross and Flag* magazine, 284 of the 300 (approx.) commisars in the original Soviet government after the 1917 revolution were from New York.
(Editor's Note: Your editor was told by a Russian nordic in Seoul, Korea in 1946: "Communism is not a native product to be exported to New York. Communism and Communist control of Russia is an import FROM New York.")

Here we have a switch from the usual charge that Communism is imported from Russia, and we are being told, in effect, that it was largely imported from the U.S.A. This, of course, is the ultimate in the irrational thinking generated by the false theory of an international Communist conspiracy. The falsehood about the 284 commissars from New York is meant to convey the idea, prevalent in anti-Semitic circles, that Communism is a Jewish plot; and the 284 commissars are supposed to be New York Jews. It doesn't say so in this particular item, but it has been stated so many times in anti-Semitic and racist journals, that the readers "catch on," without the specifics being mentioned each time. After they are told repeatedly that the Jews control New York City, it is easy for anti-Semitic dupes to equate 284 commissars from New York with 284 New York Jews.

Pertinent to our examination of Communism as an alleged foreign importation is an item in the *United States News & World Report,* November 18, 1955, which reported a Moscow radio address by Deputy Premier Lazar M. Kaganovich. In the course of his speech, the Deputy Premier quoted Lenin as having said:

There are people who believe that revolution can be brought into being to order in any country. These people are either lunatics or provocateurs.

Lenin's position was reiterated by Joseph Stalin, in an interview granted the American newspaper man, Roy Howard, in 1936:

We Marxists believe that a revolution will also take place in other countries. But it will take place only when the revolutionaries in those countries think it possible, or necessary. The export of revolution is nonsense. Every country will make its own revolution, if it wants to and if it does not want to there will be no revolution. For example, our country wanted to make a revolution and made it, and now we are building a new classless society. But to assert that we want to make a revolution in other countries, to interfere in their lives, means saying what is untrue, and what we have never advocated.

This outlook was brought up to date in a speech by Premier Nikita Khrushchev, which was broadcast on Moscow radio, January 28, 1959:

In every country the people themselves determine their fate and select the course of their development. The Soviet Union does not want to impose upon anyone the path it has chosen. We are guided wholly by the instructions of Lenin to the effect that revolutions are not exportable.

Many of the fabrications that we have discussed were also used to create the myth of the international Communist conspiracy. One of the shabbiest of these fabrications is a statement attributed to the late Communist leader, Georgi Dimitrov, who is quoted as saying:

As Soviet power grows, there will be a greater aversion to Communist parties everywhere. So we must practice the techniques of withdrawal. Never appear in the foreground; let our friends do the work. We must always remember that one sympathizer is generally worth more than a dozen militant Communists. A university professor, who without being a party member lends himself to the interests of the Soviet Union, is worth more than a hundred men with party cards. A writer of reputation, or a retired general, are worth more than 500 poor devils who don't know any better than to get themselves beaten up by the police. Every man has his value, his merit. The writer who, without being a party member, defends the Soviet Union, the union leader who is outside our ranks but defends Soviet international policy, is worth more than a thousand party members. Those who are not party members or marked as Communists enjoy greater freedom of action. This dissimulated activity which awakes no resistance is much more effective than a frontal attack by the Communists. Our friends must confuse the adversary for us, carry out our main directives, mobilize in favor of our campaign people who do not think as we do, and whom we could never reach. In this tactic we must use everyone who comes near us; and the number grows every day.

This alleged quotation appears, in condensed form, in a sleazy little pamphlet, entitled *The Truth About the American Civil Liberties Union,* issued by Organizational Research Associates, Louis Scura, Director. It operates out of a postoffice box in Garden Grove, California. The distinctive feature of this pamphlet is that it does *not* tell the truth about the American Civil Liberties Union; it smears it with phoney quotations, out-of-context quotations, and the usual unreliable items from the various Un-American Activities Committees. In 1962, Scura collaborated with Assemblyman Louis Francis in preparing and campaigning for Proposition #24, the so-called Francis Amendment to the California State Constitution. Under the guise of outlawing the Communists, this measure would have put California well on the road to becoming a Fascist state. The proposed amendment had the energetic support of the Ultra-Rightist *Fire and Police Research Association of Los Angeles,* the Birchers, Carl McIntire's American Council of Christian Churches of California, American Legion Department of California, California Real Estate Association, County Supervisors Association of California, California Society of the Daughters of the American Revolution, Los Angeles Chamber of Commerce, Orange County Associated Chamber of Commerce, Los Angeles *Herald Examiner,* Veterans of Foreign Wars California Department, Riverside County Sheriff Joe Rice, former State Senator Nelson S. Dilworth, Karl Prussion, George Putnam, Congressman James B. Utt, Rev. Paul C. Neipp, Harry Von Zell, and others.

The proposed Francis Amendment was such a dangerous measure that the *Los Angeles Times* and most of the responsible California newspapers came out against it. Even that veteran Red-hunter, Richard Nixon, joined Governor Brown in opposing it. The California State Chamber of Commerce opposed it, as did the State Chairman of the Republican Party, the State Chairman of the Democratic Party, the California Teachers Association, the San Diego Chamber of Commerce, Bishop Gerald Kennedy, Bishop James A. Pike, the California Attorney

General, and a long list of distinguished lawyers, labor leaders, scholars, and others who valued democratic rights. The Francis Amendment was soundly defeated, but it is of more than passing interest that one of the principal backers of this police state measure is using the phoney Dimitrov quotation, as part of a smear attack against the American Civil Liberties Union. In a footnote, Scura tells us that Dimitrov made those remarks in the course of giving "advice to the Lenin School of Political Warfare, as quoted in the Report of the American Bar Association Committee on Communist Tactics, Strategy and Objectives—Congressional Record, 22 August, '58, P. 17719." It should be noted that Scura uses that favorite device of the Ultra-Rightists: quoting the Congressional Record *as such*, instead of stating *who placed it in the Congressional Record*. The second point to be noted is, that Dimitrov is alleged to have made these remarks at the non-existent Lenin School of Political Warfare, a myth created by stool pigeon Joseph Kornfeder and the House Committee on Un-American Activities. It was Senator Styles Bridges who placed the Report of the American Bar Association Committee in the Congressional Record on August 22, 1958. As we mentioned in Chapter XIV, Senator Everett Dirksen placed that same Report in the Congressional Record 3½ years later, on March 1, 1962. Right-Wingers know a "good thing" when they see it, and they work hard to exploit it to the fullest degree.

Turning to the actual Report of the Bar Association Committee, we find that they quote the phoney Dimitrov remarks, and they preface the quotation with:

Georgi Dimitrov advised the Lenin School of Political Warfare how to make use of innocents and dupes in these words.

One could expect that lawyers—trained in the rules of evidence —would be able to cite a reliable source for such a quotation and for such an authoritative, prefatory statement. The only authority they give is page 2 of the 1957 annual report of the House Committee on Un-American Activities, a most dubious and unreliable source under the best of circumstances. In this instance, the irresponsibility of the lawyers' committee is shocking, because the House Committee's Report gives no source or documentation for either the quotation or their own introductory remarks: stating that Communist tactics "were concisely formulated by the former Secretary General of the Communist International, Georgi Dimitrov, at the Lenin School of revolutionary leadership in Moscow in the following words:" This is followed by the entire phoney quotation, exactly as we have quoted it.

The hate sheet, *Common Sense,* in its February 1, 1964 issue, quotes a modified version of the phoney Dimitrov remarks. It omits the first 2½ sentences and the last sentence, but at the end it *adds* the following:

Particularly, we must use ambitious politicians who need support; men who realize that we communists can clear them a path, give them publicity, and provide them with a ladder. Such men will sell their souls to the devil—and we buy souls.

*Common Sense* gives this explanation:

You have just read a quoted directive by Georgi Dimitrov, Comintern leader, 1938, as published in *The Yenan Way* by Eudocio Ravines, pp. 256-7 (Scribner's, New York, 1951).
The astounding statement quoted above was made in secret sessions held by the Comintern in Moscow, and was NEVER MEANT TO BE PUBLICIZED.

We note that the previous quoters of Dimitrov said that he delivered those remarks at the mythical Lenin School of Political Warfare, but here we are told that the remarks were made at "secret sessions held by the Comintern." Instead of the House Committee on Un-American Activities as a source, we are now given a book as authority for a statement made in "secret sessions."

The quotation attributed to Dimitrov is a weapon used by *Common Sense* in a 2½ page attack against the National Conference of Christians and Jews, which, *Common Sense* avers, is carrying out Dimitrov's conspiratorial and deceitful tactics by its sponsorship each February of BROTHERHOOD WEEK. The title of this Red-Baiting tirade is:

"BROTHERHOOD—A TRAP FOR CHRISTIANS

Is it not becoming clear why this Dimitrov quotation was fabricated by the Ultra-Rightists?

712

The Navy League of Dallas, Texas issued a brochure, entitled:

## TOO BUSY!—FOR FREEDOM?

It contains the Manuilsky Hoax, Lenin Fabrications No. 1 and No. 2, the Treaty Breaking Hoax, the "We Will Bury You" Hoax, the Stalin Fabrication No. 1, and the phoney Dimitrov quotation. The Navy League is a private organization that carries on propaganda for larger naval appropriations by Congress. For this purpose, the Red Scare lies are very useful. It may come as a shock to the reader when we disclose the fact, that the Atomic Energy Commission, Office of Technical Information Extension at Oak Ridge, Tennessee, reprinted this compendium of fabrications and distortions of truth, and shamelessly stated: "Reprinted by Permission of the Navy League, Dallas, Texas." Pursuant to our inquiry, Thomas D. Sample, Production Control Officer at the Oak Ridge plant of the Atomic Energy Commission wrote to us on May 18, 1964, regarding "Too Busy!—For Freedom?":

The USAEC has its largest operations office in Oak Ridge. Our printing plant produced quite a lot of administrative printing for them. This leaflet was printed for the Security Division for use in the security education program for employees of the USAEC and AEC contractors. Although the AEC is not a distribution point to the public for this type of material, it does print and place in the hands of each employee materials designed to make them aware of their responsibility for the protection of the National Security.

On July 15, 1965, we sent a long letter to Mr. Sample, calling to his attention 7 falsehoods in the brochure, including the lie, that the billion dollar per year pornography business is Communist-inspired, and we offered to send him overwhelming documentation of the charges, providing the Atomic Energy Commission Office would agree to distribute among its employees a disavowal of the 7 falsehoods. On August 10, 1965, Mr. S. R. Sapirie, Manager of Oak Ridge Operations, wrote us regarding the Navy League's brochure:

It is now out of stock, and we have no plans for any further printing. Accordingly we must decline your offer to review or publish the material which you have gathered.

Is it not shocking and tragic that the most powerful nation on earth requires the dissemination of lies about Lenin, Dimitrov, Stalin, Khrushchev, and the American Communists, in order to make the employees of an atomic energy plant "aware of their responsibility for the protection of the National Security"? Why cannot the truth be told as a means of insuring loyalty?

The retired oil millionaire, James R. Taylor, president of the Ultra-Rightist *Committee of Christian Laymen of Woodland Hills, California,* delivered a rambling, Red-Baiting speech at the Sixth Annual Christian Crusade Leadership School, Tulsa, Oklahoma, February 20, 1967. Taylor said:

Joseph Kornfeder was a graduate of the Lenin School of Political Warfare. Georgi Dimitrov, the Russian expert on political warfare, advised the school as follows:

This is followed by a condensed version of the Dimitrov fabrication, which Taylor attributes to the Congressional Record, August 22, 1958, page 17719, without stating *who* placed it in the Congressional Record. Incidentally, Dimitrov was a Bulgarian, not a Russian.

The December, 1967 issue of *Free Enterprise,* monthly organ of the Ultra-Rightist *We, The People,* says:

Joseph Kornfeder, a graduate of the Lenin School of Political Warfare, related how Georgi Dimitrov, the Russian expert on political warfare advised the school:

This is also followed by a condensed version of the Dimitrov fabrication, and the source given is "Congressional Record, p. 17719, Aug. 22, 1958."

The circumstantial evidence makes it pretty clear that this Dimitrov quotation is a concoction of the House Committee on Un-American Activities and its specialist in fabrication, the late Joseph Kornfeder, perpetrator of the Manuilsky Hoax. A comparison of the Manuilsky Hoax and the Dimitrov fabrication shows the use of the same style of writing, the same cadence of sentences, and the same recklessness of statements. The sheer imbecility of the alleged Dimitrov proposals would have brought his summary dismissal from his post, if he had delivered such a speech. Nowhere in any of Dimitrov's speeches and writings can one discover anything resembling either the style or the content of Kornfeder's fabrication. In response to a letter of inquiry about the alleged Dimitrov quotation, the Director of the American Institute of Marxist Studies, Dr. Herbert Aptheker, wrote to us on July 29, 1965, "that is simply out of the whole cloth; surely he never dreamed of, let alone said anything like that. I do not have any recollection of anything remotely like it."

Finally, it should be noted that, the official State Department compilation of statements by Communist leaders, does not contain that alleged Dimitrov quotation. One can be certain that, if it were a genuine item, the Cold Warriors of the State Department would have eagerly included it in their collection. Its obviously fraudulent nature made it too risky for them to use it.

## Conclusion

The evidence clearly shows that, insofar as the people of the United States of America are concerned, the menace of domestic Communism is a myth, a chimera, a delusion. Even if one proceeds from the assumption that the domestic Communists are as evil as they are portrayed by John E. Hoover, Fred Schwarz, Billy James Hargis, and the House Committee on Un-American Activities, the fact remains that the American Communist Party is very small in numbers and is heavily infiltrated with FBI stool pigeons. The splinter groups, that also call themselves Communists, are even smaller and are equally infiltrated. The "fright peddlers," as Senator Thomas H. Kuchel calls them, are accustomed to counter with the argument that Lenin was able to make a revolution in Russia with a handful of followers. This argument is usually presented with figures of the number of followers Lenin had, and it runs anywhere from exactly 14 followers to 40,000. You can take your pick of which figure, in between, suits your fancy!

The argument is incredibly stupid and/or dishonest. When an honest person uses the argument, he is indulging in two fallacies: the nonsequitur and oversimplification. Translating this into plain United States, we must point out that it does not follow that, if something happened in Russia, it will be repeated here; and revolutions are not made to order by individuals or

715

groups who agitate for revolution. If tomorrow morning, 40,000 agitators should take positions on the main thoroughfares of the principal cities of the United States and scream at the top of their lungs for the violent overthrow of the United States Government, the only thing that would probably happen, if the police did not interfere, would be that 40,000 agitators would acquire hoarse voices and would probably receive volleys of epithets and ridicule from the people passing by. The point is that there has to be widespread discontent in large segments of the population and a desperate need to eliminate oppressive conditions in order for revolutionists to succeed in their efforts. Without revolutionary conditions, revolutionists cannot effect the violent overthrow of a government. Inasmuch as there is no revolutionary situation in this country at the present time, the "fright peddlers" should be challenged to "put up or shut up." Senator Abraham Ribicoff told, on the *Meet the Press* television program, January 1, 1967, about the absence of any revolutionary situation at the present time in this country. Reporting about a series of hearings, held by a Senate Subcommittee, of which he is chairman, Senator Ribicoff said that "the interesting thing is, what comes out of these hearings is that while you have 35 million very unhappy Americans, they are not revolutionary. They want a piece of the middle class. They want in."

For all their vaunted claims to be defenders of Americanism, the "fright peddlers" seem to forget that this country was born through a revolution, that violently overthrew the control of the colonies by Great Britain. They seem oblivious to the fact that the basic "rules" of revolution were brilliantly outlined in one of the world's greatest documents of human freedom, our own Declaration of Independence:

Prudence, indeed, will dictate that Governments long established should not be changed for light and transient causes; and accordingly all experience hath shown, that mankind are more disposed to suffer, while evils are sufferable, than to right themselves by abolishing the forms to which they are accustomed. But when a long train of abuses and usurpations, pursuing invariably the same Object evinces a design to reduce them under absolute Despotism, it is their right, it is their duty, to throw off such Government, and to provide new Guards for their future security.

Perhaps it would be a great help in the process of restoring

716

political sanity to this country, if we could induce the "fright peddlers" to read occasionally the Declaration of Independence and the Constitution of the United States.

Nothing that we have said should be construed as meaning that criticism of and opposition to Communism should be stifled or that such criticism is in any way morally reprehensible. The point that we are making is that lies, hysteria, and repressive legislation pave the way for Fascism and war. The history of the twentieth century proves the correctness of this analysis, and we can ignore the lessons of history only at our peril.

There remains only for brief consideration the alleged menace of Communism from abroad. It is a measure of the extent to which the Red Scare hysteria has gripped the American people that they are acquiescing in their government's acting as gendarme of the entire world. Slowly, but surely, the American people have been conditioned to accept, and even approve, the idea that our government can invade militarily any country on the globe simply by screaming "Communism." Usually, of course, pretexts of morality are used to justify American aggression, but the reasons are bogus. Every people has a right to adopt any social order it sees fit, and we have no moral or legal right to essay the role of God and to dictate to any nation, large or small, what kind of social system or form of government it should adopt. The concept of "Amerika Über Alles" is just as repugnant and dangerous as "Deutschland Über Alles." If arguments of morality and legality do not suffice, it must then be stressed that attempts to dictate our will over the entire globe can only result ultimately in a third world war. Such a war will undoubtedly be a thermonuclear war, with the very possible extinction of the human species.

The final conclusion of this study is that Americans of good will and sound mind must move rapidly and vigorously to put an end to the Red Scare, the Cold War, and the anti-Communist Crusade. They must begin to seriously study and cope with the pressing problems of poverty, unemployment, the effects of automation, the slums, inflation, discrimination, and the alarming inroads of militarism. They must no longer be captives of the diversionary propaganda of the

*Plain Liars, Fancy Liars, and Damned Liars!*

717

# Epilogue

## An Open Letter

Dear Reader:

Cordially I press your hand and congratulate you for the patience and perseverance it took to complete the reading of this book. I am keenly aware of the fact that it was not easy to read—this is inherent in any book that presents documentation in great quantity. I offer no apologies for the large amount of quotations and documentation. Discussions with hundreds of people in all parts of the country, during the years that I was doing the research for this book, convinced me that the *truth* about what is going on in this country would tax the credulity of the reader. For this reason, I decided to present adequate documentation, which could not be open to question. I did try very hard to do an honest and useful job. I hope that I have succeeded.

You may have noticed that, in the beginning I reported personal activities by use of the singular pronoun, "I." After awhile it dawned on me that so much of my work was helped by dedicated freedom lovers, who became my volunteer researchers, that I decided it was more appropriate to write in terms of "we." Rather than rewrite portions of the manuscript to conform with this changed attitude, I have decided to leave the manuscript as originally written. This explanation is given so that no one will adopt the cynical notion that the use of "we" is tantamount to my having any royalist or aristocratic pretensions. I am, by nature, a very humble person.

Nothing would have pleased me more than to list the names of the people who were my volunteer researchers. These people are the salt of the earth. They worked patiently and quietly, without fanfare, and often at great sacrifice of personal comforts. One of the proofs of my thesis, that we face the danger of Fascism in the U.S.A., is that I dare not reveal the names

718

of my volunteer researchers and give them the public recognition that they so richly deserve. This would surely invite intimidation by Fascist elements, such as the Minutemen, Ku Klux Klan, and others; and the gentlemen who maintain "subversive" lists might be tempted to add their names.

The acid test of any theory is: Does it conform with or clash with reality? With this in mind, we will now put to the test the analysis of the Red Scare presented in this study. France, Belgium, Holland, Great Britain, Italy, Austria, Finland, Sweden, Norway, Denmark, and Iceland are all countries that are thousands of miles closer to the Soviet Union than is the United States of America. According to the Ultra-Rightists' propaganda theme, they are therefore so much closer to the fountainhead of the alleged international Communist conspiracy, with the consequently greater possibility of infiltration by all the alleged Communist spies that give John E. Hoover so many conniption fits. In none of these countries do they have such a Red Scare hysteria as we have. In none of these countries are people harassed and jailed for their *beliefs* in the Communist philosophy and program. In none of these countries do they have the counterpart of the House Committee on Un-American Activities and the committees of like nature on the State level. In great Britain there is no Un-British Committee. In France their is no Un-French Committee. In Belgium there is no Un-Belgian Committee. And there is no "Un" Committee in the rest of the countries. What is the reason that, with the highest level of prosperity in any country of the world at the present time, we are so much more fearful of Russian Communism than any other Capitalist country, with the exception of those that have already become Fascist?

Another aspect of this dilemma that has been conveniently obscured is that in France, Communists serve as members of the Chamber of Deputies, as mayors of a number of cities, and as members of many city councils. The same is true in Italy and Finland. For a number of years the Communist, Willie Gallacher, served as a member of the British Parliament. There have been no reports of anyone dying of apoplexy as a result of these Communists getting elected to public office. Furthermore, it knocks into a cocked hat the Ultra-Rightist thesis that a few Communists in strategic positions can somehow mesmerize all with whom they come in contact and take over com-

719

plete control. Thoughtful people in these countries look upon us as politically immature, childish, and reckless. At one time a couple of Communists, Pete Cacchione and Benjamin Davis, Jr., were elected to the New York City Council. Nothing of a spectacular nature took place, and the Republic survived. The hysteria that has been generated since then, however, has made it increasingly difficult for Communists to participate in election campaigns. The same people, who promote these obstacles to peaceful, legal methods, are the ones who shout the loudest that the Communists advocate change by force and violence.

We can put the purveyors of the Red Scare and the "fright peddlers" to another acid test. Nowhere in their voluminous literature can one find any meaningful proposals for coping with the problems of the rising cost of living (inflation), unemployment, slum housing, poverty, discrimination, smog, crime, corruption, and many other problems. The best you will find is an expression of pious hopes that somehow things will get better, or advice to pray for better conditions. Others will brazenly deny that these problems exist, or will make comparisons with backward countries. Nowhere in their literature will one find any meaningful approach to the crying need for progressive steps toward universal disarmament. On the contrary, they use the Treaty Breaking Hoax as a device to "prove" that any steps toward universal disarmament are Utopian, impractical, and part of a Communist plot. In fact, Ultra-Rightist literature is replete with open and disguised calls for war with the Soviet Union or with Communist China, always under the guise of repelling "aggression." Never do they show a real concern of what a third world war would mean.

The application of the acid test proves conclusively that the Red Scare is a device whereby the real enemies of the American people use *the tyranny of a word*—Communism—to paralyze the thinking of the American people. By inculcating belief in a bogeyman story, they have reduced the American people to childish levels of belief in political phantasy. Inasmuch as disorientation from reality is a form of psychosis, it is clear that the psychological climate for Fascism and a third world war is being prepared by the witch-hunters of the anti-Communism crusade. This charge is made with the utmost scientific precision, because it is a matter of historical record that Benito Mussolini, Adolph Hitler, and Francisco Franco fastened Fascism around the necks of the people by the propaganda device of an anti-Communist crusade. The same is true of dictator Salazar of Portugal, dictator Chiang Kai-shek of Formosa, and all the other Fascist dictators.

One more acid test of the anti-Communist crusaders gives us the ultimate in proof of their fraudulent nature. With the possible exception of Fred Schwarz' Christian Anti-Communism Crusade and one or two others, you will find that a good part of their propaganda thrust is aimed not at Communists, but at Liberals, people who believe in Capitalism, but also believe in making some reforms and making some concessions, in order to prolong Capitalism as a viable economic system. You will find in the literature of Billy James Hargis' Christian Crusade, Robert Welch's Birch Society, and many other anti-Communist crusaders the most vitriolic denunciations of any reform measure, including Social Security. Always they wave the scarecrow of "Communism." One concrete example, of hundreds that I could cite, will illustrate this point.

Admiral Ben Moreell, U.S. Navy (Retired), is a typical Ultra-Rightist spokesman. He is chairman of the Ultra-Rightist *Americans for Constitutional Action.* He is a member of the National Strategy Committee of the Ultra-Rightist *American Security Council* (a private organization). He participated in the July 4, 1967 New England Rally for God, Family and Country at Boston, Massachusetts. This is a yearly event run by a thinly disguised front of the John Birch Society. He is on the Board of the Ultra-Rightist *Foundation for Economic Education* and the *Intercollegiate Society of Individualists.* He is a sponsor of *American Committee for Aid to Katanga Freedom Fighters.* He is the Vice Chairman of what appears to be an Ultra-Rightist top strategy group, *The 1976 Committee.* He served as Chairman of the Board of Jones & Laughlin Steel Corporation from 1947-1958. In short, Ben Moreell is a thoroughly class-conscious Capitalist-Militarist, and he speaks with authority in expressing a fair sampling of Ultra-Rightist philosophy.

In a speech he delivered in Washington, D.C., May 27, 1967, the admiral said:[1]

Most Americans have been alerted against an undefined "Communism." But many have not been alerted against the specific measures which, taken together, *are* Communism. So, unknowingly, they accept the heart of the Communist doctrine, which is the enhancement of centralized State power at the expense of the natural rights of the individual, the right to life, the right to acquire, own, enjoy and freely dispose of one's honestly accumulated property.

Please note that the admiral confirms what I have been saying throughout this book, that the Ultra-Rightist, anti-Communist crusaders have been using the propaganda device of *obscurantism,* the confusion of issues by verbal smokescreens and by massive use of fabrications. What else does an undefined "Communism" mean? If the truth were being told, why would Communism be undefined to the extent that Moreell gives it a skeptical connotation with quotation marks? Especially after so many "exposures" of Communism, why is it still undefined?

Two paragraphs later, Moreell explains that he *recently* got around to reading a basic document of the Communist movement, the *Manifesto* drawn up in 1848 by Karl Marx and Friedrich Engels. This is quite a confession to make after a person has been an "expert" in the fight against Communism for many a moon. The admiral tells us that, after reading the Manifesto, he has concluded that "we Americans have adopted, in some degree, every plank of his [Karl Marx] platform; and this process has accelerated markedly in recent decades!"

See the point? By raising the Red Scare against the income tax, against public education, against child labor laws, against the 8-hour day, against public schools, and against other reforms advocated by Communists, you can scare many people into believing these things are dangerous because they will bring on atheism and Communism!

Moreell takes the position that the income tax and any laws regulating business practices are denials of freedom, and that they lead to slavery. In the process of making this argument, he unwittingly lays himself open to a possible charge of being a crypto-Communist, because he defines economic slavery in almost identical terms as the Communists define "wage slavery." Of course, Moreell does it demagogically, but it is good for a chuckle to give him the Robert Welch "medicine."

The demagogy of the Ultra-Rightists is made very clear in other paragraph where he slyly implies that some of the

722

powers exercised by the Federal Government (and that would include enforcement of the income tax law and the labor laws) are the cause of corruption, crime, and moral degeneration.

After many plaintive declarations, Moreell makes a strategic maneuver by the use of a common trick of salesmanship that is taught to all high-pressure salesmen: close a deal on something *tangible* by first selling your prospect on something *intangible*. He tells us that the order of priority on the American scene is the restoration of American spiritual values, and he finally winds up by inviting God to be his partner:

> *The final battle will be fought in the arena* of spiritual realities. The forces of self-disciplined, morally responsible individualism will be arrayed against those of atheistic, coercive collectivism. It is my prayer that, in this Armageddon, *Americans will be found fighting on the side of a just and merciful God.*

The night after I finished reading that last Moreell pronouncement I had a dream. I saw Moreell decked out in shining armor, riding on a beautiful white charger, and with a long sword unsheathed. Behind him were thousands of Birchers and followers of Fred Schwarz, Billy James Hargis, Carl McIntire, Clarence Manion, Kenneth Goff, C .W. Burpo, and James W. Fifield. As they approached the national capitol, the Congressmen and Senators came out to greet the paraders. Moreell raised himself high on his white horse, waved his sword towards the heavens, pointed to the Congressmen and Senators, and screamed: "God almighty, in the name of all the red-blooded American patriots, strike dead those goddam Communists who passed the income tax law!" But it was only a dream!

In the world of reality, it is crystal clear that the Ultra-Rightists are losing faith in Capitalism's ability to function as a viable economic system, especially within a framework of democratic government (however limited in form it may be). It is indeed appropriate to ask them: "Why are ye fearful, O ye of little faith?"[2] The answer, in my opinion, is that in the past Capitalism has extricated itself from economic depressions or threats of depression through "priming the pump" with war or preparations for war. But now they face the dilemma, that war is no longer feasible as a means of priming

2 From Chapter 8, verse 26, of the Gospel according to St. Matthew.

the economy. For the first time in American history, Big Business is faced with the frustration of knowing that it risks total annihilation, if it unleashes a major war. This frustration is what explains much of the Ultra-Rightist hysteria and the anti-Communist crusades, with all the phoney issues and scarecrow stories. In their desperation, they turn increasingly to police state measures, which can only lead to a Fascist dictatorship.

Once in awhile, you will find an Ultra-Rightist, who, in a moment of refreshing candor, will blurt out the truth. Such was the case with Frank S. Meyer, who wrote in *National Review*, October 19, 1965:

> The domestic Communist conspiracy is not the cause of the decay of our values, of the decline of education, of the fatuousness of the general line of our foreign policy since World War II, of the rising rate of crime, of the steady sapping of constitutional safeguards, or of most of the evils that beset us.

That is quite an admission for an Ultra-Rightist to make in a magazine for Ultra-Rightist intellectuals. Frank S. Meyer ought to know whereof he speaks, because he was once a member of the Communist Party. Apparently, he had to make one "concession" to his Ultra-Rightist associates and readers when he "let the cat out of the bag." He found it necessary to refer to a non-existent "domestic Communist conspiracy." Frank knows better.

I am sure that, as a reasonable person, you must now be asking me: "Well, where do we go from here? What can I do? What should I do?" These are fair questions, and I will do my best to give honest and practicable answers. I proceed with three assumptions: 1. That you are an anti-Fascist. 2. That you are against a third world war. 3. That you want this country to go forward to greater achievements for Life, Liberty, and the pursuit of Happiness.

The first thing that you must struggle to accomplish is an end to the anti-Communist crusade, the witch-hunt that serves as a diversionary maneuver. In the spoken and written word, you must challenge every witch-hunter to tell you exactly what he means when he babbles about Communism. You must say, as Voltaire said many years ago: "When you argue with me, Monsieur, define your terms." When the witch-hunter calls anyone a Communist, ask him what "Communist" really means? Pin him down to a definition that is without lies, without distortions of truth, without vituperation. Once you have done that, you must show him that Communism is not an issue on the American political scene at the present time; that it is not on the order of the day, at the present time. Consequently, anti-Communist crusading, in the absence of any appreciable number of Communists against whom to crusade, can only lead to disaster, because of neglect to cope with real problems.

The next thing you must do is to engage in struggle to preserve the peace. The dirty wars in Vietnam, Laos, Cambodia, and other parts of the world must be brought to an end. The interventionist policies, the meddling in other people's affairs, the global bullying, the role of world gendarme, and the arms race must be terminated. The political desperadoes and ignoramuses, who say they would "Rather be Dead than Red", should be told that no one will stop them from committing suicide, but they have no right to provoke a third world war. Granted that there are some risks in a program for progressive, universal disarmament, there are even greater risks in a continuation of the arms race. The latter will *surely* lead to mutual annihilation. As the brilliant scientist and novelist, Sir Charles P. Snow, has summarized it: "Between a risk and a certainty a sane man does not hesitate".

The third plank in your program must be to resist all attempts at curtailment of democratic rights and procedures. All attempts to cause erosion of the Bill of Rights must be fought with courage and determination. The civil rights of all minority groups must be won and protected.

The fourth and perhaps most important plank in your program must be the challenge to all citizens—Ultra-Rightist and all others—to work for positive, meaningful programs that cope with poverty, unemployment, inflation, high cost of living, health problems, smog, slaughter on the highways, and the myriad of other problems that beset us. It is so much easier to blame everything onto the Communists or the liberals, but you must bring these Ultra-Rightists down to earth and challenge them to come up with bona fide proposals for the solution of these problems.

Finally, if you agree that this book can be a powerful weapon in reversing the trend towards Fascism and a third world war, will you take steps to get it into the hands of large numbers of people?

This has been a long letter, but I considered it necessary, because of the grave situation in this country at the present time. In bidding you farewell, dear reader, I give you my pledge that, as long as there is a breath of life in me, I will continue to struggle for peace, democracy, and freedom. Will you join me in the only kind of crusade that is worthwhile? I can think of no better parting sentiments than those of the American poet, James Russell Lowell:

> Is it true Freedom but to break
> Fetters for our own dear sake
> And with leathern hearts forget
> That we owe mankind a debt?
> No! True freedom is to share
> All the chains our brothers wear
> And with heart and hand to be
> Earnest to make others free.
> They are slaves who fear to speak
> For the fallen and the weak.
> They are slaves who will not choose
> And alone in silence shrink
> From the truth they sure must think.
> They are slaves who dare not be
> In the right with two or three.

Faithfully yours,
MORRIS KOMINSKY

# INDEX

729

730

731

732

733